POLITICAL CAREERS, CORRUPTION, AND IMPUNITY

POLITICAL CAREERS, CORRUPTION, AND IMPUNITY

PANAMA'S ASSEMBLY,

1984–2009

Carlos Guevara Mann

University of Notre Dame Press

Notre Dame, Indiana

Copyright © 2011 by University of Notre Dame
Notre Dame, Indiana 46556
www.undpress.nd.edu
All Rights Reserved

Manufactured in the United States of America

Library of Congress Cataloging-in-Publication Data

Guevara Mann, Carlos.
Political careers, corruption, and impunity : Panama's assembly, 1984–2009 /
Carlos Guevara Mann.
p.   cm. — (From the Helen Kellogg Institute for International Studies)
Includes bibliographical references and index.
ISBN-13: 978-0-268-02983-8 (pbk. : alk. paper)
ISBN-10: 0-268-02983-0 (pbk. : alk. paper)
1. Panama. Asamblea Legislativa.   2. Legislative bodies—Panama—History.
3. Legislators—Panama—History.   4. Political corruption—Panama.
5. Representative government and representation—Panama.
6. Panama—Politics and government—1981–   I. Title.
JL1653.G84   2011
328.728709'049—dc23

2011036540

Contents

List of Tables   ix

Acknowledgments   xiii

Introduction   1

PART I. INSTITUTIONS

Chapter 1. Political Representation and Representative
              Assemblies   17

Chapter 2. The Party System: Parties and Actors in Panama's
              Assembly   36

Chapter 3. Formal Institutional Incentives to Behavior   65

Chapter 4. Informal Institutions and Assembly Members'
              Behavior   91

PART II. ASSEMBLY MEMBERS' GOALS, BEHAVIORS, AND ACTIVITIES

Chapter 5. Political Advancement through Reelection: Prospects and Possibilities in Panama 117

Chapter 6. Political Advancement through Reelection: The Legal and Illegal Uses of Patronage 131

Chapter 7. Political Advancement through Reelection: Party Switching and Electoral Manipulation 153

Chapter 8. Personal Enrichment through Legal Means: Assembly Members' Wages in Comparative Perspective 177

Chapter 9. Personal Enrichment through Legal Means: Expanding Emoluments and Privileges 192

Chapter 10. Personal Enrichment through Illegal Means 214

Chapter 11. Preserving Immunity through Reelection 236

Conclusion 254

APPENDICES

Appendix A. Average Freedom House (FH) Scores, Corruption Perceptions Index (CPI) Scores, and Population of Countries Classified as "Free" by Freedom House, 2008–10 268

Appendix B. Number of Members in the Representative Assemblies of All Countries Classified as "Free" by Freedom House, 2008–10 271

Appendix C. Number of Members in the Representative Assemblies of Latin America's Electoral Democracies, 2008–10 277

Appendix D.   Panama's Assembly Parties, 1984–2009   278

Appendix E.   Individuals Proclaimed by the Electoral Tribunal
                as Elected Members of Panama's Assembly,
                1984–2009   283

Appendix F.   Panama's Effective Number of Parties   295

Appendix G.   Electoral Volatility in Panama, 1984–2009   298

Appendix H.   Difference in Votes for President and
                Assembly Members in Panama (Parties and
                Electoral Coalitions), 1984–2009   300

Appendix I.   Consecutive Reelection and Party Switching
                in Panama, 1984–2009   303

Appendix J.   Age of Panama's Assembly Members, 2004–9
                and 2009–14 Terms   323

Appendix K.   Gender and Social Origins of Individuals
                Proclaimed by the Electoral Tribunal as Elected
                Members of Panama's Assembly, 1984–2009   329

Appendix L.   Geodemographic Segmentation of Panama's
                Electoral Constituencies, 1984–2009   344

Appendix M.   Deviation from Proportionality (D) in Panama's
                Elections to the Assembly, 1984–2009   348

Appendix N.   Panamanian Assembly Members' Monthly
                Wages, 1960–2008   354

Appendix O.   Panamanian Assembly Members' Expected
                Salaries, 1999   356

Appendix P.   Obligation to Attend Plenary and Committee
                Meetings in Fifty-Three Liberal Democracies,
                2008   358

Appendix Q.   Passports Used by Assembly Members in
                Fifty-Three Liberal Democracies, 2010   360

Appendix R. Constituency Funding Allocations and Assembly
Members' Reelection in Panama, 1995–99   **362**

Appendix S. Non-Liability among Assembly Members in
Fifty-Two Liberal Democracies, 2008   **365**

Appendix T. Persons Consulted   **367**

Notes   **374**

Works Cited   **400**

Other Works Consulted   **437**

Index   **440**

Tables

I.1. Goals, Activities, and Behaviors of Panama's Assembly
      Members   4

1.1. Terms and Number of Members in Panama's National
      Assembly, 1904–68   28

1.2. Number of Seats in Panama's Assembly, 1984–2009   32

1.3. Some Comparative Statistics of the Membership of
      Representative Assemblies in Liberal Democracies
      and Latin American Electoral Democracies, 2008–10   34

2.1. Total Number of Seats Obtained by Panama's Assembly
      Parties, 1984–2009   45

2.2. Classification of Party Systems Based on Effective
      Number of Parties   45

2.3. Selected Party System Institutionalization Statistics
      in Panama and Latin America, 1984–2009   49

2.4. Average Starting Age of Members of Panama's Assembly
      and the U.S. House of Representatives, 1999–2009   52

2.5.   Women in Representative Assemblies, 2008–10   53

2.6.   Urban Municipal Districts and Electoral
        Constituencies in Panama, 2006–9   61

2.7.   Ideological Preferences of Assembly Members in
        Panama and Latin America, 2000–2008   63

3.1.   Effects of Seat Allocation Formulas on Candidates'
        Electoral Strategies   68

3.2.   Assembly Membership and Electoral Constituencies
        in Panama, 1984–2009   70

3.3.   District Magnitude in Panama, 1984–2009   72

3.4.   Seat Allocation in Panama's Multimember
        Constituencies, 1994–2009   76

3.5.   Seat Allocation Formulas and Number of Seats Allotted
        According to Each Formula in Panama, 1994–2009   78

5.1.   Assembly Members' Consecutive Reelection Rates in
        Panama, 1984–2009   121

5.2.   Nonconsecutive Reelection by Panama's Assembly
        Members with Party Affiliation, 1984–2009   122

5.3.   Election to Office of Equal or Higher Rank by
        Assembly Members in Panama, 1984–2009   124

5.4.   Accession to Appointed Office of Equal or Higher
        Rank by Assembly Members in Panama, 1984–2009   125

6.1.   Allocation and Disbursement of Constituency Funds
        in Panama, 1984–99   137

6.2.   Allocation of Constituency Funds among
        Government and Opposition Assembly Members
        in Panama, 1995–99   142

6.3.   Constituency Funding Allocations and Assembly
        Members' Reelection in Panama, 1995–99   148

7.1. Switches from Extinct Parties and Affiliation Changes by Elected Independents in Panama, 1994–2009   **158**

7.2. Party Switching for Electoral Purposes in Panama, 1994–2009   **160**

8.1. Assembly Members' Monthly Wages in Panama, 1960–2008   **181**

8.2. Panamanian Deputies Absent for More Than Half the Sitting Period, September 2008   **183**

8.3. Panamanian Deputies Absent for More Than Half the Sitting Period, April 2010   **183**

8.4. Panamanian Assembly Members' Expected Salaries, 1999   **185**

8.5. Yearly Remuneration of Representatives in Selected Liberal Democracies, 2007   **188**

8.6. Monthly Remuneration of Representatives in Fifteen Latin American Republics, 2007   **190**

9.1. Obligation to Attend Plenary and Committee Meetings in Fifty-Two Liberal Democracies, 2008   **200**

Acknowledgments

I initiated this study of the political behavior of Panama's assembly members as a doctoral student at the University of Notre Dame in 1995–2000. I completed it at Notre Dame as well, as a visiting fellow at the Helen Kellogg Institute for International Studies, in the spring of 2010. In the decade that elapsed between defending the dissertation and completing the project, I engaged in various activities that permitted me to observe Panamanian and international politics from different—albeit complementary—perspectives.

A stint as an assistant to Panama's minister of foreign relations, José Miguel Alemán, in 1999–2002 allowed me to grasp, among many other notions, the inner workings of the country's bureaucracy and politics. A whole new window into Panama's electoral realities opened when the ruling coalition chose Dr. Alemán as its presidential candidate in 2004 and he asked me to assist his campaign efforts. Although he did not win, the campaign taught me lessons about the nature and dynamics of public affairs in Panama that represented an enormous personal gain. Additionally, as a boss, Dr. Alemán was humane and understanding. I am deeply grateful for his trust in my capabilities and support for this project.

For a time I also worked as credit manager for the Panama branch of Lloyds TSB Bank, a British financial entity with a long trajectory in Latin

America, going back to the nineteenth century. This position, together with an interesting year as assistant to the general manager of Caja de Ahorros—a state savings and loans bank—helped me develop analytical skills that are not only central to banking but also proved very useful in the endeavor to interpret politics. My time at these jobs coincided with the commemoration of Panama's centennial as an independent state, to which I contributed by organizing nearly twenty academic sessions throughout the country—focusing on various aspects of Panama's politics, economy, social realities, history, and culture—as a member of the Presidential Centenary Commission.

Subsequently, I embarked on an academic career, first at Florida State University, Panama Branch, where I was asked to teach a class in contemporary Panamanian history. The course had been dormant for several years, so it was my challenge to recover it. Quickly, it became my favorite class, which I am glad to continue teaching as a guest lecturer whenever the opportunity arises. Later, I moved to the University of Nevada, Reno. Teaching international and comparative politics—especially the politics of Latin America and western Europe—in Nevada between 2005 and 2010 further acquainted me with important interpretive currents and kept me abreast of developments in those fields.

At the time I also started a very fruitful connection to the United Nations system as a consultant to an international organization with important operations in Latin America and the Caribbean, which I joined as a staff member in early 2011. Because the agency works closely with governments to set up and implement social services to promote human development, the ongoing consultancy provided great insight into the workings of the public sector in many countries of the region. All along I continued to write in the Panamanian press, an activity that gives me much satisfaction. When I published my first editorials in 1994, little did I surmise that writing for the newspapers would provide such excellent learning experiences and so many valuable connections in support of this book and other scholarly pursuits. Over the past fifteen years, I have written hundreds of columns in—and served as a source of political commentary for—the country's main papers, including *Crítica Libre*, *El Panamá América*, *El Siglo*, *La Estrella de Panamá*, and *La Prensa*, where I have been a regular columnist since 2004.

Many intellectual influences contributed to the development of this extended project on the members of Panama's assembly. At Ohio University, where I studied between 1991 and 1993, Michael Grow, the Latin American historian on the faculty, transmitted his enthusiasm for history together with an emphasis on accuracy. His influence on my career was positive and enduring. At Notre Dame, Michael Coppedge was a sterling mentor who, with much patience, remarkable lucidity, and good humor, guided me through the arduous process of dissertation writing. Back in 1994–95, Guillermo O'Donnell, a towering figure of democratic theory and the comparative politics of Latin America, convinced me that Notre Dame was the right place when I was considering other options for a doctoral degree. He left a lasting theoretical imprint on me, which I gratefully acknowledge.

Scott Mainwaring, director of the Kellogg Institute, helped develop my incipient interest in representation and representatives in coherent ways. His methodological rigor was inspiring and his encouragement to publish this work most rewarding. I much valued the analytical contributions of Martha Merritt, a specialist in democratic theory and Russian politics, as well as her regard for, and brilliant command of, the English language. Mark Jones, currently at Rice University but a fellow at Kellogg at the time I submitted my dissertation, provided—and continues to provide—data and sources on Latin American congresses and elections, as well as friendly suggestions and support.

This study owes much to Panamanian anthropologist Brittmarie Janson Pérez, whose assistance in information gathering and interpretation was essential in shaping the book and who for many years has been a wonderful and generous partner in countless pursuits—some academic, others prosaic, but none devoid of meaning and excitement. My intellectual debt to her is enormous. Many colleagues in the field of political science read and commented on earlier versions of the book or parts of the manuscript, including David Altman, Rossana Castiglioni, Andreas Feldmann, Stacy Fisher, Andrew Gould, Derek Kauneckis, Andrés Mejía Acosta, Robert Ostergard, Aníbal Pérez Liñán, and Christopher Simon. Specialists in Panamanian politics and history, including Italo Antinori Bolaños, Ricardo Arias Calderón, Miguel Antonio Bernal, Betty Brannan Jaén, Mario Galindo Heurtematte, Aims McGuinness,

Ramón Morales Quijano, Sharon Phillipps Collazos, Gloria Rudolf, Salvador Sánchez González, Peter Szok, Juan Antonio Tejada Mora, and Juan Cristóbal Zúñiga, also contributed disinterestedly to this project.

I have cited only some of the experiences and conversations that influenced my analysis of the behavior of Panama's assembly members over a twenty-five-year period. I mention them in all modesty and with much gratitude in order to apprise the reader of my take on Panamanian politics and some of its professional sources. Clearly, I approach the study of assembly members from a broad comparative, essentially qualitative, perspective strongly reliant on history and political chronologies, supported by basic, easily accessible quantitative analysis. But my interest in the politics of Panama precedes the listed experiences and conversations by many years, going back to the formative influences I received during childhood and adolescence.

On both sides, my family members were involved in the country's politics for many generations. Among my paternal ancestors several were committed Liberals devoted to the cause of public education, democracy, and nationalism. Prominent Conservatives on my mother's side served as government officials going as far back as the Spanish domination, took part in the isthmus's emancipation from Spain in 1821, and contributed to founding the first independent State of Panama in 1840 as well as the Republic of Panama in 1903. Growing up during the final years of the old regime (1903–68) and the dark period of military rule (1968–89), my parents, Carlos and Teresa, strove to inculcate in their offspring the values of democracy, including respect for the popular will, human rights, and the rule of law, as well as the republican virtues of decency, probity, and devotion to the public interest at a time when these principles were devalued currency. Their support, for which I am very grateful, continued through the many years I spent abroad in graduate school and academia.

It would be an oversight not to mention other persons and entities who collaborated to bring this venture to fruition. The University of Notre Dame Press and two knowledgeable outside reviewers, Peter Siavelis and Peter Szok, made important recommendations on form and substance. The time they took to read the text carefully and provide detailed comments is much appreciated. At the press, Lowell Francis and Barbara Hanrahan navigated the intricate waters of the publication process with courtesy and efficiency, and Rebecca DeBoer and Christina Lovely provided indispensable editorial support. The staff at the Kellogg Institute, the Mathewson-IGT Knowledge Center at the University of Nevada, *La Prensa,* and *El Panamá América* assisted me in many ways. Appendix T recognizes many other contributors of data and ideas to this project.

I received instrumental financial help from the Kellogg Institute's Project Latin America 2000 and Visiting Fellows Program, the University of Notre Dame's Philip Moore Fellowship, the Leo S. Rowe Fund of the Organization of American States, and the University of Nevada, Reno's, Department of Political Science and College of Liberal Arts. Carlos Guevara Céspedes and Rita Preciado Recuero helped collect much valuable information. Other family members and special persons also supported me through the critical research and writing stages: Vivian Dutari, my late uncle Francisco Céspedes, my relatives Rita and Gabriel de Obarrio, Mireya and Gerardo Dutari, and Vilma Ponce.

My children, Francisco, Cristina, and Alvaro, provide the best reason to make a contribution to society in the form of an investigation of our country's politics. If the pages that follow serve to stimulate democratic reflection, deliberation, and reform in Panama, my daughter and two sons will live in a better country. This is the main motivation that inspired me to focus on political representation in Panama and its impact on liberal democracy.

Introduction

The scene could have hardly been more illustrative of this book's topic. On January 16, 2002, before a crowd of cameramen and reporters, Panamanian legislator Carlos Afú, then of Partido Revolucionario Democrático (PRD),[1] extracted a stack of paper money from his jacket. Those six thousand dollars, he said, were the first installment of a payment for his vote in favor of a multimillion-dollar contract between the government of Panama and a private consortium, Centro Multimodal Industrial y de Servicios (CEMIS).[2] Legislator Afú claimed to have received the money from fellow party and assembly member Mateo Castillero, chairman of the chamber's Budget Committee. Disbursement of the bribe's balance—US$14,000—was still pending. That was the only kickback he had received, claimed Afú, alluding to the accusation of another fellow party and assembly member, Balbina Herrera,[3] that Afú had received "suitcases filled with money" to approve the appointment of two government nominees to the Supreme Court.

Afú's declarations sent shock waves throughout the country and seemed to confirm the perception of Panama's political system as one in which corruption, impunity, and clientelism prevail. As political figures exchanged accusations and added more sleaze to the story, commentators, media, and civil society organizations called for a sweeping investigation of the "Afúdollars" case. But the tentacles of the CEMIS affair

1

were spread too broadly throughout Panama's political establishment. They stung not only the leadership of the opposition PRD—the political arm of the 1968–89 military dictatorship—but also the government of President Mireya Moscoso, Panama's first woman president, and her Panameñista Party (PPAN), which was founded by the military's historic adversary, Arnulfo Arias. Predictably, investigations by the Prosecutor-General's Office never succeeded. In a few months, the case was filed by the Supreme Court (Alianza Ciudadana Pro Justicia 2004).[4]

This book is about behaviors, such as those portrayed above, by members of representative assemblies in liberal democracies. Following Mayhew (1974, 8) as well as Shugart and Carey (1992), the term *representative assembly* best describes the organization with whose members this book deals. In daily usage, terms such as *legislature, parliament,* or *congress* are used interchangeably to refer to the legislative branch of government. *Representative assembly,* however, is preferable to *legislature* because discussing and enacting legislation is not the only function elected chambers perform in liberal democracies and executives in both parliamentary and presidential regimes also have important lawmaking powers.

Parliament, in turn, connotes a political system in which the survival of the government depends upon the confidence of the majority in the representative chamber. *Congress* suggests a regime type in which the branches of government have separate origin and survival, a notion that excludes those assemblies, generally called *parliaments,* upon whose confidence government survival is contingent. Thus, parliaments and congresses are the two main types of representative assemblies. In 2004 Panama's congress regained the name of *National Assembly,* which it had in 1904–68, and its members once again became known as "deputies." Between 1984 and 2004 the unicameral chamber was called the *Legislative Assembly* and consisted of "legislators."

The regime type known as *liberal democracy* comprises at least three dimensions: political representation, popular elections, and civil freedoms. The representative ingredient refers to "government by the freely elected representatives of the people" in accordance with the people's preferences (Lijphart 1984, 1; 1999, 1). In modern liberal democracies such representation is normally mediated through political parties, an indispensable component of the democratic system. For Freedom House

(2009c), the electoral dimension consists, at a minimum, of the following elements:

1. A competitive, multiparty political system;
2. Universal adult suffrage for all citizens (with exceptions for restrictions that states may legitimately place on citizens as sanctions for criminal offenses);
3. Regularly contested elections conducted in conditions of ballot secrecy and reasonable ballot security, in the absence of massive voter fraud, and that yield results that are representative of the public will;
4. Significant public access of major political parties to the electorate through the media and through generally open political campaigning.

The liberal component encompasses "a substantial array of civil liberties." These include freedom of information, expression, and belief; associational and organizational rights; the rule of law, and personal autonomy and individual rights.[5] In its classification of states, Freedom House (2009c) labels liberal democracies as "free" countries. According to the organization, Panama has been a liberal democracy or "free" state since 1994.

This book's argument is simple, even self-evident for anyone who has paid attention to congressional or parliamentary politics throughout the world. The literature on legislators' behavior, mostly based on the U.S. experience, has long assumed that representatives want to advance their careers—either through reelection (where it is allowed), appointment to political office, or election to a party position—more than anything else. By focusing on the behavior of the 309 individuals who were proclaimed as duly-elected members of Panama's assembly in the six general elections held between 1984 and 2009, this book argues that representatives' actions might also be motivated by other goals and that these additional objectives may be as attractive to assembly members as career advancement.

In Panama the most salient additional goals are getting rich and remaining free from prosecution. Other goals might be recognizable in different settings; identifying them is a challenge this book poses to the scholarship. In pursuing their objectives, Panama's assembly members undertake certain activities and engage in specific behaviors (see table I.1).

Table I.1. Goals, Activities, and Behaviors of Panama's Assembly Members

Goals	Activities	Behaviors
Political advancement	Reelection to an assembly seat	Distributing patronage Buying votes Manipulating elections Switching parties
	Appointment to government office	Supporting the incumbent executive Supporting a presidential candidate
	Election to party office	Distributing patronage Buying votes Manipulating elections
Personal enrichment	Using office for private gain through legal means	Seeking emolument increases Blocking emolument reductions Seeking assembly and committee board appointments
	Using office for private gain through illegal means	Abusing privileges Selling votes Peddling influence Misappropriating public resources
Exemption from prosecution	Manipulating immunity prerogatives	Denying immunity suspension Stretching immunity provisions
	Manipulating judicial decisions	Peddling influence with judges and prosecutors "Quid pro quo": discarding cases against Supreme Court justices in exchange for justices' discarding cases against deputies

Institutionalization

Whether or not objectives in addition to reelection can be pursued by politicians—and to what degree they complement the goal of career advancement—depends, to a large extent, on the characteristics of institutionalization in a polity. Institutionalization, as Huntington reminds us, "is the process by which organizations and procedures acquire value and stability" (1968, 12).[6] Recent scholarship recognizes two broad types of institutionalization: formal and informal (Helmke and Levitsky 2006; North 1990; O'Donnell 1996, 1998b). In those areas where formal institutionalization prevails—where codified rules constitute strong predictors of political behavior—we expect that politicians in general, and members of representative assemblies in particular, will adhere to formal rules and procedures.[7] Because most modern polities have written rules that prohibit the use of public office to obtain personal gain or exemption from prosecution, strong formal institutionalization in activity areas concerning political representation, accountability, and the rule of law does not provide an incentive to the search for the additional objectives identified in this book.

Within democratic polities, however, informal institutionalization exists alongside or instead of formal institutionalization in some areas. This type of institutionalization refers to normally unwritten rules that emerge—and are conveyed and implemented—through unofficial channels. Informal institutionalization covers a broad range of phenomena: some might complement and others may compete with (or subvert) the formal institutions of democracy (Helmke and Levitsky 2006, 5, 13–16). This book focuses on three informal institutions that have a direct impact in shaping the behavior of Panama's assembly members: corruption, impunity, and clientelism.

Goals and Behaviors and Their Impact on Democracy

In states where corruption, impunity, and clientelism are informally institutionalized, the behavior of representatives might include—in addition to efforts to secure reelection or career advancement—legal or illegal attempts to become rich and remain immune from prosecution. At a large scale, self-serving behaviors such as these are likely to have a negative impact on the quality of democracy and the strength (and even durability) of the democratic regime. As noted in a survey of Latin American political institutions, poor performance by politicians—including behaviors deemed contrary to the public interest—"appears to have contributed to growing frustration in many countries" (Mateo Díaz et al. 2007, 275).

These are the main inferences drawn from the systematic examination of the individual and collective activities of the members of Panama's assembly from 1984 to 2009 undertaken in this book. The identified behaviors are observable throughout time, under authoritarianism (1984–89), during the transitional period (1989–94), and under liberal democracy (1994–2009); in both men and women representatives (although the assembly has been overwhelmingly populated by men); in members from the upper, middle, and lower classes (even though upper-class members are a minority); in deputies from rural and urban areas (although more than half of the members represent urban areas); and in representatives from all assembly parties (though a majority of the sample belongs to PRD). On this basis, some behaviors of Panama's assembly members relate more to the nature of political institutionalization—characterized on the isthmus by the coexistence of formal and informal institutions with effects on the political system—than to regime type, gender, class, social origins, or partisan preference.[8] This finding merits cautious examination and testing in other settings.

In essence, the book accomplishes three tasks. First, it reveals some fundamental goals of the members of Panama's assembly and some activities and behaviors they undertake to attain those objectives. The goals, which supplement an understanding of representatives' behavior that has tended to focus on formal institutional factors, include advancing a political career, getting rich, and enjoying freedom from prosecution. Some activities through which Panamanian deputies procure these objectives include reelection, using the prerogatives of public office for personal gain, and manipulating immunity provisions (when they were in place in 1984–2004). Assembly members engage in several behaviors within each activity category in order to pursue their goals (see table I.1).

Second, the study underscores the differences between the behavior of the members of Panama's assembly and scholarly predictions. Although the literature is vast and not wholly homogenous, certain themes recur in most analyses of the behavior of representatives. The desire for reelection—or, more generally, political advancement—is an assumption about the behavior of assembly members most students of the topic adhere to, and patronage distribution (though not more blatant vote buying) frequently emerges as a means representatives employ in their efforts to achieve political advancement (Carey 1996; Fenno 1973; Jones 1998; Mainwaring 1999; Mayhew 1974; Morgenstern 1998; Samuels 1998). Contrariwise, the few works that mention personal enrichment only do so in passing (Fenno 1973, 1; Mayhew 1974, 16), and most have not addressed members' interest in immunity from prosecution or their recourse to vote buying, party switching, or electoral manipulation as a means to advance their careers.

Third, the book endeavors to assess the ways in which those behaviors exhibited by the members of Panama's assembly affect the democratic system, especially in democratic states where informally institutionalized corruption, impunity, and clientelism are important features of political life. Since the publication of Guillermo O'Donnell's "Illusions about Consolidation" (1996), the formally–informally institutionalized dichotomy has served as a useful tool to understand major differences in quality and performance among democratic regimes. In what directly pertains to the study of representatives, the major implication is that informal institutionalization allows or encourages behaviors not normally exhibited where there is a close fit between codified rules and politicians' actions. Political behaviors stemming from informal institutionalization have not generally been addressed in the literature, which until very recently has focused on the experience of advanced liberal democratic regimes characterized by this close fit (Helmke and Levitsky 2006).

The three tasks accomplished in this research are relevant because at least since the adoption of the U.S. Constitution (1787), the question of politicians' personal motivations has lain "at the very heart of democratic theory" (Loomis 1994). More broadly, the activities of representatives have a direct impact on the quality of democratic representation.

Since representation is one of the pillars of the modern democratic system, the ways in which representatives' behavior impacts representation is an important issue in the study of democratic states and their prospects for further democratization.

Why Panama?

Recent studies have emphasized the need to engage in "systematic institutional analysis of countries" with a view to identifying the nuances of domestic political processes, assessing their impact on policy formulation, and contributing to a broader understanding of contemporary politics (Stein et al. 2005, 257). In this regard, Helmke and Levitsky (2006, 27) suggest that "efforts to identify and measure informal institutions require substantial knowledge of the communities within which those rules are embedded." This study argues that an in-depth look at the dynamics of assembly politics in a liberal democracy such as Panama, where informally institutionalized corruption, impunity, and clientelism contribute to shaping political outcomes, will broaden our understanding of the behavior of representatives, the relevance of informal institutions in shaping their conduct, and the consequences of their behavior for the democratic system.

As noted, this book relies on the Freedom House rankings, which classify the world's independent states (as well as some other territories) into three categories: "free," "partly free," and "not free."[9] On a scale ranging from 1 ("most free") to 7 ("least free"), "free" states are those that have average scores between 1.0 and 2.5. The Freedom House classification, included in the annual *Freedom in the World* report, is broadly used throughout the scholarship to ascertain the nature of contemporary political regimes.

According to *Freedom in the World 2009*, in 2008 there were 89 liberal democracies worldwide, including Panama, out of a total of 193 independent states. Panama's ranking as a "free state" continuously since 1994 makes the isthmus the fourth longest-lived liberal democracy among Latin America's ten, mostly recent, liberal democratic regimes.[10] After a U.S. invasion dislodged the armed forces and its political arm, PRD, from power, the country returned to civilian rule in 1989. As a result of general elections held in 1994, PRD—then the main opposition party—returned to power. In 1999, 2004, and 2009 general elections also returned the opposition to the presidency and executive power was transferred without significant hurdles. In 2008 Freedom House assigned the country a Political Rights (PR) score of 1 and a Civil Liberties (CL) score of 2 (with 1 representing the highest and 7 the lowest level of freedom), averaging 1.5 (Freedom House 2009e).

In Panama elections—the archetypical formal institution of democracy—coexist alongside informally institutionalized clientelism, impunity, and systemic corruption. A broadly accepted indicator of clientelism, covering the universe of liberal democracy, is not yet readily available. But several assessments of rule of law strength have been attempted, including a measure contained in the Freedom House surveys. One of the Freedom House subscores covers such issues as independence of the judiciary, prevalence of the rule of law in civil and criminal matters, civilian control of the police, protection from political terror as well as war and insurgencies, and equality of treatment under the law for all segments of the population. In this appraisal, subscores range between 0 (weak rule of law) and 16 (strong rule of law). Panama's most recent subscore is 9 out of 16, indicating a rather weak rule of law (Freedom House 2009b).

Transparency International's Corruption Perceptions Index (CPI) is a conventional measure of corruption. The CPI "ranks countries in terms of the degree to which corruption is perceived to exist among public officials and politicians" (Transparency International 2009). Scores range between 0 (highly corrupt) and 10 (highly clean). Since 2001, when Transparency International began rating Panama on the CPI, the country's score has never exceeded 3.7, indicating a strong perception of corruption. In 2009 Panama's score of 3.4 placed the country at position 84 (alongside El Salvador, Guatemala, India, and Thailand) among the 180 countries included in the ranking.[11]

Transparency International's 2009 report provided a CPI for 76 of Freedom House's 89 liberal democracies. Among these 76 states, the median Freedom House rule of law and Transparency International CPI scores were 13 and 5.1, respectively (see appendix A). Because both phenomena (systemic corruption and a weak rule of law) overlap to some degree, the argument can be made that impunity and corruption are informally institutionalized in liberal democracies with scores under the median in both categories. In 2008–9 there were 32 such "free states," including Panama as well as older liberal democracies (for example, Italy) and much larger countries such as Brazil, India, Indonesia, and Mexico, among others. These 32 countries constituted nearly one-third (36 percent) of the world's liberal democracies and 17 percent of the world's independent states, and their aggregate population of 2 billion represented 29 percent of the planet's population of 6.9 billion in 2010 (U. N. Population Division 2009).

In the effort to acquire insights into the effects of the aforementioned informal institutions, focusing on Panama is convenient for various reasons. Except for a brief interruption (1989–90),[12] the country's National Assembly has been in continuous operation since 1984. The twenty-five-year period covered in this study (five constitutional terms, plus the beginning of a sixth term) is not too brief to prevent the analyst from making reliable claims about the behavior of Panama's deputies and not too long to excessively complicate the exercise. Similarly—as discussed in chapter 1—although Panama's assembly is one of the smallest representative chambers among contemporary liberal democracies, the number of deputies during the period under review (309) is neither too small to inhibit the formulation of causal inferences nor too large to make that objective unmanageable. The fact that the assembly was installed under military rule and its constitutional design has remained basically unchanged after the country's transition to liberal democracy helps elucidate the effects of an authoritarian legacy on the behavior of political actors. On this basis, findings from this research illustrate relevant features of political representation in liberal democracies where impunity and systemic corruption (as well as clientelism) are informally institutionalized.

An Understudied Case

Informally institutionalized corruption, impunity, and clientelism condition the behavior of Panamanian politicians, among them assembly members. Deputies in Panama thus exhibit certain behaviors that, though not predicted in the literature, are nevertheless evident in some liberal democracies where those informal institutions also operate. The members of Panama's assembly, for example, seek reelection as a means to advance their political careers—as theorized by the scholarship—but also to get rich and ensure freedom from prosecution. To obtain reelection, they distribute patronage—as theories of legislators' behavior predict they should—but also buy votes more directly (sometimes actually purchasing them for cash), switch parties, and manipulate elections. These behaviors, in turn, have clear consequences for the quality of representation because—among other effects—they distort the link between representatives and their constituents, which is essential for the proper functioning of the democratic system. For these reasons, as noted above, it is interesting and useful to study the political behavior of Panama's deputies.

Yet another reason to focus on Panama is that even though it qualifies as a liberal democracy, the country's assembly politics have not received much systematic attention in scholarly circles. In-depth studies of Panama's assembly since the transition to democracy are, indeed, scarce. A pioneering work on representation, focusing on political parties and the Legislative Assembly up to the 1994 elections, is the unpublished doctoral thesis of Italo Antinori Bolaños, who later became the country's first ombudsman. His comprehensive volume on Panamanian constitutional history also deals with the assembly's design, functions, and shortcomings (Antinori Bolaños 1995, 2000).

Alvarado (1999), Bernal (2004), González Marcos (2004), and González Montenegro and Rodríguez Robles (2001), among others, focus on additional design features of the chamber. Brown Araúz (2002, 2005, 2010), Franco (2001), Freidenberg (2010), García Diez (2003), Otero Felipe (2006, 2008), Sánchez González (1996), and Valdés Escoffery (2006b) address aspects of the party system and electoral issues relevant to the assembly since the removal of the military regime. A chapter in the three-volume *Historia general de Panamá,* composed in commemoration of Panama's centennial, explores more directly the configuration and work of the assembly in the hundred years following the foundation of the republic in 1903 (Sánchez González 2004). In recent years the *Elites Parlamentarias* initiative at the University of Salamanca (Spain) has collected and analyzed information on Panama's deputies as part of the Institute of Ibero-America's ongoing research on Latin American politics. Even so, many aspects of representation in the country remain understudied.

Political representation in Panama thus provides a fertile field for data gathering and subsequent cross-national comparative analysis. Such exercises hold promise for theory enhancement, which renewed interest in democracy and democratic development has stimulated in recent decades. They can also contribute to institutional reform and policy initiatives to strengthen democracy and ensure that the benefits of good government reach the broadest possible segments of the population.

Overview of the Book

This book achieves its objectives—examining the behavior of Panama's deputies, underscoring the differences between this behavior and the predictions of theory, and assessing the ways in which representatives' actions affect the democratic system—through comparative analysis. The study contrasts the political behavior of individual assembly members in 1984–2009. This task entails a scrutiny of 309 cases (that is, assembly members), representing eighteen political parties, over a twenty-five-year period.

In an effort to determine the effects of changing institutional features on the behavior of representatives, the study also undertakes historical institutional analysis. It compares members' actions under military dictatorship (1984–89), during the transitional period (1989–94), and under liberal democracy (1994–2009). It contrasts behaviors exhibited during the administrations of four military-appointed executives (in 1984–89)[13] as well as under Presidents Guillermo Endara (PPAN, 1989–94), Ernesto Pérez Balladares (PRD, 1994–99), Mireya Moscoso (PPAN, 1999–2004), Martín Torrijos (PRD, 2004–9), and Ricardo Martinelli (CD, 2009–14).

To the extent that it is possible in a case study, the book engages in cross-national comparisons that contrast the behavior of the members of the Panamanian assembly with the actions of representatives elsewhere.

In this endeavor, I compare Panama to (1) all other liberal democracies worldwide (states classified as "free" by Freedom House in 2008); and (2) the Latin American republics classified as electoral democracies by Freedom House in 2008 (that is, all "free" and "partly free" countries in the region).[14] On occasion, the project engages in more specific comparisons with the United States, the model for Latin America's presidential democracies, and other liberal or electoral democracies. Comparisons with Chile, especially in the descriptive sections (chapters 2 and 5), are drawn from my research at the Kellogg Institute at the University of Notre Dame in spring 2010.

The book is divided in two parts. Part one focuses on institutions, which in the framework employed here provide a partial explanation for the political behavior of assembly members. Chapter 1 examines the notion of political representation, representative assemblies generally, and the Panamanian chamber particularly, providing a historical background of the assembly. Chapter 2 looks at the party system in Panama and offers a profile of its members. Chapter 3 addresses certain formal institutions that influence representatives' behavior in Panama: the electoral system, with a special focus on seat allocation rules; district size; and the balance of power between the executive and the assembly. Chapter 4 deals with three informal institutions: systemic corruption, impunity, and clientelism. These formal and informal institutions allow representatives to pursue other ends besides just reelection (or political advancement) and encourage different means for gaining reelection. The formal and informal institutions dealt with in part one constitute what in political science terminology are referred to as "explanatory variables," or those factors that purport to explain the behaviors addressed in part two.

The second part of the book focuses on the three main goals exhibited by Panama's assembly members. While they are dealt with in separate chapters, it should be noted that these objectives are not exclusive. Quite the contrary: in the Panamanian scenario, they may be complementary. In other words, political advancement through reelection assists some representatives' efforts to continue seeking rents and remain free from prosecution, or becoming rich helps some assembly members finance their reelection campaigns. As shown in chapter 6, the allocation of *partidas circuitales,* or constituency funds, to legislators until 2001, which allowed some representatives to increase their rents and fund successful bids for reelection, illustrates the frequently complementary nature of these goals.

Chapters 5, 6, and 7 examine representatives' interest in political advancement through reelection. The fifth chapter describes the reelectoral scenario in Panama and places it in comparative perspective. Chapter 6 examines the role of patronage in procuring reelection. Patronage is one strategy the literature points out as helpful in contributing to representatives' reelection. In Panama, however, it encompasses dimensions unforeseen by theorists of representatives' behavior. Chapter 7 focuses on party switching and electoral manipulation, behaviors that the literature has not usually addressed as successful tactics for achieving reelection but that are used by Panama's assembly members.

Chapters 8 through 11 examine specific objectives of members of Panama's assembly that are not generally covered in the literature—such as personal enrichment and a desire to remain free from prosecution—and a number of behaviors these goals trigger. The motivation to get rich generates legal and illegal actions by assembly members. Chapters 8 and 9 examine legal attempts at enrichment. Chapter 10 provides examples of illegal actions toward the same objective—among them vote selling by deputies, such as in the CEMIS case mentioned at the beginning of this introduction. Chapter 11 scrutinizes seat holders' quest to ensure freedom from prosecution. The book concludes with a summary of findings as well as a reflection on the effects of assembly members' behavior on the quality of democratic representation and the prospects for further democratization of Panama's precarious liberal democracy. Appendices A through T provide supplementary information in support of the book's arguments and findings, including a list of sources and other persons consulted.

PART I

Institutions

## CHAPTER 1

Political Representation
and Representative Assemblies

The individuals on whose behavior we focus were elected to exercise political representation, a constitutional role of significant relevance in liberal democracies. These individuals exercised that role as members of representative assemblies. Accordingly, it is appropriate to give some theoretical context to the notion of political representation, the functions performed by representative assemblies, and the motivations of representatives before providing background information on the Panamanian assembly and a profile of its members.

Political Representation and Its Significance
for the Democratic Regime

The relevance of assemblies and representatives derives substantially from the significance of representation for liberal democracy. The notion of representation has been aptly dealt with by Hannah Pitkin (1967, 221–22), who defines "political representation" as "primarily a public, institutionalized arrangement involving many people and groups, and operating in the complex ways of large-scale social arrangements." It implies a "substantive acting for others" requiring "independent action in the interest of the governed, in a manner at least potentially responsive to them, yet not normally in conflict with their wishes." Political representation, therefore, is a public, generally formal arrangement, entailing action for—and accountable to—a specific and defined constituency. The public, formal nature of political representation contrasts sharply with the private, informal nature of systemic corruption, impunity, and particularism and its offshoots, including clientelism.

As noted by Dahl (1971, 169–70) the idea of representation or government through representatives formulated in the eighteenth century was key to the establishment of modern democracy. Before the concept of democratic representation was devised, democracy had been exercised directly by citizens in small political communities, an impossibility in the large nation-states that emerged in the modern era. By assigning the tasks of government to a small proportion of the political community through democratic elections, however, representation solved the problem of "how to combine democracy with the large state."

In another major work, Dahl (1989, 28–30) provides more insight into one of the most momentous discoveries of the Age of Enlightenment:

> In the eighteenth century, writers began to see what the Levellers had seen earlier, that by joining the democratic idea of rule by the people to the non-democratic practice of representation, democracy could take on a wholly new form and dimension. . . . Within a few generations of Montesquieu and Rousseau, representation was widely accepted by democrats and republicans as a solution that eliminated the ancient limits on the size of democratic states and transformed democracy from a doctrine suitable only for small and rapidly vanishing city-states to one applicable to the large nation-states of the modern age.

Among the authors who inspired Dahl's reflections on representation is John Stuart Mill, whose celebrated *Considerations on Representative Government* (1861/1958) endeavored to persuade the public about the convenience and superiority of government through elected representatives. As one of Mill's commentators has written, in chapter 3 of the *Consid-*

erations ("That the Ideally Best Form of Government Is Representative Government") the British philosopher argued that "The greatest benefits to a people are provided by a form of government where sovereignty is located in the entire community and every citizen performs a public function." In this sense, "The ultimate aim would be participation by all in the sovereign power. But as a practical matter, self-government is an impossible goal. Hence the ideally best form is representative government," defined by Mill as a system "where the whole people exercise the sovereign power through their elected deputies" (Shields 1958, xii).

Democratic Representation and Good Government

The belief that democratic representation provided a mechanism to assign the tasks of government to the best and brightest in the polity was yet another reason why the practice gained acceptance among constitution builders in the eighteenth and nineteenth centuries. Foremost among the exponents of this view was John Madison, who saw representation as a mechanism to improve popular government. Madison's aim, indeed, was to devise and promote a system that would elect "proper guardians of the public weal." "The aim of every political constitution," he wrote, "is, or ought to be, first to obtain for rulers men who possess most wisdom to discern, and most virtue to pursue, the common good of the society; and in the next place, to take the most effectual precautions for keeping them virtuous whilst they continue to hold their public trust" (Madison, Hamilton, and Jay 1987, *The Federalist,* no. 57; qtd. in Epstein 1984, 154).

For purely logical reasons, representative government was, in Madison's view, the means to democratically achieve the ancient aristocratic ideal of government by the few most virtuous individuals for the benefit of the community. Representative democracy was superior to "pure" or direct democracy because the latter system, by requiring the participation in government of every member of the political community, opened the door to the imposition of opinions (and bad public policy) by unworthy types that inevitably exist in every society. Elections in representative democracies acted as a filter against the intentions of those unworthy types. Thus, through public debate and the requirements of candidate accountability, virtue would shine and wickedness be exposed. To achieve his purpose Madison not only favored representation but, furthermore, large electoral units:

> As each representative will be chosen by a greater number of citizens in the large than in the small republic, it will be more difficult for unworthy candidates to practise with success the vicious arts, by which elections are too often carried; and the suffrages of the people being more free,[1] will be more likely to centre in men who possess the most attractive merit, and the most diffusive and established characters. (Madison, Hamilton, and Jay 1987, *The Federalist*, no. 10)

Writing toward the end of World War I, when the dangers of bureaucratic authoritarianism and totalitarianism first loomed on the horizon, Max Weber (1918/1978) emphasized the republican notion of government by the most talented politicians that had been supported by Madison and the U.S. founders over a century before.[2] Weber advocated the development of a "suitable corps" of politicians—individuals of high political caliber—through the expansion of representative government and, particularly, of the oversight functions of the assembly. He envisioned for Germany a democratic government based on a proactive representative assembly that would ensure transparency in public affairs and preserve individual liberty, while constituting an incentive system that attracted political talent and directed it usefully, to the benefit of the community. "Only a working, not a merely speech-making parliament," he wrote, "can provide the ground for the growth and selective ascent of genuine leaders, not merely demagogic talents. A working parliament, however, is one which supervises the administration by continuously sharing its work" (1416).

The Purpose of Representative Assemblies

Functional representative assemblies are, therefore, a basic pillar of liberal democracy. According to democratic theory, assemblies represent the polity—that is, they act for the collectivity—in the fulfillment of essential political functions. Although these functions vary from one con-stitutional setting to another, at a minimum all representative assemblies constitute "an arena of public debate," as Mill (1861/1958) viewed them or, as expressed by another student of the organization, "public forums for the discussion of major issues, an important function in democracies" (Loewenberg 1995, 736).

In their study of policymaking in Latin America, Stein et al. (2005, 141) are more explicit about this function when they state that "the na-tional legislature is the most natural arena for the discussion, negotiation, and enforcement of political agreements. Legislatures include broader representation than the executive branch, and as such they may serve as an arena for inter-temporal political agreements." These views cap-ture the role of assemblies as the main formally institutionalized con-tributor to peaceful conflict resolution and consensus formation through civilized and altruistic debate. Representative assemblies thus provide—in theory—the classic setting for deliberation, a dimension of democ-racy that plays a fundamental role in sustaining a high-quality regime (Benhabib 1996).

In all liberal democracies representative assemblies also engage in the process of elaborating legislation, but the magnitude of assembly in-volvement in lawmaking varies from one setting to another. In some countries most legislation originates in the representative assembly, while in others most bills originate in the executive and the competence of the congress or parliament in certain areas—such as the budget—is re-stricted (Loewenberg 1995; Shugart and Carey 1992, 148–52). But in all democracies representative assemblies exercise some lawmaking func-tion, whose origins may be traced to the ancient Roman private law prin-ciple of "that which affects everyone should be approved by everyone," taken into the canon law of medieval Catholicism and thence extended to the secular world (Finer 1997, 1030). As the representative of the whole nation, the assembly must, at a minimum, approve the laws to which all the members of the community are subject; so holds this basic principle of fairness that at an early stage became part of the Western un-derstanding of democracy.

Representative assemblies also "watch and control," another func-tion identified by Mill (1861/1958). In other words, they represent the nation in the supervision of other branches of government, especially the executive. This function, generally known as *oversight*, stems from aged notions of separation and balance of power (as laid out by Plato, Aristotle, and Polybius, among others) that crystallized into modern democratic theory during the eighteenth century through the writings of Montesquieu and the U.S. founders, notably Madison (Lakoff 1996, 78, 79; Madison, Hamilton, and Jay, *The Federalist,* nos. 10 and 51; Sabine 1973, 514). As the lawmaking capacity of representative assemblies in democracies progressively dwindles due to the ever-increasing complexities and technicalities of the legislative process, the oversight function acquires increased importance (Cox 1987; Loewenberg 1995). Max Weber (1918/1978) argued that this function is all the more significant in the modern mass bureaucratized state, where supervision of the administration by a democratically elected representative assembly constitutes the principal democratic means of safeguarding individual freedoms.

This point merits a brief reflection in the context of modern politics. Various avenues are available for oversight in contemporary democratic regimes, including independent action by magistrates, prosecutors, comptrollers, regional or municipal councils, political parties, civil society organizations, the media, and individual citizens. In a liberal democracy, however, only a popularly elected chief executive and assembly can legitimately claim to represent the entire nation. Precisely because the actions of the chief executive's administration are the object of such oversight (and because the deliberative chamber provides a broader basis for representation than a popularly chosen executive), a democratically elected assembly constitutes the primary democratic channel for supervising the administration.[3]

Deliberation, lawmaking, and oversight are valuable functions that democratic theory assigns to representative assemblies. But deliberative chambers perform other tasks as well. In parliamentary regimes, they select and sustain the government, whose members are normally drawn from the leadership of the dominant parliamentary parties (Lijphart 1999). In many liberal democracies, constituents expect representatives' help in solving problems in their districts. This activity, known as "constituency service," takes up a significant amount of assembly members' time (Cain et al. 1987; see Perea 2008 for a brief view from Panama). In all political systems where they exist, representative assemblies "attract public attention to politics" (Loewenberg 1995, 745).

Furthermore—as explained by a renowned scholar of representative bodies—assemblies "recruit and train political leaders. They provide governments with crucial information about what the public wants and what it will accept, and this affects the formulation of public policies and budgets." Last but hardly least, deliberative chambers help structure and solidify the political community by "defining the constituencies of the nation, linking these constituencies to the central government, training a political leadership as well as an opposition, and providing a symbol" of the state (Loewenberg 1995, 745). This task is particularly significant in newly independent or democratizing polities.

To sum up, representative assemblies are a fundamental institution of liberal democracy because, through the legal fiction known as representation, they allow the participation of the whole community in such important democratic tasks as peacefully sorting out political conflict, lawmaking, overseeing the administration, furnishing information about and attracting attention to politics, incorporating the public into the political debate, training political leaders, and providing a symbol for the nation. Additionally, in parliamentary regimes, representative assemblies select and sustain the government. Through representation, moreover, the tasks of government can theoretically be assigned to the most competent members of the community—at least according to the views of John Madison and Max Weber. In practice, as we shall see in Panama, political representation does not always yield this republican expectation.

The Motivations of Representatives

How well representative assemblies fulfill the important functions assigned by democratic theory—deliberation, lawmaking, oversight, political socialization, leader recruitment, information supply, and nation building—depends, to a significant degree, on the behavior of their members. Personal motivations (assumed in the literature) inspire this behavior, which institutional constraints and incentives shape into political action. Clearly, some institutional settings encourage behaviors that sustain and promote liberal democracy while others do not.

Theories of legislators' behavior assume that representatives are motivated by self-interest. Within this framework, the main motivation of members of deliberative chambers is the advancement of their political careers in the short or medium term. The specific objectives that fulfill this motivation vary according to the institutional setting. Where permitted (especially in the United States), reelection is a clear objective (Arnold 1979; Cain et al. 1987; Fenno 1973; Mayhew 1974; McCubbins and Rosenbluth 1995). Where reelection is not permitted or its possibilities are constitutionally limited, appointment or election to other political office—or promotion within the party ranks—constitute the principal goals of representatives (Carey 1996; Cox 1987; Katz 1980; Mainwaring 1999; Morgenstern 1998; Samuels 1998). Each actor individually calculates the means toward these objectives on the basis of self-interest and the institutional framework within which he or she operates.

The notion that institutions in part determine the actions of representatives derives from a standard definition of institutions as "rules and procedures that structure social interaction by constraining and enabling actors' behavior" (Helmke and Levitsky 2006, 5). The assumption that institutions shape politics, noted centuries ago by Montesquieu and held today by proponents of New Institutionalism, forms part of the literature on legislators' behavior. Montesquieu (cited in Putnam 1993, 26) observed that at the birth of new states, "leaders mold institutions, whereas afterwards institutions mold leaders." In his study of the impact of institutional change on political performance in Italy between the 1970s and the 1990s, Robert Putnam (1993, 7–8)—one of the leading scholars employing a New Institutionalist approach to political analysis—wrote:

> The rules and standard operating procedures that make up institutions leave their imprint on political outcomes by structuring political behavior. Outcomes are not simply reducible to the billiard-ball interaction of individuals nor to the intersection of broad social forces. Institutions influence outcomes because they shape actors' identities, power, and strategies.

Relevant institutional features that according to theorists help shape representatives' behavior include the electoral system, term limits, party discipline, relations between the executive and the representative assembly, the availability of political resources, and the rules for their distribution. Presuming rationality and depending on the institutional framework in which representatives operate, students of the topic predict that assembly members will seek reelection or career advancement through advertising, credit claiming, position taking, supporting their parties, distributing patronage, and accommodating the bureaucracy, among other means (Arnold 1979; Cain et al. 1987; Cox 1987; Mayhew 1974).

These theories of legislators' behavior, chiefly based on the U.S. experience, have proved an effective predictor of representatives' behavior in liberal democracies where formal institutionalization prevails (Cain et al. 1987; Morgenstern et al. 1998; Samuels 1998). But the universe of democracy includes cases where formal institutionalization does not reign supreme in all aspects of politics. In many liberal democracies, informal institutionalization operates in various spheres of political activity. These countries are liberal democracies—no doubt—because their leadership positions are periodically renewed through what according to basic criteria are considered free and fair elections, the archetypal formal institution of the democratic system, and because political rights and civil liberties are in place. At the same time, certain informal institutions—"socially shared rules, usually unwritten, that are created, communicated, and enforced outside officially sanctioned channels" (Helmke and Levitsky 2006, 5)—may be important predictors of political outcomes.

In some liberal democracies, informal norms and practices (for example, systemic corruption, impunity, clientelism) may shape political behavior more than the prescriptions of codified rules. Moreover, certain democratic institutions (such as, for example, control of the armed forces by elected officials or fair and equal access to justice) might be deficient or wholly nonfunctional. In addition, political action may frequently be oriented more toward the satisfaction of particular interests than toward promoting some consensus-based notion of the public good (O'Donnell 1996).

Because both formal and informal institutions can determine the behavior of political actors, representatives in countries where significant measures of informal institutionalization exist cannot be expected to behave in the same way as do their peers operating where formal institutionalization generally prevails. Moreover, diverse behaviors by representatives are bound to produce different effects on the performance of democratic functions, such as representation. Despite these predictable discrepancies, scholars of representative assemblies (and other organizations and procedures) in countries where there are important pockets of informal institutionalization have tended to address their subject with frameworks built to explain behavior in formally institutionalized settings (Helmke and Levitsky 2006, 1). In all likelihood, the literature has tended to neglect informal institutional incentives on the behavior of representatives because of the relative difficulty of obtaining appropriate information, the analytical hurdles involved in interpreting such data, and the general expectation among researchers that formal structures suffice to explain the actions of politicians.

Panama's Assembly in Historical Perspective

Because this book illustrates the relevance of these issues with regard to the political behavior of Panama's assembly members, some background information on the Panamanian assembly and its deputies is in order. As in the other Latin American republics, the representative chamber has a long tradition in Panama. The first popularly elected assembly to represent the people of the isthmus convened on March 1, 1841, after the establishment of the independent State of Panama in 1840.[4] The chamber actively pursued its representative functions and introduced legislation to regulate the affairs of the new state, including a constitution (independent Panama's first fundamental law) approved on June 8, 1841 (Méndez 1980). Though the first Panamanian republic was short-lived—the isthmus rejoined New Granada (present-day Colombia) in December 1841—by the early nineteenth century representative government under a republican constitution formed an integral part of the mindset of Panama's political sectors.

When the Colombian Congress approved the establishment of an autonomous state of Panama under a federal regime in 1853, a state assembly was established to represent the interests of the people of the isthmus. The federal arrangement remained in place until 1886, when the Conservative "regeneration" led by Rafael Núñez declared Colombia (including Panama) a unitary republic consisting of "departments" rather than autonomous states.[5] Despite efforts toward centralization in Bogotá (which the isthmus's politically relevant sectors strongly opposed), the Colombian constitution of 1886 created "departmental assemblies" with limited representative functions in the main political divisions of the country, including the isthmus of Panama.

The National Assembly, 1904–68

Upon secession from Colombia on November 3, 1903, Panama's Provisional Government Junta summoned a Constituent Convention, whose members were popularly elected in December 1903 and met in February 1904 to draft the republic's constitution. After approving the 1904 charter and electing one of its members—physician Manuel Amador Guerrero—as the country's chief executive for the 1904–8 term, the convention transformed itself into Panama's National Assembly, serving in that capacity for two years (1904–6). Starting in 1906, elections to fill the chamber's seats were held nonconcurrently with presidential elections, every four years, until 1918. In order to make both elections concurrent, a constitutional reform approved in 1918 prolonged the term of the assembly elected that year until 1924.

In total, there were seventeen assembly terms during the old republic (1904–68). The number of National Assembly members changed throughout the 1904–68 period owing to amendments to the electoral law (see table 1.1). Membership was constitutionally established as a proportion of total population (determined at each ten-year census), but adjustments were periodically made to avoid large increases in the number of deputies (Fábrega and Boyd Galindo 1981; Sánchez González 2004).

In 1941 a new constitution approved through a plebiscite prolonged the terms of the president and deputies to six years. The new basic law extended the terms of President Arnulfo Arias and the National Assembly, elected in 1940, until 1947. After Arias's removal in 1941, his extraconstitutional successor, Minister of Government and Justice Ricardo de La Guardia, faced rising popular agitation against his de facto rule and submissive relationship to the United States. As a solution to the political crisis confronting the country, on December 29, 1944, La Guardia revoked the 1941 constitution, dissolved the National Assembly, and

Table 1.1. Terms and Number of Members in Panama's National Assembly, 1904–68

Term	Number of Deputies	Term	Number of Deputies
1904–6	32	1940–44	42
1906–10	28	1945–48	51
1910–14	28	1948–52	42
1914–18	33	1952–56	53
1918–24	33	1956–60	53
1924–28	46	1960–64	53
1928–32	46	1964–68	42
1932–36	32	1968–72[a]	42
1936–40	32		

Source: Alemán 1982; Asamblea Nacional de Panamá 1904–40; Callejas 1933; Carles Oberto 1968; Castillero Reyes 1931; Fábrega and Boyd Galindo 1981; Pippin 1964; Pizzurno and Araúz 1996.

[a] Cut short by the military coup of October 11, 1968.

convoked the election of a constitutional convention. Elections to this representative assembly were held in May 1945 and the convention began its activities on June 15. Except for the formative period between November 1903 and February 1904, this brief, six-month interruption (December 1944–June 1945) was the only time between the foundation of the republic and the 1968 military coup when a representative assembly did not exist in Panama.[6]

After convening in June 1945, the constituent convention dismissed La Guardia and elected Enrique A. Jiménez, a prominent Liberal politician, as provisional chief executive until 1948. Subsequent to the enactment of a new constitution, on March 1, 1946, the convention rescinded its constituent powers and transformed itself into a National Assembly exercising normal legislative authority in accordance with the constitution of 1946, which reinstated the four-year term for president and deputies. In July 1948 this same assembly resolved to revert into a constituent convention; it assumed broad powers and rejected the results of the presidential election held the previous May, which Arnulfo Arias had won (see chapter 7). This coup failed when the Supreme Court declared the assembly had abused its authority and revoked the chamber's July 1948 resolution. A new assembly, elected in May, was inaugurated on October 1, 1948 (Asamblea Nacional de Panamá 1948/1998; Flores Cedeño 2008; Moscoso et al. 1945, 13–17; Pizzurno and Araúz 1996, 314–17, 321–24, 343; Sánchez González 2004).

Yet another attempt, albeit unsuccessful, to close the National Assembly occurred in May 1951, when President Arnulfo Arias issued a decree replacing the constitution of 1946 with the 1941 charter and dissolving the representative chamber. The public outcry generated by the decree forced the president to repeal his decision two days later. The assembly then voted to impeach Arias for violating the constitution. After a nine-day trial, the chamber removed him from office on May 25, 1951 (Flores Cedeño 2008; Fábrega and Boyd Galindo 1981, 340–45; Pizzurno and Araúz 1996, 369–73).

The National Assembly continued functioning, generally within constitutional parameters, for the ensuing decade and a half. In 1955 the chamber impeached and dismissed President José Ramón Guizado after a majority of deputies accused him of taking part in the conspiracy to assassinate his predecessor, José Antonio Remón. The impeachment proceedings, based on false accusations, contributed to undermining the organization's reputation. In March 1968 the National Assembly voted to impeach and sack President Marco Robles for manipulating the electoral process. The National Guard, however, dispatched a regiment commanded by Omar Torrijos, a lieutenant colonel in the force with close ties to U.S. military intelligence,[7] to prevent the deputies from installing Vice-President Max Delvalle. Robles remained in power with National Guard support after a municipal judge declared the assembly's actions unconstitutional. He would be the last popularly elected chief executive to serve out his term until the transition to democracy in 1989–1994 (Pérez Liñán 2007; Ricord 1983; Zúñiga 1980).[8]

On October 11, 1968, the National Guard overthrew Robles's successor, Arnulfo Arias, who had initiated his third period in office only ten days before. The guard acted against Arias after he took steps to undermine the influence and prerogatives of the officer corps, including their participation in illegal activities providing significant rents to the upper echelons of the force, such as "prostitution, gambling, and a little drug trafficking, mainly to cater to American military personnel," according to Naylor (1999, 215). President Robles's Liberal Party also complained that Arias had manipulated the election of deputies and municipal councilors, replacing winners with losing candidates loyal to the new chief executive. The October coup signaled the end of the old regime's assembly, which the guard immediately closed (Ricord 1983). As a symbol of the break with the "oligarchic republic" that the military claimed to have eliminated, the National Assembly archives were later set on fire (Zúñiga 2002).

The Assembly of County Representatives, 1972–84

In addition to abolishing the National Assembly, the guard officialdom implemented other repressive measures, including the suspension of the 1946 charter's bill of rights, the abolition of all political parties, and the subordination of all judges and prosecutors to the military-controlled executive, thus effectively removing all vestiges of a republican constitution and establishing an authoritarian regime. The National Guard appointed a "Provisional Government Junta," headed by the two top-ranking army officers, which took over the country's administration and legislated through cabinet decrees until 1972. In December 1968 Omar Torrijos assumed control of the National Guard, the locus of power, with Boris Martínez (the coup's initiator) as his deputy. In March 1969 Torrijos discharged Martínez, exiling him to the United States. Torrijos would remain Panama's uncontested ruler until his death in 1981 (Guevara Mann 1996, 107; Janson Pérez 1997, 172–77; Junta Provisional de Gobierno 1969; Sánchez 2007, 143–45).

In 1972 Torrijos introduced a new constitution, providing for a 505-member Assembly of County Representatives. The membership of this new assembly represented each of the country's counties (*corregimientos*), Panama's smallest political division, below both municipal districts and provinces. Despite the regime's rhetoric regarding devolution of lawmaking power to "the people," the sphere of legislative activity of the new assembly was highly constrained. From 1972 to 1984, when the system was in operation, representatives met annually for only one month.

They were empowered to (1) elect the president and vice-president of the republic once every six years;[9] (2) approve or reject international treaties negotiated by the executive;[10] (3) declare war or establish peace; (4) approve or reject reforms to the country's political subdivisions as proposed by the executive; (5) grant amnesty to political prisoners; and (6) write the assembly's own rules of procedure. Actual responsibility for issuing laws was vested in the executive-appointed Legislative Council, whose members were designated by Torrijos, in accordance with article 277 of the 1972 constitution (Fábrega and Boyd Galindo 1981, 7–97; Labrut 1982, 154; Priestley 1986, 76).[11] The Assembly of County Representatives, therefore, does not qualify as a liberal democratic deliberative chamber.

The Legislative Assembly

The approval of a constitutional amendment in a 1983 referendum meant the replacement of the Assembly of County Representatives and the Legislative Council with a popularly elected Legislative Assembly in 1984. Introduced under military rule and dominated by the armed forces and PRD throughout its first term (1984–89), the new unicameral chamber has remained Panama's legislative branch until the present. While the Legislative Assembly would engage in somewhat more substantial activities than its immediate predecessor, up to the dictatorship's demise in 1989 the military continued to determine the breadth of the chamber's activities and the composition of its membership. Methods employed toward these goals included electoral fraud (see chapter 7) as well as bribery and coercion of legislators.

This book focuses on the activities of the individuals proclaimed by the country's electoral authority (the Electoral Tribunal) as elected members of the assembly since 1984 and the impact of their behavior on the democratic regime. Between 1984 and 2004 the members of Panama's assembly were chosen in direct popular elections in their constituencies through party nomination. Independents ran for the first time in 2009, as authorized in the constitutional reform of 2004 (which also restored the Panamanian chamber's original name of "National Assembly" and

Table 1.2. Number of Seats in Panama's Assembly, 1984–2009

Period	Number of Seats
1984–89	67
1989–94	67
1994–99	72
1999–2004	71
2004–9	79
2009–14	71
Total	427

Source: Tribunal Electoral 1984a, 1984b, 1991a, 1991b, 1994b, 1994c, 1999b, 1999c, 2004a, 2004b, 2009a.

its members' designation as "deputies"). Starting in 1984 and as of the writing of this volume (May 2010), six general elections have taken place in Panama: two under the military regime (1984, 1989) and four after the dictatorship's downfall (1994, 1999, 2004, 2009). Among other positions, these elections have filled 427 seats in the Panamanian assembly, as detailed in table 1.2.

Unlike the U.S. Congress and other representative assemblies, between 1984 and 2009 the Panamanian chamber did not have a set number of seats. Prior to the 2004 constitutional reform, the fundamental law required recalculating the number of chamber seats after each ten-year census (chapter 3 explains the electoral system in more depth). Since 2009 the assembly has had a fixed number of deputies, set at seventy-one in the 2004 reform.

Panama's Assembly in Comparative Perspective

Panama has one of the smallest deliberative chambers among the world's eighty-nine liberal democracies.[12] According to appendix B, the average current membership of representative assemblies (or lower houses in the case of bicameral organizations) in all "free" countries in 2008–10 was 177, well above Panama's 71. Appendix C shows that among Latin America's electoral democracies, only Costa Rica has a smaller assembly, with 57 members in 2010. The average membership in Latin America's unicameral congresses (or lower chambers) was 165.

In addition to having one of the smaller assemblies, Panama's ratio of representatives to total population is low (1:49,000), partly due to the country's small population (an estimated 3.5 million in 2010). This statistic means that, if the total number of deputies is divided by total population, in 2010 Panama had one deputy for every 49,000 inhabitants. Among the group of all "free" independent states, the average ratio is 1:98,000, and among the Latin American republics, the average ratio is 1:131,000. In Latin America only Uruguay has a lower ratio (1:34,000). In theory, a lower ratio suggests a closer connection between representatives and constituents. In conjunction with other structural conditions, however, this closer "connectivity" may also provide an ideal breeding ground for clientelism.[13]

The duration of the mandate of Panama's deputies is longer than the average term among both the world's liberal democracies and the Latin American electoral democracies (see table 1.3). Since the constitutional reform of 1983, the members of Panama's assembly serve five-year terms. The average term in all "free" countries and Latin American republics is four years, with the duration of the mandate ranging from two to five years in both subsets of independent states (see appendices B and C). A longer mandate reduces citizens' opportunities for holding representatives accountable at the ballot box and, as a result, can encourage behaviors by deputies that are deleterious to democracy.

Summary

This chapter has taken us on a journey from the more abstract to the more concrete. We began by examining the notion of political representation and its significance for the democratic regime. We saw how democratic representation is the legal fiction, developed in the eighteenth century, allowing democracy to operate in the modern mass state. Theoretically,

Table 1.3. Some Comparative Statistics of the Membership of Representative Assemblies in Liberal Democracies and Latin American Electoral Democracies, 2008–10

	Current Number of Members	*Population Per Member*	*Length of Term (Years)*
Liberal democracies (average)	177	98,000	4
Latin American electoral democracies (average)	165	131,000	4
Panama	71	49,000	5

Source: Freedom House 2009a; IPU 2010a; U. N. Population Division 2009.

in a liberal democratic constitution no organ of government provides broader representation than the deliberative assembly, whose members are responsible for carrying out essential tasks such as legislating, overseeing the conduct of public administration, serving as a training ground for politicians and government officials, symbolizing the nation, and peacefully sorting out social conflicts, particularly through debate, consensus building, and negotiation.

How well assemblies carry out these functions depends, to a significant degree, on the behavior of their members. This behavior is influenced by personal motivations, which are in turn shaped, at least in part, by institutional constraints and incentives. Theories of legislators' behavior tell us that representatives are essentially motivated by self-interest (as are most political actors). This book argues that the means through which representatives pursue self-interest depend on the characteristics of political institutionalization in the arenas where they operate. Formal institutionalization—that is, a close fit between codified norms and actual behaviors—discourages the satisfaction of self-interest through illegal activities. But in many liberal democracies, formal institutions coexist with informal institutions, including such practices as systemic corruption, impunity, and clientelism. Where these socially accepted norms subvert or prevail over codified rules, representatives (and politicians generally) have higher incentives to engage in illicit behaviors in their desire to materialize their aspirations.

After laying out these theoretical considerations, chapter 1 presented relevant information about the Panamanian assembly and its members, whose behavior illustrates the main arguments made in the book. The assembly has a long trajectory in Panama—certainly not as long as in Europe, where representative chambers originated in the Middle Ages, but as long as elsewhere in the region. Panama's first National Assembly met in 1841, during a brief spell of independent existence from Colombia (1840–41). After the foundation of the republic in 1903, the National Assembly operated continuously since 1904, except during a fleeting interruption in 1944–45, and when it was shut down by the National Guard after the 1968 coup.

In 1972 the military dictatorship created an Assembly of County Representatives, whose functions, however, do not fit the classic rendition of a representative chamber laid out at the beginning of the chapter. Its members served six-year terms. Twelve years later—as part of a strategy to provide a democratic image for a regime that, however, remained essentially authoritarian—the military dictatorship established a Legislative Assembly more along the lines of a classic congress than the Assembly of County Representatives. But, in contrast with the old republic's National Assembly, whose deputies held office for four years, the 1984 constitutional reform set legislators' terms at five years.

The following chapter continues the institutional focus with a historical and comparative look at Panama's party system. In 1984–2009 this system may be described as weakly institutionalized, in contrast with more stable ones in the region and among advanced liberal democracies. After describing the party system, chapter 2 provides a profile of Panama's assembly members. The exercise produces an image of the typical Panamanian deputy: a male party militant in his mid-forties representing an urban constituency; he does not belong to the traditional upper class or a political dynasty, he holds somewhat more conservative views than the rest of his Latin American peers, and he has a strong belief in a paternalistic state.

## CHAPTER 2

The Party System

Parties and Actors in Panama's Assembly

Since the individuals sitting during the period under scrutiny (1984–2009) were selected through party nomination, and since party affiliation is a classification tool traditionally and broadly used in political analysis (and is extensively employed in this book), it is opportune to devote some space to explaining the configuration of Panama's party system. The following sections provide a historical background, focusing on twentieth-century Panama's three main parties: the Liberal Party (and its derivations), Partido Panameñista (PPAN), and Partido Revolucionario Democrático (PRD). We then place the Panamanian party system in comparative perspective. In contrast with other systems in the region, Panama's party system may be characterized as weakly institutionalized, although since the transition to democracy (1989–94), it has shown signs of becoming more institutionalized.

From the final sections in chapter 2 emerges a profile of the typical Panamanian assembly member. This profile is based on an analysis of the age, gender, social origins, geographical provenance, and ideological views of Panama's deputies. Although these features do not represent powerful factors in the attempt to explain the behaviors addressed in this book, focusing on them is nevertheless useful to obtain a better image of the National Assembly and its members.

The Party System

Article 150 of the Panamanian constitution stipulates that deputies "will act in the interest of the nation and represent, in the National Assembly, their respective political parties and their constituents" (República de Panamá 2004).[1] In the five elections held between 1984 and 2004, only political parties were allowed to submit candidates for deputy. Independents were first allowed to run in 2009, as a result of the 2004 constitutional reform. Of a total of thirty officially recognized political groups participating in one or more elections between 1984 and 2009, eighteen had candidates proclaimed as elected members of the representative chamber. Appendix D lists the country's assembly parties in 1984–2009.

Liberalism, Personalism, and Factionalization

As in other Latin American republics, political parties first emerged in Panama in the mid-nineteenth century. Panama, as has been noted, was then part of New Granada (present-day Colombia); as a result, Colombian political institutions and practices, including the two-party system, transferred to the isthmus. Liberalism predominated among the politically relevant portions of Panama's society, including segments of the dominant merchant class, many intellectuals, and politically involved urban popular sectors. Writing in 1912, U.S. consul general Alban Snyder noted that "Panama has always been Liberal" (Szok 2001, 88n99).

The Conservative Party had a significantly smaller following, consisting of some sectors of the urban patriciate and the rural landowning class, the importance of which progressively diminished throughout the nineteenth century due to the growth of the commercial and transit economy (Figueroa Navarro 1982). During the Colombian civil conflagration known as the "War of the Thousand Days" (1899–1902), Panama was renowned as a Liberal stronghold. Liberal Party forces twice threatened Panama City and would have captured the isthmian capital from the Conservative departmental government had U.S. troops—intervening pursuant to the Treaty of Peace, Amity, Commerce, and Navigation signed with New Granada (Colombia) in 1846—not prevented them.[2]

Initially, a two-party system remained in place after Panama's secession from Colombia in 1903. As has been noted by several authors, however, on the isthmus politics were traditionally less ideological than in Colombia (Janson Pérez 1993; Ricord 1989). A lower premium on ideology and a preference for the Liberal Party among the more significant sectors explain the quick demise of the traditional Conservative Party (members of which headed the executive in 1904–10 and, briefly, in 1920). For all practical purposes, by 1910 the bipartisan system inherited from Colombia had broken down.

Together with a weak programmatic content, the absence of a strong adversary contributed to foment intense intraparty competition and strengthen *caudillismo*—the tradition of strong personalist leadership based on charismatic authority—within the Liberal camp. Among the emerging factions the more prominent rallied around Belisario Porras, a hero of the War of the Thousand Days; he was popularly elected president of Panama in 1912–16 and 1920–24 and caretaker executive in 1918–20. Considered the country's great modernizer, Porras also promoted the factionalization and personalization of Panama's politics (Arias Calderón 2003a, 2003b, 2003c). An expression of these latter tendencies was the rise of a multiparty system by the early 1930s. Several parties claiming to represent "true" liberalism emerged at the time, for example, the "Democratic," "Doctrinaire," "National," and "Renewal" Liberal parties. In actuality, these were factions formed by traditional or aspiring Liberal leaders.[3] Between 1948 and 1968 attempts to unify all parties claiming to represent the liberal ideology under the red banner of Partido Liberal Nacional were only partly successful. Despite this partitioning of Panamanian Liberalism, of the twenty-six chief executives serving between 1904 and 1968, sixteen were members of a Liberal party at the time they acceded to the presidency. Governments headed by Liberal executives ruled Panama for almost two-thirds of the "old regime" (1903–68), that is, for forty-two of the sixty-five-year period (Guevara Mann 2003).

We saw in chapter 1 that in 1969 the military regime abolished all political parties (Junta Provisional de Gobierno 1969), including Partido Liberal Nacional, some prominent members of which had supported the coup against President Arnulfo Arias. There was no formal party activity in the country for a decade, until the promulgation of a new electoral code in 1978 once again allowed political parties to organize and, ostensibly, compete for power in an electoral arena dominated by the military. Taking advantage of this aperture, a group of Liberals registered Partido Liberal in 1979.

In the schismatic tradition of Panamanian Liberalism, however, soon other parties claiming a Liberal heritage would file with the Electoral Tribunal: Movimiento Liberal Republicano Nacionalista (MOLIRENA, 1982), Partido Liberal Auténtico (PLA, 1988), Partido Liberal Republicano (LIBRE, 1994), and Partido Liberal Nacional (PLN, 1997). Partido Liberal and Partido Liberal Auténtico became extinct in 1994, when they failed to obtain sufficient votes to survive in that year's elections.[4] Followers of Partido Liberal Auténtico registered as Partido Liberal in 1996 but lost the registry in 1999 when the party did not meet the survival threshold. Followers of the original Partido Liberal (1979–94) re-registered in 2005 under their initial label but became extinct once more in 2009.

In 1984–2009 the Electoral Tribunal allocated 58 (or 14 percent) of the assembly's 427 seats to parties claiming Liberal heritage. From that perspective, one could argue that Liberalism still has a presence in the party system. However, the fact that the Liberal parties have failed to coalesce in one single entity and that splinter groups have taken opposing sides throughout the period, together with a general environment of ideological debility, considerably reduces historic Liberalism's impact on Panama's party politics.

Panameñismo *and the Challenge to Liberal Hegemony*

The 1930s saw not only the factionalization of the Liberal Party but also, as in other republics in the region, the rise of nationalist and populist challenges to liberal hegemony (Williamson 1992, 328–34, 346–49). Panama's Partido Panameñista (PPAN) is the current expression of the political movement founded at that time by Arnulfo Arias, whose

Doctrina Panameñista, enunciated in 1939, embraced nationalism and populism.

Arias, Panama's most notable *caudillo,* had founded his first party—Coalición Nacional Revolucionaria—a few years earlier (1934). In 1935 the group changed its name to Partido Nacional Revolucionario, which remained under Arias's leadership until 1941, when the *caudillo* was removed from the presidency of the republic and went into exile. Former supporters who shifted their loyalty away from Arias maintained control of the organization through the 1940s. Upon his return to Panama, Arias registered Partido Revolucionario Auténtico in 1948 and led it until he was again deposed from the national presidency in 1951. Once more, past associates appropriated the party machinery and in 1952 merged it with other organizations to form Coalición Patriótica Nacional, which supported the candidacy and subsequent administration of National Police Commandant José Antonio Remón (1952–55). In the meantime, while Arias was impeached, imprisoned, and stripped of his political rights, loyal adherents registered Partido Panameñista in early 1952. But the party did not do well in that year's May elections after Arias asked his followers to abstain from voting. The Electoral Board cancelled Partido Panameñista's registry after President Remón had a new electoral law passed through the National Assembly in 1953 that established the survival threshold at 20 percent of total votes cast in 1952.

Upon regaining his political rights, Arias re-registered Partido Panameñista in 1960. The party continued to operate under the *caudillo*'s leadership until 1968, when Arias was overthrown from the presidency a third time and once again expelled from the country (Conte Porras 1990; Pizzurno and Araúz 1996). In addition to persecuting, jailing, and exiling its leaders, the military regime suppressed Partido Panameñista and all other political parties in March 1969 (Junta Provisional de Gobierno 1969). The dictatorship permitted Arias's return to Panama in 1978. In 1983, before the regime let Arias register his party on yet another occasion, a group of former supporters appropriated the party name and labels, received official recognition as Partido Panameñista, and allied with the military regime in the 1984 elections. Arias's immense popularity still allowed him to enroll Partido Panameñista Auténtico (PPAN) as the standard bearer of the opposition in time for the electoral contest. But after the *caudillo*'s death in 1988, the military engineered one final takeover of his organization. This new usurpation resulted in a dismal performance for the party in the 1989 elections, after which it was declared extinct.

In the 1989 elections most of Arias's followers and opposition sympathizers chose the Christian Democratic Party (PDC) ticket to express their electoral preferences. Accordingly, PDC obtained the highest percentage of the vote for president and legislators in that year's elections (40 and 36 percent, respectively). Originally founded in 1960 (and "refounded" in 1979), PDC nominated Guillermo Endara (PPAN) as presidential candidate in 1989. MOLIRENA and PLA, which coalesced with PDC, also nominated Endara. Additionally, PDC (as did MOLIRENA and PLA) allowed some PPAN candidates for deputy to run on its ticket.[5]

Arnulfo Arias's supporters reorganized as Partido Arnulfista under the leadership of the *caudillo's* widow, Mireya Moscoso, in 1991. The party returned to its previous name, Partido Panameñista, in 2005 (Conte Porras 2004; Leis 1984; Linares Gutiérrez 1989; Tribunal Electoral 2008). The tortuous history of the party up to recent times serves to illustrate the convoluted nature of Panama's twentieth-century politics. In addition, this brief account reveals the long trajectory of Partido Panameñista in a setting characterized by ephemeral parties. Indeed, after Panama's factionalized and, currently, much depreciated Liberalism, *Panameñismo* is the country's second oldest political force. Two of its members— Guillermo Endara and Mireya Moscoso—served as chief executives following the overthrow of the military regime in 1989.[6] In 2009 the party supported the presidential candidacy of Ricardo Martinelli (CD), contributing significantly to his resounding victory with 19 percent of the total presidential vote (Tribunal Electoral 2009b). Moreover, in terms of assembly contingent size, it is the second largest party, following PRD. Of the 427 chamber seats in 1984–2009, the Electoral Tribunal allocated 83 (19 percent) to PPAN (see appendix D).

Partido Revolucionario Democrático: Panama's Dominant Party

To ensure "the irreversibility of the political process that began on 11 October 1968" as well as the continued control of the political system by his family and collaborators, in 1979 Omar Torrijos, Panama's military dictator, endorsed the formation of Partido Revolucionario Democrático (PRD) (Conte Porras 2004, 332). Modeled after Mexico's Partido Revolucionario Institucional (PRI), the party adopted the discourse of social democracy and affiliated with the Socialist International, alongside other prominent Latin American organizations such as Argentina's Radical Civic Union (UCR), Brazil's Democratic Labor Party (PDT), Chile's Socialist Party, Colombia's Liberal Party, Costa Rica's National Liberation Party (PLN), the Dominican Revolutionary Party (PRD), Nicaragua's Sandinista National Liberation Front (FSLN), Peru's Aprista Party (PAP), and Venezuela's Democratic Action (AD), in addition to Mexico's PRI (Socialist International 2008).[7]

Despite the social democratic rhetoric, PRD is not strongly ideological. Rather, it has shown great resilience in accommodating to the circumstances that better suit the party's power-seeking objectives. Since its founding and until the U.S. invasion of 1989, PRD served as the political arm of the military dictatorship, organizing support for the regime's leaders (including Omar Torrijos, Rubén Paredes, Manuel Noriega, and others) and filling many of the positions of Panama's bloated bureaucracy. Of the seven titular presidents in the military-controlled executive holding office between 1978 and 1989, five were PRD members.

After the displacement of the military regime, the party adapted to the country's new political conditions, winning the 1994 and 2004 presidential elections. In the period under review, it has received between 19 and 43 percent of the presidential vote. Its share of the assembly vote has oscillated between 19 and 38 percent and, in 1984–2009, the Electoral Tribunal allocated 177 (41 percent) of the 427 chamber seats to PRD (see appendices D and G). Based on this performance as well as on membership, the party qualifies as Panama's most substantial. Its 562,684 registered members as of February 28, 2010, represented about 16 percent of Panama's estimated total population of 3.5 million. At the same date, PPAN, its closest rival in terms of membership, had 243,600 adherents (Tribunal Electoral 2010).

Assembly Parties in 1984–2009

An assembly party is a political party that over the twenty-five-year timeframe had at least one candidate officially proclaimed by the Electoral

Tribunal as an assembly seat holder following an election. Appendix D reveals important information about Panama's eighteen assembly parties in 1984–2009. The first column indicates the party's acronym, in most cases the one officially used by the party, and the second column refers to the party's current official name. In some instances I assigned a different acronym to avoid confusion with other organizations. For example, to identify Partido Solidaridad, operating between 1993 and 2007 (when it fused with Partido Liberal Nacional to form Unión Patriótica), I used the acronym PSOL, rather than PS—the short form usually employed by the party. This avoids confusion with Partido Socialista (PS), active in Panama until the 1968 coup. Partido Demócrata Cristiano (PDC), renamed Partido Popular in 2001, now uses a different acronym, but for clarity and to emphasize continuity I chose to maintain the PDC label after the name change. For Partido Panameñista I use PPAN throughout, despite the party's two name and acronym changes in 1984–2009, as explained above.

The third column indicates the ideological orientation of Panama's assembly parties along the traditional left-right spectrum. The designations are not official but rather based on a classification by Panamanian sociologist Raúl Leis (1984) and my scrutiny of the parties' programs and the policies they have advocated in power. Panama's party politics—together with those of Bolivia, Colombia, the Dominican Republic, Guatemala, Peru, and Venezuela—are the least programmatic among the electoral democracies in the region (Jones 2005; Stein et al. 2005, 34, figure 3.1). Thus, right-left labels are not very informative. For example, although the statutes of the two main parties—PRD and PPAN—advocate redistributionist policies and state intervention in the economy, both have implemented Washington Consensus programs when in power (conspicuously, PRD did so in 1994–99, under President Ernesto Pérez Balladares). One salient feature that accurately reflects Panamanian political reality, however, is that in 1984–2009 there has been no assembly party of the left.

Column 4 indicates the year in which the party received official recognition from the Electoral Tribunal, which regulates Panama's party system in accordance with the 1972 constitution and the 1983 Electoral Code. A note in parenthesis indicates if the party was originally founded prior to the 1968 coup. Column 5 shows in which of the six elections covered in this book (1984, 1989, 1994, 1999, 2004, and 2009) each party participated. The seventh and eighth columns reveal if a party became extinct (by reporting the year of extinction) and provide brief additional remarks, respectively.

The sixth column shows how many chamber seats (if any) were allocated to the assembly parties subsequent to each of the six elections. This was undoubtedly the most difficult statistic to deliver. Determining fully accurate party affiliation information for the total sample of 309 individuals is impossible. Some deputies have been reelected, which means that the total count of individuals officially proclaimed as members (309) does not coincide with the total number of seats over the period (427). In addition, a deputy belonging to or elected from a party in one period might change parties later in the period or gain reelection on another party ticket in an ensuing period (see chapter 7). The only possibility for approximating the party composition of the Panamanian assembly is to base the calculation on the total number of *seats* filled (427) at the moment of proclamation by the Electoral Tribunal, as opposed to the total number of *individuals* elected to those seats during the period under study (309). Appendix E provides the party distribution of all seats in 1984–2009 and indicates the names of all seat holders (in alphabetical order), showing how many terms each individual served. Table 2.1 provides a brief overview of the assembly parties.

Multipartism with a Dominant Party

As table 2.2 shows, the members of Panama's assembly operate in a *multiparty system with a dominant party* (PRD). This classification forms part of the typology of party systems proposed by Jean Blondel (cited in Lijphart 1999, 66–69), which consists of four categories. Party systems fit this typology according to their effective number of parties, which may be calculated on the basis of vote or assembly seat shares. Accordingly, Blondel suggests the following criteria for classifying party systems: two-party systems (2 effective parties), two-and-a-half party systems (2.6 effective parties), multiparty systems with a dominant party (3.5 effective parties), and multiparty systems without a dominant party (4.5 effective parties) (see Lijphart 1999, 67).

Table 2.1. Total Number of Seats Obtained by Panama's Assembly Parties, 1984–2009

Party	Number of Seats	Proportion of Total (%)	Party	Number of Seats	Proportion of Total (%)
PRD	177	41	UP	5	1
PPAN	83	19	PL	4	1
PDC	42	10	PRC	4	1
MOLIRENA	35	8	PR	3	1
CD	18	4	LIBRE	2	0.5
PSOL	17	4	VMP	1	0.2
PLA	11	3	MORENA	1	0.2
PALA	9	2	UDI	1	0.2
MPE	6	1	Independents (2009)	2	0.5
PLN	6	1	*Total*	427	100

Source: Tribunal Electoral 1984a, 1984b, 1991a, 1991b, 1994b, 1994c, 1999b, 1999c, 2004a, 2004b, 2008, 2009a.

Table 2.2. Classification of Party Systems Based on Effective Number of Parties

Party System	Effective Number of Parties
Two-party system	2.0
Two-and-a-half-party system	2.6
Multiparty system with a dominant party	3.5
Multiparty system without a dominant party	4.5

Source: Based on Jean Blondel's classification; adapted from Lijphart 1999, 67.

Because our focus is on the behavior of individuals holding assembly seats, seat shares are more relevant to this aspect of the study than proportion of votes (see Lijphart 1999, 68n5). Based on seats, therefore, the effective number of assembly parties in Panama over the 1984–2009 period is 4.3 (see appendix F), which is within Blondel's range for multiparty systems with a dominant party (3.5–4.5). According to Lijphart (1999, 67), examples of such multiparty systems include "pre-1990 Italy with its dominant Christian Democratic party and the three Scandinavian countries [Denmark, Norway, Sweden] with their strong Socialist parties."

Panama's 4.3 on the scale is close to the cut-off figure for multiparty systems without a dominant party (4.5), but if we take into account migrations to larger organizations by deputies belonging to extinct parties, the effective number of parties drops to at least 4.2.[8] Taking other switches into account would, presumably, further reduce the effective number of assembly parties closer to 3.5, as parties with modest electoral resources have a tendency to lose deputies to the main government party as the electoral period approaches (this is addressed in more detail in chapter 7).

Party Institutionalization in the Latin American Context

Mainwaring and Scully's (1995) criteria for party institutionalization provide another avenue to understand the nature of the party system in which Panama's deputies operate. Seeking to ascertain the degree of institutionalization of Latin America's party systems—that is, the degree to which party systems are "well established and widely known, if not universally accepted" (4)—Mainwaring and Scully take into account, among other standards, regularity of competition patterns and development of stable roots in society by parties in a sample of twelve Latin American countries (not including Panama). Following Mainwaring and Scully, a later exercise by Payne et al. (2006, 2007) procured data to cover eighteen Latin American electoral democracies. Based on these studies and on Panama's electoral statistics, we can situate the country's party system in the Latin American scenario.

Mainwaring and Scully's first criterion—competition pattern regularity—is easily captured by Pedersen's index of electoral volatility, "which measures the net change in seat (or vote) shares of all parties from

one election to the next" (Mainwaring and Scully 1995, 6). The implication is that higher volatility scores are indicative of less stable competition patterns and less institutionalized party systems. Mean volatility
scores for Panama in the six elections between 1984 and 2009, based on
votes cast for president, was 45 percent. When volatility in presidential
elections is recalculated for the liberal democratic period (1994–2009),
it drops to 38 percent. This is still a high score, however, which places
Panama among the countries with higher Pedersen's indices in presidential elections, including Ecuador (1978–2002: 46 percent), Guatemala (1985–2003: 49 percent), and Peru (1980–2001: 52 percent).
In contrast, the highest mean volatility in all the elections in thirteen
Western European countries from 1885 to 1985 was France's 15 percent
(Payne et al. 2006, 170–72).[9] Appendix G shows the volatility calculations for Panama in the period under study, based on votes for president
and deputies.

Mainwaring and Scully measure the ability of parties to develop stable
roots in society—a second criterion of institutionalization—by calculating the difference between presidential and congressional votes. The
assumption is that this difference should be less pronounced "where
parties are key actors in shaping political preferences" (Mainwaring and
Scully 1995, 9). For Panama in 1984–2009, the mean difference is
2.8 percent as calculated on the basis of shares of votes received in elections to the presidency and the National Assembly by parties, and 4.8 percent based on competing coalitions of parties (see appendix H). A comparison of coalition votes is warranted based on the fact that allied parties
nominate the same presidential candidate; thus, voters may cast a ballot
for their preferred presidential candidate using any of the party tickets
in the coalition. More often than not, however, each coalition party has
a different list of candidates to the assembly. The mean difference based
on party votes (2.8 percent) is lower in Panama that in all of the twelve
countries included in Mainwaring and Scully's sample, except Uruguay
(0.6 percent in 1971–89). On the basis of coalition votes, the mean
difference (4.8 percent) is lower in Uruguay as well as Costa Rica (3.3
in 1970–90) and Argentina (3.3 in 1983–89) (Mainwaring and Scully
1995, 10). These statistics suggest a strong to moderate tendency among
Panamanian voters to vote a straight coalition ticket in elections for
president and deputies.

A second indicator of rootedness in society is the longevity of parties. "If an institutionalized party system exists," explain Mainwaring and Scully, "more parties are likely to have longer histories than in cases of less institutionalization" (1995, 13). Consequently, for their 1995 study, the authors calculated the proportion of congressional seats held after the most recent election by parties founded by 1950. A comparable statistic for Panama's 2009 seat distribution, based on parties (or their successors) operating in the 1960s, is 31 percent. Indeed, among the parties receiving seats in 2009, only PPAN and PDC were active in the 1960s. PPAN received 21 seats (30 percent) and PDC 1 seat (1 percent). Of the twelve countries in Mainwaring and Scully's sample, Peru (29 percent in 1990), Ecuador (16 percent in 1992), and Brazil (1 percent in 1990) had lower percentages (1995, 13). This statistic suggests that in 2009 an important portion of the Panamanian chamber's seats was garnered by relatively new (or ephemeral) parties.

Another measure of longevity focuses on determining the number of years since the founding of parties holding at least one-tenth of the chamber seats. The average number, calculated from Panama's 2009 election results, is 39 years.[10] This statistic situates Panama near the middle of Mainwaring and Scully's findings, above Chile (37 years in 1993), Venezuela (33 years in 1993), Peru (33 years in 1990), Bolivia (20 years in 1993), Ecuador (19 years in 1992), and Brazil (12 years in 1990) (1995, 15, table 1.5).

This analysis indicates that Panama is close to the less institutionalized end of the spectrum (near such countries as Brazil, Ecuador, and Peru) with regard to two of the four indicators (electoral volatility and proportion of seats held by parties operating the four decades preceding the most recent election). It is close to the middle with regard to the longevity of parties holding at least 10 percent of the assembly seats and is among the party systems having less difference between presidential and congressional votes. We can conclude, then, that during the period under review Panama's party system was weakly institutionalized. Mainwaring and Scully's term for such a system is "inchoate," as opposed to the "institutionalized" party systems they identified in Chile, Costa Rica, and Uruguay. It is in this generally inchoate party system that Panama's 309 assembly members operated between 1984 and 2009. Table 2.3 summarizes the results of this comparative exercise.

Table 2.3. Selected Party System Institutionalization Statistics in Panama and Latin America, 1984–2009

	Panama		Average in Mainwaring and Scully's Twelve Countries
	2009	1984–2009 (average)	
Mean electoral volatility (Pedersen's index, votes for president)	43%	45%	33%
Mean difference between coalition votes for president and assembly	3%	5%	10%
Assembly seats held by parties operating in 1960s[a]	31%	30%	60%
Average years since founding of parties with 10 percent of assembly seats	39	29	55

Source: Based on Mainwaring and Scully (1995, 6–16). Mainwaring and Scully's sample includes Argentina, Bolivia, Brazil, Chile, Colombia, Costa Rica, Ecuador, Mexico, Paraguay, Peru, Uruguay, and Venezuela. Their table showing the difference between presidential and congressional votes excludes Brazil.

Note: Larger percentages in the first two categories (volatility and difference in presidential and congressional votes) are indicative of weaker party system institutionalization. Larger numbers in the last two categories (referring to longevity of parties holding assembly seats) are indicative of stronger party system institutionalization.

[a] 1950 in Mainwaring and Scully (1995).

Panamanian Assembly Members since 1984: A Profile

In the six constitutional terms studied in this book, 309 individuals have been proclaimed by the Electoral Tribunal as holders of the assembly's total number of seats in the 1984–2009 period (427). These 309 individuals are identified in appendix E. Members are listed in alphabetical order based on their paternal last name. In keeping with the Spanish-American tradition, I provide paternal and maternal last names (when the latter were available), as well as married names for female members of the assembly. This additional information helps identify each individual more precisely and may assist in establishing familial linkages among deputies. In line with contemporary Spanish-language usage, female deputies are consistently referred to by their paternal last name.

Not all of the 309 individuals proclaimed as elected members actually carried out representative functions throughout the terms they were elected according to the Electoral Tribunal. At least five died during their tenure: Nodier Miranda (PLA, 1989–94),[11] Miguel Peregrino Sánchez (PRC, 1994–99),[12] Carlos Alvarado (PRD, 1994–2009),[13] Agustín Escudé (PRD, 2004–9),[14] and Tomás Altamirano Mantovani (PRD, 1999–2009).[15] One—Omaira Correa (PALA, 1984–89)—left the country in 1987 on account of her persecution by the military dictatorship. Three others were concurrently elected to higher office: First Vice-President Tomás Altamirano Duque (PRD) in 1994; First Vice-President Arturo Vallarino (PALA, subsequently MOLIRENA) in 1999; and Second Vice-President Rubén Arosemena (PDC) in 2004. In accordance with Panamanian law in force during the period (Antinori 1995, 992n779), all three resigned their assembly positions and were replaced by their respective first substitutes or alternates, who are elected in tandem with the "principal" member.[16]

Yet another two lost their seats as a result of prosecution and imprisonment: Anel Ramírez (PALA)[17] at the end of the 1989–94 term, and Mario Miller (PRD)[18] at the beginning of the 1994–99 period. Both were replaced by their respective substitutes. In all other instances, however, the persons designated by the Electoral Tribunal as elected assembly members sat in the chamber for the duration of their terms. Official proclamation by the tribunal (even if the proclamation bases are not sound, transparent, fair, or legitimate) thus serves to provide a clear, common standard for inclusion in the sample.

Reelection accounts for the difference between the 427 seats filled in the assembly between 1984 and 2009 and the 309 individuals who filled those seats. Of the 309 individuals, 232 were proclaimed elected once; 46, twice; 22, three times; 8, four times; and 1, five times (Elías Castillo, PRD). These statistics, portrayed in the last column of appendix E, indicate that the typical member (75 percent of the sample) serves one term in the chamber. Although, as shown in appendix I and discussed in chapter 5, the reelection rate is low compared to the United States and— among the Latin American presidential democracies—Chile,[19] some members are more successful than others in obtaining reelection. PRD has a higher reelection rate than other parties. Additionally, access to government or privately funded constituency endowments to "buy" clientelistic support from constituents may help improve a member's reelection prospects (see chapter 6).

Age

According to article 153 (section 3) of the Panamanian constitution, deputies must be at least 21 years old when they are elected. Because only a minority of incumbents provided complete biographical data in the 2004–9 and 2009–14 terms, and biographical information was not available for previous terms at the time this text was written (May 2010), I was only able to obtain birth dates for 48 deputies serving in 2004–9 and 2009–14, out of a total of 124 individuals sitting in both terms. Though incomplete, the sample is sufficiently large to provide some insight into this section's topic.

As shown in appendix J, the average age of those 48 members at the time they first served as deputies was 46 years. The youngest deputy in the sample, Ricardo Valencia (PPAN, 2009–14), began his tenure at 21. Susana Richa (PRD, 1999–2009), a sister-in-law of military leader Omar Torrijos, was the veteran in the group: she joined the assembly in 1999 at the age of 75. The average age at the start of the 2004–9 term was 50 years. The average age at the start of the 2009–14 term was 51 years. The difference between the average age at the first proclamation, on the

Table 2.4. Average Starting Age of Members of Panama's Assembly and the U. S. House of Representatives, 1999–2009

Country	Term	Average Starting Age
Panama	1999–2004	47
	2004–9	50
	2009–14	51
United States	1999–2001	53
	2001–3	54
	2003–5	54
	2005–7	55
	2007–9	56
	2009–11	57

Source: Amer 1999, 2001, 2004, 2006, 2008; Manning 2010; Guevara Mann 2004; survey of deputies' biographical information on the National Assembly website (www .asamblea.gob.pa) carried out in 2008 and 2010.

one hand, and at the start of the 2004–9 and 2009–14 terms, on the other, is due to the fact that some of the 48 members served previous terms in the chamber. Some reporting deputies began their assembly tenure in 1999, 1994, 1989, and 1984.[20] Overall, the average starting age in Panama's 1999–2004 and 2004–9 terms is lower than in the United States House of Representatives over the same period (106th through 111th congresses), as shown in table 2.4.

Gender

Most of the 309 members of Panama's assembly between 1984 and 2009 were men. Only 32, or 10 percent of the sample, were women (see appendix K). In Chile, which transitioned to democracy approximately at the same time as Panama (1989–90), the underrepresentation of women is also a problem: of 329 individuals elected to Chile's Chamber of Deputies in 1990–2010, the proportion of females in the sample is only slightly higher (12 percent).[21]

Table 2.5. Women in Representative Assemblies, 2008–10

Representative Assembly	Proportion (%)
All liberal democracies (average)	19
All Latin American electoral democracies (average)	20
Panama (2009–14 term)	8

Source: Freedom House 2009a; IPU 2010a; Tribunal Electoral 2009a.

Female members of Panama's assembly were more likely to represent urban than rural constituencies: of the 32 women deputies, 8 sat for rural districts and 24 for urban constituencies. Twenty-four have served one term; 7, two terms; and 1—Balbina Herrera (PRD)—three terms (none have served more than three terms). The percentage of women in the assembly more than doubled between 1984 and 2004. In 1984–89 the female contingent was 6 percent. It ascended to 7 percent in 1989–94, 8 percent in 1994–99, 10 percent in 1999–2004, and 15 percent in 2004–9; the female cohort reverted to 8 percent in 2009–14, a proportion that is significantly lower than the average in all liberal democracies (19 percent) and all Latin American electoral democracies in 2008–10 (20 percent) (Freedom House 2009a; IPU 2010a; Tribunal Electoral 2009a; see also appendices B and C). These findings are summarized in table 2.5.

Women are also underrepresented with respect to Panama's total population. According to the Comptroller-General's Office, women constituted 49.6 percent of Panama's estimated population at July 1, 2006 (Contraloría General 2007). This statistic contrasts quite unfavorably with a female contingent of 8 percent in the 2009–14 assembly and even with 15 percent in the 2004–9 chamber, the highest proportion of women deputies in the period under review.

According to Jones (2010), the low proportion of women in Panama's National Assembly relates to inadequacies in the country's electoral system. A quota provision is in place, according to which at least 30 percent of each parties' candidates must be women; however, electoral system complexities, the disinterest of parties in complying with this aspect of the law, and the Electoral Tribunal's inability to enforce it account for the small number of women holding elected office in Panama. This scenario is problematic for two reasons. First, it reveals a case of inadequate representation for half of the country's population. Second, it deprives the legislative process of the "unique contributions" women can make to the design of public policies and other areas (Jones 2010).

Social Origins

Although several of Panama's deputies were or became wealthy, most of those sitting between 1984 and 2009 were not part of the traditional upper class, as indicated by membership in the Union Club, the meeting place of the country's historic families and status seekers.[22] According to my calculation, facilitated by the club secretariat, out of 309 deputies, only 35—or 11 percent—belonged to that social organization.[23] In Chile the proportion of deputies belonging to the traditional upper class in 1990–2010 was approximately 27 percent.[24] On this basis, we can safely say that in 1984–2009 the Panamanian assembly was not an upper-class domain, as most representative chambers were at their inception in the predemocratic era.[25] With the progression of time and expansion of the franchise, and as democracy became more rooted, representative assemblies lost their aristocratic character.

Deputies with membership in the Union Club are identified in appendix K, together with members of so-called political dynasties. Following Dal Bó, Dal Bó, and Snyder (2009), a "dynastic" representative is one belonging to a family that placed at least one deputy in the assembly prior to that member's tenure. For the purposes of this study, "family" refers to direct ascendants (a parent, grandparent, or great-grandparent), siblings, spouses, parents-in-law, siblings-in-law, or blood uncles, aunts, great uncles, and great aunts of 1984–2009 members who served earlier in the assembly, either between 1904 and 1968 or between 1984 and 2009. Based on historical data and information contributed by various informants, I estimated that 51 representatives (16.5 percent) were members of those political dynasties. The proportion is just slightly lower in

Chile's Chamber of Deputies in 1990–2010 (15.8 percent) based on self-reporting by members in their biographies contained in the online congressional library (Biblioteca del Congreso Nacional de Chile 2010).

The estimation for Panama in the 1984–2009 period is more than double Dal Bó, Dal Bó, and Snyder's calculation for the United States in the thirty years ranging from 1966 to 1996 (7 percent).[26] Analysis of this data suggests that membership in the isthmian assembly (as well as the Chilean Chamber of Deputies) is more concentrated among certain political families than membership in the U.S. Congress. At least part of this difference might be explained by the fact that Panama's population is nearly one hundred times smaller than that of the United States.

Furthermore, as measured by conventional indicators of modernity (GDP per capita, urbanization, literacy, etc.), Panama is a less modern society than the United States, which suggests that kinship might be a more relevant determinant of politics on the isthmus than in the North American republic. Previous studies of Panama's society and politics corroborate this insight (Biesanz and Biesanz 1955; Janson Pérez 1993). More traditional associations—such as familial links—are likely to carry weight in explaining political outcomes in inchoate party systems such as Panama's, where party labels are not overly significant. These observations help give context to the information about access to and control of political influence in the republic revealed by political dynasticism in the National Assembly. Such access and control may serve, among other purposes, to allow an individual to advance a political career, obtain or protect personal wealth, and remain free from prosecution.

Aspects of Dynasticism in Panama

Although the 1968–89 military dictatorship fractured the political status quo, it did not discard all features (or figures) of the old regime. While the military dictatorship presented itself as a new system of government—a "revolution" that was to eliminate the corrupt and discredited politics of the past—it desperately needed legitimacy. Thus, the military welcomed and even tried to co-opt prominent figures of the previous political scene. In addition, those clans that had supported the National Guard prior to 1968 retained their influence.[27]

The dictatorship curtailed several of the traditional families' access to political power, especially through the persecution of all politicians associated with the executive branch it replaced, the suppression of a representative assembly between 1968 and 1984, and the prohibition of all partisan activity between 1968 and 1978. But, through co-optation into the regime in some instances, or by holding on to previously accumulated political capital and loyalties in others, some members of Panama's political elite managed to retain their clout. These dynamics become evident from an examination of some of the assembly's political dynasties.

Based on the number of family members serving in the chamber, one of the largest clans was that of the Arias Madrid, with seven representatives beginning with Harmodio Arias Madrid, a deputy in 1924–28.[28] A renowned and clever jurist, Arias was elected to the presidency of the republic in 1932–36 and remained a highly influential newspaper publisher and political operator until his death in 1963 (Sepúlveda 1983). Harmodio Arias was, as well, older brother and political mentor to Arnulfo Arias, Panama's principal twentieth-century *caudillo* and, until his death in 1988, a potent symbol of the 1968–89 opposition to the military regime (Conte Porras 1990). The power of the Arias Madrid clan was thus based on its founders' prestige stemming from both brothers' reputation for erudition and intelligence,[29] Harmodio's ability to persuade public opinion through his media outlets, and Arnulfo's powerful personal charisma.[30] It was also—significantly—a leadership having civilian (as opposed to military) foundations.

The family did not always function as a unified political bloc—its history is punctuated by quarrels between Harmodio and Arnulfo, as well as between Harmodio's restless and ambitious sons. Additionally, the Arias Madrid dynasty lost all overt political influence when the military coup ousted Arnulfo Arias from the presidency and actively persecuted his followers.[31] This is evidenced by the election of only two of its members as deputies between 1984 and 2009 (or one every 12.5 years), as opposed to five between 1924 and 1968 (or one every 8.8 years). But the fact that the family maintained a presence in the post-1984 chamber and that this presence stemmed to a significant degree from the reputation of the Arias Madrid brothers (especially Arnulfo) validates the view of the clan as a political dynasty in the National Assembly from a historical perspective.[32]

Based on number of terms served by family members, another of the largest clans was that of the Vallarino Bartuano, with a total of fourteen terms starting with Ismael Vallarino's tenure in 1952–60 (two terms). While the Arias Madrid dynasty exemplifies the somewhat weakened continuity of political influence established on civilian foundations, intellectual prestige, influence over public opinion, and charismatic leadership, the Vallarino Bartuano clan illustrates the rise of political clout from military connections and its subsequent autonomous development, partly based on clientelism. Ismael Vallarino, nicknamed *Cucho Varilla* ("Rod Cucho") for his proclivity toward political violence (notoriously by using metal rods to beat opponents), was the eldest son of an impoverished traditional upper-class family. Vallarino owed his influence to his role as goon squad leader for the Liberal Party during the turbulent period spanning the late 1940s and early 1950s,[33] as well as to the fact that his younger brother, Bolívar, was second-in-command of the National Police from 1947 to 1951 and National Guard chief in 1951–68, a time of rising, U.S.-sponsored militarization of Panamanian politics.

Ismael's son Arturo Vallarino advanced a career in Panama's bureaucracy after the 1968 military coup and in 1984 obtained an assembly seat on the ticket of PALA, one of the parties supporting the dictatorship. After switching to the opposition MOLIRENA, Vallarino was reelected in 1989 and, subsequently, in 1994 and 1999. In the latter year, as noted above, he was concurrently elected first vice-president of the republic, whereupon he resigned his assembly seat, owing to electoral requirements in force in 1984–2009.[34]

Originally based on linkages to the armed forces, Arturo Vallarino's influence became autonomous and expanded after the collapse of the military regime, as indicated by the recruitment of additional family members as National Assembly deputies. These included brothers-in-law Héctor Aparicio (MOLIRENA, 1994–2014) and Javier Tejeira (PLN, 1999–2009) as well as sister Marylín Vallarino (PSOL, 2004–14).[35] Some six decades after *Cucho*'s rise to notoriety, in late 2007, after engaging in a fistfight with a female municipal official in her Arraiján constituency, Deputy Marylín Vallarino vindicated her recourse to violence and reminisced about the paramilitary foundations of her dynasty on the assembly floor:

When that woman [the municipal officer] tried to strike me my reaction was to defend myself, so I smacked her and she splattered on the street like a papaya . . . I know how to defend myself, Mr. Speaker . . . I practice boxing every morning at 5 a.m. I have a boxing instructor, not to hurt anyone but to preserve my health, though if the day comes when I need to defend myself I will use my fists. I shall not tolerate disrespect from corrupt officials. I am a deputy but also a regular citizen who pays her taxes . . . and a proud daughter of *Cucho* Vallarino. (Asamblea Nacional 2007)

Using links to the military to create a power base and employing those connections to erect assembly dynasties has not been unusual in Panamanian politics. In addition to the Vallarino Bartuano family, this was also the case for the Paredes Robles, González Vernaza, and—perhaps more prominently—the Altamirano Duque dynasties. All three emerged in the pre-dictatorship period, made significant progress during the military regime, and solidified their presence in the National Assembly after the demise of authoritarian rule. Up to his premature death in early 2009, Tomás Altamirano Mantovani (PRD, 1999–2009) was the current representative in the assembly of the Altamirano Duque family, whose origins go back to the first half of the twentieth century. Forbears Manuel Everardo Duque, Jorge Ramírez Duque, and José Gabriel Duque served as National Assembly deputies on four occasions between 1936 and 1968. Like the Arias Madrid clan, the Duque family flexed political leverage through their own newspapers, the *Star & Herald* and *La Estrella de Panamá*—two of the oldest printed media in the Americas, going back to 1849 and 1853, respectively. I named the dynasty, however, after Altamirano Mantovani's father, Tomás Altamirano Duque, who also began his political career prior to 1968 and advanced it during the dictatorship (which he served as agency director, cabinet minister, and Legislative Council member).

Altamirano Duque tapped his links to the military regime and his family's fiefdom in the Chepo District, east of Panama City, to secure a place in the chamber as PRD legislator in 1984–89. Elected once again as assembly member and, concurrently, as first vice-president of the republic in 1994, Altamirano Duque resigned his seat in favor of his son and first alternate, Tomás Altamirano Mantovani. With the father running as first alternate, the son subsequently secured election as legislator in 1999 and reelection in 2004.

In concluding this section, it is worthwhile to establish some relationships between social class and political dynasticism in Panama to illustrate how these variables might interact in assisting the development of assembly careers. Most deputies do not belong to political dynasties or to Panama's traditional upper-class society, and a large majority (75 percent) have served only one period in the chamber. Thus, in socioeconomic terms, membership in the National Assembly appears to be quite fluid—in other words, it does not seem overly concentrated in a few influential individuals, families, or classes. Political dynasties, however, still have a presence in the chamber. Among all members elected to the assembly in 1984–2009, around one-sixth (16.5 percent) belonged to political dynasties. And, among those 51 members, about two-fifths (21, or 41 percent) belonged to or had been incorporated into the traditional upper class.

Evidently, since 1984 it is not common for an individual of the upper class to hold a seat in the National Assembly. The upper-class foundations of dynasticism are not overly robust, either. Instead, dynasticism in the post-1984 Panamanian assembly seems to be related to other variables—such as links to the military, clientelism, influence over public opinion, or leadership trajectories—rather than membership in the traditional upper class. Some members of traditional upper-class families have achieved election as assembly members (slightly above one-tenth of the sample), and those that had dynastic connections drew on political resources accumulated by their families during both the pre-dictatorship era and the military regime to realize their aspirations.

Geo-Demographic Segmentation

Determining the geo-demographic makeup of the National Assembly, based on the rural or urban provenance of the assembly members, is a useful exercise. Generally, it might show overrepresentation of some sectors with specific political motivations, explain different approaches to policy making, or elucidate certain attitudes or behaviors associated with either an agrarian or cosmopolitan culture. In this regard, Samuels and Snyder (2001, 668) posit that overrepresentation of the countryside in some Latin American congresses "tends to favour politically-conservative rural districts at the expense of politically-progressive urban districts."

The calculation for Panama shows that slightly over half of the sample—that is, 161 of 309 members, or 52 percent—represented urban constituencies (see appendix K).[36] This percentage was computed by classifying as "urban" those municipal districts having a population density of 100 per square kilometer or higher at July 1, 2006. This threshold is reasonable given that population density for the entire republic at July 1, 2006 was 43.7 per square kilometer. On this basis, eight municipal districts and their corresponding eleven electoral constituencies qualify as urban (see table 2.6).

At July 1, 2006, the population of the country's urban municipal districts amounted to 62 percent of the republic's total population of 3.3 million (Contraloría General 2006), but only 52 percent of the 309 members sitting in 1984–2009 represented urban constituencies. This analysis reveals the overrepresentation of the rural population in the assembly, as well as the malapportionment of Panama's electoral districts, a feature studied in depth by Sonnleitner (2010).

It should be noted, however, that in some cases assembly members returned from rural constituencies actually live in urban areas, especially Panama City. Up to 2006, the Electoral Code was quite lenient in this regard, allowing citizens to register as voters and candidates in areas where they maintained a residence and "political, familial, and social relations." The 2006 reform, which entered into effect in 2007, defined residence less broadly as the location where the individual "habitually resides" (República de Panamá 2003, 2007). This modification ostensibly sought to curtail the practice of voter transportation, whereby candidates (including incumbents) mobilize large contingents of voters to constituencies other than their own, where they arguably have "political, familial, and social relations," to support a particular office seeker (see chapter 7). The provision was sued before the Supreme Court by PRD Deputies Franz Wever (1994–2009) and Freidi Torres (1999–2014), who despite voting in favor of the Electoral Code reform in 2006, later

Table 2.6. Urban Municipal Districts and Electoral Constituencies in Panama, 2006–9

Municipal District	Population Density (per square kilometer)	Constituency Number[a]	Number of Deputies Elected (2009–14 Term)
Arraiján	295.8	8.1	3
Barú	107.0	4.2	1
Chitré	543.1	6.1	1
Colón	137.0	3.1	4
David	158.9	4.1	3
La Chorrera	227.1	8.5	3
Panama City	412.2	8.7	5
		8.8	5
		8.9	3
		8.10	4
San Miguelito	6,896.3	8.6	7

Source: Contraloría General 2006; Tribunal Electoral 2009a.

Note: Population density figures are as of July 1, 2006. Electoral constituency data are for the 2009 elections.

[a] See appendix L for constituency numbers and names.

concluded that their reelectoral aspirations might be better realized under the previous, more indulgent residency rule (Flores 2007a). In April 2010 the Supreme Court upheld the stricter electoral residency rule passed in 2006, ruling it was not unconstitutional, as claimed by deputies Wever and Torres (Damián 2010).

Ideological Positioning

Although—as we have seen—a strong ideological orientation is not a salient feature of Panama's political system, when questioned about their own beliefs the members of the Panamanian assembly appear to be more conservative and authoritarian than their Latin American peers. Generally, as postulated by Samuels and Snyder (2001), the conservative bend could have some relation to rural overrepresentation in the assembly.

Based on the University of Salamanca surveys, Panama's deputies are less enthusiastic about democracy than their Latin American counterparts.[37] While 95 percent of the Latin American representatives surveyed in 2000–2008 expressed a preference for democracy over any other form of government, in 2004 the proportion of Panamanian deputies in favor of democracy was lower (87 percent). A higher percentage in Panama (13 percent) than in the whole of Latin America (5 percent) said authoritarian governments were preferable in situations of economic or political instability. The large number of deputies elected by PRD (the political arm of the military regime) in the 2004 elections—43, or 54 percent of the chamber—may help explain this stronger preference for authoritarianism in Panama than in the rest of the region.

In 2004 Panama's deputies were more strongly opposed to abortion than their Latin American peers over the 2000–2008 period. On a scale from 1 to 10, where 1 represented a preference for the penalization of abortion, the average positioning of the 2004 Panamanian sample was 3.42, versus 4.67 in Latin America as a whole. Panama's deputies also professed to be quite religious. On a spectrum ranging from minimum (1) to maximum (10) religiosity, the average positioning of the isthmian assembly members was 7.09, compared to 5.46 for the Latin American sample. Discovering how Panamanian deputies reconcile such religiosity with their notorious rent seeking and attempts to remain free from prosecution for manifest breaches of the law is fertile terrain for political psychology.

A higher proportion of Panamanian deputies than other Latin American members of congress was in favor of state intervention in the economy to provide adequate social security coverage, ensure employment, establish price controls, cover basic necessities, protect the environment, and guarantee free college education. These preferences may be linked to the clientelistic political culture promoted, in particular, by the populist military regime (1968–89), which had a strong impact on Panama's politics (see chapter 4). Ironically, however, in 2004 the average

Table 2.7. Ideological Preferences of Assembly Members in Panama and Latin America, 2000–2008

	Panama (2004)	*Latin America (2000–2008)*[a]
Overall preference for democracy	87%	95%
Preference for authoritarianism in situations of economic or political instability	13%	5%
Opposition to abortion (1, maximum; 10, minimum)	3.42	4.67
Religiosity (1, minimum; 10, maximum)	7.09	5.46
In favor of state intervention to:		
Ensure social security coverage	100%	96%
Generate employment	88%	81%
Provide housing	75%	81%
Implement price controls	69%	51%
Cover basic necessities	84%	79%
Protect the environment	100%	98%
Provide unemployment insurance	71%	72%
Guarantee free and general college education	77%	76%

Source: Universidad de Salamanca 2008.

[a] The Latin American sample includes Panama.

self-positioning of deputies on the left-right spectrum was 6.43, where 1 indicates an extreme left and 10 an extreme right position. As noted by the Salamanca survey, Panama's assembly members have a tendency to situate themselves in the center-right section of the scale, while the Latin American average in 2000–2008 veered more toward the center (5.05) (Universidad de Salamanca 2008) (see table 2.7).

Summary

Of the 309 individuals proclaimed by the Electoral Tribunal as members of Panama's assembly in 1984–2009, all except two (in 2009) were nominated by political parties, as required by Panamanian law between 1984 and 2004. At the time of their proclamation, most of them (41 percent) belonged to PRD, which is the dominant party in Panama's multiparty system. During the period under review, Panama's party system was weakly institutionalized compared to other systems in the region. This feature corresponds in certain measure to the general absence of programmatic content in the country's politics, as observed by Stein et al. (2005), as well as to the informal institutionalization of clientelism, addressed in depth in chapter 4.

The typical Panamanian deputy is a male member of PRD who was first elected to the chamber in his mid-forties. Although he may have enhanced his financial position while in office (legally or illegally, as will later be seen), the archetypal deputy does not belong to the traditional upper class; neither is he part of a political dynasty. Normally, he serves one term in the assembly and is more likely than not to represent an urban constituency. His commitment to democracy is probably less strong than among his Latin American peers, as demonstrated by the University of Salamanca surveys. The emblematic Panamanian assembly member is also more conservative in religious matters and more in favor of state intervention to regulate certain aspects of the economy than the average Latin American member of congress.

In the introduction and chapter 1 we saw that both formal and informal institutions help shape the behavior of assembly members generally and that this institutionally shaped behavior is bound to have an impact on the quality of democracy. We now turn to an analysis of some of the formal institutions that influence the conduct of Panama's deputies.

## CHAPTER 3

Formal Institutional Incentives to Behavior

Chapter 1 alluded to the role of institutions in shaping political behavior. This notion is captured by the New Institutionalist argument that "politics is structured by institutions":

> The organization of political life makes a difference, and institutions affect the flow of history . . . Actions taken within and by political institutions change the distribution of political interests, resources, and rules by creating new actors and identities, by providing actors with criteria of success and failure, by constructing rules for appropriate behavior, and by endowing some individuals, rather than others, with authority and other types of resources. Institutions affect the ways in which individuals and groups become activated within and outside established institutions, the level of trust among citizens and leaders, the common aspirations of political community, the shared language, understanding, and norms of the community, and the meaning of concepts like democracy, justice, liberty, and equality. (March and Olsen, qtd. in Putnam 1993, 17)

Following this institutionalist rationale, the literature on legislators' behavior posits that members of deliberative chambers calculate and pursue the appropriate means to achieve their objectives—essentially career advancement—on the basis of self-interest and the institutional framework within which they operate. According to Katz (1980, 13), the formal institutional environment in which assembly members function consists of two basic elements: the electoral system and the distribution of politically mobilizable resources. Other authors identify additional aspects, such as the party system and relations between the executive and the assembly, as influential in determining the behavior of representatives (Mainwaring 1999; Shugart and Carey 1992).

Several formal institutional features facilitate the achievement of Panamanian deputies' goals by permitting or encouraging them to enact certain behaviors. For instance, the fact that Panama, like all other American republics (except Costa Rica and Mexico),[1] permits the reelection of representatives without restriction gives assembly members an automatic incentive to pursue additional terms in office. Article 157 of the Panamanian constitution states that members' emoluments are determined by law, thus requiring approval by the assembly and providing a setting for rent seeking (although pay raises may only take effect in the ensuing term). Likewise, the fact that the constitutional text establishes special procedures for the prosecution of deputies (article 155)—provisions further developed in the assembly's own Rules of Procedure and the Judicial Code—creates a scenario that allows some members to pursue exemption from prosecution (República de Panamá 2004, 2010a).

The behaviors identified in this book are not attributable, in their entirety, to these formal institutional features. Codified standards interact in various ways with informal institutions (the topic of chapter 4) to produce outcomes such as vote buying to procure reelection, selling votes to become rich, or expanding immunity provisions to avoid prosecution. This chapter focuses on three formal institutional arrangements that promote personalistic politics and, as a result, reinforce Panama's clientelistic political tradition: rules for the allocation of chamber seats, the size of electoral constituencies, and the balance of power between the executive and the assembly. By promoting personalism and strengthening clientelism, these institutional arrangements contribute to creating an environment in which incumbents seek political and personal advancement through reelection, personal enrichment, and exemption from prosecution, among other behaviors.

Seat Allocation Formulas and Their Effects
on Members' Behavior

Various authors have examined the behavioral implications of formulas for the assignment of assembly seats. At the highest level of generality, these formulas fall within two types: plurality and proportional representation (PR) systems (Lijphart 1999, 143–44). Plurality systems normally operate in single-member constituencies and use the majority rule to allocate seats. PR operates in multimember constituencies, that is, those electing more than one representative. Individual winners are selected from a list of candidates submitted by the party, according to the proportion of votes received by each political organization.

In his distinction between campaigning under PR and plurality systems, Katz holds that PR generally encourages ideological campaigning while plurality systems promote personalistic, localistic candidatures:

> In PR systems, voters choose parties rather than individuals. Because candidates are obliged to say "Vote for my party" rather than "Vote for me," it is more difficult for candidates of the same party to take different political lines. The importance of the corporate identity of the party is increased, and particularly the importance of the sense that its issue stands represent a unified program rather than a number of isolated proposals of individual candidates. Correspondingly, the general organizing principles underlying a specific proposal, that is the ideology, become more important.
>
> Conversely, plurality electoral schemes encourage personalistic or localistic campaigning. Since the choice of voters is for candidates rather than for parties, candidates may attempt to minimize or even ignore their party affiliation, and the commitment to a specific platform that this implies. This naturally increases the relative importance of personality. Because local candidates are encouraged, localistic consideration will be of particular importance to some candidates (facing a local party challenge) and of some importance to most candidates (hoping to prevent such a challenge in the future). (Katz 1980, 28)

Katz and other scholars also note the differences in campaign styles depending on the type of PR—closed- or open-list systems—used to

Table 3.1. Effects of Seat Allocation Formulas on Candidates' Electoral Strategies

	Type of System		
Type of Vote Candidates Are Likely to Seek	*Plurality*	*Open-List PR*	*Closed-List PR*
Personal Vote	X	X	
Party Vote			X

Source: Adapted from Carey and Shugart (1995) and Katz (1980).

allocate seats. In closed-list systems voters may only cast a vote at the party level, without expressing any preference about the candidates listed on the ballot. In other words, "the division of the seats awarded to a party is left entirely to that party's discretion, although that discretion generally must be exercised before the election takes place." The party normally submits a candidate list "under the provision that its share of the constituency's seats will be awarded to candidates in the order in which their names appear on the list" (Katz 1980, 31). Because voters cast their ballots for parties, not individuals, the expectation is that candidates in closed-list PR systems will campaign on the basis of party label and ideology.

In contrast, open-list PR allows voters "to decide among a party's several candidates in a multimember plurality system" (Katz 1980, 31).[2] Carey and Shugart (1995) predict that one of the effects of an open-list electoral system is to encourage legislative campaigning based on personal reputations (the quality of "being personally well known and liked by voters"). According to these authors, an emphasis on personal popularity is a valuable campaign tool where candidates compete not only against aspirants in other party lists but also with co-partisans appearing on the same party ballot. Table 3.1 summarizes the literature's predictions about the effects of seat allocation formulas on candidates' behavior.

Constitutional Foundations of the Electoral System

The method for electing Panama's assembly members—contained in the Panamanian constitution and Electoral Code—is not well known in scholarly circles, and its effects have been insufficiently studied. Following the 2004 constitutional reform, article 147 (section 1) of the constitution established "the principle of proportional representation." A profusion of single-member districts, however, together with low district magnitude and the plurality rule used in the distribution of remainders in multimember districts, have given the system a predominantly majoritarian character during the period under review (1984–2009). In conjunction with these features, the open-list system utilized in the first two allocation stages in multimember districts promotes the personal vote over partisan, ideological, or programmatic appeals. Thus, the effects of Panama's electoral system coincide with the theoretical predictions about the impact of plurality and open-list systems on candidates' behavior.

The fact that a majority of seats in Panama's National Assembly are allocated according to a plurality rationale have made it, in the words of Panamanian jurist Miguel Antonio Bernal (1992) a "hybrid system." In the 2009–14 term, under this "hybrid system," the National Assembly was a unicameral chamber consisting of 71 deputies elected in 39 constituencies. Thirteen of these were multimember electoral districts and the remaining 26 were single-member constituencies. Article 141 of the constitution (prior to the 2004 reform) provided general districting benchmarks, including a population guideline of 30,000 inhabitants per constituency.[3] Owing to population increases, the number of assembly members and constituencies varied during the period under review. The 2004 constitutional reform fixed the number of deputies at 71; law 59 of 2006 reconfigured the country's constituencies accordingly. Table 3.2 shows the total membership of the assembly and the number of constituencies in each term beginning in 1984.

Assembly members are chosen concurrently with all other elected officers, including the president and vice-president of the republic,[4] 20 deputies to the Central American Parliament,[5] district mayors (75 in 2009), and municipal councilors (including 623 "county representatives" and 7 aldermen in 2009). Between 1984 and 2004, two alternates or substitutes were also elected for each member of the deliberative chamber; the 2004 constitutional reform eliminated the second alternate (Tribunal Electoral 2009e).

In five of the six elections covered in this book, Panamanians chose their assembly members in accordance with article 141 of the constitution

Table 3.2. Assembly Membership and Electoral Constituencies in Panama, 1984–2009

	Term				
	1984–89 and 1989–94	*1994–99*	*1999–2004*	*2004–9*	*2009–14*
Total Membership	67	72	71	79	71
Constituencies					
Multimember	12	14	14	14	13
Single Member	28	26	26	27	26
Total	40	40	40	41	39

Source: Tribunal Electoral 1984a, 1984b, 1991a, 1991b, 1994b, 1994c, 1999b, 1999c, 2004a, 2004b, 2009b.

(prior to the 2004 reform). The highly complex formula contained in article 141 provided demographic and political-administrative bases for delineating Panama's electoral constituencies. The municipal district was (and still is) the main unit for the configuration of those constituencies. This represented a significant departure from Panama's constitutional practice until the 1968 military coup, when constituents elected deputies at the provincial level (that is, one political-administrative level above the municipal district).

The number of electoral units in each province is, roughly, a function of the province's population. Up to the 2004 reform, the general guideline was that each province should have one constituency for every 30,000 inhabitants and an additional one for any remainder over 10,000. These electoral districts were drawn along municipal borders. To reach the population criterion, the Electoral Tribunal sometimes joined two or more small municipal districts to form a constituency. Additionally, regardless of the aforementioned population provisions, article 141 divided both the San Blas indigenous reservation and Darién Province, rural regions bordering Colombia, into two single-member electoral units. These constitutional features contribute to the rural bias in the membership of the assembly noted in chapter 2.

In other parts of the country, each municipal district having over 40,000 inhabitants formed an electoral constituency. In those electoral units, constituents elected one legislator for each 30,000 inhabitants and an additional one for any remainder above 10,000. The municipal district of Panama, the republic's capital, was constitutionally divided into four constituencies. In these multimember districts, "the proportional representation system established by law," as enunciated in article 141 of the constitution prior to the 2004 reform, was utilized to allocate seats. The section that follows describes this "proportional representation system."

The aim of the 1983 constitutional reform, which laid down these districting guidelines and created a Legislative Assembly after sixteen years of authoritarian rule, was to set up a system in which small, ideally single-member constituencies would predominate. Table 3.3 shows this effect quite clearly. In the period under review, single-member districts represented between 65 and 70 percent of all constituencies in Panama. In multimember units district magnitude (M)—the number of deputies elected per district—was low, never exceeding 8. Average M for all constituencies has never reached 2, underscoring the fact that despite the "proportional representation" rhetoric, the single-member, plurality component predominates in Panama's electoral system. Small electoral districts provided the country's military overlords more possibilities for prolonging their political control, particularly through patronage and electoral manipulation, within the context of a supposedly "democratic" electoral design. This rationale coincides with Madison's observation that it is easier to practice the "vicious arts by which elections are too often carried"—that is, vote buying and election fraud—"in the small than in the large republic" (Madison, Hamilton, and Jay 1987, *The Federalist*, no. 10).

Seat Allocation in Single- and Multimember Constituencies

Panama's seat allocation formulas in both the single- and multimember constituencies clearly promote the personal vote, an important incentive to clientelism (Katz 1980; Mainwaring 1999; McCubbins and

Table 3.3. District Magnitude in Panama, 1984–2009

District Magnitude (M)	Terms									
	1984–89 and 1989–94		1994–99		1999–2004		2004–9		2009–14	
	Districts	%	Districts	%	Districts	%	Districts	%	Districts	%
1	28	70	26	65	26	65	27	66	26	67
2	5	12.5	7	17.5	7	17.5	5	12	4	10
3	1	2.5	1	2.5	1	2.5	3	8	4	10
4	4	10	2	5	3	7.5	3	8	2	5
5	2	5	3	7.5	2	5			2	5
6			1	2.5	1	2.5	1	2		
7							1	2	1	3
8							1	2		
Total Districts	40	100	40	100	40	100	41	100	39	100
Average Magnitude (M)	1.7		1.8		1.8		1.9		1.8	
Total Members	67		72		71		79		71	

Source: Tribunal Electoral 1984a, 1984b, 1991a, 1991b, 1994b, 1994c, 1999b, 1999c, 2004a, 2004b, 2009b.

Rosenbluth 1995). Single-member constituencies employ a simple plurality formula to assign winning candidacies. In these districts, the candidate who garners the largest vote is declared the winner; s/he does not require an absolute majority, only a plurality of ballots. This methodology has contributed to make PRD dominant in Panama's assembly.

In all elections to the assembly (except in 1989, when it received 19 percent of the ballots in the vote for legislators), PRD has been the recipient of the largest minority of the vote—25 percent in 1984, 23 percent in 1994, 32 percent in 1999, 38 percent in 2004, and 36 percent in 2009. In 1989 PDC received 36 percent of the ballots in the legislative election (see appendix H). The possibilities of electoral success for PRD increase in a scenario in which it receives the largest minority of the balloting in single-member districts or constituencies with low magnitude and the rest of the suffrages are divided between several of its opponents, none of which has managed to receive more than 23 percent of the total assembly vote (except in 1989).

In multimember districts constituents elect assembly members in accordance with a preferential party-list system of proportional representation, with seats allotted initially according to a double quotient system. This formula is contained in article 326 of the Electoral Code (pursuant to the 2006 reform). The first allocation uses a simple electoral quotient. During this round, seats are allocated to parties that obtain a number of votes equivalent to at least the electoral quotient. In other words, if 100,000 votes are cast in a constituency electing five members, each party attaining at least the full quota of 20,000 votes (100,000 ÷ 5) is allotted one seat. At the subsequent allocation stage, unassigned seats are distributed to parties obtaining at least as many votes as half the electoral quotient (that is, 10,000 votes in this example). Parties obtaining full-quota seats do not participate in the distribution of half-quota seats. Remaining seats go to individual candidates receiving the highest preferences in each constituency, without regard to the share of the vote received by each party (Antinori Bolaños 1995, 574–77; IPU 2010b; República de Panamá 2004, 2007).

In each of the first two allocation stages, the identity of the winning candidates is determined on the basis of the preferences received by candidates on each party list. This feature alludes to the "open-list" nature

of the system. In addition to voting for one of the party lists, the Panamanian voter has as many preferential (or "selective") votes as there are
candidates on the elector's preferred list. To vote selectively, the elector
must tick the box next to his or her preferred candidate(s). Voters are not
obliged to cast preferential votes; if they do not issue a personal ballot, all
candidates on the ticket automatically receive a preferential vote (as if the
voter had expressed a preference for all the candidates on the list).

In their electoral campaigns candidates (including incumbent
assembly members seeking reelection) solicit preferential—that is,
personal—votes from their supporters, to the detriment of other aspirants on their party lists. In this manner, they seek to maximize their
electoral prospects. To persuade constituents about the convenience of
issuing a preferential vote, candidates implement campaign strategies
that promote their image as purveyors of public goods and personal services. Clearly, the first two allotment rounds in Panama's open-list system encourage personalistic candidatures rather than ideological or programmatic campaigning (Antinori Bolaños 1995, 727–21). The method
for distributing multimember district seats not assigned in the first and
second rounds also contributes to personalism.

The Allocation of Remainders

The tripartite electoral formula used in Panama's multimember districts
goes back to 1925, when it was introduced in the country's legislation.
The quota system has obvious similarities to the methodology devised
by Thomas Hare around the middle of the nineteenth century (the
"Hare Quota"). According to Panamanian constitutionalist César Quintero (1967), however, the quotient, half quotient, and remainder system
was formulated by Greek political scientist Nikolaus Saripolos, who presented it in *La démocratie et l'élection proportionelle* (Democracy and Proportional Elections), published in Paris in 1899. With some variations—
such as the elimination of the half quotient and oscillations in the rules
for remainder allocations—this quota system was in place in Panama in
all eleven elections to the chamber held between 1928 and 1968 (Antinori
Bolaños 1995, 731, 733). Readopted in 1983, the system was employed
for the first time, under the 1972 constitution, in the 1984 elections.

At the third stage the allotment of remaining seats in multimember constituencies employs a majoritarian formula, which departs from the principle of proportional representation established in the constitution. Since 1983 the method for assigning remainders has evolved as follows.[6] In the 1984 elections (under military rule), remaining seats were assigned to parties obtaining the higher remainders, after deducting one full quota from all parties obtaining such quota and one half quota from all parties obtaining such half quota in the preceding two rounds. At least in theory, this procedure should have promoted a more proportional distribution of assembly seats among parties participating in the election. In practice, however, multipartism (addressed in chapter 2), reduced district magnitude, and small district size (discussed below) contributed to produce highly disproportional results in the 1984 elections (see appendix M).[7]

When the 1989 electoral results were computed, after the U.S. invasion of December of that year,[8] unallocated seats after the quota distributions went to parties with higher remainders, after deducting a half quotient for parties having attained both a full and a half quotient in the preceding allocation rounds. In 1993, at the proposal of PDC—which then held a majority of the assembly seats—the chamber modified the Electoral Code to allot remaining seats to the candidates (not parties) receiving larger preferential votes. Accordingly, the Electoral Tribunal employed this seat-allocation formula in 1994, 1999, 2004, and 2009 (see table 3.4).

Evidently, the reforms introduced since the 1980s have contributed to maintaining a high deviation from proportionality in Panama's electoral results. The notion of deviation from proportionality seeks to ascertain the degree to which an electoral system departs from full proportionality between vote and seat shares.[9] An example of a perfectly proportional system is one in which a party receiving 10 percent of the popular vote also receives the exact same share of chamber seats. From the premise that proportionality is a desirable, democratic goal, PR systems endeavor to reduce deviation from proportionality as much as possible. The rationale behind this effort—which goes back to the mid-nineteenth-century proposals of Thomas Hare, John Stuart Mill, and other political reformers—is that as deviation decreases, the value of

Table 3.4. Seat Allocation in Panama's Multimember Constituencies, 1994–2009

Allocation Stage	Method
Full quota	Seats are assigned to parties receiving a number of votes equivalent to the full electoral quota, that is, the total number of valid votes in a constituency divided by the number of deputies to be elected in the district. Winning candidates are those receiving the highest number of preferential votes on each party list receiving full electoral quotas.
Half quota	Seats are assigned to parties receiving a number of votes equivalent to half the full electoral quota, that is, the total number of valid votes in a constituency divided by the number of deputies to be elected in the district, divided by two. Parties obtaining full-quota seats do not participate in the distribution of half-quota seats. Winning candidates are those receiving the highest number of preferential votes on each party list receiving half quotas.
Remainder	Seats are assigned to candidates (not parties) receiving the larger preferential votes across party lists, provided that these candidates have not been declared winners at the full- or half-quota allocation stages.

Source: República de Panamá 2007 (articles 326 and 327 of the Electoral Code).

citizens' votes as determinants of who governs increases. In a perfectly proportional system, with no deviation from proportionality, every vote cast counts toward the actual election of a representative.

Under PR elections in Europe, deviation from proportionality ranges from 4 to 8 percent. In other words, this means that between 4 and 8 percent of the total votes cast in an election are "lost," in the sense that they do not translate into the election of a representative to the deliberative chamber. The figure is much higher for plurality, winner-take-all systems based on single-member constituencies where only one candidate can be elected and votes cast for all other aspirants are "lost" (such as the United States or the United Kingdom). In the British general elections of 1992, 1997, and 2001, deviation from proportionality was 17.4, 21.1, and 22.4 percent, respectively (Beetham, Ngan, and Weir 2002). Mean deviation from proportionality in Panama's six elections since 1984 is 19 percent (see appendix M). This figure coincides with results in countries employing majority-plurality systems rather than PR, which is paradoxical given the guarantee of the "principle of proportional representation" contained in Panama's constitution.

But not only are Panama's remainders allocated according to a purely majoritarian formula, which deviates from the principle of proportionality contained in the constitution. As a result of the 1993 reform and the implementing methodology adopted by the Electoral Tribunal, votes used to allocate full- and half-quota seats are not discounted when assigning remaining seats. These votes are effectively counted twice, as party votes and preferential votes. If, following the example given above, a party obtains 24,000 votes and receives one full-quota seat, that full 20,000 quota is not deducted from the top-party candidate's preferential votes at the third, remainder allocation stage. Thus, the candidate on that party list having received the highest preferential vote, to whom a seat has not already been assigned in the preceding allotment rounds, can count the full 20,000 quota as part of his or her preferential vote, which is computed as being 24,000 instead of 4,000. This formula, which distorts the results of the election in favor of the larger parties (and reinforces the system's disproportionality), has generated complaints. It also motivated a petition before the Inter-American Commission on Human Rights (IACHR) submitted by two former PPAN legislators (Daniel Arias and José Serracín, 1994–99) and PPAN candidate Leopoldo Castillo in October 1999. As of this writing, IACHR had reportedly not yet issued an opinion on the complaint.[10]

As is readily apparent, the Electoral Tribunal employed a majoritarian formula in 1994, 1999, 2004, and 2009 to allocate remaining seats in multimember district elections. As a result of the prevalence of single-member districts (see below) and a majoritarian logic for the allotment of remainders in multimember constituencies, the majority of Panama's assembly members in 1994–2009 obtained their seats through plurality,

Table 3.5. Seat Allocation Formulas and Number of Seats Allotted According to Each Formula in Panama, 1994–2009

Formula		*Number and Percentage of Seats*							
		1994		*1999*		*2004*		*2009*	
		N	%	N	%	N	%	N	%
PR	Full quota	6	8	11	15	17	22	17	24
	Half quota	20	28	18	25	20	25	19	27
	Subtotal	26	36	29	40	37	47	36	51
Majority	Remainders (multimember districts)	19	27	16	23	14	18	9	13
	Single-member districts	26	36	26	37	27	34	26	36
	Subtotal	45	63	42	60	41	52	35	49
Article 141	Surviving parties without representation[a]	1	1	0	0	1	1	0	0
	Total	72	100	71	100	79	100	71	100

Source: Tribunal Electoral 1999d, 1999e, 2004c, 2009d.

[a] According to article 141 of the constitution prior to the 2004 reform, parties meeting the minimum survival threshold (a percentage of either the presidential, assembly, or municipal vote, determined by the Electoral Code) but not obtaining representation in the assembly had a right to a chamber seat, which went to the candidate receiving the larger number of votes among all of the party's candidates.

not PR, formulas (see table 3.5). It should be noted, however, that the share of the assembly membership elected through PR has been steadily rising, reaching 51 percent in 2009. This statistic coincides with a progressive reduction in deviation from proportionality in 1994–2009, primarily as a result of the decline in the number of parties competing in the elections. But at 10 percent in 2009 (see appendix M), deviation is still high for a self-proclaimed PR system.

The obvious conclusion from this description of the electoral system is that by privileging the plurality method rather than the system of proportional representation, in the period under review Panama's allocation rules have encouraged personalism over party label as an effective campaign device. District size is another aspect of Panama's electoral system that encourages personalistic campaigning. A better understanding of the effects of district size on the behavior of incumbents seeking reelection requires a historical approach, which the following section provides.

Size Does Matter: Personalism and Small Districts

In chapter 1 we saw that upon assuming power in a 1968 coup, Panama's military dictatorship closed the 42-member National Assembly, which had functioned continuously—except for a brief interruption in 1944–45—since the foundation of the republic six decades earlier. The power to legislate remained in the hands of the military-controlled executive until 1972, when the junta introduced a new constitution, providing for a 505-member Assembly of County Representatives. As will be recalled, counties (*corregimientos*) constitute the smallest political division in Panama, below municipal districts and provinces. Prior to 1968, municipal councils, composed of councilors (*concejales*) elected at large, operated in each district. Upon the reinstatement of elected municipal councils in 1972, a plurality system, with each county electing one representative, replaced the proportional representation formula. These representatives served in several capacities: as chairs of their respective counties' community boards and members of the revamped municipal councils, the newly created provincial councils, and the Assembly of County Representatives.

A significant feature of the new system was the drastic reduction in the size of each electoral district in terms of the number of voters in each constituency. An overwhelming majority of the new electoral districts had fewer inhabitants than the preceding regime's constituencies; most had as few as 1,000 voters, and in some the number of electors barely surpassed 100 (Koster and Sánchez Borbón 1990, 214). Though the change was publicized by the dictatorship as activating "popular power" and justified in terms of placing lawmaking authority in the hands of "the most representative community leaders" (Labrut 1982, 156), this system obviously violated basic political equality tenets (Still 1981). In an opinion piece published in *La Estrella de Panamá* (October 6, 1978), former deputy Francisco Linares Herbruger illustrated this gross inequality by comparing the tiny, 32-voter community of Playa Chiquita, in Colón Province, to the Panama City working-class *corregimiento* of Calidonia with 21,595 constituents: both had equal representation in the Assembly of County Representatives.[11]

As discussed in chapter 1, because the functions of the Assembly of County Representatives were quite restricted, it does not qualify as a truly representative assembly. Although the new regime endowed county representatives with little actual lawmaking or oversight powers at the national level, it did assign them broader responsibilities—and provided budgetary allocations—at the local level (Fábrega and Boyd Galindo 1981, 39–44, 71, 73–77; Labrut 1982, 154; Priestley 1986, 76). Funding for "community projects" at the county, municipal, and provincial levels was now available to members of the military dictatorship's assembly, inaugurating a tradition whereby the county representative assumed responsibility for building streets, distributing sports gear, giving out toys at Christmastime, obtaining scholarships, and paying for funerals, all from state coffers (Cochez 1996). Thus, the assembly's only real power lay in its control over budgetary allocations for expenditures at the local level, which contributed to forge personalistic relationships between county representatives and their constituents.

The dictatorship's strategy to downsize the country's electoral districts and emasculate the legislative branch had deleterious effects on Panama's democratic development. Between 1968 and 1984 there was no political organization in Panama capable of democratically exercising such basic functions as legislating and overseeing the executive. Owing to the structural characteristics of the small electoral districts—a majority of which were located in marginalized rural areas—most of the membership in the Assembly of County Representatives exhibited low educational levels, which restricted the chamber's capacity for performing other basic representative tasks such as deliberation, political socialization, leader recruitment, information supply, and nation building.[12] This latter aspect was a direct result of an electoral arrangement based on a proliferation of small, mostly rural, impoverished single-member constituencies. With regard to the Panamanian assembly, therefore, the most lasting legacy of the military regime was a constitutional design based on small districts and a constrained sphere of action for the representative chamber. In the Panamanian context, both features operated to further promote personalistic politics.

The image of the assembly member as a local distributor of patronage in exchange for political support had become firmly entrenched by the time the military undertook a limited process of political reform in 1978–83. A constitutional amendment approved through a referendum in 1983 replaced the Assembly of County Representatives and the Legislative Council with the Legislative Assembly. After 1983, district size increased with regard to the 1972 county representatives system due to the constitutional reform that stipulated the design of electoral constituencies along the borders of the country's municipal districts, one level above the preceding arrangement in terms of political division and population. On average, however, district size remained small in comparison to the pre-1968 regime, which was based on provincial boundaries.

While some authors argue that small constituencies favor tighter accountability and a closer connection to the voters, others maintain that reduced district size encourages personalism and, through it, clientelism.[13] This latter hypothesis traces its lineage back to James Madison's claim that it is easier to practice the "vicious arts by which elections are too often carried" in the small than in the large republic (Madison, Hamilton, and Jay 1987, *The Federalist*, no. 10). According to this reasoning, lower district size fosters electoral manipulation and renders less free the "suffrages of the people," particularly in a heavily clientelistic environment, such as Panama, that is also characterized by a strong demand for public goods triggered by skewed income distribution and a high concentration of resources (including educational and professional opportunities) in the main urban areas. Such "vicious arts" should be less viable in larger constituencies, where maintaining electorally successful personal relationships is more costly (and, consequently, less feasible) and better-informed voters are more numerous. This view is shared by Katz (1980, 30):

In districts with relatively few voters, the likelihood that a candidate will be known personally by a significant proportion of his constituents is naturally greater than in districts with many voters. Meeting large numbers of voters and appealing to them on the basis of personal acquaintance only becomes a viable strategy when the district population is reasonably small. Under these circumstances, appeal to locality also may be expected. As an empirical matter, these trends ought to be most common in rural and traditionally oriented areas, where localism and personalism are likely to be embedded in the political culture. On the other hand, as the population of a district grows, the proportion of the voters that can be known by a single candidate must shrink, and so this type of appeal must be supplemented with less direct appeals.

Given Panama's historical legacies and structural characteristics, reduced district size reinforces the clientelistic tradition. If political operators can manipulate voters in lightly populated constituencies to select their representatives not on policy or programmatic foundations but, rather, on the basis of patron-client relationships, elected officials are freer to pursue their own interests or advance the agenda of their patrons, including the executive, party leaders, and business sponsors. They can easily detach from their constituents except with regard to the continued provision of personal services, for they know that the issue at stake at reelection time is not policy but the assignment of public goods on a particularistic basis. Thus, in the Panamanian context, reduced district size reinforces clientelism and undermines the notion of democratic representation, a public arrangement requiring accountability and responsiveness to the interests of the constituency (Pitkin 1967).

Personalistic Campaign Strategies

Panamanian incumbents seeking reelection and, in general, candidates coveting a deputy's seat advertise and claim credit on the basis of their capacity to provide personal goods and services. As a close observer of Panama's electoral campaigns since 1984, I have seen candidates engage in the most peculiar activities in order to captivate the attention of their constituents. "Walking" their districts—normally in the company of family, assistants, and, on occasion, prominent supporters and music bands—is the essential campaign activity. These constituency tours allow the candidate to reveal him or herself as an accessible individual, capable of interacting with ordinary citizens to help them sort out personal problems. Candidates thus perceived can claim to deserve constituents' preferential vote on the party ballot.

During these constituency tours, aspirants to an assembly seat—especially if they are assembly members wishing to retain their seats—receive hundreds of petitions, including requests of assistance in obtaining a job or government subsidy, or even of cash handouts to overcome personal difficulties. Most candidates bring along promotional material to distribute among voters: caps, t-shirts, mugs, glasses, pens, pencils, calendars, notebooks, keyholders, umbrellas, flashlights, candy, and food items, all of which bear the aspirant's name, campaign colors, symbols, motto, party affiliation, and—quite significantly, in the case of multi-member districts—the candidate's number on the ticket so constituents know where to look for him or her on the ballot and which box to tick for a preferential vote. These constituency tours also provide an occasion for sponsoring sports events and holding raffles for home appliances, such as electric fans, radios, television sets, refrigerators, washing machines, and stoves. In addition to promoting the personal qualities of the candidates, these events help aspirants manifest their concern for the well-being of their communities.

These activities are reminiscent of campaign styles in other countries. In the novel *Noticia de un secuestro* (News of an Abduction), by Colombian Nobel laureate Gabriel García Márquez, Pacho describes "how votes were obtained in Colombia and how it was that many members of Congress were elected" in the late 1980s and early 1990s:

> Vote-buying is rampant throughout the country, especially in the coastal region.[14] Raffles of home appliances in exchange for electoral favors are common. Many of the successful candidates are elected through their recourse to political vices, such as charging commissions over public salaries and misusing constituency funds. In this manner, the same people are always elected through the same means. (García Márquez 2004, 297)

In Panama, successful performance as a provider or distributor of broadly sought goods and services is considered necessary to solicit the personal vote, making it crucial that candidates have access to public or personal resources. Incumbents who are well connected with the government or the private sector thus have an advantage over those lacking such connections. In 1989 when an opposition aspirant with no obvious links to the military regime, but considerable personal wealth and a close association with the country's main brewery, decided to run for an assembly seat representing a lower-class urban constituency, he put in motion a bread-and-circus campaign. The "bread" aspect consisted of collecting and paying constituents' power bills during the electoral campaign. The "circus" aspect consisted of providing various free beer taps at selected street corners every Friday. The candidate was not only elected in 1989 but reelected five years later (Guevara Mann 2007).

The Balance of Power between the Executive and the Assembly

A constitutional design based on executive predominance, to the detriment of the representative chamber, has consequences for the assembly's performance and provides specific incentives to members' behavior (Hartlyn 1988; Shugart and Carey 1992; Weber 1918/1978). For analytic purposes, these consequences may be grouped into two broad categories. Barred from consequential participation in the affairs of state, members of a subordinate assembly may turn to "negative" or obstructionist politics. Alternatively, they may become involved in "low" politics, that is, issues of patronage, clientelism, and corruption. Which of these two activities members of a subordinate assembly choose to engage in also depends on additional institutional incentives (both formal and informal) available to representatives.

Following Max Weber, in a highly ideological setting, such as imperial Germany, also featuring a strong, efficient bureaucracy, the expected outcome is that an assembly "excluded from positive participation in the direction of political affairs" will engage in "negative politics." Such a chamber is likely to commit to confronting the administration "as if it were a hostile power." In Weber's view, this attitude has consequences not only for the reputation of the assembly and its members but also for the legitimacy of representative government. Indeed, a "hostile" assembly

> will be given only the indispensable minimum of information and will be considered a mere drag-chain, an assembly of impotent fault-finders and know-it-alls. In turn, the bureaucracy will then easily appear to parliament and its voters as a caste of careerists and henchmen who subject the people to their annoying and largely superfluous activities. (Weber 1918/1978, 1408)

To avoid this negative outcome—as well as to make the assembly a training ground for democratic leadership—in his "Parliament and Government" essay Weber proposed increasing the powers of the German representative chamber to transform it into "a working parliament . . . one which supervises the administration by continuously sharing its work" (1416).

In passing, Weber also observed that powerlessness might have other consequences for the representative assembly. To introduce the critique of plebiscitary legislation contained in "Parliament and Government," he wrote: "the mistrust against the powerless *and therefore* corrupt parliaments of the individual American [U.S.] states has led to an expansion of direct popular legislation" (Weber 1918/1978, 1455, emphasis in original). Thus, in Weber's view, a weak, incompetent assembly undermines representative government—the "ideally best" political system, according to J. S. Mill 1861/1958—in favor of plebiscitary rule, which is prone to excess and capricious swings of opinion.

This is a logical expectation, especially in a political environment heavily influenced by clientelism and where policy matters fail to attract the attention of broad sectors of the population. In other words, in clientelistic settings, an assembly subordinated to the executive and restrained from involvement in major political issues is likely to channel its energies toward issues of "low politics." Likewise, a president interested in further reducing the autonomy of the deliberative chamber will promote the involvement of representatives in these activities.

This view coincides with Cox and Morgenstern's—expressed as one of the categories in their four-fold typology of Latin American presidents and assemblies—that a venal or parochial assembly corresponds to a nationally oriented president (Cox and Morgenstern 2002). The hypothesis also finds at least partial sustenance in the experience of pre-1991 Colombia. As noted by Hartlyn (1988, 170–71), intense centralization focused members of the Colombian Congress's attention on "electoral, patronage and brokerage matters, particularly pork-barrel funds and the placement of job holders," and fostered the delegation of "high" or national political issues to the executive.

This interpretation also holds for Panama. An institutional design promoting active assembly involvement in national affairs was never characteristic of Panama, perhaps because of what constitutional specialist César Quintero described as the "mistrust that a complex or numerous or excessively active legislative branch generated and still generates in important sectors of the country." From 1904 to 1945, under the statutes of 1904 and 1941, the assembly met every two years for a brief, ninety-day period. This changed in 1946, when that year's constitution established annual, four-month sessions. However, such features as a low number of deputies,[15] a four-year mandate (which Professor Quintero considered long), and the assembly's own lack of initiative and discretion to convene extraordinary sessions remained in place. In his view, these traits prevented the chamber from becoming "a truly popular and dynamic organ" (Quintero 1967, 473, 475, 478, 485–86).

In 1983 the military reintroduced a deliberative chamber ostensibly designed along liberal-democratic lines, but this new body was even more constrained than the old regime's National Assembly, as can be seen through comparison of the assembly's powers as stipulated in the 1946 and 1972 constitutions. Articles 118 and 120 of the 1946 constitution assigned the assembly primary responsibility for determining the organization and structure of the administration as well as the size of the national security force, managing the public debt, approving all government contracts, planning the construction of public works, appointing the prosecutor-general and solicitor-general, and scrutinizing the government's accounts. Articles 159 and 161 of the 1972 constitution, however, gives the executive and other state agencies—such as the Comptroller-General's Office—the upper hand in all these affairs.[16] Article 120 of the 1946 constitution allowed the assembly to summon cabinet ministers without major restrictions. While broadening the range of officials that the chamber may summon, article 161 of the 1972 constitution limits their activity before the assembly to responding to the specific questions that the chamber must submit to the official forty-eight hours before his or her appearance. In the realm of foreign relations, article 163 of the 1972 constitution prevents the assembly from requesting "copies of instructions issued to diplomatic agents" or "reports on confidential negotiations." Article 121 of the 1946 constitution only forbade the assembly from requesting public reports on pending confidential diplomatic negotiations. The same provision of the 1946 charter prevented the assembly from authorizing public works in addition to those approved in the respective law, except in emergency cases as declared by the chamber. According to the 1972 statute, only the executive can declare a state of emergency. Article 163 of the 1972 constitution provides a revealing summary of the restricted role of the assembly under the new regime: it forbids the chamber from "interfering through resolutions in matters within the sphere of responsibility of other branches of government." The 1946 constitution contained no similar provision.

Reduced Budgetary Powers

In no other field is this restricted role more evident than in the budgetary sphere. Article 118 of the 1946 constitution assigned the assembly authority to approve the budget bill submitted by the executive, with or without amendments. If the chamber was unable to vote on the bill before its sessions expired, responsibility for this task fell upon the Permanent Legislative Commission, a seven-member committee of deputies that sat during the assembly's eight-month recess (article 122).

In contrast, the 1972 constitution severely restricts the capacity of the chamber to modify the budget bill. To that effect, the 1983 Constitutional Reform Commission added a full new chapter to the statute (articles 267–78). Accordingly, the assembly may only eliminate or reduce expense items that do not affect debt service expenditures or previously authorized public investments; it may not increase expenditures without the approval of the executive; and it may not increase income figures without the approval of the Comptroller-General's Office. Finally, if all these requirements are met, the assembly still requires executive approval before amending any item on the budget bill. If the assembly fails to approve the bill, the executive has the prerogative of enacting its budgetary initiative through a cabinet resolution. If the assembly expressly rejects the budget bill, the executive automatically rolls over the previous year's budget with the rejected bill's appropriations for debt service and public investments (Fábrega and Boyd Galindo 1981, 150–57; República de Panamá 2004).

These restrictions on the assembly's involvement in budgetary matters responded to criticism of irresponsibility and demagoguery under the old regime (Quintero 1967, 525–28). According to Mario Galindo Heurtematte, a former minister of finance (1989–93) and director at the Panama Canal Authority who also represented the opposition party MOLIRENA on the 1983 Constitutional Reform Commission, a mistrust of the chamber's potential for decreeing inflated budgets triggered the limitation of the assembly's competence in budgetary issues under the new constitutional regime.[17] But the limitations also reflect a clear intention of the military-dominated Constitutional Reform Commission to subordinate the chamber to the executive, a decision that, unsurprisingly, contributed to disseminating the view of assembly members as recycled county representatives and, as such, little more than influence peddlers with no real role in national policy making.

On only two significant aspects does the 1972 charter grant the assembly more leeway than the 1946 statute. Article 159 of the 1972 text places limits on the exercise of extraordinary powers by the executive, expressly excluding such matters as introducing new taxes, approving international treaties, and modifying provisions on civil and political rights as well as on penalties for crimes. The 1972 constitution also extends the assembly's plenary sessions to two four-month periods interrupted by two two-month recesses (article 149)—a significant change from the 1946 rules, according to which the assembly met annually for only a brief, four-month period (article 109) (Fábrega and Boyd Galindo 1981, 147; República de Panamá 2004).

A Weak Assembly

Comparative analysis of its constitutional functions, such as was conducted by Shugart and Carey (1992, 148–52, 155), also highlights the National Assembly's weakness vis-à-vis the executive. The country's performance on Shugart and Carey's index, which attempts to assess how powerful a president is in constitutional terms, shows that Panama scores on the higher end in terms of presidential legislative powers, including package and partial vetoes, decree powers, exclusive introduction of legislation, and budgetary powers. On the basis of a recalculated score correcting original assessment inaccuracies,[18] Panama obtains 7.5 in an appraisal of presidential legislative powers across forty-three cases. This score, sixth highest on Shugart and Carey's index after Chile (1969 constitution, 12), Brazil (1988 constitution, 9), Chile (1891 and 1925 constitutions, 8), and Colombia (pre-1991 constitution, 8), is evidence of the significant checks on proactive political involvement that the 1972 constitution places on the National Assembly. On the same scale, the assembly obtains 6.0 under the 1946 constitution.

Even greater mistrust of a strong assembly than existed prior to 1968 seems to have inspired the decisions of the military-controlled Constitutional Reform Commission of 1983. Its design of the assembly was less democratic than the model adopted in 1946, not only with regard to distribution and balance of powers between the executive and the deliberative chamber but also in terms of accountability. By extending the mandate of assembly members (as well as all other elected officers) to five years, the 1983 reform added an obstacle to accountability to the electorate.[19] Moreover, as stated above, reducing the scope of the chamber's constitutional functions in a highly particularistic setting provided its members with an added incentive to engage in clientelism. While contrary to democratic theory, these developments are clearly in line with the authoritarian mentality of Panama's military regime, whose main exponent, Omar Torrijos, had a contemptuous opinion of representative assemblies. Torrijos confided this view to a U.S. reporter in a 1970 interview: "Under legislative government," he declared, "we had 42 legislators, who were 42 anchors. So we removed them and now the ship of state sails freely."[20]

Summary

Although seat allocation formulas, district size, and the balance of power between the executive and the assembly are not the only formal rules that contribute to shaping the actions of Panama's deputies, they are undoubtedly significant. All three institutional features reinforce Panama's strong clientelistic tradition. They were introduced during the military-controlled constitutional review process to promote the state-sponsored clientelism on which the military regime and its party, PRD, relied to continue dominating the country's politics.

These institutional arrangements have other consequences that undermine possibilities for further democratization in Panama. Seat allocation rules that place a premium on personalism further debilitate the weak ideological element in Panama's politics. Low district size helps prevent the election of individuals with solid national reputations as representatives, an issue that prevents the system of democratic representation from entrusting the tasks of government to the most competent members of the political community. Low district magnitude, an associated (but not directly correlated) feature, contributes to generate acute deviation from proportionality, contradicting the notion of political equality and discounting the votes of a considerable portion of the electorate. Centralization of government powers in the executive precludes the participation of the assembly in meaningful political issues. Such centralization also conflicts with the notion of balance of power and the need for democratic oversight that, according to Montesquieu, Madison, J. S. Mill, Weber, and other authors, constitute important safeguards against tyranny.

Personalism, the unsuitability of many deputies, political inequality, and lack of accountability may be traced at least partly to the formal institutional arrangements outlined in this chapter. But they are also related to informal institutional features that also have an impact on the behavior of political actors. Chapter 4 addresses the more salient informal institutions of Panama's political system that interact with formal institutions to stimulate the behavior of assembly members.

CHAPTER 4

Informal Institutions and Assembly Members' Behavior

Institutions do not require formal codification to be considered as such. Informal practices that guide action and create expectations—such as systemic corruption, impunity, and clientelism—might become institutionalized just like rules and procedures that are created according to formal parameters (Helmke and Levitsky 2006; North 1990). As distinct manifestations of the phenomenon of informal institutionalization, systemic corruption, impunity, and clientelism share similarities. All three, for instance, contradict democratic expectations and constitute violations of the legal-rational norm that actions by state officials should be impartial and universalistic (Weber 1922/1978, 217–26).

The abuse of office for personal gain, exemption from justice, and the assignment of particularistic benefits in exchange for political support effectively creates privileges in favor of certain individuals or groups, to the detriment of the notion of political equality. These phenomena may be complementary: impunity might provide protection from legal action against those who commit corrupt and particularistic actions that are illegal according to the letter of the law. Above all, in what concerns this study, the expectation of corruption, impunity, and clientelism encourages certain behaviors by Panamanian political actors in general and, specifically, by assembly members. These behaviors would not normally be tolerated in liberal democracies with more strongly institutionalized rule of law and more programmatic politics—at least not to the extent exhibited in the Panamanian case.

Systemic Corruption

Systemic corruption is one of the informal institutions that guides representatives' behavior in Panama. Transparency International (2010) defines corruption as "the abuse of entrusted power for private gain," including such activities as bribing public officials, providing kickbacks in government procurement, and embezzling public funds. Systemic corruption occurs when this abuse of power pervades a political system. Under such circumstances, it constitutes a "competing" informal institution, that is, one that coexists with nonfunctional formal institutional arrangements. Helmke and Levitsky (2006, 15) write that "competing informal institutions trump their formal counterparts, generating outcomes that diverge markedly from what is expected from the formal rules."

Many assessments of Panama's politics emphasize the pervasiveness of corruption. Freedom House (2009e) argues that "corruption remains widespread" in the country's politics, and Panama's Corruption Perceptions Index score in 2009 was 3.4, indicating a strong perception of the phenomenon (Transparency International 2009). The 2009 State Department report on human rights in Panama contends that corruption is a serious governance problem (U.S. Department of State 2010). A January 2008 *Economist Intelligence Unit* analysis of conditions on the isthmian republic asserts that "lack of progress on improving security and tackling corruption are seen as the main weaknesses of the government." "Corruption of public functionaries at all levels of government" is one of the country's main problems, according to the Bertelsmann Transformation Index report. This assessment notes that "Panamanian citizens perceive all branches of government as corrupt . . . The rise of crime and the corrupt nature of the judiciary have led to further disillusionment, which could lead to a significant decline in the popular support for democracy" (Bertelsmann Transformation Index 2008).

As an informal institution in Panama (and elsewhere), systemic corruption rests on unwritten, socially shared norms created, communicated, and enforced extra-officially (Helmke and Levitsky 2006, 5, 15). One basic norm relates to bribery and can be stated as follows: To get an officeholder to do something in one's interest or prevent the officeholder from carrying out an action against one's interest, one needs to bribe the officeholder. Government officials at all levels expect to receive bribes and interested parties expect to have to provide them, whether to a policeman to avoid a traffic citation or to a cabinet minister to secure a government contract. Such is the strength of bribery as a social norm that an online real estate and travel information site posted a guide to foreigners with information about how to proceed in encounters with traffic policemen:

Corruption: Panama's Police Bribed
Anyone that owns a car in Panama and regularly drives it either inside or outside of Panama City has come into contact with Panama's Finest at least a time or two. Maybe you were stopped for disobeying a nonexistent sign, maybe you were stopped because you were going 55 in a 50, or maybe you were just stopped because the cop was bored. Either way, we've all been there. Long story short, regardless of what law you supposedly broke, if you drive away with a ticket in hand, then you're a sucker.
Money talks in this country, and cops are always looking for a little extra cheddar. But unless you handle it correctly, they'll end up writing you a ticket that will cost you at least half a day to pay, even if it's only the $60.00 infraction for talking on the cell phone.
Let's be honest here. When you are deep in the interior of the country, driving along the highway minding your own damn business, and you see a cop on the side of the road with a radar detector, if you are human you'll naturally glance down at the odometer and check to see how fast you are going. Funny thing is, this guy is already waving you down, and attempting to pull you over from the side of the road. Odds are he probably doesn't even have batteries in his damn radar gun, but he's still in uniform and therefore may have other *compadres* up the road that are ready to bolt after your car if you pass this lookout guy . . .
A good metric is to include US$0.50 for every KM you were going over 10KM above what is supposedly the legal speed limit. Fold up a

$5.00 bill and put it in with your passport. That should have you off and running in no time.[1]

A case involving Legislator Haydée Milanés (PSOL, later PPAN, 1994–2004) illustrates the socially shared norm of bribery at a higher level. In September 2008 Milanés publicly accused Legislator Balbina Herrera (PRD, 1989–2004) of attempting to bribe her, nine years earlier, with US$750,000. The purpose of the payment offer was to persuade Milanés to remain a PRD ally and thus deny President Mireya Moscoso (PPAN, 1999–2004) a majority in the Legislative Assembly (Boyd Marciacq 2008). Needless to say, the Public Prosecutor's Office did not follow up on the allegation.

Another basic norm of corruption relates to patrimonialism, "a situation in which political rulers treat the state as if it were their own property" (Mainwaring 1999, 179). In Panama it is a widespread norm for officeholders to utilize their offices to obtain personal and family benefits. For example, it was claimed that Legislator Miguel Bush (PRD, 1989–2004) used part of his constituency fund to build a private road in his father-in-law's property (Pérez Jaramillo 1999a). According to Panamanian sociologist Raúl Leis (2004), such behaviors by politicians reveal "the effect in Panama of the patrimonialist culture, by which politics is conceived of and managed as an extension of private space." In liberal democratic regimes, most patrimonialist activities are considered instances of corruption, although loopholes might exist that allow the discretionary use of public resources with significant latitude.

Corruption has a very long history in Panama, going back to the Spanish domination. A lucrative contraband trade flourished in Panama through bribery of royal officials on the isthmus, especially during the decline of the imperial monopolistic commercial system in the eighteenth century. In 1722, for example, English smugglers "bribed the governor, the royal prosecutor," and other Panama City officials to ensure a place for their wares at that year's Portobello Fair (Guevara Mann 1996, 7). Figueroa Navarro's (1982) captivating study of isthmian society in the nineteenth century contains references to the enrichment of government officials and the creation of personal fortunes among some traditional families as a result of graft and embezzlement. A confidential official file on longtime bureaucrat Ramón Vallarino Jiménez, excerpts of which Figueroa Navarro reproduces, insinuates that Vallarino, Panama City's customs administrator in 1844, had become wealthy by appropriating customs duties. Appointments to Panama's bureaucracy were "based more on nepotism and personalism than on the intellectual merits of the officials . . . The particularistic character of recruitment engendered an environment of intrigues, machinations, and scheming" (Figueroa Navarro 1982, 180, 204).

When the urban patriciate decided to sever Panama's links with Madrid in 1821 as well as with Bogotá in 1903, they bribed the local garrison to guarantee that the occupying army would not derail their plans. Thus, independence was obtained without bloodshed and Panama's foundation was intimately linked to corruption.[2] Mariano Arosemena, one of the country's founding fathers, described the events of 1821 as follows:

> The garrison was the only sworn enemy of our enterprise [that is, independence] and an obstacle to our welfare. A sudden uprising against that brutal mercenary force would have been risky. We had to adopt measures that would lead to our objective. After profound meditations, good judgment advised undermining the army by encouraging its soldiers to desert, with the purpose of isolating their chiefs, and popularizing the independence ideal by creating political societies among the masses.
>
> Citizens Blas, Mariano, and Gaspar Arosemena . . . as well as José María Barrientos . . . assumed the sensitive mission of disbanding the troops, leaving their officers without a single armed soldier on which to rely to continue supporting the cause of His Catholic Majesty [the Spanish monarch]. These citizens paid deserters from their personal funds . . . Patriots paid each deserting soldier ten pesos. A soldier turning in his weapon received a larger emolument (15 pesos). (Arosemena 1949, 126–27)

Corruption gained strength in Panama throughout the twentieth century and, significantly, after the 1968 military coup.[3] During his ephemeral third administration (October 1–11, 1968), President Arnulfo Arias's restructuring of the National Guard appeared to threaten the officer corps' active participation in corrupt activities, including the drug trafficking, prostitution, and gambling enterprises in which the guard had been involved since the 1940s (Bernal 1986, 3; Naylor 1999, 215). In response, the guard overthrew Arias and inaugurated an era of direct rule by the military. In its unchecked exercise of power, the guard broadened its criminal involvement and subjected the institutions of the state to its rent-seeking interests.

Under the military regime corruption was facilitated by an abundance of economic resources in the form of bank loans, the proceeds of illicit activities that flowed into the country's financial sector, and valuable property turned over to the state by the United States between 1979 and 1999, after the 1977 Panama Canal Treaty entered into effect. These resources were available for plunder under an authoritarian regime subject to no vertical or horizontal controls. The military dictatorship secured loyalty through a system of graft and corruption that included extensive participation in the international arms and narcotics trade. The scheme was based on a military monopoly of these activities, including drugs transshipment and money laundering (Ropp 1992). Institutionalized illegality financed the flamboyant lifestyle of the dictators and their staff and strengthened their firm grip on power.

Especially in its latter phase, under the leadership of Manuel Noriega (1983–89), the military regime that ruled Panama in 1968–89 approximated the ideal construct of "sultanism," as defined by Chehabi and Linz (1998a). First identified as a regime type by Weber (1922/1978), sultanism is a system of domination "based on personal rulership." Loyalty to the ruler, however, "is motivated not by his embodying or articulating an ideology, nor by a unique personal mission, nor by any charismatic qualities, but by a mixture of fear and rewards to his collaborators." A sultanistic ruler exercises power "without restraint, at his own discretion and above all unencumbered by rules or by any commitment to an ideology or value system." Under sultanism, the rule of law is "constantly subverted by arbitrary personal decisions of the ruler, which he does not feel constrained to justify in ideological terms. As a result corruption reigns supreme at all levels of society" (Chehabi and Linz 1998a, 7–8).

Sultanistic regimes include Haiti under the Duvaliers, Cuba under Batista, the Dominican Republic under Trujillo, Nicaragua under the Somozas, Reza Pahlevi's rule in Iran, and Marcos's dictatorship in the

Philippines. Chehabi and Linz (1998b, 45, 47) posit that the powerful legacy of sultanism, especially in terms of "the corruption of society and the illegitimacy of individuals and institutions," leaves deep scars in a nation's polity that prevent the development of democratic institutions, notably the rule of law. This is certainly true of Panama, where not only is the rule of law defective (as discussed in the following section) but corruption is the name of the game in national politics. Indeed, as emphasized in the Bertelsmann Transformation Index 2008 report,

> Although the public views corruption as one of the most urgent problems facing the country, little has been done to address this problem in recent years. Corrupt officeholders are still not prosecuted adequately under the law. The [Martín] Torrijos Administration [PRD, 2004–9], which had promised to fight corruption, was itself widely perceived as corrupt. In October 2006, the newspaper *El Siglo* revealed that Torrijos engaged in nepotism, appointing several family members as ambassadors or consuls.

Impunity

O'Donnell (1996, 43) notes that "In many countries of the global East and South, there is an old and deep split between the *pays réel* and the *pays legal*"—that is, between how individuals operate on a daily basis and what the law stipulates. This split is reflected in such features as a denial of justice for marginalized sectors and impunity for those who have influence to escape law enforcement. Despite what legal codes may prescribe, justice is not fulfilled partly because, in an expression of informal institutionalization, some members of the political community— particularly those with resources to penetrate the judicial process— succeed in remaining free from prosecution (O'Donnell 1998a).

The informal norm regarding impunity encourages influential individuals to manipulate the judicial system to their advantage with the purpose of remaining beyond the reach of justice. Paraphrasing the author of the traffic guidelines in the preceding section, only suckers and losers are subject to the stringencies of the law. O'Donnell (1999, 312) illustrates the rationale and implications of this informal rule: "When a shady businessman recently [1997] said in Argentina, 'To be powerful is to have (legal) impunity,' he expressed a presumably widespread feeling that, first, to voluntarily follow the law is something that only idiots do and, second, that to be subject to the law is not to be the carrier of enforceable rights but rather a sure signal of social weakness."

The informal institutionalization of impunity creates expectations and in part determines the behavior of political actors in Panama, as in other countries of the "global East and South." The U.S. State Department's *Report on Human Rights Practices* for Panama in 2007 indicates that "although the law provides for an independent judiciary, the judicial system was susceptible to corruption and outside influence, including manipulation by other branches of government" (U.S. Department of State 2008). The 2009 Freedom House entry on Panama concurred when it stated that the judiciary "remains overburdened, inefficient, politicized, and prone to corruption" (Freedom House 2009e). In actuality, individuals enjoying influence and money have the certainty that they will not be prosecuted for the illegalities they may commit.

Informally institutionalized impunity facilitates corruption and clientelism and has consequences for the behavior of political actors, among them assembly members. In liberal democracies with strong rule of law, the certitude—or near certitude—that transgressions of legality, if discovered, will be punished contributes to keeping illegal behavior under control. Where, as in Panama, the certainty is that judicial authorities will not prosecute violations of the law by influential individuals, political actors are free to operate with significantly lesser constraints on their actions.

The Military Boost to Impunity, 1968–89

A fair degree of impunity was prevalent in Panama prior to 1968, as expected in a setting where social networks and patron-client relationships were the basic units of political interaction (Janson Pérez 1993, 12–13). Columbia University sociologists John Biesanz and Mavis Hiltunen Biesanz, who conducted a broad study of isthmian society in the early 1950s, remark that while the press occasionally accused officials of graft, "arrest or punishment for misappropriation of public funds" was uncommon (Biesanz and Biesanz 1955, 145). Perhaps the most notorious instance of impunity during the old regime occurred in 1955, when the dominant political sectors succeeded in covering up the assassination of President José Antonio Remón (1952–55). On this occasion, political maneuvering not only resulted in the obstruction of justice but also in the removal and infamous conviction of First Vice-President José Ramón Guizado, who was unjustly charged with the killing's intellectual authorship (Pippin 1964; Zúñiga 1980; see also chapter 1).

The old regime was inadequate in ensuring justice and fairness, but it was the military dictatorship that provided the most significant impulse for Panama's present "unrule" of law. An editorial in *El Panamá América* (April 11, 2000) supports this view:

> A culture of concealment, cover-ups, indifference, and disregard developed in our country over recent decades, even with respect to flagrant violations of the Constitution and laws supposedly in force . . . The authorities discover a container full of several million dollars, a worker falls from a scaffold as a result of inappropriate security measures, a repugnant homicide is committed, thieves rob money custody agencies, government checks are falsified, abuses of power or bribery occur, and the community finds out through the media, which covers the events for a few days, after which everything falls into a black hole in the community's conscience and the mind of the authorities.
>
> Without a doubt, this decay in the rule of law gained strength and became consolidated during the 21 years of military preeminence. At that time, family or friendship relations—or simply money—allowed military officers to discontinue an investigation, bend the will of a jury, or arrange with a prosecutor, judge, or prison warden the removal of penalties or the silencing of the media.
>
> Unfortunately, the reestablishment of democracy has not produced much improvement. We can even say that in some aspects, things have deteriorated in the last years. It is high time for civil society to become more watchful and militant in demanding the prosecution and punishment of crimes and transgressions of the law.

As conveyed by the editorialist, the military regime subverted whatever weak rule of law there was in Panama in 1968. Upon assuming power, the National Guard "suspended" several provisions of the 1946 constitution, notably the guarantees of individual rights contained in the charter (Organization of American States 1978, 12–13). Pursuant to its "Provisional Government Statute," which acquired supremacy over the 1946 constitution, the armed forces appointed a military junta and a cabinet, exercised legislative authority, and nominated compliant individuals to the Supreme Court and the Prosecutor-General's Office (Bernal 1986, 46, 21–22, 82–83). Predictably, police, investigative, and intelligence operations remained strictly dependent upon the National Guard commandant.

To replace the 1946 charter, the dictatorship put through its own constitution, which entered into force on October 11, 1972, the fourth anniversary of the military coup. Article 2 provided for the exercise of public power by the executive, legislative, and judicial branches acting in "harmonic collaboration" with the "public force," that is, the military. Article 277 recognized the leadership of Omar Torrijos and confirmed his sweeping authority over national affairs, including the power to appoint Supreme Court justices, the prosecutor-general, and the officers of the National Guard (Fábrega and Boyd Galindo 1981, 7, 96–97). Although this clause expired in 1978, judicial nominations remained the monopoly of the guard's commandant throughout the regime. By appointing the judiciary's high officials, the country's military rulers effectively influenced the entire law-enforcement sector, all members of which owed their nominations to their immediate superiors (Organization of American States 1978, 15, 69).

The Effects of Militarism on the Rule of Law

A policy of removing the criminal activities of the military dictatorship from the judicial sphere had crippling effects on Panama's law-enforcement organizations. Twenty years after the demise of authoritarian rule, the country's judicial authorities have not yet successfully prosecuted the vast majority of crimes and incidents of corruption occurring in 1968–89. Moreover, throughout the regime, the judiciary served to grant pseudo-legal validity to the arbitrary actions of the dictatorship. For instance, in early 1976, after a number of human rights activists sued the government for exiling several prominent opponents, the Supreme

Court dismissed the plea, even though the 1972 constitution expressly forbade exile.

In 1977 the Inter-American Commission on Human Rights reported the dictatorship's highly arbitrary exercise of power and its numerous interferences with the judicial process. The organization also recommended that the government take measures to assure the effective independence of the judiciary and order all officials of the executive branch—including officers of the National Guard—to comply with judicial decisions (Organization of American States 1978, 99–100, 110–11). The dictatorship, however, not only ignored these recommendations but stepped up its brutality and illegality, especially after Manuel Noriega assumed command of the Panamanian Defense Forces (PDF) in 1983.[4]

Active military engagement in illicit activities such as torture, political assassinations and "disappearances," embezzlement, bribery, contraband, and narcotics and arms trafficking undermined the moral basis of the law and promoted these manifestations of criminal behavior as a practicable way of life. For National Guard officers, PRD leaders, government officials, and—in general—supporters of the military regime, illegality protected by impunity provided a viable means of acquiring wealth quickly, rising in economic status, and achieving a measure of social advancement. State-fostered illegality became, in effect, the trademark of military-controlled Panama. In addition, intrusion by the armed forces in public affairs promoted the isthmian variant of militarism, combining corruption, violence, and a disregard for human rights, as a viable modus vivendi. These traits, operating in sharp contradiction with the letter and spirit of the law, characterized Panamanian society under military rule (Bernal 1986, 47–50, 62–63, 82–84; Naylor 1999, 215–24).

Liberal Democracy and the Unrule of Law

Panama returned to civilian rule in 1989–90 burdened by the trauma of the U.S. invasion and contaminated by a culture of violence, impunity, and corruption. Although the invasion crushed the PDF and put an end to its control of the state, it represented no solution for the country's acute structural crisis. Addressing these issues was the responsibility of

Panama's new rulers. But, contrary to public expectations, which called for a complete overhaul of the constitutional, judicial, and administrative systems, the government of President Guillermo Endara (PPAN, 1989–94) decided to abide by the military regime's legal framework, including the 1972 constitution, as amended in 1983.

In addition to Endara's failure to democratize Panama's juridical structure and his adherence to the dictatorship's constitution, the apathy of judicial authorities in seeking indictments against those accused of numerous illegal acts committed during the military regime was particularly demoralizing (Furlong 1993). Interventions by the executive to forestall the course of justice were also detrimental to the consolidation of an effective and transparent judicial system. The most blatant of these interventions took the form of presidential pardons. Although article 184 (section 12) of the constitution stipulates that this executive function only applies to political (not criminal) offenses, Panama's presidents have used them to protect influential individuals from prosecution in criminal cases as well.

In June 1994, a few weeks before the expiration of his term, Endara used the prerogative to pardon 542 civilian collaborators of former dictator Manuel Noriega accused of political offenses (Ministerio de Gobierno y Justicia 1994a, 1994b, 1994c, 1994d). Based on this precedent, the Pérez Balladares administration (PRD, 1994–99) issued at least three pardon decrees covering 390 individuals, among them some conspicuous collaborators of the military dictatorship whose offenses the executive interpreted as having a "political" nature. Among those exonerated from criminal responsibility were several former PDF officers accused of gross human rights violations, notorious appropriators of public resources, and the architects of the military regime's electoral frauds (Ministerio de Gobierno y Justicia 1994e, 1995; Rohter 1995; U.S. Department of State 2000).

Reflecting on this abuse of executive authority, an editorial in *El Panamá América* (August 31, 1999) condemned the "shameful" practice of "abusing, denaturalizing, and prostituting" the prerogative of presidential pardons in order "to release common criminals." "In five years of government by PRD," added the editorial, "more than a thousand criminals have been exonerated and set free." According to the daily, the list included "looters of the public treasury," "coward assassins," "embezzlers of the worst breed," "torturers," and "rapists," among other types.

The proclivity to exempt criminals from justice did not, however, remain a monopoly of PRD administrations. Toward the end of her term, President Mireya Moscoso (PPAN, 1999–2004) also issued various pardon decrees. One of them covered four individuals convicted of plotting to assassinate Cuban leader Fidel Castro during a visit to Panama in 2000. The most prominent of these was Luis Posada Carriles, a notorious anti-Castro activist alleged to have participated in a 1976 conspiracy to explode a Cuban airplane en route from Caracas to Havana, resulting in the death of seventy-three passengers (Campbell 2006).

During his administration, President Martín Torrijos (PRD, 2004–9) granted pardons to persons convicted for various felonies (Flores 2009b). In addition, individuals linked to abuses during the military period received appointments during his tenure. The most alarming of these appointments was that of Daniel Delgado Diamante, a former National Guard officer facing an investigation into the killing of a military subordinate. Delgado served in sensitive positions, including those of customs chief and, later, Minister of Government and Justice (2007–8) in charge of domestic security. Torrijos eventually sacked Delgado, replacing him with a former justice in the dictatorship's "discredited Supreme Court" (Jackson 2008).

The practice of readmitting collaborators of the military regime continued under President Ricardo Martinelli (CD, 2009–14), who appointed as police chief an officer in Noriega's vicious "antiterrorist" unit (UESAT). During the latter years of the dictatorship, UESAT served to smother pro-democracy dissidents, and at the time of the U.S. invasion it reportedly carried out abductions and assassinations of civilians (Jackson 2009a). In May 2010 President Martinelli issued a round of pardons exonerating forty-seven policemen for various excesses, including killings (Mendoza 2010). Shockingly, the chief executive also admitted feeling "sorry" for former dictator Noriega, who at the time had just been arraigned for money laundering charges before a judge in France. The president said Noriega had already paid his dues to society and deserved to return to Panama to serve the remainder of his sentence time under house arrest (EFE 2010).

As this narration demonstrates, in addition to the sultanistic legacy of the military regime, a weak commitment to the universalistic foundations of liberal democracy as well as to the rule of law by Panama's civilian leaders has further eroded the cause of justice and legality. The generalized climate of impunity described in this section conditions the behavior of Panama's political actors, including members of the National Assembly. Politicians inclined to illicit behavior are likely to participate in illegalities if they know that with appropriate connections or for the right fee they can get away with unlawful activities.

In the case of Panama's assembly members, a long, five-year mandate, coupled with the nonexistence of citizen initiatives such as recall and referenda, serve to further promote impunity. Only parties, which are for the most part controlled by closed cliques, possess recall mechanisms.[5] Citizens are able to hold deputies accountable only at election time, once every five years. Additionally, between 1984 and 2004 members of the assembly enjoyed a broad "legislative" immunity—the topic of chapter 11—that they transmuted into an institution protecting them from prosecution in nearly all cases. Indeed, as long as deputies follow the party line, they have a free hand in personal enrichment and other particularistic activities during incumbency.

Clientelism

Lemarchand (qtd. in Taylor-Robinson 2006, 109) defines clientelism "as a mode of social stratification in which clients and patrons are tied to one another in a mutually beneficial but unequal exchange relationship." Mainwaring (1999, 177) identifies four defining features in this patron-client relationship: "an unequal character, uneven reciprocity, a noninstitutionalized nature, and a face-to-face character." Here we may substitute "noninstitutionalized" with "informally institutionalized" for, as recent scholarship has shown, clientelism may be considered an informal institution to the extent that it constitutes an unwritten set of rules around which actors' expectations converge (Helmke and Levistky 2006).

The basic norm of clientelism is that the weaker party to the transaction provides political support (chiefly—but not exclusively in a democracy—votes) in exchange for desired resources provided by, or through, a more powerful agent. According to Mainwaring (1999, 178), "Clientelistic relationships are not based on codified rules or universal criteria. Instead, the exchange is personalized and individualized, based on bargaining (implicit or explicit) between the two sides." Clientelism involves the assignment of public goods "as though they were personal favors to clienteles in return for supporting their political patron. Political criteria (allegiance to a person or party) and personal connections prevail over other possible modes of selection of beneficiaries (universal entitlement, random selection, meritocracy, efficiency, etc.)."

We have seen that although some clientelistic practices may involve illegal acts, clientelism and corruption are not synonymous. Mainwaring (1999, 180) points out that "some forms of clientelism constitute legitimate political practices." There is no doubt, however, that clientelism undermines the quality of democratic representation. Its private, particularistic nature contradicts the public essence of representation, as defined by Pitkin (1967, 221–22). Its hierarchical character countervails the principle of political equality that is at the root of liberal democracy and reduces possibilities for the exercise of democratic accountability. Constituents "bought" by politicians through clientelistic favors are unlikely to hold those politicians accountable when they fail to act in the public interest. Moreover, where the democratic system requires civic engagement and active involvement in public affairs, clientelism breeds passivity and conformism. As observed by O'Donnell (1996), clientelism may coexist with democracy; however, it reduces the possibilities for advancing toward a deeper democratization that, according to Dahl (1998), is the challenge for all liberal democracies.

The Ancient Lineage of Clientelism

Clientelism is a form of particularism, which refers to behavior by state officials oriented toward the satisfaction of particular needs (rather than some notion of the public good). In addition to clientelism, particularism encompasses patrimonialism, patronage, and other "actions that, under the formal rules of the institutional package" of democracy, "would be considered corrupt" (O'Donnell 1996). But although particularism is not entirely coterminous with corruption, significant overlap exists between both activities. In broad terms, patronage—another expression of particularism—refers to "the use or distribution of state resources on a nonmeritocratic basis for political gain" (Mainwaring 1999, 177). Goods distributed in exchange for support traditionally included jobs in the government bureaucracy. After the expansion in state activity experienced in most countries in the course of the twentieth century, however, today patronage additionally encompasses "public sector services and works projects, state contracts and concessions, and state investments" (Mainwaring 1999, 177). Political scientist Frank Sorauf has best expressed the concept "as an incentive system—a political currency with which to 'purchase' political activity and political responses" (Mainwaring 1999, 177).

When deputies procure bureaucratic appointments for political supporters or organizers (or their dependents or relatives) who are not qualified for such jobs, they engage in patronage. As an assistant to Panama's Minister of Foreign Relations (1999–2002), I witnessed several instances of assembly members and other well-placed political actors seeking appointments to benefit political allies. Such patronage might constitute corruption if the "broker" who seeks the appointment or the decision-making government official receives a bribe for making the appointment or award. Otherwise, it might violate regulations requiring a meritocratic or universalistic assignment of state resources. Oftentimes, however—while clearly not in the public interest—patronage can be legal if the allocating authority enjoys discretionary leeway.

Patron-client relationships have an ancient lineage going back at least to Roman times. The *Encyclopædia Britannica* entry on "clientship" defines the practice as a "relationship between a man of wealth and influence (patron) and a free client; the client acknowledged his dependence on the patron and received protection in return." Moreover, in ancient Rome,

> The patron might support his client in the courts or supply him with daily food, often converted into cash (*sportula*). The client was expected to show deference to his patron, especially by calling upon him each morning (*salutatio*) and by aiding him in his private and public life. The political in-

fluence exercised by patrons over their clients was of considerable importance in the voting conducted in the public assemblies (*comitia*) under
the republic. (*Encyclopædia Britannica* 2008)

Clientelism had a prominent role in many political systems throughout history. To cite just one example, alongside such associated features
as a "strongly hierarchical society" and particularism, clientelism was—
according to Finer (1997, 1311)—one of the "forces" that maintained
French absolutism in operation: "The king kept his nobles sweet by grants
of honours, lands, pensions, appointments, and the power to distribute
minor appointments to their followings. In their turn, these great nobles
dispensed these favours to their dependants, high and low, like so many
Mafia 'Godfathers,' and so guaranteed the Crown their allegiance and
service."

The practice became part of Latin American politics during the Ibe-
rian domination and, after the surge of electoral politics, gained a principal expression in vote buying (Williamson 1992, 146–47, 237–38,
280). Private and public resources may serve to finance clientelistic activities; when public resources are employed, clientelism may overlap
with patronage, depending on whether the relationship is hierarchically
unequal and unevenly reciprocal. Variants of clientelism operate, for example, when Panamanian deputies seeking reelection buy constituents'
votes or when assembly members obtain cash rewards from the executive in exchange for passing a government-sponsored bill. Though these
activities are illegal and penalized by Panamanian law, they are nevertheless widely prevalent, as this study shows.

As noted, not all particularistic behaviors constitute instances of ex-
ploiting public trust for private benefit. For instance, although their activities might violate the universalistic criterion that is part and parcel
of our understanding of democracy, representatives who orchestrate the
assignment of state resources in their constituencies on a nonuniversal-
istic or nonmeritocratic basis—for example, to friends or supporters, as
is common in some liberal democracies—do not necessarily engage in
corruption. But, as was also mentioned before, corruption and particularism intersect at certain points. Such intersection occurs, for example,
when deputies accept bribes to cast votes in certain ways, use assembly

staff allocations to appoint family members or close associates who do not perform their functions, or misappropriate, for personal gain, constituency funding provided by the state.

A Time-Honored Clientelistic Tradition

Clientelism—a paradigmatic informal institution—historically had strong influence on Panama's politics, a characteristic noted by students of isthmian society and political culture (Biesanz and Biesanz 1955; Janson Pérez 1993; Guevara Mann 2007). Janson Pérez emphasizes the "face-to-face" nature of social, economic, political, and religious interactions, which she explains on the basis of a historically low population density. "In terms of social organization," she adds, "the social network and patron/client relationships became the basic units above the level of the family . . . In asymmetrical relations, the patron/client relationship—called *compadrazgo* and *padrinazgo* in the Panamanian political scenario—prevailed as the basic relation for survival and upward mobility" (Janson Pérez 1993, 12–13).

In Janson Pérez's view, the gradual erosion of ideology experienced after Panama's secession from Colombia in 1903 reinforced clientelism. "Personalism, reliance on networks, and pragmatism tended to stunt the growth of parties based on principles over personalities." Furthermore,

> In a society where pragmatism reigned, principled leaders were discouraged, removed, or isolated. Defense of principles was anathema in a culture which relied on personal relationships to obtain desired goods and ends.
>
> Financed by special interests, larger political parties were but higher-level structures built upon personalism, family, network, and patron/client relationships for the purpose of enhancing and protecting these interests.
>
> Thus, the concept of the political party as an instrument of political patronage was entrenched. Voting behavior in terms of supporting a party in the expectation that, when in power the party would provide jobs, was generalized. Individuals put enormous pressure upon government officials to provide jobs and special favors. Conversely, it was not only politically but socially disastrous for an office holder to fail to meet his network obligations, or for a party to neglect its own while in power. (Janson Pérez 1993, 23–26)

Biesanz and Biesanz concur with Janson Pérez's notions about the lack of ideology and the pervasiveness of clientelism in the old regime, which they argue, conforms to the "Latin American pattern." In their view, party labels meant little: "The party is not . . . a group of like-thinking citizens advocating a certain platform to be fulfilled by a certain candidate. It is a personalized affair, a feudal system in miniature in which the candidate is the 'Gran señor,' and his vassals support him with the expectation of receiving protection and favors in return" (Biesanz and Biesanz 1955, 144).

According to a practice already well established at the time of Biesanz and Biesanz's writing, party leaders would "court the local caciques, or chiefs (also called *gamonales*)." These "ward heelers" of Panama—landowners or merchants who frequently held public office as provincial deputies, governors, or mayors—"control blocks of votes, and no party leader dares ignore them. They are the foundation stones of party organization, particularly in the rural districts" (1955, 151–52). Panamanian intellectual Gil Blas Tejeira,[6] cited by Biesanz and Biesanz, explains the dynamics of a political system deeply permeated by clientelism:

> Many are the *gamonales* who owe their power and influence to the fact that they always have their purses open to take care of a need which they know exists and to their willingness always to help a friend in an administrative matter. Naturally when election day draws near . . . the farmer . . . prefers to go to the cacique for advice, offering his vote. For the only thing which really interests him is to be able to go on counting on the aid and protection of the *gamonal,* with the money in his pocketbook when necessary, and with the letter for the governor or the assemblyman or the high functionary so they will give heed to his requests.
>
> The *campesino* and even the city man who has no considerable wealth nor independent position is accustomed to depend on the influential friend in order to have his rights respected, tranquility to keep the things he possesses and even to secure those little favors which are denied to those who do not have such relationship. (Biesanz and Biesanz 1955, 151–52)

Anthropologist Gloria Rudolf offers yet another depiction of clientelism in the old regime. Her study of a small highland community in central Panama covers the dynamics of client-patron relationships that constituted the basis of rural politics prior to 1968. Although the text employs fictitious names to protect confidentiality, it is illustrative not only of the support-buying mentality of politicians but also of voters' expectations of candidates and deputies wishing to retain their assembly seats:

> I remember when Lelo Conte ran for Deputy in the old National Assembly. When he started he was rich, when he ended he was richer. At election time he came to Copé and sent word up to us that there would be food. We all climbed down to get some, but there wasn't even much to eat. My mother didn't get any. Later, after the election, she saw him once and asked him for something in return for her vote. He said, "No," mentioning that he had already given much. He did nothing for us. A little later Choncho Sosa campaigned in Copé and he got us to vote with the promise of meat . . . By the time I got there it was all gone, but we collected big sacks of sugar. After the vote we never saw Sosa again. Then there was Juan Arango who distributed money. (Rudolf 1999, 129)

Military Clientelism through Control of State Resources

Janson Pérez, Biesanz and Biesanz, and Rudolf agree that electoral results in old regime Panama were highly determined by asymmetrical patron-client relationships. As exercised by National Assembly aspirants or deputies seeking reelection, clientelism constituted a highly visible informal institution in the sense that it guided political life more effectively than codified rules, as theorized by O'Donnell (1996). Because in their quest for political gain candidates relied significantly on private resources, however, the practice was not entirely coterminous with patronage, or "the use or distribution of state resources on a nonmeritocratic basis for political gain" (Mainwaring 1999, 177).

This characteristic would change with the exponential growth in state activity in the 1960s and 1970s, particularly after the 1968 military coup, as well as with the military regime's heavy reliance on state resources to buy political support. Beginning with the U.S. Alliance for Progress initiative and, later, with the expansion in the availability of international finance and development capital, the Panamanian state became eligible for—and made use of—large amounts of funding (Koster and Sánchez Borbón 1990, 122, 138, 147). A strong legacy of clientelism, in addition to the authoritarian, particularistic, and venal nature of the military regime and the lax funding criteria applied by international donors and financiers, naturally resulted in a heightened use of state funds to cultivate political clienteles. Janson Pérez writes:

> The funds obtained from outside sources by the military-controlled governments were detoured into the pockets of office-holders, no doubt. They were also employed to accentuate paternalism and patron/client relationships.
>
> Instead of being converted into goods and services in the form of "rights" or entitlements, the military-controlled government converted these inputs into "gifts." Already existing paternalism and patron/client relations systems of political adaptation were thus strengthened. (Janson Pérez 1993, 357)

The military regime's efforts to build clienteles targeted low-income urban dwellers and the peasantry. Outside funding allowed the creation of Banco Hipotecario Nacional, a state mortgage bank, in 1973, which provided an opportunity for assigning housing loans through political intermediaries as personal favors of dictator Omar Torrijos. Drivers' unions aligned with the regime gained access to fuel subsidies, and student leaders responsive to the military obtained scholarships, as did poor families who pledged support to the dictatorship. The expansion of the state allowed the use of the public payroll to favor political clients through government jobs in a manner that far surpassed the tradition of the old regime, under which the practice was customary (Biesanz and Biesanz 1955, 145–46; Pereira 1979, 136, 176–77; Priestley 1986, 129; Vásquez 1989, 215, 317).

Responsive rural communities—easier to manipulate than more informed and populated urban districts—also received benefits during the military period (Koster and Sánchez Borbón 1990, 214). Torrijos would frequently carry out what he called "domestic patrolling": tours of the countryside during which he personally supplied the needs of the local population—through immediate cash handouts, when required—and ordered improvements for the benefit of receptive communities (Wong 2001). In exchange for political support, the regime created and sponsored dozens of agricultural cooperatives and provided their leaders with easy access to credit, thereby channeling large amounts of public funding to the cooperatives. Their directing boards, most of whose members also drew salaries from the state, mismanaged a considerable proportion of these funds (Koster and Sánchez Borbón 1990, 151–52; Pereira 1979, 136–37; Priestley 1986, 60). Rudolf illustrates the dynamics of the new, state-financed clientelism as they affected a remote rural community in Coclé Province:

> To gain support of the peasantry, but keep control centralized in his office, Torrijos designed top-down, authoritarian, and male-controlled operations. He built them on patron-client relationships that reinforced existing economic, political, and gender inequalities. This meant that important decisions made at the political top in Panama City flowed downward through a system of patronage. Eventually, they would get to the level of military men like Fernando García who, in turn, selected a few local people as his client-allies . . .
>
> García tapped these men and their wives and families sometimes for economic assistance . . . He also turned to some of them for dependable political support. Carlos Rocha, for example, who had wide political networks in the region due to his years of work as a *regidor*,[7] acted often as García's political eyes, ears and mouth in the region. García groomed him as a candidate for municipal representative in the national elections of August of 1972, a position that Carlos won. (Rudolf 1999, 131)

As expected in a country with acute income inequality[8]—and as a result, strong, stable demand for public goods—clientelism succeeded in generating support for the military regime. At the polls, the regime's party, PRD, received no less than 19 percent of the assembly vote in the six elections between 1984 and 2009; the period average is 29 percent (see chapters 2 and 3 and appendix H). More significantly, widespread, state-sponsored clientelism became pervasive in Panama's political system. This feature falls in line with Chehabi and Linz's prediction that if a sultanistic regime is replaced by democracy, "chances are that this new democracy will display strong clientelistic tendencies, with the democratically elected leaders using the resources of their office to build nationwide patron-client relationships" (1998b, 45). Indeed, with regard to the behavior of Panamanian legislators, this strong legacy of clientelism encouraged the design and use of *partidas circuitales*—large constituency funds directly administered by members of the assembly—as a principal element in their reelection aspirations, especially in 1999.[9]

Summary

At least three informal institutions prevalent in Panama help create an environment that encourages assembly members to seek other ends besides career advancement through reelection and promotes the use of reelectoral devices seldom dealt with by analysts of assembly politics. A strong historical legacy of corruption, impunity, and clientelism, which received impetus during the 1968–89 military regime, fosters actions that, while not generally addressed in the literature, are central to understanding the behavior of representatives in some liberal democracies and the undemocratic performance of deliberative chambers in these settings. Assemblies constituted on the basis of corruption, impunity, and clientelism are bound to have difficulties in producing democratic effects because these informal traits violate the very essence of the liberal democratic system.

By encouraging bribery, embezzlement, and related corrupt activities; exempting certain individuals from justice (impunity); and manipulating voters through the particularistic assignment of public goods (clientelism), all three traits contradict the notions of political equality and universalism that are central to the idea of democracy. They also undermine the democratic requisites of the rule of law, transparency, and accountability, according to which the actions of government officials should unfold in compliance with the provisions of the law and the citizenry has a right to dismiss those officers who act illegally or unethically.

These traits also distort the notion of democratic representation, a legal fiction whereby the whole community participates in the fulfillment of such basic democratic functions as deliberation, lawmaking, and oversight and that additionally aims to assign the functions of government to the most competent members of the community. Members of deliberative chambers who obtain their seats by partaking in corrupt, illegal, or clientelistic activities hardly possess the necessary credentials to act substantively in the interest of the governed because these informal institutions pollute the link between constituents and their representatives. Democratic representation requires a free, fluid connection between representatives and constituents, a connection obstructed by the informal traits that condition the selection of Panama's deputies. Individuals who manipulate the political system to remain free from prosecution are hardly fit to act as anticipated by Madison, that is, as "proper guardians of the public weal." Last but not least, corruption, clientelism, and impunity may prevent the members of the political community from participating in the process of discussing, elaborating, and enacting measures that affect all, yet another key ingredient of the democratic system.

Clientelism in Panama is reinforced by at least three other formal institutional traits—seat allocation formulas, district size, and the balance of power between the executive and the assembly. The preceding chapter examined these institutional arrangements and showed how they foster personalism and patron-client relationships. The institutional arrangements covered in chapters 2 and 3 provide incentives to specific behaviors by Panama's assembly members. The remainder of the book addresses some of the more salient behaviors by Panamanian deputies that are at least partly stimulated by the institutional features addressed thus far.

PART II

Assembly Members' Goals,
Behaviors, and Activities

CHAPTER 5

Political Advancement through Reelection

Prospects and Possibilities in Panama

Theories of legislators' behavior, built primarily on the U.S. experience, portray representatives as self-interest maximizers whose main goal is to secure reelection (Fenno 1973; Mayhew 1974). Fenno (1973, 1) initially suggested that members of the U.S. Congress are motivated by three basic goals (reelection, obtaining influence within the representative assembly, and formulating good public policy) and two additional objectives (pursuing higher office and securing private gain). Since the publication of Mayhew's *Congress: The Electoral Connection,* the scholarship has considered representatives in the United States primarily as "single-minded seekers of reelection" (Mayhew 1974, 5). Indeed, between 1946 and 1998, an average of 92 percent of members of the House of Representatives and 83 percent of Senate incumbents sought reelection in each electoral cycle (Ornstein et al. 2000, 57–58). In 1982–2004 the averages were 91 and 81 percent, respectively (Renka 2007).

The literature assumes that members of representative assemblies want reelection because they are interested in pursuing a political career. Within this framework, representatives are generally motivated by what Joseph Schlesinger (1966, 10) labeled "static ambition," that is, a desire to build "a long-run career out of a particular office," which theorists view as "a marked goal of many American [U.S.] congressmen and senators." Satisfying this objective through a congressional seat has become increasingly possible, as demonstrated by the high reelection rates enjoyed by members of the U.S. Congress. "Over the course of the past 100 years," wrote Loomis in 1998, "the Congress has developed into an institution that fosters long careers." In the mid-1990s, approximately 15 percent of House members had served twenty years, and the average member had spent ten years in the lower chamber. In the Senate the average length of service was eleven years, or roughly two terms (Loomis 1998, 63).

On average, 93 percent of the members of the House seeking reelection achieved their goal in 1964–2006. "Few things in life are more predictable than the chances of an incumbent member of the U.S. House of Representatives winning reelection," claimed the Center for Responsive Politics. "With wide name recognition, and usually an insurmountable advantage in campaign cash, House incumbents typically have little trouble holding onto their seats." For senators, the average in 1964–2006 was 82 percent—a somewhat lower percentage than for House members but still overwhelmingly in favor of incumbents (Center for Responsive Politics 2010).

Reelection, therefore, permits the continued exercise of political office. In the United States it is a *sine qua non* for members of Congress motivated by static political ambition. A congressional seat guarantees a place in the public arena, gives representatives a role in decision making as well as in the allocation of resources, and assigns responsibility for policy making and oversight, all of which constitute important activities for building and maintaining political careers. As a result, Mayhew's assertion that "successful pursuit of a career requires continual reelection" has become a fundamental premise of the literature on U.S. members' behavior (Mayhew 1974, 15–16).

This model travels well to other liberal democracies where there are no restrictions on the reelection of representatives and where an assembly seat actually provides interesting opportunities for career advancement (as it does in the United States). Recent studies have examined its applicability to other democratic states where reelection is forbidden or uncommon. Authors thus engaged have also started from the premise that representatives everywhere seek political advancement. They have concluded, however, that in countries where reelection is restricted—or where more attractive opportunities for pursuing advancement exist in arenas other than the deliberative assembly—representatives seek to advance their careers through appointment or election to other political offices or promotion within the party bureaucracy (Carey 1996; Jones 1998; Mainwaring 1999; Morgenstern 1998; Samuels 1998).

In Costa Rica, for example, where the immediate reelection of deputies is forbidden, representatives endeavor to increase their standing with party leaders (particularly the presidential candidate) and their popularity with constituents in an attempt to maximize their chances of obtaining a political appointment in the ensuing term (Carey 1996, 94–101). In Argentina and Brazil, where unrestricted reelection is allowed, deputies frequently use their congressional experiences as "springboards" to more politically gainful employment. After serving their terms in the congress, Argentine and Brazilian deputies aspire to national- or state-level positions such as minister, senator, governor, state or provincial secretary, state or provincial representative, or mayor (Jones 1998; Samuels 1998). As observed by Samuels (1998) in Brazil, representatives in these contexts exhibit "progressive" ambition—that is, "a desire to build a political career outside of the Chamber of Deputies following election as deputy"—as opposed to the "static" ambition revealed by most members of the U.S. Congress, who aspire to build a career within the House of Representatives or the Senate.

Assembly Members' Reelection in Panama

In Panama there is no restriction on the reelection of members of the National Assembly. If we apply the assumptions of the literature on the U.S. Congress to the Panamanian case, Panama's deputies should reveal an interest in maintaining their political careers through reelection. They do indeed, having increasingly sought to retain their seats since the reintroduction of the assembly in 1984. At the end of the 1984–89 term, 54 percent of the chamber, or 36 of a total of 67 legislators, ran for reelection. Five years later, the figure rose to 67 percent, or 45 of 67 legislators. In the 1999 elections, 63 of 72 legislators, or 88 percent of the chamber, campaigned to retain their seats; in 2004 the figure was 59 of 71 members, or 83 percent. The proportion of incumbents seeking reelection dropped to 72 percent in 2009 (57 of 79 deputies) (see appendix I).

Although reelection rates rose in Panama over the past quarter century, they are much lower than in the United States or even Chile, the Latin American republic that transitioned to democracy simultaneously (in 1989–90) to Panama and where the consecutive reelection of members of congress is allowed. In 1990–2010, 78 percent of Chile's deputies sought reelection. On average, 80 percent of those seeking reelection succeeded.[1] In Panama only 22 percent of those members of the assembly who sought to continue in office achieved their objective in 1989. At that time, a low reelection rate may have been a function of the massive opposition vote against the military dictatorship, which—chiefly through the "vicious arts" criticized by Madison—had succeeded in obtaining a majority of seats in the 1984 elections (Ricord 1991, 85–86; see also chapter 7). Only one of twenty-four incumbents aligned with the military regime who sought reelection accomplished his objective.[2]

In 1994—five years after the overthrow of the military regime—the return rate among members seeking reelection rose only slightly, to 27 percent. More likely than not, this was also the result of general disappointment with the performance of the parties that had opposed the dictatorship and the absence of material incentives to vote for incumbents. In the 1989–94 term under President Guillermo Endara (PPAN), state expenditures in constituencies were subject to more rigorous controls than during the military dictatorship or the ensuing governments of the liberal democratic period.[3]

A significant rise to 49 percent, however, took place in 1999. This was initially interpreted as resulting from a considerable increase in the availability and expenditure of constituency funds known as *partidas circuitales* (examined in detail in chapter 6). While these funds doubtless played a role in buying support for incumbents, the fact is that the reelection rate remained at 49 percent in 2004, two years after direct constituency funding to legislators was suspended and—allegedly—replaced by other, indirect, and less evident forms of patronage. The rate dropped a little, to 46 percent, in 2009 (see table 5.1).

Table 5.1. Assembly Members' Consecutive Reelection Rates in Panama, 1984–2009

	1989	1994	1999	2004	2009	Average
Percentage of total membership seeking reelection	54	67	88	83	72	73
Percentage of those seeking reelection who succeeded (reelection rate of incumbents)	22	27	49	49	46	39
Percentage of total membership achieving reelection (reelected incumbents prevalence rate)	12	18	43	41	33	29

Source: Tribunal Electoral 1984a, 1991a, 1994a, 1994b, 1999a, 1999b, 2004a, 2004b, 2009a, 2009c.

Political Advancement Along Other Paths

Evidence from the period under review shows that, on average, seven out of ten Panamanian deputies sought consecutive reelection. Of those seeking to retain their seats in the immediately ensuing term, however, less than four out of ten achieved their goal. This statistic seems quite low, especially when compared to the reelection rates of members of the U.S. Congress or deputies from Chile. If Panama's assembly members are interested in pursuing political careers, are there other possibilities open to them in addition to consecutive reelection to a chamber seat?

Returning to the assembly at a later date is an option; however, based on the 1984–2009 electoral record, the likelihood of such a return is even lower than of retaining the seat in the immediately ensuing election. As shown in table 5.1, on average 29 percent of the total chamber (not just members seeking reelection) held on to their seats. Comparatively, the average proportion achieving nonconsecutive reelection in 1984–2009 was 4.5 percent—14 out of 309 individuals in the sample, as shown in appendix E (see table 5.2).

Accession to other elected office is also a possibility, including president and vice-presidents of the republic,[4] county representatives, municipal

Table 5.2. Nonconsecutive Reelection by Panama's Assembly Members with Party Affiliation, 1984–2009

Assembly Member	1984–89	1989–94	1994–99	1999–2004	2004–9	2009–14
Tomás Altamirano Duque	PRD		PRD			
Abelardo Antonío		PRD	PRD	PRD		PRD
Leopoldo Benedetti			PPAN		PSOL	
Marcos González				PPAN		CD
Camilo Gozaine	PRD			PRD		
Aristides de Icaza			PRC		PSOL	CD
Mario Miller			PRD			CD
César Pardo	PRD		PRD	PRD	PRD	
Juan Peralta			LIBRE		PRD	
Benicio Robinson		PRD	PRD		PRD	PRD
Jorge Alberto Rosas			MOLIRENA			MOLIRENA
Jacobo Salas	PPAN			PPAN		
Noriel Salerno			PSOL	PSOL		UP
Jerry Wilson	PRD			PRD	PRD	

Source: Tribunal Electoral 1984a, 1991a, 1994a, 1994b, 1999a, 1999b, 2004a, 2004b, 2009a, 2009c.

mayors (since 1994),[5] and Central American deputies (in 1999–2009).[6] Among these offices, the analysis takes into consideration those of president, vice-president, Central American deputy, and mayor of major provincial capitals, which are at the same or higher rank as National Assembly member. The likelihood of acceding to one of these offices is only slightly higher than of achieving nonconsecutive reelection to the chamber: only 15 assembly members out of 309 (5 percent) achieved another elected office of equal or higher rank. No assembly member between 1984 and 2009 has yet acceded to the presidency of the republic. This finding contrasts starkly with the old regime's record: of Panama's twenty-six chief executives between 1904 and 1968, at least thirteen (50 percent) had prior experience as deputies either in the National Assembly or the departmental chamber under Colombian rule (Guevara Mann 2004). As discussed in chapter 2, Legislators Tomás Altamirano

Duque, Arturo Vallarino, and Rubén Arosemena were concurrently elected as vice-presidents of the republic in 1994, 1999, and 2004, respectively. After serving in the chamber, twelve deputies were elected as Central American deputies in 1999–2009; one of these members had been elected mayor of Panama City in 1994 (see table 5.3).

As in other liberal democracies, the possibility of acceding to appointed office of equal or higher rank is also open to former assembly members. In Panama the likelihood of such appointment depends on the strength of connections with the nominating authority, more often than not the chief executive. Some former members have obtained appointment to very desirable offices, such as Supreme Court justice, prosecutor-general, cabinet minister, national agency administrator, or ambassador[7] that are of equivalent or higher rank than National Assembly member. Though several deputies have returned to public service through appointments to lesser office, such as heads of ministerial departments, provincial governors, or foreign-service posts below ambassador, this analysis focuses on accession to offices that seem to provide career advancement at an equivalent or higher level.[8]

An online search of assembly members' career paths conducted in March 2008 and April 2010 indicated that the chances of obtaining such executive appointment is just a little higher than of returning to the National Assembly at a later time or obtaining other elected office. According to the exercise, twenty-nine former deputies (9 percent of the sample) received appointments of this type (see table 5.4).[9] The percentage of those receiving appointments is still lower than the average proportion of the total membership achieving consecutive reelection (29 percent).

In sum, opportunities for career advancement through avenues other than consecutive reelection are available to Panama's deputies. Assembly members may return to the chamber in a later term, obtain election to another office, or receive appointment to executive office; however, in 1984–2009 the viability of advancing a political career along these other paths was lower than through consecutive reelection. This contributes, in part, to explaining the attraction of reelection in Panama, which, on average, was sought by 73 percent of all assembly members in 1984–2009. To increase their prospects for reelection in a highly

Table 5.3. Election to Office of Equal or Higher Rank by Assembly Members in Panama, 1984–2009

Assembly Member	Party and Term(s)	Subsequent Elected Office and Party	Terms
Tomás Altamirano Duque	PRD (1984–89)	First Vice-President (PRD)	1994–99
Eliseo Alvarez	MOLIRENA (1989–94)	Central American Deputy (MOLIRENA)	1999–2004
David Arce	PPAN (1984–89)	Central American Deputy (PSOL)	2004–14
Argentina Arias	PPAN (2004–9)	Central American Deputy (PPAN)	2009–14
Rubén Arosemena	PDC (1994–2009)	Second Vice-President (PDC)	2004–9
Camilo Brenes	PDC (1989–94)	Central American Deputy (PDC)	1999–2009
Omaira Correa	PALA (1984–89)	Mayor of Panama City (MOLIRENA)	1994–99
		Central American Deputy (PSOL)	2004–14
Dorindo Cortés	PRD (2004–9)	Central American Deputy (PRD)	2009–14
Hugo Giraud	PRD (1984–89)	Central American Deputy (PRD)	1999–2009
Gerardo González[a]	PRD (1989–99)	Central American Deputy (PRD)	2004–9
Jílmer González[b]	PLA (1989–94)	Central American Deputy (PPAN)	1999–2004
José Hill	PDC (1989–94)	Central American Deputy (PDC)	1999–2004
Danis Montemayor	PPAN (2004–9)	Central American Deputy (PPAN)	2009–14
Franklyn Rivera	PRD (1984–89)	Central American Deputy (PRD)	2004–9
Arturo Vallarino	PALA (1984–89), MOLIRENA (1989–2004)	First Vice-President (MOLIRENA)	1999–2004

Source: Loo Pinzón 2010; Tribunal Electoral 1991a, 1994b, 1999b, 2004b.

[a] Died in 2006.

[b] Elected as first substitute of Nodier Miranda in 1989, González acceded to Miranda's seat at the latter's death in 1991.

Table 5.4. Accession to Appointed Office of Equal or Higher Rank by Assembly Members in Panama, 1984–2009

Assembly Member	Party and Term(s)	Subsequent Appointed Office	Tenure
Marco Alarcón[a]	PPAN (1984–89)	Minister of Education	1991–94
		Ambassador to Cuba	1999–2003
Alfredo Arias	PPAN (1994–99)	Administrator-General, Inter-Oceanic Regional Authority	2000–2004
Mario Boyd Galindo	MOLIRENA (1989–94)	Ambassador to Brazil	2002–4
		Ambassador to Argentina	2009–
Felipe Cano	PRD (1999–2004)	Vice-Minister of Social Development	2006–7
		Vice-Minister of Labor	2007–9
Celso Carrizo	PRD (1984–89)	Ambassador to Guatemala	2004–9
Omar Chen	PRD (1999–2004)	Director-General, National Lottery	2004–6
Gisela Chung	MOLIRENA (1989–94)	Commercial Representative to China[b]	1999–2002
Alberto Cigarruista	PLA (1989–99), PPAN (1999–2004)	Supreme Court Justice	2002–12
Luis Carlos Cleghorn	PPAN (2004–9)	Ambassador to Cuba	2009–
Guillermo Cochez	PDC (1984–94)	Ambassador to the Organization of American States (OAS)	2009–
Omaira Correa	PALA (1984–89)	Mayor of Panama City	1991–93
		Governor of the Province of Panama	2009–
Enrique Garrido	PPAN (1994–99, 2004–9), PDC (1999–2004)	Ambassador to Bolivia	2009–
Luis Gómez	PRD (1984–89)	Ambassador to Cuba	2008–9
Balbina Herrera	PRD (1989–2004)	Minister of Housing	2004–8
Euribíades Herrera	MOLIRENA (2004–9)	National Director, Community Development Program	2009–
Raymundo Hurtado	MOLIRENA (1994–99)	Ambassador to Paraguay	1999–2002
Mariela Jiménez	MPE (1994–99)	Director-General, Civil Service	2009–
Gloria Moreno	PDC (1989–94)	Director-General, National Customs Authority	2009–
Oydén Ortega	PRD (1994–99)	Supreme Court Justice	2008–18
Bolívar Pariente	PPAN (1994–99)	General Manager, National Bank of Panama	1999–2004

Table 5.4. (continued)

Assembly Member	Party and Term(s)	Subsequent Appointed Office	Tenure
Luis Posse	PPAN (1994–99)	Minister of Agriculture	1999–2000
		General Manager, Agricultural Development Bank	2009
Pablo Quintero Luna	PPAN (1994–99)	Executive Secretary, Public Security and National Defense Council	1999–2001
		Director-General, Transit and Terrestrial Transportation Authority	2001–4
Olgalina Rodríguez	PRD (1999–2004)	Governor of the Province of Colón	2004–6
		Ambassador to Ecuador	2006–9
Olimpo Sáez	MOLIRENA (1989–94)	Ambassador to Brazil	1999–2002
		Ambassador to Vietnam	2002–4
		Ambassador to Nicaragua	2009–11
Jacobo Salas	PPAN (1984–89, 1999–2004)	Minister of Government and Justice	1993–94
Eric Santamaría	PDC (1989–94)	Vice-Minister of Agriculture	2005–9
José Sossa	PDC (1989–94)	Prosecutor-General	1995–2005
Jerry Wilson	PRD (1984–89, 1999–2009)	Supreme Court Justice	1988–89
Teresita Yániz[c]	PDC (1999–2009)	National Secretary, Nutritional Feeding Program	2004–7

Source: Based on online research conducted by the author in March 2008 and April 2010.

[a] Died in 2003.

[b] This position is equivalent to that of ambassador, except for the fact that Panama does not maintain diplomatic relations with the People's Republic of China.

[c] Yániz ran for reelection in 2004. Although her party did not obtain a full or half quota in her constituency and her share of the selective vote was not sufficient to guarantee election, she claimed she deserved a place in the chamber based on the constitutional provision whereby parties that had survived but not elected a deputy had a right to an assembly seat (article 141 prior to the 2004 reform; see chapter 3). The Electoral Tribunal disagreed and the case was brought before the Supreme Court, which did not rule in Yániz's favor until February 2009, four months before the 2004–9 term was over. Thus, although an elected deputy, Yániz did not exercise her representative function until the end of the term. In 2004–7, when it was not certain that her reelectoral aspirations would be recognized, she served as National Secretary of the Presidency of the Republic's Nutritional Feeding Program under President Martín Torrijos (PRD), a close political ally.

clientelistic environment, incumbents engage in patronage distribution through very creative activities, which the literature on legislators' behavior has not generally addressed. Chapter 6 focuses on patronage distribution by Panamanian deputies interested in reelection.

Requirements for Reelection

In their quest to preserve their assembly seats, Panamanian deputies are subject to the regulations applicable to candidates generally. These rules are contained in the constitution and the Electoral Code.[10] The most significant of these regulations address issues of citizenship, age, residency, occupation, legal status, and nomination. According to the constitution's article 153, only Panamanian citizens by birth or naturalization (with fifteen years of residency after naturalization) may obtain nomination as candidates to the National Assembly. Individuals who have renounced Panamanian citizenship, acquired another nationality (other than by birth), or entered the service of an enemy state are not eligible, according to article 9 of the Electoral Code. Article 153 of the constitution stipulates an age requirement of twenty-one years at the moment of election and residency in the constituency beginning at least one year prior to nomination. The charter's article 45 bans members of the clergy of any religious denomination from serving as state employees (except as educators, researchers, or social service providers), and article 27 of the Electoral Code specifies that certain functionaries in the executive, judiciary, and other branches of government (including members of the security forces) holding office within six months of the election are prohibited from being nominated.

As a condition for becoming a deputy, article 153 of the constitution requires that individuals be in full exercise of their citizenship rights and not currently under sentence for a felony entailing a prison term of five years or more. Between 1984 and 2004 this latter condition covered sentencing for embezzlement with prison terms of any duration as well as electoral crimes, but—significantly—the 2004 constitutional reform dropped these prohibitions. Article 9 of the Electoral Code prevents candidatures of individuals subject to judicial interdiction.

Presumably, if they are incumbents, deputies seeking reelection met all these conditions when they were elected; however, as in other realms of public activity, in Panama's electoral scenario codified norms are not always a reliable blueprint for political outcomes. In the 2004 elections, for instance, the Electoral Tribunal did not prevent the candidacy of Manuel Ruiz, an Evangelical minister who aspired to become a deputy in one of the larger Panama City constituencies, despite the constitutional prohibition on clerical candidatures. It was rumored that the tribunal's magistrates wished to avoid the maledictions likely to be cast upon them if they banned the preacher's candidacy. The tribunal's leniency and Ruiz's reputation as a miraculous healer, however, were insufficient to get him elected as an assembly member on the MOLIRENA ticket (Jackson 2004; Tejera 2007).

From 1984 to 2004 only political parties recognized by the Electoral Tribunal could nominate candidates to a National Assembly seat (article 140 of the constitution before the 2004 reform). The 2004 constitutional reform allowed independent candidatures to the assembly beginning in the 2009 electoral cycle (article 146 of the constitution including the 2004 reform). But, as per article 251 of the Electoral Code, the official requirements of these candidatures are not easy to meet. Independents seeking to become candidates must submit a list of adherents numbering no less than 4 percent of the valid votes for deputy issued in the constituency in the immediately preceding election. These adherents cannot be members of political parties, a significant hurdle given that more than half of Panama's citizens are registered party members (53 percent in 2010) (República de Panamá 2007; Tribunal Electoral 2010). Two independents were elected in 2009: Yanibel Ábrego and Carlos Afú. Afú, of CEMIS fame (see chapter 10), was first elected in 1994 on the PALA ticket and secured reelection as a PRD candidate in 1999 and in 2004 on the PPAN list. When PPAN refused to nominate him in 2009, Afú decided to go it alone.

In most of the elections covered in this study, the provision requiring party nomination, which prevailed in 1984–2004, stimulated interesting behaviors in members seeking reelection. This is consistent with the predictions of the literature, which attributes elected officials' behavior partly to the candidate selection rules prevailing in a polity (Otero Felipe 2008). For most of the period under review, nomination was a prerogative of the leadership in all Panamanian parties. Slowly, however, political organizations began adopting primaries as the mode of selecting their candidates to the assembly. The trend began with PRD, which held primary elections for National Assembly candidates (and all other candidatures) in 1999, 2004, and 2009. In 2009 PPAN, CD, UP, and VMP also selected their respective assembly nominees through primaries. In a few cases, however, certain winning aspirants were forced to resign their candidacies after their parties entered into electoral alliances with other political organizations and the coalition terms required submitting a unified list in certain constituencies (Freidenberg 2010; Otero Felipe 2008).

Thus, because the leadership played such a relevant role in determining candidatures in all parties for most of this period, some incumbents interested in serving a subsequent period sought to remain on good terms with the party bosses (as predicted by the literature). Those who quarreled with the leadership opted to switch parties and gain nomination by another entity. Party switching, which remains an understudied feature of legislators' behavior, is facilitated in Panama by the clientelistic nature of the party system, as well as by the aforementioned constitutional provision requiring party sponsorship of candidatures in 1984–2004, which was formalized in the constitution until the 2004 reform created the possibility of independent candidacies. Chapter 7 deals with party switching in more detail.

Summary

Where they are allowed to serve several terms, members of representative assemblies are likely to seek reelection, whether to advance their political careers or pursue other goals (or both), as allowed by the institutional context. In Panama a majority of incumbents in 1984–2009 (73 percent) sought consecutive reelection, although overall only 39 percent of those who tried to retain their seats actually succeeded. Even though the likelihood of retaining an assembly seat in Panama is low compared to that in the United States, other advanced liberal democracies, and some Latin American republics (such as Chile), it is higher than advancing a political career along other paths, including nonconsecutive reelection to the National Assembly, election to another position, or appointment to government office of equal rank.

Panama's deputies follow the assumptions of legislators' behavior theory with regard to achieving reelection to a significant extent. As predicted by Mayhew (1974), they advertise and claim credit and some even take political positions, despite the fact that they operate in an environment with very low programmatic content (see chapter 2). In their endeavor to gain reelection, many deputies support the party line, as expected by some authors. This is predictable, given the relevance of the party leadership in determining candidatures, although several parties have recently adopted primaries as a mode of selecting their candidates to the National Assembly (and other elected offices). To retain their seats, however, other incumbents see fit to switch parties (see chapter 7). As noted in the scholarship on legislators' behavior (Cain, Ferejohn, and Fiorina 1987), assembly members seeking reelection also distribute patronage; the legal and illegal uses of patronage for electoral gain in Panama are examined in chapter 6.

## CHAPTER 6

Political Advancement through Reelection

The Legal and Illegal Uses of Patronage

Representatives in many democracies engage in patronage-related activities, such as securing the construction of public works in key localities and obtaining state funding for specific groups and projects in their constituencies. In this capacity, members of representative assemblies assume the role of intermediaries between the executive branch and their constituents in the process of allocating state resources. In the United States, for example, this activity—labeled "allocation responsiveness" by some and, more colloquially, "pork barrel" politics by others—takes up a substantial amount of representatives' time and energy. Members of Congress introduce legislation to ensure that their districts receive "a fair share of government projects, programs, and expenditures" (Cain, Ferejohn, and Fiorina 1987, 3–4). Although it is undertaken with a clear electoral objective in mind, in most advanced democracies "allocation responsiveness" does not comprise direct access to constituency funds by representatives for the provision of goods and services to constituents with the express purpose of creating electoral clienteles. This is certainly not true in the United States and Great Britain, the cases studied by Cain, Ferejohn, and Fiorina in their 1987 discussion of allocation and service responsiveness.

Once incumbents to the Panamanian assembly obtain nomination by a duly recognized political party, they may seek reelection. As predicted by legislators' behavior theory, to aid their reelectoral ambitions Panamanian assembly members also resort to patronage. In Panama, however, patronage encompasses dimensions that the literature on legislators' behavior has not yet fully addressed. Members of the Panamanian assembly engage in a much more straightforward particularistic distribution of public goods and services with an unmistakable electoral connection in mind, and they use state resources to purchase political support in both legal and illegal ways.

Legal Distribution of Patronage through *Partidas Circuitales*

Partidas circuitales, or "constituency funds," were budget funds assigned directly to legislators for discretionary use in their districts in 1985–87 and 1993–2001. Inspired by Panama's clientelistic tradition, conceived toward the end of the old regime (1903–1968), instituted during the military regime (1968–89), revived—after the overthrow of the dictatorship—toward the end of the Endara administration (PPAN, 1989–94), and maximized during the government of Ernesto Pérez Balladares (PRD, 1994–99), *partidas circuitales* were a means that helped some Panamanian legislators surmount a low reelection rate.

The rise in the availability of *partidas circuitales* was promoted by President Pérez Balladares in an attempt to render the assembly even less effective than prescribed by the Panamanian constitution. In this way, the president ensured the uncontested application of his agenda and legislators were guaranteed funding to cultivate electoral clienteles (Cochez 2000). The policy had adverse consequences for the democratic system, especially with regard to the balance of power, oversight of the government, and quality of representation. In the pursuit of the objectives of Pérez Balladares as well as of the members of Panama's assembly, however, it proved successful.

Old Republic Origins

The practice of allocating "development" funds directly to representatives can be traced to the inception of the military dictatorship's constitution in 1972 (see chapter 2). Additional antecedents are found not only in the clientelistic approach to politics that was a legacy of the old regime (see chapter 4) but also in an initiative by assembly member Ovidio Díaz (1964–68, 1984–89), who in 1965 proposed the allocation of state resources directly to members of the assembly for the construction of public works (Pérez Jaramillo 2000).

Ovidio Díaz was first elected deputy in 1964, on the Partido Republicano (PR) ticket, in representation of his native Los Santos Province. In an essay responding to heightened criticism of *partidas circuitales,* former assemblyman Díaz explained that the proposal was a reaction to his own disillusion "after I became aware of my incapacity to satisfy the most urgent basic needs of the community and my friends in the constituency who had faith and hope in my mandate." As chairman of the assembly's Public Works Committee, Ovidio Díaz secured the inclusion in the 1966 budget of a US$30,000 fund for each deputy, with the exception of two other members and Díaz himself who, as originator of the initiative, received a higher amount.[1] In his account Díaz underscores the electoral connection implicit in the establishment of these deputy funds:

> As every good idea, this one took root and continued to be utilized in 1966, 1967, and 1968 to build public works, some of which were completed by the military government. *The prize I received was my reelection as deputy in the following period* [1968]. *From the communities of Los Santos, which were satisfied with their deputy's work, I not only received votes but also money and goods as contributions to my electoral campaign.* The result was that for the first time the opposition won in the Province of Los Santos, despite the enormous persecution unleashed by the government of Marco Robles [1964–68]. (O. Díaz 2000, emphasis added)

Constituency Funding during the Military Regime (1984–89)

In 1984 Ovidio Díaz was elected legislator in representation of a constituency in Los Santos Province as a member of PRD, the military regime's party, with which he collaborated after the 1968 coup. As a result of the 1960s experience with deputy funds, Diaz explained that

> it was not difficult to sell my idea once again, now as chairman of the Budget Committee. Owing to the changes introduced in the 1983

constitutional reform, particularly in articles 269 and 270 [of the constitution], I had to negotiate with Nicolás Ardito Barletta,[2] then President of the Republic, who authorized the necessary funding that allocated $200,000 to each government legislator and $100,000 to each opposition member. It was pressure from some of my party's leaders that prevented the distribution of the same amount to all legislators, as I wished. (O. Díaz 2000)

As indicated by Díaz, the executive allocated different amounts to government and opposition members in 1985, 1986, and 1987 under the so-called Programa Multiagencial de Proyectos Comunitarios (Multiagency Program), as *partidas circuitales* were then designated. But, according to the Comptroller-General's Office—and contrary to Díaz's recollection—in 1985 allocations ranged from US$59,000 to US$166,000 for government legislators and from US$20,000 to US$40,000 for opposition members. In 1986 members of the pro-dictatorship bloc received from US$151,000 to US$301,000, and opposition legislators obtained from US$10,000 to US$70,000. In 1987 government members received from US$30,000 to US$200,000; opposition legislators received no funding. The total amount disbursed among members of the assembly under the Multiagency Program in 1985–87 reached US$17.4 million (current dollars; Contraloría General 1987).

Knowledgeable sources confirmed that the Multiagency Program was suspended after 1987 owing to the dismal state of government finances during the last years of the military regime. Reportedly, however, legislators aligned with the dictatorship received indirect and irregular payments for personal, political, and "allocation responsiveness" purposes in 1987, 1988, and 1989.[3] In 1990 the Comptroller-General's Office initiated an investigation into the use of some US$4.3 million assigned to members of the assembly under the Multiagency Program during the 1984–89 term (see chapter 10 for additional discussion of the Multiagency Program).

Partidas Circuitales *in the Transitional Period (1989–94)*

After the removal of the military regime, financial constraints and a stricter management of state resources initially prevented a return to the practice of allotting constituency funds, despite the fact that legislators insisted on their assignment. But constituency funds were once again included in the 1993 budget as a device to generate support for the governing parties and incumbent members of the assembly in the upcoming (1994) elections.[4] According to the Comptroller-General's Office, US$83.6 million were assigned to "parliamentary [sic] initiatives" in the 1993 budget, specifically in the Planning Office's budget.

As was the case previously, pro-government members and certain "collaborating" legislators across party lines received substantially higher amounts than opposition members. In 1993 allocations to pro-government legislators ranged between US$1.7 million and US$3.7 million. Opposition members received up to US$960,000; at least four assembly members reportedly did not receive any funding at all (Contraloría General 1994). In 1993, however, legislators did not have direct access to these resources and the Comptroller-General's Office did not authorize any disbursement of funds unless projects were specifically contemplated in the budget bill. Funds were normally channeled through the Ministry of Public Works under strict supervision by the Comptroller-General's Office.[5] For this reason, of the hefty allocations assigned in 1993, approximately one-third of the US$83.6 million, or US$28.5 million, remained undisbursed. This figure roughly coincides with the *partidas* amount allocated in the 1994 budget (US$28.9 million), almost 100 percent of which was disbursed in that election year. Presumably, therefore, funding not used in 1993 was redistributed in 1994, albeit unequally, among the full membership of the assembly. Although many legislators in the government bloc obtained substantially more funding than their opposition peers, no clear pattern was discernible in the 1994 allotment, in which all legislators obtained *partidas circuitales* ranging between US$79,000 and US$1.2 million (Contraloría General 1994).

The difference between allocated and disbursed amounts points to an important matter in *partidas* politics: the issue of state control over expenditures. According to the Comptroller-General's Office, legislators disbursed the entire constituency funding allocated in the 1984–89 period (US$17.4 million). At a time of extreme corruption and military manipulation of the political process (as described in chapters 4 and 7), this is a revealing fact that suggests lax supervision of expenditures by the Comptroller-General's Office.[6] This deduction is substantiated by the fact that after the return to constitutional rule, a more independent Comptroller-General's Office opened investigations into the use of Multiagency Program funds, as a result of which at least one former legislator, Anselmo Guainora (PRD, 1984–89), was convicted of misappropriation of public resources (see chapter 10).

In the 1989–94 period—again, according to the Comptroller-General's Office—total disbursements of US$84 million represented 75 percent of the full amount allocated in the period (US$112.6 million). As noted above, the difference between authorized and disbursed amounts was more evident in 1993, when total disbursements (US$55.1 million) added up to two-thirds of the appropriated sum (US$83.6 million). In 1994, an electoral year, the disbursement rate neared 100 percent. Presumably, either projects were approved the previous year or the Comptroller-General's Office applied a more flexible disbursement procedure in an effort to facilitate legislators' electoral aspirations.

The Apogee of Constituency Funding (1994–99)

Closer oversight of *partidas circuitales* under the Endara administration contrasts with lax supervision under President Ernesto Pérez Balladares, otherwise known for his strong-handed approach to government. Legislators were assigned abundant constituency funding in each fiscal year of the Pérez Balladares administration. Moreover, new, more "flexible" disbursement procedures were introduced under a new comptroller-general, Aristides Romero, who happened to be a first cousin to Pérez Balladares. This made it easier for assembly members to spend the allocated amounts and claim credit for the projects undertaken through constituency appropriations.

Instead of directing constituency activities through the Ministry of Public Works, which required holding public bids with the participation of a minimum of three bidders, Pérez Balladares allowed legislators to channel funds through the Emergency Development Fund (Fondo de Emergencia Social, or FES).[7] As an agency of the Presidency of the Republic for emergency relief, FES was authorized to assign its projects directly without holding public bids. During the Pérez Balladares ad-

Table 6.1. Allocation and Disbursement of Constituency Funds in Panama, 1984–99

Year	Funds Allocated	Funds Disbursed	Disbursement as a Percentage of Allocation
1985	3.6	3.6	100
1986	9.4	9.4	100
1987	4.4	4.4	100
1988	0	0	n.a.
1989	0	0	n.a.
1990	0	0	n.a.
1991	0	0	n.a.
1992	0	0	n.a.
1993	83.6	55.1	66
1994	28.9	28.9	100
1995	21.8	20.9	96
1996	39.2	36.8	94
1997	43.6	43.2	99
1998	45.9	45.3	99
1999	37.6	23.4	62

Source: Contraloría General 1987, 1994, 1998a, 1999a, 2000.

Note: Funds are given in millions of current U.S. dollars. n.a. indicates data not applicable; disbursement of constituency funds was suspended in 1988–92.

ministration, a practice developed whereby legislators' set up their own nongovernmental organizations (NGOs), which applied for and received funds directly from FES with the ostensible objective of carrying out development projects in their constituencies.[8]

These policies contributed to a disbursement rate of over 90 percent under the Pérez Balladares administration, reaching almost 100 percent in 1997 and 1998. Ironically, it dropped to 62 percent in the election year of 1999, but we can presume that by this time the benefits of "efficient" and regular disbursement of constituency funds had already accrued. Table 6.1 shows the allocation and disbursement of *partidas* during the period under review.

As during the Endara administration, under Pérez Balladares *partidas circuitales* were included in the Planning Office's budget. In July 1999, after the election—but before the inauguration—of President Mireya Moscoso (PPAN), the PRD-controlled Legislative Assembly voted to remove the constituency appropriations from the Planning Office's budget and incorporate them into the assembly's own budget, under the chamber's "investments" account. This move responded to President Moscoso's campaign promise that once in office she would "revise" the allocation of constituency funds, hinting at their elimination or transfer to the municipal councils or county representatives.[9] In order to prevent the eradication of a major public resource to which many of its members attributed their reelection in 1999, the assembly instituted article 16 of the hastily approved Law no. 35 of 1999, which amended the chamber's Organic Law, to further stipulate that the assembly's budget should be equivalent to at least 2 percent of the central government's current income and that this budget would increase every year proportionally according to the increase in the government's budget.[10] Furthermore, the amendment determined that henceforth the assembly would "design and administer" its own budget and that in no case would the global amount for *partidas circuitales* be less than the previous year's appropriation for this item (Asamblea Legislativa 1999, 82–83 [article 267-A]).

Much to the legislators' chagrin, however, the Moscoso administration succeeded in eliminating the funds beginning in 2002. Deputies have complained bitterly about the unavailability of *partidas circuitales* ever since. In response to these complaints, in March 2008 assembly president Pedro González (PRD, 1999–2009) promised to introduce legislation to reestablish constituency funding on a permanent basis (Cumbrera 2007; Prieto Barreiro 2008). As of May 2010 the chamber had not passed a law restoring the funds, though the idea of allocating public resources to deputies for constituency projects remains popular among assembly members in the 2009–14 term.

More broadly, whether through formally codified *partidas circuitales* or other means, deputies belonging to parties across the spectrum have proven unyielding in their pursuit of state monies to finance their reelectoral ambitions (and acquire personal wealth). In January 2010 an extensive investigative report in *La Prensa* uncovered a subterfuge employed by assembly members, in the absence of *partidas circuitales,* to obtain ample funding from the government ostensibly for programs in their constituencies. According to *La Prensa,* with government acquiescence at least nineteen deputies during both the Moscoso (1999–2004) and Martín Torrijos (2004–9) administrations siphoned approximately US$12 million from the Social Investment Fund (FIS, successor to FES). Deputies used resources to reward campaign supporters, relatives, and business partners. In exchange, the Moscoso and Torrijos administrations secured these deputies' loyal support in the chamber (Unidad Investigativa de *La Prensa* 2010).

Constituency Funding in Comparative Perspective

The previous section underscored two key elements that in part explain the perceived electoral value of Panama's *partidas circuitales:* size and lack of control over their disbursement. Although the direct assignment of funds to assembly members—especially such generous funding as was the custom in Panama—for discretionary particularistic use violates the norm that legislation should be impartial and universalistic (Weber 1922/1978, 217–26), Panama is by no means the only Latin American country where such practice has existed.[11] At least in Argentina, Ecuador, Costa Rica, and Colombia, representatives had direct access to state funds. In Argentina members of the lower chamber "receive a base amount of resources for the granting of subsidies to non-profit and governmental institutions (approximately US$18,000–20,000 in 1998), of pensions to individuals (approximately US$1,200 per month in total, including medical coverage), and of a small number of modest scholarships to university students" (Jones 1998, 31n46).

In Ecuador deputies were formerly assigned budget funds (*partidas presupuestarias*) to carry out projects in their constituencies. Owing to complaints of corruption and clientelism, the 1998 constituent convention eliminated these funds and inserted a clause in the constitution explicitly prohibiting deputies from "offering, dealing with, receiving, or managing budget resources, except for those assigned to the operation of the Congress."[12] Costa Rican deputies also had access to similar funding sources called *partidas específicas,* "small pork-barrel appropriations targeted at specific communities" (Carey 1996, 107). Whereas in Argentina constituency funds are distributed evenly among representatives, in Costa Rica they were assigned almost exclusively to members of the government party. In response to accusations of mismanagement, in May 1998 the Costa Rican Legislative Assembly approved a law that placed *partidas específicas* under stricter government control and channeled such resources through the municipalities, thus placing constraints on the discretionary use of these funds by deputies (Leis 1999).

The Colombian equivalent of funding assigned to members of congress for projects in their districts, called *auxilios parlamentarios,* was in existence at least from 1968 to 1991.[13] Reportedly, *auxilios* were a part of the package that President Alberto Lleras Restrepo (1966–70) negotiated to placate members who were reluctant to go along with his proposals to increase the executive's budgetary powers vis-à-vis the congress and formalize the status of several decentralized agencies.[14] Through constituency funding the Colombian congress ensured it would exercise latitude in the provision of goods and services to constituencies after losing initiative in all other budgetary matters under the 1968 constitutional reform.[15] This development speaks directly to the hypothesis advanced in chapter 3 suggesting that, in a clientelistic setting, a representative assembly denied involvement in issues of "high" politics is likely to direct its energies toward patronage and related activities.

Because of their electoral use, *auxilios parlamentarios* stood out as "the most viable mechanism to guarantee a legislator's reelection." As in Panama, this use was facilitated by lack of adequate controls in their assignment and disbursement. This feature contributed to the abuse of *auxilios* for personal enrichment (Behar and Villa 1991, 63–70).[16] Complaints of maladministration and widespread graft prompted action by the 1991 constituent convention to eliminate them (Archer and Shugart 1997, 135–36). As a result, the 1991 Colombian constitution specifically forbids *auxilios.* In their stead, *proyectos de co-financiación,* involving negotiations between members of the congress, departmental or municipal governments, and the National Planning Office, emerged in the Colombian political scenario. Rather than outright grants to members of the congress, *proyectos de co-financiación* were projects approved by the Planning Office at the request of congressional members. Primarily because of the financial difficulties of the national government, the Pastrana administration (1998–2002) suspended the program.[17]

Size and Lack of Control: The Electoral Connection

As this modest comparative survey shows, the assignment of constituency funds to representatives is not unique to Panama. Panamanian *partidas,* however, were significantly larger than their counterparts elsewhere, and their use appears to have been subject to much less oversight. These features underscore the electoral value of *partidas circuitales.* The size of the fund, which was generally higher for government members, together with lack of control over its disbursement helped determine assembly members' reelection possibilities.

Analysis of the figures allotted as *partidas* during each fiscal year of the government of Ernesto Pérez Balladares, when the constituency funds were allocated continuously, indicates the intensification of size and lack of control. These two factors explain the interest of assembly members in constituency funding. For the purposes of this analysis, fiscal years 1995 through 1999 coincide with the term of Pérez Balladares, given that the constitutional term began on September 1 and ended on August 31 and the fiscal year starts on January 1 and concludes on December 31.[18] In other words, legislators elected in May 1994 took the oath on September 1, 1994, and received funding beginning on January 1, 1995, through August 31, 1999—that is, for twelve months in 1995, 1996, 1997, and 1998 and for eight months in 1999. This accounts for a lower *partidas* budget in the election year of 1999. When calculated as a monthly figure, however, the 1999 *partidas* amount is higher than in any other year during Pérez Balladares's presidency.

Constituency funding increased continuously during the 1994–99 term: from US$21.8 million in 1995, it rose to US$39.2 million in 1996, US$43.6 million in 1997, US$45.9 million in 1998, and US$37.6 million for the first eight months of 1999, amounting to a grand total of US$188.1 million. As a monthly average, during the Pérez Balladares

Table 6.2. Allocation of Constituency Funds among Government and Opposition Assembly Members in Panama, 1995–99

	Number of Legislators	%	Total Partidas Allotted (in US$)	%
Government	43	60	142,530,836	76
Opposition	29	40	45,605,113	24
Total	72	100	188,135,949	100

Source: Contraloría General 1998b, 1999b.

Note: Given the party switches by assembly members throughout the term, the figures reflect the adherence of members to the government and opposition blocs as of September 1998.

administration the figure allotted to legislators "initiatives" (as members' projects were euphemistically called) rose from US$1.8 million in 1995 to US$3.9 million in 1999, which represents a 171 percent increase over the five-year period.[19]

How were allocation amounts determined?[20] Prior to submittal of the annual budget bill to the chamber in September or October of each year, the assembly leadership and the executive negotiated to set a global figure for "parliamentary initiatives." The assembly leadership then apportioned *partidas circuitales* to legislators based on political criteria. The directing board allocated funds among legislators according to three basic guidelines: adherence to the government bloc, membership in the Budget Committee, and performance of a formal or informal leadership role within the assembly.[21] Consequently, the allotment of *partidas circuitales* was highly skewed against opposition members, as shown in table 6.2.

After determining the global amount for "parliamentary initiatives," the assembly leadership decided how much corresponded to each legislator. A baseline was then set for opposition and government members. In 1997–98, the last two full fiscal years during which the Pérez Balladares administration allocated *partidas circuitales,* this baseline was US$300,000 for opposition (or pseudo-opposition) legislators and US$650,000 for members formally adhering to the government bloc. Depending on the degree of influence they exercised within the assembly, some legislators received larger funds. In 1997 the opposition's ceiling was US$540,000, the amount received by the seven opposition members that belonged to the Budget Committee in the 1996–97 legislature. The 1998 opposition ceiling was US$500,000, allotted to Rubén Arosemena (PDC),[22] then an opposition member of the Budget Committee. After this, the leadership assigned the highest amounts in the opposition bloc to other Budget Committee members and two of five Movimiento Papa Egoró (MPE) legislators, who, although not formally belonging to the government coalition at that time, regularly gave support to the executive's agenda in the assembly. In 1997 average and modal funding for opposition members was US$367,059 and US$300,000, respectively. In 1998 the same indicators were US$360,006 and US$300,000, respectively. Given that the total allocation increased in 1998, a lower average for opposition members in the latter year indicates a more biased distribution in favor of government legislators.

While in 1997 average and modal funding for government members was US$817,886 and US$850,000, respectively, the same indicators in 1998 were US$859,013 and US$850,000, respectively. The directing board set aside the highest amounts for government members of the Budget Committee and the assembly leaders, consisting of the chamber's president, the two vice-presidents, key committee chairs, and government majority leaders (who do not have an official position per se within the chamber, except as *jefes de fracción,* or bloc coordinators). The highest amount assigned in 1997 was US$1,110,000, allocated to assembly president César Pardo (PRD). Seven other legislators, including the two vice-presidents, the chair and certain members of the Budget Committee, and Balbina Herrera (PRD), a past president and government whip, received over one million dollars in 1997.

The ceiling reached US$1,605,000 in 1998, allocated to Budget Committee chair Carlos Alvarado (PRD). Assembly president Gerardo González (PRD) and the vice-chair of the Budget Committee received over one million dollars each. Eleven other legislators, including the chamber's two vice-presidents, all government members of the Budget Committee, and Balbina Herrera (PRD) received over US$900,000 in 1998.[23]

Lack of Control over Disbursement

In addition to size, lack of effective government control over the disbursement of *partidas circuitales* explains their attraction to assembly members. Members of the Panamanian chamber were able to use the funds to support whatever activity they wished. As in Costa Rica and Colombia (Carey 1996, 111–12; Hartlyn 1988, 173), Panama's assembly members directed constituency allocations toward two principal activities: infrastructure improvement and "social support."[24] The first included building or repair of roads, bridges, schools, health centers, housing complexes, churches, marketplaces, airstrips, docks, aqueducts, power plants, drainage systems, slaughterhouses, and other public facilities. At times, however, legislators channeled *partidas* to infrastructure activities not wholly within the public sphere. In 1996, for example, a number of government and opposition legislators pooled their funding to contribute to the renovation of the influential National Bar Association (Colegio Nacional de Abogados) (Cochez 1998). At the time the association was headed by Gerardo Solís (PRD), director of President Pérez Balladares's FES, the government office through which most legislators channeled their constituency funds. Gerardo Solís subsequently served in electorally sensitive capacities as housing minister (1998), electoral prosecutor (1999–2006), and Electoral Tribunal magistrate (2006–). Under "social support," on the other hand, fell such activities as distributing food, school supplies, and toys; providing scholarships; purchasing vehicles (such as buses, police cars, trucks, and ambulances) for community use; financing nutritional and substance-control programs; funding cooperatives and land surveying efforts; setting up maternity wards and senior-citizen clinics; and providing disaster relief.[25]

Legislators claimed direct credit for all these activities by publicizing them in the newspapers through press releases or paid advertisements and erecting highly visible signs indicating their sponsorship of projects. They frequently referred to "social support" uses of *partidas* as "donations" from legislators. The legislator's name was normally affixed to sports uniforms or painted on vehicles purchased through the member's *partida*. One legislator, Edgardo ("Galo") Alvarez (PRD, 1994–99), sponsored the construction of a housing complex that was later named *Villa*

Galo after him. Others, for example, advertised their pooling of funds to contribute to the continued operation of the local hospital morgue (Cordero 1999; Fonseca 1994).

In response to criticism pointing to the nonrational use of public monies through *partidas circuitales,* legislators argued that constituency funds allowed them to satisfy certain social needs that the highly centralized Panamanian state is unable to fulfill, particularly in distant rural areas. For instance, in 1999 Legislator Laurentino Cortizo (PSOL), elected president of the chamber in September 2000, asserted that without *partidas circuitales* the constituents of his rural district would most likely not have had access to scholarships, roads, "and many other public works." Opposition member Mario Quiel (PL, 1994–99) claimed that constituency projects were "legislators' answers to the basic and priority needs of their communities."[26]

Critics protested that leaving allocation decisions wholly to individual legislators prevented the optimal use of state resources to satisfy socioeconomic needs. One political observer remarked: "Hundreds of scholarships are distributed according to political criteria instead of serving to alleviate the needs of sectors that require them most but, unfortunately, do not represent votes" (Leis 1999). Others highlighted the fact that legislator allocation decisions frequently did not coincide with the country's priorities, as assembly members normally assigned funds with an electoral objective in mind (Blandón Figueroa 1999; Cochez 1996; Lewis Galindo 1999). Still others protested that the discretionary use of funds promoted corruption, for legislators could choose to devote *partidas* to private uses without major restrictions.[27] During the electoral campaign leading to the 1999 elections, Camilo Gozaine (PRD), who served as assembly president during the 1984–89 period and returned to the chamber in 1999–2004, declared that *partidas circuitales* had served to "enrich bad politicians" (Pérez Jaramillo 1999a).

Lenient Supervision by the Comptroller-General's Office

As allocations and expenditures of state resources, *partidas* were theoretically subject to the oversight of the Comptroller-General's Office, according to article 280 of the Panamanian constitution (Contraloría

General 1999b, 46). During the administration of Pérez Balladares, however, supervision of these funds was lax. Although complaints of irregularities in the management of *partidas* were widespread, no substantive action was taken against any legislator.

In November 1998 Comptroller-General Gabriel Castro[28] declared that he had ordered the suspension of disbursements under one legislator's *partida circuital* after discovering a mismatch between the amount of the expenditure and the value of the goods to be purchased. The identity of the legislator was not disclosed, however, and nobody was brought to trial for the alleged misconduct. In early 1999 the Comptroller-General's Office revealed that it was investigating between five and ten legislators for irregularities in the management of *partidas*. After loud protests from the assembly, however, the office apparently abandoned interest in further pursuing the matter (Gálvez 1999; Pérez Jaramillo 1999a).

A lack of transparency by the Comptroller-General's Office regarding constituency funding continued in later administrations, despite the fact that the Moscoso administration suspended the program beginning in 2002. With the purpose of reconfirming the information I had collected at a previous research stage, in 2007 I asked Comptroller-General Carlos Vallarino (PRD) to indicate the "parliamentary initiatives" amounts allocated to each legislator going back to 1985. I based my petition on article 41 of the constitution (on the right of petition) and Law no. 6 of 2002, Panama's freedom of information act, which provides broad access to official data and establishes penalties for not complying with citizens' requests (República de Panamá 2002).

Despite the enacted penalty for failing to provide timely responses, Vallarino missed the constitutionally established deadline to answer information requests. Eventually, under pressure from the Panama Chapter of Transparency International, which reiterated my petition, the comptroller-general responded that his office was not the appropriate agency from which to solicit the information (even though, as my letter noted, previous reports from the Comptroller-General's Office contained the data). By refusing to release data in the custody of his office, Vallarino may have been trying to avoid stirring up a hornets' nest at a time when some of his fellow party members in the National Assembly— including the influential Pedro González (PRD, 1999–2009), who proposed a bill to permanently restore funding while chamber president in 2007–8—were insisting on the reinstatement of constituency funding (Prieto Barreiro 2008). More broadly, the incident illustrates the culture of concealment and informality prevailing in the country, where the stipulations of codified law are not reliable predictors of conduct by state officials.

The direct allocation of state funds to legislators for their discretionary expenditure, with little or no transparency or control by the relevant authorities, provided members of Panama's assembly with a convenient electoral connection. *Partidas circuitales* supplied the necessary capital for creating and fostering electoral clienteles that were likely to vote for their incumbent "benefactors" under the expectation of continuing to receive the goods and services delivered by their patrons. Additionally, direct, discretional, and uncontrolled access to funding provided opportunities to claim credit, that is, "acting so as to generate a belief in a relevant political actor (or actors) that one is personally responsible for causing the government, or some unit thereof, to do something that the actor (or actors) considers desirable" (Mayhew 1974, 52–53). According to Mayhew, credit claiming is one activity in which representatives find it electorally useful to engage:

> The political logic of [credit claiming], from the congressman's point of view, is that an actor who believes that a member can make pleasing things happen will no doubt wish to keep him in office so that he can make pleasing things happen in the future. The emphasis here is on individual accomplishment (rather than, say, party or governmental accomplishment) and on the congressman as doer (rather than as, say, expounder of constituency views). Credit claiming is highly important to congressmen, with the consequence that much of congressional life is a relentless search for opportunities to engage in it. (1974, 53)

Evidence from the May 1999 elections provides some grounds to conclude that patronage distribution through *partidas circuitales* had a favorable effect on the reelection prospects of legislators. The available data shows that the group of legislators receiving larger *partidas* in 1995–99 was reelected at higher rates than the group receiving less

Table 6.3. Constituency Funding Allocations and Assembly Members'
Reelection in Panama, 1995–99

Size of Disbursement	Members Seeking Reelection	Members Reelected	Reelection Rate
Under US$2M	31	11	35%
Above US$2M	32	20	63%
Total	63	31	49%

Source: Contraloría General 1999b.

funding. Presumably, as well as allowing higher visibility and name recognition, larger *partidas* translated into heightened constituent loyalty, which in turn yielded better results at the ballot box.

Of 63 legislators seeking reelection in 1999, 32 (all pro-government) received allocations above US$2 million between 1995 and 1999. Twenty of these, or 63 percent, were reelected. These results are well above the average reelection rate for all 63 individuals who ran for reelection in 1999 (49 percent; see table 5.1). For the 31 aspirants who received under US$2 million, 11 (35 percent) achieved reelection (Contraloría General 1999b). Appendix R presents full data on constituency allocations for these 63 members seeking reelection in 1999. Although the small number of cases reduces the statistical significance of the analysis, these findings are nevertheless suggestive of the role of larger, unsupervised *partidas circuitales* in procuring the reelection of Panama's legislators.

Seeking Reelection through Illegal Distribution of Patronage

In addition to distributing patronage through legal means, such as *partidas circuitales* when they were in place (1985–87, 1993–2001), Panamanian deputies have also illegally employed state resources in an effort to obtain constituent support and promote their electoral aspirations. In 1990, shortly after the removal of the military regime, investigators found a government truck painted with the PRD label at state property assigned to the former Panamanian Defense Forces. Inscribed on the truck was electoral propaganda that read "Carlos Duque, President; César Pardo, Legislator: he delivers!"[29] Membership in the governing party and close links to power-holding sectors facilitated this use of state assets to further the reelectoral ambitions of Legislator Pardo (PRD, 1984–89, 1994–2009).[30] Recurrence of the practice after the transition to liberal democracy substantiates the fact that the activity is commonplace in Panama.

The PARVIS Housing Subsidy Case (1997–99) represents just one of many allegations of use of public funds for electoral purposes during the twenty-five-year period extending from 1984 to 2009. The Rapid Help Program for Social Interest Housing (Programa de Ayuda Rápida para Viviendas de Interés Social, or PARVIS) was a US$34.5 million low-income housing improvement project.[31] With the Inter-American Development Bank (IDB) providing half the funding (US$17.25 million), PARVIS began in mid-1997 and was scheduled to continue through 2001. The program was designed to provide up to US$1,000-worth of construction materials (blocks, sand, cement, zinc sheets, and others) to individuals having legal title over their properties but whose monthly income was under US$300.

During the last two years of the Pérez Balladares administration, government supporters directed PARVIS materials toward electoral and private gain. The latter included appropriation for sale or personal construction projects by public employees and government sympathizers. It is estimated that PARVIS materials worth a total of US$1.2 million were misused between 1997 and 1999. The immediate goal of PARVIS was to generate support for President Pérez Balladares's proposed constitutional change that would allow his immediate reelection in 1999. After the proposal was defeated in a referendum held on August 30, 1998, the program was recycled to provide illegal electoral assistance to certain pro-government politicians with privileged access to the Ministry of Housing, who sought nomination in the October ruling party primary and reelection to office in the May 1999 general elections. The scheme basically consisted in appropriating materials from Housing Ministry warehouses throughout the country and distributing them in exchange for a commitment to vote for a ruling party (PRD) candidate to office. A more sophisticated version that provided a stronger incentive to vote for the issuing candidate and promote his/her candidacy among family and friends in the constituency included distributing PARVIS certificates promising to supply materials after the election was over.

Allegedly, in addition to Minister Francisco Sánchez Cárdenas (PRD), Vice-Minister Rogelio Paredes (PRD), a son of ex-assembly member Rigoberto Paredes, was also involved in the scheme.[32] As vice-minister of housing (1994–98), the younger Paredes served briefly as acting minister in 1998 and then quit to become an unsuccessful assembly candidate for the PRD in the May elections. Also mentioned in the PARVIS irregularities were PRD legislators Gerardo González (at the time president of the ruling party as well as of the Legislative Assembly) and Benicio Robinson, both of whom sought reelection but failed;[33] Pedro González, a son of Gerardo who pursued and won an assembly seat;[34] Cecilia Monteza, a former Housing Ministry officer who quit to run unsuccessfully as PRD candidate for legislator in the same district as Gerardo González; and several other PRD activists and candidates to elective office.

The state agencies responsible for clearing up the PARVIS irregularities failed to pursue this objective diligently. Disgruntled former legislator Enrique Riley (PRD, 1994–99), an opponent of Pedro González after losing the PRD primary to him and switching to another party (CD), presented criminal charges against González for illegal use of state resources, but the case was dismissed. Although the electoral use of PARVIS was publicly known at least since June 1998, when PRD legislator Abelardo Antonío took the assembly floor to deplore not being among those representatives enjoying favored access to construction materials for electoral purposes, the Electoral Prosecutor's Office and the Electoral Tribunal failed to intervene at any point to prevent the illegal use of government resources for campaign purposes.

After the May 1999 elections the Prosecutor-General's Office conducted an official investigation into the PARVIS scandal. With two exceptions, however, the indictment produced in early January 2000 did not call for the prosecution of any of the major figures involved in the case. Among PRD celebrities, former vice-minister Paredes was indicted for "infringing his duties as a public servant," a petty charge. Former candidate Monteza—a minor star in the PRD constellation—was charged with a serious crime: misappropriation of public resources.

The indictment against Cecilia Monteza was widely regarded as retaliation by PRD and assembly president Gerardo González. As an adversary of González for an assembly seat, the former housing official had gained the enmity of the chamber's presiding officer. In addition to Monteza and Paredes, Prosecutor Cecilia López's report implicated twelve other individuals in the PARVIS irregularities. Most of these were middle- and lower-rank Housing Office staff, among them ex-legislator Francisco Solís (PRD, 1984–89), who had secured a position in that department during the administration of President Pérez Balladares.[35]

After a preliminary hearing in April 2000, the Panama City circuit judge in charge of the procedure declined to hear the cases against eight of the fourteen defendants, among them Rogelio Paredes, whose legal action he downgraded and reassigned to a municipal judge. The six remaining defendants, including ex-PRD candidate Monteza, went to trial in October 2000. On November 29, 2000, the circuit judge absolved three defendants and sentenced three others to imprisonment. Cecilia Monteza was among those condemned. She received a seven-year prison sentence and was fined US$3,000 for forgery and embezzlement. Later, the municipal judge hearing Rogelio Paredes's case absolved him. In 2004 Paredes ran again and was elected deputy on the PRD ticket to represent the Arraiján constituency (no. 8.1) in the National Assembly. He obtained reelection in 2009.

Summary

In most advanced democracies, representatives' role in the distribution of patronage is limited to that of intermediaries between the state and their constituents. In Panama, however, many assembly members have secured roles, through both legal and illegal means, as direct providers of goods and services to their constituencies. As suggested by the Social Investment Fund and PARVIS scandals, with a view to attaining reelection some Panamanian assembly members—particularly those with privileged access to the government—may channel state resources to electoral activities in illicit ways. Legislators also formally instituted recourse to state funding in support of their reelectoral ambitions through the *partidas circuitales* implemented in 1985–87 and 1993–2001. Access to these funds gave them an electoral advantage over nonincumbents.

Legal and illegal distribution of patronage for electoral gain has consequences for democratic representation. By creating an electoral clientele, patronage distribution corrupts the free link that, ideally, should exist between representatives and constituents. Conditioning constituents to provide electoral support in exchange for the goods and services directly delivered by assembly members restricts voters' right to cast their ballots on the basis of principles and platforms. Under liberal democracy, the exercise of this right is also a prerequisite for maintaining a high-quality regime.

Privileged access to government resources for electoral purposes also violates the idea of equality that is at the basis of the democratic system. Constituency funding, together with other forms of legal and illegal electoral use of state resources, creates a subsidy in favor of incumbents. This discriminates against candidates who do not have such access and—as it may increase the likelihood of reelection—reduces the chances of holding incumbents accountable for their performance in office. The executive's use of constituency funding as a tool to bribe deputies into inaction is yet another detrimental consequence of patronage politics in the Panamanian context.

Panamanian deputies employ other means to increase their reelection prospects. Among these are switching parties and manipulating the electoral process, topics rarely addressed by the literature. Chapter 7 addresses both mechanisms.

CHAPTER 7

Political Advancement through Reelection
Party Switching and Electoral Manipulation

This chapter continues the focus on some activities Panamanian assembly members carry out to gain reelection that the literature on legislators' behavior has not yet fully explored. The initial section deals with party switching. When a Panamanian political party fails to reach the mandated electoral threshold for survival and is thus declared "extinct," formal institutional features provide an incentive to party switching. More frequently, however, label changes occur when deputies interested in securing reelection fail to obtain endorsement by their original parties or calculate that their prospects for remaining in office are higher if they switch to another party. In their bids to ensure reelection, some of Panama's assembly members have also attempted to manipulate citizen preferences (through vote buying, for example) or alter election results. While these activities were commonplace during the authoritarian period (1968–89), they have also taken place under liberal democracy. These strategies to obtain election to an assembly seat (or reelection, in the case of incumbents) are seldom addressed in the scholarship. Highlighting these electoral tactics employed by Panama's deputies will broaden our understanding not just of representatives' behavior but also of its repercussions on the quality of democratic representation.

Party Switching

According to some analysts of representatives' behavior, supporting their parties is one of the means assembly members employ to advance their political careers (Cox 1987). The underlying logic is that ballot control, especially in closed-list systems, renders parties crucial in ensuring nomination to office (Carey and Shugart 1995). Most Panamanian deputies follow this prediction, especially those belonging to the more disciplined parties, such as PRD.

An important feature ensuring this support is the recall mechanism included in the constitution (article 151), which establishes that parties may revoke a deputy's mandate under certain circumstances. One of these is that the party's statutes must specifically contain the recall mechanism (República de Panamá 2004). Other requirements, added in early 2010, stipulate that parties must submit all recalls approved by their boards to the recalled deputy's constituents. In the respective constituency, recalls need approval by two-thirds of the district's voters before they are effective (República de Panamá 2010b; see chapter 4, note 5).

Even as they support their parties, some Panamanian assembly members—indeed, a substantial minority—also change labels. This behavior, which occurs elsewhere in the region as well, remains an understudied trait of Latin American congressional politics. In Ecuador Mejía Acosta (1999) estimated that, on average, 12 percent of representatives changed parties in every legislative period between 1979 and 1996. In Brazil, according to Desposato (2006, 63), "more than a third of deputies switch party during their terms, some as many as seven times."

Although party switching is also intense in Panama, the rate is difficult to calculate. Many switches remain informal due to legislators failing to register with the new party they choose to vote with in the chamber or that nominates them for reelection. Moreover, the assembly does not keep records of representatives' "migrations." For example, in December 2008 the assembly website still contained the original seat distribution emanating from the 2004 proclamations, despite the fact that two parties (PLN and PSOL) had merged to form a new one (Unión Patriótica) and various deputies had formally changed their affiliations (Asamblea Nacional 2008c).

Additionally, the analyst must distinguish between switching for purely electoral purposes and affiliation changes forced upon deputies by rules on party survival or "emergency" situations. In a fragmented and volatile multiparty environment such as Panama's, it is not uncommon for parties to "disappear" after each election, especially where survival thresholds are in place. Following the 1994 elections, for example, seven of fifteen parties failed to reach the 5 percent survival threshold in force at the time (LIBRE, PALA, PL, PLA, UDI, Movimiento de Unidad Nacional [MUN], and Partido Panameñista Doctrinario [PPD]). Thus, the Electoral Tribunal cancelled their registries. In the aftermath of the May 1999 voting, five of twelve parties participating in the contest were declared extinct (MORENA, MPE, PL, PRC, and Partido Nacionalista Popular [PNP]). All seven parties participating in the 2004 elections survived, but the configuration of the party system changed afterward with the recognition of (yet another mutation of) Partido Liberal (2005) and Vanguardia Moral de la Patria (2007), as well as with the merger of Partido Solidaridad and Partido Liberal Nacional to form Unión Patriótica (2006). Subsequent to the 2009 elections, the Electoral Tribunal rescinded the inscription of Vanguardia Moral de la Patria (VMP) and Partido Liberal (PL), which failed to reach the voting threshold of 4 percent of ballots cast for president, deputies, mayors, or municipal councilors (Guevara Mann 2010). These developments illustrate the fleeting nature of many of Panama's parties and the country's weakly institutionalized party system (see discussion in chapter 2).

Switching from "Extinct" Parties

The provision on survival requires that parties reach a certain electoral threshold at election time in order to maintain their official registry. The threshold has changed during the twenty-five-year period under review. In the 1984 and 1989 elections it was 3 percent; in the 1994 and 1999 elections it was 5 percent; and since the 2002 electoral reform it has been 4 percent (Antinori Bolaños 1995, 937–41; República de Panamá 2003). The party survival requirement promotes switching by deputies from parties not meeting the threshold and thus declared "extinct" by the Electoral Tribunal. A member elected by a party that "disappears" immediately after the election has at least three options at hand. One is to declare him or herself "independent," which complicates committee assignments in the chamber and nomination for reelection, both of which were party-based features during the period under review (except for independent candidatures in 2009, as noted in chapter 5). A second, related possibility is to join the re-registry efforts of the extinct party leadership; if a decision is made to register the party anew, the party must obtain the affiliation of a proportion of the citizenry equivalent to the party survival threshold. In this scenario the deputy remains unaffiliated until the recognition requisites are met at some point during the constitutional, five-year term of office. The third and easiest option is to switch to a surviving party.

The extinction rule and the incentives it creates contradict the logic of proportional representation, which seeks to provide minorities with a voice in the deliberative chamber. A threshold is convenient to limit the number of parties in a system and facilitate governance, but if a party representing a platform and the principles behind it obtains a sufficient number of votes to elect one or more of its deputies to the assembly, the party should survive, even if it does not meet the threshold. The party's deputies, who stand for the group's platform and principles, should not be forced to migrate to organizations postulating different programs — not even in Panama, where the programmatic content of party politics is not, as we saw in chapter 2, particularly strong. However, the fact that only the threshold rationale — and not the logic of proportional representation — applies under such circumstances underscores the hybrid nature of Panama's electoral system, combining plurality and PR features (see chapter 3).

Because, as noted above, the National Assembly does not keep records of deputies' party movements, I was only able to systematically determine party switches by comparing the list of winning candidates proclaimed by the Electoral Tribunal with the official list of candidates in the ensuing election. Based on this methodology, the exercise that follows provides party switching information for incumbents seeking reelection in 1994, 1999, 2004, and 2009. This reduced sample of 224 members is still sufficiently large to provide statistical significance to the analysis results.[1]

Party extinction affected deputies' affiliation in at least ten instances (4 percent of the subset of 224) during the period under review. Additionally, the two independents elected in 2009 quickly signed up with President Martinelli's party, CD. Their shift calls into question the convenience of allowing independent candidatures—presumably, voters elected them at least in part because of their autonomous stances. Be that as it may, of the twelve switches identified in this section (ten members of extinct parties and two independents), eight occurred in 1994, one in 1999, and three in 2009.

Three members of extinct parties joined the successor party and nine other deputies affiliated with different parties. The main beneficiary of this type of switch was Partido Panameñista (PPAN), the country's second largest party in 1984–2009, which added four new members to its contingent (three in 1994 and one in 1999). CD, the president's party after the 2009 elections, added three members (see table 7.1). When these switches are taken into account, the effective number of parties (4.4) drops slightly to 4.2, thus reinforcing Panama's nature as a multiparty system with a dominant party (see chapter 2 and appendix F).

Going Back Home after "Emergency" Switches

The vicissitudes of Panama's party politics have sometimes prevented candidates from running on their own party tickets. In 1983, for example, the military dictatorship engineered the takeover of the opposition Partido Liberal (PL). A similar maneuver occurred in 1988, after Arnulfo Arias's death, with Partido Panameñista Auténtico (PPAN). As a result, the "true" followers and candidates of these opposition parties were not able to use the party labels in the 1984 and 1989 elections, respectively. "True" Liberal candidates in the 1984 elections, such as Mario J. de Obaldía and Marco Alarcón, ran as Panameñista candidates, and in 1989 "true" Panameñista candidates, such as Francisco Artola, Nodier Miranda, and Lucas Zarak, ran as Liberal Auténtico candidates. The creation of an "authentic" Liberal Party in 1988—that is, one not aligned with the military dictatorship—allowed Obaldía and Alarcón to seek reelection on a Liberal ticket. After Arnulfo Arias's followers re-registered in 1991 (as Partido Arnulfista), Artola, Zarak, and Jílmer González (who

Table 7.1. Switches from Extinct Parties and Affiliation Changes by Elected Independents in Panama, 1994–2009

Deputy Name	Election Year[a]	Extinct Party	Surviving or New Party
Carlos Afú	1994	PALA	PRD
Rogelio Alba	1994	LIBRE	PLN[b]
Alberto Cigarruista	1994	PLA	PPAN
Jaime Loré	1994	PL	PSOL
Juan Peralta	1994	LIBRE	PLN[b]
Mario Quiel	1994	PLA	PL[c]
Orestes Vásquez	1994	UDI	PPAN
Lenín Sucre[d]	1994	PL	PPAN
José Carreño	1999	PRC	PPAN
Hernán Delgado	2009	VMP	CD
Carlos Afú	2009	Independent	CD
Yanibel Ábrego	2009	Independent	CD

Source: Based on comparison of the list of winning candidates proclaimed by the Electoral Tribunal with the official list of candidates in the ensuing election.

[a] This year corresponds to the first year of the election term in which the deputies' party was declared extinct.

[b] Members of LIBRE joined other extinct party members to form PLN in 1996 (see appendix D).

[c] Partido Liberal (PL) was the name adopted by the extinct PLA when it re-registered in 1996 (see appendix D). This Partido Liberal once again became extinct in 1999.

[d] Legislator Sucre first adhered to MOLIRENA but subsequently sought reelection on the PPAN ticket. He was reelected and joined PPAN.

replaced Nodier Miranda after the latter's death during the term) ran for reelection as candidates of their original party. Of these five members, only Zarak obtained reelection.

A peculiar case occurred in 1994, when Joaquín Franco's own PLA missed the Electoral Tribunal's candidate registration deadline. Fortunately for Franco, he had negotiated co-sponsorship of his candidacy with Partido Arnulfista (PPAN), which did file on time. Franco was elected on the PPAN ticket in representation of the rural, single-member San Carlos–Chame constituency. Because his party did not meet the survival threshold, he re-registered his group as Partido Liberal in 1996. In 1999 he ran for reelection on this party's slate but failed to succeed, and Partido Liberal once again lost its registry.

Party Switching: The Electoral Connection

We have thus far examined cases in which deputies are forced to switch parties owing to emergency circumstances or the application of electoral legislation concerning party survival. But most of the label changes observable in Panama may be attributed to other, more clearly electoral machinations. Such migrations may follow a private calculation about reelection possibilities or a public quarrel with the party leadership that would make it difficult for assembly members to receive nomination by their parties. My analysis of the trajectories of the 224 deputies who sought reelection in 1994–2009 reveals that 21 percent of the sample switched parties. This party switching rate does not capture migrations by deputies who did not seek reelection, as well as movements among parties by members who switched more than once during their terms. Significantly, however, even while not capturing the entire phenomenon of party switching in Panama, the rate is higher than Mejía Acosta's (1999) average estimation for Ecuador in the 1979–96 period (12 percent). My speculation is that if all other changes could be systematically accounted for, Panama's switching rate would be close to or higher than Brazil's 33 percent, as reported by Desposato (2006). However, a 21 percent switching rate is high enough to indicate that electorally motivated migrations have an important presence in Panama's assembly politics and—additionally—implications for the quality of democracy.

In 1994–2009, 48 assembly members elected by a party meeting the survival threshold ran for immediate reelection as candidates of a different party (see table 7.2). Of the 48 individuals who switched, 19 renewed their mandates, representing a reelection rate of 40 percent—slightly below the average reelection rate among members seeking reelection in 1994–2009 (43 percent, see table 5.1).

At first sight, given that the overall consecutive reelection rate among deputies seeking reelection is slightly higher than the immediate reelection rate for switchers, party switching for electoral purposes does not seem to provide an advantage to incumbents. Disaggregating the data,

Table 7.2. Party Switching for Electoral Purposes in Panama, 1994–2009

		Reelection Bid			
Name	Election Party	Year	Party	Party Size[a]	Election Achieved
Marco Ameglio	MORENA	1999	PPAN	Larger	Yes
Gloria Young	MPE	1999	PPAN	Larger	Yes
Sergio Gálvez	CD	2004	PPAN	Larger	Yes
Enrique Garrido	PDC	2004	PPAN	Larger	Yes
José Varela	PDC	2004	PPAN	Larger	Yes
José Fábrega	PSOL	2009	PRD	Larger	Yes
Aristides de Icaza	PSOL	2009	CD	Larger	Yes
Abraham Martínez	PSOL	2009	PRD	Larger	Yes
José Muñoz	PSOL	2009	CD	Larger	Yes
Marylín Vallarino	PSOL	2009	CD	Larger	Yes
Marco Ameglio	PLA	1994	MORENA	Similar	Yes
Enrique Garrido	PPAN	1999	PDC	Smaller	Yes
Carlos Santana	PPAN	1999	PDC	Smaller	Yes
José Varela	PPAN	1999	PDC	Smaller	Yes
Carlos Afú	PRD	2004	PPAN	Smaller	Yes
José Fábrega	PPAN	2004	PSOL	Smaller	Yes
José Muñoz	PPAN	2004	PSOL	Smaller	Yes
Sergio Gálvez	PPAN	2009	CD	Smaller	Yes
Carlos Afú	PPAN	2009	Independent	n.a.	Yes
Herman Gnaeggi	PLA	1994	MOLIRENA	Larger	No
Olmedo Guillén	PRC	1999	PDC	Larger	No
Aristides de Icaza	PRC	1999	PSOL	Larger	No
Víctor Méndez	MPE	1999	MOLIRENA	Larger	No
Haydée Milanés	PSOL	2004	PPAN	Larger	No
Carlos Santana	PDC	2004	PPAN	Larger	No

Table 7.2. (continued)

Name	Election Party	Year	Party	Party Size[a]	Election Achieved
			Reelection Bid		
Rogelio Alba	PLN	2009	CD	Larger	No
Juvenal Martínez	CD	2009	PRD	Larger	No
Wigberto Quintero	MOLIRENA	2009	CD	Larger	No
Javier Tejeira	PLN	2009	PPAN	Larger	No
Carlos Escobar	PDC	1994	MORENA	Similar	No
Gloria Moreno	PDC	1994	MORENA	Similar	No
Raymundo Hurtado	MOLIRENA	1999	CD	Similar	No
Mariela Jiménez	MPE	1999	PRC	Similar	No
Noriel Salerno	PSOL	2004	PLN	Similar	No
Alonso Fernández	MOLIRENA	1994	PRC	Smaller	No
Leo González	MOLIRENA	1994	MORENA	Smaller	No
Domiluis Montenegro	MOLIRENA	1994	MORENA	Smaller	No
Daniel Arias	PPAN	1999	PDC	Smaller	No
Leopoldo Benedetti	PPAN	1999	PRC	Smaller	No
Rodrigo Jované	PPAN	1999	PL	Smaller	No
Manuel Ortiz	PPAN	1999	PDC	Smaller	No
Enrique Riley	PRD	1999	CD	Smaller	No
José Serracín	PPAN	1999	PDC	Smaller	No
Lucas Zarak	PPAN	1999	PDC	Smaller	No
Arcelio Batista	PRD	2004	PPAN	Smaller	No
Manuel de La Hoz	PRD	2004	PPAN	Smaller	No
Mireya Lasso	PSOL	2009	VMP	Smaller	No
Euribíades Herrera	MOLIRENA	2009	Independent	n.a.	No

Source: Tribunal Electoral 1994a, 1994b, 1999a, 1999b, 2004a, 2004b, 2009a, 2009c.

Note: Highlighted members did not win reelection.

[a] Compared to former party.

however, provides more relevant information. The results, while not statistically significant (owing to the small number of cases), are nevertheless informative.

Deputies who migrated to larger parties (that is, parties having more affiliates) appear to have greater success in gaining reelection than their peers moving to smaller organizations or parties of a similar size. This outcome may be related to bigger parties' ability to obtain a larger share of the vote and to a somewhat significant tendency among voters to vote a straight ticket (as noted in chapter 2), which is likely to be more prevalent among electors who are party members. Of the 20 deputies who switched to larger parties, 10 secured reelection. Five of these reelected assembly members moved to PPAN, 3 to CD, and 2 to PRD. Comparatively, of those twenty who moved to smaller parties, 7 (35 percent) were reelected. Of those 6 who switched to similarly sized organizations, only 1 returned to office.

From another perspective, PPAN was the party that experienced both the largest number of defections (13) and additions (11), followed by PDC (5 and 8, respectively). CD, the party of President Ricardo Martinelli (2009–14), suffered 2 defections but gained 8 incumbents from other parties. These statistics relate to weak party discipline, a feature linked to the low programmatic content of Panama's politics and an inchoate party system (previously noted in chapter 2). Nine of the 13 defections from PPAN took place during the 1994–99 term, when the party was in opposition. After the Panameñista presidential primary in March 1998, a majority of the party's legislators broke with Mireya Moscoso's leadership, choosing to support the defeated candidate in the primary (Alberto Vallarino) and form their own assembly bloc. Although the party expelled the rebels, they remained in the assembly and coalesced around their own, informal trademark (*saltamontes,* or "grasshoppers").

At the beginning of the 1999 political campaign, 7 of these PPAN dissidents, who were keen on retaining their seats, secured the support of PDC: Daniel Arias, Enrique Garrido, Manuel Ortiz, Carlos Santana, José Serracín, José Varela, and Lucas Zarak.[2] Although only three "grasshoppers" secured reelection—Garrido, Santana, and Varela—nomination of the defectors benefited PDC. After its poor performance at the polls in 1994, Panama's Christian Democratic Party was particularly worried about its prospects for survival. The votes pooled by the Panameñista dissidents helped PDC surpass the survival threshold in the 1999 elections.

Eight of the 11 migrations to PPAN occurred in the 1999–2004 term, when the party controlled the executive. During this period, the party not only attracted the three "grasshoppers" who had gained reelection in 1999 on the PDC slate. Legislator Haydée Milanés (PSOL), who had collaborated very closely with the administration of President Mireya Moscoso (PPAN), also migrated to the president's Panameñista Party, as did Sergio Gálvez, elected on the CD ticket in 1999. Additionally, PPAN attracted three deputies from the PRD, reportedly the most disciplined of Panama's parties: Arcelio Batista, Manuel de La Hoz, and—last but hardly least—Carlos Afú, the main protagonist in the CEMIS affair (see introduction and chapter 10), who moved to the government bloc after exchanging pungent accusations with the PRD leadership.

Though not strongly conclusive, these trends fall in line with two aspects of Panama's politics addressed before: a weakly institutionalized party system and strong presidentialism. Panamanian parties are often unable to maintain discipline among their assembly contingents. In this regard, in early 2008 a prominent member of MOLIRENA (who served in the chamber in 1989–94) complained to this author that his party's deputies "do as they please" ("*hacen lo que les da la gana*").[3] In contrast, the power of the purse gives the executive significant influence among the assembly membership, to the point of attracting independents or deputies from opposition parties to its assembly bloc. The analysis of constituency allocations (see chapter 6) and this discussion of party switching shows that such has been the case in the administrations of Pérez Balladares (PRD, 1994–99), Moscoso (PPAN, 1999–2004), Martín Torrijos (PRD, 2004–9), and Martinelli (CD, 2009–14). Pérez Balladares and Moscoso initially did not have absolute majorities in the chamber, but they succeeded in enlarging their blocs by attracting members from other parties. Torrijos and Martinelli, who had absolute majorities from the start of their administrations, also drew independents or opposition members to their camps. In 2004–9 Torrijos formally added three deputies to his bloc: Juvenal Martínez (CD), Abraham Martínez (PSOL), and José Fábrega (PSOL) (Flores 2007b).

In the months elapsed since President Martinelli's inauguration (July 1, 2009) and the writing of this text (May 2010), several PRD mayors and municipal councilors switched to CD. Party leaders bitterly complained about these "migrations" and the recurrent support Gabriel Méndez (PRD, 2009–14), among other PRD assembly members, offered the government in the chamber. PRD secretary-general Mitchell Doens angrily referred to Méndez as "a Trojan horse," insisting it was time "PRD stop counting Méndez as one of its members" (Lara 2010). When the party threatened to revoke the mandate of Méndez and other elected PRD migrants, the government bloc in the National Assembly passed Law no. 14 of 2010, which attached further requirements to the recall provision, making it more difficult to apply (see above and chapter 4, note 5). Subsequently, Rony Araúz and José Lozada (both PRD, 2009–14) switched to CD, and PRD leaders accused the main government party of "buying" Araúz's registration.[4]

Party switching has significant consequences for the democratic system, especially for political representation and vertical accountability. Because parties are the means of organizing and aggregating citizens' political preferences in mass liberal democracies, particularly at election time, in theory they constitute an important vehicle for representing the views of their constituents and holding political leaders accountable. But, as noted by Mainwaring (1999, 6) in the Brazilian case,

> where party labels change frequently, where major parties disappear and others come on the scene, where politicians switch parties with impunity, where party discipline is limited, and where interparty electoral alliances are common but neither national nor enduring, electoral accountability through parties is hampered.

Electoral Manipulation

In some democracies—such as Panama—electoral outcomes do not result entirely from procedures established in codified rules. Although holding free and fair elections regularly is a condition for electoral (and liberal) democracy, some measure of vote fraud may persist even in these regimes. Alongside transparent voting, illegal practices such as vote rigging may also play a role in determining who assumes office, especially in settings where there is a tradition of electoral manipulation and impunity is informally institutionalized.

Widespread vote fraud was a traditional feature of Panamanian politics. In *The People of Panama*, Biesanz and Biesanz begin their section on electoral politics by indicating that to "assure the outcome of an election and achieve the tantalizing prizes of political office, candidates employ all the old Tammany devices." At the time they wrote, mechanisms for election rigging had "only slightly refined since Colombian days, when many voters approached the booths time after time and some districts ran up a vote two or three times the number of its voters" (Biesanz and Biesanz 1955, 149).

In Panama, as in Colombia and elsewhere, the maxim *quien escruta, elige* ("he who counts, elects") was long in vogue. Up to 1968 it was common for members of the National Vote Counting Board to discard whole blocks of suffrages on various pretexts. Perhaps the most notorious instance of electoral fraud prior to the military regime occurred in 1948. Biesanz and Biesanz (1955, 150–51) provide a lively description of the events surrounding the presidential election of that year:

> It is generally conceded that Arnulfo Arias, then at the peak of his popularity, had polled a plurality of votes. But the government had backed Domingo Díaz, in spite of numerous sanctimonious vows that *this time* there would be no "official" candidate. They dragged out the count through the summer, playing a waiting game to see if they could get away with throwing out district after district of Arnulfista votes on the grounds of fraud. They finally decided they could and declared the septuagenarian Díaz, who had wanted the office all his adult life, President of Panama. Then in November, 1949, when Police Chief Remón fell out with the administration and in a vengeful spirit put Arnulfo Arias back into power, the elections board amiably announced within an hour that they had made a mistake in the count, and Arnulfo had really been the popular choice. Thus are revolutions "constitutionalized."

Two decades later, at the last elections held under the old regime and with Arnulfo Arias again as a principal protagonist, the government of President Marco Robles, the coalition of parties supporting the official candidate, and the National Guard attempted to thwart Arias's return to power in the general election of May 12. As documented by Brittmarie Janson Pérez (1993, 32–33), in addition to setting up the electoral machinery to favor the government's choice,

> their tactics included intimidation and violence. In the attacks staged by paramilitary contingents against Arias' supporters, two persons were killed. Voters were prevented from casting their ballots. After the votes were cast, ballot boxes in areas where Arias was known to be strong, were destroyed. The vote count was delayed for days, presumably to engineer a last-minute fraud.

In May 1968, however, pressure from civil society, led by Archbishop Tomás Clavel, produced a change in the attitude of the National Guard, which ultimately resulted in the recognition of Arnulfo Arias's victory and his short-lived third administration until he was deposed by the military ten days after assuming office on October 1, 1968.

Under the old regime as well as afterwards, fraud affected elections not only to the presidency but to other offices as well. After the proclamation of Arias's triumph in 1968, the Robles administration concentrated its attention on assembly elections, maneuvering to control the provincial election boards and delay the vote count. Arnulfo Arias responded by exerting pressure on the electoral authorities, with the aim of engineering a majority in the National Assembly and the municipal councils. Results for the assembly were not reported until the eve of inauguration day (October 1), by which time it became evident that President Arias had deprived a number of opposition deputies of their credentials (Janson Pérez 1993, 33–34).

The Fraudulent Tradition of the Military Regime

During the military period recourse to vote rigging escalated to heights unexplored by the *caciques* (political bosses) of the old regime, particularly as a result of the application of electronic devices to fraudulent purposes (Arias de Para 1984). The regime's stratagem of purporting to generate international legitimacy on the basis of elections made vote fraud an important element in the dictatorship's attempts to remain in power against the will of the majority of the population. At that time the Electoral Tribunal, the military, and PRD (as well as satellite parties supporting the dictatorship), assisted by individual candidates to office, engaged in widespread vote rigging with the purpose of fabricating electoral victories for the military regime. Janson Pérez (1993, 168–69) offers a telling account of the events surrounding the general election of 1984, which once again featured Arnulfo Arias as the opposition presidential candidate:

> As soon as Arnulfo Arias' victory at the polls became apparent, in a two-pronged strategy which it would repeat in the presidential elections of 1989, the military-controlled government delayed the vote count and used violence.
>
> On 7 May 1984, the day after the elections, a PRD paramilitary squad reportedly organized by former Vice-President Gerardo González Vernaza[5] and Humberto López Tirone fired upon a crowd of opposition demonstrators who were pressuring the National Vote Counting Board to speed up the counting process. Two men died and about 40 persons were wounded . . .
>
> By 7 May in the morning the Electoral Tribunal knew that Arnulfo Arias had won by 13,000 votes, and the scramble started . . .
>
> Two years later, highly placed sources in the White House admitted to Seymour M. Hersh of *The New York Times* that there was never any doubt that the elections had been fraudulent. The CIA had complete reports to that effect, and the night of the elections the [U.S.] embassy knew that Noriega had stopped the vote count to prepare the fraud. Nevertheless, the Reagan administration did nothing because it felt that Noriega would not have responded to U.S. pressure to recognize Arias' victory.

The military's scheme not only resulted in the fraudulent election of PRD presidential nominee Nicolás Ardito Barletta but also the improper assignment of legislative seats to several pro-dictatorship legislative candidates: Rafael Ábrego (PRD), Pedro Brin Martínez (PRD), Ebén Chi (PRD), Santiago Curabo (PRD), Hugo Giraud (PRD), Anselmo Guainora (PRD), Harmodio Icaza (PALA), Guillermo Jiménez (PRD),

Rigoberto Paredes (PRD), Hugo Torrijos (PRD), and perhaps others as well. In this manner, these candidates assumed legislative office and the regime ensured a majority in the assembly that enabled it to pass laws and take action in accordance with "democratic" principles.[6]

In 1989 the dictatorship and its supporting parties, led by PRD, attempted similar actions. Because the opposition vote was massive, however, not even the ingenious artifices of the military-controlled Electoral Tribunal and PRD leaders were capable of overturning the victory of the opposition slate, led by Guillermo Endara (PPAN), a follower of Arnulfo Arias (who had died the previous year). In the face of these developments, the regime opted for annulling the elections and de facto prolonging its rule, which lasted until the U.S. invasion of December 1989.[7]

Blatant, overt fraud as described here was not an issue in 1994–2009. After the overthrow of the military regime in 1989, the most vicious features of electoral politics under military control were eliminated through the abolition of the army, the restoration of civilian rule, and the acquisition of a somewhat greater measure of autonomy by the Electoral Tribunal. Electoral irregularities, however, continue to occur, stimulated by the weakness of the rule of law and the strength of impunity as an informal institution in Panamanian politics. Since 1990 Panamanian assembly members seeking reelection have applied specific devices to engineer favorable electoral outcomes, including using their influence to alter voter records, delivering money in exchange for a promise to vote (or not to vote), and exercising influence to manipulate the vote count, among others. These practices, which have roots in political habits anteceding the inauguration of liberal democracy, presumably have had some effect in determining which candidates effectively assume office and, in particular, which deputies remain in the assembly and which must face retirement.

Voter Transportation

Maintaining accurate voter records is the responsibility of the Electoral Tribunal. Especially under military rule, however, the tribunal manipulated these records to favor official candidates, including aspirants to assembly seats. In 1984 and 1989, for example, officials reassigned known opponents to far away precincts or dropped their names from the registry, thus preventing them from exercising their right to vote. At the same time, the tribunal enfranchised several thousand persons who for various reasons (age restrictions, failure to notify residence changes on time, etc.) did not appear on the electoral registry and issued special credentials to public employees allowing them to vote at any precinct (and, thus, repeatedly). It is estimated that this maneuver cost the opposition approximately 100,000 ballots in 1984 (Arias de Para 1984, 72–75; Koster and Sánchez Borbón 1990, 305–6; Ricord 1991, 84, 85).[8]

While such large-scale fraud is no longer the case, the liberal democratic period has seen complaints of voter list alterations at the district level to include sympathizers of incumbents or "official" candidates. In May 1994 Laurentino Cortizo, at the time a candidate to the assembly on the PSOL ticket, protested that activists of PLA (then part of the government coalition) transported several hundred voters from other districts to support the Liberal candidate in his constituency. These individuals presumably employed special credentials issued by the Electoral Tribunal to vote outside their districts. On this occasion the tribunal held new elections, after which Cortizo was declared the winner (Murillo Muñoz 1994b).

Reportedly, in 1999 certain candidates to the assembly, in collusion with electoral authorities, "transplanted" voters to their constituencies. Candidate Renato Pereira (PRD) complained before the electoral prosecutor about the presence in his Panama City district of between three and four thousand voters from other precincts who had been transported to support incumbent PRD Legislators Elías Castillo, Manuel de La Hoz, and Olivia de León (all three reelected). Estranged PRD Legislator Enrique Riley, the candidate of CD in a remote district of Veraguas Province, protested that PRD candidate Pedro González, a son of assembly president Gerardo González (PRD), introduced more than eight hundred voters from other constituencies to guarantee the younger González's victory at the polls.[9]

Several months prior to the election, Legislator Pablo Quintero Luna (PPAN), from a rural constituency in the Province of Herrera, accused PRD activists of bloating his district's register with approximately two thousand "new" voters (Quintero de León 1998). Quintero lost his seat to Mateo Castillero of PRD. After the May 1999 elections, community leaders in Darién Province indicated they would complain before several international human rights organizations about the inclusion of "thousands" of Panama City residents in the local voting rosters. The leaders argued that the Electoral Tribunal was well aware of the irregularity but neglected to take any action, ostensibly to contribute to the reelection of one of the province's legislators, then-influential Haydée Milanés (PSOL), as well as to the election of a PRD candidate, Sergio Tócamo (both of whom realized their aspirations) (Castro 1999).

The Ombudsman's Office received complaints of illegal changes in voter registries in the district of Chepo, where incumbent Tomás Altamirano Mantovani (PRD), a son of First Vice-President Tomás Altamirano Duque (PRD), was declared the winner in the contest against Panameñista challenger Hernán Delgado (Defensoría del Pueblo 1999; Salas Céspedes 1999). Delgado, who ran again in 2004 and 2009, attained victory on the latter occasion, despite numerous alleged irregularities to favor the candidacy of the former vice-president and PRD candidate in that constituency.[10] In 2009 Kayra Harding, PRD assembly candidate in the district of Arraiján, protested that the number of voters in several precincts exceeded the number of constituents registered to vote. She insinuated that alterations in the registry contributed to the reelection of Rogelio Paredes (PRD, 2004–14) (Paredes 2009).[11]

Vote Buying

Allegedly, buying votes (or abstentions) is another fraudulent mechanism employed by assembly members to preserve their seats. In 1984 there was widespread vote buying in the San Blas Indigenous Reservation as well as in the rural provinces of Herrera and Los Santos, where the price of a ballot ranged between US$5 and US$20. Together with money, candidates with close links to the military regime who additionally had privileged access to the Electoral Tribunal gave vote sellers the "right" ticket—that is, they handed voters a party ballot before the voter entered the precinct.

Renting voting cards (*cédulas*) is a variant of this behavior that was employed in the 1984 elections and on subsequent occasions as well.[12] Candidates pay voters a certain sum in exchange for their voting cards, which the aspirant retains until the election is over. This mechanism not only prevents would-be followers of an opponent from supporting him/her at the ballot box but also potentially provides the candidate who "rents" the *cédula* with an extra vote. The rented voting card is given to a supporter, who may thus vote more than once for the candidate of his/her preference. In 1984 and 1989 lax controls at the precincts, which were mostly staffed by supporters of the military regime who condoned such illegalities, facilitated multiple voting (Arias de Para 1984, 75–77; Ricord 1991, 83–88).

After the overthrow of the military regime, some degree of vote buying has persisted, albeit through more subtle devices. During the 1994 political campaign and elections, newspaper articles repeatedly reported on vote buying and described it as an expected political practice. Complaints about the inclination of candidates to pay in exchange for purported support at the polls marred elections to the assembly in several precincts in Herrera, Coclé, and Darién provinces, among others. Lamenting the prevalence of the practice in his district, one political commentator wrote that vote buying had completely distorted the principle of representation in Darién (Brannan Jaén 1994a; Castillo 1994; Rodríguez 1994; Sanchiz 1994).

On election day in 1999, Franz Wever (PRD) allegedly distributed as much as US$25,000 in low-denomination (US$10) supermarket coupons to constituents. Alberto Alemán Boyd (PRD), who ran for re-election in the same district as Wever but failed to retain the assembly seat he had held since 1984, accused the latter of vote buying by supposedly devoting part of his *partida circuital* to financing the coupons. Reports of ballot purchasing also came from the impoverished Ngobe-Buglé Indigenous Reservation (where a major fraud occurred in 1984), the rural district of Antón (Coclé Province), and low-income sectors of Panama City.[13] In the highland region of Veraguas Province, PRD candidate Pedro González was accused of distributing large quantities of food and counterfeit US$20 bills to voters during the elections. In reference to González's activities, the U.S. State Department *Country Report on Human Rights Practices* for 1999 asserted: "Domestic and international observers characterized the [1999] elections as generally free and fair; however, several local contests were marred by reports of vote buying and in extreme cases, voter intimidation. Legislative District 9-3, in Veraguas Province, was criticized widely for such electoral interference"

(U.S. Department of State 2000).[14] In 2004 Marcos González (PPAN) complained that his incumbent party fellow Francisco Alemán traded supermarket coupons for votes. Alemán was eventually cleared. Teresita Yániz (PDC) objected to similar practices in her constituency that— according to her denunciations—affected her electoral results.

Electoral prosecutor Gerardo Solís indicted Legislator Haydée Milanés, who switched from PSOL to PPAN ahead of the 2004 elections, for using state funds to buy suffrages in Darién Province. Milanés protested that the accusation was motivated by PRD spite—she was allied to that party in 1994–99 before supporting President Mireya Moscoso (PPAN) in 1999–2004 (see chapter 4). But the Electoral Tribunal admitted Solís's case, annulled Milanés's victory, and called new elections in her constituency. In the new contest, incumbent Milanés was defeated by Geovany Castillo, the PRD nominee, who enjoyed strong support from his party and President-Elect Martín Torrijos (PRD) (Alfaro 2004; Arosemena 2004; Fernández 2004).

In 2009 the Electoral Prosecutor's Office received several accusations of vote buying throughout the country. One of the complainants accused incumbent Ezequiel Ramírez (PRD, 2004–9), a deputy from Darién Province, of paying voters in exchange for their support at the polls (Fiscalía General Electoral 2009a). In any event, candidate Salvador Real (UP) defeated Ramírez. In Chiriquí Province, former legislator Edwin Aizpurúa (PPAN, 1999–2004) alleged that incumbent and fellow party member Miguel Fanovich (PPAN, 2004–14) secured his reelection through vote buying in the constituency of David, through which means—according to the complainant—Fanovich ensured his reelection (Valdés 2009).

Rigging the Vote Count

Exercising influence to manipulate the vote count is another mechanism to which some deputies resort in an effort to maintain their seats. This influence is a function of their individual standing with the Electoral Tribunal authorities as well as their rank in the party, the strength of the party in national politics, their links to the executive, and the degree of executive involvement in electoral affairs. As expected, this type of fraud was much more prevalent during the military period.

In 1984, for example, the "victory" of several pro-regime candidates to the assembly was based on results featured on "corrected" tally sheets that had been audaciously written over at the PRD-controlled scrutiny boards. On instructions from the military command and with the additional purpose of securing their continuation in office, Alberto Alemán Boyd and Rigoberto Paredes attempted to make "corrections" of similar or greater magnitude in 1989. Telephone conversation recordings that circulated widely at the time revealed their efforts to violate tally sheets with the purpose of concocting at least fifteen assembly seats for government supporters, including incumbent legislators.[15]

In a different context and to a lesser degree, in 1994–2009 tally sheets have also "disappeared" and "reappeared," sometimes with curious additions. In 1994 the press reported "grave irregularities" in electoral computations pertaining to Panama City precincts as well as to voting places in Chiriquí and Darién provinces. In the latter region, candidate Abraham Pretto (MOLIRENA), a Tercer Partido Nacionalista deputy under the old regime during the 1960–64 and 1964–68 terms, complained that the tally sheets had been purposely altered to favor Haydée Milanés of PSOL (Otero 1994c). In 1999 over one hundred vote records pertaining to several Panama City precincts remained at undisclosed locations for approximately two days after the May 2 elections. After they were finally retrieved, candidates complained that figures did not match the data immediately reported at the end of the vote.[16] In addition, the Ombudsman's Office received complaints of tally sheet alterations in the district of La Chorrera. These changes ostensibly favored incumbent Roberto Ábrego (PRD), to the detriment of challenger Leopoldo Castillo (PPAN) (Defensoría del Pueblo 1999). In 2004 PRD candidate Maribel Coco protested that some persons in her constituency had been offered "up to US$1,000 for changing the election results." She accused incumbent Franz Wever of masterminding the payments (Flórez 2004).

Objecting to Adverse Electoral Results

During the military period another device employed to assign seats to favored individuals included accepting all legal objections (*impugnaciones*) presented by pro-government candidates, who consistently impugned adverse voting results. Accordingly, only votes cast in precincts in which pro-regime candidates won were taken into consideration in the final count (Arias de Para 1984, 78–82). The dictatorship implemented a similar strategy in 1989 before annulling the elections (Ricord 1991, 91–99).

While the practice of impugning adverse electoral results continues under liberal democracy, the Electoral Tribunal has revealed less inclination to go along with it. In 1994–2009 the tribunal dismissed most formal objections to vote counts. Furthermore, the cost of presenting electoral suits has risen considerably, as the tribunal requires the deposit of a substantial bail before considering them and, on occasion, has resorted to fining the promoters of legal actions against candidates declared to have won. While these restrictions have been criticized as constituting an obstacle to justice, they have also reduced incentives to attempt to manipulate the distribution of assembly seats on the basis of purported legal actions.

The Endurance of Localized Irregularities

Panama's liberal democracy appears to have overcome the practice of governments resorting to large-scale, blatant electoral fraud to ensure their continuation in power. But localized irregularities, linked to the informal institutionalization of impunity and aimed at guaranteeing the election and reelection of certain candidates (among them deputies) remain an issue. The 1999 electoral experience provides testimony in support of this affirmation. Shortly after the elections, Ombudsman Ítalo Antinori Bolaños reported receiving an "avalanche" of complaints about lack of transparency.[17] Reflecting on the persistence of manipulative practices, an editorial in *El Panamá América* insisted that the elections of May 1999 had been "the most irregular of those held since the middle of the century."[18] According to the daily, "vote-buying, violence, spurious records, altered tally sheets, and irregular counts" characterized a process resulting in the "questionable assignment of at least one dozen Assembly seats, mainly to the ruling PRD . . . without any arithmetic relationship to the total amount of votes cast in the legislative election." A decade later, such "vicious arts" continued to plague Panamanian electoral processes. In 2009 the Electoral Prosecutor's Office initiated eighty-one investigations into electoral irregularities. Thirty-nine of these cases concerned vote buying. The illegal use of state resources, another anomaly prevalent in Panama, was the object of eleven complaints throughout the country (Fiscalía General Electoral 2009b).

Summary

Switching parties and manipulating elections, in which Panama's deputies engage, as we have seen, are not among the electoral behaviors predicted by the literature. Although most Panamanian assembly members support their parties, many of them also change labels. They do so because their own parties become extinct and because they hold differences with the leadership, but they also have a clear electoral connection in mind. Toward the end of their terms, at election time, many shift parties because opportunities for securing candidacy are few or nonexistent in their own parties or because they believe they have higher reelection prospects under different labels. The available evidence suggests more success in achieving reelection among deputies who change to larger parties and less likelihood of holding on to a seat among those who shift to smaller parties.

Switching parties has negative effects on representation and accountability. Party switching releases representatives from the commitment of upholding the program their constituents voted for when they opted for a certain party label (assuming, of course, that constituents voted on a programmatic basis). Moreover, it reduces opportunities for accountability through elections because it complicates voters' possibilities for effectively rewarding or punishing politicians and parties at the ballot box.

Electoral manipulation is another activity Panama's deputies undertake with the purpose of securing reelection. To promote their continuation in office, some assembly members modify voting records, buy votes from constituents, and distort electoral computations. Although much more widespread under the military dictatorship (1968–89), these practices have continued—albeit to a lesser degree—under liberal democracy. Due to their irregular nature, it is difficult to estimate how much they influence the reelection of deputies. Based on the available evidence, however, it seems fair to say that at least some assembly members owe their continuation in office to the manipulation of voter preferences.

Party switching and electoral manipulation, promoted by an informal institutionalization that also encourages a much broader use of patronage than is the case in consolidated liberal democracies, have not merited much scholarly attention by students of legislators' behavior. Panamanian assembly members seek reelection through these and other means to advance their political careers but also to get rich and preserve their freedom from prosecution. Chapter 8 begins to examine deputies' interest in personal enrichment.

## CHAPTER 8

Personal Enrichment through Legal Means

Assembly Members' Wages in Comparative Perspective

The establishment of democracy gives rise to certain expectations among the members of the political community. One is that action by government leaders be oriented toward some version of the public good (O'Donnell 1996), given that an intrinsic quality of the democratic regime as a political system is that it is completely (or almost completely) responsive to all its citizens (Dahl 1971, 2). Naturally, such a regime is an ideal type; absolute or near-absolute responsiveness, although possible conceptually, is materially unattainable. Even so, the democratic rhetoric—"government of the people, by the people, for the people"—legitimizes an ideal that, among other things, repudiates behavior by public officials oriented toward the satisfaction of private objectives.

This universalistic expectation is embedded in a republican tradition with deep roots in Western political thinking. The moral philosophers of antiquity exalted civic virtue, which they understood as unselfish dedication to the *res publica*. Renaissance and Enlightenment thinkers identified patriotism, conceptualized as the suppression of personal ambition and unswerving devotion to the public welfare, as an essential element in maintaining a vigorous political regime. In *The Spirit of the Laws* Montesquieu (1748/1966) argued that sustaining the democratic regime required the prevalence of a generalized "sensation" of civic virtue among its members.

These theoretical admonitions notwithstanding, behavior by public officials oriented toward private gain is present in all liberal democracies. There are, however, significant variations in the degree of particularism that different democratic regimes exhibit or tolerate. Clearly, there is less of it where a universalistic rule of law is strongly institutionalized—that is, where written laws are generally a reliable predictor of the behavior of political actors. Where corruption, impunity, and clientelism serve as better predictors of politicians' behavior, a drive toward private gain is more evident in their actions.

This is the first of three chapters focusing on private gain as a motivation for the actions of Panama's deputies. Based on the premise that representatives are self-interested rational actors, getting rich may well be a reason for obtaining or maintaining an assembly seat. Analysts of representatives' behavior, however, have only mentioned this goal in passing. While "private gain" is one of five goals of representatives mentioned in his 1973 study of congressional committees, Fenno clarified on the book's first page that this objective "will not be treated at all." Mayhew (1974, 16)—another major theorist of representatives' behavior— wrote that some members of the U.S. Congress may "try to get rich in office, a quest that may or may not interfere with reelection," but he did not elaborate the idea further.

Concerning politicians generally, Samuels (1998) observed that "many politicians may seek office for other reasons" than obtaining reelection, "such as promoting good policy or to become rich." Despite these cursory references, the scholarship has not examined the private gain objective and its implications in sufficient depth. At least one analyst describes this as a potential weakness, for representatives "do their work within environments that are increasingly populated by the affluent—ranging from corporate executives to high-powered lobbyists to many wealthy peers with similar backgrounds and experiences" (Loomis 1994, 348).

In the analysis of Panamanian deputies' behavior from 1984 onwards, acquiring wealth emerges as an important motivation for seeking reelection. In 1999 an acute observer of Panamanian politics, former electoral tribunal member and supreme court magistrate César Quintero, explained the "excess" of assembly candidates principally as a function of the high salaries and ample prerogatives enjoyed by chamber members.[1] This chapter situates the emoluments received by Panama's assembly members in comparative perspective, showing how—according to various criteria—they are very well paid. As a result, obtaining and retaining a deputy's seat constitute a legal means to securing and maintaining access to a high income.

Assembly Members' Wages

For their services to the state, public officials, including representatives, should receive adequate compensation. In many countries the low remuneration received by officers of the state is frequently cited as an explanation for public sector corruption. In this context, increasing public officials' salaries could be judged positively if the pay raise is meant to rectify income inequality and discourage illegal enrichment.[2] If, however, wage structures are not based on merit or job responsibility, or fail to address salary injustices and dissuade illicit rent seeking, they lose significance in democratic terms. In Panama, as this and the following two chapters show, deputies' preoccupation with increasing their earnings has little to do with the aforesaid democratic objectives. On the contrary, they relate to a desire for personal enrichment, partly induced by the informal institutions discussed in chapter 4 as well as by the military regime's sultanistic legacy.

In a constitutional analysis volume published toward the end of the old regime, César Quintero (1967, 474) complained of the "evident tendency towards the increase of deputies' salaries, diets, allowances, and privileges." From 1904 to 1932 Panama's assembly members only received payment during sessions. Under the 1904 constitution, the assembly met every two years for a four-month period, and Law no. 3 of 1904 established their salary at 400 pesos (approximately US$200) per month during sessions (Convención Nacional 1906). At one point before 1932, and after the adoption of the U.S. dollar as legal tender in Panama (pursuant to the Legal Tender Agreement of June 20, 1904[3]), the salary was set at US$300 per session month. In 1932 lawmakers added to the US$300 monthly sessional allowance a US$150 payment for each month during which the assembly was in recess.

This double remunerative scale was abrogated in 1956, when pursuant to a constitutional amendment deputies' salaries increased to US$750 per month throughout the year. An additional allowance of US$1,000 per extraordinary session was also introduced at this time. In 1964 the US$750 allowance was enhanced with a US$250 monthly supplementary stipend, which in effect signified an increase in deputies' salaries to US$1,000 per month. At the time, Quintero (1967, 476–78) judged this emolument "excessive." In his opinion, "a deputy should not be paid more than a schoolteacher or a high-school instructor. If he has no personal supplementary income, he can live on such salary; if he has additional income, such salary will allow him to maintain his habitual lifestyle."

Overpaid Deputies?

This payment was modest, however, compared to the emolument legislators approved for themselves after the 1983 constitutional reform went into effect. At the time of the new assembly's inauguration, in 1984, members set their monthly remuneration at US$7,000.[4] Despite members' attempts to increase their wages, as of this writing the emolument remains at that level. The US$7,000 figure still contrasts sharply, however, with the minimum monthly wage in the private service sector, which the Martinelli administration set at US$218.40 in December 2009, or with the minimum monthly wage for public employees, set at US$375 in April 2010 (Flores 2008; Ministerio de Trabajo y Desarrollo Laboral 2009; Ministerio de la Presidencia 2010).

In real dollars the basic salary of a legislator in 1984, when Panama's assembly was restored under military rule, was nearly three times the income of a deputy in 1968, when the chamber was shut down by the National Guard. Using 1960 as a base year and adjusting assembly members' income for cost of living in Panama, as reported in the World Bank's World Development Indicators Database, the US$1,000 monthly wages of deputies in 1968 represented US$924.44 in 1960 dollars. When the assembly was reintroduced in 1984, the monthly US$7,000 income of legislators represented US$2,700.49 in 1960 dollars, or 2.92 times the wages of a deputy in 1968 (adjusted for 1960 prices) (see table 8.1).[5]

Table 8.1. Assembly Members' Monthly Wages in Panama, 1960–2008

Year	Real Emolument (in US$)[a]	Year	Real Emolument (in US$)[a]
1960	750.00	1985	2,673.05
1961	745.42	1986	2,674.83
1962	739.60	1987	2,648.44
1963	736.28	1988	2,638.96
1964	958.58	1989	2,633.54
1965	954.17	1990	2,613.42
1966	952.33	1991	2,581.00
1967	939.40	1992	2,534.75
1968	924.44	1993	2,523.30
1969	n.a.	1994	2,491.69
1970	n.a	1995	2,467.16
1971	n.a.	1996	2,436.57
1972	n.a.	1997	2,404.72
1973	n.a	1998	2,391.35
1974	n.a.	1999	2,361.89
1975	n.a.	2000	2,326.01
1976	n.a.	2001	2,319.89
1977	n.a.	2002	2,296.79
1978	n.a.	2003	2,287.83
1979	n.a.	2004	2,283.66
1980	n.a.	2005	2,213.24
1981	n.a.	2006	2,167.80
1982	n.a.	2007	2,081.05
1983	n.a.	2008	1,913.46
1984	2,700.49		

Source: Quintero 1967; Flores 2008; World Bank 2010. See also appendix N in this volume.

Note: Data are not provided for 1969–83, during which the national assembly did not operate owing to its closure by the military in 1968.

[a] Emoluments given in 1960 prices.

As shown in table 8.1, an assembly member's job was much more lucrative in 1984–2009 than under the old regime. The comparison is not only significant in real terms but also with regard to members' workload. Admittedly, the sitting period in the plenum increased from four months under the 1946 constitution to eight months beginning in 1984. In addition, starting in 1984, committees are supposed to meet during the chamber's two recesses (though committees are loath to meet at those times). But, although comparative data were not available at the time of this writing, we can safely say that absenteeism is high under the current regime. Consider, for instance, attendance statistics for September 2008 (presented in table 8.2), which I had the opportunity to procure and analyze during one of this project's research stages. There were eighteen sittings that month. Twenty-three deputies (30 percent of the membership) failed to show up for more than nine days (that is, half the sitting period), either because they were "on leave" or absent without excuse.

There were a total of 1,404 deputy sittings in September 2008,[6] but National Assembly attendance statistics indicate that actual deputy sittings that month amounted to just 887, or 63 percent of the total (Asamblea Nacional 2008b), which implies a loss of 517 deputy sittings (37 percent). Based on the monthly bill for deputies' emoluments (US$7,000 x 78 = US$546,000), this 37 percent loss cost Panama US$202,020 in September 2008. Although some absentee members authorize their alternates to act on their behalf, this does not minimize the loss since substitutes receive a monthly salary of US$2,000 regardless of whether they replace their principals or not.[7]

In April 2010 there were 17 assembly sittings. Thirteen deputies (18 percent of 71 members) were absent without excuse or "on leave" nine days or more, that is, for more than 50 percent of the meetings (see table 8.3).

If we repeat the exercise carried out above for September 2008, there were 1,207 deputy sittings in April 2010, but the actual deputy sittings that month amounted to 865, or 72 percent of the total (Asamblea Nacional 2010c), a loss of 342 deputy sittings (28 percent). Based on the monthly expenditure for members' wages, this 28 percent loss cost Panama US$139,160 in April 2010.

Table 8.2. Panamanian Deputies Absent for More Than Half the Sitting Period, September 2008

Name	Party	Number of Days Absent	Name	Party	Number of Days Absent
Sergio Gálvez	PPAN	17	Yasmina Guillén	PSOL	12
Tomás Altamirano Mantovani	PRD	16	Javier Tejeira	PLN	12
			Eloy Zúñiga	PRD	12
José Brown	CD	15	Pedro González	PRD	11
Iván López	PRD	15	Antonio Rodríguez	PRD	11
José Muñoz	PSOL	15	Elías Castillo	PRD	10
Rubén Beitía	PSOL	14	Bernardo Ábrego	PRD	10
Héctor Alemán	PRD	14	Arturo Araúz	PLN	10
Yassir Purcait	PRD	13	Benito Cases	PRD	10
Geovany Castillo	PRD	13	Olivares Frías	PRD	10
Rogelio Alba	PLN	12	Euribíades Herrera	MOLIRENA	10
José Baruco	PRD	12	Maricruz Padilla	PRD	10

Source: Asamblea Nacional 2008b.
Note: There were eighteen assembly sittings in September 2008.

Table 8.3. Panamanian Deputies Absent for More Than Half the Sitting Period, April 2010

Name	Party	Number of Days Absent	Name	Party	Number of Days Absent
Rony Araúz	PRD	17	Rogelio Paredes	PRD	10
Ricardo Valencia	PPAN	15	Benicio Robinson	PRD	10
Sergio Gálvez	CD	12	Freidi Torres	PRD	10
Abelardo Antonío	PRD	12	Víctor Juliao	CD	10
Raúl Pineda	PRD	11	Héctor Aparicio	MOLIRENA	9
José Lozada	PRD	11	Abraham Martínez	PRD	9
Leopoldo Archibold	CD	10			

Source: Asamblea Nacional 2010c.
Note: There were seventeen assembly sittings in April 2010.

Absenteeism in April 2010 declined compared to September 2008, perhaps as a result of a new provision included in the assembly's Rules of Procedure in February 2010 stipulating the loss of wages for "unjustified" absences (though not for leaves) (Asamblea Nacional 2010a). Reportedly, assembly president José Luis Varela (2009–10) insisted on members' attendance. In a May 2010 interview granted to *La Prensa*, Deputy José Muñoz Molina (CD, 2009–14; PSOL, 2004–9; PPAN, 1999–2004) said Varela had succeeded in instilling a sense of "responsibility" among members. Molina, chosen by his government bloc peers to succeed Varela in the assembly presidency during the 2010–11 term, confessed that previously, he "never went" to the chamber (Mizrachi Angel 2010). As this exercise shows, however, absenteeism remains a costly problem in Panama's deliberative chamber.

Other considerations substantiate the assertion that deputies are overpaid, in real terms, with regard to old-regime assembly members. As explained in chapter 3, pre-1968 deputies represented larger territorial constituencies. Despite population growth between 1968 and 1984, some of the old electoral districts had more inhabitants than the new constituencies created under the 1983 regime. Access to those larger electoral districts was, generally, more complicated. Moreover, under the 1946 statute the assembly had broader constitutional functions.

An additional element to consider in determining if Panama's deputies seek to obtain (or retain) an assembly seat for legal enrichment purposes is whether or not their professional qualifications would entitle them to similar incomes in the Panamanian labor market.[8] A review of members' CVs for the 1999–2004 term[9] revealed that at that time, most legislators would not have been able to receive gross annual wages of US$84,000 had they not been assembly members. In 2000, when the analysis was undertaken, 67 of the 71 legislators elected in 1999 had provided their resumes. In accordance with a survey of international prices and wages published by the Union Bank of Switzerland (Gutmann and Frey 2000), most respondents (73 percent) could have expected to receive gross annual salaries of less than US$27,000 had they held legitimate employment commensurate with their professional and educational backgrounds. Slightly over one-fourth (27 percent) could have expected to receive gross annual salaries above US$27,000. Forty percent of the

Table 8.4. Panamanian Assembly Members' Expected Salaries, 1999

Salary Category	Number of Members	Percentage
Less than US$10,000	22	33
US$10,000–20,000	0	0
US$20,000–27,000	27	40
Over US$27,000	18	27
	67	100

Source: Gutmann and Frey 2000; legislators' CVs available at the Legislative Assembly website (http://www.asamblea.gob.pa) in 2000.

Note: There were 71 members of the assembly in 1999, but resumes for only 67 were available for analysis.

responding legislators would probably have received gross annual salaries in the US$20,000–US$27,000 range, and one-third likely would have earned a salary under US$10,000 per annum (see table 8.4 and appendix O for calculation details). These findings support the claim that some members of Panama's National Assembly seek reelection to maintain their high-income jobs.

Additional Allowances

As do members who exercise leadership roles in other representative assemblies, the Panamanian chamber's president and two vice-presidents receive supplementary allowances.[10] From 1984 to 1994 the president (speaker) of the assembly received an additional monthly stipend of US$2,500 and each of the two vice-presidents an extra US$1,250 monthly allowance. After 1994 these supplementary payments increased to US$5,000 and US$3,000 per month, respectively.[11] Later, these extra emoluments rose to US$7,000 for the chamber president and US$5,000 for each of the two vice-presidents (Flores 2009a). Reportedly, the supplementary monthly allowances for the assembly president and vice-presidents dropped to US$3,000 in July 2009 (Flores 2009c).

A desire to obtain such generous additional compensation partly explains the commotion surrounding the annual election of the assembly's directing board, when influential deputies belonging to the majority lobby their peers (as well as the executive) in an effort to obtain election to it. In 2010, for instance, Rogelio Baruco (CD, 2009–14) and José Muñoz Molina competed for the presidency of the chamber. At one point during the struggle for his fellow members' votes, Baruco publicly insinuated that President Martinelli (CD, 2009–14) would decide which of the party representatives would be assembly president in the 2010–11 term (Cordero 2010). The fact that such interference by the chief executive would be a gross violation of the notion of separation of powers in a presidential regime seemed to escape Baruco in his quest for the leading position in the chamber. When the government bloc announced that it would nominate Molina, it was not disclosed if Martinelli had intervened on Molina's behalf or if his improved attendance (see above) had favorably impressed the assembly members aligned with the government.

Deputies who perform as officers in the chamber's twenty-one committees (reduced to fifteen in 2010) also receive additional stipends. The plenum elects these officers on an annual basis. In 2008 an opposition member confided to the author that the amount of committee officers' supplementary allowances remained "one of the Assembly's best kept secrets."[12] In 1998 committee presidents reportedly received a US$1,250 "special monthly diet." Vice-presidents were paid an extra US$1,000, and secretaries (who are also deputies) received a supplementary US$750 stipend per month (Janson Pérez 1998a). This extra remuneration is likely to remain at the same level, if it has not increased since 1998.

In addition to the US$7,000 monthly emolument, in 1984 members received a US$4,000 fixed staff allocation, which they still obtain (Flores 2008). Theoretically, this allocation exists for personnel appointment purposes and is not part of a deputy's monthly paycheck. For that reason, it is not considered part of a member's basic remuneration, although abuses occur, particularly through the time-honored practice of appointing relatives or supporters who pay kickbacks to deputies in exchange for those appointments. A complaint against Deputy Rogelio Alba (PLN, previously LIBRE) submitted at the Prosecutor-General's

Office in 2005 accused him of this type of illegality (Otero 2005; see chapter 10).

Members also have access to additional funding to appoint "activists" and "advisors" in their constituencies or to the assembly bureaucracy. This undisclosed additional staff allocation is generally not distributed equally among members; normally, those belonging to the majority obtain higher allotments. For this purpose, in 1999–2000 all members of the chamber received an extra US$4,000 (on top of the fixed staff allocation mentioned above). Funding thus obtained is used to reward family, friends, and loyal followers. Members also had access to *partidas circuitales* in 1985–89 and 1993–2001.[13]

Emoluments in Comparative Perspective

Payments received by Panama's deputies are not only well above the earnings of most of the country's citizens; they also compare favorably to the remuneration received by assembly members in other liberal and electoral democracies. Table 8.5 presents a comparative analysis using data on representatives' salaries in selected liberal democracies included in the 2008 British government report on parliamentary pay, pensions, and allowances. Note that even though Panama has significant human development needs to meet (as indicated by its Human Development Index [HDI] ranking of 62), in 2007 the country paid its deputies higher wages than Norway (HDI rank 1), Sweden (7), Spain (15), and New Zealand (20), all more developed and wealthier states.

Another comparative assessment of members' emoluments considers the average number of inhabitants represented by each deputy. There is an expectation that the effort, responsibility, and prestige of representation rise with the increase in the number of constituents; therefore, this ratio provides a standard for appropriate compensation that is more commensurate to the demands and stature of each position.[14] Based on this criterion, in 2007 the wages of a Panamanian deputy cost each individual in his or her constituency £1.23 per annum, significantly more than in such highly developed countries as the United States (£0.15), Spain (£0.23), Australia (£0.40), Germany (£0.43), France (£0.54), the

Table 8.5. Yearly Remuneration of Representatives in Selected Liberal Democracies, 2007

Country and Currency	Annual Salary in National Currency	Purchasing Power Parity (PPP)	Equivalent in UK£	UNDP Human Development (HDI) Rank (2007)[a]	Number of Members in the Lower or Single Chamber (2007)	Population in Millions (2007)	Population per Lower/ Single- Chamber Member in Thousands	Cost per Inhabitant in UK£
Ireland (€)	95,363	1.62	58,866	5	166	4.4	27	2.18
Sweden (SKr)	634,800	14.83	42,805	7	349	9.1	26	1.64
Norway (NKr)	612,000	14.03	43,621	1	169	4.7	28	1.56
New Zealand (NZ$)	122,500	2.38	51,471	20	120	4.2	35	1.47
Panama (US$)	84,000	1.62[b]	51,852	62	78[c]	3.3	42	1.23
Italy (€)	140,444	1.39	101,039	18	630	59.4	94	1.07
Canada (C$)	150,800	1.99	75,779	4	308	33.0	107	0.71
UK (£)	60,675	1.00	60,675	21	646	61.0	94	0.65
Netherlands (€)	90,070	1.40	64,336	6	150	16.4	109	0.59
France (€)	83,435	1.44	57,941	8	577	61.8	107	0.54
Germany (€)	84,108	1.42	59,231	22	598	82.3	138	0.43
Australia (A$)	127,060	2.25	56,471	2	150	21.0	140	0.40
Spain (€)	36,249	1.24	29,233	15	350	44.9	128	0.23
USA (US$)	165,200	1.62	101,975	13	435	302.7	696	0.15

Source: Annual salaries and PPP are taken from U. K. Review Body on Senior Salaries (2008), which uses 2007 data. The number of members in each chamber comes from a review of the IPU PARLINE Database in 2008. Population figures were taken from the World Bank's World Indicators Database in 2008. Using these data produced slightly different results from those reported in UK Review (2008). The Human Development Index rankings were obtained from UNDP (2009), which correspond to rankings in 2007.

Note: As in the original source (UK Review 2008), the monetary equivalent is presented in pounds sterling (£). Converting the monetary equivalent to U. S. dollars would have required using a different PPP factor and was unnecessary for the purpose of the exercise, which is to show how the remuneration of Panama's deputies compares to wages paid to representatives in a selected group of liberal democracies with high human development, regardless of what currency is used to represent those wages.

[a] HDI rankings closer to 1 indicate higher human development.

[b] Since the U. S. dollar is legal tender in Panama, I used the same PPP factor for both the United States and the isthmian republic, although there are differences in the overall cost of living in the two countries that may be blurred by using the same factor.

[c] The actual number of deputies in Panama's National Assembly in 2007 was 78 since the Supreme Court had not yet ruled in favor of Teresita Yániz's claim that she deserved a seat based on the 2004 electoral results.

Netherlands (£0.59), the United Kingdom (£0.65), Canada (£0.71), and Italy (£1.07). One could argue, based on the comparison between representatives' wages in Panama and selected liberal democracies, that the isthmian republic should direct resources from wages paid to deputies (and other high-ranking officials as well) toward more explicit human development purposes.

A comparison of the emoluments of Panama's deputies to remuneration received by representatives in other Latin American republics demonstrates that Panama's deputies are well-remunerated (see table 8.6). An EFE cable dated April 10, 2007, provided this information (in US dollars) for all the republics except Costa Rica, the Dominican Republic, Haiti, and Peru (Barros 2007).[15] Adjusting the salaries for inflation as reported by the World Bank shows that, at the time, members were better paid in only two countries of the set (Mexico and Colombia). In 2007 deputies in Panama received heftier emoluments than representatives in some countries of the region having higher human development indices, including Argentina, Chile, and Uruguay. Furthermore, the cost of a Panamanian deputy's remuneration per inhabitant was the highest in the set.

Despite their ample remuneration, Panamanian deputies have on several occasions attempted to increase their income. So have representatives in other countries, such as El Salvador and Nicaragua; however, deputies in these nations do not earn as much as members of Panama's National Assembly. In 1998, for example, a bill providing a US$1,000 monthly increase in deputies' emoluments to US$4,500 was submitted to the Nicaraguan National Assembly. The chamber's president, Iván Escobar Fornos, justified the proposed pay raise as a measure to avoid "bribery" and as a reward for the assembly's "efficiency." Such increases would be justifiable if in fact low pay was the reason for corruption in the first place. But, as critics complained, deputies' salaries were already disproportionate to the remuneration earned by less influential public sector employees, such as physicians, schoolteachers, and policemen, who on average received monthly salaries of US$200, US$80, and US$70, respectively.[16] A decade later, the members of El Salvador's Legislative Assembly introduced a new salary scheme representing a pay raise between US$1,840 and US$2,920. Faced with overwhelming public criticism, however, the measure was rescinded.[17]

Table 8.6. Monthly Remuneration of Representatives in Fifteen Latin American Republics, 2007

Country	Annual Salary in US$	Inflation Factor[a]	Adjusted Remuneration	UNDP Human Development (HDI) Rank (2007/ 2008)[b]	Number of Members in the Lower or Single Chamber	Population in Millions	Population per Lower/ Single- Chamber Member in Thousands	Cost per Inhabitant
Panama	7,000	1.00	7,000	62	78[c]	3.3	42	0.17
El Salvador	4,000	1.05	3,800	106	84	6.9	82	0.05
Chile (net)	7,414	1.29	5,750	44	120	16.6	138	0.04
Mexico (net)	6,980	0.84	8,289	53	500	105.3	211	0.04
Uruguay	2,736	2.24	1,223	50	99	3.3	33	0.04
Colombia	7,660	1.00	7,660	77	166	46.1	278	0.03
Ecuador	4,800	1.24	3,881	80	100	13.3	133	0.03
Guatemala	3,254	1.50	2,169	122	158	13.3	84	0.03
Nicaragua	3,222	2.08	1,550	124	92	5.6	61	0.03
Brazil	8,100	1.18	6,840	75	513	191.2	373	0.02
Honduras	2,000	1.79	1,118	112	128	7.1	55	0.02
Paraguay	3,466	2.26	1,531	101	80	6.1	76	0.02
Argentina	2,884	3.71	777	49	257	39.5	154	0.01
Bolivia	1,312	1.95	674	113	130	9.5	73	0.01
Venezuela	2,064	3.68	560	58	167	27.5	165	0.00

Source: Adapted from Barros (2007) using UNDP (2009) and data retrieved from the Inter-Parliamentary Union (IPU) and the World Bank websites in 2008.

[a] Panama = 1.

[b] HDI rankings closer to 1 indicate higher human development.

[c] The actual number of deputies in Panama's National Assembly in 2007 was 78 since the Supreme Court had not yet ruled in favor of Teresita Yániz's claim that she deserved a seat based on the 2004 electoral results.

Summary

In addition to pursuing reelection for career maintenance or advancement, as held by theories of legislators' behavior, representatives may seek successive terms in office for other reasons. Evidence from Panama shows that some members of deliberative chambers use legal or illegal means at their disposal in order to increase their personal wealth. Chapter 8 began a focus on Panamanian deputies' attempts to ensure personal enrichment through legal means. In Panama the high remuneration and ample privileges with economic value enjoyed by deputies provide a clear incentive for office seeking. Analysis provided in this chapter shows that members of the National Assembly receive abundant emoluments, both according to contemporary and historical Panamanian standards as well as in comparison to representatives in other countries. High absenteeism, added to the fact that most members vehemently oppose initiatives to reduce their remuneration, indicate that some deputies are more interested in the economic rewards they can obtain from holding office than in building political careers in the chamber or adequately representing the interests of their constituents through the promotion of good policies.

The public has criticized Panamanian deputies' efforts to maximize their remuneration. Even so, members of Panama's assembly have tried to raise their salaries, directly or through indirect legal subterfuges, on at least three occasions during the period under review. In another three, they resolutely resisted attempts to curtail their emoluments. Chapter 9 describes these episodes.

## CHAPTER 9

Personal Enrichment through Legal Means

Expanding Emoluments and Privileges

This chapter describes and classifies some attempts at personal enrichment through legal means by Panama's assembly members. In the present context, personal enrichment is understood as a political actor's efforts at enhancing his/her economic status directly through legal or illegal means. While in some cases Panama's assembly members have attempted to augment their personal wealth through means constituting transgressions of the law, they have also attempted to do so legally (though perhaps not morally) through formal institutional mechanisms. Some of these, such as the legislative process and recourse to Supreme Court rulings, may allow representatives to increase their remuneration and establish or expand prerogatives with economic value.

Other avenues for accumulating personal wealth include efforts to prevent salary decreases and increase emoluments—described in the six "episodes" immediately following, in which assembly members across the political spectrum participated actively—as well as efforts to expand and abuse the postal, telephone, and telegraph franking privileges and a tax exemption on the purchase of vehicles.

Attempts to Change Legislators' Emoluments

Episode 1: Legislators' Refusal to Accept the General Salary Reduction (1990)

Upon assuming office after the U.S. invasion of December 1989, the administration of President Guillermo Endara (PPAN) found the government's finances in a chaotic state.[1] In consequence, Endara introduced a series of measures to restore fiscal order that included salary cuts for top government officials. Cabinet Decree no. 22 of February 2, 1990, fixed the president's emoluments at US$7,000 per month and that of second-level officials, including ministers, Supreme Court magistrates, and legislators, at US$5,000 per month. In the case of the members of the Legislative Assembly, this measure represented a monthly cut of US$2,000 in their paychecks. It was estimated at the time that the salary reduction in the higher government levels would produce annual savings of approximately US$2.1 million.

The salary decree cutting government wages was introduced pursuant to the "Statute of Immediate Return to Constitutional Order" issued on December 21, 1989, which assigned all legislative functions to the executive until the Legislative Assembly was able to meet. After the conclusion of a dubious electoral review process,[2] the assembly met for the first time on March 1, 1990. Shortly thereafter, legislators began to complain that the executive had acted illegally by including them in the salary reduction decree. Legislator Milton Henríquez (PDC), president of the Budget Committee, summed up the complaints of his fellow members by reminding the executive and the public that in accordance with article 157 of the constitution, legislators' emoluments were established by law. In consequence, the executive had no authority to reduce members' salaries: only the assembly could change them through the legislative process.

The chamber's attempts to resist the reduction of members' salaries were highly unpopular and contributed significantly to the erosion of public confidence in the assembly. Nearly three years of political turmoil and U.S. economic sanctions, added to the destruction brought about by the U.S. invasion, had devastated the country's economy and caused widespread deprivation. Even in the face of extensive criticism, however, the assembly succeeded in maintaining the remuneration of legislators at their higher, pre-1990 level.

*Episode 2: Legislators' Attempt to Secure Payment
for "Vacations" (1994–96)*

In May 1994 assembly president Arturo Vallarino (MOLIRENA, previously PALA)[3] wrote to Comptroller-General José Chen Barría to request payment of vacation benefits to the chamber's sixty-seven legislators.[4] Vallarino argued that as public employees and in accordance with Panamanian law, legislators were entitled to receive one month's full payment for every eleven months' work. The bill for legislators' vacation payments amounted to approximately US$1.3 million.

The comptroller-general requested a legal opinion from Solicitor-General Donatilo Ballesteros, who rejected the claim. Payment of vacation benefits required continuous, uninterrupted service for at least eleven months, which was not the case of legislators who met twice a year during four-month periods separated by two two-month recesses. In actuality, said the solicitor-general, legislators were paid during twelve months every year when they only worked during eight months. Quoting the poor attendance record of many legislators, indignant observers added that the assembly only met four days a week during sessions. The assembly countered Ballesteros's opinion by claiming that legislators' duties continued during recess. During these four months they attended committee meetings and carried out constituency service. In response, the solicitor-general expressed the view that—according to the constitution—attendance at committee meetings and performance of constituency service during recess were optional and not directly linked to the official duties of members. Because the assembly insisted on obtaining payment and the comptroller-general refused, the matter was submitted to the Supreme Court.

It took the magistrates almost two years to resolve the issue. In February 1996 the court basically reiterated the solicitor-general's argument and ruled that legislators were not entitled to receive vacation payments. The ruling emphasized that legislators received additional pay during extraordinary sessions and did not enjoy immunity against criminal prosecution during recess (see chapter 11). These facts, said the court, clearly demonstrated that members were not required to work during recess. In other words, they enjoyed a "holiday" period of four months per year while the rest of the working population was only entitled to a one-month yearly vacation. Although the assembly's membership had changed by the time the court issued its verdict, the chamber was dismayed by the result. Many in the new assembly were counting on a favorable ruling from the court and an increase in income. Legislator Miguel Bush (PRD) took the floor to lambast the court for snubbing the "popular class" represented in the chamber by denying its representatives payment of what he claimed was legally due them. Government and opposition legislators added that the unfavorable decision would undermine relations between the assembly and the court.

Episode 3: Legislators Repeatedly Reject a Salary Reduction Proposal (1994–96)

In response to complaints about the high level of compensation awarded to legislators, their ample privileges, and their poor attendance records, a "Movement for a Purge in the Assembly" (*Movimiento de Depuración Legislativa*) emerged during the 1994 political campaign.[5] The proposal included a US$2,000 salary reduction to US$5,000 per month, the abolition of the vehicle tax exemption privilege (which allowed the tax-free purchase of three vehicles per term for legislators' personal use, reduced to two vehicles in 2010), the obligation to submit a yearly declaration of assets, the suspension of allowances for failure to attend meetings, and an obligation to resign six months prior to elections for those members seeking reelection. Several legislative candidates joined the movement, including incumbent Marco Ameglio (originally PLA, then MORENA, subsequently PPAN).

Once the new assembly met, in September 1994, Legislator Olmedo Guillén (PRC) took the reformist banner to the assembly floor and submitted a bill setting a US$5,600 limit on members' remuneration. The proposal included using the savings generated by the salary reduction for the creation of a special fund against poverty and drug consumption. Together with the proposed cut, Guillén also submitted a bill restricting the automobile tax exemption privilege (see below). The chamber shelved both proposals, however. At the beginning of the next legislative period, in October of 1995, Guillén once again presented the bills.[6] On this occasion several members attributed demagogic motivations to Guillén. Legislator Raymundo Hurtado (MOLIRENA), for example, said the salary reduction proposal was "yet another act of demagoguery, because he [Guillén] knows it will not be approved." Hurtado added: "The salary we earn is not sufficient; in my case, I have to share it with my constituency and all the country's unemployed" (Rodríguez Bernal 1995). The comments by Hurtado are indicative of some members' claim that they require ample remuneration and access to state funding (such as *partidas circuitales*) to finance public works and provide clientelistic favors. There is no doubt that members channel funds toward these objectives (see chapter 6); as the record shows, however—and as is demonstrated by specific behaviors described in this chapter—the urge for salary increases and additional funding also responds to a desire for personal enrichment exhibited by some members of Panama's assembly.

As before, Guillén's salary reduction plan was not considered in the appropriate committee during the fall 1995 session of the Legislative Assembly, and the following year Guillén resubmitted his proposal. Once again, members dismissed it as demagoguery. Legislator César Pardo (PRD) declared he wished he could have access to "a one million dollar allowance," so as to satisfy all the needs of his constituency (Quintero de León 1996).[7] Legislator Alberto Cigarruista (then PLA, later PPAN) suggested that the proposal was illegal because the Rules of Procedure stipulated that members' remuneration should be equivalent to the salary of cabinet ministers, which had recently been increased to US$10,000 per month. After this third attempt, the issue was ostensibly dropped by Guillén.

Episode 4: Legislators Attempt a Pay Increase (1995–97)

The ministerial pay increase to US$10,000 went into effect on October 1, 1995.[8] Because the constitution (article 213) and certain laws require an equivalence between the salaries of ministers of state and several other high-level officers, including the magistrates of the Supreme Court and the Electoral Tribunal, the prosecutor-general, the solicitor-general, and the electoral prosecutor, these high-ranking officials immediately requested a salary adjustment. During the last three months of 1995 the increase was charged to a "Global Expenses" account controlled by the executive. In this manner President Ernesto Pérez Balladares (PRD, 1994–99) avoided presenting a budgetary amendment request before the assembly.

The budget bill for fiscal year 1996 (January 1–December 31, 1996), submitted by the executive to the assembly in the last quarter of 1995, contemplated the increase in the salaries of ministers, magistrates, and other high-level officers. It also provided a 140 percent increase in alternates' monthly emoluments, from US$250 to US$600.[9] The assembly approved the bill in December 1995. Pérez Balladares's salary changes were highly unpopular and heavily criticized in the press as well as by the Catholic Church and other civil society groups. The assembly reacted to this criticism by demanding a US$3,000 increase in the salaries of its seventy-two members, whose emoluments—in accordance with article 229 of the chamber's Rules of Procedure—must equal those paid to ministers of state. The demands came from both government and opposition members. Legislator Elías Castillo (PRD) complained that ministers were paid more than legislators when in theory both categories of officeholders should earn the same pay. On October 20 the press quoted the reminder of Legislator Lucas Zarak (then PPAN, later PDC) to Pérez Balladares that an increase in the salaries of ministers triggered an automatic rise in the remuneration of the seventy-two assembly members, the nine Supreme Court justices, the three Electoral Tribunal magistrates, and other high-level officials.

The executive, however, declined to adjust legislators' paychecks. It based its decision on article 157 of the constitution, which stipulates that any increase in legislators' salaries can only take effect in the subsequent term (República de Panamá 2004). The executive also cited budgetary constraints—a US$3,000 per month pay increase for legislators represented an additional US$2.6 million yearly expenditure, which the 1996 budget bill, approved by the chamber at the end of 1995, did not include. Furthermore, at the time a decision was pending on a December 1995 suit presented before the Supreme Court by a pro-government attorney, who asked the magistrates to declare unconstitutional the provision establishing an equivalence between legislators' and ministers' salaries. Despite Miguel Bush's threats to sue the government before the Supreme Court, in practice there was little the assembly could do to further its cause but await a decision by the justices.

In a verdict issued on December 5, 1996, the court ruled that the Rules of Procedure provision establishing the equivalence of "prerogatives, emoluments, and allowances" enjoyed by legislators and ministers of state (article 229) was not unconstitutional. At the same time, it emphasized the constitutional provision whereby legislation providing salary increases enters into effect after the conclusion of the term of the assembly that approved it (article 157). With regard to the specific issue in question, the ruling was ambiguous because it was the executive, not the chamber, that had ordered a wage increase that benefited certain categories of officers, including assembly members.

A few days earlier, on December 3, the assembly had approved a bill submitted by Legislator Alberto Alemán Boyd (PRD) presumably in support of the equivalence provision. Although the bill concentrated on matters of protocol—stipulating, for instance, that legislators and alternates should occupy the same order of precedence on state occasions as cabinet ministers and that their families should be granted preferential treatment in official functions—it was insistently rumored that the real intention of the assembly was to further its claim to the salary increment. The "honors" bill passed the third reading with thirty-five votes in favor and four abstentions. Only four members opposed it: Olmedo Guillén (PRC), Víctor Méndez Fábrega (MPE), and the substitutes for Lenín Sucre (PL, subsequently PPAN) and Rubén Arosemena (PDC).

Believing its claim had been boosted by the Supreme Court ruling and the "honors" bill of early December, the assembly now proceeded to insist on a pay adjustment for its members. By early 1997, however, the government was already immersed in a campaign to ensure the approval of a constitutional amendment allowing the chief executive's consecutive reelection. The public uproar caused by the increase in ministers' salaries and the approval of Alemán's "honors bill" was certain to intensify with a US$3,000 increase in the emoluments of all seventy-two legislators. Citizen indignation would have disastrous effects on the government's image and, consequently, on Pérez Balladares's reelection campaign.

To bring the matter temporarily to a close, in July of 1997—one year before the referendum on reelection—Pérez Balladares ordered a reduction in ministers' monthly salary to US$7,000, the same amount earned by the members of the assembly. Sensing that their chances for a pay increase had vanished, some legislators reacted angrily. Alberto Cigarruista criticized the decrease as "arbitrary" and demanded that the president submit a bill to the chamber regulating the issue of high-level government salaries. Predictably, no such bill was submitted.

Episode 5: Legislators Refuse to Consent to Loss of Allowances for Unjustified Absences (1998)

Between 1984 and 2004 Panamanian deputies were elected concurrently with two substitutes.[10] This changed to one alternate, starting in 2009, pursuant to the 2004 constitutional reform. Substitutes are meant to replace their principals when the latter cannot be present at assembly meetings (República de Panamá 2004 [article 147]). Despite the existence of alternates, as noted before, absenteeism is a chronic problem in the Panamanian assembly (see tables 8.2 and 8.3). Many committee and plenary sessions cannot be held because deputies repeatedly fail to show up and neglect to send their substitutes to the meetings. Between 1984 and 2005 Panamanian deputies had no obligation to be present at assembly sessions and were not penalized for failing to attend. A "Parliamentary Ethics and Honor Code" adopted in 2005 made turnout at committee and plenary meetings compulsory and provided for the regular publication of attendance lists. But deputies who failed to attend sittings received no disciplinary or, much less, pecuniary sanctions (República de Panamá 2005). This changed with the reform of the assembly's Rules of Procedure in 2010, which authorizes loss of allowances for "unjustified" absences (Asamblea Nacional 2010a [article 86]).

The absence of an obligation to attend meetings in Panama in 1984–2009 contrasted with practices in other democratic regimes. Within a dataset of 52 liberal democracies that by the end of 2008 had provided information to the Inter-Parliamentary Union (IPU) about this issue, attendance was compulsory at either plenary or committee meetings (or both) for representatives in 37 countries (71 percent of the sample) and noncompulsory in 15 states (29 percent). Had Panama

Table 9.1. Obligation to Attend Plenary and Committee
Meetings in Fifty-Two Liberal Democracies, 2008

	Sanctions	
Attendance	*Yes*	*No*
Compulsory	29	8
Noncompulsory	10	5

Source: IPU PARLINE database search in December 2008.

furnished information to the IPU at the time (2008), it would have
classified with the former group. Regardless of whether attendance was
compulsory or not, representatives in 39 countries (75 percent) were
subject to some type of sanction for not showing up at meetings. These
ranged from disciplinary measures (that is, call to order, reprimand,
suspension) to loss of indemnities, committee membership, or mandate (see table 9.1 and appendix P).

In response to widespread public criticism for absenteeism, in 1993
Legislator José Hill (PDC) submitted a bill that penalized legislators with
suspension of allowances for unjustified absences.[11] The proposal was
never considered. In 1994, as a result of heightened absenteeism at election time, assembly president Arturo Vallarino threatened members who
failed to attend with loss of allowances. The measure, however, was never
implemented, despite Vallarino's assurances to the contrary. In the following term (1994–99) Legislator Víctor Méndez Fábrega submitted a
new bill stipulating salary discounts for unjustified absences. Predictably,
it did not even reach the discussion stage at the committee level and was
dropped from the agenda at the end of the legislative period. In September 1998, after submitting the bill five times and in response to the public outcry that blatant absenteeism had triggered, Miguel Bush, chairman of the assembly's Rules Committee, finally agreed to place it on
the agenda. The proposal passed the first reading on October 22 with
the Rules Committee's recommendation that it be urgently processed

by the plenum. There, however, it was received with disdain and never scheduled for the second reading.

Most legislators preferred either to remain silent or express their agreement with the measure. Some, however, were surprisingly candid about their feelings toward the prospect of losing allowances for failing to attend assembly meetings. Bush, who presided over the first reading of the bill in 1998, called it a "chimerical" project submitted by a "clown" (Méndez) interested in ensuring his own reelection.[12] Legislator Benicio Robinson (PRD) also belittled the initiative as "a political show" organized by Méndez. Gerardo González (PRD), president of the chamber from 1997 to 1999, claimed it was "unconstitutional" and "ridiculous" (*un disparate*) to propose a salary discount for unjustified absences. "The issue of attendance at sessions is one of civic responsibility. Whoever wishes to attend shows up. Legislators have the right to attend or not to attend meetings," explained the chamber's presiding officer (Jordán 1997b).

*Episode 6: Legislators Attempt to Ensure a
Retroactive Salary Adjustment, 2000*

In February 2000 the press reported some members' intention to obtain a retroactive salary adjustment for the 1994–99 group of legislators.[13] The attempt was based on the Supreme Court ruling of December 5, 1996, declaring that the provision mandating an equivalence between ministers' and legislators' salaries was constitutional. The adjustment would cover eighteen months of the period during which cabinet ministers' emoluments exceeded legislators' salaries by US$3,000 (see above).[14] The cost of the requested adjustment added up to approximately US$3.6 million. If effective, it would benefit 31 of the 71 members of the assembly elected in 1999, or 44 percent of the chamber, who were also legislators between 1994 and 1999, with a payment of over US$50,000 per legislator.

On June 22, 2000, assembly president Enrique Garrido (at the time PDC, previously and subsequently PPAN) requested authorization from the Comptroller-General's Office to pay the salary adjustment. Comptroller-General Alvin Weeden refused to authorize the payment, arguing that the 1996 court ruling did not constitute an instruction to satisfy the legislators' claim. He further added that funding for this purpose was not included in the budget and that such an expenditure would place the government in difficulties.

Assembly sources held different opinions. Garrido, president of the chamber from 1999 to 2000, held the view that the adjustment should be paid but recognized the competence of the Supreme Court to clear the matter. Like almost half of his peers, Garrido had served in the previous assembly. Francisco Alemán (PPAN), a new member who served as Budget Committee chairman in 1999–2000, argued that the 1996 ruling meant the adjustment had to be paid. Recognizing that funds had not been appropriated for this purpose, he suggested that the Assembly Board could decide whether to allocate funds from the chamber's own 2000 budget. Pursuant to a 1999 reform of the assembly's Rules of Procedure, explained Alemán, the chamber had the power to administer its own resources. Legislator Haydée Milanés (PSOL, later PPAN)—like Garrido, a reelected member and the chamber's first vice-president—insisted that the court ruling paved the way for the retroactive salary adjustment. She expressed her intention of accepting retroactive payment because legislators had a "right" to the adjustment and "rights cannot be relinquished" (Santos Barrios 2000a).

As a result of the controversy between the assembly and the Comptroller-General's Office, the matter was brought before the Supreme Court. On January 25, 2001, the court declared that the adjustment should not be paid. The ruling was based on article 157 of the constitution, which stipulates that any rise in deputies' salaries only takes effect in the ensuing period.

Expansion and Abuse of Deputies' Ample Privileges

To assist in the performance of their duties, members of deliberative chambers in most countries enjoy certain prerogatives. With the purpose of facilitating communication with constituents, for example, they normally have postal franking privileges. Likewise, members of representative assemblies frequently receive diplomatic, official, or special passports that allow preferential migratory treatment (and, in the case of diplomatic passports, immunity abroad under the 1961 Vienna Convention on Diplomatic Relations). These specific identity documents facilitate travel in which modern-day members of assemblies increasingly engage in the fulfillment of their representative duties. Within a group of 53 liberal democracies that in early 2010 had provided information to the IPU on the subject, 24 (45 percent) reported assigning diplomatic passports to representatives. Another 17 (32 percent) reported assigning them official or special passports, while representatives in eleven countries (21 percent) traveled on their own, regular passports (see appendix Q). Article 230 of the assembly's Rules of Procedure grants Panamanian deputies diplomatic passports as well as franking and other privileges (Asamblea Nacional 2010a). The Panamanian assembly has, however, expanded these privileges in ways that are not directly linked to the fulfillment of its members' representative functions but appear to relate more to a collective aspiration for status aggrandizement or, when the privileges in question have economic value, personal enrichment.

Franking Privileges

The deputies' postal franking privilege within Panamanian territory was included in the Rules of Procedure adopted by the new assembly in 1984. As indicated in article 230 of these rules (2010 version), together with this prerogative legislators also instituted in their favor a telephone and telegraph frank within Panamanian territory (Asamblea Legislativa 1999).[15] Although members of the National Assembly are not known for communicating with their constituents through massive newsletter and bulletin mailings—as are their counterparts in the United States and other countries—it does make sense to recognize the postal frank as a mechanism that might help deputies procure a closer link between the electorate and their representatives. Theoretically, the telephone frank also fulfils the same purpose.

It is practical to assign prerogatives to members of deliberative chambers as long as they assist in the achievement of the representative function—a collective good. But when privileges merely establish a personal benefit (as opposed to a collective good) they are no longer functional in democratic terms. To expand personal prerogatives such as these makes even less sense in the context of a democratic constitution. But this is precisely what Panamanian legislators did in 1992, when a reform of the Rules of Procedure extended the postal, telephone, and telegraph franking privileges to alternates at all times, even when they did not act in their principals' stead (República de Panamá 1992 [article 95]). As was previously emphasized, alternates fulfill no representative (or, for that matter, official) function whatsoever except in the absence of their principals. For purposes of better representation, substitutes temporarily operating as deputies should be able to use their principals' franking privileges. Otherwise, the nature of their position does not warrant the usufruct of such prerogatives.

The trend toward the expansion of special prerogatives for personal economic gain once again became evident in June 1995, when the assembly attempted to introduce a mobile telephone privilege. The proposal was submitted by members of all parties, including Benicio Robinson (PRD), Yadira González (PRD), Roberto Ábrego (PRD), Carlos Afú (PALA, later PRD, subsequently PPAN, later independent), Edgardo Alvarez (PRD), Carlos Alvarado (PRD), Enrique Montezuma (PRD), Jaime Loré (PL, later PSOL), Gloria Young (MPE, later PPAN), Mariela Jiménez (MPE), and Rodrigo Arosemena (MOLIRENA). Public disapproval became so widespread after the measure passed the third reading, by a 40-7 vote, that assembly president Balbina Herrera (PRD) asked President Pérez Balladares to veto the new privilege. Provided with an opportunity to present himself as a champion against particularistic politics, the chief executive obligingly consented (Vega and Álvarez Cedeño 1995).

It is difficult to estimate the economic significance of the postal and telephone frank to deputies and substitutes. In May 1999 the telephone franking privilege consisted of a US$200 monthly telephone bill credit. Legislators representing districts other than Panama City's constituencies had access to a national long distance line at their assembly offices (Bouche 1999). By August 2005 the telephone credit had risen to US$500 for the use of up to three telephone lines per deputy with local or long-distance service. The assembly also provided each member with a mobile phone with 1,200 free monthly minutes, not exceeding a cost of US$90 per month (López 2005).

Diplomatic Passports

Observers tend to agree that a generalized interest among assembly members and their substitutes for accumulating personal privileges—particularly if they have monetary value—has driven the expansion of members' prerogatives, not only with respect to the postal, telephone, and telegraphic frank but in other regards as well.[16] In 1984 the assembly decreed a generous assignment of diplomatic passports, which deputies took care to expand. Article 206 of the 1984 Rules of Procedure provided for the use of diplomatic passports by legislators. Members' dependents and alternates who acted for their principals were also eligible for the privilege. In 1992 diplomatic passports were assigned to substitutes, whether or not they had ever replaced their principals, as well as to alternates' spouses. A 1998 amendment to the Rules of Procedure included alternates' dependents among the beneficiaries of diplomatic travel documents (Asamblea Legislativa 1984, 1992, 1998).

While giving representatives diplomatic passports when they travel abroad on official duty is justified, there is no reason to assign them to substitutes (unless they replace their principals or otherwise act in an official capacity abroad) or to representatives' or alternates' dependents, who fulfill no representative function whatsoever. Aside from constituting an unnecessary privilege, it lends itself to abuse, such as in the case of an alternate who requested a diplomatic passport for her thirty-four-year-old son, claiming (despite the son's age) he was still her "dependent."[17] Developments in this sense can only be understood in the context of personal privilege expansion for economic or status motivations.

With regard to economic gain, the immunity enjoyed by bearers of diplomatic passports can constitute a convenient aid in attempts to introduce or export illicit goods for profit. Bearers of diplomatic passports are frequently granted expeditious passage through ports of entry as well as other courtesies, such as freedom from customs inspections. Although no Panamanian assembly member has ever been convicted of using his/her diplomatic immunity to introduce illegal goods into Panama or other countries, at least one has been accused of using his influence and immunity in Panama to assist in drug export operations. As described in more detail in chapter 11, in 1994 Legislator Anel Ramírez (PALA) was caught in a sting operation in Miami and accused of conspiring to organize drug shipments from Panama to the United States (Brannan Jaén 1994b, 1994c, 1994d, 1994e).

Moreover, bearers of Panamanian diplomatic (or consular) passports have been involved in contraband. In 1997 the Panamanian consul-general in New York, Frank Iglesias, a relation of President Pérez Balladares,[18] conspired to introduce a highly valuable Peruvian archaeological piece into the United States and sell it for US$1.6 million. According to the indictment issued by a U.S. federal grand jury in 1998, Iglesias used his diplomatic privileges to smuggle or help smuggle the artifact. Reportedly, he also took advantage of his diplomatic status to escape arrest and return to safety in Panama (Atwood 2004; Brannan Jaén 1998).

An Obsession with Status

Yet another way of understanding the access to diplomatic passports enjoyed not only by deputies but also by their families, substitutes, and substitutes' families is as a sui generis conception of honor shared by many members of the assembly. Although not central to this study, it is nevertheless instructive to focus briefly on deputies' constant preoccupation with matters of protocol and their insistence on public recognition. When referring to him/herself, for example, a Panamanian deputy will say "I am 'the honorable' so-and-so," as if election to the assembly automatically transformed one into an "honorable" individual and this condition accompanied the deputy throughout incumbency, regardless of performance.

This obsession with status was more likely than not an additional important reason behind the "honors bill" submitted by Alberto Alemán Boyd in 1996 (see above). During discussions of the bill and after its approval, in response to intense public criticism, many members provided revealing information about their concern for and ideas about personal honor. In defense of the bill, Alemán said his "intention was not to grant legislators new rights above the rest of the citizenry, but to give legislators the treatment they deserve as genuine representatives of the people, who arrived at this branch of government through popular election."[19] Enrique Garrido, president of the assembly in 1999–2000, explained that he voted in favor of the "honors bill" in 1996 because "on many public occasions I have a place to sit but my wife is left standing, so I am forced to withdraw in embarrassment" (Otero 1996).

These comments by Alemán and Garrido shed some light on the reasons behind the assignment of diplomatic passports to members, alternates, and all their dependents, although this privilege does not make sense within the logic of liberal democracy. Some analysts of Panamanian politics share this view. In May 2000 former legislator Guillermo Cochez (PDC, 1984–94) and attorney Víctor Martínez presented an unconstitutionality suit before the Supreme Court against the Rules of Procedure articles establishing the telephone frank, the diplomatic passport privilege, and other prerogatives of legislators and alternates, such as the automobile tax exemption privilege (discussed below). In a press summary of their action, the plaintiffs wrote that these benefits "constitute privileges in favor of a special group of persons, owing to their political condition, in violation of article 19 of the constitution, which prohibits establishing privileges on the basis of race, birth conditions, social class, gender, religious affiliation, or political ideas" (Cochez and Martínez 2000). The court did not find in favor of the complainants.[20]

Expansion and Abuse of the Automobile
Tax Exemption Privilege

As in other countries (such as the United States), each member of the Panamanian assembly has the right to a special vehicle license plate. Panamanian deputies share this privilege with their substitutes.[21] Because traffic policemen are hesitant to stop automobiles exhibiting "legislative" plates, some observers believe they allow members and their substitutes to avoid citations (and fines) for traffic violations. Moreover, in 1984–2009 the assembly's Rules of Procedure gave deputies the right to purchase one vehicle every two years free of import duties and "all other taxes." The 2010 reform to the Rules of Procedure determined that deputies could only acquire two vehicles under this provision; previously, members purchased up to three vehicles in their five-year terms (Asamblea Nacional 2010a). The rationale behind this privilege is that as representatives, assembly members must remain in close contact with their constituents, for which purpose they require efficient means of transportation. Hence, to facilitate their efforts in procuring this collective good (adequate representation), the state should somehow compensate representatives for their transportation costs and the deterioration of their vehicles due to constant travel to their districts.

Panama is not the only country where this special prerogative was instituted. In El Salvador deputies had the right to import a vehicle with value up to US$25,000 tax free; this prerogative was abolished beginning in 1997 (Martínez Peñate 1997).[22] In Uruguay, pursuant to a law adopted in 1955, deputies and senators (as well as other elected national officials) were allowed to "import a new car, free of all normal tariffs, every two years." The law was popularly christened *Ley de colas chatas,* or "Law of the flat-tailed cars," after the large, U.S.-manufactured sedans apparently favored by members of the Uruguayan Congress. During the existence of the tax exemption in Uruguay, it was common for newly elected representatives to receive loans from dealers to import vehicles. At the end of the biennium, the lending-dealer bought the automobile back from the representative, "at the market price, subtracting his loan." At the time, representatives made from US$5,000 to US$7,000 on the deal "while having a car without personal expense during the period." Although the purpose of this privilege was to encourage representatives to "maintain their contacts in the interior," the public considered the automobile tariff exemption "an abuse of privilege" (Taylor 1962, 73, 197n27).[23] Reportedly, the exemption was in effect until the demise of the constitutional regime in 1973 and was not reinstated after the transition to democracy culminating in 1985.[24]

A Tax Exemption for Luxury Vehicles

Up to 2010, the provision allowing Panamanian deputies to purchase an automobile every two years free of import tax was interpreted as meaning that representatives had the right to purchase three import tax-free vehicles at any time during their five-year terms. Members share the tax exemption with other high-ranking public officials, such as Supreme Court magistrates, as well as with their own substitutes (Mendieta 1994b). Article 206 of the 1984 Rules of Procedure stipulated that only substitutes who had stood in for their principals were eligible for the privilege, which they could only exercise once during the term (Asamblea Legislativa 1984). In accordance with an amendment introduced in 1992, alternates who at any point replaced their principals could exercise the privilege once every three years (Asamblea Legislativa 1992, article 95). In other words, they were allowed to purchase two duty-free vehicles during their principals' term. The 2010 reform limited alternates' privilege to one vehicle per term. Article 230 of the Rules of Procedure currently in force (2010 version) also assigns deputies and alternates the prerogative of replacing an exempted automobile lost through accident or theft with a new, tax-free vehicle (Asamblea Nacional 2010a).

As did some Uruguayan representatives during the existence of the *Ley de colas chatas,* some Panamanian deputies abused the import tax exemption for personal economic advantage. *La Prensa* published a description of the procedure employed to obtain profits through the exploitation of this privilege.[25] According to the account, a car dealer would "sell" a high-priced vehicle, tax-free, to a deputy (or alternate), who would subsequently resell the automobile to a third party. The cost for the third party would be higher than the original "sale" price, that is, the price at which the assembly member (or substitute) supposedly bought the vehicle, but still substantially lower than what it would cost the third party to acquire the car at the regular market price, including taxes.

The difference between the original, or gross import, price of the automobile and the tax-free resale price of the vehicle provided a profit that was split between the deputy (or alternate) and the dealer. For example, a luxury automobile having an import price (prior to tariffs) of US$40,000 and a market price (including taxes) of US$80,000 would be sold through a deputy for US$60,000. The buyer saved US$20,000 and both the dealer and the assembly member (or substitute) split the US$20,000 profit. On occasion, the original "sale" to the deputy (or substitute) occurred only on paper, that is, the vehicle never actually came into the assembly member's possession.

According to the initial design of the vehicle tax exemption, at the time of resale the purchaser of an exempted vehicle was required to pay all duties that the original proprietor (deputy, substitute, magistrate, diplomat, or other) was exempted from paying. Article 540 of the Fiscal Code stipulated that upon transfer (that is, sale or donation) to a third party not enjoying the privilege, goods imported under tax exemption prerogative would be subject to taxation at the normal rates. In December 1991, however, the assembly unanimously approved an amendment to the Fiscal Code whereby purchasers of vehicles owned by foreign diplomats assigned to Panama, Panamanian diplomats concluding their missions abroad, and members of the judicial branch and the assembly enjoying exemption privileges were not subject to payment of the appropriate duties.[26] In 2006 a new amendment to the code was introduced that exempted deputies from paying sales tax on their imported vehicles (Ng 2006).

In 1994 the comptroller-general's annual report indicated that between January 1990 and December 1993 legislators and substitutes had purchased 349 tax-free vehicles. This figure represents approximately 75 percent of the total number of vehicles that would have been bought from 1989 to 1994 if all legislators and alternates had made maximum use of the privilege, that is, 469 automobiles.[27] The total value of the exemptions reported up to December 1993 exceeded US$4 million— in other words, as reported in the press, the state failed to receive over US$4 million in taxes as a result of legislators' and alternates' exercise of the exemption privilege between 1990 and 1993 (Vergara 1994). All legislators (and most substitutes) had exercised the privilege at least once, but some clearly took more advantage of it than others.

According to a report in *La Prensa*,[28] Legislator Edilberto Culiolis (PRD) had the highest investment in vehicles during this period. From 1991 (when he assumed office in that year's by-elections) to 1993, he received an exemption of US$91,000 on his acquisition of one Mercedes Benz and two BMW automobiles with a total original market value of nearly US$190,000. Culiolis was a member for Darién Province, a remote jungle region on the border with Colombia with poor road infrastructure, generally inaccessible to luxury sedans. Other important beneficiaries of the tariff frank from 1990 to 1993 included Melquíades Riega (PL), who received an US$80,000 exemption on his acquisition of one Lexus and two Mercedes Benz vehicles with a total market price of US$173,500, and Miguel Bush, who obtained a US$89,000 exemption on his purchase of one Jaguar and one Mercedes Benz jointly valued at US$157,000. Mario Rognoni (PRD), who acquired two Mercedes Benz and one Mitsubishi Galant vehicles for a total of US$135,000, received an exemption of US$80,000. Gerardo González (PRD), another major recipient of the benefit, reportedly paid US$132,000 for three Infiniti automobiles and obtained an exemption of US$62,000 (Vergara 1994).

Resistance to the Curtailment of Privileges

The publication of the comptroller-general's 1994 report with details about the exercise of the exemption privilege by legislators generated significant indignation and calls for regulation. Assembly secretary-general Rubén Arosemena (PDC), who was elected as legislator in 1994 and re-elected in 1999 and 2004, declared it was necessary to revise the existing legislation to avoid tax evasion by consumers (Figueroa 1994a); however, Arosemena also functioned as attorney and member of the board of the BMW dealership where many legislators and substitutes purchased their vehicles.[29]

In March 1994 the PDC majority faction submitted a bill that placed a US$5,000 limit on exemptions under the vehicle tariff frank. Although the press reported that legislators agreed it was necessary to approve the limitation, the bill never passed the first reading (Vega and Álvarez Cedeño 1994). As indicated above, during the ensuing term (1994–99) Olmedo Guillén presented a proposal with the same purpose on three different occasions, but his initiative did not prosper. Shortly after the May 1999 election, a major car dealership set up an exhibit of its newest models at the Legislative Assembly premises, ostensibly to facilitate the purchase of vehicles by the incoming group of legislators.[30]

After the 1994 incident, the Comptroller-General's Office has been reluctant to provide information on exemptions granted to assembly members. In 2002, based on the public information law adopted in January of that year (see chapter 6), a reporter from *La Prensa* asked the office to provide an updated list of all exonerated vehicles registered by legislators. Comptroller-General Alvin Weeden refused to release the data, arguing that the government had not yet provided enabling regulations for the public information law (IAPA 2002).

Between 2000 and 2004 legislators and alternates imported 340 tax-free vehicles, which under normal circumstances would have resulted in a total of US$3.5 million in import duties (Sánchez González 2004). A new vehicle sale and tax evasion scandal broke out in mid-2005, involving not only National Assembly members and substitutes but also deputies to the Central American Parliament (PARLACÉN) and their alternates, who enjoy the same privileges as the members of Panama's deliberative chamber. In response, on July 21 assembly president Jerry Wilson (PRD) ordered the "suspension" of the privilege. This measure did not last long, however: incoming chamber president Elías Castillo (PRD) restored the tax break in October, albeit with a US$10,000 ceiling. As a result, deputies received exemptions for nearly US$56,000 in 2006 and US$122,000 between January and July 2007 (Alfaro 2006; DPA 2005; Estrada 2005; Flores 2007b).

In February 2010 the assembly amended its Rules of Procedure to prohibit the use of exonerated vehicles for "unauthorized purposes" and stipulate that resale of cars acquired by deputies and occurring less than three years after their initial purchase are subject to import and other taxes. Prior to the adoption of this rule, however, the new cohort had already begun to take advantage of the vehicle subsidy. In the first nine months of the 2009–14 constitutional term, chamber members imported thirty-two vehicles collectively valued at US$1.2 million. The fiscal exoneration for these acquisitions exceeded US$260,000 (Cumbrera 2010).

Summary

Panama's assembly members enjoy wide-ranging privileges with significant economic value, including a postal, telephone, and telegraphic frank, access to diplomatic passports, and a tax exemption on vehicle purchases that deputies transformed into a lucrative business operation. Political influence and control over the legislative process facilitate members' attempts to increase their remuneration and expand their prerogatives. Personal enrichment by representatives has clear implications for the democratic regime, principally because the establishment of democracy gives rise to certain expectations among the population regarding the behavior of public officers. In a democratic regime, citizens expect that state officials will act to procure the public good. As state employees, representatives require adequate compensation, especially if the public aspiration is an assembly consisting of members who—as hoped by Weber (1919/1946)—will live "for" politics. A strong impulse toward personal enrichment by representatives, however, violates the theoretical underpinnings of the modern democratic system and also undermines public trust in liberal democracy, increasing the populace's alienation from the political system. Juan Linz (1978) explored the detrimental consequences of this alienation. More than any other type of regime, democracy depends on popular support and legitimacy. Behavior by politicians that does not coincide with the universalistic expectations of the population undermines democratic legitimacy and contributes to democratic deterioration or even breakdown.

To increase their personal wealth, members of representative assemblies may also engage in illicit activities, which undermine public trust in democracy even more than do attempts to legally increase public officials' personal wealth. As a breach of the law, illegal enrichment violates the democratic requirement of "adherence to the rules of the game by both a majority of the voting citizens and those in positions of authority, as well as trust on the part of the citizenry in the government's commitment to uphold them" (Linz 1978, 17). Chapter 10 examines this additional facet of the personal enrichment objective.

```
┌─────────────────┐
│   CHAPTER 10    │
└─────────────────┘
```

Personal Enrichment through
Illegal Means

Between 1984 and 2004, when the official name for members of Panama's chamber was *legisladores* ("legislators"), the public often referred to them as *legisladrones*,[1] a hybrid of the terms *legislador* and *ladrón* ("thief"). This use is indicative of a popular perception that in addition to attempting to get rich through legal means—that is, through emolument increases, the expansion of franking privileges, and the sale of vehicles—assembly members engage in illegal means to enhance their personal economic situation.[2] Institutionalization of such informal practices as corruption and impunity, which were boosted by the military regime, has encouraged some Panamanian deputies' involvement in illegal acts aimed at increasing their personal wealth. The military dictatorship's sultanistic style, to which many of its supporters were socialized during its prolonged, two-decade tenure, in part explains why, although this behavior occurs among assembly members across the political spectrum, it is especially observable among members with stronger links to the 1968–89 military regime and its supporting parties, especially PRD. Electoral rules, corruption, impunity, clientelism, vote fraud, and an efficient political machine with a countrywide presence helped PRD and its allies obtain majorities in the 1984–89, 1994–99, 1999–2004, and 2004–9 assemblies.[3]

Even within the generalized context of democratic malfunctioning that prevailed during the period under scrutiny (1984–2009), the Panamanian experience reveals assembly members more easily fulfilled their enrichment aspirations when such agencies as the judiciary, the Electoral Tribunal, the Prosecutor-General's Office, and the Comptroller-General's Office enjoyed less autonomy, as in 1984–89 and in 1994–2009. Conversely, attempts to check members' rent-seeking ambitions occurred when these organizations were able to exercise somewhat increased autonomy, such as in 1989–94. Only occasionally, however, did these efforts succeed.

Because some Panamanian deputies have been accused of employing illicit means to increase their personal wealth, we need to question the assumption that representatives essentially seek reelection or career advancement. In liberal democracies where corruption, impunity, and clientelism are informally institutionalized, describing illegal personal enrichment poses a methodological difficulty. In these settings, suspected offenses by public officials are seldom investigated transparently. In Panama, of 309 individuals serving in the assembly in 1984–2009, four were convicted of wrongdoing. The first—Rigoberto Paredes— was a close collaborator of the military regime with an extensive record of illegalities. The remaining three—Anselmo Guainora, Anel Ramírez, and Mario Miller—were marginal politicians linked to the military regime. Two others—Elías Castillo (PRD) and Otilio Miranda (PALA)— spent some time in preventive detention for embezzlement and other offenses but eventually regained their freedom through political influence. Chapter 11 describes the circumstances surrounding the detention of Elías Castillo; Miranda's tale is told later in this chapter.

In July 1991 Rigoberto Paredes, a former Tercer Partido Nacionalista deputy (1964–68) and PRD legislator (1984–89) closely connected to dictator Manuel Noriega, received sentencing for human rights violations.[4] Other accusations included homicide, abuse of authority, and personal violence. Although critics also linked Paredes to cases of embezzlement and misappropriation, apparently he was never tried for these crimes. He spent a total of four years in jail before receiving a pardon from President Ernesto Pérez Balladares (PRD) in September 1994 (Ministerio de Gobierno y Justicia 1994e). In September 1993 Anselmo Guainora (PRD, 1984–89), a legislator for Darién Province, was tried for misappropriation and falsification of public documents. A Panama City circuit judge condemned him to forty-four months of imprisonment in March 1994 (Mendieta 1994a). In October 1993 agents of the U.S. Drug Enforcement Administration (DEA) arrested another legislator for Darién Province, Anel Ramírez (PALA, 1989–94), in Miami for conspiring to introduce narcotics to the United States. A U.S. federal judge sentenced Ramírez to six years' imprisonment in January 1995 (Brannan Jaén 1994e, 1997a). Mario Miller (PRD), elected as legislator for Bocas del Toro Province in May 1994, was arrested for extortion the following November, stripped of his immunity, and convicted in 1997. In July 2000, however, the Supreme Court repealed the conviction (Díaz 2000b; Janson Pérez 2000b; Otero 2000a). He ran again on the CD ticket for an assembly seat in 1999, 2004, and 2009, obtaining nonconsecutive reelection on the last occasion. Chapter 11 examines the cases of Ramírez and Miller in further detail.

The absence of conclusive evidence (that is, judicial rulings or other formal institutional procedures) of additional enrichment by deputies relates to the pervasiveness of informally institutionalized impunity in Panama (as discussed in chapter 4, influential politicians can normally obtain freedom from prosecution). Lacking such definitive confirmation, this chapter offers examples of attempts at illegal enrichment drawn from newspaper reports, including instances of selling votes, exercising political influence to obtain business advantages or personal benefits, and misappropriating public resources. Certainly, members of Panama's National Assembly share accusations of undue acquisition of wealth with representatives in other settings, as illustrated with coverage of analogous incidents in other countries.

Vote Selling

Vote selling by members of representative assemblies is a phenomenon in some democracies. Representatives use bribes thus received for personal enrichment or to build up reelection chests. In 1997 the press disclosed that at least five Brazilian deputies received nearly US$190,000 each in exchange for their votes in favor of the constitutional amendment allowing the consecutive reelection of the country's executive officers, including President Fernando Henrique Cardoso (Schemo 1997a, 1997b). In neighboring Peru, the release of a video in 2000 that showed Peruvian spy chief Vladimiro Montesinos handing opposition congressman Alberto Kouri a US$15,000 bribe to join the government bloc in the Congress triggered extensive demands for the resignation of President Alberto Fujimori, who had just begun serving a third (fraudulent) term in office, as well as for the prosecution of Montesinos. Critics of the Fujimori regime seized the opportunity to emphasize that vote buying was standard practice in the Peruvian chamber under his rule. The congressional bribery scandal accentuated the Peruvian political crisis, ultimately resulting in the chief executive's departure from office in late November 2000 (Brooke 2000; Krauss 2000d, 2000e; Vargas Llosa 2000).

In August 2000 as many as eleven of the seventy-two members of the Argentine Senate were implicated in a bribe-taking scandal according to which some senators received payments to facilitate the approval of a controversial labor reform bill the previous April. As in Peru, this incident triggered a political crisis that severely tainted the reputation of President Fernando de La Rúa's administration and sparked the resignation of Vice-President Carlos Álvarez, who protested that the government's fight against corruption was not sufficiently energetic (Krauss 2000a, 2000b, 2000c). These and even more serious political incidents contributed to the decline in President La Rúa's prestige, eventually leading to his downfall in December 2001. In 2006 Colombian congresswoman Yidis Medina accepted favors in exchange for her vote in support of a constitutional amendment enabling President Álvaro Uribe's reelection. The Supreme Court tried Medina and found her guilty in June 2008. She received a forty-month house detention sentence (Romero 2008).

Vote Selling by Panamanian Deputies

Some Panamanian deputies allegedly obtain payments in cash or other personal rewards to vote as requested by strong political actors, which may include the executive or important economic groups. Naturally, not all legislative votes are bought or sold. Politically unpopular measures or bills in the approval of which strong actors have a vested interest are more likely objects of monetary transactions than is legislation offering opportunities for position taking and other electorally gainful activities. In Panama the practice whereby deputies sell their votes goes back to the pre-1984 period. Under the military regime it was apparently common to resort to cash payments in an effort to encourage the approval of legislation the executive wished to pass through the Assembly of County Representatives or the National Legislative Council. On November 25, 1984, an opinion piece in *La Prensa* claimed the defunct National Legislation Council, in existence from 1978 to 1984, "charged" a "fee" of US$250,000 for passing urgent legislation. This allegation is reminiscent of a statement made in a World Bank report about parliamentary practices in Poland: "In 1992 a fee for blocking amendments to the law on gambling was $500,000 but recently rose to the zloty equivalent of $3m," according to the report.[5]

It has long been rumored that the executive bribes Panamanian deputies to obtain support for important bills, such as the annual budget bill. When *partidas circuitales* were in effect, especially in 1994–99, increasing constituency allocations was one way of ensuring approval of the budget initiative every December. Providing cash rewards is another mechanism employed for the same purpose. "Christmas envelopes" (*sobrecitos de Navidad*) supposedly received by deputies at year-end are a well-understood means of executive influence (Harrington 1994). Cash, however, is not the only means used by the executive to pay for votes. A confidential informant apprised this author of the use of government concessions—specifically, for the exploitation of marine beds—to third parties linked to a deputy in exchange for that member's support for the government's legislative agenda. Reportedly, quarrying, mining, hydroelectric, and other concessions also serve similar purposes.

The "Cartier" Incident, 1999

In December 1999 President Mireya Moscoso (PPAN) reportedly secured the passage of the budget bill and other important legislation through a combination of constituency funding and personal gifts to members of the chamber.[6] Legislators of the opposition PRD agreed to support the executive after the government promised it would guarantee each member access to at least US$300,000 in constituency funding throughout 2000.[7] Additionally, at a year-end luncheon held in the presidential house, the chief executive gave each legislator an expensive Cartier wristwatch and accessory jewelry.

While newspaper reports estimated that legislators' Christmas gifts had cost approximately US$150,000, President Moscoso insisted that she had paid for the jewelry from private funds. To criticism that her initiative might be construed as bribery, the president replied that her predecessors also distributed presents at the year-end reception for members of the Legislative Assembly and that nobody ever complained. Comptroller-General Alvin Weeden certified that no public funds were employed in the purchase of the gifts and explained that the jewelry had been distributed "as a show of gratitude for the months of work legislators have put into guaranteeing the country's governance" (Sucre Serrano and Domínguez 2000). The president's chief of staff, Ivonne Young, added that it was customary to give presents during the Christmas season. In a roundabout reference to the chamber's high absenteeism rate, Young added that the Cartier wristwatches would facilitate legislators' punctual arrival at assembly sessions.

Most members were not troubled by the many complaints voiced in the media about the executive's practice of presenting gifts to members of the chamber. Legislator Carlos Smith (PRD) declared that he personally found nothing "sinful" in the idea and that the president's gift should not be considered as an attempt to "buy" assembly members' responsiveness to the president. Legislators José Luis Fábrega (PPAN, subsequently PSOL, later PRD) and Felipe Cano (PRD) coincided in their appraisal of the action as a "good gesture of the president at a time of love and reconciliation."[8] Teresita Yániz (PDC) was the only member to return the gift, explaining in a letter to President Moscoso that the chief executive's actions might be interpreted in ways that could affect the image of the government and the assembly.

Public objections to the distribution of expensive year-end presents to assembly members triggered a change in the executive's approach to this tradition. In the next holiday season, the president's Christmas gift consisted of a "modest" wine basket for each of the country's seventy-one legislators. At least one member publicly complained about the change in the practice, which under President Pérez Balladares had included giving legislators engraved gold fountain pens and costly leather brief-cases. Accustomed to more generous gifts under the previous executive, Elías Castillo criticized Moscoso for yielding to public pressure in an "extreme" manner that resulted in the presentation of "a very common gift," compared to the "attractive present" received in 1999.

Powerful Vote Buyers Outside the Executive

Important economic sectors also seek deputies' votes.[9] In 1994 an opinion editorial in *La Prensa* complained that legislators received payment to reject a bill regulating the sale of spare automobile parts. In 1997–98 the press reproduced accusations that a U.S. construction conglomerate had distributed up to US$5 million in bribes among legislators and other high government officials to obtain a contract for the construction of a new assembly building, valued at US$30.4 million.[10]

In 1995 former president Guillermo Endara (PPAN) attributed the PRD bloc's insistence on passing an amnesty law to the prospect of re-ceiving a kickback from the bill's beneficiaries. The proposed law ex-tinguished all pending legal actions against supporters of the military dictatorship and returned all illegally acquired property to its most re-cent holders. Endara publicly denounced Legislator Alberto Alemán Boyd (PRD) as the mastermind behind an operation that would give back approximately US$78 million in liquid assets and properties to their military regime holders, allegedly for a commission to be paid to the bill's supporters in the assembly. In retaliation, Alemán angrily threat-ened to sue Endara for slander. The suit never materialized, however, as the former chief executive declared he was prepared to provide proof of mismanagement involving PRD figures. The amnesty bill eventually disappeared from the legislative agenda, under pressure from local and international human rights groups.

In 2006 a fiscal reform proposed by the government that reduced the tax liability on stock sales from 30 to 5 percent passed the assembly with an overwhelming majority of votes by deputies across party lines. The reform reportedly reduced the government's receipts in an interna-tional financial entity's acquisition of a local bank by almost US$400 million. Rumors spread that high officials in the executive branch and National Assembly deputies had received kickbacks for designing and approving the fiscal law, which was condemned by critics as strongly detrimental to the national interest.

Selling Votes in Support of Contracts with the State

Contracts between the state and private companies, some of which require approval by the assembly in accordance with the constitution's article 159, provide yet another opportunity for selling votes.[11] In December 1992 allegations circulated that Refinería Panamá, a Texaco subsidiary, paid a number of legislators to ensure approval of an agreement signed with the Panamanian government a few months before. When the assembly postponed discussion of the highly polemic contract, Legislator Miguel Bush (PRD, 1989–2004), who favored the agreement, explained that some members opposed the contract for "conceptual" reasons while others were expecting money from Refinería Panamá in order to vote in favor of the deal.

The bribery allegations were never confirmed because the appropriate state agencies did not investigate them. After initially procrastinating, the assembly hurriedly approved the contract before the legislative period expired on December 31, 1992. In Panama, as in other countries, a large percentage of all legislation passes on the eve of adjournment. In the context of personal enrichment described here, this phenomenon might be understood on the basis of the higher bribes that deputies can extract from interested parties when only a few days or hours are left before the legislative period concludes.[12]

A similar accusation of vote selling came before the Rules Committee in 1994. Legislator Balbina Herrera (PRD, 1989–2004) accused the Chiriquí Land Company, a Chiquita Brands subsidiary, of delivering nearly ten thousand cases of bananas to an undisclosed number of legislators in order to promote the approval of a contract with the company. Because the charge was never formally investigated, the public remained ignorant of the use given the bananas, that is, for personal consumption, sale, or distribution among constituents. While an agreement with Chiriquí Land Company did not pass in 1994, when a new contract was finally achieved in 1998 it was not reported if donations of produce contributed to the assembly's approval.

The CEMIS Scandal (2002)

In December 2001 President Mireya Moscoso appointed two close collaborators, Minister of Government and Justice Winston Spadafora (PPAN) and Legislator Alberto Cigarruista (PPAN, previously PLA), as Supreme Court magistrates. As stipulated by the constitution (article 161, section 4), such appointments require approval by the chamber. But Moscoso was a few votes short in the Legislative Assembly, where PRD and its allies, totaling thirty-seven members, outnumbered the bloc supporting her administration, consisting of thirty-four legislators from PPAN, MOLIRENA, PLN, PSOL, CD, and PRC. The government was intent on avoiding a defeat in the assembly, such as had occurred two years earlier, when Moscoso's nomination of former president Guillermo Endara to the Supreme Court failed to garner the support of a majority of legislators.

When the vote came up at an extraordinary session convened especially for the purpose of considering the appointments, Spadafora and Cigarruista received the support of the government bloc as well as of three PRD dissenters: Deputies Carlos Afú and Carlos Alvarado and alternate Tomás Altamirano Duque, who acted on behalf of his son, Tomás Altamirano Mantovani. The PRD leadership, which had ordered its members to reject the nominations, was incensed at this departure from the party line. The leadership especially targeted Afú. Balbina Herrera accused him of taking a US$1.5 million bribe to vote in favor of Spadafora and Cigarruista. In response to these accusations, on January 16, 2002, Afú claimed that he voted in conscience for Moscoso's nominees. He denied selling his vote on the Supreme Court nominations but admitted to accepting US$20,000 from PRD bloc coordinator Mateo Castillero to support another initiative: a US$400 million development contract in Colón Province favoring Centro Multimodal Industrial y de Servicios (CEMIS). The chamber approved the CEMIS contract just two days prior to the assembly's closing session, on December 29, 2001. According to Afú, Castillero provided an advance payment of US$6,000 on the bribe and promised to disburse the balance shortly afterwards.

Afú additionally declared that other PRD members had received bribes to ensure their backing for the CEMIS contract.

Although the Prosecutor-General's Office initiated an investigation for corruption, its actions came to naught. An audit by an umbrella civil society organization, Alianza Ciudadana Pro Justicia, concluded that the prosecutor-general's investigations were notoriously deficient. Furthermore, on June 30, 2003, the chamber issued a resolution nullifying all inquiries into the case, supposedly on the basis of existing provisions on assembly members' immunity—which covered them during the sitting period as well as five days before and after the opening and closing dates of plenary sessions. At the moment the allegations first surfaced (January 16, 2002), however, assembly members were not protected by immunity; the extraordinary meetings had ended on January 10, so the five-day "grace period" had already expired. Even so, the Supreme Court confirmed the assembly's resolution and closed the case.

The press and civil society organizations protested strongly against the Supreme Court's decision. Alianza Ciudadana Pro Justicia warned that the justices' resolution would generate "even more uneasiness and mistrust towards the institutions of democracy, especially the administration of justice." It also called for the resignation of magistrates Spadafora and Cigarruista and demanded a reopening of the case (Alianza Ciudadana Pro Justicia 2004). In 2005 Prosecutor-General Ana Gómez petitioned the Supreme Court in this regard. More than four years passed before the court granted her petition to reopen the case in December 2009. Because the 2004 constitutional reform eliminating deputies' immunity required assembly members' trial by the Supreme Court, the court retained the part of the CEMIS scandal involving incumbent deputies and sent the portion dealing with justices Spadafora and Cigarruista to the National Assembly. Hearing cases against Supreme Court magistrates is one of the chamber's judicial functions, in keeping with article 160 of the constitution. Accordingly, in April 2010 the assembly's Rules Committee met to consider the allegations. Its verdict, approved by the plenum, was that the file contained no evidence of wrongdoing by either Spadafora or Cigarruista. At the time this text was submitted, the court had not initiated hearings on alleged transgressions by deputies in the CEMIS case (Asamblea Nacional 2010d; Jackson 2009b; Navarro 2010; Otero 2010).

Exercising Political Influence to Obtain Particularistic Benefits

Some Panamanian deputies use their contacts with high officials in the executive branch—or other forms of political influence—to obtain benefits for themselves or for third parties (for a fee). Charges of this type have also tarnished the reputation of representative assemblies elsewhere. In that paragon of liberal democracy—the United States—the justice system has tried members of Congress for this sort of illegality. In recent years a well-publicized case involved Representative Randy "Duke" Cunningham (R-California), who was found guilty of taking up to US$2.4 million in bribes from defense contractors and sentenced to eight years and four months' imprisonment. Cunningham exercised his clout with the Department of Defense to secure contracts in favor of his benefactors.[13]

In Panama during the 1994–99 period, several pro-government legislators, among other PRD leaders, reportedly used their influence to obtain leases on prized property built under U.S. administration in the former Canal Zone. In addition to cabinet ministers, Supreme Court magistrates, and other high government officials, assembly president Gerardo González (PRD) and legislators Balbina Herrera (PRD), César Pardo (PRD), César Sanjur (PRD), Felipe Serrano (PRD), Abel Rodríguez (PRD), and a substitute of Carlos Alvarado (PRD) received valuable houses in the area. Furthermore, in 1999 the assembly passed a law granting the occupants of these houses the first right of purchase, an entitlement not previously recognized to tenants of those properties.[14]

A World of Business Opportunities

Political influence also helps deputies take advantage of business opportunities to which they might not otherwise have access. In 1994–99, under the Pérez Balladares administration (PRD), the Transit Authority assigned Legislator Benicio Robinson (PRD) several lucrative taxi operation permits in his native Bocas del Toro Province. After the end of the term in 1999, members of the local drivers' unions complained before the new authorities of what they deemed a "political" assignment and demanded the invalidation of the permits (Henry 1999a, 2000).

In 1994 assembly president Arturo Vallarino (MOLIRENA, previously PALA) was accused of attempting to manipulate the bidding process for the assignment of a slot-machine concession contract.[15] Legislator Vallarino was the attorney for the company that since 1981 had operated the slot machines at Panama's casinos, a state monopoly until 1998. The company that provided and operated the machines received between 20 and 25 percent of the earnings, estimated at approximately US$77 million per year. After complaints of irregularities in the bidding process surfaced, President Endara (PPAN) decided to expropriate the slot machines. Vallarino, who achieved reelection in May 1994, accused the president of arbitrariness, called him a "crook," and appealed the expropriation decree before the new (PRD) government, which assumed power on September 1, 1994. Allegedly, to further his claims, he voted for the PRD candidate to the presidency of the new assembly, Balbina Herrera, thus breaking with the party line. The Pérez Balladares administration, however, resolved to abide by Endara's decision and retained ownership of the slot machines.

The Association of Ex-Legislators

In July 1999 twenty-four government and opposition legislators who failed to achieve reelection formed the "Association of Ex-Legislators of the Republic." This "nonprofit organization" was constituted with the stated purpose of transmitting former members' "experience and expertise" to the incoming assembly in order "to strengthen the democratic system." Through Law no. 35 of 1999, the PRD-controlled Legislative Assembly officially recognized the Ex-Legislators Association as an "advisory" organization providing "support to the parliamentary process" for the "democratic and institutional strengthening of the Legislative branch" (Asamblea Legislativa 1999 [article 242-A]). Some observers commented that the real purpose of the organization was to promote the appointment of lame-duck legislators as advisors and to other lucrative offices in the assembly bureaucracy in the ensuing term.

Several former members—not all of them founding fathers of the Ex-Legislators Association, however—obtained jobs as "advisors" to the new assembly. An updated list published in *El Siglo* on April 24, 2000, gave the names of seven ex-legislators reputedly serving in an advisory capacity from September 1, 1999 to August 31, 2000, with monthly salaries of US$4,000 each. The list included Daniel Arias (PPAN, 1994–99), Mariela Jiménez (MPE, 1994–99), Raúl Ossa (PDC, 1984–94), Mario Quiel (PLA, 1994–99), José Serracín (PPAN, 1994–99), José Torres (PDC, 1989–94), and Lucas Zarak (PPAN, 1989–99). An eighth ex-legislator, Alfredo Oranges (PRD, 1984–89), also received an appointment to the assembly staff but was asked to resign when confronted with prosecution in Italy in a money-laundering case (Jordán Serrano 2000a). After obtaining control of the assembly in September 2000, the opposition PRD, in alliance with PDC, allegedly sacked these "advisors." The new assembly governing board, presided over by Legislator Laurentino Cortizo (PSOL), replaced them with politicians closely linked to the military regime, such as puppet presidents Manuel Solís Palma (PRD, 1988–89) and Francisco Rodríguez (PRD, 1989) (Chéry 2000; Muñoz 2000).

In 1999–2000 membership in the fledgling Ex-Legislators Association, together with influence with the faction controlling the presidency of the chamber, helped past members renew their presence in the assembly. Chamber president Enrique Garrido (PDC, formerly and subsequently PPAN) explained that in exchange for support for the government's legislative agenda, the executive agreed to surrender control of the presidency and all appointments in the assembly bureaucracy to Garrido's faction, consisting of PPAN defectors as well as members of PDC and the extinct PL, PRC, and Partido Nacionalista Popular (PNP).[16] While not strictly illegal, the appointment of former legislators as "advisors" garnered strong criticism as an act of corruption. Political commentator Maribel Cuervo captured the public mood regarding the appointment of ex-assembly members to the chamber's bureaucracy when she wrote:

> to create expensive advisory positions paid for with government funds, with the sole intention of allowing ex legislators and former candidates who have been rejected by the popular vote to generate sufficient income so as to balance their personal financial statements, or to hire unemployed politicians with the purpose of keeping them alive in the political arena

and thus postpone their irreversible transit towards the annals of the insignificant, generates repugnance and profound disappointment. (Cuervo de Paredes 1999)

Misappropriating Public Resources

Some representatives in electoral or liberal democracies may also try to get rich by misappropriating public resources. In 1999 detractors accused former Ecuadorian president Fabián Alarcón of misappropriation during his tenure as president of the Congress in 1995. Alarcón allegedly approved nearly 2,000 fictitious appointments to the congressional payroll between 1995 and 1998 (Canahuate 2006). A corruption scandal publicized in March 2000 involved the speaker of the Colombian House of Representatives, Armando Pomárico, as well as other deputies, in the approval of approximately US$2.5 million in dubious contracts for improvements in the congressional building.[17]

Based on observed behaviors, the Panamanian public associates assembly members with misappropriation of public funds. One example is the PARVIS housing subsidy scandal, addressed in chapter 6, in which incumbents misdirected funds toward electoral and personal use. Widespread perception of corruption also surrounded the assignment and use of *partidas circuitales,* a reelection mechanism also described in chapter 6. Particularistic decision making in the allocation and disbursement of those constituency funds, as well as the lack of efficient state control over their management, fed these perceptions.

Especially since the transition to liberal democracy, the press reports broadly on enrichment by assembly members. Legislator Felipe Serrano (PRD, 1994–99) supposedly misdirected up to US$500,000 of his constituency fund toward personal use. Miguel Bush, chair of the Rules Committee between 1994 and 1999, was mentioned in connection with the alleged disappearance of approximately US$1 million in constituency funds. At the same time, he was accused of devoting part of his constituency fund to building a private road on family property. Still another legislator of the main government party during the Pérez Balladares administration, Roberto Ábrego (PRD, 1994–2004), was supposedly involved in the misuse of two vehicles acquired through his constituency allocation that ended up in the hands of a relative and a political associate. Newspaper coverage also indicated that Ábrego had used $8,500 of his *partida circuital* toward a relative's wedding.[18]

In October 1996 the two alternates of Legislator Rogelio Alba (PLN, previously LIBRE) accused him of irregular practices in the management of his constituency fund.[19] The substitutes charged that the legislator falsified the signatures of at least forty scholarship beneficiaries to collect their stipends and misrepresented the identities of the participants in a public bid to build libraries in his district. The alternates also denounced Alba for maintaining a payroll of false employees, who only showed up on payday to collect their salaries and gave the assemblyman a percentage of their earnings (Otero 2005). Legislator Alba denied the charges and threatened to eliminate the substitutes from his payroll as well as to initiate proceedings for slander. Predictably, the alternates retracted their accusation, after which the Rules Committee of the assembly dismissed the case.

Despite widespread allegations of misappropriation, only once has the Panamanian judiciary undertaken a concerted effort to settle accusations of this type.[20] This occurred during the 1989–94 administration of Guillermo Endara, which was characterized by slightly increased opportunities for the exercise of horizontal accountability. Notwithstanding the political mistakes incurred by the Endara administration (some of which are addressed in chapter 4), a careful review of the historical record shows that in 1989–94, the judiciary, the Electoral Tribunal, the Prosecutor-General's Office, and the Comptroller-General's Office were less dependent on the executive than during the military regime or the Pérez Balladares, Moscoso, Torrijos, and Martinelli administrations (1994–2009).

Endara was elected as a result of massive opposition to the military dictatorship, whose misdeeds remained strongly embedded in the country's collective memory. Additionally, several of the civilian government's closest collaborators maintained strong stances against military authoritarianism and corruption and suffered abuse from the dictatorship's henchmen. Respecting the constitutional separation of powers and supporting corruption investigations was also a means of distinguishing the new, civilian administration from despotic rule by the armed forces and PRD. Even so, the strength of Panama's informal institutionalization and the pervasiveness of the military regime's sultanistic legacy prevented the thorough cleanup hoped for by many sectors.

In 1990, at the request of Legislator José Antonio Sossa (PDC),[21] the Comptroller-General's Office initiated an investigation over the use of funds allocated to members of the 1984–89 assembly under the legislator's Multiagency Program (Programa Multiagencial de Proyectos Comunitarios, as *partidas circuitales* were then called). Although the comptroller-general identified several irregularities, political pressures — which intensified after the return of PRD to office in 1994 — prevented the satisfactory conclusion of the investigations. In January 1990 the Comptroller-General's Office announced that an estimated US$4.3 million allocated to members of the assembly under the Multiagency Program remained unaccounted for. The authorities called on legislators who received these funds to explain their use of state resources or face prosecution. In July 1992 the Comptroller-General's Office reported that only five of seventeen legislators involved in the Multiagency Program irregularities had submitted documents explaining the use of allocated funds to the office's satisfaction. An audit revealed that over US$2 million of the program was directed toward "fictitious" operations by pro-dictatorship legislators. The scheme involved issuing checks to ghost companies linked to assembly members, supposedly for payment of services that were never rendered. Some, if not most, of these misdirected funds served for personal enrichment.

The seventeen legislators listed in the report by the Comptroller-General's Office included Lorenzo Alfonso (PRD), the beneficiary of a US$275,000 allocation; Alberto Alemán Boyd (PRD, US$265,000); Anselmo Guainora (PRD, US$216,000); Moisés Melamed (PRD, US$165,505); Fabio Juárez (PRD, US$160,000); Ebén Chi (PRD, US$146,000); Magdalena Rodríguez (PRD, US$140,500); Guillermo Jiménez (PRD, US$127,000); and Francisco Solís (PRD, US$88,195). Reportedly, Rafael Ábrego (PRD), Jorge Simons (PRD), Hugo Torrijos (PRD), Alicio Rivera (PRD), Gustavo Collado (PALA), Carlos Barsallo (PRD), and Romelia Esquivel (PRD) were also under investigation. While indicating that it also had legislators opposed to the dictatorship under scrutiny, the Comptroller-General's Office promised it would act to recover the misappropriated funds.

The investigative zeal of the Comptroller-General's Office decreased with the return of the PRD to power in 1994. In consequence, most former legislators accused of misappropriating state resources remain unpunished and retain possession of the allegedly embezzled funds. As mentioned at the beginning of this chapter, the only reported instance in which a former member of the assembly received punishment for misappropriation occurred in 1993–94, when ex-legislator Anselmo Guainora was prosecuted and sentenced for appropriating a state vehicle presumably acquired with funds from the Multiagency Program. But President Pérez Balladares pardoned him and President Martín Torrijos (PRD, 2004–9) appointed him governor of the Emberá Indigenous Reserve (Ministerio de Gobierno y Justicia 1994e, 2008).

At a May 1996 hearing before the assembly's Budget Committee, Comptroller-General Aristides Romero, a cousin of Pérez Balladares, reported that from 1990 to 1995, his office returned approximately $9 million in funds previously seized from embezzlement suspects. Confiscated funds were restored to their "rightful" owners because the Comptroller-General's Office received reimbursement for misappropriated assets in some cases or, in others, determined that no misappropriation had occurred. The comptroller further informed the assembly that 1996 had seen a "high" rate in the return of seized funds. This was a particularly sensitive topic for the PRD-controlled assembly, given that several of its members experienced confiscation of assets for irregularities committed during the 1968–89 military dictatorship.

Enrichment and Immunity

Otilio Miranda (PALA, 1984–89) was one of the former legislators who succeeded not only in remaining unaccountable and in retaining most of the properties he allegedly acquired during the dictatorship, but also in returning to public office after being implicated in gross misappropriation.[22] The case of Miranda is revealing not only as an example of the interest in personal enrichment that drives some Panamanian deputies' quest for reelection and the purported illegalities some of them incur in the pursuit of this objective. It also illustrates the degree of impunity that prevails in the political system and allows many current and former assembly members to avoid responsibility for their misdeeds. Additionally, the case demonstrates the powerful effect the military regime's sultanistic style exerts on post-dictatorship Panama, encouraging illegal enrichment and freedom from prosecution for transgressors of the law. Such features corroborate the thesis of Chehabi and Linz (1998b, 45, 47) about the long-lasting consequences of sultanism on a country's political society, extending beyond the replacement of authoritarian rule.

A former schoolteacher, Otilio Miranda was a close collaborator of dictator Manuel Noriega. In October 1999 an anonymous letter received in the Prosecutor-General's Office mentioned Miranda as one of the members of a "special commando" that in 1971 abducted Father Héctor Gallego from his parish in Veraguas Province (Otero 1999b; Pérez González and Domínguez 1999). The body of Father Gallego, a Catholic priest who advocated liberation theology, was never found. Investigations conducted after the fall of the military regime suggested that he was tortured to death. In his column of February 6, 1990, award-winning journalist Guillermo Sánchez Borbón included Miranda's name among those involved in the 1985 assassination of Hugo Spadafora, an outspoken critic of Noriega.

Between 1984 and 1989, as a member of PALA, a PRD satellite closely linked to the dictatorship, Miranda represented his native province of Chiriquí in the Legislative Assembly, from where he actively supported the dictatorship's agenda. At the same time, he reportedly served as a front for Noriega's several businesses in Chiriquí Province and elsewhere. In 1994 a piece in *La Prensa* (March 23) described him as "financial advisor" to the dictator. Whatever his professional capacity, he was accused of expropriating a large rural estate and a tanning plant for Noriega.

Miranda sought reelection in 1989. The military regime's vote-rigging strategy (in which Alberto Alemán Boyd and Rigoberto Paredes played a prominent role, as described in chapter 7) determined that Miranda would retain his seat. But annulment of the May elections, ordered by Noriega, frustrated his reelection. After the U.S. invasion of December 20, 1989, Miranda went into hiding and later fled the country. Arrested in New Orleans on May 15, 1990, he was deported to Panama in mid-July. Upon his arrival, judicial authorities placed him in preventive detention while he awaited trial for at least five cases the Prosecutor-General's Office had submitted against him, four of them for embezzlement. Miranda allegedly used his influence as a member of Noriega's entourage and his privileged access to state resources as a pro-regime legislator to increase his personal wealth. In January 1990 education minister Ada López (also a PDC legislator) implicated him, together with other former members of the assembly, in the misappropriation of over US$100,000 of the ministry's contingency fund. Presumably, former legislators Miranda, Hugo Giraud (PRD), and Camilo Gozaine (PRD) employed funds and materials meant for the refurbishment of public schools to complete the construction of private residences and pay for holiday travel.[23]

The inventory of assets allegedly appropriated by Miranda during his term included several properties and houses, a milk processing plant, a corn mill, a water tank, four hundred rolls of fence wire, several hundred head of cattle, telegraph posts, processed wood, galvanized steel pipes, tractors, railroad tracks, and approximately two hundred archaeological items, all of which was valued at several million dollars. Miranda presumably took control of some of these properties and goods on instructions from Noriega, but allegedly he kept some for personal use. Additionally, the former legislator was accused of participating in a US$7 million fraud against the National Bank (Banco Nacional de Panamá). For these offenses, the Prosecutor-General's Office and the Comptroller-General's Office seized bank accounts and property registered in his name.

Aided by contacts in the security forces and the Prosecutor-General's Office, on October 31, 1990 — after little more than three months in preventive detention — Miranda escaped prison. When a plot to overthrow the government that the former legislator had participated in disintegrated, he fled to Costa Rica on November 7. From there he issued threats against the custodian of one of the Chiriquí properties the government had confiscated from him.

Police recaptured Miranda in late 1993 as he attempted to cross the border and imprisoned him at the public jail in David, the capital of Chiriquí Province. Claiming poor health, in March 1994 he requested home imprisonment. In September 1994 a judge granted his request. At the same time, newly inaugurated president Pérez Balladares pardoned

Miranda, together with a number of former collaborators of the military regime (Ministerio de Gobierno y Justicia 1994e; see also chapter 4).

Upon his release, arguing that the presidential pardon foreclosed any responsibility he had for misappropriation, Miranda immediately proceeded to one of the rural properties he took hold of during his term in the assembly and expelled the government custodians at gunpoint. The Comptroller-General's Office ordered Miranda's eviction, but the police did not execute the order until the end of February 1995. Some time later, the Comptroller-General's Office inexplicably appointed Miranda's attorney as the official custodian of the ex-legislator's properties. Miranda was able to re-occupy them after December 30, 1995, when his attorney delegated custody on the former legislator himself.

On February 18, 1995, the Comptroller-General's Office determined that Miranda and other associates should be held responsible for misappropriation of funds assigned to the former legislator under the 1984–89 Multiagency Program. In March 1998 the same office concluded that Miranda was accountable for embezzling nearly US$190,000 of an aqueduct construction project in Chiriquí Province, and in August 1998 it decided that six properties valued at approximately US$500,000, which were illegally transferred to private companies following Miranda's instructions, should revert to the state. While the office succeeded in restoring some of the misappropriated assets, most of the irregularities Miranda was accused of were not clarified due to negligence by the authorities as well as to the presidential pardon granted by Pérez Balladares in 1994.

In May 1999 Miranda attempted to win an assembly seat for the Chiriquí constituency he represented as a PALA legislator from 1984 to 1989. This time he stood as a candidate of Partido Cambio Democrático (CD), headed by Ricardo Martinelli,[24] one of the four parties in the alliance that supported the candidacy of President Mireya Moscoso, the leader of the opposition to the PRD government (and, by implication, to the military regime Miranda had served). Unsuccessful in his bid, Miranda accused his main contender, Carlos Alvarado (PRD), of ensuring his reelection victory through "voter transportation" and vote buying by means of the PARVIS subsidy (topics addressed in chapters 7 and 6, respectively).

Alvarado described Miranda as "a criminal and a liar" and threatened to sue him for slander. Manifesting indignation at the fact that "an individual who stole six million dollars remains free," Alvarado also promised he would initiate legislation aimed at reviewing Pérez Balladares's pardon decree (Rivera 1999). But Alvarado failed to keep his promise, presumably because so many of his co-partisans were among the beneficiaries of Pérez Balladares's various pardons. The Moscoso administration rewarded Miranda's support during the electoral campaign by appointing him Panama's consul-general in Santo Domingo, Dominican Republic. In 2004 he again attempted to gain election to the assembly on the CD ticket as a member for his Chiriquí constituency but lost a second time to Carlos Alvarado.

Summary

Informally institutionalized corruption, impunity, and clientelism were furthered by the military regime's sultanistic approach to politics in Panama and promoted some assembly members' involvement in illegal enrichment activities. Deputies in Panama, as in some other liberal democracies, sell their votes, exercise influence to obtain benefits for themselves or others, and appropriate state resources. Because—as this chapter shows—members of Panama's assembly are not alone in their efforts to get rich, the rent-seeking objective remains a promising area for further scholarly research.

Apart from constituting a breach of the law, illegal enrichment by representatives violates the notion of democratic representation, one of the pillars of the modern democratic regime. When members of deliberative chambers are overly concerned with increasing their personal wealth, they become more responsive to those actors who have the power to increase their income, such as the executive or large private interests. They are also prone to cross party lines in contravention of the platforms on which they acceded to office. Concurrently, they become less responsive to their own constituents, whose views they are supposed to represent and in whose interest they are supposed to act (Pitkin 1967).

Distorted responsiveness also affects the balance of power in democratic regimes, one of the basic safeguards against tyranny (Montesquieu 1748/1966). As illustrated by the Panamanian case, executives interested in imposing their own agenda over the public interest may do so consti-

tutionally by buying the approval of the chamber through personal rewards such as constituency appropriations or cash handouts. Likewise,
assemblies concerned with ensuring impunity for illegal enrichment
may twist the law to attain their objectives, undermine the judiciary or
other agencies exercising democratic control, or collude with them in
covering up mutual wrongdoing.

These reflections lead directly to the issue of accountability. If personal enrichment by representatives so violates the basic norms of the
democratic system, why do constituents tolerate it? One reason is that in
informally institutionalized democratic regimes, institutions responsible
for ensuring horizontal accountability do not operate under the conditions of autonomy needed to satisfactorily accomplish their objectives
(O'Donnell 1998b). As noted in this chapter, the enrichment aspirations
of Panamanian legislators were more easily fulfilled when such agencies
as the judiciary, the Electoral Tribunal, the Prosecutor-General's Office,
and the Comptroller-General's Office enjoyed less autonomy, such as
during the military regime (1968–89) and the Pérez Balladares, Moscoso, Torrijos, and Martinelli administrations (1994–2009). The only
significant (albeit modest) attempt to investigate illegal enrichment by
members of the assembly occurred during the Endara administration
(1989–94), when these institutions were able to exercise somewhat increased autonomy.

Institutional obstacles to the exercise of vertical accountability—that
is, accountability exercised by voters—constitute another explanation
for the toleration and recurrence of legal and illegal enrichment practices by legislators. In the case of Panama, such features as electoral fraud,
a highly disproportional electoral system, and the prevalence of clientelism significantly distort the will of the electorate. In 1999, 2004, and
2009, for example, they contributed to ensure the reelection of a higher
percentage of incumbents (49, 49, and 46 percent, respectively) than expected based on previous electoral experiences (1989, 1994). As reported
in this chapter, according to press coverage some reelected deputies participated in ethically ambiguous practices. Chapter 11 examines what for
the larger part of the period under study was a major formal obstacle to
accountability in Panama: the practice of "parliamentary" or "legislative"
immunity.

## CHAPTER 11

Preserving Immunity through Reelection

In most countries, members of representative assemblies enjoy immunity, a "grant of exception from certain civil and criminal penalties accorded to parliamentarians for the duration of their service in the chamber, and sometimes beyond their service, in order to ensure their freedom to perform their duties as representatives" (Kurian 1998, 5). Some assembly members—most likely those involved in unlawful activities—may be interested in reelection to retain immunity or in initial election to gain immunity. This particularly may be the case in countries where the grant of exception is broad and guarantees that representatives will in most cases remain free from prosecution, despite the gravity of the misdeeds they may commit. Representatives may want this immunity to prevent arrest or to ensure that they will be able to continue to commit illegal acts with impunity. In 1997 the Honduran Catholic Church criticized the "sale" of congressional candidacies to persons wishing to avoid prosecution for criminal acts, indebtedness, corruption, or even to escape responsibility for alimony payments. "The assignment of candidacies in exchange for money is a proven and reproachable fact," said an editorial in the church's official newspaper.[1]

Between 1984 and 2004 Panamanian legislators instituted and expanded broad immunity provisions that ensured that most wrongdoing by assembly members would be free from prosecution. These provisions guaranteed their freedom from asset seizures in civil cases from the moment of their election to the end of the mandate and their freedom from arrest in criminal cases from five days before the start of ordinary and extraordinary sessions to five days after the close of the sittings. Additionally, immunity stipulations required the plenum's authorization to initiate investigations against, and prosecute, any member. The 2004 constitutional reform eliminated deputies' inviolability in criminal cases and the requirement of assembly authorization to investigate and prosecute members. Responsibility for investigating, prosecuting, and trying members was vested in the Supreme Court. This reform, however, has failed to guarantee deputies' equal treatment under the law.

Evidence from Panama—especially in 1984–2004, when the broader immunity provisions were in place—indicates that some assembly members were eager to retain and exercise their freedom from justice. This was particularly the case for members implicated in illegal acts, especially corrupt activities (but also more serious criminal actions). Immunity is thus intimately linked to illegal personal enrichment as a major incentive for seeking office or ensuring reelection. In 1984–2004 extensions of immunity gained easy approval by the chamber with the support of members from all political parties, in addition to, as we might expect, those legislators publicly involved in wrongdoing. Beneficiaries of "legislative" immunity also gained election to leadership positions in the assembly. Yet another compelling proof that the majority of the chamber values this privilege is that in 1984–2004 immunity was lifted only twice and, on both occasions, only as a result of strong outside pressure on the chamber. These developments relate to the general climate of impunity that prevails in Panama, which prevents the prosecution and punishment of politically influential offenders.

Representatives' Immunity in Comparative Perspective

Parliamentary immunity originally rose in pre-democratic times as a safety measure against the obstacles that powerful political actors, notably the executive, could place on the activity of representative assemblies (Moscote 1943, 240).[2] Its purpose is to prevent politically motivated legal actions against members that would render them unable to fulfill their representative duties and thus would violate the will of the electorate as well as the idea of democratic representation. This tradition, therefore, is a remnant from a pre-democratic past. It makes sense to retain such traditions when their existence contributes to strengthening and broadening the scope of liberal democracy. But when they weaken important dimensions of the democratic regime, such as the rule of law or legal equality, their endurance warrants close scrutiny.

Non-Liability

Non-liability and inviolability are the two basic types of immunity granted to representatives. Non-liability (also called non-accountability) allows members to express their opinions and exercise their mandates freely without facing suits for declarations or votes emitted as part of their official functions (Kurian 1998, 6). Within the sample of 51 liberal democracies that by the end of 2008 had responded to the Inter-Parliamentary Union (IPU) survey on the subject, all recognized the non-liability of representatives (see appendix S).[3]

Forty-five of these countries indicated whether non-liability is limited to words written and spoken by representatives and votes cast by them in the chamber, or if it applied to their declarations outside the representative assembly as well. In 19 of these countries (42 percent), non-accountability referred to words written and spoken by members both within and outside the chamber, provided that these statements related to their duties as representatives. In 26 states (58 percent), non-liability applied only within the assembly. Panamanian deputies also enjoy non-liability. According to article 154 of the constitution, they are not legally responsible for the opinions and votes they issue in the exercise of their office (República de Panamá 2004). The provision is interpreted as providing assembly members with unrestricted freedom to express views on any subject or person.

Inviolability

Inviolability, the second basic type of immunity, protects members of deliberative assemblies from arrest or other restrictions of their freedom to which they could be liable on account of acts performed outside the exercise of their functions (Kurian 1998, 5; IPU 2010a). Inviolability may safeguard representatives against prosecution or arrest in criminal cases, from civil suits, or both. Between 1984 and 2004 Panama provided constitutional protection against criminal cases and confiscation in civil suits. According to a survey in the IPU PARLINE database carried out in 1999, when Panama's legislators enjoyed both constitutional safeguards, most responding countries gave members of their representative assemblies some type of inviolability.

The less-privileged representatives in the IPU PARLINE dataset were those in three liberal democracies that did not grant any type of inviolability to their representatives (Namibia, the Netherlands, and New Zealand). Members in other liberal democracies, including Australia, Canada, India, the United Kingdom, and the United States, only recognized inviolability in civil suits. Representatives in most liberal democratic states, including Austria, Belgium, Chile, France, Japan, Spain, Sweden, and Switzerland, only enjoyed immunity in criminal cases. The most privileged members of deliberative chambers were those in states recognizing immunity in both civil and criminal cases, such as Argentina, Costa Rica, Denmark, Finland, Israel, Norway, and Uruguay.

According to article 149 of the version of the constitution in force in 1999, Panamanian legislators enjoyed inviolability in criminal cases during sessions as well as five days before the start and five days after the close of each session. During this period members of the Legislative Assembly could not be prosecuted or arrested for criminal or police cases without the chamber's prior authorization, except when caught *in flagrante delicto* or when a member voluntarily renounced immunity.[4] Article 149 allowed civil suits against legislators but prohibited asset seizures from members' until the expiration of their terms (República de Panamá 1994/1995).

Partly in response to the uproar caused by the CEMIS case described in chapter 10, the 2004 constitutional reform amended the provision on criminal prosecution, but protection against seizures in civil cases remains in place, as stipulated in article 155 of the constitutional text currently in force (República de Panamá 2004). Moreover, deputies seeking reelection enjoy inviolability during the electoral process as well. According to the Electoral Code, candidates cannot be arrested or prosecuted without Electoral Tribunal authorization (except when caught *in flagrante delicto*) during the electoral period, which runs from four months prior to election day to three months after the Electoral Tribunal completes the task of issuing winners' credentials (República de Panamá 2007 [articles 143, 219, 200]).[5] In addition to the constitutional and electoral immunity provisions, supplementary legislation (especially in the assembly's Rules of Procedure)—as well as the assembly's own handling of most cases against members—rendered legislators practically unbound from the law, especially in 1984–2004.

Over the two decades following the establishment of the Legislative Assembly, the chamber approved laws developing the immunity theme considerably. As a result, Panama's legislators became much more privileged than would have appeared from a reading of the constitution. As revealed by the ensuing chronological survey, legislators consistently expanded and defended their inviolability in ways that transformed this privilege into an incentive to secure reelection, especially in cases of wrongdoing by members.

The 1990–92 Struggle for Immunity

Concerted action by the assembly during the 1990s to strengthen legislators' inviolability prerogatives shows the high value members assign to immunity. Early in the decade, from 1990 to 1992, the assembly reacted resolutely to the attempts of a more autonomous Prosecutor-General's Office to hold legislators accountable for common crimes. Action by the prosecutor-general against officers of the state was a new development in Panama, where during the 1968–89 regime public officials, including legislators, generally enjoyed de facto immunity owing to the prosecuting agency's subordination to the military-controlled executive.

The case in point between 1990 and 1992 was the protracted effort by the Prosecutor-General's Office to act against three PRD legislators: Alberto Alemán Boyd, Elías Castillo, and Balbina Herrera. At the time of their proclamation as elected legislators, shortly after the U.S. invasion of December 20, 1989, but prior to the first sitting of the new Legislative Assembly on March 1, 1990, all three members were under investigation. Alberto Alemán Boyd was accused of embezzlement and electoral fraud, Elías Castillo of embezzlement, and Balbina Herrera of conspiring to commit murder.[6]

When press reports suggested that ongoing investigations might disqualify the three PRD leaders from membership in the assembly, officials of the new government quickly replied that they could only be prosecuted and tried if authorized by the assembly. This interpretation was constructed on the basis of the above-mentioned Electoral Code provision that recognized candidates' inviolability (currently, article 143). It did not take into account, however, that widespread irregularities occurred during the 1989 electoral campaign that grossly vitiated the elections (see chapter 7).[7]

On June 26 (four days before adjournment), when the Prosecutor-General's Office completed its investigation and asked the chamber to suspend the immunity of Alemán Boyd, Castillo, and Herrera, assembly officers complained that Prosecutor-General Rogelio Cruz had waited until the last moment to file his request. In the absence of legal precedents, handling the cases would be time consuming, they explained, for this was the first time the assembly had received a formal request for immunity suspension. The chamber was now too busy to consider the request, said assembly president Carlos Arellano Lennox (PDC),[8] but Cruz could order any arrest after July 5, when the immunity period expired. Before the end of the immunity period, however, at least two of the accused legislators left the country, only to return after they were once again legally immune.[9]

Over recess, the Rules Committee of the assembly met to consider the prosecutor-general's request. The committee decided in favor of suspending the PRD legislators' immunity and presented the plenum with this recommendation after the chamber reconvened on September 1.[10] In the meantime, however, a row about the distribution of the directing positions of the assembly developed within the governing coalition. PDC, which held a relative majority of seats, wished to retain control of the presidency of the chamber, while the other government parties advocated rotation of the office among the coalition members.[11] When PDC refused, the remaining parties in the coalition struck a deal with its erstwhile opponents. As it turned out, PRD cast the decisive vote for Alonso Fernández Guardia (MOLIRENA) to assume the presidency of the assembly, presumably in exchange for guarantees of immunity for its troubled legislators.[12]

Heated controversies over legislators' immunity characterized the beginning of this new legislative period. When discussion of the Rules Committee report requesting immunity suspension began, PRD legislators argued that the petition not only was unconstitutional but also demonstrated the Endara administration's proclivity toward political persecution. The party's representatives engaged in filibuster and blackmail tactics, accusing legislators in the governing coalition of an assortment of crimes, from embezzlement to rape.

The newly elected assembly president, Fernández Guardia, declared a permanent session until the matter was decided. Meanwhile, the debate dragged on endlessly and bitterly. At one point Alemán Boyd, Castillo, and Herrera voluntarily renounced their immunity; Prosecutor-General Cruz, however, later explained in public that the waivers were not valid due to a legal technicality. When Alemán Boyd and Herrera (but not Castillo) "corrected" their waivers, Raúl Ossa (PDC), chairman of the Rules Committee, requested a vote to confirm the suspension of immunity. The PRD bloc then walked out of the assembly hall and broke the quorum. This blunt action concluded the debate, for according to the chamber's Rules of Procedure a break in quorum automatically brought a permanent session to an end.[13]

New Rules, Expanded Inviolability

Even though the assembly failed to decide on the issue of legislative inviolability, Cruz ordered the arrest of Castillo after the immunity period ended on January 5, 1991. Throughout Castillo's detention the PRD bloc in the assembly repeatedly demanded his release on constitutional and legal bases. In response to these protests and, more generally, in reiteration of the importance members of the assembly assign to their immunity prerogatives, the chamber introduced substantial elaborations to the inviolability thesis as part of the wide-ranging reform of the assembly's Rules of Procedure approved in May 1992. As corollary to this approval, in June 1992 Castillo was set free and reassumed his legislative seat.[14]

The 1992 reform of the Rules of Procedure considerably strengthened legislators' inviolability. The law was now rewritten to say that while either citizens or the prosecutor-general could request the prosecution of a legislator, a suit against a member required presentation of proof of wrongdoing. Suits by citizens further required depositing an unspecified bail bond with the Prosecutor-General's Office.[15] These new conditions significantly obstructed the process of holding legislators accountable in civil cases and for criminal offenses.

As stipulated by the 1992 reform, upon receipt of an accusation against a legislator, the prosecutor-general was immediately required to file the complaint with the assembly, which assigned it to the Rules Committee. If the committee believed the charge merited a formal investigation, it could recommend a suspension of immunity to the plenum. Otherwise, the committee rejected and filed the complaint. The same procedure applied when, acting *sua sponte,* the prosecutor-general requested immunity suspension for investigative purposes (República de Panamá 1992 [articles 77, 78, 80]). The 1992 reform also nullified any judicial process in which an accused legislator had not previously waived his/her immunity or the assembly had not authorized the proceedings. For investigative purposes, the plenum could only suspend a legislator's immunity for a maximum period of two and a half months. The Prosecutor-General's Office had to conclude the investigation and the Supreme Court had to issue an indictment within this period. Otherwise, the process was rendered null and void (República de Panamá 1992 [article 94]).[16] Given the overburdening of Panama's judicial system, it was highly unlikely that the court could formalize an indictment within such a short term. Furthermore, the Prosecutor-General's Office required authorization from the assembly before it could begin investigation of a legislator's activities. Once the investigation concluded, the report had to be sent to the assembly before the case was tried. Once the chamber authorized the trial and after formalizing the indictment, the Supreme Court was required to rule within a one-month period. Except as a result of a judicial ruling or when caught *in flagrante delicto,* a legislator could not be arrested unless expressly authorized by the assembly (República de Panamá 1992 [articles 79, 81]).

The Case of Elías Castillo

The January 1991 arrest of Legislator Elías Castillo proved to be the high point in the battle between the Prosecutor-General's Office and the Legislative Assembly.[17] Thereafter, several factors combined to assert legislative inviolability. Among these were PRD's renewed belligerence, the party's acquisition of a majority of the seats filled in the January 1991 partial legislative election,[18] enlistment of foreign support for their cause,[19] an erosion in the credibility of the Prosecutor-General's Office, and the breakdown of the governing coalition in April 1991, which prompted further cooperation between the remaining government parties and PRD.[20]

Above and beyond these variables, the most significant factor explaining the expansion of inviolability was the general interest among both government and opposition legislators for upholding the "principle" of "legislative" immunity. Castillo, as noted above, remained in prison for a year and a half, after which he returned to the assembly. In his specific case, the chamber retroactively applied the Rules of Procedure amendment requiring prior assembly authorization for any investigation against a member. This requirement was not met in Castillo's case because it was not in force at the time of his arrest. For that reason, charges against him were dismissed.[21] After his return to the assembly, Castillo successfully ran for reelection in 1994, 1999, 2004, and 2009. He is the only individual to have served five terms in the Legislative Assembly. In 2005–7 he was the chamber's presiding officer, and he chaired the Rules Committee in 2008–9 (Asamblea Nacional 2008a).

Although Prosecutor-General Cruz requested the indictment of Balbina Herrera, the cases against her were eventually dropped, ostensibly for lack of strong evidence. She was reelected in 1994 and 1999, served as housing minister in the Torrijos administration (2004–9), and was her party's presidential candidate in 2009. The accusations against Alemán Boyd were left dormant; he gained reelection in 1994 but did not succeed in 1999.

Variations on the Immunity Theme

In the face of attempts to hold legislators accountable for transgressions of the law, the Panamanian assembly has consistently sprung to the defense of its members, protecting them through collective action against prosecution. The chamber repeatedly held that its members enjoyed a special legal status and acted firmly to maintain it. Through 2004, under four different administrations, the Rules Committee recurrently dismissed charges against both government and opposition legislators.[22] In other instances it neglected to consider serious complaints. No action was taken, for example, in June 1991 when the acting mayor of Panama City complained that Alemán Boyd had obstructed a police operative and assaulted a local *corregidor* (county magistrate). Such permissiveness was also demonstrated toward Balbina Herrera after authorities accused her of inciting violent disturbances during the official visit of President George H. W. Bush in June 1992.[23]

Members of the Panamanian assembly also maintained that immunity was transferable to a legislator's property. When the house of Gerardo González (PRD) was searched under warrant in 1992, the chamber issued a statement protesting violation of González's "immunity." In reply, Prosecutor-General Cruz contended that inviolability did not apply to a legislator's property or belongings.[24] But the "transfer of immunity" argument has held: when in 1992 police at a roadblock stopped the automobile of Miguel Bush (PRD) for suspicion of carrying contraband, the legislator defended his immunity, as well as that of his vehicle, at gunpoint. An automobile reportedly owned by the same member was involved in a similar incident in 1997.[25]

In fact, only under pressure from more powerful external actors did the assembly acquiesce in suspending the immunity of its members. The details of pressure exertion and resistance by the chamber give additional support to the view that exercising and protecting inviolability is a major concern of Panama's deputies. Thus, at least some Panamanian assembly members are interested in reelection not only to advance their political careers, as held by the literature on representatives' behavior, but also to increase their personal wealth and remain free from prosecution. Only two examples exist of immunity suspension by the assembly. Both occurred in 1994, in response to strong demands the chamber was unable to resist. In the first case, there is ample reason to suspect that pressure by agencies of the U.S. government, notably the Drug Enforcement Administration (DEA) and the Justice Department, affected the outcome. In the second case, pressure applied by President Ernesto Pérez Balladares (PRD) had the same effect.

In November 1993 the DEA arrested Anel Ramírez (PALA, a PRD ally) in a sting operation in Miami.[26] Before a U.S. federal judge, the legislator for Darién Province confessed he had employed public funds to purchase 150 kilograms of cocaine, stored the narcotics in his house, and used his vehicle to transport the drugs. Covert DEA agents participating in the operation testified that Ramírez "repeatedly offered to use his immunity to 'protect' illegal shipments and operations."[27] When questioned during the trial (which took place after his term in the assembly expired in 1994), the ex-assemblyman admitted that he had personally carried five parcels of cocaine in his car because his "immunity as a legislator ensured that no police officer would search" his automobile (Brannan Jaén 1997a). Due to the international implications of the case, but only after lengthy procrastination, the assembly voted to strip Ramírez of immunity in April 1994. It was the first time the chamber suspended the immunity of one of its members.

In November 1994 Mario Miller (PRD) was reportedly caught *in flagrante delicto* by Panamanian police officers in an attempt to extort money from a group of businessmen.[28] Although the intervention of fellow legislator Aristides de Icaza (PRC, subsequently PSOL, later CD) initially prevented his arrest, Miller turned himself in hours later. Claiming it had the right to determine the flagrancy of a crime,[29] the assembly immediately demanded the transfer of Miller's case from the Prosecutor-General's Office. Balbina Herrera, at that time president of the assembly, and Miguel Bush, then chair of the Rules Committee, were among the most vocal defenders of the arrested member's immunity. The tenor of their demands and the leadership positions held by these advocates of the imprisoned legislator suggest the relevance immunity provisions held for the assembly membership.

The same day Miller surrendered, however, President Pérez Balladares asked his party's National Executive Committee to expel Miller and revoke his mandate, which would have the same effect as stripping him of immunity. Though Pérez Balladares used the case as proof that he would prosecute corruption in his administration, political observers believed that Miller had incurred the chief executive's personal wrath on account of his outspoken statements about the administration and that the president wished to use him as an example of what was in store for legislators who entertained thoughts of independent action. Certainly, only at the president's insistence did the chamber eventually agree to the suspension of Miller's immunity.

Miller was convicted in December 1997 and a Panama City circuit judge sentenced him to forty-four months' imprisonment for extortion and conspiracy to commit crimes. The judge also barred him from exercising public office for the same period. At that time, however, the former legislator received a parole because he had already served most of his prison sentence in preventive detention. In 1999 Miller stood as an assembly candidate for Bocas del Toro Province on the Cambio Democrático (CD) ticket but failed to win back the assembly seat he had held briefly in 1994. In July 2000—ten months after the end of Pérez Balladares's administration—the Supreme Court repealed the 1997 conviction. Miller ran once more as a CD candidate in 2004 and 2009, winning an assembly seat in the latter election.

Inviolability: The Electoral Connection

The preceding discussion substantiates the view that Panamanian legislators were keenly interested in exercising and expanding their immunity. A case illustrating the connection between inviolability and election to an assembly seat is that of Pedro González. Although he was elected for the first time in 1999, the González case lends support to the view that some candidates who strive for a seat in the chamber are motivated by a strong desire to remain free from prosecution.

On June 10, 1992—the eve of a visit to Panama by President George H. W. Bush—an attack on a U.S. military vehicle in the outskirts of Panama City killed one U.S. soldier and severely wounded another. Eyewitnesses identified Pedro González, son of PRD president and legislator Gerardo González, as one of three assailants. The younger González had reportedly participated in subversive activities from 1990 to

1992 (Abad n.d.). Panamanian investigators later found the attackers' automobile at a nearby property owned by González and one of the murder weapons at the workplace of a daughter of the legislator (Garvin 1997a).

Before the police could execute an arrest warrant, however, González left the country incognito, presumably to Cuba.[30] He remained abroad until after the return of PRD to power, in September 1994. At a press conference held in the presidential house on January 25, 1995, González—accompanied by his father and the rest of the family, as well as Prosecutor-General José Antonio Sossa (PDC)—"surrendered" to President Pérez Balladares. Imprisoned under privileged conditions in an air-conditioned private cell with a television set, a cellular phone, a fax machine, and a computer—facilities denied to the rest of Panama's prison population—González pursued a political career while in jail, securing election as undersecretary of the PRD's youth organization (Garvin 1997a, 1997b, 1997c).

While prosecutors and judicial authorities put off the trial for as long as they could, Gerardo González ostensibly exercised his political influence to derail the case. Pérez Balladares dismissed Jaime Abad, the police chief who had investigated the attack, and González charged Abad with forging an FBI ballistics test unfavorable to his son. Another charge claimed that Abad had concealed a Panamanian police ballistics test that was less damaging to the younger González. While the forgery charge was dismissed after the U.S. embassy in Panama authenticated the results, the judge in the case upgraded Abad's concealment charge from a misdemeanor to a felony (Garvin 1997c).

On October 7, 1997, Pedro González was finally tried. A jury consisting of public employees who owed their jobs to the PRD government pronounced him not guilty on November 1, 1997. The U.S. government, which had repeatedly expressed an interest in González's conviction and offered a US$100,000 reward for his capture, did not hesitate to manifest its deep displeasure. Washington spokesmen complained bitterly about the lack of transparency of Panama's judicial system. The State Department's *Panama Country Report on Human Rights Practices for 1997* reproduced these complaints:

> In November a jury acquitted Pedro Miguel Gonzalez, son of Legislative
> Assembly president Gerardo Gonzalez (also president of the ruling Demo-

cratic Revolutionary Party—PRD), and two other defendants, Amado
Sanchez Ortega and Roberto Garrido, who were accused of the politically
motivated 1992 killing of U.S. serviceman corporal Zak Hernandez and
intent to kill U.S. army sergeant Ronald Terrell Marshall. Gonzalez was
freed; Sanchez must still serve a 7-year prison term for a prior murder
conviction; and Garrido had still not been located at year's end. Gonzalez
was acquitted despite clear evidence of his guilt and in the wake of improper actions by his father in this case and a separate case against a police
official, Jaime Abad. Gonzalez's trial was subject to political interference,
manipulation, and intimidation of the judge and jury. (U.S. Department
of State 1998)

Rumors that González might be abducted by U.S. authorities and
placed on trial in the United States began to circulate at the time. This
expectation was not far-fetched based on the precedent set by the 1989
U.S. invasion—one of the justifications for which was bringing Noriega to the United States to face drug trafficking indictments—and on
the existence of an indictment for terrorism against González, issued
by a District of Columbia grand jury in mid-1992.[31]

While Pedro González enjoyed de facto inviolability under the PRD
government, U.S. pressures against him made continued immunity a necessity in his case. Elections scheduled for 1999 might return an opposition government more responsive to U.S. requirements and thus trigger
a reopening of his case. In this context, González launched his candidacy for a single-member rural district in Veraguas Province, where his
family had exerted political influence for many years and solidified its
control during the military dictatorship.

In the October 1998 PRD primary, González faced incumbent PRD
legislator Enrique Riley. Subsequent to González's proclamation by the
Electoral Tribunal as the winning candidate, Riley complained that his
opponent had been involved in widespread vote buying and tally-sheet
alterations. After losing the ensuing legal battle, Riley switched labels
and accepted nomination by CD, one of the parties supporting the
candidacy of President Mireya Moscoso (PPAN, 1999–2004).[32]

During the 1999 electoral campaign, Riley repeatedly denounced
González for propaganda destruction, illegal use of PARVIS subsidies
to attract voters, and other forms of vote buying (see chapters 6 and 7).

González retorted by complaining that Riley used vehicles purchased through the member's *partida circuital* to promote his candidacy. After the elections Riley accused González of voter transportation, intimidation, and vote buying through the distribution of construction materials, food, and cash, including counterfeit US$20 bills. Despite the obvious occurrence of irregularities, Gerardo Solís, the electoral prosecutor and a member of PRD with close links to President Pérez Balladares—neglected to conduct any investigations, thus opening the way for the Electoral Tribunal's endorsement of González's "victory."[33] In August 1999—again amidst denunciations of fraud—González secured his election as regional president of the PRD in Veraguas Province (Hernández 1999).

González's public declarations as legislator-elect emphasized his fear of action by U.S. authorities and thus the importance of securing criminal inviolability and political influence through an assembly seat. On May 18, 1999, he accused former police chief Jaime Abad of colluding with the U.S. embassy in a kidnapping attempt aimed at sending him to trial in Washington, D.C. *El Panamá América* reported him as saying that "officials of the U.S. Embassy and the FBI were involved in the false proceedings" initiated against him. He further added that U.S. officials "had set up a strategy" with the purpose of creating for him an "image of a villain to facilitate his abduction." Citing the precedent of Legislator Anel Ramírez (PALA, 1989–94), he claimed the strategy contemplated his capture "before the inauguration of the new administration, to take advantage of the climate of uncertainty that would prevail" until the swearing-in ceremony on September 1.[34] Later he said that "only as a dead man" would he leave Panama to stand trial in the United States (Quintero de León 1999). As he was well aware, only in Panama would he continue to enjoy immunity from prosecution as legislator in the 1999–2004 term. Only in Panama, as well, could González have such a successful political career. In 2004 he won reelection for the Veraguas constituency, and in 2007 he gained election to the presidency of the National Assembly.

The U.S. government was not amused. On September 1, 2007, the Department of State expressed the Bush administration's "deep disappointment" that "from all its members," Panama's deputies had chosen González as assembly president. Alluding to the indictment against González in the killing of Serviceman Hernández and the attempted murder of Sergeant Marshall, the statement emphasized the interest of the United States in bringing to justice those responsible for the crimes (U.S. Department of State 2007).

Reportedly in retaliation for the assembly's poor choice, the U.S. Congress shelved approval of the Trade Promotion Agreement with Panama, signed in December 2006. As of May 2010 Congress still had not considered the treaty.[35] With regard to González, in 2009 he ran for reelection but lost to opposition candidate Francisco Brea (PPAN). Despite his membership in the government bloc, the damage caused to the Torrijos administration's foreign agenda through the rise of González to the presidency of the National Assembly likely alienated the legislator from top party leaders and supporters in his constituency.

The 2004 Constitutional Reform on Immunity

The 2004 constitutional reform abolished the requirement of assembly authorization to investigate and prosecute deputies accused of criminal offenses. Such investigations and prosecutions are now authorized by the Supreme Court, which also conducts inquiries and tries accused deputies (República de Panamá 2004 [article 155]). This amendment has failed to bring about better justice in Panama, however. Observers suggested that because the constitution (articles 155, 160) stipulates that the assembly is the competent authority to prosecute and try Supreme Court magistrates—and the Supreme Court is the competent authority to prosecute and try National Assembly deputies—justices and assembly members protect each other.

In 2010, as noted in chapter 10, the assembly swiftly exonerated Supreme Court magistrates Spadafora and Cigarruista from any wrongdoing in the CEMIS case. Prior to his nomination to the Supreme Court for a ten-year term, Cigarruista was a legislator in 1989–94 (PLA), 1994–99 (PLA), and 1999–2004 (PPAN). He resigned his seat in 2002 to assume his new position in the court. As of May 2010 the Supreme Court had not yet made a decision on whether any of the seventeen incumbent deputies also serving in 1999–2004 held responsibility in the CEMIS scandal.[36]

At the end of 2009, when the latest update before submitting this text was available, the Supreme Court reported receiving 116 cases against National Assembly deputies and their substitutes—as well as Panamanian members of the Central American Parliament (PARLACÉN) and their alternates, who enjoy the same prerogatives as National Assembly members—since 2002. These cases included accusations for drug trafficking, personal attacks, document and electoral fraud, misappropriation and embezzlement, domestic violence, rape, and other crimes. At the time (December 2009), deputies with the largest number of accusations included Franz Wever (PRD, 7 cases), Rogelio Alba (PLN, previously LIBRE, 6 cases), Jerry Wilson (PRD, 5 cases), José Varela (PPAN, previously PDC, 5 cases), Osman Gómez (PPAN, 4 cases), José Carreño (PPAN, 3 cases), Javier Tejeira (PLN, 3 cases), Miguel Fanovich (PPAN, 3 cases), and Danis Montemayor (PPAN, 3 cases). Among the 116 lawsuits, the Supreme Court had only tried one: that of Fausto Misselis, substitute of Enrique Garrido (PPAN, 1994–2009), who was convicted of possessing illegal drugs in June 2009 (Palm 2009; Pérez González 2008).

Ostensibly to clear this case buildup and ensure that, in the future, accusations against deputies would not accumulate, in March 2010 the assembly Committee on Government, Justice, and Constitutional Affairs proposed a reform to the Penal Procedure Code. The bill would give the Supreme Court a one-month term to investigate accusations against deputies. Defendant deputies who believe that investigations have prolonged "unjustifiably" would have the option of petitioning the court to order a final, ten-day term to finalize the inquiry. If the court fails to act in eight days after receiving such petition, or if the prosecutor fails to submit the results of the inquiry within the ten-day term, the case would become extinct (Asamblea Nacional 2010b). This proposal, included in the agenda for the July 2010 session of the assembly, provides further evidence that in the pursuit of mechanisms to facilitate their freedom from justice, the imagination of Panama's deputies knows few bounds.

Summary

The record indicates that Panama's assembly, including members from across the political spectrum, shows a firm determination to uphold the inviolability of its members. In 1984–2004 the chamber legislated to make it practically impossible to hold members accountable for misdeeds, dismissed complaints against members on the occasions that they made their way to the Rules Committee, and even claimed the extension of the principle of inviolability to include legislators' property. The chamber, moreover, elected some of the most notorious beneficiaries of immunity to positions of leadership, a development that indicates a lenient approach toward impunity among its membership. Only when coerced by more powerful political actors, such as the executive or agencies of the U.S. government, did the assembly acquiesce in lifting members' immunity. This occurred only twice, in the cases of Legislators Anel Ramírez (PALA, 1994) and Mario Miller (PRD, 1994).

In Panama de jure or de facto immunity is a privilege that deputies appreciate highly and wish to preserve through reelection. To retain immunity from prosecution through reelection or initial election, some candidates and members of the assembly—particularly those troubled by accusations of wrongdoing—actively engage in electoral politics through patronage distribution and other mechanisms described in chapters 6 and 7. This was the case of PRD candidate Pedro González, whose election to a legislator's seat and reelection in 2004 was a safety measure against potential imprisonment.

Evidence presented in this chapter supports the assumption that an interest in remaining free from prosecution also motivated the reelectoral ambitions of other legislators at odds with the law, such as PRD members Alberto Alemán Boyd, Balbina Herrera, Miguel Bush, and Elías Castillo. Such de jure or de facto freedom from prosecution as enjoyed by Panamanian legislators is a significant obstacle to the democratic requirements of accountability and impartial, universalistic application of the law.

Conclusion

This book argued that in some liberal democracies, informally institutionalized corruption, impunity, and clientelism, together with formal institutions such as the electoral system and the constitutional distribution of power among the executive and legislative branches, motivate assembly members to seek other goals outside reelection or, more generally, career advancement. Informally institutionalized corruption, impunity, and clientelism also encourage different means toward reelection besides those predicted by scholars of representatives' behavior. This argument derives from a close examination and analysis of the behavior of assembly members in Panama in 1984–2009; Panamanian legislators demonstrate a desire to pursue political careers—as predicted by the literature—but also seek enrichment and immunity from prosecution. To achieve reelection—which in this context serves not only as a means for political advancement but also for getting rich and remaining free from the reach of justice—representatives distribute patronage much more broadly and directly than their peers in liberal democracies where such formal features as the rule of law are strongly institutionalized. Panama's deputies also exhibit behaviors that the literature has not considered sufficiently, such as switching parties and manipulating elections as well as electoral rules.

These findings are significant because they illustrate ways in which informal institutions contribute to shaping the behavior of the members of representative assemblies. They underscore the need for approaching the study of representatives from a broader perspective than has usually been the case. The literature holds that assembly members are rational actors concerned with advancing their political careers as permitted by the formal institutional context in which they operate, and it normally approaches the examination of representatives' behavior from this assumption. This is a valid expectation in those liberal democratic settings where there is a close fit between the letter of the law and political actors' behavior. But where some informal institutions are better predictors of actors' behavior than written rules or formal procedures, it is reasonable to expect that informal features—such as, in Panama, systemic corruption, impunity, and clientelism—allow representatives to pursue other objectives in addition to those encouraged by formal institutions. The book's findings are also valuable because they enhance our understanding of the effects of representatives' behavior on the quality of the democratic regime and, particularly, on the quality of democratic representation. The following sections approach this topic from the perspective of democratic theory.

Fairness

The establishment of liberal democracy gives rise to certain expectations among the population. These expectations relate to properties of the democratic system and to citizens' ideas of what democracy supposedly means. According to Dahl (1989, 221), democracy (or "polyarchy") "is a political order distinguished by the presence of seven institutions, all of which must exist for a government to be classified as a polyarchy." Dahl further states that "the institutions of polyarchy are necessary to democracy"; in other words, they are required for the "highest feasible attainment of the democratic process in the government of a country" (1989, 222). These institutions, which in essence constitute the electoral and liberal dimensions of democracy, are (1) elected officials; (2) free and fair elections; (3) inclusive suffrage; (4) the right to run for office; (5) freedom of expression; (6) alternative information; and (7) associational autonomy. As explained by O'Donnell (1996), the first four institutions relate to an essential characteristic of democracy: inclusive, fair, and competitive elections. The final three attributes address "political and social freedoms that are minimally necessary not only during but also between elections as a condition for elections to be fair and competitive" (O'Donnell 1996, 35).

Fairness is thus a precondition for democratic elections. Citizens of a democratic state expect that fairness will also prevail not only in the electoral realm but, additionally, in other spheres of political life, such as in policy making and implementation as well as in the administration of justice. This universalistic expectation derives from the notion of political equality, a cornerstone of democratic thought, according to which each member of the community has equal political rights and responsibilities and no one should enjoy special advantages or privileges in their relationship to the community.

Fairness requires that action by government leaders be universalistic, that is, oriented toward some consensus-based version of the public good (O'Donnell 1996). The republican tradition in which this view is embedded requires unselfish dedication to the *res publica* by those who exercise public office and rejects the use of political office for private gain. Under a republican constitution, citizens in general and officeholders in particular are expected to sacrifice their personal interests to the benefit of the community. The republican tradition further holds that public officeholders "should subject themselves to the law no less and even more than ordinary citizens . . . Republicanism is damaged if public officials, elected or not, refuse to subject themselves to the law, or prefer private interest to public duty" when the two conflict (O'Donnell 1998b, 118). In accordance with this view, it is unfair for officers of the state to influence the political process for personal benefit because such actions violate the republican basis of liberal democracy as well as the notions of equality and universalism that are central to the democratic regime.

Some behaviors by Panamanian legislators described in this book contravene the ideas of fairness and universalism that are at the root of citizens' democratic expectations. Vote fraud and, in general, attempts to manipulate the electorate's will through legal or illegal measures that render useless the ballots of an appreciable portion of the voting population constitute a violation of citizens' basic right to participate in the political process through free and fair election of their representatives. The prevalence of fraudulent electoral practices at the local level in Panama (as well as in other liberal democracies) poses a challenge to students of contemporary democracy. At a minimum, it encourages scholars to refine their assessments of democratic regimes in ways that, while remaining analytically useful, are also sensitive to significant variance in electoral practices.

The establishment and expansion of broad prerogatives in favor of representatives, including franking, diplomatic passport, and tax exemption privileges as well as wide-ranging immunities from prosecution, also violate notions of equality and fairness. It is practical to assign prerogatives to members of deliberative chambers as long as such facilities assist in the achievement of democratic representation—a public good. But when privileges merely establish a personal benefit (as opposed to a public good), they are no longer functional in democratic terms. Expanding these personal prerogatives—as Panamanian deputies have done since the reestablishment of the assembly in 1984—makes even less sense in a democratic context. Members of Panama's National Assembly transgressed this public-private boundary by—among other activities—legislating to broaden personal privileges with economic value. Chapter 9 reviewed the amendments to the chamber's Rules of Procedure and other legislation that authorized the use of diplomatic passports by deputies' families, alternates, and alternates' family members; allowed free telephone access to substitutes; and permitted the sale of tax-exempt vehicles, giving rise to a lucrative "legislative trade" in automobiles. Chapter 10 explained how some members engage in unethical enrichment practices by selling their legislative votes, exercising undue influence to obtain personal or particularistic benefits, and appropriating public resources for personal or electoral use. Chapter 11 traced the legislative process that permitted deputies to remain virtually free from prosecution for offenses through the expansion of the so-called legislative or parliamentary immunity.

Legislating with the express intent of enabling a minority to remain above the rule of law is particularly contradictory to democratic theory. In some liberal democracies, influential individuals can achieve this goal through informal channels. In Panama, however, assembly members went even further in 1984–2004, securing for themselves a legal license to remain free from prosecution by incorporating into the assembly's Rules of Procedure provisions that made it impossible, in most cases, to prosecute legislators for breaches of legality.

Personal enrichment by representatives has clear implications for the democratic regime. Under liberal democracy citizens expect that the officers of the state will act to procure the public good, not to gain personal advantages. When legislators seek enrichment through illegal means and remain unpunished for it, they also undermine the rule of law. Furthermore, a strong impulse toward both legal and illegal personal enrichment by representatives not only violates the theoretical underpinnings of the modern democratic system. It also weakens public trust in democracy, alienating the population from the democratic system. Juan Linz (1978) has explored in depth the detrimental consequences of this alienation. More than any other regime type, liberal democracy depends on popular support and democratic legitimacy. Behavior by politicians that does not coincide with the universalistic expectations of the population undermines democratic legitimacy and, by breeding cynicism and discontent among the citizenry, provides an added element toward democratic deterioration and breakdown.

Accountability and Representation

Under liberal democracy the notion of accountability implies that citizens can punish officeholders who do not live up to democratic standards of fairness and universalism through removal from office and, when warranted, through judicial procedures. Democratic constitutions contain accountability mechanisms, the ideal purpose of which is to keep rulers "virtuous whilst they continue to hold their public trust" (Madison, Hamilton, and Jay 1987, *The Federalist*, no. 57). More realistically, these mechanisms seek "to prevent, or at any rate sanction, improper actions by officeholders" (O'Donnell 1998b, 119).

The behavior of Panamanian legislators has important consequences for accountability, both vertical and horizontal. Voters exercise vertical accountability particularly at election time. Some constitutions also allow citizens to activate other vertical accountability initiatives, such as recalls or referenda, between elections. Horizontal accountability refers to "actions ranging from routine oversight to criminal sanctions or impeachment" that specific political institutions are allowed to take "in relation to possibly unlawful actions or omissions by other agents or agencies of the state" (O'Donnell 1998b, 117). Using the lens of vertical and horizontal accountability provides an opportunity for considering the effects of Panamanian deputies' behavior on the democratic system—and, particularly, on democratic representation—along two different dimensions: at the constituent-representative and the executive-assembly levels.

Representation is the legal fiction that enables the entire community to be present in the democratic decision-making process, and it forms an integral part of our contemporary notion of democracy. Hannah Pitkin, whose *Concept of Representation* (1967) remains the most thorough treatment of the subject, defines this legal fiction as "primarily a public, institutionalized arrangement involving many people and groups, and operating in the complex ways of large-scale social arrangements." It implies a "substantive acting for others" requiring "independent action in the interest of the governed, in a manner at least potentially responsive to them, yet not normally in conflict with their wishes" (Pitkin 1967, 221–22). This definition offers insights into what the link between constituents and representatives ideally should look like. Democratic representation is a public—not private, or particularistic—institution. The substantive action it implies requires a transparent, public link between constituents and representatives based on trust and responsiveness. Clientelistic practices, including the widespread use of patronage for electoral purposes, as is the norm in Panama, or—worse still—the outright purchase of votes with cash or other public or private resources, distorts this link. Democratic representation requires a free, fluid connection between representatives and constituents, a connection obstructed by the informal traits that condition the selection of Panama's deputies. Patronage and other clientelistic devices allow representatives to "buy" their release from the social contract that links them to their constituents and stipulates responsiveness to their collective views and wishes.

Party switching operates in a similar way to twist the concept of democratic representation. When members change parties, constituents cannot expect them to act in accordance with the political option voters selected at the polls. In the absence of vertical accountability initiatives (for example, popular recall) and effective horizontal accountability mechanisms between elections, clientelism and party switching allow members to neglect their duties as representatives during their terms. Moreover, by fostering the creation of electoral clienteles, clientelism allows representatives to overcome the barriers that periodic elections impose on unresponsive and inadequate behavior. The considerable increase in Panamanian assembly members' reelection rate in 1999, and sustained in 2004 and 2009, supports this appraisal.

In reaction to criticism of clientelism, particularly through their access to *partidas circuitales* through 2001, some Panamanian legislators argued that the practice of engaging in constituency work through *partidas* is a response to high demand for public services in a context of skewed income distribution.[1] This is a weak justification for clientelistic practices that absorb an excessive amount of legislators' time, energy, and resources and, furthermore, assume proportions that significantly undermine the democratic system in Panama. As conceptualized by Cain, Ferejohn, and Fiorina (1987, 2–3), democratic representation encompasses at least three dimensions. The first is policy responsiveness, or how "faithfully" representatives "respond to the wishes of the district in words and deeds." Allocation responsiveness, or the representative's efforts "to ensure that his or her district gets a fair share of government projects, programs, and expenditures," is a second component. Democratic representation also includes service responsiveness: members' work in response to "individual and group requests for assistance in dealing with the government bureaucracy."

When representatives engage in allocation responsiveness, democratic theory suggests they should strive to ensure the distribution of public goods on a universalistic basis. In Panama, however, intense particularism characterized the implementation of "legislators' initiatives" through constituency funding. Universal entitlement, efficiency, or meritocratic criteria were not normally employed to assign public goods through constituency funding. More often than not, particularistic, electoral, or arbitrary standards provided a basis for decision making. Furthermore, even if their access to and use of *partidas circuitales* was interpreted as allocation responsiveness, Panamanian legislators' overriding preoccupation with this activity caused them to neglect other important facets of representation, notably policy responsiveness.

Weak Policy Responsiveness

The general unfitness of Panama's assembly also makes it difficult for the chamber to engage in universalistic policy responsiveness. Formal institutional factors that promote personalism and clientelism explain in part the lack of a "suitable corps" of representatives in the National Assembly. In particular, low district size prevents the election of individuals with solid, policy-based national reputations, an issue that further prevents the system of democratic representation from entrusting the tasks of government to the most competent members of the political community.

A concern with personal enrichment, securing freedom from prosecution, and obtaining reelection through clientelistic means also affects the assembly's performance as an agent of horizontal accountability. In Panama such concerns make deputies responsive to actors who have the power and resources through which to obtain personal wealth, immunity, and a continued presence in the chamber, especially the executive. Moreover, an executive concerned with implementing its program without opposition actively promotes these behaviors in exchange for the assembly's rubber stamp on its agenda. This undermines the chamber's capacity for overseeing the activities of the executive, a basic function within the democratic system's balance of power.

Disconnection between Constituents and Representatives

Several instances in recent Panamanian political history demonstrate the negative effects that the constituent-representative disconnection and the manipulation of the assembly by the executive have on the country's democratic development. The dynamics of a constitutional process attempting to authorize the consecutive reelection of the president, in 1997–98, illustrates this phenomenon better than any other episode. A proposal allowing the chief executive to stand for immediate reelection was not one of the issues contemplated in PRD's electoral platform in 1994. Even so, shortly after the presidential inauguration, it became obvious that President Ernesto Pérez Balladares (PRD, 1994–99) aspired to serve at least two five-year terms in office. At the president's instigation, his party drafted a consecutive reelection proposal that Legislator Balbina Herrera (PRD, 1989–2004) submitted to the assembly on October 20, 1997.[2]

In those Latin American republics where the checks and balances of the democratic system do not succeed in effectively forestalling abuses of power by the executive, the ban against consecutive presidential reelection is one of the few functional safeguards against the prolongation of self-seeking and authoritarian rule. Most of the region's constitutions, therefore, continue to contain this ban, despite setbacks in Peru (1993),[3] Argentina (1994), Brazil (1997), Venezuela (1999), Dominican Republic (2002), Colombia (2004), Ecuador (2008), and Bolivia (2009). Article 178 of Panama's constitution allows a president to seek reelection only after two consecutive terms have elapsed since his or her departure from office. Article 313 stipulates that amendments to this or any other constitutional provision require approval by two consecutively elected assemblies or endorsement by the chamber in two successive session periods. In the latter case, after the assembly's approval the proposal must also go before the electorate in a binding referendum (República de Panamá 2004). Because Pérez Balladares was interested in seeking reelection in May 1999, he opted for the second procedure.

Panama's opposition politicians, political commentators, and independent observers immediately warned of the harmful consequences that might derive from permitting a president to serve successive terms. Referring to the requirement that legislation should be universalistic, jurist Mario Galindo Heurtematte cautioned that the proposal's sole aim was to satisfy the personal ambition of Pérez Balladares. The prohibition against reelection, Galindo explained, "purports to overcome the rooted inclination of our politicians to hold on to power with tenacity worthy of better causes." No one could ignore, he added, that in a centralized state such as Panama, where the executive exerts such overwhelming influence on all government institutions, "the participation of President Pérez Balladares as a candidate in the 1999 elections would tilt the electoral balance in favor of the government and contaminate the electoral process, casting doubt over it or, even worse, annulling its legitimacy" (Galindo Heurtematte 1997).

More significantly, at the time Herrera presented the constitutional reform proposal before the assembly, public opinion clearly opposed the immediate reelection of the president. An internal opinion poll conducted by PRD in September 1997 revealed that 40 percent of respondents supported the proposal while a majority opposed it.[4] Quarterly polls published by *La Prensa* between March 1997 and March 1998 indicated that the percentage of respondents supporting the reelection initiative never exceeded 39 percent and the proportion that opposed it never dropped under 54 percent.[5] Capturing the prevailing mood against Pérez Balladares's initiative, an editorial in *El Panamá América* (October 21, 1997) predicted that the government would lose the following year's reelection referendum "to a massive 'No' vote," which "neither abstentions, nor discarded ballots, nor computer manipulation" would prevent.

The government majority in the assembly, however, failed to take note of popular opposition to immediate presidential reelection. At the end of both discussion periods, the constitutional amendment passed the third reading with the affirmative vote of forty legislators, or 56 percent of the chamber.[6] Before the electorate, however, the reelection proposal suffered a stunning defeat, as forecasted by opinion polls and political commentators. Despite the widespread use of state resources to promote Pérez Balladares's personal aspirations and numerous electoral irregularities, the referendum held on August 30, 1998, returned a 64 percent popular majority against the constitutional amendment, versus only 34 percent in favor.[7]

The presidential reelection initiative provides a telling example of the acute disconnection between voters and representatives in Panama. In this case, policy responsiveness required a rejection of Pérez Balladares's reelection scheme by the assembly. The chief executive's ample use of government resources to put together a majority coalition, however, succeeded in overcoming any meaningful opposition to his objective in the chamber. Through executive largesse, particularly manifested in larger constituency appropriations for loyal legislators, the president rendered a majority of the assembly responsive to his personal agenda, as opposed to the wishes of the governed. The fact that, despite intense opposition to the constitutional amendment, 50 percent of the assembly members who voted in favor of the reform bill achieved reelection is indicative of Panamanian deputies' ability to overcome the hurdle of unresponsiveness through personalism and clientelism. It also shows the ways in which these practices place an obstacle on vertical accountability. These electorally successful members were among those rewarded with larger *partidas circuitales*.

A Constrained Assembly

In Panama in 1997 and 1998, a proactive assembly, consisting of members adequately representing the policy views of the electorate, would have prevented unnecessary polarization and the misuse of state resources in a needless political adventure.[8] The informal incentives to focus on "low politics" as well as the formal constraints on its meaningful participation in national affairs prevented the assembly from playing this role. Max Weber stands out among the authors that studied the negative effects of these constraints on the representative assembly from a broad, historically informed perspective. In his 1918 essay entitled "Parliament and Government in a Reconstructed Germany," Weber reflects on the role of the representative assembly in preserving individual freedom in the modern mass bureaucratized state. "In view of the growing indispensability of the state bureaucracy and its corresponding increase in power," he wrote, "how can there be any guarantee that any powers will remain which can check and effectively control the tremendous influence of this stratum?" (Weber 1918/1978, 1403). Weber's solution is placing ultimate responsibility for the tasks of government in the hands of politicians (as opposed to bureaucrats) trained in and accountable to a representative chamber.

Weber's essay is particularly useful because it provides a sharp criticism of a weak, incompetent chamber as much as of those commentators who discredit the representative assembly "in favor of other political powers"—namely, the executive (an authoritarian monarchy in Germany at the time Weber wrote). A weak representative chamber is a consequence of authoritarianism—specifically, in Germany, "a legacy of Prince Bismarck's long domination and of the nation's attitude toward him since the last decade of his chancellorship." Bismarck's emasculation of the German parliament produced "a nation without any political sophistication" (1385). A similar critique can be made about Panama.

In Weber's view, accountability to the representative chamber is the only means of safeguarding individual freedoms. The bureaucracy, therefore, must answer to the assembly. According to his formula, a proactive assembly is the democratic state's best defense against improvisation, impulsiveness, and imprudence. For this reason, his objective was to strengthen the representative chamber as an organ of administrative supervision and an agency for the recruitment of capable leaders. The "decisive question," in Weber's considerations, is "How can parliament be made fit to govern?" (1426). Weber advocates, above all, the development of a "suitable corps" of representatives. According to his scheme, this goal can best be achieved by transforming the representative chamber into an institution that attracts political talent to its ranks. Such transformation requires reforms aimed at making the assembly a factor of "positive politics." "Parliament must be completely reorganized in order to produce such leaders and to guarantee their effectiveness" (1428). In this endeavor, Weber—as does John Stuart Mill—clearly favors a representative form of government.

Weber's reflections provide a convenient starting point for a "democratic critique of democracy," a necessity in all contemporary liberal democracies but especially in many polities where democratic development shows little progress beyond regular elections (O'Donnell qtd. in Verbitsky 2000). Without a doubt, the political situation of these countries is preferable to the conditions of authoritarianism that prevailed until recently. Critiques of liberal democracy should therefore be construed in such a way as to make it patently clear that democracy is superior to other, nondemocratic forms of political organization.

Contemporary assessments of democracy should also highlight features that prevent further democratization, such as—among many others—behaviors by representatives that undermine the democratic system. These critiques should point to the endurance of authoritarian traits that place an obstacle on democratic development, including—in the case of Panama—the military regime's sultanistic approach to politics; the informal institutionalization of corruption, impunity, and clientelism; and a constitutional design promoting particularism while centralizing power in the executive. Democratic development requires overcoming these formal and informal features, initially through a broad, consensus-based process of institutional reform. However difficult it may be to overcome the legacies of the past, Panama should not postpone this task any longer.

APPENDICES

Appendix A. Average Freedom House (FH) Scores, Corruption Perceptions Index (CPI) Scores, and Population of Countries Classified as "Free" by Freedom House, 2008–10

Country	Average FH Score, 2008[a]	FH Subscore, Rule of Law Question, 2008	CPI Score, 2009	Population, 2010[b]
Sweden	1.0	16	9.2	9.3
Finland	1.0	16	8.9	5.3
Iceland	1.0	16	8.7	0.3
Norway	1.0	16	8.6	4.9
Luxembourg	1.0	16	8.2	0.5
Barbados	1.0	16	7.4	0.3
Malta	1.0	16	5.2	0.4
New Zealand	1.0	15	9.4	4.3
Switzerland	1.0	15	9.0	7.6
Netherlands	1.0	15	8.9	16.7
Canada	1.0	15	8.7	33.9
Germany	1.0	15	8.0	82.1
Ireland	1.0	15	8.0	4.6
Austria	1.0	15	7.9	8.4
Japan	1.5	15	7.7	127.0
Belgium	1.0	15	7.1	10.7
France	1.0	15	6.9	62.6
Chile	1.0	15	6.7	17.1
Uruguay	1.0	15	6.7	3.4
Cyprus (Greek)	1.0	15	6.6	0.9
Dominica	1.0	15	5.9	0.1
Portugal	1.0	15	5.8	10.7[c]
Taiwan	1.5	15	5.6	23.0
Kiribati	1.0	15	2.8	0.1
Denmark	1.0	14	9.3	5.5
Australia	1.0	14	8.7	21.5
United Kingdom	1.0	14	7.7	61.9
United States of America	1.0	14	7.5	317.6
Estonia	1.0	14	6.6	1.3
Slovenia	1.0	14	6.6	2.0
Spain	1.0	14	6.1	45.3
Cape Verde	1.0	14	5.1	0.5

Appendix A. (continued)

Country	Average FH Score, 2008[a]	FH Subscore, Rule of Law Question, 2008	CPI Score, 2009	Population, 2010[b]
Czech Republic	1.0	14	4.9	10.4
Lithuania	1.0	14	4.9	3.3
St. Vincent & The Grenadines	1.5	13	6.4	0.1
Botswana	2.0	13	5.6	2.0
South Korea	1.5	13	5.5	48.5
Mauritius	1.5	13	5.4	1.3
Costa Rica	1.0	13	5.3	4.6
Hungary	1.0	13	5.1	10.0
Israel	1.5	11	6.1	7.3
St. Lucia	1.0	12	7.0	0.2
Poland	1.0	13	5.0	38.0
Samoa	2.0	13	4.5	0.2
Latvia	1.5	12	4.5	2.2
Slovakia	1.0	12	4.5	5.4
Italy	1.5	12	4.3	60.1
Ghana	1.5	12	3.9	24.3
Greece	1.5	12	3.8	11.2
Belize	1.5	12	2.9	0.3
Sao Tome & Principe	2.0	12	2.8	0.2
Mongolia	2.0	12	2.7	2.7
South Africa	2.0	11	4.7	50.5
Bulgaria	2.0	11	3.8	7.5
Romania	2.0	11	3.8	21.2
Lesotho	2.5	11	3.3	2.1
Benin	2.0	11	2.9	9.2
Namibia	2.0	10	4.5	2.2
Croatia	2.0	10	4.1	4.4
Trinidad & Tobago	2.0	10	3.6	1.3
Vanuatu	2.0	10	3.2	0.2
Dominican Republic	2.0	10	3.0	10.2
Argentina	2.0	10	2.9	40.7
Ukraine	2.5	10	2.5	45.4
Suriname	2.0	9	3.7	0.5
Serbia	2.5	9	3.5	9.9

Appendix A. (continued)

Country	Average FH Score, 2008[a]	FH Subscore, Rule of Law Question, 2008	CPI Score, 2009	Population, 2010[b]
India	2.5	9	3.4	1,124.5
Panama	1.5	9	3.4	3.5
Brazil	2.0	8	3.7	195.4
Peru	2.5	8	3.7	29.5
Guyana	2.5	8	2.6	0.8
El Salvador	2.5	7	3.4	6.2
Jamaica	2.5	7	3.0	2.7
Indonesia	2.5	7	2.8	232.5
Mali	2.5	7	2.8	13.3
Mexico	2.5	6	3.3	110.6
Average (arithmetic mean)	1.5	12.5	5.4	40.1
Median (middle number of the group)	1.5	13.0	5.1	6.8
Mode (number most frequently occurring)	1.0	15.0	2.8	0.2
Statistics for 32 countries with Rule of Law and CPI scores below the median:				
Average (arithmetic mean)	2.0	9.8	3.5	63.5
Median (middle number of the group)	2.0	10.0	3.4	8.4
Mode (number most frequently occurring)	2.0	12.0	4.5	2.2

Source: Freedom House 2009a, 2009b; Transparency International 2009; U.N. Population Division 2009.

Note: N = 76. Highlighted countries have Rule of Law and CPI scores below the median.

[a] The average Freedom House Score is determined by (PR x CL)/2, where PR = Political Rights and CL = Civil Rights in the Freedom House assessment.

[b] Population is based on the U.N. Population Division Estimate.

[c] The population estimate for Taiwan comes from U.S. Central Intelligence Agency 2010.

Appendix B. Number of Members in the Representative Assemblies of All Countries Classified as "Free" by Freedom House, 2008–10

Country	Structure of the Representative Assembly^a	Chamber Name	Current Number of Members, 2010	Population, 2010 (millions)	Population per Member (thousands)	Term (years)	Women #	Women %
Andorra	Unicameral	General Council	28	0.1	4	4	10	36
Antigua & Barbuda	Bicameral	House of Representatives	19	0.1	5	5	2	11
Argentina	Bicameral	Chamber of Deputies	257	40.7	158	4	99	39
Australia	Bicameral	House of Representatives	150	21.5	143	3	41	27
Austria	Bicameral	National Council	183	8.4	46	5	51	28
Bahamas	Bicameral	House of Assembly	41	0.3	7	5	5	12
Barbados	Bicameral	House of Assembly	30	0.3	10	5	3	10
Belgium	Bicameral	House of Representatives	150	10.7	71	4	57	38
Belize	Bicameral	House of Representatives	32	0.3	9	5	0	0
Benin	Unicameral	National Assembly	83	9.2	111	4	9	11
Botswana	Unicameral	National Assembly	63	2.0	32	5	5	8
Brazil	Bicameral	Chamber of Deputies	513	195.4	381	4	45	9
Bulgaria	Unicameral	National Assembly	240	7.5	31	4	50	21
Canada	Bicameral	House of Commons	308	33.9	110	4	68	22
Cape Verde	Unicameral	National Assembly	72	0.5	7	5	13	18
Chile	Bicameral	Chamber of Deputies	120	17.1	143	4	17	14
Costa Rica	Unicameral	Legislative Assembly	57	4.6	81	4	22	39
Croatia	Unicameral	Parliament	153	4.4	29	4	32	21
Cyprus (Greek)	Unicameral	House of Representatives	56	0.9	16	5	8	14
Czech Republic	Bicameral	Chamber of Deputies	200	10.4	52	4	31	16

Appendix B. (continued)

Country	Structure of the Representative Assembly[a]	Chamber Name	Current Number of Members, 2010	Population, 2010 (millions)	Population per Member (thousands)	Term (years)	Women #	Women %
Denmark	Unicameral	Parliament	179	5.5	31	4	68	38
Dominica	Unicameral	House of Assembly	25	0.1	4	5	5	20
Dominican Republic	Bicameral	Chamber of Deputies	178	10.2	57	4	35	20
El Salvador	Unicameral	Legislative Assembly	84	6.2	74	3	16	19
Estonia	Unicameral	Parliament	101	1.3	13	4	23	23
Finland	Unicameral	Parliament	200	5.3	27	4	80	40
France	Bicameral	National Assembly	577	62.6	108	5	107	19
Germany	Bicameral	Federal Diet	622	82.1	132	4	204	33
Ghana	Unicameral	Parliament	230	24.3	106	4	19	8
Greece	Unicameral	Parliament	300	11.2	37	4	52	17
Grenada	Bicameral	House of Representatives	15	11.2	747	5	2	13
Guyana	Unicameral	National Assembly	70	0.8	11	5	21	30
Hungary	Unicameral	National Assembly	386	10.0	26	4	43	11
Iceland	Unicameral	Parliament	63	0.3	5	4	27	43
India	Bicameral	House of the People	545	1,124.5	2,063	5	59	11
Indonesia	Unicameral	House of Representatives	560	232.5	415	5	101	18
Ireland	Bicameral	House of Representatives	165	4.6	28	5	23	14
Israel	Unicameral	Parliament	120	7.3	61	4	23	19
Italy	Bicameral	Chamber of Deputies	630	60.1	95	5	134	21

Appendix B. (continued)

Country	Structure of the Representative Assembly[a]	Chamber Name	Current Number of Members, 2010	Population, 2010 (millions)	Population per Member (thousands)	Term (years)	Women #	Women %
Jamaica	Bicameral	House of Representatives	60	2.7	45	5	8	13
Japan	Bicameral	House of Representatives	480	127.0	265	4	54	11
Kiribati	Unicameral	House of Assembly	46	0.1	2	4	2	4
Latvia	Unicameral	Parliament	100	2.2	22	4	22	22
Lesotho	Bicameral	National Assembly	120	2.1	18	5	29	24
Liechtenstein[b]	Unicameral	Diet	25	0.0	2	4	6	24
Lithuania	Unicameral	Parliament	141	3.3	23	4	27	19
Luxembourg	Unicameral	Chamber of Deputies	60	0.5	8	5	12	20
Mali	Unicameral	National Assembly	147	13.3	90	5	15	10
Malta	Unicameral	House of Representatives	69	0.4	6	5	6	9
Marshall Islands	Unicameral	Parliament	33	0.1	3	4	1	3
Mauritius	Unicameral	National Assembly	70	1.3	19	5	12	17
Mexico	Bicameral	Chamber of Deputies	500	110.6	221	3	131	26
Micronesia[c]	Unicameral	Congress	14	0.1	7	2	0	0
Monaco[d]	Unicameral	National Council	23	0.0	1	5	6	26
Mongolia	Unicameral	State Great Hural	76	2.7	36	4	3	4
Namibia	Bicameral	National Assembly	78	2.2	28	5	21	27
Nauru[e]	Unicameral	Parliament	18	0.0	1	3	0	0
Netherlands	Bicameral	House of Representatives	150	16.7	111	4	63	42

Appendix B. (continued)

Country	Structure of the Representative Assembly[a]	Chamber Name	Current Number of Members, 2010	Population, 2010 (millions)	Population per Member (thousands)	Term (years)	Women #	Women %
New Zealand	Unicameral	House of Representatives	122	4.3	35	3	41	34
Norway	Unicameral	Parliament	169	4.9	29	4	67	40
Palau[f]	Bicameral	House of Delegates	16	0.0	1	4	0	0
Panama	Unicameral	National Assembly	71	3.5	49	5	6	8
Peru	Unicameral	Congress of the Republic	120	29.5	246	5	33	28
Poland	Bicameral	Sejm	460	5.0	11	4	92	20
Portugal	Unicameral	Assembly of the Republic	230	10.7	47	4	65	28
Romania	Bicameral	Chamber of Deputies	334	21.2	63	4	38	11
Samoa	Unicameral	Legislative Assembly	49	0.2	4	5	4	8
San Marino[g]	Unicameral	Great and General Council	60	0.0	1	5	10	17
Sao Tome & Principe	Unicameral	National Assembly	55	0.2	4	4	4	7
Serbia	Unicameral	National Assembly	250	9.9	40	4	54	22
Slovakia	Unicameral	National Council	150	5.4	36	4	27	18
Slovenia	Bicameral	National Assembly	90	2.0	22	4	13	14
South Africa	Bicameral	National Assembly	400	50.5	126	5	178	45
South Korea	Unicameral	National Assembly	299	48.5	162	4	44	15
Spain	Bicameral	Congress of Deputies	350	45.3	129	4	128	37

Appendix B. (continued)

Country	Structure of the Representative Assembly[a]	Chamber Name	Current Number of Members, 2010	Population, 2010 (millions)	Population per Member (thousands)	Term (years)	Women #	Women %
St. Kitts & Nevis	Unicameral	National Assembly	15	0.1	7	5	1	7
St. Lucia	Bicameral	House of Assembly	18	0.2	11	5	2	11
St. Vincent & Grenadines	Unicameral	House of Assembly	22	0.1	5	5	4	18
Suriname	Unicameral	National Assembly	51	0.5	10	5	13	25
Sweden	Unicameral	Parliament	349	9.3	27	4	162	46
Switzerland	Bicameral	National Council	200	7.6	38	4	58	29
Taiwan[b]	Unicameral	Legislative Yuan	112	23.0	205	4	n.a.	n.a.
Trinidad & Tobago	Bicameral	House of Representatives	41	3.6	88	5	11	27
Tuvalu[i]	Unicameral	Parliament	15	0.0	1	4	0	0
Ukraine	Unicameral	Parliament	450	45.4	101	5	36	8
United Kingdom	Bicameral	House of Commons	646	61.9	96	5	126	20
United States of America	Bicameral	House of Representatives	435	317.6	730	2	73	17
Uruguay	Bicameral	House of Representatives	99	3.4	34	5	15	15
Vanuatu	Unicameral	Parliament	52	0.2	4	4	2	4

Appendix B. (continued)

Country	Structure of the Representative Assembly[a] Chamber Name	Current Number of Members, 2010	Population, 2010 (millions)	Population per Member (thousands)	Term (years)	Women #	Women %
Average (arithmetic mean)		177		98	4	38	19
Median (middle number of the group)		120		32	4	23	18
Mode (number most frequently occuring)		150		4	4	2	0

Source: Freedom House 2009a; IPU 2010a; U.N. Population Division 2009.

Note: N = 89.

[a] Data for the lower chambers of bicameral assemblies are presented here.

[b] Population estimated at 0.04 in 2010.

[c] Term is two years except for four at-large senators elected for four years.

[d] Population estimated at 0.03 in 2010.

[e] Population estimated at 0.01 in 2010.

[f] Population estimated at 0.02 in 2010.

[g] Population estimated at 0.03 in 2010.

[h] Information on Taiwan comes from Legislative Yuan 2008 and U.S. Central Intelligence Agency 2010. Data concerning gender was not available at the time of this research.

[i] Population estimated at 0.01 in 2010.

Appendix C. Number of Members in the Representative Assemblies of Latin America's Electoral Democracies, 2008–10

Country	Structure of the Legislative Branch[a]	Chamber Name	Number of Members	Population (millions)	Population per Member (thousands)	Term (years)	Women #	Women %
Argentina	Bicameral	Chamber of Deputies	257	40.7	158	4	99	39
Bolivia	Bicameral	Chamber of Deputies	130	10.0	77	5	33	25
Brazil	Bicameral	Chamber of Deputies	513	195.4	381	4	45	9
Chile	Bicameral	Chamber of Deputies	120	17.1	143	4	17	14
Colombia[b]	Bicameral	House of Representatives	166	46.3	279	4	n.a.	n.a.
Costa Rica	Unicameral	Legislative Assembly	57	4.6	81	4	22	39
Dominican Republic	Bicameral	Chamber of Deputies	178	10.2	57	4	35	20
Ecuador	Unicameral	National Assembly	124	13.8	111	4	40	32
El Salvador	Unicameral	Legislative Assembly	84	6.2	74	3	16	19
Guatemala	Unicameral	Congress of the Republic	158	14.4	91	4	19	12
Haiti	Bicameral	Chamber of Deputies	98	10.2	104	4	4	4
Honduras	Unicameral	National Congress	128	7.6	59	4	23	18
Mexico	Bicameral	Chamber of Deputies	500	110.6	221	3	131	26
Nicaragua	Unicameral	National Assembly	92	5.8	63	5	19	21
Panama	Unicameral	National Assembly	71	3.5	49	5	6	8
Paraguay	Bicameral	Chamber of Deputies	80	6.5	81	5	10	13
Peru	Unicameral	Congress of the Republic	120	29.5	246	5	33	28
Uruguay	Bicameral	House of Representatives	99	3.4	34	5	15	15
Venezuela	Unicameral	National Assembly	166	29.0	175	5	29	17
Average (arithmetic mean)			165		131	4	33	20
Median (middle number of the group)			124		91	4	23	19
Mode (number most frequently occurring)			120		n.a.	4	33	n.a.

Source: Freedom House 2009a; IPU 2010a; U.N. Population Division 2009.

Note: N = 19.

[a] Data for the lower chambers of bicameral assemblies are presented here.
[b] Data concerning gender not available for Colombia.

Appendix D. Panama's Assembly Parties, 1984–2009

Acronym	Name	Ideological Orientation	Year Recognized[a]	Electoral Participation (year)	Assembly Members (#)	Declared Extinct (year)	Remarks
CD	Partido Cambio Democrático	Right	1998	1999 2004 2009	2 3 13		Political instrument of businessman Ricardo Martinelli. Main party supporting his election to the presidency in 2009.
LIBRE	Partido Liberal Republicano	Right	1993	1994	2	1994	Founded by members of the extinct Liberal and Republicano parties, operating in the 1960s and 1980s.
MOLIRENA	Movimiento Liberal Republicano Nacionalista	Right	1982	1984 1989 1994 1999 2004 2009	3 18 5 3 4 2		Founded by members of the former Partido Liberal, Movimiento de Liberación Nacional, Partido Republicano, Partido Acción Democrática, and Tercer Partido Nacionalista, operating in the 1960s.
MORENA	Movimiento de Renovación Nacional	Right	1993	1994 1999	1 0	1999	Political instrument of businessman Joaquín J. Vallarino.
MPE	Movimiento Papa Egoró	Center	1993	1994 1999	6 0	1999	Political instrument of singer Rubén Blades.
PALA	Partido Laborista	Right	1983 (pre-1968)	1984 1989 1994	7 1 1	1994	Founded by members of Partido Laborista Agrario, operating in the 1960s, prior to the 1968 military coup. Aligned with the military regime in 1984 and 1989.

Appendix D. (continued)

Acronym	Name	Ideological Orientation	Year Recognized[a]	Electoral Participation (year)	Assembly Members (#)	Declared Extinct (year)	Remarks
PDC	Partido Demócrata Cristiano (Partido Popular after 2001)	Center-Right	1979 (pre-1968)	1984 1989 1994 1999 2004 2009	6 28 1 5 1 1		Successor to the Christian Democratic Party operating between 1960 and 1968. Changed its name to Partido Popular in 2001. After opposing the military dictatorship, Partido Popular aligned with PRD in 2000–2009.
PL	Partido Liberal	Right	1979 (pre-1968)	1984 1989 1994	1 1 2	1994	Successor to the traditional Liberal Party operating since the mid-1800s, during the period of union with Colombia (1821–1903). Aligned with the military regime in 1984 and 1989.
PLA	Partido Liberal Auténtico (Partido Liberal in 1996–99)	Right	1988	1989 1994 1999	9 2 0	1994 1999	A scion of Partido Liberal, led by Legislator Arnulfo Escalona (1984–89), who opposed the party's alignment with the military regime. Became extinct in 1994 but re-registered in 1996 as Partido Liberal. Became extinct once again in 1999.

Appendix D. (continued)

Acronym	Name	Ideological Orientation	Year Recognized[a]	Electoral Participation (year)	Assembly Members (#)	Declared Extinct (year)	Remarks
PLN	Partido Liberal Nacional	Right	1997	1999 2004	3 3		Founded by Deputy Raúl Arango Gasteazoro (1960–68) after the extinction of Partido Liberal Republicano in 1994. Merged with Partido Solidaridad to form Partido Unión Patriótica in 2006.
PPAN	Partido Panameñista (Partido Panameñista Auténtico in 1983–89) (Partido Arnulfista in 1991–2005)	Center-Right	1983 (pre-1968)	1984 1989 1994 1999 2004 2009	13 0 14 19 16 21		Successor to Arnulfo Arias's various parties, the first of which was founded in 1934. Registered in 1983 as Partido Panameñista Auténtico. After Arias's death in 1988, the military regime engineered a takeover of the party, resulting in a massive electoral loss. Reorganized as Partido Arnulfista under the leadership of Arias's widow, Mireya Moscoso, in 1991, the party returned to its previous name, Partido Panameñista, in 2005.

Appendix D. (continued)

Acronym	Name	Ideological Orientation	Year Recognized[a]	Electoral Participation (year)	Assembly Members (#)	Declared Extinct (year)	Remarks
PR	Partido Republicano	Right	1983 (pre-1968)	1984 1989	3 0	1991	Successor to Partido Republicano, operating between 1960 and 1968. Aligned with the military regime in 1984 and 1989. Declared extinct in 1991, at the conclusion of the 1989 electoral process.
PRC	Partido Renovación Civilista	Right	1993	1994 1999	3 1	1999	Formed by business and civic leaders who participated in the 1987–89 civil resistance movement against the military dictatorship.
PRD	Partido Revolucionario Democrático	Center	1979	1984 1989 1994 1999 2004 2009	34 10 30 34 43 26		Political arm of the military regime between 1979 and 1989, created by dictator Omar Torrijos. Dominant party in Panama in 1984–2009.
PSOL	Partido Solidaridad	Right	1993	1994 1999 2004	4 4 9		Political instrument of businessman Samuel Lewis Galindo. Merged with Partido Liberal Nacional to form Partido Unión Patriótica in 2006.

Appendix D. (continued)

Acronym	Name	Ideological Orientation	Year Recognized[a]	Electoral Participation (year)	Assembly Members (#)	Declared Extinct (year)	Remarks
UDI	Unión Democrática Independiente	Right	1993	1994	1	1994	Founded by attorney Jacinto Cárdenas.
UP	Partido Unión Patriótica	Right	2006	2009	5		Merger of Partido Liberal Nacional and Partido Solidaridad.
VMP	Partido Vanguardia Moral de la Patria	Right	2007	2009	1	2009	Founded by former president Guillermo Endara after quarrelling with the leadership of Partido Panameñista, to which he belonged.
Independents				2009	2		Independent candidacies were first allowed in 2009.
Totals	18				427		

Source: Conte Porras 2004; Leis 1984; Tribunal Electoral 1984a, 1984b, 1991a, 1991b, 1994b, 1994c, 1999b, 1999c, 2004b, 2008, 2009a.

Note: Parties having at least one member in the National Assembly in the period 1984–2009 included.

[a] Parties that were in existence prior to the 1968 military coup are indicated by "(pre-1968)."

Appendix E. Individuals Proclaimed by the Electoral Tribunal as Elected Members of Panama's Assembly, 1984–2009

	Name				Terms						Number
	First/ Second	Paternal Last	Maternal Last	Married	1984– 1989	1989– 1994	1994– 1999	1999– 2004	2004– 2009	2009– 2014	of Terms
1	Bernardo	ÁBREGO	Jiménez						PRD		1
2	Yanibel Yineva	ÁBREGO	Smith							IND	1
3	Roberto	ÁBREGO	Torres				PRD	PRD			2
4	Rafael Clemente	ÁBREGO			PRD						1
5	Lorenzo	ACOSTA					PRD				1
6	Crispiano	ADAMES	Navarro							PRD	1
7	Carlos Agustín	AFÚ	Decerega				PALA	PRD	PPAN	IND	4
8	Emiliano	AGUILAR			PPAN						1
9	Edwin Alexis	AIZPURÚA						PPAN			1
10	Ramón	AIZPURÚA				PDC					1
11	Marco	ALARCÓN	Palomino		PPAN						1
12	Rogelio	ALBA	Filós				LIBRE	PLN	PLN		3
13	Aurelio A.	ALBA	Villarreal			PLA					1
14	Miguel	ALEMÁN	Alegría						PRD	PRD	2
15	Alberto	ALEMÁN	Boyd		PRD	PRD	PRD				3
16	Héctor Bolívar	ALEMÁN	Estévez					PRD	PRD		2
17	Francisco José	ALEMÁN	Mendoza					PPAN	PPAN	PPAN	3
18	Lorenzo Sotero	ALFONSO	Govea		PRD						1
19	Tomás Gabriel	ALTAMIRANO	Duque				PRD	PRD			2
20	Tomás Gabriel	ALTAMIRANO	Mantovani			PDC			PRD		2
21	Alcibíades	ALVARADO	A.			PDC					1
22	Carlos Ramón	ALVARADO	Acosta				PRD	PRD	PRD		3
23	Jorge Enrique	ALVARADO	Real						PRD		1
24	Edgardo	ALVAREZ					PRD				1
25	Eliseo	ALVAREZ				PLA					1
26	Marco Antonio	AMEGLIO	Samudio			MOLIRENA	MORENA	PPAN			3

Appendix E. (continued)

First/ Second	Paternal Last	Maternal Last	Married	1984– 1989	1989– 1994	1994– 1999	1999– 2004	2004– 2009	2009– 2014	Number of Terms
27	Francisco José	AMEGLIO	Samudio					PPAN			1
28	Abelardo Enrique	ANTONÍO	Quijano			PRD	PRD	PRD		PRD	4
29	Héctor Eduardo	APARICIO	Díaz				MOLIRENA	MOLIRENA	MOLIRENA	MOLIRENA	4
30	Rony Ronald	ARAÚZ	González							PRD	1
31	Arruro Bolívar	ARAÚZ	Urriola					PLN	PLN		2
32	David	ARCE	Merel		PPAN						1
33	Denis	ARCE	Morales				PRD	PRD	PRD	PRD	4
34	Leopoldo Angelino	ARCHIBOLD	Hooker							CD	1
35	Antonio	ARDINES			PRD						1
36	Carlos Alejo	ARELLANO	Lennox		PDC	PDC					2
37	Antonio Manuel	ARIAS	Campagnani		PPAN						1
38	Alfredo	ARIAS	Grimaldo				PPAN				1
39	Argentina Anabel	ARIAS	Torres						PPAN		1
40	Daniel	ARIAS					PPAN				1
41	Gabriel	AROSEMENA	Jaén			PDC					1
42	Rodrigo	AROSEMENA	de Roux				MOLIRENA				1
43	Juan Carlos	AROSEMENA	Valdés						PRD	PRD	2
44	Rubén Eloy	AROSEMENA	Valdés				PDC	PDC	PRD		3
45	Jorge Iván	ARROCHA	Rosario							PPAN	1
46	Francisco	ARTOLA	Araúz		PPAN	PLA					2
47	Florencio	ASPRILLA	Chávez		PALA						1
48	Leandro	ÁVILA							PRD	PRD	2
49	Alexis	AYALA				PDC					1
50	Iracema	AYARZA	Parra	de Dale					PPAN		1
51	Alberto Efraín	BARRANCO	Pérez							PRD	1
52	Carlos	BARSALLO			PRD						1

Appendix E. (continued)

#	First/Second	Paternal Last	Maternal Last	Married	1984–1989	1989–1994	1994–1999	1999–2004	2004–2009	2009–2014	Number of Terms
53	Rogelio Agustín	BARUCO	Mojica							CD	1
54	José Belisario	BARUCO	Villarreal						PRD		1
55	Arcelio	BATISTA	Rivera					PRD			1
56	Anastasio	BATISTA	Z.			PDC					1
57	Robustiano	BEITÍA	Lezcano		PPAN						1
58	Rubén Darío	BEITÍA	Vásquez						PSOL		1
59	Leopoldo Luis	BENEDETTI	Milligan				PPAN		PSOL		2
60	Heriberto Orlando	BERNAL	Marín		PRD						1
61	Dalia Mirna	BERNAL	Yáñez	de Gracia					CD	CD	2
62	Samuel	BINNS	Villagra					CD			1
63	José Isabel	BLANDÓN	Figueroa					PPAN	PPAN	PPAN	3
64	Mario	BOYD	Galindo			MOLIRENA					1
65	Francisco Javier	BREA	Clavel							PPAN	1
66	Camilo	BRENES	Pérez			PDC					1
67	Pedro Teodoro	BRIN	Martínez		PRD						1
68	José	BROWN	Cuanwater						CD		1
69	Miguel	BUSH	Ríos			PRD	PRD	PRD			3
70	Felipe Antonio	CANO	González					PRD			1
71	Miguel A.	CÁRDENAS	Sandoval			MOLIRENA					1
72	José Olmedo	CARREÑO	Araúz					PRC	PPAN		2
73	Fernando Guillermo	CARRILLO	Silvestri							UP	1
74	Carlos E.	CARRIZO	Alba			PDC					1
75	Celso Gustavo	CARRIZO			PRD						1
76	Benito	CASES	Jiménez						PRD		1
77	Dana Daris	CASTAÑEDA	Guardia							UP	1
78	Mateo	CASTILLERO	Castillo					PRD			1

Appendix E. (continued)

| | Name | | | | Terms | | | | | | Number |
	First/ Second	Paternal Last	Maternal Last	Married	1984– 1989	1989– 1994	1994– 1999	1999– 2004	2004– 2009	2009– 2014	of Terms
79	Alberto Magno	CASTILLERO	M.				PSOL	PSOL			2
80	Geovany Abad	CASTILLO	Berrío						PRD		1
81	Julio César	CASTILLO	Gómez					PPAN			1
82	Elías Ariel	CASTILLO	González			PRD	PRD	PRD	PRD	PRD	5
83	Jorge Ernesto	CASTRO	de Gracia					PRD			1
84	Omar E.	CHENG	Chang					PRD			1
85	Ebén	CHI	Rodríguez		PRD						1
86	Gisela	CHUNG	A.			MOLIRENA					1
87	Alberto	CIGARRUISTA	Cortés			PLA	PLA		PPAN		3
88	Luis Carlos	CLEGHORN	Palomino					PPAN			1
89	Guillermo A.	COCHEZ	Farrugia		PDC	PDC					2
90	Manuel	COHEN	Salerno		PALA						1
91	Gustavo Nelson	COLLADO	López							PPAN	1
92	Milciades Abdiel	CONCEPCIÓN							PRD		1
93	Ernesto	CÓRDOBA	Campos		PR						1
94	Omaira Judith	CORREA	Delgado		PALA						1
95	Justo	CORTÉS	Duarte		MOLIRENA						1
96	Dorindo Jayan	CORTÉS	Marciaga						PRD		1
97	Laurentino	CORTIZO	Cohen				PSOL	PSOL			2
98	Héctor	CRESPO	Barría			MOLIRENA					1
99	Edilberto	CULIOLIS	Carrión			PRD					1
100	Santiago	CURABO	Ábrego		PRD						1
101	Hernán	DELGADO	Quintero							VMP	1
102	Juan	DELGADO					PRD				1
103	Raúl E.	DEIVALLE	Henríquez		PR						1
104	Ovidio	DÍAZ	Vásquez		PRD						1

Appendix E. (continued)

#	First/ Second	Paternal Last	Maternal Last	Married	1984– 1989	1989– 1994	1994– 1999	1999– 2004	2004– 2009	2009– 2014	Number of Terms
105	Jorge	DÍAZ					MPE				1
106	Renaúl Alcónides	DOMÍNGUEZ	Villarreal							PRD	1
107	Argénida Cecilia	DUMANOIR		de Barrios	PALA						1
108	Alfredo	EHLERS				PDC					1
109	Pacífico Manuel	ESCALONA	Ávila						PPAN		1
110	Arnulfo	ESCALONA	Ríos			PLA					1
111	Carlos F.	ESCOBAR	R.			PDC					1
112	Sebastián	ESCOBAR				PDC					1
113	Agustín	ESCUDÉ	Saab	de Pardo					PRD		1
114	Romelia	ESQUIVEL			PRD						1
115	José Luis	FÁBREGA	Polleri					PPAN	PSOL	PRD	3
116	Miguel Ángel	FANOVICH	Tijerino						PPAN	PPAN	2
117	Alonso	FERNÁNDEZ	Guardia			MOLIRENA					1
118	Jaime Ricardo	FERNÁNDEZ	Urriola		MOLIRENA						1
119	Guillermo Antonio	FERRUFINO	Benítez							CD	1
120	Mario	FORERO	Mojica			MOLIRENA	MOLIRENA				2
121	Joaquín Fernando	FRANCO	Vásquez				PPAN				1
122	Rubén Darío	FRÍAS	Ortega							PRD	1
123	Olivares	FRÍAS							PRD		1
124	Irene	GALLEGO	Carpintero							PDC	1
125	Sergio Rafael	GÁLVEZ	Evers					CD	PPAN	CD	3
126	Alcibíades	GARCÍA	C.			PDC					1
127	Hernán	GARCÍA	Franceschi		PPAN						1
128	Vidal	GARCÍA	Ureña							CD	1
129	Roberto A.	GARIBALDO	Soto			MOLIRENA					1
130	Enrique	GARRIDO	Arosemena				PPAN	PDC	PPAN		3

Appendix E. (continued)

	Name				Terms						Number of Terms
	First/ Second	Paternal Last	Maternal Last	Married	1984– 1989	1989– 1994	1994– 1999	1999– 2004	2004– 2009	2009– 2014	
131	Hugo Heberto	GIRAUD	Vernaza		PRD						1
132	Ernesto	GIRÓN	M.			PDC					1
133	Herman	GNAEGGI	Urriola			PLA					1
134	Luis Antonio	GÓMEZ	Pérez		PRD						1
135	Osman Camilo	GÓMEZ						PPAN	PPAN	PPAN	3
136	Leo A.	GONZÁLEZ	Delgado			MOLIRENA					1
137	Marcos Aurelio	GONZÁLEZ	González					PPAN		CD	2
138	Elpidio	GONZÁLEZ	González					PPAN			1
139	Pedro Miguel	GONZÁLEZ	Pinzón					PRD	PRD		2
140	Gerardo	GONZÁLEZ	Vernaza			PRD	PRD				2
141	Yadira	GONZÁLEZ					PRD				1
142	Camilo	GOZAINE	Gozaine		PRD			PRD			2
143	Manuel María	GRIMALDO	Cañas						PPAN		1
144	Anselmo Lino	GUAINORA			PRD						1
145	Tomás Rafael	GUERRA	Caballero		PPAN						1
146	Yasmina Benilda	GUILLÉN	Anguizola	de O'Brien					PSOL		1
147	Gustavo G.	GUILLÉN	Peralta				PRC				1
148	Olmedo	GUILLÉN				PLA					1
149	Zulay del Carmen	GUTIÉRREZ	Rodríguez	de Vásquez					PRD		1
150	Milton Cohen	HENRÍQUEZ	Sasso			PDC					1
151	Raúl Antonio	HERNÁNDEZ	López							UP	1
152	Juan	HERNÁNDEZ	Morales						PRD		1
153	Elizabeth	HERNÁNDEZ	Romero	de Quirós					PRD		1
154	Balbina del Carmen	HERRERA	Araúz			PRD	PRD	PRD			3
155	Absalón	HERRERA	García							PRD	1
156	José Ismael	HERRERA	González					PRD			1

Appendix E. (continued)

	Name				Terms						Number of Terms
	First/ Second	Paternal Last	Maternal Last	Married	1984– 1989	1989– 1994	1994– 1999	1999– 2004	2004– 2009	2009– 2014	
157	Euríbiades Vladimir	HERRERA	de León						MOLIRENA		1
158	José María	HERRERA	Ocaña							PPAN	1
159	José Rafael	HILL	Williams			PDC					1
160	Sylvan Keith	HOLDER	Lay			PDC					1
161	Raymundo	HURTADO	W.				MOLIRENA				1
162	Alberto T.	IBÁÑEZ				MOLIRENA					1
163	Aristides	de ICAZA	Hidalgo				PRC		PSOL	CD	3
164	Francisco Harmodio	ICAZA	Sánchez		PALA						1
165	Nelson	JACKSON	Palma						PRD	PRD	2
166	Guillermo	JIMÉNEZ	Miranda		PRD						1
167	Mariela	JIMÉNEZ					MPE				1
168	Rodrigo	JOVANÉ					PPAN				1
169	Fabio Elías	JUÁREZ			PRD						1
170	Víctor Nelson	JULIAO	Toral							CD	1
171	Manuel J.	de LA HOZ	Martínez	de Francis		PDC	PRD				2
172	Raquel	LANUZA	Pinzón	de Solís				PRD			1
173	Mireya del Carmen	LASSO	Milanés						PSOL		1
174	Luis Eduardo	LAY	Návalo							PPAN	1
175	Mario Augusto	LÁZARUS								CD	1
176	Rubén	de LEÓN	Sánchez				PRD	PRD		PRD	3
177	Olivia	de LEÓN		de Pomares				PRD	PRD		2
178	Dámaso	LOMBARDO	Bennett		PRD						1
179	Eddy E.	LONDOÑO	G.					PRD			1
180	Iván Javier	LÓPEZ	Pérez			PDC					1
181	Ada Luz	LÓPEZ		de Gordón					PRD		1
182	Víctor	LÓPEZ					PRD				1

Appendix E. (continued)

| | Name | | | Terms | | | | | | Number |
	First/Second	Paternal Last	Maternal Last	Married	1984–1989	1989–1994	1994–1999	1999–2004	2004–2009	2009–2014	of Terms
183	Jaime E.	LORÉ					PL				1
184	José Manuel	LOZADA	Morales							PRD	1
185	Vicente	MAGALLÓN	Arcia					PRD			1
186	Rolando H.	MARTINELLI	Della Togna			MOLIRENA					1
187	Juvenal	MARTÍNEZ	Castillo						CD		1
188	Juan Antonio	MARTÍNEZ	Díaz							PRD	1
189	Abraham	MARTÍNEZ	Montilla						PSOL	PRD	2
190	Berrilo	MEJÍA	Ortega		PDC						1
191	Moisés	MELAMED			PRD						1
192	Victor	MÉNDEZ	Fábrega				MPE				1
193	Gabriel Enrique	MÉNDEZ	de La Guardia							PRD	1
194	Erasmo	MÉNDEZ	Mérida			PDC					1
195	Haydée del Carmen	MILANÉS		de Lay			PSOL	PSOL			2
196	Mario	MILLER					PRD			CD	2
197	Nodier	MIRANDA	Morales			PLA					1
198	Otilio	MIRANDA			PALA						1
199	Jorge Elías	MONTEMAYOR	Ábrego		PDC	PDC					2
200	Danis Mireya	MONTEMAYOR	Cedeño						PPAN		1
201	Raúl de Jesús	MONTENEGRO	Diviazo		PRD						1
202	Domiluis	MONTENEGRO				MOLIRENA					1
203	Librado	MONTENEGRO				MOLIRENA					1
204	Patricio	MONTEZUMA	González				PRD				1
205	Enrique	MONTEZUMA	Moreno					PRD	PRD		2
206	Hugo Alvin	MORENO	González							PPAN	1
207	Gloria Maritza	MORENO		de López		PDC					1
208	José	MORRIS	Quintero		PRD						1

Appendix E. (continued)

#	First/ Second	Paternal Last	Maternal Last	Married	1984– 1989	1989– 1994	1994– 1999	1999– 2004	2004– 2009	2009– 2014	Number of Terms
209	Marcelino Antonio	MUDARRA	Velásquez						MOLIRENA		1
210	José	MUÑOZ	Molina					PPAN	PSOL	CD	3
211	Adolfo Elías	NAME	Tuñón				PRD				1
212	Luis Fidel	NARVÁEZ				MOLIRENA					1
213	Luis	NAVAS	Pájaro		PRD						1
214	Mario J.	de OBALDÍA	Miranda		PPAN						1
215	Alfredo Armando	ORANGES	Bustos		PRD						1
216	Oydén	ORTEGA	Durán				PRD				1
217	Manuel H.	ORTIZ	S.				PPAN				1
218	Raúl J.	OSSA	de La Cruz	de Donado	PDC	PDC					2
219	Maricruz Edith	PADILLA	Castillo						PRD		1
220	César Augusto	PARDO	Rivera		PRD		PRD	PRD	PRD		4
221	Rogelio Enrique	PAREDES	Robles						PRD	PRD	2
222	Rigoberto	PAREDES	Solís		PRD						1
223	Bolívar	PARIENTE	Castillero				PPAN				1
224	Juan Manuel	PERALTA	Ríos				LIBRE		PRD		2
225	Hermisenda	PEREA	González						PRD		1
226	Ricardo	PÉREZ	C.			PDC					1
227	Bernabé	PÉREZ	Frachiola				MPE				1
228	Raúl Gilberto	PINEDA	Vergara							PRD	1
229	Emiliano José	PONCE	Arze		PPAN						1
230	Luis Alejandro	POSSE	Martinz				PPAN				1
231	Crescencia	PRADO	García							PRD	1
232	Yassir Aboobeker	PURCAIT	Saborío						PRD	PRD	2
233	Mario	QUIEL					PLA				1
234	Olmenares	QUIJANO	G.			MOLIRENA					1

Appendix E. (continued)

#	First/Second	Paternal Last	Maternal Last	Married	1984–1989	1989–1994	1994–1999	1999–2004	2004–2009	2009–2014	Number of Terms
235	Wigberto Esteban	QUINTERO	Gutiérrez						MOLIRENA		1
236	Pablo	QUINTERO	Luna				PPAN				1
237	Luis Eduardo	QUIRÓS	Bernal							PPAN	1
238	Simón	QUIRÓS	y Quirós		PPAN						1
239	Ezequiel	RAMÍREZ	Madero						PRD		1
240	Anel José	RAMÍREZ				PALA					1
241	Salvador	REAL	Chen							UP	1
242	Francisco A.	REYES	Rodríguez					PPAN			1
243	Susana Eugenia	RICHA	Humbert	de Torrijos				PRD	PRD		2
244	Melquíades	RIEGA	Wong			PL					1
245	Enrique	RILEY	Puga				PRD				1
246	Juan Miguel	RÍOS	González							PPAN	1
247	Alicio Atilio	RIVERA	L.		PRD						1
248	Franklin	RIVERA				PRD					1
249	Benicio Enacio	ROBINSON	Grajales			PRD	PRD		PRD	PRD	4
250	Raúl Eugenio	RODRÍGUEZ	Araúz						PRD		1
251	Antonino	RODRÍGUEZ	Gutiérrez						PRD		1
252	Tito	RODRÍGUEZ	Mena							PPAN	1
253	Magdalena	RODRÍGUEZ		de Durán	PRD						1
254	Olgalina Marisín	RODRÍGUEZ		de Quijada				PRD			1
255	Abel	RODRÍGUEZ					PRD				1
256	Mario	ROGNONI				PRD					1
257	Donato	ROSALES	Ortega				PRD				1
258	Jorge Rubén	ROSAS	Ábrego		MOLIRENA	MOLIRENA					2
259	Jorge Alberto	ROSAS	R.					MOLIRENA		MOLIRENA	2
260	Virgilio Antonio	SÁENZ	Sandoval		PL						1

Appendix E. (continued)

	First/ Second	Paternal Last	Maternal Last	Married	1984– 1989	1989– 1994	1994– 1999	1999– 2004	2004– 2009	2009– 2014	Number of Terms
261	Olimpo A.	SÁEZ	Marcucci			MOLIRENA					1
262	Jacobo Lorenzo	SALAS	Díaz		PPAN			PPAN			2
263	Miguel Lorenzo	SALAS	Oglesby							PPAN	1
264	Noriel	SALERNO	Estévez				PSOL	PSOL		UP	3
265	Serafín	SÁNCHEZ	González					PPAN			1
266	Miguel Peregrino	SÁNCHEZ					PRC				1
267	César	SANJUR					PRD				1
268	Eric Fidel	SANTAMARÍA				PDC					1
269	Carlos E.	SANTANA	Aizprúa				PPAN	PDC			2
270	Carlos Alberto	SANTANA	Rodríguez							PPAN	1
271	José del Carmen	SERRACÍN	Acosta				PPAN				1
272	Vianor E.	SERRACÍN			PDC						1
273	Felipe	SERRANO			PRD						1
274	Martín	SERRANO			PRD						1
275	Jorge Emilio	SIMMONS	Saldaña				PRD				1
276	Carlos José	SMITH	Smith				PRD	PRD			2
277	Rogelio	SOLANILLA	Tejeira		PPAN						1
278	Francisco Javier	SOLÍS			PRD						1
279	José Antonio	SOSSA				PDC					1
280	Lenín	SUCRE	Benjamín				PL	PPAN			2
281	Hirisnel	SUCRE	Serrano					PRD			1
282	Javier Filemón	TEJEIRA	Pulido					PLN	PLN		2
283	Sergio	TÓCAMO						PRD			1
284	José D.	TORRES	A.			PDC					1
285	Freidi Martín	TORRES	Díaz					PRD	PRD	PRD	3
286	Hugo	TORRIJOS	Herrera		PRD						1

Appendix E. (continued)

	Name				Terms						Number
	First/ Second	Paternal Last	Maternal Last	Married	1984– 1989	1989– 1994	1994– 1999	1999– 2004	2004– 2009	2009– 2014	of Terms
287	José Francisco	URRUTIA	B.					PPAN			1
288	Adolfo Tomás	VALDERRAMA	Rodríguez							PPAN	1
289	Ricardo Alejandro	VALENCIA	Arias							PPAN	1
290	Marylín Elizabeth	VALLARINO	Bartuano	de Sellhorn					PSOL	CD	2
291	Arturo Ulises	VALLARINO	Bartuano		PALA	MOLIRENA	MOLIRENA	MOLIRENA			4
292	Alejandro	VANEGAS	Rosero						PRD		1
293	José Luis	VARELA	Rodríguez				PPAN	PDC	PPAN	PPAN	4
294	Pablo	VARGAS	Caballero							PPAN	1
295	Alcibíades	VÁSQUEZ	Velásquez					PPAN	PPAN	PPAN	3
296	Orestes	VÁSQUEZ					UDI				1
297	Andrés	VEGA	Cedeño					PRD			1
298	Francisco Eloy	VEGA								PRD	1
299	Alonso O.	VILLARREAL	Pinzón			PDC					1
300	Franz Olmedo	WEVER	Zaldívar				PRD	PRD	PRD		3
301	Roberto	WILL	Guerrero				MPE				1
302	Jerry Vicente	WILSON	Navarro		PRD			PRD	PRD		3
303	Teresita de Jesús	YÁNIZ	Alonso	de Arias				PDC	PDC		2
304	Gloria del Carmen	YOUNG	Chizmaar				MPE	PPAN			2
305	José	YOUNG	Rodríguez		PR						1
306	Lucas Ramón	ZARAK	Linares			PLA	PPAN				2
307	Mayra Delania	ZÚÑIGA	Díaz						PRD		1
308	Eloy Antonio	ZÚÑIGA	Him						PRD		1
309	Edwin Alberto	ZÚÑIGA	Mencomo							PPAN	1

427

Source: Tribunal Electoral 1984a, 1984b, 1991a, 1991b, 1994b, 1994c, 1999b, 1999c, 2004b, 2009a.

Appendix F. Panama's Effective Number of Parties

Effective Number of Parties (ENP) in Panama's Assembly, 1984–2009

Party	Seats	Share (%)	Share^2	ENP
PRD	177	41	0.171826753	
PPAN	83	19	0.037783348	
PDC	42	10	0.009674819	
MOLIRENA	35	8	0.006718624	
CD	18	4	0.001777007	
PSOL	17	4	0.001585047	
PLA	11	3	0.000663636	
PALA	9	2	0.000444252	
MPE	6	1	0.000197445	
PLN	6	1	0.000197445	
UP	5	1	0.000137115	
PL	4	1	8.77535E-05	
PRC	4	1	8.77535E-05	
PR	3	1	4.93613E-05	
LIBRE	2	0	2.19384E-05	
VMP	1	0	5.48459E-06	
MORENA	1	0	5.48459E-06	
UDI	1	0	5.48459E-06	
Independents	2	0	2.19384E-05	
Total	427	100	0.23126875	4.323973724

Note: The formula for the effective number of assembly parties is: $1/S_i^2$, where S_i is the proportion of seats of each party that obtained a seat in the assembly (Lijphart 1999, 68). Accordingly, the fourth column gives the square of the share of seats for each party. The sum of the squares gives the denominator of the operation. The number 1 is then divided by this denominator to provide the ENP.

Appendix F. (continued)

Adjusted Effective Number of Parties (ADJ ENP) in Panama's National Assembly, 1984–2009

Party	Seats	Share (%)	Share2	ENP
PRD	178	42	0.173773783	
PPAN	87	20	0.04151287	
PDC	42	10	0.009674819	
MOLIRENA	35	8	0.006718624	
CD	21	5	0.002418705	
PSOL	18	4	0.001777007	
PLA	9	2	0.000444252	
PALA	8	2	0.000351014	
PLN	8	2	0.000351014	
MPE	6	1	0.000197445	
UP	5	1	0.000137115	
PL	3	1	4.93613E-05	
PRC	3	1	4.93613E-05	
PR	3	1	4.93613E-05	
MORENA	1	0	5.48459E-06	
Total	427	100	0.237510215	4.210345226

Note: The formula for the effective number of assembly parties is: $1/S_i^2$, where S_i is the proportion of seats of each party that obtained a seat in the assembly (Lijphart 1999, 68). Accordingly, the fourth column gives the square of the share of seats for each party. The sum of the squares gives the denominator of the operation. The number 1 is then divided by this denominator to provide the ENP. The ADJ ENP results from identifying the parties from and to which deputies of extinct parties migrated.

Appendix F. (continued)

Shifts from Extinct Parties (or Switches by Independents) in Panama,
1984–2009

Deputy Name	Year of Migration	From (extinct party)	To (surviving or new party)
Carlos Afú	1994	PALA	PRD
Rogelio Alba	1994	LIBRE	PLN
Alberto Cigarruista	1994	PLA	PPAN
Jaime Loré	1994	PL	PSOL
Juan Peralta	1994	LIBRE	PLN
Mario Quiel	1994	PLA	PL[a]
Orestes Vásquez	1994	UDI	PPAN
Lenín Sucre[b]	1994	PL	PPAN
José Carreño	1999	PRC	PPAN
Hernán Delgado	2009	VMP	CD
Carlos Afú	2009	Independent	CD
Yanibel Ábrego	2009	Independent	CD

Note: Factoring in these changes causes a drop in the ENP from 4.3 to 4.2.

Sources for all tables: A search through electronic newspaper archives of *Crítica Libre, El Siglo, El Panamá América, La Estrella de Panamá,* and *La Prensa* revealed these migrations; Lijphart 1999; Tribunal Electoral 1984a, 1984b, 1991a, 1991b, 1994b, 1994c, 1999b, 1999c, 2004b, 2008, 2009a.

[a] Partido Liberal (PL) was the name adopted by the extinct PLA when it re-registered in 1996. On this basis, Legislator Quiel actually remained in his original party.

[b] Legislator Sucre first adhered to MOLIRENA but subsequently sought reelection on the PPAN ticket. He was reelected and joined PPAN.

Appendix G. Electoral Volatility in Panama, 1984–2009

Electoral Volatility in Presidential Elections (Based on Votes), 1984–2009

Political Party	1984 Votes	1984 %	1989 Votes	1989 %	1994 Votes	1994 %	1999 Votes	1999 %	2004 Votes	2004 %	2009 Votes	2009 %	Electoral Volatility (%) 1984–1989	1989–1994	1994–1999	1999–2004	2004–2009	Mean Volatility (%)
PRD	175,749	27	120,564	19	326,095	31	403,649	32	649,157	43	553,974	35	4	6	1	6	4	4
CD							36,068	3	79,491	5	509,986	32				1	13	5
PPAN	221,363	34	2,750	0	211,780	20	367,865	29	162,830	11	293,554	19	17	10	4	9	4	9
MOLIRENA	30,738	5	132,011	20	115,478	11	140,240	11	60,106	4	94,841	6	8	5	0	3	1	3
UP											53,952	3					2	2
VMP											36,867	2					1	1
PDC	46,974	7	261,598	40	25,476	2	141,283	11	62,007	4	35,459	2	16	19	4	3	1	9
PL	28,597	4	12,718	2	46,775	4					7,794	0	1	1	2		0	1
PSOL					9,120	1	23,524	2	462,824	31					0	15	15	8
PLN							36,111	3	22,632	2						1	1	1
PRC					23,592	2	45,192	4							1	2		1
MORENA					32,122	3	28,544	2							2	1		1
PLA			69,779	11	43,797	4	25,579	2						1	1	1		2
MPE					182,405	17	20,217	2						8	9	1		6
PNP	15,992	2					10,196	1					1			0		1
PALA	46,726	7	35,264	5	17,046	2							1	2	1	1		1
LIBRE					12,166	1								1	1			1
MUN					9,304	1								0	0			0
UDI					8,020	1								0	0			0
PPD					3,668	0								0	0			0
PR	34,235	5	5,584	1									2	0				1
PP	11,595	2	5,533	1									0	0				0
PPR			2,919	0									0	0				0
PAN			1,463	0									0	0				0
PDT			855	0									0	0				0
PAPO	13,784	2											1					1
FRAMPO	5,327	1											0					0
PdP	4,600	1											0					0
PRT	3,973	1											0					0
PST	2,085	0											0					0
Totals	641,738	100	651,038	100	1,066,844	100	1,278,468	100	1,499,047	100	1,586,427	100	55	59	27	43	43	45

Appendix G. (continued)

Electoral Volatility in Elections for Assembly Members (Based on Votes), 1984–2009

Political Party	1984 Votes	%	1989 Votes	%	1994 Votes	%	1999 Votes	%	2004 Votes	%	2009 Votes	%	1984–1989	1989–1994	1994–1999	1999–2004	2004–2009	Mean Volatility (%)
PRD	153,182	25	114,741	19	236,319	23	393,356	32	549,948	38	537,426	36	3	2	5	3	1	3
CD			3,015	0			66,841	5	107,511	7	352,319	23			3	1	8	4
PPAN	124,562	20			150,217	15	266,030	22	279,560	19	334,282	22	10	7	4	1	1	5
UP											85,609	6					3	3
MOLIRENA	50,936	8	122,974	20	116,833	11	92,711	8	125,547	9	70,457	5	6	4	2	1	2	3
PDC	69,998	11	219,944	36	66,411	6	107,179	9	86,727	6	55,598	4	12	15	1	1	1	6
PL	36,040	6	17,712	3	35,516	3					18,111	1	2	0	2			1
VMP											14,760	1					0	0
PSOL					67,306	7	71,860	6	227,604	16				3		5	8	4
PLN							75,866	5	76,191	5						0	3	2
MORENA					68,581	7	42,996	3						3	2	2		2
PLA			61,916	10	31,045	3	41,588	3						3	0	2		2
PRC					57,590	6	37,705	3						4	1	2		1
MPE					99,760	10	21,841	2						5	4	1		3
PNP	12,596	2					11,506	1					1		0	0		1
PALA	74,430	12	47,775	8	28,172	3							2	3	1			2
MUN					27,017	3								1	1			1
LIBRE					24,979	2								1	1			1
UDI					13,106	1								1	1			1
PPD					10,720	1								1	1			1
PR	51,103	8	8,602	1									3	1				2
PdP	7,315	1	4,988	1									0					0
PPR			3,572	1									0					0
PAN			2,917	0									0					0
PDT			1,075	0									0					0
PAPO	8,471	1											1					1
PP	8,063	1											1	0				0
FRAMPO	7,813	1											1					1
PRT	3,545	1											0					0
PST	1,283	0											0					0
Independents											35,793	2					1	1
Totals	609,337	100	609,231	100	1,033,572	100	1,229,479	100	1,453,088	100	1,504,355	100	43	51	31	19	29	35

MEAN VOLATILITY IN ELECTIONS FOR PRESIDENT AND DEPUTIES 40%

Note: Thirty parties took part in all six elections held.

Sources for both tables: Comité de Apoyo 1989; Nohlen 1993; Tribunal Electoral 1984a, 1984b, 1991a, 1991b, 1994a, 1994b, 1994c, 1999b, 1999c, 2004b, 2009b, 2009c.

Appendix H. Difference in Votes for President and Assembly Members in Panama (Parties and Electoral Coalitions), 1984–2009

		1984				
Coalition	Political Party	President Votes	%	Deputies Votes	%	Absolute Difference (%)
Unión Nacional Democrática	PRD	175,749	27.0	153,182	25.1	1.9
(UNADE)	PALA	46,726	7.2	74,430	12.2	5.0
	PL	28,597	4.4	36,040	5.9	1.5
	PR	34,235	5.3	51,103	8.4	3.1
	PP	11,595	1.8	8,063	1.3	0.5
	FRAMPO	5,327	0.8	7,813	1.3	0.5
	PdP	4,600	0.7	7,315	1.2	0.5
1		306,829	47.1	337,946	55.5	8.3
Alianza Democrática de	PPAN	221,363	34.0	124,562	20.4	13.6
Oposición (ADO)	PDC	46,974	7.2	69,998	11.5	4.3
	MOLIRENA	30,738	4.7	50,936	8.4	3.6
2		299,075	45.9	245,496	40.3	5.6
3	PNP	15,992	2.5	12,596	2.1	0.4
4	PAPO	13,784	2.1	8,471	1.4	0.7
5	PRT	3,973	0.6	3,545	0.6	0.0
6	PST	2,085	0.3	1,283	0.2	0.1
Totals/Average Difference (parties)		641,738	100.0	609,337	100.0	2.5
Totals/Average Difference (coalitions)		641,738	100.0	609,337	100.0	2.5

		1989/1991				
Coalition	Political Party	President Votes	%	Deputies Votes	%	Absolute Difference (%)
Coalición de Liberación	PRD	120,564	18.5	114,741	18.8	0.3
Nacional (COLINA)	PALA	35,264	5.4	47,775	7.8	2.4
	PL	12,718	2.0	17,712	2.9	1.0
	PR	5,584	0.9	8,602	1.4	0.6
	PdP	5,533	0.8	4,988	0.8	0.0
	PPR	2,919	0.4	3,572	0.6	0.1
	PAN	1,463	0.2	2,917	0.5	0.3
	PDT	855	0.1	1,075	0.2	0.0
1		184,900	28.4	201,382	33.1	4.7
Alianza Democrática de	PDC	261,598	40.2	219,944	36.1	4.1
Oposición Civilista	MOLIRENA	132,011	20.3	122,974	20.2	0.1
(ADO-Civilista)	PLA	69,779	10.7	61,916	10.2	0.6
2		463,388	71.2	404,834	66.5	4.7
3	PPAN	2,750	0.4	3,015	0.5	0.1
Totals/Average Difference (parties)		651,038	100.0	609,231	100.0	0.8
Totals/Average Difference (coalitions)		651,038	100.0	609,231	100.0	3.2

Appendix H. (continued)

		1994				
	Political	President		Deputies		Absolute
Coalition	Party	Votes	%	Votes	%	Difference (%)
Pueblo Unido	PRD	326,095	30.6	236,319	22.9	7.7
	PALA	17,046	1.6	28,172	2.7	1.1
	LIBRE	12,166	1.1	24,979	2.4	1.3
1		355,307	33.3	289,470	28.0	5.3
Alianza Democrática	PPAN	211,780	19.9	150,217	14.5	5.3
	PL	46,775	4.4	35,516	3.4	0.9
	PLA	43,797	4.1	31,045	3.0	1.1
	UDI	8,020	0.8	13,106	1.3	0.5
2		310,372	29.1	229,884	22.2	6.9
3	MPE	182,405	17.1	99,760	9.7	7.4
Cambio '94	MOLIRENA	115,478	10.8	116,833	11.3	0.5
	MORENA	32,122	3.0	68,581	6.6	3.6
	PRC	23,592	2.2	57,590	5.6	3.4
4		171,192	16.0	243,004	23.5	7.5
5	PDC	25,476	2.4	66,411	6.4	4.0
Concertación Nacional	MUN	9,304	0.9	27,017	2.6	1.7
	PSOL	9,120	0.9	67,306	6.5	5.7
6		18,424	1.7	94,323	9.1	7.4
7	PPD	3,668	0.3	10,720	1.0	0.7
Totals/Average Difference (parties)		1,066,844	100.0	1,033,572	100.0	3.0
Totals/Average Difference (coalitions)		1,066,844	100.0	1,033,572	100.0	5.6

		1999				
	Political	President		Deputies		Absolute
Coalition	Party	Votes	%	Votes	%	Difference (%)
Nueva Nación	PRD	403,649	31.6	393,356	32.0	0.4
	PLN	36,111	2.8	75,866	6.2	3.3
	MPE	20,217	1.6	21,841	1.8	0.2
	PSOL	23,524	1.8	71,860	5.8	4.0
1		483,501	37.8	562,923	45.8	8.0
Unión por Panamá	PPAN	367,865	28.8	266,030	21.6	7.1
	MOLIRENA	140,240	11.0	92,711	7.5	3.4
	MORENA	28,544	2.2	42,996	3.5	1.3
	CD	36,068	2.8	66,841	5.4	2.6
2		572,717	44.8	468,578	38.1	6.7
Acción Opositora	PDC	141,283	11.1	107,179	8.7	2.3
	PLA	25,579	2.0	41,588	3.4	1.4
	PRC	45,192	3.5	37,705	3.1	0.5
	PNP	10,196	0.8	11,506	0.9	0.1
3		222,250	17.4	197,978	16.1	1.3
Totals/Average Difference (parties)		1,278,468	100.0	1,229,479	100.0	2.2
Totals/Average Difference (coalitions)		1,278,468	100.0	1,229,479	100.0	5.3

Appendix H. (continued)

		2004				
	Political	President		Deputies		Absolute
Coalition	Party	Votes	%	Votes	%	Difference (%)
Patria Nueva	PRD	649,157	43.3	549,948	37.8	5.5
	PDC	62,007	4.1	86,727	6.0	1.8
1		711,164	47.4	636,675	43.8	3.6
Visión de País	PPAN	162,830	10.9	279,560	19.2	8.4
	MOLIRENA	60,106	4.0	125,547	8.6	4.6
	PLN	22,632	1.5	76,191	5.2	3.7
2		245,568	16.4	481,298	33.1	16.7
3	PSOL	462,824	30.9	227,604	15.7	15.2
4	CD	79,491	5.3	107,511	7.4	2.1
Totals/Average Difference (parties)		1,499,047	100.0	1,453,088	100.0	5.9
Totals/Average Difference (coalitions)		1,499,047	100.0	1,453,088	100.0	9.4

		2009				
	Political	President		Deputies		Absolute
Coalition	Party	Votes	%	Votes	%	Difference (%)
Un País para Todos	PRD	553,974	34.9	537,426	35.7	0.8
	PDC	35,459	2.2	55,598	3.7	1.5
	PL	7,794	0.5	18,111	1.2	0.7
1		597,227	37.6	611,135	40.6	3.0
Alianza por el Cambio	CD	509,986	32.1	352,319	23.4	8.7
	PPAN	293,554	18.5	334,282	22.2	3.7
	MOLIRENA	94,841	6.0	70,457	4.7	1.3
	UP	53,952	3.4	85,609	5.7	2.3
2		952,333	60.0	842,667	56.0	4.0
3	VMP	36,867	2.3	14,760	1.0	1.3
4	Independents	0	0.0	35,793	2.4	2.4
Totals/Average Difference (parties)		1,586,427	100.0	1,504,355	100.0	2.5
Totals/Average Difference (coalitions)		1,586,427	100.0	1,504,355	100.0	2.7

Note: The period average of absolute difference for parties is 2.8, and for coalitions is 4.8.

Sources for all tables: Comité de Apoyo 1989; Nohlen 1993; Tribunal Electoral 1984a, 1984b, 1991a, 1991b, 1994b, 1994c, 1999b, 1999c, 2004b, 2009b, 2009c.

Appendix I. Consecutive Reelection and Party Switching in Panama, 1984–2009

Seated Assembly Members Seeking Reelection

	Name				1984–1989 Term			Reelection	
	First/Second	Paternal Last	Maternal Last	Married	Election Party Acronym	Survived?	Sought?	Party	Achieved
1	Rafael Clemente	ÁBREGO			PRD	Yes	No		
2	Emiliano	AGUILAR			PPAN	Yes	Yes	PPAN	No
3	Marco	ALARCÓN	Palomino		PPAN	Yes	Yes	PLA	No
4	Alberto	ALEMÁN	Boyd		PRD	Yes	Yes	PRD	Yes
5	Lorenzo Sotero	ALFONSO	Govea		PRD	Yes	No		
6	Tomás Gabriel	ALTAMIRANO	Duque		PRD	Yes	Yes	PRD	No
7	David	ARCE	Merel		PPAN	Yes	Yes	PPAN	No
8	Antonio	ARDINES			PRD	Yes	No		
9	Carlos Alejo	ARELLANO	Lennox		PDC	Yes	Yes	PDC	Yes
10	Antonio Manuel	ARIAS	Campagnani		PPAN	Yes	Yes	PDC	No
11	Francisco	ARTOLA	Araúz		PPAN	Yes	Yes	PLA	Yes
12	Florencio	ASPRILLA	Chávez		PALA	Yes	Yes	PALA	No
13	Carlos	BARSALLO			PRD	Yes	No		
14	Robustiano	BEITÍA	Lezcano		PPAN	Yes	No		
15	Heriberto Orlando	BERNAL	Marín		PRD	Yes	No		
16	Pedro Teodoro	BRIN	Martínez		PRD	Yes	No		
17	Celso Gustavo	CARRIZO			PRD	Yes	Yes	PRD	No
18	Ebén	CHI	Rodríguez		PRD	Yes	No		
19	Guillermo A.	COCHEZ	Farrugia		PDC	Yes	Yes	PDC	Yes
20	Gustavo Nelson	COLLADO			PALA	Yes	No		
21	Ernesto	CÓRDOBA	Campos		PR	Yes	Yes	PR	No
22	Omaira Judith	CORREA	Delgado		PALA	Yes	No		

Seated Assembly Members Seeking Reelection (continued)

	Name			1984–1989 Term				
				Election Party			Reelection	
First/Second	Paternal Last	Maternal Last	Married	Acronym	Survived?	Sought?	Party	Achieved
23 Justo	CORTÉS	Duarte		MOLIRENA	Yes	Yes	MOLIRENA	No
24 Santiago	CURABO	Ábrego		PRD	Yes	No		
25 Raúl E.	DELVALLE	Henríquez		PR	Yes	No		
26 Ovidio	DÍAZ	Vásquez		PRD	Yes	No		
27 Argénida Cecilia	DUMANOIR		de Barrios	PALA	Yes	Yes	PALA	No
28 Romelia	ESQUIVEL		de Pardo	PRD	Yes	Yes	PRD	No
29 Jaime Ricardo	FERNÁNDEZ	Urriola		MOLIRENA	Yes	No		
30 Hernán	GARCÍA	Franceschi		PPAN	Yes	Yes	PLA	No
31 Hugo Heberto	GIRAUD	Vernaza		PRD	Yes	No		
32 Luis Antonio	GÓMEZ	Pérez		PRD	Yes	Yes	PRD	No
33 Camilo	GOZAINE	Gozaine		PRD	Yes	Yes	PRD	No
34 Anselmo Lino	GUAINORA			PRD	Yes	Yes	PRD	No
35 Tomás Rafael	GUERRA	Caballero		PPAN	Yes	No		
36 Francisco Harmodio	ICAZA	Sánchez		PALA	Yes	Yes	PALA	No
37 Guillermo	JIMÉNEZ	Miranda		PRD	Yes	No		
38 Fabio Elías	JUÁREZ			PRD	Yes	No		
39 Dámaso	LOMBARDO	Bennett		PRD	Yes	Yes	PRD	No
40 Bertilo	MEJÍA	Ortega		PDC	Yes	Yes	PDC	No
41 Moisés	MELAMED			PRD	Yes	Yes	PRD	No
42 Otilio	MIRANDA			PALA	Yes	Yes	PALA	No
43 Jorge Elías	MONTEMAYOR	Abrego		PDC	Yes	Yes	PDC	Yes
44 Raúl de Jesús	MONTENEGRO	Diviazo		PRD	Yes	No		
45 José	MORRIS	Quintero		PRD	Yes	Yes	PRD	No

Seated Assembly Members Seeking Reelection (continued)

| | Name | | | | 1984–1989 Term | | | | |
| | First/Second | Paternal Last | Maternal Last | Married | Election Party | | | Reelection | |
					Acronym	Survived?	Sought?	Party	Achieved
46	Luis	NAVAS	Pájaro		PRD	Yes	No		
47	Mario J.	de OBALDÍA	Miranda		PPAN	Yes	Yes	PLA	No
48	Alfredo Armando	ORANGES	Bustos		PRD	Yes	No		
49	Raúl J.	OSSA	de La Cruz		PDC	Yes	Yes	PDC	Yes
50	César Augusto	PARDO	Rivera		PRD	Yes	Yes	PRD	No
51	Rigoberto	PAREDES	Solís		PRD	Yes	Yes	PRD	No
52	Emiliano José	PONCE	Arze		PPAN	Yes	No		
53	Simón	QUIRÓS	y Quirós L.		PPAN	Yes	No		
54	Alicio Atilio	RIVERA			PRD	Yes	No		
55	Magdalena	RODRÍGUEZ		de Durán	PRD	Yes	No		
56	Jorge Rubén	ROSAS	Ábrego		MOLIRENA	Yes	Yes	MOLIRENA	Yes
57	Virgilio Antonio	SÁENZ	Sandoval		PL	Yes	No		
58	Jacobo Lorenzo	SALAS	Díaz		PPAN	Yes	No		
59	Vianor E.	SERRACÍN			PDC	Yes	No		
60	Martín	SERRANO			PRD	Yes	Yes	PRD	No
61	Jorge Emilio	SIMMONS	Saldaña		PRD	Yes	No		
62	Rogelio	SOLANILLA	Tejeira		PPAN	Yes	No		
63	Francisco Javier	SOLÍS			PRD	Yes	Yes	PRD	No
64	Hugo	TORRIJOS	Herrera		PRD	Yes	Yes	PRD	No
65	Arturo Ulises	VALLARINO	Bartuano		PALA	Yes	Yes	MOLIRENA	Yes
66	Jerry Vicente	WILSON	Navarro		PRD	Yes	No		
67	José	YOUNG	Rodríguez		PR	Yes	Yes	PR	No
Total (N)							36		8
Total (%)							54		22

Seated Assembly Members Seeking Reelection (continued)

	Name				1989–1994 Term Election Party			Reelection	
	First/Second	Paternal Last	Maternal Last	Married	Acronym	Survived?	Sought?	Party	Achieved
1	Ramón	AIZPURÚA			PDC	Yes	No		
2	Aurelio A.	ALBA	Villarreal		PLA	Yes	No		
3	Alberto	ALEMÁN	Boyd		PRD	Yes	Yes	PRD	Yes
4	Alcibíades	ALVARADO	A.		PDC	Yes	Yes	PDC	No
5	Eliseo	ALVAREZ			MOLIRENA	Yes	Yes	MOLIRENA	No
6	Marco Antonio	AMEGLIO	Samudio		PLA	Yes	Yes	MORENA	Yes
7	Abelardo E.	ANTONÍO	Quijano		PRD	Yes	Yes	PRD	Yes
8	Carlos Alejo	ARELLANO	Lennox		PDC	Yes	No		
9	Gabriel	AROSEMENA	Jaén		PDC	Yes	Yes	PDC	No
10	Francisco	ARITOLA	Araúz		PLA	Yes	Yes	PPAN	No
11	Alexis	AYALA			PDC	Yes	No		
12	Anastasio	BATISTA	Z.		PDC	Yes	Yes	PDC	No
13	Mario	BOYD	Galindo		MOLIRENA	Yes	No		
14	Camilo	BRENES	Pérez		PDC	Yes	Yes	PDC	No
15	Miguel	BUSH	Ríos		PRD	Yes	Yes	PRD	Yes
16	Miguel A.	CÁRDENAS	Sandoval		MOLIRENA	Yes	No		
17	Carlos E.	CARRIZO	Alba		PDC	Yes	No		
18	Elías Ariel	CASTILLO	González		PRD	Yes	Yes	PRD	Yes
19	Gisela	CHUNG	A.		MOLIRENA	Yes	Yes	MOLIRENA	No
20	Alberto	CIGARRUISTA	Cortés		PLA	Yes	Yes	PLA	Yes
21	Guillermo A.	COCHEZ	Farrugia		PDC	Yes	Yes	PDC	No
22	Héctor	CRESPO	Barría		MOLIRENA	Yes	Yes	MOLIRENA	No
23	Edilberto	CULIOLIS	Carrión		PRD	Yes	No		
24	Alfredo	EHLERS			PDC	Yes	Yes	PDC	No

Seated Assembly Members Seeking Reelection (continued)

		Name			Election Party			Reelection	
	First/Second	Paternal Last	Maternal Last	Married	Acronym	Survived?	Sought?	Party	Achieved
25	Arnulfo	ESCALONA	Ríos		PLA	Yes	No		No
26	Carlos F.	ESCOBAR	R.		PDC	Yes	Yes	MORENA	No
27	Sebastián	ESCOBAR			PDC	Yes	No		
28	Alonso	FERNÁNDEZ	Guardia		MOLIRENA	Yes	Yes	PRC	No
29	Mario	FORERO	Mojica		MOLIRENA	Yes	Yes	MOLIRENA	Yes
30	Alcibíades	GARCÍA	C.		PDC	Yes	Yes	PDC	No
31	Roberto A.	GARIBALDO	Soto		MOLIRENA	Yes	Yes	MOLIRENA	No
32	Ernesto	GIRÓN	M.		PDC	Yes	Yes	PDC	No
33	Herman	GNAEGGI	Urriola		PLA	Yes	Yes	MOLIRENA	No
34	Leo A.	GONZÁLEZ	Delgado		MOLIRENA	Yes	Yes	MORENA	No
35	Gerardo	GONZÁLEZ	Vernaza		PRD	Yes	Yes	PRD	Yes
36	Gustavo G.	GUILLÉN	Peralta		PLA	Yes	No		
37	Milton Cohen	HENRÍQUEZ	Sasso		PDC	Yes	Yes	PDC	No
38	Balbina del Carmen	HERRERA	Araúz		PRD	Yes	Yes	PRD	Yes
39	José Rafael	HILL			PDC	Yes	Yes	PDC	No
40	Sylvan Keith	HOLDER	Williams		PDC	Yes	No		
41	Alberto T.	IBÁÑEZ	W.		MOLIRENA	Yes	No		
42	Raquel	LANUZA		de Francis	PDC	Yes	Yes	PDC	No
43	Ada Luz	LÓPEZ		de Gordón	PDC	Yes	Yes	PDC	No
44	Rolando H.	MARTINELLI	Della Togna		MOLIRENA	Yes	No		
45	Erasmo	MÉNDEZ	Mérida		PDC	Yes	No		
46	Nodier	MIRANDA[a]	Morales		PLA	Yes	Yes	PPAN	No
47	Jorge Elías	MONTEMAYOR	Abrego		PDC	Yes	No		
48	Domiluis	MONTENEGRO			MOLIRENA	Yes	Yes	MORENA	No

1989–1994 Term

Seated Assembly Members Seeking Reelection (continued)

	Name				Election Party			Reelection	
						1989–1994 Term.			
	First/Second	Paternal Last	Maternal Last	Married	Acronym	Survived?	Sought?	Party	Achieved?
49	Librado	MONTENEGRO			MOLIRENA	Yes	Yes	MOLIRENA	No
50	Gloria Maritza	MORENO		de López	PDC	Yes	Yes	MORENA	No
51	Luis Fidel	NARVÁEZ			MOLIRENA	Yes	No		
52	Raúl J.	OSSA	de La Cruz		PDC	Yes	No		
53	Ricardo	PÉREZ	C.		PDC	Yes	No		
54	Olmenares	QUIJANO	García		MOLIRENA	Yes	Yes	MOLIRENA	No
55	Anel José	RAMÍREZ			PALA	Yes	No		
56	Melquíades	RIEGA	Wong		PL	Yes	Yes	PL	No
57	Franklin	RIVERA			PRD	Yes	Yes	PRD	No
58	Benicio Enacio	ROBINSON	Grajales		PRD	Yes	Yes	PRD	Yes
59	Mario Adolfo	ROGNONI			PRD	Yes	Yes	PRD	No
60	Jorge Rubén	ROSAS	Abrego		MOLIRENA	Yes	Yes	MOLIRENA	No
61	Olimpo A.	SÁEZ	Marcucci		MOLIRENA	Yes	Yes	MOLIRENA	No
62	Eric Fidel	SANTAMARÍA			PDC	Yes	Yes	PDC	No
63	José Antonio	SOSSA	Rodríguez		PDC	Yes	Yes	PDC	No
64	José D.	TORRES	A.		PDC	Yes	No		
65	Arturo Ulises	VALLARINO	Bartuano		MOLIRENA	Yes	Yes	MOLIRENA	Yes
66	Alonso O.	VILLARREAL	Pinzón		PDC	Yes	No		
67	Lucas Ramón	ZARAK	Linares		PLA	Yes	Yes	PPAN	Yes
Total (N)							45		12
Total (%)							67		27

a Legislator Miranda died before the expiry of the term. He was replaced by his alternate, Jílmer González, who sought reelection in 1994 but did not succeed. Thus, for the purposes of this analysis, the name Nodier Miranda represents both Miranda and his alternate seeking reelection.

Seated Assembly Members Seeking Reelection (continued)

	Name				Election Party			Reelection	
						1994–1999 Term			
	First/Second	Paternal Last	Maternal Last	Married	Acronym	Survived?	Sought?	Party	Achieved
1	Roberto	ÁBREGO	Torres		PRD	Yes	Yes	PRD	Yes
2	Lorenzo	ACOSTA			PRD	Yes	No	PRD	Yes
3	Carlos Agustín	AFÚ	Decerega		PALA	No	Yes	PRD	Yes
4	Rogelio	ALBA	Filós		LIBRE	No	Yes	PLN	Yes
5	Alberto	ALEMÁN	Boyd		PRD	Yes	Yes	PRD	No
6	Tomás Gabriel	ALTAMIRANO[a]	Duque		PRD	Yes	Yes	PRD	Yes
7	Carlos Ramón	ALVARADO	Acosta		PRD	Yes	Yes	PRD	Yes
8	Edgardo	ALVAREZ			PRD	Yes	Yes	PRD	No
9	Marco Antonio	AMEGLIO	Samudio		MORENA	Yes	Yes	PPAN	Yes
10	Abelardo E.	ANTONIO	Quijano		PRD	Yes	Yes	PRD	Yes
11	Héctor Eduardo	APARICIO	Díaz		MOLIRENA	Yes	Yes	MOLIRENA	Yes
12	Denis	ARCE	Morales		PRD	Yes	Yes	PRD	Yes
13	Alfredo	ARIAS	Grimaldo		PPAN	Yes	Yes	PPAN	No
14	Daniel	ARIAS			PPAN	Yes	Yes	PDC	No
15	Rodrigo	AROSEMENA	de Roux		MOLIRENA	Yes	No		
16	Rubén Eloy	AROSEMENA	Valdés		PDC	Yes	Yes	PDC	Yes
17	Leopoldo Luis	BENEDETTI	Milligan		PPAN	Yes	Yes	PRC	No
18	Miguel	BUSH	Ríos		PRD	Yes	Yes	PRD	Yes
19	Alberto Magno	CASTILLERO	M.		PSOL	Yes	Yes	PSOL	Yes
20	Elías Ariel	CASTILLO	González		PRD	Yes	Yes	PRD	Yes
21	Alberto	CIGARRUISTA	Cortés		PLA	No	Yes	PPAN	Yes

Seated Assembly Members Seeking Reelection (continued)

		Name			Election Party			Reelection	
	First/Second	Paternal Last	Maternal Last	Married	Acronym	Survived?	Sought?	Party	Achieved
22	Laurentino	CORTIZO	Cohen		PSOL	Yes	Yes	PSOL	Yes
23	Juan	DELGADO			PRD	Yes	No		No
24	Jorge	DÍAZ			MPE	Yes	Yes	MPE	No
25	Mario	FORERO	Mojica		MOLIRENA	Yes	Yes	MOLIRENA	No
26	Joaquín Fernando	FRANCO	Vásquez		PPAN	Yes	Yes	PL	No
27	Enrique	GARRIDO	Arosemena		PPAN	Yes	Yes	PDC	Yes
28	Gerardo	GONZÁLEZ	Vernaza		PRD	Yes	Yes	PRD	No
29	Yadira	GONZÁLEZ			PRD	Yes	Yes	PRD	No
30	Olmedo	GUILLÉN			PRC	Yes	Yes	PDC	No
31	Balbina del Carmen	HERRERA	Araúz		PRD	Yes	Yes	PRD	Yes
32	Raymundo	HURTADO	Lay		MOLIRENA	Yes	Yes	CD	No
33	Aristides	de ICAZA	Hidalgo		PRC	Yes	Yes	PSOL	No
34	Mariela	JIMÉNEZ			MPE	Yes	Yes	PRC	No
35	Rodrigo	JOVANÉ			PPAN	Yes	Yes	PL	No
36	Manuel J.	de LA HOZ	Martínez		PRD	Yes	Yes	PRD	Yes
37	Olivia	de LEÓN		de Pomares	PRD	Yes	Yes	PRD	Yes
38	Víctor	LÓPEZ			PL	No	Yes	PRD	No
39	Jaime E.	LORÉ			MPE	Yes	Yes	PSOL	No
40	Víctor	MÉNDEZ	Fábrega		MPE	Yes	Yes	MOLIRENA	No
41	Haydée del Carmen	MILANÉS		de Lay	PSOL	Yes	Yes	PSOL	Yes
42	Mario Lewis	MILLER[b]	Byrnes		PRD	Yes	No		Yes

1994–1999 Term

Seated Assembly Members Seeking Reelection (continued)

	Name				Election Party		Sought?	Reelection	
	First/Second	Paternal Last	Maternal Last	Married	Acronym	Survived?		Party	Achieved
43	Enrique	MONTEZUMA	Moreno		PRD	Yes	Yes	PRD	Yes
44	Adolfo Elías	NAME	Tuñón		PRD	Yes	No		
45	Oydén	ORTEGA	Durán		PRD	Yes	No		
46	Manuel H.	ORTIZ	S.		PPAN	Yes	Yes	PDC	No
47	César Augusto	PARDO	Rivera		PRD	Yes	Yes	PRD	Yes
48	Bolívar	PARIENTE	Castillero		PPAN	Yes	Yes	PPAN	No
49	Juan Manuel	PERALTA	Ríos		LIBRE	No	Yes	PLN	No
50	Bernabé	PÉREZ	Frachiola		MPE	Yes	Yes	MPE	No
51	Luis Alejandro	POSSE	Martinz		PPAN	Yes	No		
52	Mario	QUIEL			PLA	No	Yes	PL	No
53	Pablo	QUINTERO	Luna		PPAN	Yes	Yes	PPAN	No
54	Enrique	RILEY	Puga		PRD	Yes	Yes	CD	No
55	Benicio Enacio	ROBINSON	Grajales		PRD	Yes	No	PRD	No
56	Abel	RODRÍGUEZ			PRD	Yes	Yes		
57	Donato	ROSALES	Ortega		PRD	Yes	Yes	PRD	No
58	Noriel	SALERNO	Estévez		PSOL	Yes	Yes	PSOL	Yes
59	Miguel Peregrino	SÁNCHEZ[c]			PRC	Yes	Yes	PRC	Yes
60	César	SANJUR			PRD	Yes	Yes	PRD	No
61	Carlos E.	SANTANA	Aizprúa		PPAN	Yes	Yes	PDC	Yes
62	José del Carmen	SERRACÍN	Acosta		PPAN	Yes	Yes	PDC	No
63	Felipe	SERRANO			PRD	Yes	No		

Seated Assembly Members Seeking Reelection (continued)

	Name				Election Party			Reelection	
	First/Second	Paternal Last	Maternal Last	Married	Acronym	Survived?	Sought?	Party	Achieved
						1994–1999 Term			
64	Carlos José	SMITH	Smith		PRD	Yes	Yes	PRD	Yes
65	Lenín	SUCRE	Benjamín		PL	No	Yes	PPAN	Yes
66	Arturo Ulises	VALLARINO	Bartuano		MOLIRENA	Yes	Yes	MOLIRENA	Yes
67	José Luis	VARELA	Rodríguez		PPAN	Yes	Yes	PDC	Yes
68	Orestes	VÁSQUEZ			UDI	No	Yes	PDC	No
69	Franz Olmedo	WEVER	Zaldívar		PRD	Yes	Yes	PRD	Yes
70	Roberto	WILL	Guerrero		MPE	Yes	Yes	MPE	No
71	Gloria del Carmen	YOUNG	Chizmaar		MPE	Yes	Yes	PPAN	Yes
72	Lucas Ramón	ZARAK	Linares		PPAN	Yes	Yes	PDC	No
Total (N)							63		31
Total (%)							88		49

[a] In 1994 Legislator Altamirano was concurrently elected as first vice-president of the republic. He resigned his seat in favor of his alternate (and son), Tomás Altamirano Mantovani, who sought and achieved reelection in 1999. Thus, for the purposes of this analysis, the name Tomás Altamirano Duque represents both Altamirano Duque and his alternate seeking reelection.

[b] Legislator Miller was tried and unseated in 1994. He was replaced by substitute Eleutería Baker, who did not seek reelection. Miller ran again in 1999, 2004, and 2009, winning reelection on this latter occasion.

[c] Legislator Sánchez died before the expiry of the term. He was replaced by his alternate, José Carreño, who sought and achieved election in 1999. Thus, for the purposes of this analysis the name Miguel Peregrino Sánchez represents both Sánchez and his alternate seeking reelection.

Seated Assembly Members Seeking Reelection (continued)

| | Name | | | 1999–2004 Term | | | | |
| | | | | Election Party | | | Reelection | |
First/Second	Paternal Last	Maternal Last	Married	Acronym	Survived?	Sought?	Party	Achieved
1 Roberto	ÁBREGO	Torres		PRD	Yes	Yes	PRD	No
2 Carlos Agustín	AFÚ	Decerega		PRD	Yes	Yes	PPAN	Yes
3 Edwin Alexis	AIZPURÚA			PPAN	Yes	Yes	PPAN	No
4 Rogelio	ALBA	Filós		PLN	Yes	Yes	PLN	Yes
5 Héctor Bolívar	ALEMÁN	Estévez		PRD	Yes	Yes	PRD	Yes
6 Francisco José	ALEMÁN	Mendoza		PPAN	Yes	Yes	PPAN	Yes
7 Tomás Gabriel	ALTAMIRANO	Mantovani		PRD	Yes	Yes	PRD	Yes
8 Carlos Ramón	ALVARADO	Acosta		PRD	Yes	Yes	PRD	Yes
9 Francisco José	AMEGLIO	Samudio		PPAN	Yes	Yes	PPAN	No
10 Marco Antonio	AMEGLIO	Samudio		PPAN	Yes	No		
11 Abelardo E.	ANTONÍO	Quijano		PRD	Yes	Yes	PRD	No
12 Héctor Eduardo	APARICIO	Díaz		MOLIRENA	Yes	Yes	MOLIRENA	Yes
13 Arturo Bolívar	ARAÚZ	Urriola		PLN	Yes	Yes	PLN	Yes
14 Denis	ARCE	Morales		PRD	Yes	Yes	PRD	No
15 Rubén Eloy	AROSEMENA	Valdés		PDC	Yes	Yes	PDC	Yes
16 Arcelio	BATISTA	Rivera		PRD	Yes	Yes	PPAN	No
17 Samuel	BINNS	Villagra		CD	Yes	No		
18 José Isabel	BLANDÓN	Figueroa		PPAN	Yes	Yes	PPAN	Yes
19 Miguel	BUSH	Ríos		PRD	Yes	No		
20 Felipe Antonio	CANO	González		PRD	Yes	Yes	PRD	No

Seated Assembly Members Seeking Reelection (continued)

	Name				Election Party			Reelection	
	First/Second	Paternal Last	Maternal Last	Married	Acronym	Survived?	Sought?	Party	Achieved
21	José Olmedo	CARREÑO	Araúz		PRC	No	Yes	PPAN	Yes
22	Mateo	CASTILLERO	Castillo		PRD	Yes	No		
23	Alberto Magno	CASTILLERO	M.		PSOL	Yes	Yes	PSOL	No
24	Julio César	CASTILLO	Gómez		PPAN	Yes	Yes	PPAN	No
25	Elías Ariel	CASTILLO	González		PRD	Yes	Yes	PRD	Yes
26	Jorge Ernesto	CASTRO	de Gracia		PRD	Yes	Yes	PRD	No
27	Omar E.	CHENG	Chang		PED	Yes	No		
28	Alberto	CIGARRUISTA	Cortés		PPAN	Yes	No		
29	Laurentino	CORTIZO	Cohen		PSOL	Yes	No		
30	José Luis	FÁBREGA	Polleri		PPAN	Yes	Yes	PSOL	Yes
31	Sergio Rafael	GÁLVEZ	Evers		CD	Yes	Yes	PPAN	Yes
32	Enrique	GARRIDO	Arosemena		PDC	Yes	Yes	PPAN	Yes
33	Osman Camilo	GÓMEZ			PPAN	Yes	Yes	PPAN	Yes
34	Elpidio	GONZÁLEZ	González		PPAN	Yes	Yes	PPAN	No
35	Pedro Miguel	GONZÁLEZ	Pinzón		PRD	Yes	Yes	PRD	Yes
36	Marcos Aurelio	GONZÁLEZ			PPAN	Yes	Yes	PPAN	No
37	Camilo	GOZAINE	Gozaine		PRD	Yes	Yes	PRD	No
38	Balbina del Carmen	HERRERA	Araúz		PRD	Yes	No		
39	José Ismael	HERRERA	González		PRD	Yes	Yes	PRD	No
40	Manuel J.	de LA HOZ	Martínez		PRD	Yes	Yes	PPAN	No

1999–2004 Term

Seated Assembly Members Seeking Reelection (continued)

1999–2004 Term

	Name			Election Party			Reelection	
First/Second	Paternal Last	Maternal Last	Married	Acronym	Survived?	Sought?	Party	Achieved
41 Rubén	de LEÓN	Sánchez		PRD	Yes	Yes	PRD	Yes
42 Olivia	de LEÓN		de Pomares	PRD	Yes	Yes	PRD	No
43 Eddy E.	LONDOÑO	G.		PRD	Yes	Yes	PRD	No
44 Vicente	MAGALLÓN	Arcia		PRD	Yes	Yes	PRD	No
45 Haydée del Carmen	MILANÉS		de Lay	PSOL	Yes	Yes	PPAN	No
46 Enrique	MONTEZUMA	Moreno		PRD	Yes	No		
47 José	MUÑOZ	Molina		PPAN	Yes	Yes	PSOL	Yes
48 César Augusto	PARDO	Rivera		PRD	Yes	Yes	PRD	Yes
49 Francisco A.	REYES	Rodríguez		PPAN	Yes	Yes	PPAN	No
50 Susana Eugenia	RICHA	Humbert	de Torrijos	PRD	Yes	Yes	PRD	Yes
51 Olgalina M.	RODRÍGUEZ		de Quijada	PRD	Yes	Yes	PRD	No
52 Jorge Alberto	ROSAS	R.		MOLIRENA	Yes	Yes	MOLIRENA	No
53 Jacobo Lorenzo	SALAS	Díaz		PPAN	Yes	Yes	PPAN	No
54 Noriel	SALERNO	Estévez		PSOL	Yes	Yes	PLN	No
55 Serafín	SÁNCHEZ	González		PPAN	Yes	Yes	PPAN	No
56 Carlos E.	SANTANA	Aizprúa		PDC	Yes	Yes	PPAN	No
57 Carlos José	SMITH	Smith		PRD	Yes	Yes	PRD	No
58 Lenín	SUCRE	Benjamín		PPAN	Yes	Yes	PPAN	No
59 Hirisnel	SUCRE	Serrano		PRD	Yes	No		No
60 Javier Filemón	TEJEIRA	Pulido		PLN	Yes	Yes	PLN	Yes

Seated Assembly Members Seeking Reelection (continued)

1999–2004 Term

	First/Second	Paternal Last	Maternal Last	Married	Acronym	Survived?	Sought?	Party	Achieved
		Name				Election Party		Reelection	
61	Sergio	TÓCAMO			PRD	Yes	No	PRD	Yes
62	Freidi Martín	TORRES	Díaz		PRD	Yes	Yes	PPAN	No
63	José Francisco	URRUTIA	B.		MORENA	No	Yes		
64	Arturo Ulises	VALLARINO[a]	Baruano		MOLIRENA	Yes	Yes	MOLIRENA	Yes
65	José Luis	VARELA	Rodríguez		PDC	Yes	Yes	PPAN	Yes
66	Alcibíades	VÁSQUEZ	Velásquez		PPAN	Yes	Yes	PPAN	Yes
67	Andrés	VEGA	Cedeño		PRD	Yes	No		
68	Franz Olmedo	WEVER	Zaldívar		PRD	Yes	Yes	PRD	Yes
69	Jerry Vicente	WILSON	Navarro		PRD	Yes	Yes	PRD	Yes
70	Teresita de Jesús	YÁNIZ	Alonso	de Arias	PDC	Yes	Yes	PDC	Yes
71	Gloria del Carmen	YOUNG	Chizmaar		PPAN	Yes	Yes	PPAN	No
	Total (N)					59			29
	Total (%)					83			49

[a] In 1999 Legislator Vallarino was concurrently elected as first vice-president of the republic. He resigned his seat in favor of his alternate, Wigberto Quintero, who sought and achieved election in 2004. Thus, for the purposes of this analysis the name Arturo Vallarino represents both Vallarino and his alternate seeking reelection.

Seated Assembly Members Seeking Reelection (continued)

	Name				Election Party			Reelection	
							2004–2009 Term		
	First/Second	Paternal Last	Maternal Last	Married	Acronym	Survived?	Sought?	Party	Achieved
1	Bernardo	ÁBREGO	Jiménez		PRD	Yes	Yes	PRD	No
2	Carlos Agustín	AFÚ	Decerega		PPAN	Yes	Yes	IND	Yes
3	Rogelio	ALBA	Filós		PLN	Yes	Yes	CD	No
4	Héctor Bolívar	ALEMÁN	Estévez		PRD	Yes	No		Yes
5	Miguel	ALEMÁN	Alegría		PRD	Yes	Yes	PRD	Yes
6	Francisco	ALEMÁN	Mendoza		PPAN	Yes	Yes	PPAN	Yes
7	Tomás Gabriel	ALTAMIRANO[a]	Mantovani		PRD	Yes	Yes	PRD	No
8	Jorge	ALVARADO	Real		PRD	Yes	Yes	PRD	No
9	Carlos Ramón	ALVARADO[b]	Acosta		PRD	Yes	No		
10	Héctor	APARICIO	Díaz		MOLIRENA	Yes	Yes	MOLIRENA	Yes
11	Arturo Bolívar	ARAÚZ	Urriola		PLN	Yes	Yes	UP	No
12	Denis	ARCE	Morales		PRD	Yes	Yes	PRD	Yes
13	Argentina Amabel	ARIAS	Torres		PPAN	Yes	No		
14	Juan Carlos	AROSEMENA	Valdés		PRD	Yes	Yes	PRD	Yes
15	Rubén Eloy	AROSEMENA[c]	Valdés		PDC	Yes	Yes	PDC	No
16	Leandro	ÁVILA			PRD	Yes	Yes	PRD	Yes
17	Alberto Efraín	BARRANCO	Pérez		PPAN	Yes	Yes	PPAN	No
18	José Belisario	BARUCO	Villarreal		PRD	Yes	No		
19	Rubén Darío	BEITÍA[d]	Vásquez		PSOL	Yes	Yes	UP	No
20	Leopoldo	BENEDETTI[d]	Milligan		PSOL	Yes	Yes	UP	No
21	Dalia Mirna	BERNAL	Yáñez		CD	Yes	Yes	CD	Yes
22	José Isabel	BLANDÓN	Figueroa		PPAN	Yes	Yes	PPAN	Yes
23	José	BROWN	Cuanwater		CD	Yes	Yes	CD	No

Seated Assembly Members Seeking Reelection (continued)

		Name			Election Party			Reelection	
	First/Second	Paternal Last	Maternal Last	Married	Acronym	Survived?	Sought?	Party	Achieved
24	José Olmedo	CARREÑO	Araúz		PPAN	Yes	Yes	PPAN	No
25	Benito	CASES	Jiménez		PRD	Yes	No		
26	Geovany Abad	CASTILLO	Berrío		PRD	Yes	No		
27	Elías Ariel	CASTILLO	González		PRD	Yes	Yes	PRD	Yes
28	Luis Carlos	CLEGHORN	Palomino		PPAN	Yes	Yes	PPAN	No
29	Milciades Abdiel	CONCEPCIÓN	López		PRD	Yes	No		
30	Dorindo Jayan	CORTÉS	Marciaga		PRD	Yes	No		
31	Pacífico	ESCALONA	Ávila		PPAN	Yes	No		
32	Agustín	ESCUDÉ^e	Saab		PRD	Yes	No		
33	José Luis	FÁBREGA	Polleri		PSOL	Yes	Yes	PRD	Yes
34	Miguel	FANOVICH	Tijerino		PPAN	Yes	Yes	PPAN	Yes
35	Olivares	FRÍAS			PRD	Yes	No		
36	Sergio	GÁLVEZ	Evers		PPAN	Yes	Yes	CD	Yes
37	Enrique	GARRIDO	Arosemena		PFAN	Yes	Yes	PPAN	No
38	Osman Camilo	GÓMEZ			PFAN	Yes	Yes	PPAN	Yes
39	Pedro Miguel	GONZÁLEZ	Pinzón		PRD	Yes	Yes	PRD	No
40	Manuel	GRIMALDO	Cañas		PPAN	Yes	Yes	PPAN	No
41	Yasmina Benilda	GUILLÉN	Anguizola	de O'Brien	PSOL	Yes	No		
42	Zulay	GUTIÉRREZ		de Vásquez	PRD	Yes	Yes	PRD	No
43	Juan	HERNÁNDEZ	Morales		PRD	Yes	Yes	PRD	No
44	Elizabeth	HERNÁNDEZ	Romero	de Quirós	PRD	Yes	Yes	PRD	No
45	Euribíades Vladimir	HERRERA	de León		MOLIRENA	Yes	Yes	IND	No
46	José Rafael	HILL			PRD	Yes	No		

2004–2009 Term

Seated Assembly Members Seeking Reelection (continued)

		Name			Election Party		Reelection		
	First/Second	Paternal Last	Maternal Last	Married	Acronym	Survived?	Sought?	Party	Achieved
47	Aristides	de ICAZA	Hidalgo		PSOL	Yes	Yes	CD	Yes
48	Nelson	JACKSON	Palma		PRD	Yes	Yes	PRD	Yes
49	Mireya del Carmen	LASSO	Pinzón	de Solís	PSOL	Yes	Yes	VMP	No
50	Rubén	de LEÓN	Sánchez		PRD	Yes	Yes	PRD	Yes
51	Iván Javier	LÓPEZ	Pérez		PRD	Yes	No		
52	Juvenal	MARTÍNEZ	Castillo		CD	Yes	Yes	PRD	No
53	Abraham	MARTÍNEZ	Montilla		PSOL	Yes	Yes	PRD	Yes
54	Danis Mireya	MONTEMAYOR	Cedeño		PPAN	Yes	No		
55	Patricio	MONTEZUMA	González		PRD	Yes	Yes	PRD	No
56	Marcelino Antonio	MUDARRA	Velásquez		MOLIRENA	Yes	No		
57	José	MUÑOZ	Molina		PSOL	Yes	Yes	CD	Yes
58	Maricruz Edith	PADILLA	Castillo	de Donado	PRD	Yes	Yes	PRD	No
59	César Augusto	PARDO	Rivera		PRD	Yes	No		
60	Rogelio Enrique	PAREDES	Robles		PRD	Yes	Yes	PRD	Yes
61	Juan Manuel	PERALTA	Ríos		PRD	Yes	No		
62	Hermisenda	PEREA	González		PRD	Yes	Yes	PRD	No
63	Yassir Abbobeker	PURCAIT	Saborío		PRD	Yes	Yes	PRD	Yes
64	Wigberto Esteban	QUINTERO	Gutiérrez		MOLIRENA	Yes	Yes	CD	No
65	Ezequiel	RAMÍREZ	Madero		PRD	Yes	Yes	PRD	No
66	Susana	RICHA	Humbert	de Torrijos	PRD	Yes	Yes	PRD	No
67	Benicio Enacio	ROBINSON	Grajales		PRD	Yes	Yes	PRD	Yes
68	Raúl Eugenio	RODRÍGUEZ	Araúz		PRD	Yes	Yes	PRD	No
69	Antonio	RODRÍGUEZ	Gutiérrez		PRD	Yes	No		

2004–2009 Term

Seated Assembly Members Seeking Reelection (continued)

	Name			Election Party		Sought?	Reelection	
First/Second	Paternal Last	Maternal Last	Married	Acronym	Survived?		Party	Achieved
70 Javier Filemón	TEJEIRA	Pulido		PLN	Yes	Yes	PPAN	No
71 Freidi Martín	TORRES	Díaz		PRD	Yes	Yes	PRD	Yes
72 Marylín Elizabeth	VALLARINO	Bartuano		PSOL	Yes	Yes	CD	Yes
73 Alejandro	VANEGAS	Rosero		PRD	Yes	Yes	PRD	No
74 José Luis	VARELA	Rodríguez		PPAN	Yes	Yes	PPAN	Yes
75 Alcibíades	VÁSQUEZ	Velásquez		PPAN	Yes	Yes	PPAN	Yes
76 Franz Olmedo	WEVER	Zaldívar		PRD	Yes	No		
77 Jerry	WILSON	Navarro		PRD	Yes	Yes	PRD	No
78 Teresita de Jesús	YÁNIZ[f]	Alonso	de Arias	PDC	Yes	No		
79 Eloy Antonio	ZÚÑIGA	Him		PRD	Yes	No		
Total (N)						57		26
Total (%)						72		46
Average (%) (1989, 1994, 1999, 2004, 2009)						73		39

[a] Deputy Altamirano died in 2009, in the midst of his reelection campaign. He was replaced as a deputy (and candidate) by his alternate, Tomás Altamirano Duque (his father), who lost the election. Thus, for the purposes of this analysis, the name Tomás Altamirano Mantovani represents both Altamirano Mantovani and his substitute seeking reelection.

[b] Deputy Alvarado died in 2008. He was succeeded by his alternate, Omar Chavarría, who did not run for election in 2009.

[c] In 2004 Deputy Arosemena was concurrently elected as second vice-president of the republic. He resigned his National Assembly seat but ran again for deputy in 2009. On this occasion he lost.

[d] PLN and PSOL merged in 2006 to form UP. Deputies from PLN and PSOL who ran for reelection on the UP ticked are counted as remaining in their original party. PLN and PSOL deputies migrating to other parties are counted as having switched.

[e] Deputy Escudé died in 2009. He was replaced by his alternate, Ramiro Villarreal, who did not run for election in 2009.

[f] After a prolonged lawsuit, the Supreme Court validated the reelection of Deputy Yániz in February 2009. She thus only served five months of the five-year term ending on June 30, 2009.

Parry Switches at Election Time

1989–1994 Term

#	First/Second	Name Paternal Last	Maternal Last	Married	Election Party Acronym	Survived?	Sought?	Reelection Party	Party Size
1	Marco Antonio	AMEGLIO	Samudio		PLA	Yes	Yes	MORENA	Similar
2	Carlos F.	ESCOBAR	R.		PDC	Yes	Yes	MORENA	Similar
3	Alonso	FERNÁNDEZ	Guardia		MOLIRENA	Yes	Yes	PRC	Smaller
4	Herman	GNAEGGI	Urriola		PLA	Yes	Yes	MOLIRENA	Larger
5	Leo A.	GONZALEZ	Delgado		MOLIRENA	Yes	Yes	MORENA	Smaller
6	Domiluis	MONTENEGRO			MOLIRENA	Yes	Yes	MORENA	Smaller
7	Gloria Maritza	MORENO		de López	PDC	Yes	Yes	MORENA	Similar

1994–1999 Term

#	First/Second	Name Paternal Last	Maternal Last	Married	Election Party Acronym	Survived?	Sought?	Reelection Party	Party Size
1	Marco Antonio	AMEGLIO	Samudio		MORENA	Yes	Yes	PPAN	Larger
2	Daniel	ARIAS			PPAN	Yes	Yes	PDC	Smaller
3	Leopoldo Luis	BENEDETTI	Milligan		PPAN	Yes	Yes	PRC	Smaller
4	Enrique	GARRIDO	Arosemena		PPAN	Yes	Yes	PDC	Smaller
5	Olmedo	GUILLÉN			PRC	Yes	Yes	PDC	Larger
6	Raymundo	HURTADO	Lay		MOLIRENA	Yes	Yes	CD	Similar
7	Aristides	de ICAZA	Hidalgo		PRC	Yes	Yes	PSOL	Larger
8	Mariela	JIMÉNEZ			MPE	Yes	Yes	PRC	Similar
9	Rodrigo	JOVANÉ			PPAN	Yes	Yes	PL	Smaller
10	Victor	MÉNDEZ	Fábrega		MPE	Yes	Yes	MOLIRENA	Larger
11	Manuel H.	ORTIZ	S.		PPAN	Yes	Yes	PDC	Smaller
12	Enrique	RILEY	Puga		PRD	Yes	Yes	CD	Smaller
13	Carlos E.	SANTANA	Aizprúa		PPAN	Yes	Yes	PDC	Smaller
14	José del Carmen	SERRACÍN	Acosta		PPAN	Yes	Yes	PDC	Smaller
15	José Luis	VARELA	Rodríguez		PPAN	Yes	Yes	PDC	Smaller
16	Gloria del Carmen	YOUNG	Chizmaar		MPE	Yes	Yes	PPAN	Larger
17	Lucas Ramón	ZARAK	Linares		PPAN	Yes	Yes	PDC	Smaller

Party Switches at Election Time (continued)

1999–2004 Term

	Name				Election Party			Reelection	
	First/Second	Paternal Last	Maternal Last	Married	Acronym	Survived?	Sought?	Party	Party Size
1	Carlos Agustín	AFÚ	Decerega		PRD	Yes	Yes	PPAN	Smaller
2	Arcelio	BATISTA	Rivera		PRD	Yes	Yes	PPAN	Smaller
3	José Luis	FÁBREGA	Polleri		PPAN	Yes	Yes	PSOL	Smaller
4	Sergio Rafael	GÁLVEZ	Evers		CD	Yes	Yes	PPAN	Larger
5	Enrique	GARRIDO	Arosemena		PDC	Yes	Yes	PPAN	Larger
6	Manuel J.	de LA HOZ	Martínez		PRD	Yes	Yes	PPAN	Smaller
7	Haydée del Carmen	MILANÉS	de Lay		PSOL	Yes	Yes	PPAN	Larger
8	José	MUÑOZ	Molina		PPAN	Yes	Yes	PSOL	Smaller
9	Noriel	SALERNO	Estévez		PSOL	Yes	Yes	PLN	Similar
10	Carlos E.	SANTANA	Aizprúa		PDC	Yes	Yes	PPAN	Larger
11	José Luis	VARELA	Rodríguez		PDC	Yes	Yes	PPAN	Larger

2004–2009 Term

	Name				Election Party			Reelection	
	First/Second	Paternal Last	Maternal Last	Married	Acronym	Survived?	Sought?	Party	Party Size
1	Carlos Agustín	AFÚ	Decerega		PPAN	Yes	Yes	IND	Smaller
2	Rogelio	ALBA	Filós		PLN	Yes	Yes	CD	Larger
3	José Luis	FÁBREGA	Polleri		PSOL	Yes	Yes	PRD	Larger
4	Sergio	GÁLVEZ	Evers		PPAN	Yes	Yes	CD	Smaller
5	Euribíades Vladimir	HERRERA	de León		MOLIRENA	Yes	Yes	IND	Smaller
6	Aristides	de ICAZA	Hidalgo		PSOL	Yes	Yes	CD	Larger
7	Mireya del Carmen	LASSO	Pinzón	de Solís	PSOL	Yes	Yes	VMP	Smaller
8	Abraham	MARTÍNEZ	Montilla		PSOL	Yes	Yes	PRD	Larger
9	Juvenal	MARTÍNEZ	Castillo		CD	Yes	Yes	PRD	Larger
10	José	MUÑOZ	Molina		PSOL	Yes	Yes	CD	Larger
11	Wigberto Esteban	QUINTERO	Gutiérrez		MOLIRENA	Yes	Yes	CD	Larger
12	Javier Filemón	TEJEIRA	Pulido		PLN	Yes	Yes	PPAN	Larger
13	Marylín Elizabeth	VALLARINO	Bartuano		PSOL	Yes	Yes	CD	Larger

Source for entire appendix: Tribunal Electoral 1984a, 1984b, 1991a, 1991b, 1994b, 1994c, 1999b, 1599c, 2004b, 2009b, 2009c.

Appendix J. Age of Panama's Assembly Members, 2004–9 and 2009–14 Terms

	First/Second	Paternal Last	Maternal Last	Married	Born	Started First Term	First Term Served	2004 Term	2009 Term
1	Bernardo	ÁBREGO	Jiménez		n.d.	2004			
2	Yanibel Yineva	ÁBREGO	Smith		1978	2009	31		31
3	Carlos Agustín	AFÚ	Decerega		1949	1994	45	55	60
4	Crispiano	ADAMES	Navarro		1961	2009	48		48
5	Rogelio	ALBA	Filós		1956	1994	38	48	
6	Francisco José	ALEMÁN	Mendoza		1955	1999	44		54
7	Héctor Bolívar	ALEMÁN	Estévez		n.d.	1999			
8	Miguel	ALEMÁN	Alegría		n.d.	2004			
9	Tomás Gabriel	ALTAMIRANO	Mantovani		1959	1999	40	45	
10	Carlos Ramón	ALVARADO	Acosta		1943	1994	51	61	
11	Jorge Enrique	ALVARADO	Real		1969	2004	35	35	
12	Abelardo Enrique	ANTONÍO	Quijano		n.d.	1989			
13	Héctor Eduardo	APARICIO	Díaz		1951	1994	43	53	58
14	Arturo Bolívar	ARAÚZ	Urriola		n.d.	1999			
15	Rony Ronald	ARAÚZ	González		n.d.	2009			
16	Denis	ARCE	Morales		1937	1994	57	67	72
17	Leopoldo Angelino	ARCHIBOLD	Hooker		n.d.	2009			
18	Argentina Amabel	ARIAS	Torres		1965	2004	39	39	
19	Rubén Eloy	AROSEMENA	Valdés		1960	1994	34	44	
20	Juan Carlos	AROSEMENA	Valdés		1963	2004	41		46
21	Jorge Iván	ARROCHA	Rosario		n.d.	2009			
22	Leandro	ÁVILA			n.d.	2004			
23	Iracema	AYARZA	Parra	de Dale	n.d.	2009			

Appendix J. (continued)

| | Name | | | | Year | | First Term | Age at Beginning of | |
	First/Second	Paternal Last	Maternal Last	Married	Born	Started First Term	Served	2004 Term	2009 Term
24	Alberto Efraín	BARRANCO	Pérez		n.d.	2004			
25	José Belisario	BARUCO	Villarreal		1961	2004	43	43	
26	Rogelio Agustín	BARUCO	Mojica		1940	2009	69		69
27	Rubén Darío	BEITÍA	Vásquez		1937	2004	67	67	
28	Leopoldo Luis	BENEDETTI	Milligan		1944	1994	50	60	
29	Dalia Mirna	BERNAL	Yáñez	de Gracia	1954	2004	50		55
30	José Isabel	BLANDÓN	Figueroa		n.d.	1999			
31	Francisco Javier	BREA	Clavel		n.d.	2009			
32	José	BROWN	Cuanwater		n.d.	2004			
33	José Olmedo	CARREÑO	Araúz		n.d.	1999			
34	Fernando Guillermo	CARRILLO	Silvestri		1965	2009	44		44
35	Benito	CASES	Jiménez		n.d.	2004			
36	Dana Daris	CASTAÑEDA	Guardia		n.d.	2009			
37	Elías Ariel	CASTILLO	González		n.d.	1989			
38	Geovany Abad	CASTILLO	Berrío		n.d.	2004			
39	Luis Carlos	CLEGHORN	Palomino		n.d.	2004			
40	Manuel	COHEN	Salerno		n.d.	2009			
41	Milciades Abdiel	CONCEPCIÓN	López		n.d.	2004			
42	Dorindo Jayan	CORTÉS	Marciaga		n.d.	2004			
43	Hernán	DELGADO	Quintero		1940	2009	69		69
44	Renaúl Alcónides	DOMÍNGUEZ	Villarreal		n.d.	2009			
45	Pacífico Manuel	ESCALONA	Ávila		n.d.	2004			
46	Agustín	ESCUDÉ	Saab		1960	2004	44	44	

Appendix J. (continued)

	Name				Year		Age at Beginning of		
	First/Second	Paternal Last	Maternal Last	Married	Born	Started First Term	First Term Served	2004 Term	2009 Term
47	José Luis	FÁBREGA	Polleri		n.d.	1999			
48	Miguel Angel	FANOVICH	Tijerino		n.d.	2004			
49	Guillermo Antonio	FERRUFINO	Benítez		1974	2009	35		35
50	Olivares	FRÍAS			n.d.	2004			
51	Rubén Darío	FRÍAS	Ortega		n.d.	2009			
52	Sergio Rafael	GÁLVEZ	Evers		n.d.	1999			
53	Irene	GALLEGO	Carpintero		1960	2009	49		49
54	Vidal	GARCÍA	Ureña		n.d.	2009			
55	Enrique	GARRIDO	Arosemena		n.d.	1994			
56	Osman Camilo	GÓMEZ			n.d.	1999			
57	Marcos Aurelio	GONZÁLEZ	González		n.d.	1999			
58	Pedro Miguel	GONZÁLEZ	Pinzón		1965	1999	34	39	
59	Manuel María	GRIMALDO	Cañas		1960	2004	44	44	
60	Yasmina Benilda	GUILLÉN	Anguizola	de O'Brien	n.d.	2004			
61	Zulay del Carmen	GUTIÉRREZ	Rodríguez	de Vásquez	1957	2004	47	47	
62	Elizabeth	HERNÁNDEZ	Romero	de Quirós	1954	2004	50	50	
63	Juan	HERNÁNDEZ	Morales		n.d.	2004			
64	Raúl Antonio	HERNÁNDEZ	López		1949	2009	60		60
65	Absalón	HERRERA	García		n.d.	2009			
66	Euribíades Vladimir	HERRERA	de León		n.d.	2004			
67	José María	HERRERA	Ocaña		n.d.	2009			
68	Aristides	de ICAZA	Hidalgo		1941	1994	53	63	68
69	Nelson	JACKSON	Palma		1966	2004	38	38	43

Appendix J. (continued)

	First/Second	Paternal Last	Maternal Last	Married	Born	Started First Term	First Term Served	2004 Term	2009 Term
		Name				Year		Age at Beginning of	
70	Victor Nelson	JULIAO	Toral	de Solís	1957	2009	42		42
71	Mireya del Carmen	LASSO	Pinzón	de Solís	n.d.	2004			
72	Luis Eduardo	LAY	Milanés		n.d.	2009			
73	Mario Augusto	LÁZARUS	Návalo		n.d.	2009			
74	Rubén	de LEÓN	Sánchez		1965	1999	34	39	44
75	Iván Javier	LÓPEZ	Pérez		n.d.	2004			
76	José Manuel	LOZADA	Morales		n.d.	2009			
77	Juan Antonio	MARTÍNEZ	Díaz		n.d.	2009			
78	Juvenal	MARTÍNEZ	Castrillo		n.d.	2004			
79	Abraham	MARTÍNEZ	Montilla		n.d.	2004			
80	Gabriel Enrique	MÉNDEZ	de La Guardia		n.d.	2009			
81	Mario Lewis	MILLER	Byrnes		n.d.	1994			
82	Danis Mireya	MONTEMAYOR	Cedeño		n.d.	2004			
83	Patricio	MONTEZUMA	González		n.d.	2004			
84	Hugo Alvin	MORENO	González		1957	2009	52	52	
85	Marcelino Antonio	MUDARRA	Velásquez		n.d.	2004			
86	José	MUÑOZ	Molina		n.d.	1999			
87	Maricruz Edith	PADILLA	Castrillo	de Donado	n.d.	2004			
88	César Augusto	PARDO	Rivera		n.d.	1984			
89	Rogelio Enrique	PAREDES	Robles		1957	2004	47	47	52
90	Juan Manuel	PERALTA	Ríos		n.d.	1994			

Appendix J. (continued)

	First/Second	Paternal Last	Maternal Last	Married	Born	Started First Term	First Term Served	2004 Term	2009 Term
		Name				Year		Age at Beginning of	
91	Hermisenda	PEREA	González		1959	2004	45	45	
92	Raúl Gilberto	PINEDA	Vergara		n.d.	2009			
93	Crescencia	PRADO	García		n.d.	2009			
94	Yassir Aboobeker	PURCAIT	Saborío		n.d.	2004			
95	Wigberto Esteban	QUINTERO	Gutiérrez		n.d.	2004			
96	Luis Eduardo	QUIRÓS	Bernal		1964	2009	45		45
97	Ezequiel	RAMÍREZ	Madero		n.d.	2004			
98	Salvador	REAL	Chen		n.d.	2009			
99	Susana Eugenia	RICHA	Humbert	de Torrijos	1924	1999	75	80	
100	Juan Miguel	RÍOS	González		1951	2009	58		58
101	Benicio Enacio	ROBINSON	Grajales		n.d.	1989			
102	Antonino	RODRÍGUEZ	Gutiérrez		n.d.	2004			
103	Raúl Eugenio	RODRÍGUEZ	Araúz		n.d.	2004			
104	Tito	RODRÍGUEZ	Mena		n.d.	2009			
105	Jorge Alberto	ROSAS	Rodríguez		n.d.	1999			
106	Miguel Lorenzo	SALAS	Oglesby		n.d.	2009			
107	Noriel	SALERNO	Estévez		n.d.	1994			
108	Carlos Alberto	SANTANA	Rodríguez		n.d.	2009			
109	Javier Filemón	TEJEIRA	Pulido		1964	1999	35	40	
110	Freidi Martín	TORRES	Díaz		1965	1999	34	39	
111	Adolfo Tomás	VALDERRAMA	Rodríguez		n.d.	2009			44

Appendix J. (continued)

#	First/Second	Paternal Last	Maternal Last	Married	Born	Started First Term	First Term Served	2004 Term	2009 Term
112	Ricardo Alejandro	VALENCIA	Arias		1988	2009	21		21
113	Marylín Elizabeth	VALLARINO	Bartuano	de Sellhorn	1956	2004	48	48	53
114	Alejandro	VANEGAS	Rosero		1956	2004	48	48	
115	José Luis	VARELA	Rodríguez		1952	1994	32	42	47
116	Pablo	VARGAS	Caballero		n.d.	2009			
117	Alcibíades	VÁSQUEZ	Velásquez		1962	1999	37	42	47
118	Francisco Eloy	VEGA			n.d.	2009			
119	Franz Olmedo	WEVER	Zaldívar		n.d.	1994			
120	Jerry Vicente	WILSON	Navarro		1943	1984	41	61	
121	Teresita de Jesús	YÁNIZ	Alonso	de Arias	1943	1999	56	61	
122	Edwin Alberto	ZÚÑIGA	Mencomo		n.d.	2009			
123	Eloy Antonio	ZÚÑIGA	Him		1947	2004	57	57	
124	Mayra Delania	ZÚÑIGA	Díaz		n.d.	2004			
	Averages						46	50	51

Source: Deputies biographies retrieved from National Assembly website on June 3, 2008, and March 31, 2010 (http://www.asamblea.gob.pa); newspaper searches (*La Prensa, El Panamá América, La Estrella de Panamá, El Siglo, Crítica Libre*); Tribunal Electoral 2004a, 2009a.

Note: Based on data from deputies who provided biographical information in the 2004–9 and 2009–14 terms. n.d. indicates that no biographical information was available for the deputy on the retrieval dates.

Appendix K. Gender and Social Origins of Individuals Proclaimed by the Electoral Tribunal as Elected Members of Panama's Assembly, 1984–2009

	Name					Constituency (Rural/Urban)	Membership in Union Club (Y = Yes)	Political Dynasty Member (Y = Yes)	Number of Terms Served
	First/Second	Paternal Last	Maternal Last	Married	Gender				
1	Bernardo	ÁBREGO	Jiménez		M	R			1
2	Yanibel Yineva	ÁBREGO	Smith		F	R			1
3	Roberto	ÁBREGO	Torres		M	U			2
4	Rafael Clemente	ÁBREGO			M	R			1
5	Lorenzo	ACOSTA			M	U			1
6	Crispiano	ADAMES	Navarro		M	U			1
7	Carlos Agustín	AFÚ	Decerega		M	R		Y	4
8	Emiliano	AGUILAR			M	U			1
9	Edwin Alexis	AIZPURÚA			M	U			1
10	Ramón	AIZPURÚA			M	U			1
11	Marco	ALARCÓN	Palomino		M	U			1
12	Rogelio	ALBA	Filós		M	R			3
13	Aurelio A.	ALBA	Villarreal		M	R			1
14	Miguel	ALEMÁN	Alegría		M	U		Y	2
15	Alberto	ALEMÁN	Boyd		M	U			3
16	Héctor Bolívar	ALEMÁN	Estévez		M	U			2
17	Francisco José	ALEMÁN	Mendoza		M	U	Y	Y	3
18	Lorenzo Sotero	ALFONSO	Govea		M	R			1
19	Tomás Gabriel	ALTAMIRANO	Duque		M	R	Y	Y	2
20	Tomás Gabriel	ALTAMIRANO	Mantovani		M	R	Y	Y	2
21	Alcibíades	ALVARADO	A.		M	R			1

Appendix K. (continued)

| | Name | | | | | Constituency | Membership in Union Club | Political Dynasty Member | Number of |
---	First/Second	Paternal Last	Maternal Last	Married	Gender	(Rural/Urban)	(Y = Yes)	(Y = Yes)	Terms Served
22	Carlos Ramón	ALVARADO	Acosta		M	R			3
23	Jorge Enrique	ALVARADO	Real		M	U	Y		1
24	Edgardo	ALVAREZ			M	U			1
25	Eliseo	ALVAREZ			M	U			1
26	Francisco José	AMEGLIO	Samudio		M	U	Y	Y	1
27	Marco Antonio	AMEGLIO	Samudio		M	U	Y		3
28	Abelardo Enrique	ANTONÍO	Quijano		M	R-U			4
29	Héctor Eduardo	APARICIO	Díaz		M	R		Y	4
30	Rony Ronald	ARAÚZ	González		M	R			1
31	Arturo Bolívar	ARAÚZ	Urriola		M	R			2
32	David	ARCE	Merel		M	U			1
33	Denis	ARCE	Morales		M	U			4
34	Leopoldo Angelino	ARCHIBOLD	Hooker		M	R			1
35	Antonio	ARDINES			M	R			1
36	Carlos Alejo	ARELLANO	Lennox		M	U			2
37	Antonio Manuel	ARIAS	Campagnani		M	U	Y	Y	1
38	Alfredo	ARIAS	Grimaldo		M	R	Y	Y	1
39	Argentina Amabel	ARIAS	Torres		F	U			1
40	Daniel	ARIAS			M	U			1
41	Gabriel	AROSEMENA	Jaén		M	R			1
42	Rodrigo	AROSEMENA	de Roux		M	U	Y	Y	1
43	Juan Carlos	AROSEMENA	Valdés		M	U	Y	Y	2

Appendix K. (continued)

	Name				Gender	Constituency (Rural/Urban)	Membership in Union Club (Y = Yes)	Political Dynasty Member (Y = Yes)	Number of Terms Served
	First/Second	Paternal Last	Maternal Last	Married					
44	Rubén Eloy	AROSEMENA	Valdés		M	U	Y	Y	3
45	Jorge Iván	ARROCHA	Rosario		M	R			1
46	Francisco	ARTOLA	Araúz		M	R			2
47	Florencio	ASPRILLA	Chávez		M	U			1
48	Leandro	ÁVILA			M	U			2
49	Alexis	AYALA			M	R			1
50	Iracema	AYARZA	Parra	de Dale	F	U			1
51	Alberto Efraín	BARRANCO	Pérez		M	U			1
52	Carlos	BARSALLO			M	R			1
53	Rogelio Agustín	BARUCO	Mojica		M	U			1
54	José Belisario	BARUCO	Villarreal		M	U			1
55	Arcelio	BATISTA	Rivera		M	R			1
56	Anastasio	BATISTA	Z.		M	U			1
57	Robustiano	BEITÍA	Lezcano		M	R			1
58	Rubén Darío	BEITÍA	Vásquez		M	R			1
59	Leopoldo Luis	BENEDETTI	Milligan		M	U	Y		2
60	Heriberto Orlando	BERNAL	Marín		M	R			1
61	Dalia Mirna	BERNAL	Yáñez	de Gracia	F	U			2
62	Samuel	BINNS	Villagra		M	R			1
63	José Isabel	BLANDÓN	Figueroa		M	U			3
64	Mario	BOYD	Galindo		M	R	Y	Y	1

Appendix K. (continued)

	Name					Membership in Union Club (Y = Yes)	Political Dynasty Member (Y = Yes)	Number of
	First/Second	Paternal Last	Maternal Last	Married	Gender	Constituency (Rural/Urban)		Terms Served
65	Francisco Javier	BREA	Clavel		M	R		1
66	Camilo	BRENES	Pérez		M	U		1
67	Pedro Teodoro	BRIN	Martínez		M	R		1
68	José	BROWN	Cuanwater		M	R		1
69	Miguel	BUSH	Ríos		M	U		3
70	Felipe Antonio	CANO	González		M	U		1
71	Miguel A.	CÁRDENAS	Sandoval		M	R		1
72	José Olmedo	CARREÑO	Araúz		M	R		2
73	Fernando Guillermo	CARRILLO	Silvestri		M	U		1
74	Carlos E.	CARRIZO	Alba		M	R	Y	1
75	Celso Gustavo	CARRIZO			M	R		1
76	Benito	CASES	Jiménez		M	R		1
77	Dana Daris	CASTAÑEDA	Guardia		F	R		1
78	Mateo	CASTILLERO	Castillo		M	R		1
79	Alberto Magno	CASTILLERO	M.		M	U		2
80	Geovany Abad	CASTILLO	Berrío		M	R		1
81	Julio César	CASTILLO	Gómez		M	R		1
82	Elías Ariel	CASTILLO	González		M	U		5
83	Jorge Ernesto	CASTRO	de Gracia		M	R		1
84	Omar E.	CHENG	Chang		M	R		1
85	Ebén	CHI	Rodríguez		M	R		1

Appendix K. (continued)

	First/Second	Paternal Last	Maternal Last	Married	Gender	Constituency (Rural/Urban)	Membership in Union Club (Y = Yes)	Political Dynasty Member (Y = Yes)	Number of Terms Served
86	Gisela	CHUNG	A.		F	U			1
87	Alberto	CIGARRUISTA	Cortés		M	R			3
88	Luis Carlos	CLEGHORN	Palomino		M	U			1
89	Guillermo A.	COCHEZ	Farrugia		M	U	Y		2
90	Manuel	COHEN	Salerno		M	U		Y	1
91	Gustavo Nelson	COLLADO			M	U			1
92	Milciades Abdiel	CONCEPCIÓN	López		M	U			1
93	Ernesto	CÓRDOBA	Campos		M	U			1
94	Omaira Judith	CORREA	Delgado		F	U			1
95	Justo	CORTÉS	Duarte		M	U			1
96	Dorindo Jayan	CORTÉS	Marciaga		M	U			1
97	Laurentino	CORTIZO	Cohen		M	R	Y		2
98	Héctor	CRESPO	Barría		M	R		Y	1
99	Edilberto	CULIOLIS	Carrión		M	R			1
100	Santiago	CURABO	Ábrego		M	R			1
101	Hernán	DELGADO	Quintero		M	R			1
102	Juan	DELGADO			M	R			1
103	Raúl E.	DELVALLE	Henríquez		M	R	Y	Y	1
104	Ovidio	DíAZ	Vásquez		M	R			1
105	Jorge	DíAZ			M	U			1
106	Renaúl Alcónides	DOMÍNGUEZ	Villarreal		M	R			1

Appendix K. (continued)

	First/Second	Paternal Last	Maternal Last	Married	Gender	Constituency (Rural/Urban)	Membership in Union Club (Y = Yes)	Political Dynasty Member (Y = Yes)	Number of Terms Served
107	Argénida Cecilia	DUMANOIR		de Barrios	F	U			1
108	Alfredo	EHLERS			M	U			1
109	Pacífico Manuel	ESCALONA	Ávila		M	U		Y	1
110	Arnulfo	ESCALONA	Ríos		M	U		Y	1
111	Carlos F.	ESCOBAR	R.		M	U			1
112	Sebastián	ESCOBAR			M	R			1
113	Agustín	ESCUDÉ	Saab		M	U			1
114	Romelia	ESQUIVEL		de Pardo	F	U			1
115	José Luis	FÁBREGA	Polleri		M	U	Y	Y	3
116	Miguel Angel	FANOVICH	Tijerino		M	U			2
117	Alonso	FERNÁNDEZ	Guardia		M	U		Y	1
118	Jaime Ricardo	FERNÁNDEZ	Urriola		M	U	Y	Y	1
119	Guillermo Antonio	FERRUFINO	Benítez		M	U			1
120	Mario	FORERO	Mojica		M	R			2
121	Joaquín Fernando	FRANCO	Vásquez		M	R	Y		1
122	Rubén Darío	FRÍAS	Ortega		M	U			1
123	Olivares	FRÍAS			M	R			1
124	Irene	GALLEGO	Carpintero		M	R			1
125	Sergio Rafael	GÁLVEZ	Evers		M	U			3
126	Alcibíades	GARCÍA	C.		M	R			1
127	Hernán	GARCÍA	Franceschi		M	R			1

Appendix K. (continued)

| | Name | | | | | | Membership in Union Club | Political Dynasty Member | Number of |
	First/Second	Paternal Last	Maternal Last	Married	Gender	Constituency (Rural/Urban)	(Y = Yes)	(Y = Yes)	Terms Served
128	Vidal	GARCÍA	Ureña		M	U			1
129	Roberto A.	GARIBALDO	Soto		M	R			1
130	Enrique	GARRIDO	Arosemena		M	R			3
131	Hugo Heberto	GIRAUD	Vernaza		M	R			1
132	Ernesto	GIRÓN	M.		M	R			1
133	Herman	GNAEGGI	Urriola		M	R			1
134	Luis Antonio	GÓMEZ	Pérez		M	U			1
135	Osman Camilo	GÓMEZ			M	U			3
136	Leo A.	GONZÁLEZ	Delgado		M	U	Y		1
137	Elpidio	GONZÁLEZ	González		M	U			1
138	Pedro Miguel	GONZÁLEZ	Pinzón		M	R		Y	2
139	Gerardo	GONZÁLEZ	Vernaza		M	U		Y	2
140	Yadira	GONZÁLEZ			F	U			1
141	Marcos Aurelio	GONZÁLEZ			M	U			2
142	Camilo	GOZAINE	Gozaine		M	U			2
143	Manuel María	GRIMALDO	Cañas		M	U			1
144	Anselmo Lino	GUAINORA			M	R			1
145	Tomás Rafael	GUERRA	Caballero		M	U			1
146	Yasmina Benilda	GUILLÉN	Anguizola	de O'Brien	F	R			1
147	Gustavo G.	GUILLÉN	Peralta		M	R			1
148	Olmedo	GUILLÉN			M	U			1

Appendix K. (continued)

	First/Second	Paternal Last	Maternal Last	Married	Gender	Constituency (Rural/Urban)	Membership in Union Club (Y = Yes)	Political Dynasty Member (Y = Yes)	Number of Terms Served
149	Zulay del Carmen	GUTIÉRREZ	Rodríguez	de Vásquez	F	R			1
150	Milton Cohen	HENRÍQUEZ	Sasso		M	U	Y		1
151	Raúl Antonio	HERNÁNDEZ	López		M	R	Y		1
152	Juan	HERNÁNDEZ	Morales		M	U			1
153	Elizabeth	HERNÁNDEZ	Romero	de Quirós	F	U			1
154	Balbina del Carmen	HERRERA	Araúz		F	U			3
155	Absalón	HERRERA	García		M	R			1
156	José Ismael	HERRERA	González		M	R			1
157	Euriblades Vladimir	HERRERA	de León		M	U			1
158	José María	HERRERA	Ocaña		M	R		Y	1
159	José Rafael	HILL			M	U			1
160	Sylvan Keith	HOLDER	Williams		M	U			1
161	Raymundo	HURTADO	Lay		M	U			1
162	Alberto T.	IBÁÑEZ	W.		M	R			1
163	Aristides	de ICAZA	Hidalgo		M	U			3
164	Francisco Harmodio	ICAZA	Sánchez		M	U			1
165	Nelson	JACKSON	Palma		M	R			2
166	Guillermo	JIMÉNEZ	Miranda		M	R			1
167	Mariela	JIMÉNEZ			F	U			1
168	Rodrigo	JOVANÉ			M	R			1

Appendix K. (continued)

	Name						Membership in Union Club (Y = Yes)	Political Dynasty Member (Y = Yes)	Number of Terms Served
	First/Second	Paternal Last	Maternal Last	Married	Gender	Constituency (Rural/Urban)			
169	Fabio Elías	JUÁREZ			M	R			1
170	Víctor Nelson	JULIAO	Toral		M	U		Y	1
171	Manuel J.	de LA HOZ	Martínez		M	U			2
172	Raquel	LANUZA		de Francis	F	U			1
173	Mireya del Carmen	LASSO	Pinzón	de Solís	F	U	Y		1
174	Luis Eduardo	LAY	Milanés		M	R		Y	1
175	Mario Augusto	LÁZARUS	Návalo		M	U			1
176	Rubén	de LEÓN	Sánchez		M	R			3
177	Olivia	de LEÓN		de Pomares	F	U			2
178	Dámaso	LOMBARDO	Bennett		M	R			1
179	Eddy E.	LONDOÑO	G.		M	R			1
180	Iván Javier	LÓPEZ	Pérez		M	R			1
181	Ada L.	LÓPEZ		de Gordón	F	U			1
182	Víctor	LÓPEZ			M	U			1
183	Jaime E.	LORÉ			M	R			1
184	José Manuel	LOZADA	Morales		M	R			1
185	Vicente	MAGALLÓN	Arcia		M	U			1
186	Rolando H.	MARTINELLI	Della Togna		M	R	Y	Y	1
187	Juvenal	MARTÍNEZ	Castillo		M	R			1
188	Juan Antonio	MARTÍNEZ	Díaz		M	R			1

338 | Appendix K

Appendix K. (continued)

	Name				Gender	Constituency (Rural/Urban)	Membership in Union Club (Y = Yes)	Political Dynasty Member (Y = Yes)	Number of Terms Served
	First/Second	Paternal Last	Maternal Last	Married					
189	Abraham	MARTÍNEZ	Montilla		M	U			2
190	Berrilo	MEJÍA	Ortega		M	U			1
191	Moisés	MELAMED			M	R			1
192	Víctor	MÉNDEZ	Fábrega		M	U	Y	Y	1
193	Gabriel Enrique	MÉNDEZ	de La Guardia		M	U	Y	Y	1
194	Erasmo	MÉNDEZ	Mérida		M	R		Y	1
195	Haydée del Carmen	MILANÉS		de Lay	F	R			2
196	Mario	MILLER			M	R			2
197	Nodier	MIRANDA	Morales		M	R		Y	1
198	Otilio	MIRANDA			M	R			1
199	Jorge Elías	MONTEMAYOR	Ábrego		M	R			2
200	Danis Mireya	MONTEMAYOR	Cedeño		F	R			1
201	Raúl de Jesús	MONTENEGRO	Diviazo		M	U	Y		1
202	Domiluis	MONTENEGRO			M	R			1
203	Librado	MONTENEGRO			M	U			1
204	Patricio	MONTEZUMA	González		M	R			1
205	Enrique	MONTEZUMA	Moreno		M	R			2
206	Hugo Alvin	MORENO	González		M	R			1
207	Gloria Maritza	MORENO		de López	F	U			1
208	José	MORRIS	Quintero		M	U			1
209	Marcelino Antonio	MUDARRA	Velásquez		M	R			1

Appendix K. (continued)

	First/Second	Paternal Last	Maternal Last	Married	Gender	Constituency (Rural/Urban)	Membership in Union Club (Y = Yes)	Political Dynasty Member (Y = Yes)	Number of Terms Served
210	José	MUÑOZ	Molina		M	U			3
211	Adolfo Elías	NAME	Tuñón		M	R			1
212	Luis Fidel	NARVÁEZ			M	R			1
213	Luis	NAVAS	Pájaro		M	U			1
214	Mario J.	de OBALDÍA	Miranda		M	U	Y	Y	1
215	Alfredo Armando	ORANGES	Bustos		M	U			1
216	Oydén	ORTEGA	Durán		M	U			1
217	Manuel H.	ORTIZ	S.		M	R			1
218	Raúl J.	OSSA	de La Cruz		M	U			2
219	Maricruz Edith	PADILLA	Castillo	de Donado	F	U			1
220	César Augusto	PARDO	Rivera		M	R			4
221	Rogelio Enrique	PAREDES	Robles		M	U		Y	2
222	Rigoberto	PAREDES	Solís		M	U			1
223	Bolívar	PARIENTE	Castrillero		M	R			1
224	Juan Manuel	PERALTA	Ríos		M	R			2
225	Hermisenda	PEREA	González		F	U			1
226	Ricardo	PÉREZ	C.		M	U			1
227	Bernabé	PÉREZ	Frachiola		M	U			1
228	Raúl Gilberto	PINEDA	Vergara		M	U			1
229	Emiliano José	PONCE	Arze		M	R	Y	Y	1
230	Luis Alejandro	POSSE	Martinz		M	R	Y		1

Appendix K. (continued)

	First/Second	Paternal Last	Maternal Last	Married	Gender	Constituency (Rural/Urban)	Membership in Union Club (Y = Yes)	Political Dynasty Member (Y = Yes)	Number of Terms Served
231	Crescencia	PRADO	García		F	R			1
232	Yassir Aboobeker	PURCAIT	Saborío		M	U			2
233	Mario	QUIEL			M	R			1
234	Olmenares	QUIJANO	G.		M	R			1
235	Wigberto Esteban	QUINTERO	Gutiérrez		M	U			1
236	Pablo	QUINTERO	Luna		M	R			1
237	Luis Eduardo	QUIRÓS	Bernal		M	U		Y	1
238	Simón	QUIRÓS	y Quirós		M	U			1
239	Ezequiel	RAMÍREZ	Madero		M	R			1
240	Anel José	RAMÍREZ			M	R			1
241	Salvador	REAL	Chen		M	R			1
242	Francisco A.	REYES	Rodríguez		M	U			1
243	Susana Eugenia	RICHA	Humbert	de Torrijos	F	U		Y	2
244	Melquíades	RIEGA	W.		M	R			1
245	Enrique	RILEY	Puga		M	R			1
246	Juan Miguel	RÍOS	González		M	R			1
247	Alicio Atilio	RIVERA	I.		M	R			1
248	Franklyn	RIVERA			M	U			1
249	Benicio Enacio	ROBINSON	Grajales		M	R			4
250	Raúl Eugenio	RODRÍGUEZ	Araúz		M	R			1
251	Antonino	RODRÍGUEZ	Gutiérrez		M	R			1

Appendix K. (continued)

	First/Second	Name Paternal Last	Maternal Last	Married	Gender	Constituency (Rural/Urban)	Membership in Union Club (Y = Yes)	Political Dynasty Member (Y = Yes)	Number of Terms Served
252	Tito	RODRÍGUEZ	Mena		M	U			1
253	Magdalena	RODRÍGUEZ		de Durán	F	R			1
254	Olgalina M.	RODRÍGUEZ		de Quijada	F	U			1
255	Abel	RODRÍGUEZ			M	U			1
256	Mario	ROGNONI			M	U	Y		1
257	Donato	ROSALES	Ortega		M	U			1
258	Jorge Alberto	ROSAS	Rodríguez		M	R		Y	2
259	Jorge Rubén	ROSAS			M	R			2
260	Virgilio Antonio	SÁENZ	Sandoval		M	R			1
261	Olimpo A.	SÁEZ	Marcucci		M	U			1
262	Jacobo Lorenzo	SALAS	Díaz		M	U			2
263	Miguel Lorenzo	SALAS	Oglesby		M	U		Y	1
264	Noriel	SALERNO	Estévez		M	R			2
265	Serafín	SÁNCHEZ	González		M	R			1
266	Miguel Peregrino	SÁNCHEZ			M	R			1
267	César	SANJUR			M	U			1
268	Eric Fidel	SANTAMARÍA			M	R			1
269	Carlos E.	SANTANA	Aizprúa		M	R			1
270	Carlos Alberto	SANTANA	Rodríguez		M	R			1
271	José del Carmen	SERRACÍN	Acosta		M	U			1
272	Vianor E.	SERRACÍN			M	U			1

Appendix K. (continued)

	Name			Gender	Constituency (Rural/Urban)	Membership in Union Club (Y = Yes)	Political Dynasty Member (Y = Yes)	Number of Terms Served
	First/Second	Paternal Last	Maternal Last	Married					
273	Felipe	SERRANO			M	R			1
274	Martín	SERRANO			M	R			1
275	Jorge Emilio	SIMMONS	Saldaña		M	U			1
276	Carlos José	SMITH	Smith		M	U			2
277	Rogelio	SOLANILLA	Tejeira		M	R			1
278	Francisco Javier	SOLÍS			M	R			1
279	José Antonio	SOSSA			M	U			1
280	Lenín	SUCRE	Benjamín		M	U	Y	Y	2
281	Hirisnel	SUCRE	Serrano		M	R		Y	1
282	Javier Filemón	TEJEIRA	Pulido		M	R		Y	2
283	Sergio	TÓCAMO			M	R			1
284	José D.	TORRES	A.		M	U			1
285	Freidi Martín	TORRES	Díaz		M	R			3
286	Hugo	TORRIJOS	Herrera		M	U		Y	1
287	José Francisco	URRUTIA	B.		M	R			1
288	Adolfo Tomás	VALDERRAMA	Rodríguez		M	U			1
289	Ricardo Alejandro	VALENCIA	Arias		M	U		Y	1
290	Marylín Elizabeth	VALLARINO	Baruano	de Sellhorn	F	U		Y	2
291	Arturo Ulises	VALLARINO	Baruano		M	U		Y	4
292	Alejandro	VANEGAS	Rosero		M	U			1
293	José Luis	VARELA	Rodríguez		M	R	Y	Y	4
294	Pablo	VARGAS	Caballero		M	R			1

Appendix K. (continued)

	Name				Gender	Constituency (Rural/Urban)	Membership in Union Club (Y = Yes)	Political Dynasty Member (Y = Yes)	Number of Terms Served
	First/Second	Paternal Last	Maternal Last	Married					
295	Alcibíades	VÁSQUEZ	Velásquez		M	U			3
296	Orestes	VÁSQUEZ			M	R			1
297	Andrés	VEGA	Cedeño		M	U			1
298	Francisco Eloy	VEGA			M	R			1
299	Alonso O.	VILLARREAL	Pinzón		M	U			1
300	Franz Olmedo	WEVER	Zaldívar		M	U			3
301	Roberto	WILL	Guerrero		M	U			1
302	Jerry Vicente	WILSON	Navarro		M	U			3
303	Teresita de Jesús	YÁNIZ	Alonso	de Arias	F	U	Y		2
304	Gloria del Carmen	YOUNG	Chizmaar		F	U			2
305	José	YOUNG	Rodríguez		M	U			1
306	Lucas Ramón	ZARAK	Linares		M	U	Y	Y	2
307	Mayra Delania	ZÚÑIGA	Díaz		F	U		Y	1
308	Eloy Antonio	ZÚÑIGA	Him		M	R		Y	3
309	Edwin Alberto	ZÚÑIGA	Mencomo		M	U		Y	1
Total Women					32				
Total Urban						160			
Total Union Club Members							35		
Total Political Dynasty Members								51	
Total Seats									427

Source: Marlina Morán, email to the author, March 2, 2007; Rita Preciado Recuero, email to the author, April 28, 2010; Tribunal Electoral 1984a, 1984b, 1991a, 1991b, 1994b, 1994c, 1999b, 1999c, 2004b, 2008, 2009a.

Appendix L. Geodemographic Segmentation of Panama's Electoral Constituencies, 1984–2009

			Member			
	Constituency	*Urban/*	*1984–1989*		*1989–1994*	
Number	*Name*	*Rural*	*Name*	*Party*	*Name*	*Party*
1.1	Changuinola, parts of Bocas del Toro District (all of Bocas del Toro Province in 2004 and after)	Rural	Francisco ARTOLA	PPAN	Francisco ARTOLA	PPAN
1.2	Chiriquí Grande, parts of Bocas del Toro District	Rural	Santiago CURABO	PRD	Benicio ROBINSON	PRD
2.1	Penonomé	Rural	Rogelio SOLANILLA	PPAN	Alberto IBÁÑEZ	MOLIRENA
			César PARDO	PRD	Gabriel AROSEMENA	PDC
2.2	Antón	Rural	Emiliano PONCE	PPAN	Mario BOYD	MOLIRENA
2.3	La Pintada, Olá, Natá	Rural	Virgilio SÁENZ	PL	Herman GNAEGGI	PLA
2.4	Aguadulce	Rural	Raúl DELVALLE	PR	Luis NARVÁEZ	MOLIRENA
3.1	Colón	Urban	Jaime FERNÁNDEZ	MOLIRENA	Alonso FERNÁNDEZ	MOLIRENA
			Argénida DUMANOIR	PALA	Alfredo EHLERS	PDC
			Jacobo SALAS	PPAN	Raquel LANUZA	PDC
			Luis NAVAS	PRD	Miguel BUSH	PRD
3.2	Chagres, Donoso, Portobelo, Santa Isabel	Rural	Antonio ARDINES	PRD	Abelardo ANTONÍO	PRD
4.1	David	Urban	Bertilo MEJÍA	PDC	José TORRES	PDC
			Tomás GUERRA	PPAN	Librado MONTENEGRO	MOLIRENA
			Camilo GOZAINE	PRD	Camilo BRENES	PDC
4.2	Barú	Urban	José MORRIS	PRD	Ricardo PÉREZ	PDC
			Vianor SERRACÍN	PDC	Ramón AIZPURÚA	PDC
4.3	Bugaba	Rural	Hernán GARCÍA	PPAN	Alexis AYALA	PDC
			Martín SERRANO	PRD	Eric SANTAMARÍA	PDC
4.4	Indigenous areas of Remedios, San Félix, San Lorenzo, Tolé	Rural	Guillermo JIMÉNEZ	PRD	Ernesto GIRÓN	PDC
4.5	Alanje, Boquerón, Renacimiento (4.4 in 2009)	Rural	Robustiano BEITÍA	PPAN	Gustavo GUILLÉN	PLA
4.6	Boquete, Dolega, Gualaca (4.5 in 2009)	Rural	Otilio MIRANDA	PALA	Nodier MIRANDA	PLA
4.7	Remedios, San Félix, San Lorenzo, Tolé (4.6 in 2009)	Rural	Jorge Rubén ROSAS	MOLIRENA	Jorge Rubén ROSAS	MOLIRENA
5.1	Chepigana, Sambú	Rural	Pedro BRIN	PRD	Edilberto CULIOLIS	PRD
5.2	Pinogana, Cémaco	Rural	Anselmo GUAINORA	PRD	Anel RAMÍREZ	PALA
6.1	Chitré	Urban	Gustavo COLLADO	PALA	Arnulfo ESCALONA	PLA
6.2	Parita, Los Pozos, Pesé	Rural	Lorenzo ALFONSO	PRD	Héctor CRESPO	MOLIRENA
6.3	Ocú, Santa María, Las Minas	Rural	Celso CARRIZO	PRD	Aurelio ALBA	PLA
7.1	Las Tablas, Pocrí (Guararé, Las Tablas, Pocrí, and Pedasí in 2009)	Rural	Francisco SOLÍS	PRD	Miguel CÁRDENAS	MOLIRENA
7.2	Los Santos, Guararé (Los Santos, Macaracas and Tonosí in 2009)	Rural	Magdalena RODRÍGUEZ	PRD	Alberto CIGARRUISTA	PLA
7.3	Macaracas, Tonosí, Pedasí	Rural	Ovidio DÍAZ	PRD	Sebastián ESCOBAR	PDC
8.1	Arraiján	Urban	Rigoberto PAREDES	PRD	José HILL	PDC
8.2	Capira	Rural	Carlos BARSALLO	PRD	Domiluis MONTENEGRO	MOLIRENA
8.3	Chame, San Carlos	Rural	Heriberto BERNAL	PRD	Melquíades RIEGA	PL
8.4	Chepo, Chimán, Balboa, Taboga	Rural	Tomás ALTAMIRANO D.	PRD	Roberto GARIBALDO	MOLIRENA
8.5	La Chorrera	Urban	Raúl OSSA	PDC	Raúl OSSA	PDC
			Hugo TORRIJOS	PRD	Anastasio BATISTA	PDC

	Member							
1994–1999		1999–2004		2004–2009		2009–2014		
Name	Party	Name	Party	Name	Party	Name	Party	Seats[a]
Felipe SERRANO	PRD	Arcelio BATISTA	PRD	José BROWN	CD	Mario MILLER	CD	10
Mario MILLER	PRD	Omar CHENG	PRD	Benicio ROBINSON	PRD	Benicio ROBINSON	PRD	
Benicio ROBINSON	PRD	Samuel BINNS	CD					4
Mario QUIEL	PLA	Hirisnel SUCRE	PRD	Eloy ZÚÑIGA	PRD	Jorge ARROCHA	PPAN	12
César PARDO	PRD	César PARDO	PRD	César PARDO	PRD	Renaúl DOMÍNGUEZ	PRD	
Bolívar PARIENTE	PPAN	Javier TEJEIRA	PLN	Javier TEJEIRA	PLN	Raúl HERNÁNDEZ	UP	6
Juan PERALTA	LIBRE	José URRUTIA	PPAN	Juan PERALTA	PRD	Dana CASTAÑEDA	UP	6
Noriel SALERNO	PSOL	Noriel SALERNO	PSOL	Juvenal MARTÍNEZ	CD	Noriel SALERNO	UP	6
Jorge DÍAZ	MPE	Olgalina RODRÍGUEZ	PRD	Leopoldo BENEDETTI	PSOL	Mario LÁZARUS	CD	24
Abelardo ANTONÍO	PRD	Abelardo ANTONÍO	PRD	Alejandro VANEGAS	PRD	Abelardo ANTONÍO	PRD	
Leopoldo BENEDETTI	PPAN	Jacobo SALAS	PPAN	Manuel GRIMALDO	PPAN	Miguel SALAS	PPAN	
Miguel BUSH	PRD	Miguel BUSH	PRD	Dorindo CORTÉS	PRD	Iracema AYARZA	PRD	
Laurentino CORTIZO	PSOL	Laurentino CORTIZO	PSOL	Nelson JACKSON	PRD	Nelson JACKSON	PRD	6
Denis ARCE	PRD	Denis ARCE	PRD	Denis ARCE	PRD	Denis ARCE	PRD	18
Edgardo ALVAREZ	PRD	Edwin AIZPURÚA	PPAN	Miguel FANOVICH	PPAN	Miguel FANOVICH	PPAN	
Lorenzo ACOSTA	PRD	Camilo GOZAINE	PRD	Agustín ESCUDÉ	PRD	Rogelio BARUCO	CD	
Yadira GONZÁLEZ	PRD	Osman GÓMEZ	PPAN	Osman GÓMEZ	PPAN	Osman GÓMEZ	PPAN	11
Carlos SMITH	PRD	Carlos SMITH	PRD	José BARUCO	PRD			
Luis POSSE	PPAN	Julio CASTILLO	PPAN	Rubén BEITÍA	PSOL	Pablo VARGAS	PPAN	12
Alfredo ARIAS	PPAN	José HERRERA	PRD	Yasmina GUILLÉN	PSOL	Rony ARAÚZ	PRD	
Enrique MONTEZUMA	PRD	Enrique MONTEZUMA	PRD					4
Miguel SÁNCHEZ	PRC	José CARREÑO	PRC	José CARREÑO	PPAN	José LOZADA	PPAN	6
Carlos ALVARADO	PRD	Carlos ALVARADO	PRD	Carlos ALVARADO	PRD	Hugo MORENO	PPAN	6
Rodrigo JOVANÉ	PPAN	Jorge Alberto ROSAS	MOLI-RENA	Raúl RODRÍGUEZ	PRD	Jorge Alberto ROSAS	MOLI-RENA	6
Haydée MILANÉS	PSOL	Haydée MILANÉS	PSOL	Geovany CASTILLO	PRD	Luis LAY	PPAN	6
Jaime LORÉ	PL	Sergio TÓCAMO	PRD	Ezequiel RAMÍREZ	PRD	Salvador REAL	UP	6
Alberto CASTILLERO	PSOL	Alberto CASTILLERO	PSOL	Pacífico ESCALONA	PPAN	Manuel COHEN	PPAN	6
José VARELA	PPAN	José VARELA	PDC	José VARELA	PPAN	José VARELA	PPAN	6
Pablo QUINTERO	PPAN	Mateo CASTILLERO	PRD	Antonio RODRÍGUEZ	PRD	Juan RÍOS	PPAN	6
Carlos AFÚ	PALA	Carlos AFÚ	PRD	Carlos AFÚ	PPAN	Carlos AFÚ	IND	6
Alberto CIGARRUISTA	PLA	Alberto CIGARRUISTA	PPAN	Olivares FRÍAS	PRD	Francisco VEGA	PRD	6
Juan DELGADO	PRD	Jorge CASTRO	PRD	Marcelino MUDARRA	MOLI-RENA			5
Abel RODRÍGUEZ	PRD	Vicente MAGALLÓN	PRD	Rogelio PAREDES	PRD	Rogelio PAREDES	PRD	13
Lenín SUCRE	PL	Lenín SUCRE	PPAN	Argentina ARIAS	PPAN	Ricardo VALENCIA	PPAN	
				Marylín VALLARINO	PSOL	Marylín VALLARINO	CD	
				Mayra ZÚÑIGA	PRD			
Orestes VÁSQUEZ	UDI	Serafín SÁNCHEZ	PPAN	Zulay GUTIÉRREZ	PRD	Yanibel ÁBREGO	IND	6
Joaquín FRANCO	PPAN	Arturo ARAÚZ	PLN	Arturo ARAÚZ	PLN	José HERRERA	PPAN	6
Tomás ALTAMIRANO D.	PRD	Tomás ALTAMIRANO M.	PRD	Tomás ALTAMIRANO M.	PRD	Hernán Delgado	VMP	6
Aristides de ICAZA	PRC	Roberto ÁBREGO	PRD	Aristides de ICAZA	PSOL	Aristides de ICAZA	CD	14
Roberto ÁBREGO	PRD	Susana RICHA	PRD	Susana RICHA	PRD	Rubén FRÍAS	PRD	
				Alberto BARRANCO	PPAN	Guillermo FERRUFINO	CD	

Appendix L. (continued)

			Member			
	Constituency	Urban/	1984–1989		1989–1994	
Number	Name	Rural	Name	Party	Name	Party
8.6	San Miguelito	Urban	Justo CORTÉS	MOLIRENA	Eliseo ALVAREZ	MOLIRENA
			Francisco ICAZA	PALA	Gisela CHUNG	MOLIRENA
			Emiliano AGUILAR	PPAN	Carlos ESCOBAR	PDC
			Jorge SIMMONS	PRD	Alonso VILLARREAL	PDC
			Luis GÓMEZ	PRD	Balbina HERRERA	PRD
8.7	San Felipe, El Chorrillo, Santa Ana,	Urban	David ARCE	PPAN	Lucas ZARAK	PPAN
	Calidonia, Curundú (Panama City)		Marco ALARCÓN	PPAN	José SOSSA	PDC
	(San Felipe, El Chorrillo, Santa Ana,		Romelia ESQUIVEL	PRD	Franklyn RIVERA	PRD
	Calidonia, Curundú, Bella Vista, Ancón		Alberto ALEMÁN	PRD	Alberto ALEMÁN	PRD
	Bethania, Pueblo Nuevo in 2009)					
8.8	Bella Vista, Ancón, Bethania, Pueblo	Urban	Omaira CORREA	PALA	Ada LÓPEZ	PDC
	Nuevo (Panama City)					
	(San Francisco, Parque Lefevre, Río		Carlos ARELLANO	PDC	Carlos ARELLANO	PDC
	Abajo, Juan Díaz in 2009)		Mario de OBALDÍA	PPAN	Marco AMEGLIO	PLA
			Alfredo ORANGES	PRD	Mario ROGNONI	PRD
8.9	San Francisco, Parque Lefevre, Río	Urban	Florencio ASPRILLA	PALA	Olimpo SÁEZ	MOLIRENA
	Abajo, Juan Díaz (Panama City)		Guillermo COCHEZ	PDC	Guillermo COCHEZ	PDC
	(Chilibre, Las Cumbres in 2009)		Antonio ARIAS	PPAN	Gloria MORENO	PDC
			José YOUNG	PR	Milton HENRÍQUEZ	PDC
			Raúl MONTENEGRO	PRD	Elías CASTILLO	PRD
8.10	Pedregal, Tocumen, Pacora, San Martín,	Urban	Arturo VALLARINO	PALA	Arturo VALLARINO	MOLIRENA
	Las Cumbres o Alcalde Díaz, Chilibre					
	(Panama City) (Pedregal, Pacora, San		Simón QUIRÓS	PPAN	Leo GONZÁLEZ	MOLIRENA
	Martín, Tocumen, Las Mañanitas,		Ernesto CÓRDOBA	PR	Keith HOLDER	PDC
	December 24, 2009)		Jerry WILSON	PRD	Gerardo GONZÁLEZ	PRD
9.1	Santiago de Veraguas	Rural	Ebén CHI	PRD	Erasmo MÉNDEZ	PDC
			Moisés MELAMED	PRD	Carlos CARRIZO	PDC
9.2	Soná, La Mesa (Soná, La Mesa, Las Palmas	Rural	Rafael ÁBREGO	PRD	Rolando MARTINELLI	MOLIRENA
	in 2009)					
9.3	Santa Fe, Calobre, San Francisco (Santa Fe,	Rural	Hugo GIRAUD	PRD	Alcibíades GARCÍA	PDC
	Calobre, San Francisco, Cañazas in 2009)					
9.4	Montijo, Río de Jesús, La Atalaya, Mariato	Rural	Fabio JUÁREZ	PRD	Mario FORERO	MOLIRENA
9.5	Las Palmas, Cañazas	Rural	Jorge MONTEMAYOR	PDC	Jorge MONTEMAYOR	PDC
10.1	Narganá, parts of Ailigandí, Madungandí	Rural	Dámaso LOMBARDO	PRD	Alcibíades ALVARADO	PDC
10.2	Parts of Ailigandí, Tubualá, Puerto Obaldía,	Rural	Alicio RIVERA	PRD	Olmenares QUIJANO	MOLIRENA
	Wargandí					
12.1	Kankintú	Rural				
12.2	Besiko	Rural				
12.3	Muna	Rural				
Total Seats		427		67		67

Source: Tribunal Electoral 1984a, 1984b, 1991a, 1991b, 1994b, 1994c, 1999b, 1999c, 2004b, 2009a.

[a] This column indicates the total number of deputies elected in each constituency throughout the 1984–2009 period.

				Member				
1994–1999		1999–2004		2004–2009		2009–2014		
Name	Party	Name	Party	Name	Party	Name	Party	Seats[a]
Raymundo HURTADO	MOLI-RENA	Francisco ALEMÁN	PPAN	Vladimir HERRERA	MOLI-RENA	Marcos GONZÁLEZ	CD	36
Gloria YOUNG	MPE	Gloria YOUNG	PPAN	Dalia BERNAL	CD	Dalia BERNAL	CD	
José SERRACÍN	PPAN	Marcos GONZÁLEZ	PPAN	Francisco ALEMÁN	PPAN	Francisco ALEMÁN	PPAN	
César SANJUR	PRD	Elpidio GONZÁLEZ	PPAN	Milcíades CONCEPCIÓN	PRD	Raúl PINEDA	PRD	
Balbina HERRERA	PRD	Balbina HERRERA	PRD	Leandro ÁVILA	PRD	Leandro ÁVILA	PRD	
Víctor LÓPEZ	PRD	Felipe CANO	PRD	Miguel ALEMÁN	PRD	Miguel ALEMÁN	PRD	
				Abraham MARTÍNEZ	PSOL	Abraham MARTÍNEZ	PRD	
Lucas ZARAK	PPAN	Sergio GÁLVEZ	CD	Sergio GÁLVEZ	PPAN	Sergio GÁLVEZ	CD	24
Mariela JIMÉNEZ	MPE	Francisco REYES	PPAN	Hermisenda PEREA	PRD	Adolfo VALDERRAMA	PPAN	
Franz WEVER	PRD	Franz WEVER	PRD	Franz WEVER	PRD	Crispiano ADAMES	PRD	
Alberto ALEMÁN	PRD	Andrés VEGA	PRD			Víctor JULIAO	CD	
						José BLANDÓN	PPAN	
Rodrigo AROSEMENA	MOLI-RENA	José BLANDÓN	PPAN	José BLANDÓN	PPAN	Luis QUIRÓS	PPAN	26
Rubén AROSEMENA	PDC	Rubén AROSEMENA	PDC	Rubén AROSEMENA	PDC	Elías CASTILLO	PRD	
Marco AMEGLIO	MOLI-RENA	Marco AMEGLIO	PPAN	Mireya LASSO	PSOL	Fernando CARRILLO	UP	
Oydén ORTEGA	PRD	Héctor ALEMÁN	PRD	Héctor ALEMÁN	PRD	José FÁBREGA	PRD	
Víctor MÉNDEZ	MPE					Gabriel MÉNDEZ	PRD	
Manuel de LA HOZ	PRD	Manuel de LA HOZ	PRD	Juan HERNÁNDEZ	PRD	Yassir PURCAIT	PRD	29
Bernabé PÉREZ	MPE	Teresita YÁNIZ	PDC	Teresita YÁNIZ	PDC	Vidal GARCÍA	CD	
Olmedo GUILLÉN	PRC	José FÁBREGA	PPAN	José FÁBREGA	PSOL	Tito RODRÍGUEZ	PPAN	
Olivia de LEÓN	PRD	Olivia de LEÓN	PRD	Luis CLEGHORN	PPAN			
Elías CASTILLO	PRD	Elías CASTILLO	PRD	Elías CASTILLO	PRD			
				Jorge ALVARADO	PRD			
Arturo VALLARINO	MOLI-RENA	Arturo VALLARINO	MOLI-RENA	Wigberto QUINTERO	MOLI-RENA	Edwin ZÚÑIGA	PPAN	30
Daniel ARIAS	PPAN	Alcibíades VÁSQUEZ	PPAN	Alcibíades VÁSQUEZ	PPAN	Alcibíades VÁSQUEZ	PPAN	
Roberto WILL	MPE	José MUÑOZ	PPAN	José MUÑOZ	PSOL	José MUÑOZ	CD	
Gerardo GONZÁLEZ	PRD	Jerry WILSON	PRD	Jerry WILSON	PRD	Juan C. AROSEMENA	PRD	
Donato ROSALES	PRD	Francisco AMEGLIO	PPAN	Juan C. AROSEMENA	PRD			
				Elizabeth HERNÁNDEZ	PRD			
				Maricruz PADILLA	PRD			
				Yassir PURCAIT	PRD			
Carlos E. SANTANA	PPAN	Carlos E. SANTANA	PDC	Iván LÓPEZ	PRD	Carlos A. SANTANA	PPAN	12
Adolfo NAME	PRD	Rubén de LEÓN	PRD	Rubén de LEÓN	PRD	Rubén de LEÓN	PRD	
Héctor APARICIO	MOLI-RENA	Héctor APARICIO	MOLI-RENA	Héctor APARICIO	MOLI-RENA	Héctor APARICIO	MOLI-RENA	6
Enrique RILEY	PRD	Pedro GONZÁLEZ	PRD	Pedro GONZÁLEZ	PRD	Francisco BREA	PPAN	6
Mario FORERO	MOLI-RENA	Freidi TORRES	PRD	Freidi TORRES	PRD	Freidi TORRES	PRD	6
Manuel ORTIZ	PPAN	Eddy LONDOÑO	PRD	Mireya MONTEMAYOR	PPAN			5
Enrique GARRIDO	PPAN	Enrique GARRIDO	PDC	Enrique GARRIDO	PPAN	Juan MARTÍNEZ	PRD	6
Rogelio ALBA	LIBRE	Rogelio ALBA	PLN	Rogelio ALBA	PLN	Absalón HERRERA	PRD	6
				Bernardo ÁBREGO	PRD	Leopoldo ARCHIBOLD	CD	2
				Patricio MONTEZUMA	PRD	Irene GALLEGO	PDC	2
				Benito CASES	PRD	Crescencia PRADO	PRD	2
	72		71		79		71	427

Appendix M. Deviation from Proportionality (D) in Panama's Elections to the Assembly, 1984–2009

	1984	

Remainder Rule: Allocated to parties with largest remainders after deducting full or half quotas from parties allotted full-quota or half-quota seats, respectively (1983 electoral code)

Relative Proportionality of Allocation Rule: More proportional than subsequently

Electoral Environment: Blatant fraud

Consecutive Reelection Rate: Not applicable (first election)

	Political Party	*Seats*	*%*	*Votes*	*%*	*D*
1	PRD	34	51	153,182	25	26
2	PPAN	13	19	124,562	20	1
3	PALA	7	10	74,430	12	2
4	PDC	6	9	69,998	11	3
5	PR	3	4	51,103	8	4
6	MOLIRENA	3	4	50,936	8	4
7	PL	1	1	36,040	6	4
8	PNP	0	0	12,596	2	2
9	PAPO	0	0	8,471	1	1
10	PP	0	0	8,063	1	1
11	FRAMPO	0	0	7,813	1	1
12	PdP	0	0	7,315	1	1
13	PRT	0	0	3,545	1	1
14	PST	0	0	1,283	0	0
	Total	67	100	609,337	100	26

Appendix M. (continued)

1989

Remainder Rule: Allocated to parties with largest remainders after deducting
a half quota from parties allotted full-quota or half-quota seats, respectively.
Parties not allotted quota seats did not participate in remainder allocation
(1988 electoral code)

Relative Proportionality of Allocation Rule: Less proportional than in 1984

Electoral Environment: Major attempt to rig elections; elections annulled;
distribution determined on the basis of incomplete records and partial
elections in 1991

Consecutive Reelection Rate: 22%

	Political Party	Seats	%	Votes	%	D
1	PDC	28	42	219,944	36	6
2	MOLIRENA	18	27	122,974	20	7
3	PRD	10	15	114,741	19	4
4	PLA	9	13	61,916	10	3
5	PALA	1	1	47,775	8	6
6	PL	1	1	17,712	3	1
7	PR	0	0	8,602	1	1
8	PdP	0	0	4,988	1	1
9	PPR	0	0	3,572	1	1
10	PPAN	0	0	3,015	0	0
11	PAN	0	0	2,917	0	0
12	PDT	0	0	1,075	0	0
Total		67	100	609,231	100	16

Appendix M. (continued)

1994

Remainder Rule: Allocated to candidates receiving higher preferences,
  without regard to party, after allotting full- and half-quota seats
  (1993 electoral code)
Relative Proportionality of Allocation Rule: Less proportional than in 1989
Electoral Environment: Localized irregularities
Consecutive Reelection Rate: 27%

	Political Party	Seats	%	Votes	%	D
1	PRD	30	42	236,319	23	19
2	PPAN	14	19	150,217	15	5
3	MOLIRENA	5	7	116,833	11	4
4	MPE	6	8	99,760	10	1
5	MORENA	1	1	68,581	7	5
6	PSOL	4	6	67,306	7	1
7	PDC	1	1	66,411	6	5
8	PRC	3	4	57,590	6	1
9	PL (1979–1994)	2	3	35,516	3	1
10	PLA	2	3	31,045	3	0
11	PALA	1	1	28,172	3	1
12	MUN	0	0	27,017	3	3
13	LIBRE	2	3	24,979	2	0
14	UDI	1	1	13,106	1	0
15	PPD	0	0	10,720	1	1
	Total	72	100	1,033,572	100	24

Appendix M. (continued)

1999

Remainder Rule: Allocated to candidates receiving higher preferences, without regard to party, after allotting full- and half-quota seats (1997 electoral code, which did not change allocation rules)
Relative Proportionality of Allocation Rule: Same as in 1994
Electoral Environment: Localized irregularities
Consecutive Reelection Rate: 49%

	Political Party	Seats	%	Votes	%	D
1	PRD	34	48	393,356	32	16
2	PPAN	19	27	266,030	22	5
3	PSOL	4	6	71,860	6	0
4	MOLIRENA	3	4	92,711	8	3
5	CD	2	3	66,841	5	3
6	PDC	5	7	107,179	9	2
7	PLN	3	4	75,866	6	2
8	MORENA	0	0	42,996	3	3
9	PL (1997–1999)	0	0	41,588	3	3
10	PRC	1	1	37,705	3	2
11	MPE	0	0	21,841	2	2
12	PNP	0	0	11,506	1	1
Total		71	100	1,229,479	100	21

Appendix M. (continued)

2004

Remainder Rule: Allocated to candidates receiving higher preferences,
  without regard to party, after allotting full- and half-quota seats
  (2003 electoral code, which did not change allocation rules)
Relative Proportionality of Allocation Rule: Same as in 1994, 1999
Electoral Environment: Localized irregularities
Consecutive Reelection Rate: 49%

	Political Party	Seats	%	Votes	%	D
1	PRD	43	54	549,948	38	17
2	PPAN	16	20	279,560	19	1
3	PSOL	9	11	227,604	16	4
4	MOLIRENA	4	5	125,547	9	4
5	CD	3	4	107,511	7	4
6	PDC	1	1	86,727	6	5
7	PLN	3	4	76,191	5	1
Total		79	100	1,453,088	100	18

Appendix M. (continued)

2009

Remainder Rule: Allocated to candidates receiving higher preferences, without regard to party, after allotting full- and half-quota seats (2007 electoral code, which did not change allocation rules)

Relative Proportionality of Allocation Rule: Same as in 1994, 1999, 2004

Electoral Environment: Localized irregularities

Consecutive Reelection Rate: 46%

	Political Party	Seats	%	Votes	%	D
1	PRD	26	37	537,426	36	1
2	PPAN	21	30	334,282	22	7
3	CD	13	18	352,319	23	5
4	UP	5	7	85,609	6	1
5	MOLIRENA	2	3	70,457	5	2
6	PDC	1	1	55,598	4	2
7	VMP	1	1	14,760	1	0
8	PL	0	0	18,111	1	1
9	Independents	2	3	35,793	2	0
	Total	71	100	1,504,355	100	10

Sources for all tables: Comité de Apoyo 1989; Nohlen 1993; Tribunal Electoral 1984a, 1984b, 1991a, 1991b, 1994b, 1994c, 1999b, 1999c, 2004b, 2009b, 2009c.

Note: The formula for $D = (1/2)$ SUM [ABS $(S_i - V_i)$], where S represents seats and V stands for votes. Mean deviation from proportionality in 1984–2009 was 19 percent.

Appendix N. Panamanian Assembly Members' Monthly Wages, 1960–2008

Year	Consumer Price Index (CPI)[a]	Deflator[b]	Nominal Income (US$)	Real Income (US$)	% Variation since 1960
1960	31.6177	1	750	750.00	
1961	31.8118	1.006139	750	745.42	−0.61
1962	32.0624	1.014065	750	739.60	−1.39
1963	32.2067	1.018629	750	736.28	−1.83
1964	32.984	1.043213	1,000	958.58	27.81
1965	33.1363	1.04803	1,000	954.17	27.22
1966	33.2004	1.050057	1,000	952.33	26.98
1967	33.6572	1.064505	1,000	939.40	25.25
1968	34.2021	1.081739	1,000	924.44	23.26
1969	34.8271	1.101506	n.a.	n.a.	n.a.
1970	35.901	1.135472	n.a.	n.a.	n.a.
1971	36.5901	1.157266	n.a.	n.a.	n.a.
1972	38.5695	1.219871	n.a.	n.a.	n.a.
1973	41.214	1.30351	n.a.	n.a.	n.a.
1974	47.9187	1.515566	n.a.	n.a.	n.a.
1975	50.7368	1.604696	n.a.	n.a.	n.a.
1976	52.7409	1.668081	n.a.	n.a.	n.a.
1977	55.1594	1.744573	n.a.	n.a.	n.a.
1978	57.4764	1.817855	n.a.	n.a.	n.a.
1979	62.068	1.963078	n.a.	n.a.	n.a.
1980	70.6383	2.234138	n.a.	n.a.	n.a.
1981	75.7966	2.397284	n.a.	n.a.	n.a.
1982	79.0184	2.499182	n.a.	n.a.	n.a.
1983	80.68	2.551735	n.a.	n.a.	n.a.
1984	81.9569	2.592121	7,000	2,700.49	260.07
1985	82.7983	2.618733	7,000	2,673.05	256.41
1986	82.7433	2.616993	7,000	2,674.83	256.64
1987	83.5678	2.64307	7,000	2,648.44	253.12

Appendix N. (continued)

Year	Consumer Price Index (CPI)[a]	Deflator[b]	Nominal Income (US$)	Real Income (US$)	% Variation since 1960
1988	83.868	2.652565	7,000	2,638.96	251.86
1989	84.0406	2.658024	7,000	2,633.54	251.14
1990	84.6873	2.678478	7,000	2,613.42	248.46
1991	85.7512	2.712126	7,000	2,581.00	244.13
1992	87.3158	2.761611	7,000	2,534.75	237.97
1993	87.7121	2.774145	7,000	2,523.30	236.44
1994	88.8247	2.809335	7,000	2,491.69	232.23
1995	89.7078	2.837265	7,000	2,467.16	228.96
1996	90.8342	2.872891	7,000	2,436.57	224.88
1997	92.0372	2.910939	7,000	2,404.72	220.63
1998	92.5518	2.927215	7,000	2,391.35	218.85
1999	93.7061	2.963723	7,000	2,361.89	214.92
2000	95.1107	3.008147	7,000	2,327.01	210.27
2001	95.4027	3.017383	7,000	2,319.89	209.32
2002	96.3623	3.047733	7,000	2,296.79	206.24
2003	96.7397	3.059669	7,000	2,287.83	205.04
2004	96.9164	3.065258	7,000	2,283.66	204.49
2005	100	3.162785	7,000	2,213.24	195.10
2006	102.0959	3.229074	7,000	2,167.80	189.04
2007	106.3519	3.363682	7,000	2,081.05	177.47
2008	115.6669	3.658296	7,000	1,913.46	155.13

Source: Quintero 1967; Flores 2008; World Bank 2010.

Note: All figures in 1960 prices. Data not applicable for 1969–83, when the assembly was suspended under military rule.

[a] World Bank, 2005 = 100.

[b] World Bank, 1960 = 1.

Appendix O. Panamanian Assembly Members' Expected Salaries, 1999

To determine the wages members would receive if they had other employment based on their professional qualifications, I classified the 67 legislators in the 1999–2004 cohort that had posted their CVs to the assembly website in 2000 according to their backgrounds. Total membership in the 1999–2004 assembly consisted of 71 legislators. Members' resumes were available at the time at the Legislative Assembly website (http://www.asamblea.gob.pa). Marcela Endara assisted in downloading the CVs.

Based on each legislator's profile, including education and all jobs held, with the exception of their positions as legislators, I classified each member in one of the categories in Gutmann and Frey (2000), which provides average salary information for Panama City in 1999. This survey of international wages had twelve categories:

1. Saleswoman
2. Female industrial worker
3. Building laborer
4. Skilled industrial worker
5. Automobile mechanic
6. Primary schoolteacher
7. Bus driver
8. Secretary
9. Cook (chef)
10. Engineer
11. Department manager
12. Bank credit clerk

I added a thirteenth category—higher-income job—for cases in which a legislator's profile appeared to qualify him or her for a better-paid job than bank credit officer.

Appendix O. (continued)

Panamanian Assembly Members Expected Salaries, 1999

Gutmann and Frey Categories	Matching Categories in Legislators' Profiles	Expected Annual Salary (in US$)
Saleswoman		4,200
Female industrial worker		4,500
Building laborer		4,700
Skilled industrial worker		5,800
Automobile mechanic		6,100
Primary schoolteacher		6,200
Bus driver	Taxi driver	9,800
Secretary	Accountant, agricultural technician, business clerk, public sector clerk, high school professor, medical technician, reporter	9,900
Cook (chef)		18,900
Engineer	Agricultural engineer, chemical engineer, driver-entrepreneur, engineering technician, public sector administrator, rural dentist, rural physician, university professor, veterinarian	20,100
Department manager	Commercial farmer, pilot, industry supervisor	24,800
Bank credit clerk	Bank administrator, business administrator	26,800
Higher-income job	Attorney, businessman, urban physician	Above 27,000

Source: Gutmann and Frey 2000; legislators' CVs available at the Legislative Assembly website in 2000 (http://www.asamblea.gob.pa).

Appendix P. Obligation to Attend Plenary and Committee Meetings in Fifty-Three Liberal Democracies, 2008

	Country	Compulsory Attendance at Meetings		Sanction		
		Plenary	*Committees*	*Pecuniary Loss*	*Mandate or Committee Membership Suspension or Loss*	*Other Disciplinary Action*
1	Andorra	Y	n.d.	Y	N	N
2	Argentina	Y	Y	Y	N	Y
3	Australia	N	N	N	Y	N
4	Austria	Y	Y	N	Y	N
5	Belgium	N	N	N	N	N
6	Benin	Y	Y	Y	N	Y
7	Botswana	Y	Y	N	Y	N
8	Bulgaria	Y	Y	Y	N	N
9	Canada	N	N	Y	N	N
10	Cape Verde	Y	Y	N	Y	N
11	Chile	Y	Y	Y	N	N
12	Costa Rica	Y	Y	Y	N	Y
13	Croatia	Y	Y	N	N	N
14	Cyprus (Greek)	Y	Y	Y	N	N
15	Czech Republic	Y	Y	Y	N	N
16	Denmark	N	N	N	N	N
17	Estonia	Y	Y	N	N	N
18	Finland	N	n.d.	Y	Y	N
19	France	N	N	Y	N	N
20	Germany	Y	Y	Y	N	N
21	Greece	Y	Y	Y	N	N
22	Grenada	Y	Y	N	Y	N
23	Hungary	Y	Y	Y	N	N
24	Iceland	N	N	N	N	N
25	India	N	N	N	Y	N
26	Indonesia	Y	Y	N	N	N
27	Israel	N	N	Y	N	Y
28	Italy	Y	Y	Y	N	N
29	Jamaica	N	N	N	Y	N

Appendix P. (continued)

	Country	Compulsory Attendance at Meetings		Sanction		
		Plenary	Committees	Pecuniary Loss	Mandate or Committee Membership Suspension or Loss	Other Disciplinary Action
30	Japan	Y	Y	N	N	Y
31	Latvia	Y	Y	Y	Y	N
32	Lesotho	Y	Y	N	N	Y
33	Liechtenstein	Y	Y	N	N	N
34	Luxembourg	N	N	Y	N	N
35	Mali	N	Y	Y	Y	N
36	Namibia	N	N	N	Y	N
37	Netherlands	N	N	N	N	N
38	New Zealand	Y	Y	N	N	N
39	Norway	Y	Y	N	Y	N
40	Panama[a]	Y	Y	N	N	N
41	Poland	Y	Y	Y	N	Y
42	Portugal	Y	Y	Y	Y	Y
43	Senegal[b]	Y	Y	N	Y	N
44	Slovakia	Y	Y	Y	N	N
45	South Korea	Y	Y	N	N	N
46	Spain	Y	Y	N	N	N
47	Sweden	N	N	N	N	N
48	Switzerland	Y	Y	Y	N	N
49	Trinidad & Tobago	N	N	N	Y	N
50	Ukraine	Y	Y	Y	Y	Y
51	United Kingdom	N	Y	N	N	Y
52	United States	Y	Y	N	N	N
53	Uruguay	Y	Y	N	Y	Y

Source: Asamblea Nacional 2010a; Freedom House 2009a. Data on attendance requirements comes from a survey of the IPU PARLINE database conducted at the end of 2008.

Note: Y = Yes; N = No; n.d. = information not available.

[a] Panama was added to the original dataset of fifty-two countries that provided information to IPU at the time the survey was conducted.

[b] Senegal was classified as a liberal democracy in Freedom House's 2008 report but not subsequently.

Appendix Q. Passports Used by Assembly Members in Fifty-Three Liberal Democracies, 2010

	Country	Type	Remarks
1	Andorra	D	
2	Argentina	R	
3	Australia	O	
4	Austria	R	Members receive diplomatic passports if requested
5	Belgium	S	Passport with a "protection arrangement"
6	Benin	D	
7	Botswana	D	
8	Bulgaria	D	
9	Canada	S	
10	Cape Verde	D	
11	Chile	D	
12	Costa Rica	D	
13	Croatia	D	
14	Cyprus	R	Diplomatic passport for certain members, including those attending regularly meetings of international parliamentary organizations
15	Czech Republic	D	
16	Denmark	O	Certain MPs may apply for diplomatic passports
17	Estonia	D	
18	Finland	O	
19	France	R	
20	Germany	D	
21	Greece	D	
22	Grenada	R	Diplomatic passport at request and under special conditions
23	Hungary	D	
24	Iceland	O	
25	India	D	
26	Indonesia	D	
27	Israel	O	

Appendix Q. (continued)

	Country	Type	Remarks
28	Italy	O	
29	Jamaica	D	
30	Japan	O	
31	Latvia	D	
32	Lesotho	O	
33	Liechtenstein	R	Diplomatic or official passport on request
34	Luxembourg	R	Diplomatic passport for deputies who belong to an international parliamentary assembly
35	Mali	D	
36	Mexico	O	
37	Namibia	O	
38	Netherlands	R	Diplomatic passport for some members
39	New Zealand	O	
40	Norway	S	
41	Panama[a]	D	
42	Poland	O	
43	Portugal	D	
44	Samoa	D	
45	Slovakia	D	
46	Spain	R	
47	Sweden	S	
48	Switzerland	R	Diplomatic passport, upon request, for members of international delegations
49	Trinidad & Tobago	O	
50	Ukraine	D	
51	United Kingdom	R	
52	United States	O	
53	Uruguay	D	

Source: IPU 2010a; República de Panamá 2010a.

Note: D = Diplomatic; O = Official; S = Special; R = Regular.

[a] Panama was added to the original dataset of fifty-two countries that provided information to IPU at the time the survey was conducted.

Appendix R. Constituency Funding Allocations and Assembly Members' Reelection in Panama, 1995–99

Assembly Member	Constituency Funding Allocations (in US$)					Total	Reelected[a]
	1995	1996	1997	1998	1999		
1 Carlos Alvarado	411,000	1,438,000	1,060,000	1,605,000	1,425,000	5,939,000	Yes
2 Gerardo González	400,000	1,084,818	1,100,000	1,080,000	1,397,100	5,061,918	No
3 Olivia de León de Pomares	321,000	1,080,000	1,100,000	900,000	900,000	4,301,000	Yes
4 Balbina Herrera	358,000	820,000	1,100,000	900,000	900,000	4,078,000	Yes
5 Tomás Altamirano Mantovani	400,000	930,000	750,000	1,030,000	900,000	4,010,000	Yes
6 Manuel de La Hoz	450,000	715,000	1,042,716	850,000	925,000	3,982,716	Yes
7 Carlos Afú	450,000	715,000	1,100,000	850,000	825,000	3,940,000	Yes
8 César Pardo	321,000	705,000	1,110,000	900,000	900,000	3,936,000	Yes
9 Juan Peralta	420,000	930,000	692,900	925,000	900,000	3,867,900	No
10 Haydée Milanés de Lay	321,000	715,000	1,100,000	845,050	800,000	3,781,050	Yes
11 Franz Wever	321,000	930,000	750,000	850,000	800,000	3,651,000	Yes
12 Elías Castillo	321,000	600,000	850,000	900,000	900,000	3,571,000	Yes
13 Carlos Smith	400,000	715,000	650,000	900,000	900,000	3,565,000	Yes
14 Laurentino Cortizo	321,000	600,000	850,000	850,000	900,000	3,521,000	Yes
15 Jaime Loré	321,000	600,000	850,000	850,000	900,000	3,521,000	No
16 Alberto Castillero	345,725	600,000	750,000	913,950	909,896	3,519,571	Yes
17 Noriel Salerno	450,000	600,000	750,000	900,000	800,000	3,500,000	Yes
18 Alberto Alemán Boyd	321,000	600,000	750,000	900,000	900,000	3,471,000	No
19 Denis Arce	450,000	600,000	750,000	850,000	800,000	3,450,000	Yes
20 Benicio Robinson	321,000	715,000	750,000	850,000	800,000	3,436,000	No
21 Donato Rosales	321,000	600,000	850,000	850,000	800,000	3,421,000	No
22 Victor Lopez	302,944	607,250	774,063	850,000	800,000	3,334,257	No

Appendix R. (continued)

	Assembly Member	Constituency Funding Allocations (in US$)						Reelected[a]
		1995	1996	1997	1998	1999	Total	
23	Abelardo Antonío	321,000	600,000	750,000	850,000	800,000	3,321,000	Yes
24	Miguel Bush	321,000	600,000	750,000	850,000	800,000	3,321,000	Yes
25	Edgardo Alvarez	321,000	600,000	750,000	850,000	800,000	3,321,000	No
26	César Sanjur	321,000	600,000	650,000	900,000	850,000	3,321,000	No
27	Rogelio Alba	321,000	600,000	650,000	909,871	800,000	3,280,871	Yes
28	Roberto Abrego	321,000	600,000	750,000	850,000	700,000	3,221,000	Yes
29	Enrique Montezuma	321,000	600,000	650,000	650,000	946,375	3,167,375	Yes
30	Yadira González	321,000	600,000	750,000	850,000	592,290	3,113,290	No
31	Enrique Riley Puga	321,000	600,000	750,000	850,000	200,000	2,721,000	No
32	Bernabé Pérez	302,944	600,000	400,000	400,000	300,000	2,002,944	No
33	Alfredo Arias	680,055	300,000	300,000	450,000	200,000	1,930,055	No
34	Jorge Díaz	302,944	350,000	450,000	450,000	350,000	1,902,944	No
35	Roberto Will	302,944	350,000	400,000	491,000	350,000	1,893,944	No
36	Mario Quiel	381,944	300,000	390,400	300,000	500,000	1,872,344	No
37	Aristides de Icaza	181,944	350,000	400,000	400,000	500,000	1,831,944	No
38	Héctor Aparicio	181,944	372,650	419,999	540,000	290,000	1,804,593	Yes
39	Miguel P. Sánchez (José Carreño)	210,388	600,000	400,000	300,000	200,000	1,710,388	Yes
40	Víctor Méndez Fábrega	302,944	350,000	300,000	540,000	200,000	1,692,944	No
41	Arturo Vallarino	420,944	370,000	344,000	300,000	200,000	1,634,944	Yes
42	Lucas Zarak	253,944	300,000	420,000	300,000	320,000	1,593,944	No
43	José Luis Varela	181,944	607,500	300,000	300,000	200,000	1,589,444	Yes
44	José Serracín	181,944	600,000	300,000	300,000	200,000	1,581,944	No

Appendix R. (continued)

Assembly Member	Constituency Funding Allocations (in US$)						
	1995	1996	1997	1998	1999	Total	Reelected[a]
45 Lenín Sucre	181,944	300,000	350,000	540,000	200,000	1,571,944	Yes
46 Mario Forero	181,944	480,000	339,000	300,000	270,000	1,570,944	No
47 Olmedo Guillén	274,500	300,000	300,000	300,000	392,814	1,567,314	No
48 Bolívar Pariente	401,944	300,000	325,000	300,000	200,000	1,526,944	No
49 Enrique Garrido	181,944	300,000	422,811	300,000	320,000	1,524,755	Yes
50 Alberto Cigarruista	181,944	300,000	300,000	540,000	200,000	1,521,944	Yes
51 Carlos Santana	181,944	300,000	300,000	540,000	200,000	1,521,944	Yes
52 Orestes Vásquez	181,944	300,000	300,000	540,000	200,000	1,521,944	No
53 Leopoldo Benedetti	181,944	300,000	420,000	300,000	320,000	1,521,944	No
54 Manuel Ortiz	181,944	300,000	420,000	300,000	320,000	1,521,944	No
55 Rodrigo Jované	181,944	300,000	420,000	300,000	320,000	1,521,944	No
56 Pablo Quintero Luna	381,944	300,000	300,000	300,000	227,250	1,509,194	No
57 Joaquín Franco	181,944	600,000	300,000	300,000	125,000	1,506,944	No
58 Rubén Arosemena	181,944	300,000	500,000	300,000	200,000	1,481,944	Yes
59 Mariela Jiménez	302,944	350,000	300,000	300,000	200,000	1,452,944	No
60 Daniel Arias	181,944	600,000	300,000	300,000	53,625	1,435,569	No
61 Raymundo Hurtado	302,944	300,000	339,000	300,000	186,577	1,428,521	No
62 Gloria Young	181,944	350,000	300,000	300,000	200,000	1,331,944	Yes
63 Marco Ameglio	181,944	300,000	350,000	300,000	200,000	1,331,944	Yes

Source: Contraloría General 1999b.

Note: Highlighted members belonged to the opposition (or pseudo-opposition) bloc in September 1998.

[a] Sixty-three of seventy-two assembly members sought reelection in 1999.

Appendix S. Non-Liability among Assembly Members in Fifty-Two Liberal Democracies, 2008

	Country	Within the Chamber	Outside the Chamber
		Non-Liability	
1	Andorra	Y	n.d.
2	Argentina	Y	Y
3	Australia	Y	N
4	Austria	Y	Y
5	Belgium	Y	N
6	Benin	Y	Y
7	Botswana	Y	N
8	Bulgaria	Y	Y
9	Canada	Y	Y
10	Cape Verde	Y	Y
11	Chile	Y	N
12	Costa Rica	Y	Y
13	Croatia	Y	N
14	Cyprus (Greek)	Y	N
15	Czech Republic	Y	N
16	Denmark	Y	Y
17	Estonia	Y	N
18	Finland	Y	n.d.
19	France	Y	N
20	Germany	Y	N
21	Greece	Y	Y
22	Grenada	Y	n.d.
23	Hungary	Y	Y
24	Iceland	Y	n.d.
25	India	Y	N
26	Indonesia	Y	n.d.
27	Israel	Y	n.d.
28	Italy	Y	Y
29	Jamaica	Y	N
30	Japan	Y	N

Appendix S. (continued)

Country	Non-Liability Within the Chamber	Outside the Chamber
31 Latvia	Y	Y
32 Lesotho	Y	N
33 Luxembourg	Y	Y
34 Mali	Y	Y
35 Namibia	Y	N
36 Netherlands	Y	N
37 New Zealand	Y	N
38 Norway	Y	N
39 Panama[a]	Y	Y
40 Poland	Y	Y
41 Portugal	Y	Y
42 Senegal[b]	Y	N
43 Slovakia	Y	Y
44 South Korea	Y	N
45 Spain	Y	N
46 Sweden	Y	N
47 Switzerland	Y	Y
48 Trinidad & Tobago	Y	N
49 Ukraine	Y	N
50 United Kingdom	Y	N
51 United States	Y	N
52 Uruguay	Y	Y

Source: Freedom House 2009a; República de Panamá 2004. Data on non-liability comes from a survey of the IPU PARLINE database conducted at the end of 2008.

Note: Y = Yes; N = No; n.d. = information not available.

[a] Panama was added to the original dataset of fifty-one countries that provided information to IPU at the time the survey was conducted.

[b] Senegal classified as a liberal democracy in Freedom House's 2008 report but not subsequently.

Appendix T. Persons Consulted

The following persons provided information, shared ideas, or offered critique toward completion of this study of Panama's assembly members. Unless otherwise indicated, however, the author is solely responsible for interpretations offered in the book.

Manuel Alcántara Sáez, Professor of Political Science, University of Salamanca

José Miguel Alemán, Vice-Minister of Government and Justice (1994); Minister of Foreign Relations (1999–2003); presidential candidate (PPAN, MOLIRENA, PLN, 2004)

David Altman, Associate Professor, Pontificia Universidad Católica de Chile

Marco Ameglio, Legislator (PLA, 1989–94; MORENA, 1994–99; PPAN, 1999–2004); President of PPAN (2005–6)

Italo Antinori Bolaños, National Ombudsman (Defensor del Pueblo de la República de Panamá, 1997–2001)

Carlos Arellano Lennox, Legislator (PDC, 1984–94); President of the Legislative Assembly (1990)

Mercedes Arias Brostella, journalist

Ricardo Arias Calderón, President of PDC (1980–93); President of the Christian Democratic Organization of the Americas (ODCA, 1981–85); Vice-President of Panama (1989–92); Minister of Government and Justice (1989–91); President of the Christian Democratic International (1995–98, 1999)

Rosario Arias de Galindo, President, Editora *Panamá América* (1989–2010)

Alfredo Arias Grimaldo, Minister of Public Works (1991–93); Legislator (PPAN, 1994–99); Administrator-General of the Inter-Oceanic Regional Authority (ARI, 2000–2004)

Juan Arias Zubieta, Publisher, *La Prensa* (1995–2000)

Roberto Arosemena Jaén, philosopher

Judy Bartlett, web design specialist, Helen Kellogg Institute for International Studies, University of Notre Dame

Fernando Berguido Guizado, Truth Commission member (2001–2); President, Panama Chapter of Transparency International (2000–2004); Publisher, *La Prensa* (2004–)

Miguel Antonio Bernal, Professor of Law, University of Panama

José Blandón Figueroa, Legislator (PPAN, 1999–)

Felipe Botero, Associate Professor of Political Science, Universidad de Los Andes, Colombia

Betty Brannan Jaén, Washington correspondent of *La Prensa*

Daniel Brinks, Associate Professor of Political Science and Concurrent Associate Professor of Law, University of Notre Dame

Rubén Darío Carles Jr., Minister of Finance (1956–58); Minister of Agriculture and Commerce (1965–67, 1968); Comptroller-General (1989–93); presidential candidate (MOLIRENA, MORENA, PRC, 1994)

Rossana Castiglioni, Associate Professor of Political Science, Universidad Diego Portales, Chile

Gilda Cedeño de Tedman, bank manager

Francisco S. Céspedes, Director, Department of Educational Affairs, Organization of American States (1957–73) (deceased)

José Chen Barría, Comptroller-General (1993–94); Administrator-General of the Inter-Oceanic Regional Authority (ARI, 1994)

Richard E. Clinton Jr., College Counselor, American School of Guatemala

Guillermo A. Cochez, Legislator (PDC, 1984–94); Mayor of Panama City (1989–91); Ambassador to the Organization of American States (OAS, 2009–11)

Michael Coppedge, Associate Professor of Political Science, University of Notre Dame

Hernán Delgado, President of the National Bar Association (1980–84); alternate Supreme Court Justice (1983); Deputy (VMP, 2009–)

Ovidio Díaz, Deputy (PR, 1964–68) and Legislator (PRD, 1984–89)

I. Roberto Eisenmann Jr., Publisher, *La Prensa* (1980–95); President, Panama Chapter of Transparency International (1995–2000)

María Alejandra Eisenmann, attorney and Secretary-General, Ministry of Foreign Relations (1999–2003)

Guillermo Endara, Constitutional Reform Commission member for PPAN (1983); President of Panama (PPAN, 1989–94); presidential candidate (PSOL, 2004, VMP, 2009) (deceased)

Marcela Endara, Director of the Office of the First Lady, Presidency of the Republic (1990–94); official in the Ministry of Foreign Relations (1999–2003)

Andreas Feldmann, Associate Professor of Political Science, Pontificia Universidad Católica de Chile

Myra Fernández Guardia, administrator and retired bank manager

Stacy Fisher, Associate Professor of Political Science, University of Nevada, Reno

Robert Fishman, Professor of Sociology, University of Notre Dame

Flavia Freidenberg, Professor of Political Science and Assistant Director, Institute of Ibero-America, University of Salamanca

Mario Galindo Heurtematte, Constitutional Reform Commission member for MOLIRENA (1983); Minister of Finance (1989–93); Presidential Advisor (1999–2002); member of the Board of Directors of the Panama Canal Authority (2001–10)

Alexandra García Iragorri, Professor of Law and Political Science, Universidad del Norte, Colombia

Francisco Gómez, National Director for Fiscal Control, Comptroller-General's Office (1996–2002)

Andrew Gould, Associate Professor of Political Science, University of Notre Dame

Michael Grow, Associate Professor of History, Ohio University (retired)

Gloria Guardia, writer and member of the Panamanian, Nicaraguan, Colombian, and Spanish Academies of Language

Olmedo Guillén, Legislator (PRC, 1994–99)

Jonathan Hartlyn, Professor of Political Science, University of North Carolina at Chapel Hill

Gary Hoskin, Professor of Political Science, Universidad de Los Andes, Colombia

Scott van Jacob, Latin American Bibliographer, Theodore M. Hesburgh, C.S.C., Library, University of Notre Dame (deceased)

Brittmarie Janson Pérez, anthropologist and writer

Mark Jones, Professor of Political Science, Rice University

Derek Kauneckis, Associate Professor of Political Science, University of Nevada, Reno

Richard Koster, writer

Mireya Lasso, Deputy (PSOL, 2004–9)

Beatriz Lyons de López, bank manager

Juan Carlos Machado, attorney and doctoral candidate in government, University of Sussex

Scott Mainwaring, Professor of Political Science and Director, Helen Kellogg Institute for International Studies, University of Notre Dame

Guillermo Márquez Amado, Director of Consular Affairs, Ministry of Finance (1989–90); Electoral Tribunal Magistrate (1990–97)

Salvador Martí i Puig, Professor of Political Science, University of Salamanca

Angélica Maytín, Executive President, Panama Chapter of Transparency International (2005–)

James E. McDonald, C.S.C., priest; Associate Vice President and Counselor to the President, University of Notre Dame

Mark G. McGrath, C.S.C., Archbishop of Panama (1969–94) (deceased)

Aims McGuinness, Associate Professor of History, University of Wisconsin, Milwaukee

Andrés Mejía Acosta, Research Fellow, Institute of Development Studies, University of Sussex

Bertilo Mejía Ortega, Legislator (PDC, 1984–89)

Víctor Méndez Fábrega, Legislator (MPE, 1994–99)

Juan Méndez Salazar, Division Head and Secretary-General, Ministry of Foreign Relations (1999–2003)

Gonzalo Menéndez Franco, Director-General of the National Police (1991); Patrimonial Responsibility Tribunal Magistrate (1991–94) (deceased)

Martha Merritt, political scientist; Associate Dean for International Education, University of Chicago

Jorge Mitchell, Chief Archivist, *La Prensa*

Coralia Montenegro, bank officer; Compliance Officer, Executive Secretariat, National Council for Transparency against Corruption (2010–11)

Juan Esteban Montes, political scientist; Director, Notre Dame–Chile Program

Ramón Morales Quijano, retired insurance manager; Consul-General in Yokohama (1960–63) and Port Said (1963); Chargé d'Affaires in Egypt (1964–67); Ambassador to El Salvador (1967–68); President of the Board of Directors, Caja de Ahorros (1990–93); President, MOLIRENA (1995–97); Ambassador to the United Nations (1999–2004)

Marlina Morán, Secretary to the Board of Directors, Union Club of Panama

Eugenio Morice, attorney

María Cristina Mosquera, retired bank officer

Guillermo O'Donnell, Professor Emeritus, Senior Fellow, Helen Kellogg Institute for International Studies, University of Notre Dame

Robert Ostergard, Associate Professor of Political Science, University of Nevada, Reno

César Pereira Burgos, member of the Legislative Council (elected, 1980–84); Ambassador to the United Nations (1989–92); Minister of Agriculture (1992–94); Presidential Advisor (1999–2000); Supreme Court Magistrate (2000–2004) (deceased)

Ernesto Pérez Balladares, Legislative Council member (designated, 1975–76); Minister of Finance (1976–81); Minister of Planning (1981–82); President of Panama (PRD, 1994–99)

Rafael Pérez Jaramillo, journalist and human rights activist

Aníbal Pérez Liñán, Associate Professor of Political Science, University of Pittsburgh

Sharon Phillipps Collazos, sociologist

Vonda Polega, Senior Library Specialist, Kellogg Information Center, University of Notre Dame

Emiliano Ponce Arze, Legislator (PPAN, 1984–89)

Rita Preciado Recuero, retired budget officer, U.S. Army South

César Quintero, Professor of Law, University of Panama; Electoral Tribunal Magistrate (1982–84); Supreme Court Magistrate (1989–92) (deceased)

Pablo Quintero Luna, Legislator (PPAN, 1994–99); Executive Secretary, Public Security and National Defense Council (1999–2001); Director-General, Transit and Terrestrial Transportation Authority (2001–4)

Alberto Quirós Guardia, Professor of Economics, Universidad Católica Santa María La Antigua, Panama (retired)

Eduardo Quirós, Alternate Legislator (PPAN, 1999–2004); Vice-Minister of Finance (2000–2003); Minister of Public Works (2003–4)

Patrick Ragains, Business and Government Librarian, Mathewson-IGT Knowledge Center, University of Nevada, Reno

Alejandro von Rechnitz, S.J., priest

Humberto E. Ricord, Professor of Law, University of Panama; Constitutional Reform Commission member (1983) (deceased)

Julieta Romero, chief archivist, *El Panamá América*

Jaime Ros, Professor of Economics, University of Notre Dame

Ana Cecilia de Roux, bank manager

Jorge Rubén Rosas, Deputy (MLN, 1960–68); Legislator (MOLIRENA, 1984–94); Minister of Labor and Social Welfare (1989–93)

Gloria Rudolf, anthropologist

Olimpo Sáez, Legislator (MOLIRENA, 1989–94) and Ambassador to Brazil (1999–2002), Vietnam (2002–4), and Nicaragua (2009–)

Sebastián Saiegh, Associate Professor of Political Science, University of California, San Diego

David J. Samuels, Professor of Political Science, University of Minnesota

Guillermo Sánchez Borbón, writer and member of the Panamanian Language Academy

Salvador Sánchez González, Legislative Director of the National Assembly (2006–9); Legal and Technical General Director of the National Assembly (2009–)

Peter Siavelis, Associate Professor of Political Science, Wake Forest University

Christopher A. Simon, Professor of Political Science, University of Nevada, Reno

Peter A. Szok, Associate Professor of History, Texas Christian University

Juan Antonio Tejada Mora, attorney; alternate Supreme Court Justice (1990–2000); Truth Commission member (2001–2)

Otilia Tejeira de Koster, human rights activist

Berta Ramona Thayer, journalist

Eduardo Valdés Escoffery, Electoral Tribunal Magistrate (1990–)

Jorge Vargas Cullel, Deputy Director, Programa *Estado de la Nación,* Costa Rica

Alvin Weeden, Comptroller-General (2000–2005)

Carlos Iván Zúñiga, Professor of Law, University of Panama; Deputy (Partido Socialista, 1964–68); presidential candidate (Partido Acción Popular, 1984); President, Universidad de Panamá (1991–94) (deceased)

Juan Cristóbal Zúñiga, Professor of Law, University of Panama; Presidential Advisor (1990–94); Legal Counsel, Ministry of Foreign Relations (1999–2004)

Notes

Introduction

1. For a list of assembly parties having at least one member in the National Assembly in 1984–2009 (and their acronyms), see appendix D.

2. Approving or rejecting contracts with the government is a function of the National Assembly, according to article 159, section 15 of the Panamanian constitution (República de Panamá 2004).

3. Balbina Herrera (PRD), mayor of the San Miguelito municipality in 1984–89, legislator in 1989–2004, and minister for housing in 2004–8, was her party's presidential candidate in the May 2009 elections. She lost to Ricardo Martinelli, who was supported by a coalition of parties led by his own Cambio Democrático (CD), PPAN, MOLIRENA, UP.

4. Chapter 10 addresses the CEMIS case in more detail.

5. Freedom House's "personal autonomy and individual rights" category includes absence of state control over travel or choice of residence, employment, or institution of higher education; the right to private property; gender equality; the right to choose marriage partners and determine size of family; equality of opportunity; and the absence of economic exploitation (Freedom House 2009d).

6. Political institutionalization, both formal and informal, is the subject of part 1 (especially chapters 3 and 4).

7. According to O'Donnell (1996), three basic features characterize formal institutionalization: an explicit formalization of democratic institutions

in constitutions and auxiliary legislation, a close fit between formal rules and actual behavior, and a universalistic orientation to some consensus-based notion of the public good.

8. I thank Gloria Rudolf for suggesting possible connections between the identified behaviors and such analytical categories as gender and class.

9. For Freedom House classifications, methodology, and country narratives, see Freedom House 2009c.

10. Since 1972, when Freedom House's ratings began, Panama's rankings are as follows: "not free" in 1972–77; "partly free" in 1978–87; "not free" in 1988–89; "partly free" in 1990–93; and "free" in 1994–present. The country was under a military regime continuously from 1968 to 1989.

Among the twenty Latin American republics, Freedom House (2009a) classified the following ten as "free" in 2008. These states have been uninterrupted liberal democracies since the dates indicated in parenthesis: Costa Rica (pre-1972), Uruguay (1985), Chile (1990), Panama (1994), El Salvador (1997), Dominican Republic (1998), Mexico (2000), Peru (2001), Brazil (2002), and Argentina (2003).

11. For the CPI methodology and country scores, see Transparency International (2009).

12. In May 1989 the military-controlled Electoral Tribunal annulled the elections held that month, which had resulted in a massive victory for the opposition. The 1984–89 constitutional term expired on August 31, 1989. That day the "General Council of State," another organ subordinated to the military, appointed a "provisional government" to assume executive functions until new elections were held (at an undefined time). The Legislative Assembly ceased to operate and the General Council of State appointed a forty-one-member "Legislation Commission" to exercise legislative functions (Consejo General de Estado 1989a, 1989b).

The December 1989 U.S. invasion dismantled this unconstitutional structure and permitted the rise to power of Guillermo Endara (PPAN), the rightful winner of the May 1989 presidential election. Subsequently, a commission was appointed to review the 1989 election results for the Legislative Assembly and municipal councils. Based on the commission's findings, the Electoral Tribunal proclaimed the election of fifty-eight legislators, who assumed office on March 1, 1990. Thus, the Legislative Assembly did not operate in the six-month period between September 1, 1989, and March 1, 1990. In 1991 the Electoral Tribunal held elections for nine unfilled assembly seats, after which the process to determine the composition of the sixty-seven-member chamber finally concluded (Ricord 1991).

13. A military-orchestrated electoral fraud ensured the election of Nicolás Ardito Barletta (PRD) to the presidency and a Legislative Assembly majority

for the PRD in 1984, the first time popular elections for the executive and an assembly were held in Panama since 1968. The military deposed Ardito in 1985. He was succeeded by (fraudulent) First Vice-President Eric Delvalle (PR), who was impeached by the Legislative Assembly and unseated in February 1988 after he issued a decree dismissing Manuel Noriega as commander of the Panamanian Defense Forces. On orders from Noriega, the Legislative Assembly bypassed constitutional succession by (fraudulent) Second Vice-President Roderick Esquivel (PL) and installed Manuel Solís Palma (PRD), a minister in Delvalle's cabinet, as "acting president." When the 1984–89 constitutional term expired, on August 31, 1989, the General Council of State instated Comptroller-General Francisco Rodríguez (PRD) as "provisional president." Rodríguez remained "provisional president" until the U.S. invasion of December 20, 1989, removed him from the presidential house (Ricord 1991).

14. According to Freedom House (2009a), nineteen Latin American independent states (that is, all except Cuba) classified as electoral democracies in 2008: Argentina, Bolivia, Brazil, Chile, Colombia, Costa Rica, Dominican Republic, Ecuador, El Salvador, Guatemala, Haiti, Honduras, Mexico, Nicaragua, Panama, Paraguay, Peru, Uruguay, and Venezuela.

Chapter 1. **Political Representation and Representative Assemblies**

1. Presumably, the suffrages of the people would be "more free" in larger districts because the "vicious arts"—which might include buying votes in various ways—are less practicable on a large scale. One could also suppose that because in larger constituencies personal attachments through family, friendship, business, or patron-client relationships are less widespread, people are more free to vote according to their consciences. I thank Martha Merritt for this observation.

2. I am grateful to Guillermo O'Donnell for pointing to the relevance of Weber's essay on parliamentary government.

3. I thank Salvador Sánchez for directing my attention to this point.

4. Through its own means, without outside assistance, on November 28, 1821, the *cabildo* (municipal council) of Panama City declared the isthmus's independence from Spain and its union with Simón Bolívar's Republic of Colombia (comprising present-day Colombia, Ecuador, and Venezuela). When Bolívar's Colombia disintegrated in 1830, Panama separated from Bogotá. After reuniting with New Granada (present-day Colombia), Panama again seceded, for a brief period, in 1831. The independent State of Panama, proclaimed on November 18, 1840, lasted thirteen months and obtained diplomatic recognition from Costa Rica.

5. The term *department*, still in use in Colombia, follows the French designation of *département*, the administrative division created after the 1789 Revolution under the centralized authority of the state.

6. I thank Ricardo Arias Calderón for directing my attention to the 1944–45 interlude.

7. According to a U.S. National Security Council information memorandum dated October 14, 1977, in 1955 Torrijos was recruited as a paid "confidential informant" of the U.S. Army's 470th Counterintelligence Corps (CIC). In exchange for intelligence information, he continued to receive money and in-kind payments from the CIC through at least 1970 (U.S. National Security Council 1977).

8. President Robles's electoral credentials were questionable. Observers argued that Arnulfo Arias won the 1964 elections but was deprived of the presidency by the incumbent Chiari administration and the National Guard, with U.S. support (Pizzurno and Araúz 1996, 476–78).

9. The Assembly of County Representatives never exercised this power autonomously. On the two occasions when it met to elect the president and vice-president, it simply rubber-stamped Omar Torrijos's choice for the office: Demetrio Lakas in 1972 and Aristides Royo in 1978 (*El Matutino,* September 2, 1978, text obtained through Brittmarie Janson Pérez; Koster and Sánchez Borbón 1990, 215–16, 223).

10. Ironically, in the sole instance when the Assembly of County Representatives attempted to reject a treaty negotiated by the military-controlled executive, the National Guard occupied the chamber and forced its members to approve the agreement. This occurred in November 1980, during assembly deliberations on the so-called Treaty of Montería, which granted Colombian warships exemption from payment of Panama Canal tolls (Azcárate 2000; *La Prensa,* November 13, 1980, and May 13, 1981).

11. Article 277 "recognized" Torrijos as "maximum leader of the Panamanian revolution" and granted him authority to coordinate all public administration tasks; appoint and dismiss cabinet ministers, members of the Legislative Council, and all other executive-appointed officers of the state; negotiate contracts and loans; direct the country's foreign affairs; and attend the meetings of the cabinet, the Legislative Council, the Assembly of County Representatives, the provincial councils, and the local community boards. The Legislative Council became partly elective in 1980, as a result of the 1978 constitutional reform (Fábrega and Boyd Galindo 1981, 45–46, 96–97).

12. In conducting this exercise, I used the standard methodology, which compares unicameral assemblies with lower chambers of bicameral congresses.

13. Appendices B and C do not provide robust evidence in support of this claim. Clientelism is generally considered to be more prevalent in Brazil, India,

and Indonesia—some of the countries with the highest ratio of representatives to total population—than in some of the states with the lower ratios, such as Andorra, Denmark, Finland, Iceland, Liechtenstein, Luxembourg, Norway, San Marino, and Sweden.

Chapter 2. The Party System: Parties and Actors in Panama's Assembly

1. This and all other quotes from Spanish-language sources are the author's translation.

2. Known in Colombia and Panama as the Mallarino-Bidlack Treaty, in this bilateral agreement New Granada (Colombia) granted the United States the right of free transit through the isthmus of Panama. In exchange, the United States assumed the "duty" of preserving the neutrality and security of the transit zone as well as New Granada's sovereignty over the isthmus (McCullough 1977, 136).

3. Examples include Rodolfo Chiari Robles (president in 1924–28), chief of the National Liberal Party, and his son Roberto Chiari Remón (president in 1960–64); Enrique A. Jiménez (president in 1945–48), leader of the Liberal Democratic Party; Domingo Díaz Arosemena (president in 1948–49), who led the Doctrinaire Liberal Party; and Francisco Arias Paredes, presidential hopeful in 1932 and 1945, head of the Renewal Liberal Party.

4. On party survival and extinction, see chapter 7.

5. Following its resounding electoral victory in 1989, in 1994 PDC's share of the presidential and assembly votes suffered a precipitous drop to 2 and 6 percent, respectively. Its assembly contingent declined from twenty-eight legislators in 1989–94 to one (Rubén Arosemena) in 1994–99.

6. Guillermo Endara was president in 1989–2004. Mireya Moscoso was chief executive in 1999–2004.

7. The Socialist International suspended Panama's PRD in 1989 as a result of its collaboration with the military regime of Manuel Noriega. The International reinstated PRD in the 1990s after the removal of the authoritarian system.

8. I calculated this adjusted effective number of assembly parties based on Electoral Tribunal data on party extinction, winning candidate proclamations, candidate lists, and personal interviews. On this basis, I estimated that during the period under review, PPAN received at least four additional members from extinct parties; CD, three; PLN, two; PRD, one; and PSOL, one (see appendix F).

9. Note, however, that volatility figures for Western European countries are based mostly on parliamentary elections, as opposed to Latin America's presidential elections.

10. As shown in appendix M, in 2009 only three parties held at least 10 percent of the seats in the assembly: PRD, founded in 1979; PPAN, originally established in 1934; and CD, founded in 1998.

11. Legislator Miranda died in 1991 and was replaced by Jílmer González, alternate legislator.

12. Legislator Sánchez died in 1997 and was replaced by José Carreño, alternate legislator.

13. Deputy Alvarado died in 2008 and was replaced by Omar Chavarría, alternate deputy.

14. Deputy Escudé died in 2009 and was replaced by Ramiro Villarreal, alternate deputy.

15. Deputy Altamirano Mantovani died in 2009 and was replaced by Tomás Altamirano Duque (his father), alternate deputy.

16. In May 2010 the Supreme Court declared unconstitutional the provision requiring candidates elected to two positions to opt for one of the two within ten days of the proclamation (Órgano Judicial 2010).

17. In September 1993 U.S. officials arrested Anel Ramírez in Miami at the culmination of a sting operation (see chapter 11). His substitute, Antonio Ramírez, should have taken his place in the assembly for the remainder of the 1989–94 term (September 1993–August 1994). Press reports, citing the Comptroller-General's Office, indicated that Antonio did not show up in the assembly (Otero 1994a).

18. Alternate Eleuteria Baker (PRD) replaced Legislator Miller. For more details of Miller's case, see chapter 11.

19. The average proportion of assembly members who sought reelection in 1989, 1994, 1999, 2004, and 2009 was 73 percent. The average proportion of deputies who achieved reelection was 39 percent. Reelection rates (based on the proportion of members seeking reelection) rose from 22 percent in 1989 to 27 percent in 1994 and 49 percent in both 1999 and 2004, before declining slightly to 46 percent in 2009 (see appendix I). Despite the increases, Panama's reelection rates are lower than in the United States where, on average, 95 percent of House members seeking reelection between 1990 and 2004 succeeded (Thirty-thousand.org 2006). Comparatively in Latin America, 80 percent of Chilean deputies seeking reelection in 1989–2009 succeeded (statistic compiled from Gobierno de Chile 2010 and Servicio Electoral de Chile 2008).

20. Although during the final writing stages I was not able to broaden the sample to include the age of all 309 members, in previously published research I provided the average age at the start of the 1945–48 and 1999–2004 periods (45 and 47 years, respectively) (Guevara Mann 2004). Thus, the average starting age at the dawn of the twenty-first century is slightly higher than in the mid-1940s, as is to be expected given the general increase in life expectancy.

21. Statistics compiled from Gobierno de Chile (2010) and Servicio Electoral de Chile (2008).

22. For brief reference to the club and its role in Panamanian society, see Simons (1999).

23. Marlina Morán, secretary to the board of directors of the club, provided information about membership in 2007. I updated the data in 2010 and corroborated the information with valuable help from Rita Preciado Recuero.

24. The basis for calculating this statistic was different in Chile. Instead of focusing on social club membership (an indicator that was not available for Chile at the time I completed this research), I focused on schools attended by 308 Chilean deputies, out of 329 in 1990–2010, who provided this information in their biographies (obtained at Biblioteca del Congreso Nacional de Chile 2010). Upper-class schools were identified with valuable assistance from Andreas Feldmann and Juan Esteban Montes. Classifications are available from the author.

25. As political historians have often emphasized, representative assemblies emerged in western Europe during medieval and modern times generally as political organizations representing the most influential socioeconomic sectors or "estates," including the landed nobility, the clergy, and—later—the propertied and commercial urban interests. Many of these assemblies remained the domain of the upper classes well into the modern era, up until the emergence of mass democracy in the late nineteenth and early twentieth centuries. In Great Britain, for example, Finer explains that while membership in the House of Lords consisted exclusively of titled nobility, the House of Commons was initially (up to the early eighteenth century) populated by representatives of the untitled landed gentry and, subsequently (up to the nineteenth century), by younger sons of peers who were not eligible to succeed to their fathers' seats in the Lords (Finer 1997, 1024 ff, 1337, 1356–57).

26. Dal Bó, Dal Bó, and Snyder's (2009) study covers the period from 1789 to 1996 (207 years). They observe that "while 11 percent of legislators were dynastic between 1789 and 1858, only 7 percent were dynastic after 1966" (119).

27. Brittmarie Janson Pérez, email to the author, June 15, 2008.

28. Adding deputies related by marriage to Harmodio Arias Madrid would have increased the Arias Madrid clan to at least nine members. These would have included Arias's father-in-law Aurelio Guardia Ponce (a deputy in 1904–16) and brother-in-law Aurelio Guardia Vieto (a deputy in 1936–40). I left them out of the Arias Madrid family tree because these members of the Guardia family were not closely related to Gerardo and Alfredo Arias Grimaldo (nephews of Harmodio and Arnulfo Arias Madrid), who were elected deputies in 1968 and 1994, respectively.

29. At a time when educational levels in Panama were quite precarious, Harmodio and Arnulfo Arias held advanced degrees from prestigious universities. Harmodio did undergraduate work at the University of Cambridge and in 1911 received a doctoral degree in law from the London School of Economics. Arnulfo obtained his bachelor's degree at the University of Chicago and a doctorate in medicine from Harvard University in 1924 (Szok 2001, 85n91, 110). The fact that both brothers overcame their rural middle-class backgrounds to obtain higher education at prominent universities served to enhance their prestige (Brittmarie Janson Pérez, email to the author, June 15, 2008).

30. Brittmarie Janson Pérez, email to the author, June 15, 2008.

31. For instance, upon seizing power in 1968 the military regime expropriated the Arias family's Editora Panamá América, which published three widely circulating newspapers: *El Panamá América, La Hora* (replaced by *El Matutino* during military rule), and the popular tabloid *Crítica*. The dictatorship retained control of these media until the 1989 U.S. invasion provided the Arias family with an opportunity to recover them after twenty-one years of military control (Sepúlveda 1983).

32. In the 1984 political campaign, Antonio Arias Campagnani's television and printed advertisements ingeniously positioned him alongside his great-uncle Arnulfo Arias (author's recollection). The strategy paid off when Arias Campagnani, who had no previous political experience, obtained a seat in the Legislative Assembly.

33. Pizzurno and Araúz (1996, 341, 354, 359) allude to the activities of the Liberal Party goon squads (*pie de guerra*) led by Ismael Vallarino. Novelist Gloria Guardia's *Lobos al anochecer* provides a vivid narration of these activities in the context of Panama's political and institutional degradation during the late 1940s and early 1950s (see Guardia 2006).

34. Vallarino's seat was filled by first alternate Wigberto Quintero (MOLIRENA), who was elected as a "principal" deputy in 2004.

35. It was joked that Arturo Vallarino had his own "party" bloc in the 2004–9 assembly, consisting of sister Marylín and brothers-in-law Javier Tejeira and Héctor Aparicio. Deputy Tejeira later quarreled with his wife, Carlota Vallarino, who filed family violence charges against the assembly member (Gálvez 2007).

36. Appendix K shows 160 members from urban constituencies, excluding the borderline case of Abelardo Antonío (PRD), elected in a rural constituency in 1989 but, subsequently, reelected three times by an urban district (1994, 1999, and 2009). Adding Legislator Antonío to the group of urban legislators increases the number of urban deputies to 161.

37. I am grateful to Manuel Alcántara and Mark Jones for emphasizing the relevance of the University of Salamanca surveys to this project.

Chapter 3. **Formal Institutional Incentives to Behavior**

1. In 1979–84 Ecuador forbade the consecutive reelection of deputies (Mejía Acosta 2004). The Venezuelan constitution of 1999 allows a maximum of two consecutive reelections. For the texts of the American constitutions, see Georgetown University (1995–2010).

2. Especially in the Spanish-speaking world, the type of system in which voters can select candidates within one party list (but not across lists) is also known as "closed, non-blocked list PR," to distinguish it from systems in which voters are allowed to choose candidates from all lists participating in the election (called "open lists" in this terminology). In this regard, see Antinori Bolaños (1995).

3. There were several exceptions to this general guideline, which are treated below.

4. Two vice-presidents of the republic were elected in 1984, 1989, 1994, 1999, and 2004; one vice-president is elected starting in 2009.

5. The Central American Parliament consists of twenty deputies from each of the following countries: Dominican Republic, El Salvador, Guatemala, Honduras, Nicaragua, and Panama. Costa Rica is not a member. The parliament was established through an international treaty in 1987 and began functioning in 1991. Panama joined in 1994 and elected its first Central American deputies in 1999. The parliament's decisions have no binding power; the chamber is meant to serve as a consultative, consensus-building entity that deflates conflict and provides general guidelines to the governments of its member states (PARLACÉN 2010). In 2009 Panama made a decision to withdraw from the Central American Parliament effective in November 2010 (Arcia Jaramillo 2010; Jackson 2009c).

6. This chronology is based on a review of the Electoral Code and its reforms. Antinori Bolaños (1995, 736–49) offers a much more detailed description, based on the decrees issued by the Electoral Tribunal to regulate vote tallying in the 1984, 1989, and 1994 elections.

7. As will be seen in chapters 4 and 7, fraud, clientelism, and regime-sponsored intimidation tarnished the 1984 election and contributed to fabricate a majority of votes for PRD. These phenomena, however, would not have produced PRD dominance in the chamber had it not been for such features as high multipartism (fourteen parties competed in the election) as well as small district size and magnitude. As a result, PRD received thirty-four chamber seats—twice the number it was entitled to had the system been perfectly proportional (see appendix M).

8. The elections, held on May 7, 1989, were annulled by the military-controlled Electoral Tribunal on May 10 as a result of the overwhelming vote in

favor of the opposition coalition led by Guillermo Endara. On December 26 — six days after the U.S. invasion — the same Electoral Tribunal revoked the annulment decree of May 10 and formed a commission to determine the composition of the assembly for the 1989–94 term, based on votes cast in the elections of May 7.

The commission included representatives of political parties participating in the 1989 elections and based its count on incomplete tally sheets. These tallies had numerous irregularities that were never cleared. Additionally, several of the parties that competed in the elections and were convoked to conduct the count had obtained their registries through illegal means. Furthermore, many potential candidates were prevented from freely participating in the 1989 elections through intimidation or violence.

Despite these serious issues, the new government and the Electoral Tribunal accepted the commission's report. On February 23, 1990, the Electoral Tribunal proclaimed the election of fifty-eight legislators and decided to hold a new vote to fill the remaining nine seats, representing districts that had returned insufficient electoral information. Thus constituted, the new assembly met for the first time on March 1, 1990. Partial elections to complete the chamber took place in 1991. As a result, the electoral process that began in 1989 finally concluded in 1991 (Ricord 1991, 565–68; Valdés Escoffery 2006a).

9. The general formula for deviation from proportionality (D) is: $D = (1/2) \sum |si - vi|$, in which si represents the percentage of seats obtained by each party and vi stands for the percentage of votes obtained by each party. See Taagepera and Shugart (1989, 104–8).

10. Eugenio Morice, email to the author, December 27, 2008; Morice (2000).

11. Editorial obtained through Brittmarie Janson Pérez. Francisco Linares Herbruger was a deputy for the province of Panama in 1940–44, 1952–56, and 1964–68. In each term he represented the party led at the time by his brother-in-law, Arnulfo Arias, that is, Partido Nacional Revolucionario (1940–44) and Partido Panameñista (1952–56 and 1964–68).

12. Brittmarie Janson Pérez, email to the author, November 27, 2000.

13. Small constituencies can actually achieve both sets of objectives, although the accountability and connection with voters fostered by clientelism is hardly the type that enhances the quality of democracy.

14. Geographically and culturally, the coastal region of Colombia shares common features with Panama.

15. See chapter 1, especially table 1.1.

16. The article numbers used in reference to the 1972 constitution correspond to the text after its most recent modification (2004).

17. Mario Galindo Heurtematte, personal interview with the author, January 4, 1999.

18. I changed the scores Shugart and Carey (1992) assigned Panama on "exclusive introduction of legislation" and "budgetary initiative" in accordance with the constitution of 1972, as reformed in 1983. With regard to the first aspect, Shugart and Carey assigned Panama a zero to indicate that the executive had no exclusive power for introducing legislation (apart from the executive budgetary initiative). According to my calculations, Panama scores at least 1 on this count, for only the executive may introduce legislation on government salaries and the structure of the national administration. I am grateful to Salvador Sánchez González for his views on this matter (email to the author, September 7, 1998).

In terms of budgetary initiative, I changed Panama's score from Shugart and Carey's zero, indicating no restriction on legislative amendment of the executive's budget proposal, to 1.5, in accordance with article 271 of the 1972 constitution, which indicates that the assembly may eliminate or reduce budget expense items except for debt service expenditures; may not increase expenditures without the approval of the cabinet; and may not increase income figures without the approval of the Comptroller-General's Office. If all these requirements are met, cabinet approval is still required to modify the budget bill.

19. While the five-year term introduced in 1983 is longer than the old regime's four-year period, it does represent an improvement over the six-year term during which county representatives were in office from 1972 to 1984. The 1941 constitution also stipulated a six-year term for elected officers (see chapter 1). I thank Ricardo Arias Calderón for drawing my attention to this point.

20. *El Panamá América*, July 27, 1970; editorial obtained through Brittmarie Janson Pérez.

Chapter 4. **Informal Institutions and Assembly Members' Behavior**

1. *Panama Report*, November 21, 2008.

2. U.S. support for Panama's emancipation from Colombia in 1903 also contributed to the success of the secessionist movement.

3. For eloquent treatments of corruption during the military regime, see Dinges (1990), Koster and Sánchez Borbón (1990), Naylor (1999), Ricord (1991), Ropp (1992), Velásquez (1993), and Zimbalist and Weeks (1991).

4. In 1983 the National Guard (*Guardia Nacional de Panamá*) was renamed "Panamanian Defense Forces" (*Fuerzas de Defensa de Panamá*). On the transformation of Panama's armed force, see Guevara Mann (1996).

5. Law no. 14 of 2010 requires that parties submit recalls they approve to the recalled deputy's constituents. Two-thirds of the constituency's voters must support the measure before it becomes effective (República de Panamá 2010b).

6. Gil Blas Tejeira was a deputy in the 1945–48 assembly.

7. *Regidor* refers to the unpaid deputy of a *corregidor,* or county magistrate, in an isolated locality.

8. The most recent Gini coefficient (a measure of inequality in income or consumption distribution) available for Panama at the time of this writing was 0.549. On a scale from 0 to 1, in which 0 represents perfect equality and 1 represents perfect inequality, Panama was the sixth most unequal society in Latin America, according to the United Nations Development Programme's 2009 *Human Development Report.*

9. Chapter 6 addresses this phenomenon in detail.

Chapter 5. **Political Advancement through Reelection: Prospects and Possibilities in Panama**

1. Statistics compiled by the author in February 2010 from Gobierno de Chile (2010) and Servicio Electoral de Chile (2008).

2. This was Alberto Alemán Boyd (PRD), legislator between 1984 and 1999.

3. Harrington (1994); see also opinion editorials in *La Prensa* on January 12, 1994; February 16, 1994; and May 17, 1994.

4. One vice-president is elected starting in 2009, pursuant to the 2004 constitutional reform.

5. Municipal mayors were elected in 1984 (but not in 1989) and, subsequently, in 1994, 1999, 2004, and 2009. Thus, election to this office was an available option for assembly members in the 1984–2009 sample beginning in 1994.

6. On the Central American Parliament (PARLACÉN), see chapter 3, note 5.

7. The appointment of incumbent deputies as Supreme Court justices, prosecutor-general, or solicitor-general was constitutionally banned in the 2004 reform.

8. Admittedly, strict application of this standard might be somewhat misleading. Appointment as provincial governor or head of an important office within a ministry may provide the officeholder with significant political clout. Within the foreign service, appointment to a merchant marine consulate might supply very attractive opportunities for enrichment, depending on the revenue-generating potential of the office. According to Panamanian law, as an incentive to promote maritime business certain consuls are entitled to appropriate 8 percent of the consulate's monthly revenues up to US$20,000; 9 percent of any excess up to US$50,000; and, beyond that figure, 10 percent (Castrellón

2009). However, in the interest of parsimony and with the purpose of conducting the most systematic analysis possible based on the predictions of the literature on legislators' behavior, which focuses on the career (not rent-seeking) aspirations of members of representative assemblies, I decided to focus on positions ranking equal to or higher than deputy in the public sector hierarchy.

9. This exercise focuses on appointments received (1) after the end of the representative mandate; and (2) during but exceeding the term of the mandate, such as those of Jerry Wilson (PRD) and Alberto Cigarruista (PPAN, previously PLA), who were appointed Supreme Court justices during their membership in the assembly for terms exceeding their representative mandates. It does not cover appointments to executive office during the representative mandate. At least three deputies have served as ministers during their assembly terms (permitted in Panama, as in other presidential republics, though not in the United States): Jorge Rubén Rosas (MOLIRENA, 1984–94), who was Minister of Labor in 1989–93; Héctor Alemán (PRD, 1999–2009), Minister of Government and Justice in 2004–6; and Guillermo Ferrufino (CD, 2009–14), appointed Minister of Social Development in 2009. Likewise, between 1989 and 1991, when municipal mayors were designated by the executive branch, Guillermo Cochez (PDC, 1984–94) served as mayor of Panama City, a substantial position given the visibility and budgetary resources of the office.

10. The 1972 constitution was amended in 1978, 1983, 1994, and 2004. The 1983 and 2004 reforms addressed the electoral system for assembly members. The 1983 Electoral Code was amended in 1984, 1988, 1992, 1993, 1997, 2002, 2006, 2007, and 2010.

Chapter 6. Political Advancement through Reelection: The Legal and Illegal Uses of Patronage

1. According to Díaz, the other two deputies were Jorge Rubén Rosas, a brother of Comptroller-General Olmedo Rosas, and Virgilio Schuverer, "who were not satisfied with their allocation and demanded a higher sum. We finally acceded to their wishes to prevent the destruction of this happy initiative" (O. Díaz 2000). Jorge Rubén Rosas served two terms as Movimiento de Liberación Nacional (MLN) deputy (1960–68) for Chiriquí Province and two additional terms as MOLIRENA legislator (1984–94); he also served as Labor Minister in 1989–93. Virgilio Schuverer served as Partido Acción Radical (PAR) deputy for Bocas del Toro Province (1964–68).

2. Ardito Barletta was fraudulently installed in the presidency by the Noriega dictatorship in 1984. See the introduction (note 13) as well as Arias de Para (1984).

3. Carlos Arellano Lennox, interview with the author, August 31, 2000. A protest leaflet distributed in late June 1987 claimed that one pro-dictatorship legislator was receiving US$300,000 monthly for distribution among other assembly members, including at least six opposition "sold legislators" (*legisladores vendidos*) (Panama protest leaflet, 1987, obtained through Brittmarie Janson Pérez).

4. Cochez (2000); see also articles in *El Panamá América,* January 1 and 3, 1993; *El Siglo,* January 3 and 16, 1993; and *La Prensa,* January 2 and 5, 1993.

5. Cochez (2000); Francisco Gómez, telephone conversation with the author, September 4, 2000.

6. Conceivably, it might also suggest transparent and efficient management of constituency funds by legislators, but this is unlikely given the sultanistic context that characterized military rule in Panama (see chapter 4).

7. Francisco Gómez, telephone conversation with the author, September 4, 2000. FES was renamed Fondo de Inversión Social, or FIS, at the beginning of President Mireya Moscoso's administration (1999–2004).

8. See an editorial in *El Panamá América,* September 10, 2000; *El Siglo,* September 6, 2000; Martínez (2000b); Otero (2000b); and Pérez Jaramillo (1999a).

9. See Cádiz (1999); Pérez Jaramillo (1999a); and articles in *El Panamá América,* June 14, 1999; *La Prensa,* May 6, 1999.

10. In 1999 the central government's current income amounted to US$1.7 billion (Contraloría General 2000, 31).

11. But, contrary to what some Panamanian assembly members seem to believe, the practice of allocating constituency funds to representatives is by no means widespread, least of all in advanced liberal democracies; the assignment of government resources on a particularistic basis clearly violates one of the defining characteristics of such democracies: "universalistic orientations to some version of the public good" (O'Donnell 1996, 40). In a meeting held on January 9, 1999, in support of the candidacy of Mireya Moscoso (PPAN), former legislator Gloria Moreno (PDC) declared her failure to understand the "fuss" over *partidas circuitales,* when (according to her) representatives everywhere, including U.S. senators and House members, "also have access to constituency funds" (author's personal recollection). In 2009 President Ricardo Martinelli appointed Moreno as director-general of the National Customs Authority (see table 5.4).

12. Michael Coppedge, email to the author, March 19, 1999; Bertilo Mejía Ortega, email to the author, December 27, 2008.

13. The quote from writer Gabriel García Márquez in chapter 3 refers to these funds.

14. Gary Hoskin, email to the author, August 14, 2000.

15. Jonathan Hartlyn, email to the author, August 14, 2000.

16. I am grateful to Aníbal Pérez Liñán for providing this reference.

17. Gary Hoskin, email to the author, August 14, 2000.

18. In the 2004 reform the constitutional term of office was modified to begin on July 1 and end on June 30, starting in 2009.

19. See Contraloría General (1999b, 58, 64) and articles in *El Panamá América* on December 4, 1995 and October 30, 1998.

20. This description of the allocation procedure for *partidas circuitales* comes from newspaper coverage, as indicated in the text; from analysis of the "Parliamentary Initiatives Program" breakdown for 1997 and 1998, included in Contraloría General (1998a, 1998b, 1999a, 1999b, 2000); and Miguel Antonio Bernal, email to the author, December 30, 1997; José Blandón Figueroa, email to the author, January 6 and 9, 1998; Guillermo A. Cochez, email to the author, March 1, 1999; and Francisco Gómez, telephone conversation with the author, September 4, 2000. All figures represent current U.S. dollars.

21. *El Panamá América,* October 30, 1998.

22. In 2004 Arosemena obtained reelection to his assembly seat and concurrent election as second vice-president of the republic on the presidential ticket headed by Martín Torrijos (PRD).

23. Blandón Figueroa (1998b); Contraloría General (1999b, 58, 64); Pérez Jaramillo (1999a); see also articles in *El Panamá América,* August 27, 1997, and October 30, 1998; and *El Siglo,* September 8, 1998.

24. Description of these uses comes from a review of *Crítica Libre, El Panamá América, El Siglo,* and *La Prensa* covering events between 1990 and 1999.

25. Cochez (1996); article *El Panamá América,* December 18, 1996; and Pérez Jaramillo (1998).

26. *El Panamá América,* February 9, 1999, and December 3, 1998.

27. Miguel Antonio Bernal, email to the author, December 30, 1997; Blandón Figueroa (1998b).

28. In 1998 Gabriel Castro, an attorney with close personal links to President Pérez Balladares, replaced Aristides Romero as comptroller-general after the latter's death (Castro and Berguido 2007).

29. *La Prensa,* July 17, 1990. Carlos Duque was PRD's presidential candidate in 1989, supported by the military regime and PRD satellite parties.

30. Pardo represented the constituency of Penonomé, the capital of Coclé Province. He failed to retain his seat in 1989 but returned to the assembly in 1994 and achieved reelection in 1999 and 2004 (see appendix E). He was assembly president between 1996 and 1997.

31. This summary of the PARVIS case is based on information obtained from Defensoría del Pueblo (1999); IDB (1997); Pérez Jaramillo (2000); and a review of PARVIS coverage in *El Panamá América* (1998–2000), *El Siglo* (1999–2000), and *La Prensa* (1998–2000).

32. Rigoberto Paredes was a PR deputy in 1964–68 and a PRD legislator in 1984–89. See chapter 10 for additional information about his relationship to the military dictatorship. Rogelio Paredes was elected deputy on the PRD ticket in 2004 and reelected in 2009 (see appendix E).

33. Gerardo González was elected Central American deputy in 2004 and died in 2006; Benicio Robinson was reelected for a third (nonconsecutive) term in 2004 and once again in 2009 (see appendix E).

34. Reelected in 2004, Pedro González became president of the National Assembly in 2007.

35. In 1990 a report by the Comptroller-General's Office mentioned Francisco Solís in connection with the Multiagency Program irregularities (see chapter 10). Solís received a pardon from Pérez Balladares in 1994 (Ministerio de Gobierno 1994e).

Chapter 7. Political Advancement through Reelection: Party Switching and Electoral Manipulation

1. Because the subset of 224 members includes deputies who achieved reelection, some names are repeated in the sample.

2. As indicated in table 7.2, the remaining two—Leopoldo Bendedetti and Rodrigo Jované—obtained nomination from PRC and PL, respectively.

3. Olimpo Sáez, email to the author, April 6, 2008.

4. Bocharel (2010); *El Panamá América,* June 8, 2010.

5. Gerardo González served two terms as PRD legislator (1989–94, 1994–99) and two terms as Legislative Assembly president (1997–98, 1998–99).

6. Arias de Para (1984); Carrasco (1987); Brittmarie Janson Pérez, email to the author, April 19, 1998; Guillermo A. Cochez, email to the author, September 4, 1998; *El Siglo,* June 10, 1987.

7. *El Siglo,* April 28 and 29, 1999; Ricord (1991, 97–108); see also notes 12 and 13 in the introduction.

8. At the time, Panama's electoral population was approximately 917,000.

9. Batista and Torres (1999); Berroa and Jordán (1999); *La Prensa,* May 8, 1999.

10. In a public letter to President Martín Torrijos dated April 2, 2009, opposition aspirant Hernán Delgado listed a number of alleged instances of use of government resources to support PRD candidate Tomás Altamirano Duque (Delgado Quintero 2009).

11. As vice-minister of housing in 1994–98, Rogelio Paredes was allegedly involved in the PARVIS affair (see chapter 6).

12. *El Siglo,* May 7, 1999.

13. Defensoría del Pueblo (1999); Ehrman (1999); *El Siglo,* May 6, 7, and 13, 1999; Torres (1999b, 1999c).

14. The U.S. government accused Pedro González, a son of assembly president Gerardo González (PRD) and a candidate in legislative district 9-3, of the killing of a U.S. serviceman. Chapter 11 describes the irregularities characterizing González's election in more detail.

15. *El Siglo,* April 28 and 29, 1999.

16. Ábrego (1999); *El Siglo,* May 4 and 5, 1999; *La Prensa,* May 5, 1999; Torres and Jordán (1999).

17. *El Siglo,* May 7, 1999.

18. *El Panamá América,* June 6, 1999.

Chapter 8. Personal Enrichment through Legal Means: Assembly Members' Wages in Comparative Perspective

1. *El Panamá América,* February 7, 1999. Nearly 560 candidates competed for the 71 chamber seats disputed in 1999, which represents an average of approximately 8 candidates per seat (Tribunal Electoral 1999a). While this may in part be attributed to the large number of parties competing in the election—twelve registered organizations participated in the process—it also indicates a strong desire among politicians for obtaining an assembly seat.

2. I am grateful to Martha Merritt for this insight.

3. For the text of the agreement, see U.S. Department of State (1972, 681–83).

4. This amount consists of a US$1,800 "salary"; "representation expenses" in the amount of US$3,200; a US$1,000 fuel allowance; and a US$1,000 "diet." In the period under review (1984–2009), deputies received the full amount of US$7,000 (less income tax and Social Security contributions) in their monthly paychecks, regardless of attendance or whether they incurred representation or fuel expenses. A reform of the Rules of Procedure adopted in February 2010 stipulates the loss of wages for "unjustified" absences. Article 229 of the assembly's Rules of Procedure requires that deputies obtain "the same prerogatives, emoluments, and allowances received by ministers of State" (Asamblea Nacional 2010a). A cabinet minister's monthly salary is US$7,000.

5. Appendix N provides the full data used for calculating these statistics. I am grateful to Jaime Ros for his assistance in carrying out this exercise.

6. The total number of deputy sittings is determined by multiplying the number of deputies at the time (78) by the number of assembly sessions (18). The number of deputies in 2004–9 was 79, but in September 2008 the Supreme Court had not yet ruled in favor of Teresita Yániz's claim that she had won a deputy's seat. Thus, the actual number of deputies at the time was 78.

7. See chapter 9, note 9.

8. I am grateful to Scott Mainwaring for suggesting this assessment of assembly members' income levels.

9. I was able to analyze the CVs at an earlier stage of research for this volume.

10. Together with the secretary-general, who is not a deputy, the president and two vice-presidents constitute the assembly board, or *Junta Directiva*. See article 13 of the Rules of Procedure in Asamblea Nacional (2010a).

11. Marco Ameglio, email to the author, September 11, 1998.

12. Mireya Lasso, email to the author, December 5, 2008.

13. José Blandón Figueroa, interview with the author, August 8, 2000; *El Siglo,* April 28 and May 3, 2000; see also chapter 6.

14. I thank Michael Coppedge for this observation.

15. Cable obtained through Juan Carlos Machado.

16. *El Panamá América,* September 3, 1998.

17. *América Económica,* January 30, 2008.

Chapter 9. **Personal Enrichment through Legal Means: Expanding Emoluments and Privileges**

1. The government bloc involved in this dispute was comprised of PDC, MOLIRENA, PLA (and PPAN under reorganization). This section is based on *La Prensa*'s editorial of February 20, 1990; Quintero de León (1990); Ricord (1991, 571–72); Rodríguez Jované (1990); and Vernaza (1990).

2. For details, see chapter 3, note 8.

3. The government bloc involved in this episode was PPAN and PLA in 1994 and PRD and PSOL in 1994–96. Arturo Vallarino, legislator for PALA (1984–89) and MOLIRENA (1989–2004), was elected four times to the National Assembly. In 1999, in addition to attaining reelection, Vallarino was elected first vice-president of the republic (see chapter 2).

4. This section is based on *El Panamá América,* February 7, 8, and 9, 1996; Figueroa (1994b); *La Prensa,* July 15, 1994; Mendieta and Otero (1994); Murillo Muñoz (1994c); Otero (1994b); Quintero de León (1994a); and Sucre Serrano (1994b).

5. The government bloc involved in this episode was comprised of PRD and PSOL. This section is based on *El Panamá América,* October 18, 1995; Olmedo Guillén, email to the author, April 16, 2000; Martínez Dettore (1994a, 1994b); Quintero de León (1994b, 1996); Rodríguez Bernal (1995); and Rujano (1994).

6. Blandón Figueroa (1998a); Víctor Méndez Fábrega, email to the author, April 27, 2000.

7. Pardo actually received such an allowance in 1997 in the form of US$1.1 million in constituency funding (see appendix R).

8. The government bloc involved in this dispute was comprised of PRD, PSOL, PLN, part of MPE, and two "independents." This section is based on Álvarez Cedeño (1996); Álvarez Cedeño and Rodríguez Bernal (1996); *El Panamá América,* October 24, 1995, November 24 and 26, 1995, December 2, 5, 9, 11, and 12, 1995, February 9, 1996, November 27 and 28, 1996, December 2–30, 1996; García Rivas (1996); Herrera y Franco (1996); Jordán (1996, 1997a); *La Prensa,* September 29, 1994, October 2, 19, and 20, 1996, December 6, 1996; Obaldía (1997); Otero (1996, 1997); Otero and Jordán (1996); Otero and Quintero de León (1997); Pérez González (2000a); Rodríguez Bernal (1996a, 1996b); Rodríguez Bernal and Sucre Serrano (1996); Rujano (1995); and Vega (1995).

9. At some point after 1996, alternates' salaries increased to US$1,000 and, later, US$1,500. Beginning in April 2000 substitutes' emoluments increased again to US$2,000. Alternates do not perform any service to the state in exchange for this payment. Deputies and parties thus compensate substitutes from the public treasury for their role as political activists (Jordán 2000; Víctor Méndez Fábrega, email to the author, April 10 and 27, 2000).

10. The government bloc involved in this episode was comprised of PRD, PSOL, PLN, part of MPE, and two "independents."

11. This section is based on Álvarez Cedeño (1994, 1998); Delgado (1998); *El Panamá América,* October 23, 27, and 30, 1998, May 21, 1999; Jordán (1996, 1997b); Jordán Serrano (1998a, 1998b); *La Prensa,* March 23, 1994, April 27, 1997, September 26, 1997, October 22, 1998, March 1, 1999; Víctor Méndez Fábrega, email to the author, April 10, 2000; Murillo Muñoz (1994a); Murillo Muñoz and Vega (1994); Otero (1994a, 1999a); Pérez González (1999); Quijano (1999); Reyes (1994); Rodríguez Bernal (1996b); Sucre Serrano (1994a); and Torres (1999a, 1999d).

12. Incidentally, Méndez failed to achieve reelection.

13. The government bloc involved in this episode was comprised of PPAN, MOLIRENA, CD, PSOL, PLN, and PDC. This section is based on Chéry (2001); Cordero (2000b); Díaz (2000a); Martínez (2000a); Pérez González (2000a, 2000b, 2000c); Santos Barrios (2000a, 2000b); Sucre Serrano (2001).

14. It is unclear why the claim covered eighteen instead of twenty-one months, that is, between October 1, 1995, when the ministerial pay increase became effective, and June 30, 1997, after which it was revoked.

15. The telegraph privilege was rescinded in 2010, with the decline in telegraphic communications.

16. Marco Ameglio, email to author, September 11, 1998; Miguel Antonio Bernal, email to the author, September 6, 1998; Guillermo A. Cochez, email to the author, September 4, 1998.

17. I fielded this request when serving as acting vice-minister of foreign affairs, November 2–6, 1999. I refused to sign the passport.

18. Frank Iglesias is the father of one of Pérez Balladares's sons-in-law.

19. *El Panamá América,* November 27, 1996.

20. Guillermo A. Cochez, email to the author, December 11, 2008.

21. Other public officials, such as county representatives or councilors, also have special plates.

22. I am grateful to Mark Jones for this reference.

23. I am grateful to Aníbal Pérez Liñán for this reference.

24. David Altman, email to the author, April 8, 2000.

25. *La Prensa,* May 3, 1994.

26. Ibid.

27. At the time there were 67 legislators and 134 substitutes in the assembly. The total number of exempted vehicles legislators were allowed to purchase was 201 (67 x 3). The total for alternates was 268 (134 x 2), giving a grand total for the period of 469.

28. *La Prensa,* March 19, 1994.

29. *La Prensa,* May 3, 1994. *La Prensa* reported that Bavarian Motors, of whose board Rubén Arosemena was a member, had sold forty-five BMWs to legislators and substitutes between 1990 and 1993. In addition to his election as legislator and second vice-president of the republic (2004), Arosemena was elected PDC president in 1995 (Otero and Hernández 1995).

30. *La Prensa,* May 27, 1999.

Chapter 10. **Personal Enrichment through Illegal Means**

1. Bernal (2000); *El Panamá América,* August 28, 2000; *El Siglo,* August 7, 2000.

2. The term is also used in other Latin American countries to refer to members of legislative bodies. In Panama it was popularized by Pedro Altamiranda, a well-known composer and singer, with his 2004 theme *Los legisladrones o relevo generacional* (*Crítica Libre,* March 28, 2004).

3. Chapter 3 explains the effect of electoral laws on the makeup of the assembly. Chapter 4 addresses the consequences of informally institutionalized corruption, impunity, and clientelism on assembly members' behavior. Chapter 7 describes the 1984 electoral fraud, gross irregularities in the 1989 elections, and more subtle means of manipulating the popular vote in 1994–2009, which worked to some parties' advantage, including PRD.

4. Information on the prosecution and sentencing of Rigoberto Paredes comes from articles in *La Prensa* on the following dates: February 10, 1990; March 19, 1990; January 14, 1991; March 14, 1991; July 18, 1991; September 2, 1991; February 23, 1994; September 24, 1994; and January 10, 1996.

5. *The Economist Intelligence Unit*, April 3, 2000.

6. This section is based on Berroa (2000); Berroa and Jordán (2000); Cordero (2000a); *El Panamá América*, January 3–13, 2000, January 25, 2000; Janson Pérez (2000a); *La Prensa*, January 5, 2000; Ortega Luna (2000); Pérez González and Rodríguez (2000); Rodríguez (2000); Sucre Serrano and Domínguez (2000); and Sucre Serrano and Jordán (2000).

7. For a detailed discussion of the dynamics of constituency funds, see chapter 6.

8. *El Panamá América*, January 3–13, 2000.

9. This section is based on *El Panamá América*, November 28, 1995, December 2–5, 1995, December 20, 1995, May 11, 1998; Jackson (2006); *La Prensa*, December 6, 1995, December 10, 1995, September 26, 1997, October 15–17, 1997, October 21, 1997, November 22, 1997, December 1, 1997, May 9, 1998, June 2, 1998; July 1, 1998, July 31, 1998, September 13, 1999; and Quintero Jiménez (1994).

10. The assembly did not grant the contract. A bidding process for the construction of a new building began in 2010 (Muñoz Aragón 2010).

11. This section is based on *La Estrella de Panamá*, June 18, 1993; and *La Prensa*, November 27, 1992, December 10, 1992, December 29, 1992, December 31, 1992, May 1, 1994, June 30, 1994, and January 23, 1998.

12. I thank Michael Coppedge for this observation.

13. "Crooked Congressman Going to Prison," *CNN.com*, March 3, 2006, http://articles.cnn.com/2006-03-03/justice/cunningham.sentenced_1_congressman-cunningham-jason-forge-mitchell-wade?_s=PM:LAW.

14. Cochez (1999); *El Panamá América*, June 17, 1999; *La Prensa*, May 23 and June 17, 1999.

15. The description of the slot machine case is based on *La Prensa*, February 22–24, 1994, June 16, 1994, June 29, 1994, July 2, 1994, July 30, 1994, August 13, 1994, August 16–17, 1994, August 22, 1994, and October 3–12, 1994.

16. *El Panamá América*, February 11, 2000; *La Prensa*, July 2, 1999.

17. Miranda (2000); *The Economist Intelligence Unit*, April 10, 2000.

18. *El Panamá América*, March 8 and 11, 1999; Pérez Jaramillo (1998, 1999); and Rafael Pérez Jaramillo, personal conversations with the author, March 12, 17, and 18, 1999.

19. The Alba case is based on *El Panamá América*, October 26–29, 1996, November 7–13, 1996; and *La Prensa*, October 25–29, 1996, November 7–11, 1996, and August 21, 1997.

20. This section is based on *La Prensa*, January 27, 1990, July 29, 1992, March 7, 1994, May 16, 1996, and June 3, 1999.

21. In 1994 Pérez Balladares appointed Sossa as prosecutor-general for a ten-year term (1995–2005).

22. This section is based on *Crítica,* December 19, 1984, June 18, 1987, July 8, 1986, July 11, 1987; *El Matutino,* July 29, 1986, August 7, 1986; *El Panamá América,* May 23, 1996, September 25 and 28, 1997; *El Siglo,* January 4, 1990, February 10, 1990; Figueroa (1999); Henry (1999b); Brittmarie Janson Pérez, email to the author, April 14, 2000; *La Prensa,* January 12, 1990, January 20, 1990, February 13, 1990, February 22–24, 1990, March 7–10, 1990, April 30, 1990, May 9, 1990, May 16, 1990, May 24, 1990, June 28, 1990, July 12, 1990, September 9, 1990, October 27, 1990, October 30–31, 1990, November 1–3, 1990, November 8–16, 1990, December 6, 1990, December 14, 1990, August 12, 1991, February 7, 1994, March 17, 1994, March 23, 1994, April 8, 1994, September 12, 1994, October 4–8, 1994, October 13, 1994, November 7, 1994, November 10, 1994, November 28, 1994, February 18, 1995, February 28, 1995, November 2, 1995, December 30, 1995, January 1 and 26, 1996, July 7, 1996, August 12, 1996, September 22, 1996, September 27–28, 1997, October 2–4, 1997, March 27, 1998, August 11–12, 1998; *La República,* December 19, 1984, June 14, 1987; Bertilo Mejía Ortega, email to the author, December 27, 2008; Rivera (1999, 2004); and Sánchez Borbón (1992, 1994a, 1994b).

23. Hugo Giraud was elected as deputy to the Central American Parliament (PARLACÉN) on the PRD ticket in 1999 and reelected in 2004. In October 2000 he was elected president of PARLACÉN (Cordero 2000c). Camilo Gozaine competed for an assembly seat on the PRD ticket and obtained reelection, after two terms, in May 1999. In 2004 he tried to hold on to his seat but was defeated.

24. Ricardo Martinelli was elected president of Panama in 2009 as a candidate of his own CD, PPAN, UP, and MOLIRENA.

Chapter 11. **Preserving Immunity through Reelection**

1. *La Prensa,* September 29, 1997.

2. This historical interpretation is originally Hans Kelsen's, as expressed in *Vom Wessen und Wert der Demokratie* (Tübingen, 1929).

3. Panama did not respond to the IPU questionnaire by the close of 2008. I added the country to the sample based on the relevant information contained in the constitution (República de Panamá 2004).

4. As in most other countries where inviolability applies, the assembly also held the exclusive right to decide whether a legislator would be prosecuted, in which case it had to authorize the trial. While deliberative chambers traditionally grant their members certain privileges and immunities in order to guarantee the effective performance of representative duties (as indicated, for

example, in article 1, section 6 of the U.S. Constitution), the Panamanian case stands out for the breadth of these prerogatives in 1984–2004, as specified in the assembly's Rules of Procedure and exemplified by custom and practice.

5. This provision also applies to presidents, vice-presidents, and secretaries and subsecretaries of officially recognized political parties, as well as to several officers of the Electoral Tribunal.

6. The Prosecutor-General's Office did not formalize the case against a fourth PRD legislator, Mario Rognoni.

7. Marco Ameglio, email to the author, September 11, 1998; Miguel Antonio Bernal, email to the author, September 6, 1998; Guillermo A. Cochez, email to the author, September 4, 1998; email to the author from a confidential source, 1998; *El Panamá América,* February 7, 1990; Janson Pérez (1998b); *La Prensa,* February 4, 1990; Guillermo Márquez Amado, email to the author, September 3, 1998.

8. Arellano Lennox broke with the PDC leadership in 1993. After the 1994 elections, he joined PPAN.

9. *La Prensa,* June 27, 1990, July 2, 1990, September 4, 1990.

10. *La Prensa,* July 13 and 25, 1990. The nine members of the Rules Committee were Raúl Ossa, Gloria Moreno, and Raquel Lanuza of PDC; Miguel Cárdenas, Domiluis Montenegro, and Leo González of MOLIRENA; Aurelio Alba and Marco Ameglio of PLA; and Alberto Alemán Boyd of PRD. All except Alemán Boyd voted in favor of recommending immunity suspension (Marco Ameglio, email to the author, September 11, 1998; *La Prensa,* July 25, 1990).

11. In September 1990 the government coalition in the Legislative Assembly consisted of PDC, MOLIRENA, and PLA. Some PLA legislators were members of PPAN who had switched for "emergency" reasons (see chapter 7). Together, these parties held fifty-one of the still incomplete assembly's fifty-eight seats. PRD members held all seven opposition seats.

12. *La Prensa,* September 4 and 8, 1990. Alonso Fernández Guardia joined PPAN after the 1994 elections. The September 1990 deal set the stage for productive collaboration between the PRD bloc and the MOLIRENA and PLA contingents in the chamber. Thanks to PRD support, MOLIRENA, PLA, and PPAN (which re-registered as Partido Arnulfista in 1991) obtained control of the directing positions of the assembly in 1990–91, 1992–93, and 1993–94 (Marco Ameglio, email to the author, September 11, 1998; *La Prensa,* December 30, 1992; *Latin American Newsletters* wire, September 24, 1992).

13. *La Prensa,* September 4–20, 1990.

14. Miguel Antonio Bernal, email to the author, September 6, 1998; email to the author from a confidential source, 1998; *La Prensa,* January 5, 1991, February 26, 1991, March 12, 1991, April 23, 1991, April 28, 1991, May 3, 1991, June 5, 1992; República de Panamá (1992); Salvador Sánchez González, email to the author, September 7, 1998.

15. República de Panamá (1992 [article 78]); Salvador Sánchez González, email to the author, September 7, 1998.

16. At the prosecutor-general's request, the Supreme Court had the option of requesting a once-only, two-and-a-half-month extension to broaden the case. The assembly had the right to approve or reject the extension request.

17. This section is based on Marco Ameglio, email to the author, September 11, 1998; Miguel Antonio Bernal, email to the author, September 6, 1998; Guillermo A. Cochez, email to the author, September 4, 1998; email to the author from a confidential source, 1998; and *La Prensa,* December 29, 1990, February 26, 1991, March 12, 1991, April 28, 1991, June 6, 1992, September 3, 1996.

18. As a result of electoral irregularities in May 1989 and the overthrow of the military regime following the U.S. invasion in December 1989, partial elections to complete the membership of the assembly were held in January 1991. The PRD and its allies (PALA, PL) acquired five of the nine contested seats in the elections of January 27, 1991 (*La Prensa,* January 30, 1991).

19. In March 1991 Humberto Peláez, president of the Latin American Parliament (PARLATINO), and Deputy Walter Márquez, member of the Human Rights Subcommittee of the Venezuelan Congress, visited Castillo in prison (*La Prensa,* March 12, 1991).

20. In April 1991 PDC withdrew from the government coalition. MOLIRENA, PLA, and PPAN (which re-registered as Partido Arnulfista in 1991) remained in the coalition until the beginning of the 1994 electoral campaign. At that time, MOLIRENA withdrew from the alliance.

21. *La Prensa,* June 6, 1992. Castillo's attorney asserted this decision was legal because the constitution authorizes the retroactive application of a law when it benefits an accused or convicted individual.

22. *La Prensa,* October 7, 1994, August 29, 1995, December 23, 1995, August 20, 1997.

23. *La Prensa,* June 15, 1991, June 16, 1992; UPI wire, July 6, 1992.

24. *La Prensa,* June 23, 1992.

25. *La Prensa,* June 16, 1992, April 4, 1997, April 20, 1997.

26. This section is based on Brannan Jaén (1994b, 1994c, 1994d, 1994e, 1997a); *La Prensa,* December 27, 1993, February 24, 1994, March 15, 1994, April 6, 1994, August 29, 1994; and Reuters wires, October 20 and 25, 1993, April 6, 1994.

27. *La Prensa,* August 30, 1994.

28. This section is based on Marco Ameglio, email to the author, September 11, 1998; Miguel Antonio Bernal, email to the author, September 6, 1998; email to the author from a confidential source, 1998; J. M. Díaz (2000b); *El Panamá América,* December 3 and 26, 1997; Janson Pérez (2000b) and email to the author, May 8, 2000; Jordán Serrano (2000b); *La Prensa,* November 22

and 24, 1994, November 29–December 3, 1994, March 24, 1995, November 22–24, 1995, December 8, 1995; Guillermo Márquez Amado, email to the author, September 3, 1998; Otero (2000a); and Sagel and Díaz (2000).

29. An editorial in *La Prensa* (May 17, 1995) complained that a recent amendment to the Judicial Code had given the assembly the right to determine the flagrancy of a crime imputed to one of its members.

30. *La Prensa,* May 23 and 24, 1994.

31. Brannan Jaén (1997b); *El Panamá América,* November 5, 1997; Garvin (1997a); *La Prensa,* November 25, 1997.

32. *El Panamá América,* October 28–31, 1998, November 11–12 and 24–27, 1998, December 2 and 3, 1998.

33. *El Panamá América,* April 1, 1999; *El Siglo,* May 8–18, 1999; *La Prensa,* March 31, 1999, May 16, 1999.

34. *El Panamá América,* May 18, 1999.

35. *Latin Business Chronicle,* March 17, 2008.

36. Incumbents in 2009–14 who served in 1999–2004, during which the CEMIS case took place, include Carlos Afú (independent, previously PPAN, PRD, PALA), Francisco Alemán (PPAN), Abelardo Antonío (PRD), Héctor Aparicio (MOLIRENA), Denis Arce (PRD), José Blandón (PPAN), Elías Castillo (PRD), José Fábrega (PRD, previously PSOL and PPAN), Sergio Gálvez (CD, previously PPAN), Osman Gómez (PPAN), Rubén de León (PRD), José Muñoz (CD, previously PSOL and PPAN), Jorge Rosas (MOLIRENA), Noriel Salerno (UP, previously PSOL), Freidi Torres (PRD), José Varela (PPAN), and Alcibíades Vásquez (PPAN).

Conclusion

1. In an opinion editorial published in *La Prensa,* Legislator Teresita Yániz (PDC, 1999–2009) attributed Panamanian assembly members' emphasis on service and allocation responsiveness through *partidas circuitales* "to the lack of political culture which we suffer as a nation, the result of 21 years of military hegemony," in addition to "the harsh reality faced by the majority of the population, burdened with concrete and urgent problems." She added: "The wish to solve problems and provide assistance . . . is a genuine preoccupation of many legislators, who live in close contact with their constituents. Abandoned by the executive, constituents demand attention in the areas of health, education, transportation, and employment. *Partidas circuitales* serve to address these needs. Clientelism exists and prospers because there are clients who need urgent attention" (Yániz de Arias 2000).

2. *El Panamá América,* October 21, 1997; *La Prensa,* October 21, 1997.

3. In 2000 Peru reintroduced the ban on consecutive presidential reelection (see the Peruvian constitution in Georgetown University [1995–2010]).

4. *El Panamá América,* September 29, 1997.

5. *La Prensa,* June 24, 1998.

6. *El Panamá América,* November 26, 1997, May 19, 1998.

7. Defensoría del Pueblo (1998); *El Panamá América,* August 31, 1998.

8. The cost of organizing the presidential reelection referendum reportedly amounted to US$5 million (*El Panamá América,* October 21, 1997). This figure does not include amounts expended for publicity or other "incentives" provided by the government to build up popular support for reelection.

Works Cited

Abad, Jaime. n.d. "Cronología del asesinato de un soldado y el linchamiento de un ex-policía." Unpublished pamphlet.

Ábrego, Aris. 1999. "Fiscalía investiga pérdida de 163 actas electorales." *El Panamá América,* May 4. http://www.pa-digital.com.pa/ (accessed May 17, 2000, through the electronic archive).

Alemán, Alfredo. 1982. *Mayor Alemán: Memorias.* Panama: Ministerio de Educación, 1982.

Alfaro, Julio. 2004. "Milanés de Lay pierde curul." *La Prensa,* September 13. http://mensual.prensa.com/mensual/contenido/2004/09/13/hoy/pdf/Portada.pdf (accessed May 16, 2010).

———. 2006. "Nueva demanda contra exoneración de carros." *La Prensa,* February 24. http://mensual.prensa.com/mensual/contenido/2006/02/24/hoy/panorama/513731.html (accessed May 16, 2010).

Alianza Ciudadana Pro Justicia. 2004. *Justicia independiente: una exigencia ciudadana.* Panama: Alianza Ciudadana Pro Justicia.

Alvarado, José Manuel. 1999. "La modernización de la Asamblea Legislativa de Panamá." In *Experiencias de modernización legislativa en América Central y República Dominicana,* ed. Ronny Rodríguez. San José: Instituto Interamericano de Derechos Humanos. http://www.oas.org/sap/publications/1999/experiencias_modernizacion/doc/pbl_experiencias_modernizacion_99_spa.pdf (accessed May 16, 2010).

Álvarez Cedeño, Manuel. 1994. "Continúa el ausentismo legislativo." *La Prensa,* March 4. http://biblioteca.prensa.com/contenido/1994/batch02/santi-0000131.html (accessed May 16, 2010).

―――. 1996. "Alemán Boyd acusa a medios de 'tergiversar' ley." *La Prensa*, December. http://biblioteca.prensa.com/contenido/1996/batch11/animal-000 0748.html (accessed May 16, 2010).

―――. 1998. "Asamblea sesionó solo dos días esta semana por falta de quórum." *La Prensa*, September 11. http://biblioteca.prensa.com/contenido/1998/ 09-septiembre/19b40054.html (accessed May 16, 2010).

Álvarez Cedeño, Manuel, and Rolando Rodríguez Bernal. 1996. "Exige el legislador Bush: Tenemos que ganar igual que ministros." *La Prensa*, February 2. http://biblioteca.prensa.com/contenido/1996/batch01/busha-000 0091.html (accessed May 16, 2010).

Amer, Mildred. 1999. "Membership of the 106th Congress: A Profile." CRS Report for Congress, RS20013. Washington, DC: Congressional Research Service, Library of Congress.

―――. 2001. "Membership of the 107th Congress: A Profile." CRS Report for Congress, RS20760. Washington, DC: Congressional Research Service, Library of Congress. http://digital.library.unt.edu/govdocs/crs/permalink/ meta-crs-1517:1 (accessed May 16, 2010).

―――. 2004. "Membership of the 108th Congress: A Profile." CRS Report for Congress, RS21379. Washington, DC: Congressional Research Service, Library of Congress. http://www.senate.gov/reference/resources/pdf/ RS21379.pdf (accessed May 16, 2010).

―――. 2006. "Membership of the 109th Congress: A Profile." CRS Report for Congress, RS22007. Washington, DC: Congressional Research Service, Library of Congress. (http://www.senate.gov/reference/resources/pdf/ RS22007.pdf (accessed May 16, 2010).

―――. 2008. "Membership of the 110th Congress: A Profile." CRS Report for Congress, RS22555. Washington, DC: Congressional Research Service, Library of Congress. (http://www.senate.gov/reference/resources/pdf/ RS22555.pdf (accessed May 16, 2010).

Antinori Bolaños, Italo. 1995. "La representación política en Panamá: partidos políticos y sistema electoral." Ph.D. diss., Universidad Complutense de Madrid. http://www.ucm.es/BUCM/tesis/19911996/S/0/S0018201.pdf (accessed May 16, 2010).

―――. 2000. *Panamá y su historia constitucional (1808–2000)*. Panama: Defensoría del Pueblo de la República de Panamá.

Archer, Ronald, and Matthew Soberg Shugart. 1997. "The Unrealized Potential of Presidential Dominance in Colombia." In *Presidentialism and Democracy in Latin America*, ed. Scott Mainwaring and Matthew Soberg Shugart, 110–59. Cambridge: Cambridge University Press.

Arcia Jaramillo, O'Higgins. 2010. "Secretario del SICA respeta la salida de Panamá del Parlacen." *La Prensa*, May 10. http://www.prensa.com/hoy/ panorama/2183285.asp (accessed May 16, 2010).

Arias Calderón, Ricardo. 2003a. "Recordando el futuro: política y gobernantes. Establecimiento de la República, 1903–1931: conservadores y liberales." *El Panamá América,* June 1.

———. 2003b. "Recordando el futuro: política y gobernantes. Establecimiento de la República, 1902–1931: Belisario Porras." *El Panamá América,* June 8.

———. 2003c. "Recordando el futuro: política y gobernantes. Establecimiento de la República, 1903–1931. Porras y el porrismo." *El Panamá América,* June 15.

Arias de Para, Raúl. 1984. *Así fue el fraude.* Panama: Imprenta Edilito.

Arnold, R. Douglas. 1979. *Congress and the Bureaucracy: A Theory of Influence.* New Haven, CT: Yale University Press.

Arosemena, Mariano. 1949. *Apuntamientos históricos (1801–1840).* Panama: Ministerio de Educación, 1949 [manuscript originally completed in 1868].

Arosemena, Víctor. 2004. "Más denuncias electorales." *La Prensa,* May 8. http://biblioteca.prensa.com/contenido/2004/05/08/8-4a-fotonota.html (accessed May 16, 2010).

Asamblea Legislativa de Panamá. 1984. *Ley 49 del 4 de diciembre de 1984; Ley 50 del 12 de diciembre de 1984.* Vol. 5 of *Leyes aprobadas por la Asamblea Legislativa, 1984.* Panama: Asamblea Legislativa.

———. 1992. "Ley No. 7 de 27 de mayo de 1992, por la cual se reforma la Ley No. 49 de 4 de diciembre de 1984, que dicta el Reglamento Orgánico del Régimen Interno de la Asamblea Legislativa." *Gaceta Oficial* no. 22.044, May 28. http://www.asamblea.gob.pa/APPS/LEGISPAN/PDF_GACETAS/1990/1992/22044_1992. PDF (accessed June 3, 2008).

———. 1998. "Ley No. 16 de 17 de febrero de 1998, por la que se reforma el Texto Unico del Reglamento Orgánico del Régimen Interno de la Asamblea Legislativa." *Gaceta Oficial* no. 23.486, February 19.

———. 1999. *Reglamento orgánico del régimen interno de la Asamblea Legislativa* [Rules of Procedure]. Panama: Asamblea Legislativa.

Asamblea Nacional de Panamá. 1904–40. *Anales de la Asamblea Nacional.* Panama: Asamblea Nacional.

———. 1948/1998. "Resolución por la cual la Asamblea Nacional se declara Asamblea Constituyente." *Estudios Políticos* 1 (January–March 1998): 34–36.

———. 2007. "Acta de la sesión ordinaria de la Asamblea Nacional correspondiente al 12 de septiembre de 2007." http://www.asamblea.gob.pa/actas/actas-2007/SEPTIEMBRE/ACTA_09_12_07.pdf (accessed May 16, 2010).

———. 2008a. "Miembros de las comisiones por bancadas (2008–2009)." http://www.asamblea.gob.pa/COMISIONES%202008-2009.pdf (accessed December 28, 2008).

————. 2008b. "Cuadro de Asistencia Mensual de Honorables Diputados y Suplentes" (September). http://www.asamblea.gob.pa/transparencia/asistencia/ASISTENCIASEPTIEMBRE08.pdf (accessed May 16, 2010).

————. 2008c. "Curules de la Asamblea Nacional." http://www.asamblea.gob.pa/asamblea/curules-diputados.pdf (accessed May 16, 2010).

————. 2010a. *Reglamento orgánico del régimen interno de la Asamblea Nacional* [Rules of Procedure]. Panama: Asamblea Nacional. http://www.asamblea.gob.pa/main/LinkClick.aspx?fileticket=smg-o5j5U0U%3d&tabid=123 (accessed May 16, 2010).

————. 2010b. "Proyecto de Ley #131, por el cual se modifican, adicionan y derogan disposiciones del Código Procesal Penal adoptado por la Ley #63 de 2008." http://www.asamblea.gob.pa/actualidad/proyectos/2010/2010_P_131.pdf (accessed May 16, 2010).

————. 2010c. "Cuadro de asistencia mensual de honorable diputados y suplentes" (April). http://www.asamblea.gob.pa/main/LinkClick.aspx?fileticket=wNjIHu1J4aY%3d&tabid=136 (accessed May 16, 2010).

————. 2010d. "Resolución #132 de 30 de abril de 2010, por la cual se ratifica la decisión de la Comisión de Credenciales, Justicia Interior, Reglamento y Asuntos Judiciales, de no admitir el expediente contentivo de la denuncia relativa a la ratificación de los nombramientos de dos magistrados de la Corte Suprema de Justicia, Alberto Cigarruista Cortés y Winston Spadafora Franco y de archivar el expediente." *Gaceta Oficial* no. 26,530-A, May 11. http://www.gacetaoficial.gob.pa/pdfTemp/26530_A/27479.pdf (accessed May 16, 2010).

Atwood, Roger. 2004. *Stealing History: Tomb Raiders, Smugglers, and the Looting of the Ancient World.* New York: Macmillan.

Azcárate, Fermín. 2000. "Recordando a Julio E. Linares." *El Panamá América,* April 22.

Barros, Laura. 2007. "Los diputados en toda América devengan salarios escandalosos." *Agencia EFE,* April 10. http://www.radiolaprimerisima.com/noticias/12246 (accessed December 16, 2008).

Batista, Juan, and Víctor Torres. 1999. "Según abogado de Riley Puga: El fraude del 9-3 fue bien planificado." *La Prensa,* May 16. http://biblioteca.prensa.com/contenido/1999/05/25g45247.html (accessed May 16, 2010).

Beetham, David, Pauline Ngan, and Stuart Weir. 2002. "Democratic Audit: An Inauspicious Year for Democracy." *Parliamentary Affairs* 55 (2): 400–415.

Behar, Olga, and Ricardo Villa. 1991. *Penumbra en el Capitolio.* Santafé de Bogotá: Planeta Colombiana Editorial.

Benhabib, Seyla, ed. 1996. "Toward a Deliberative Model of Democratic Legitimacy." In *Democracy and Difference: Contesting the Boundaries of the Political,* ed. Seyla Benhabib. Princeton, NJ: Princeton University Press.

Bernal, Miguel Antonio. 1986. *Militarismo y administración de justicia.* Panama: Ediciones Nari.

———. 1992. *¿Reformas o constituyente?* Panama: Ediciones Nari.

———. 2000. "Partidas circuitales." *El Panamá América,* September 11.

———. 2004. "Las inconsultas reformas constitucionales." *Investigación y pensamiento crítico* 2:51–63. http://www.usma.ac.pa/web/DI/images/IPC%20No.%202/p.51-63%20_Bernal_%20corregido.pdf (accessed May 16, 2010).

Berroa, Gerardo. 2000. "De los Cartier al Concha y Toro." *La Prensa,* December 23. http://mensual.prensa.com/mensual/contenido/2000/12/23/hoy/portada/index.htm (accessed May 16, 2010).

Berroa, Gerardo, and Gionela Jordán. 1999. "Denuncian 'trasplante' de electores en el circuito 8–9." *La Prensa,* May 7. http://biblioteca.prensa.com/contenido/1999/05/25734503.html (accessed May 16, 2010).

———. 2000. "Obsequio de los Cartier fue un gesto inoportuno: Guardia." *La Prensa,* January 8. http://mensual.prensa.com/mensual/contenido/2000/01/08/sabado/portada.html (accessed May 16, 2010).

Bertelsmann Transformation Index. 2008. "Panama Country Report." http://www.bertelsmann-transformation-index.de/1396.0.html?&L=1 (accessed May 16, 2010).

Biblioteca del Congreso Nacional de Chile. 2010. "Reseñas parlamentarias." http://biografias.bcn.cl/pags/biografias/index.php (accessed May 20, 2010).

Biesanz, John, and Mavis Hiltunen Biesanz. 1955. *The People of Panama.* New York: Columbia University Press.

Blandón Figueroa, José. 1998a. "Hacia una nueva Asamblea." *La Prensa,* October 18.

———. 1998b. "Las partidas circuitales." *La Prensa,* November 29.

———. 1999. "Reelección y partidas circuitales." *El Panamá América,* March 10.

Bocharel, Flor. 2010. "Diputado abandona las filas del PRD y se va al CD." *La Prensa,* May 10. http://mensual.prensa.com/mensual/contenido/2010/05/10/hoy/nacionales/2182937.asp (accessed May 16, 2010).

Boyd Marciacq, Carmen. 2008. "Haydeé Milanés de Lay acusa a Balbina de tratar de sobornarla." *El Siglo,* September 4. http://www.elsiglo.com/ (accessed April 27, 2010, through the electronic archive).

Brannan Jaén, Betty. 1994a. "La cobertura internacional de las elecciones." *La Prensa,* February 23. http://biblioteca.prensa.com/contenido/1994/batch02/bety23.000-0000296.html (accessed May 16, 2010).

———. 1994b. "Ramírez ofreció inmunidad para proteger cargamentos de drogas." *La Prensa,* August 30. http://biblioteca.prensa.com/contenido/1994/batch10/bety30.001-0001316.html (accessed May 16, 2010).

———. 1994c. "Grabaciones comprometen a Ramírez." *La Prensa,* August 31. http://biblioteca.prensa.com/contenido/1994/batch10/bety31.000-000 1527.html (accessed May 16, 2010).

———. 1994d. "El juicio de Anel Ramírez." *La Prensa,* September 4. http:// biblioteca.prensa.com/contenido/1994/batch07/bety4.000-0000330 .html (accessed May 16, 2010).

———. 1994e. "Anel Ramírez se declara culpable." *La Prensa,* November 16. http://biblioteca.prensa.com/contenido/1994/batch09/betty-0003846 .html (accessed May 16, 2010).

———. 1997a. "El retorno de Anel Ramírez." *La Prensa,* January 5. http:// biblioteca.prensa.com/contenido/1997/batch07/betty5.html (accessed May 16, 2010).

———. 1997b. "El caso González no se ha cerrado aún." *La Prensa,* November 23. http://biblioteca.prensa.com/contenido/1997/batch04/be23-000 0038.html (accessed May 16, 2010).

———. 1998. "El caso de un contrabando consular," *La Prensa,* August 16. http://biblioteca.prensa.com/contenido/1998/08-agosto/18g33322.html (accessed May 16, 2010).

Brooke, James. 2000. "Peru's President Calls an Election and Will Not Run." *New York Times,* September 17. http://query.nytimes.com/gst/fullpage .html?res=9901E1D81F38F934A2575AC0A9669C8B63 (accessed May 16, 2010).

Brown Araúz, Harry. 2002. "Hacia la Consolidación del Sistema de Partidos Políticos Panameños (1990–1999)." *Revista Tareas* 111:5–26.

———. 2005. "Las elecciones desviadas de Panamá en 2004." *Nueva Sociedad* 195 (January–February): 4–17. http://www.insumisos.com/lectura sinsumisas/Elecciones%20en%20Panama%202004.pdf (accessed May 16, 2010).

———. 2010. "La política de la reforma electoral en Panamá." In *Las reformas electorales en Panamá: claves de desarrollo humano para la toma de decisiones,* ed. Harry Brown Araúz, 13–71. Panama: United Nations Development Programme and Tribunal Electoral de Panamá.

Cádiz, Vielka. 1999. "Rechazan traspaso de partidas circuitales." *El Panamá América,* August 22. http://www.pa-digital.com.pa/periodico/ edicion-anterior/nacion-interna.php?story_id=298293 (accessed May 16, 2010).

Cain, Bruce, John Ferejohn, and Morris Fiorina. 1987. *The Personal Vote: Constituency Service and Electoral Independence.* Cambridge, MA: Harvard University Press.

Callejas, Santander. 1933. *Resumen político de la administración del Dr. Manuel Amador Guerrero, 1904–1908.* Panama: Imprenta Nacional.

Campbell, Duncan. 2006. "U.S. Embarrassed by Terror Suspect." *Guardian* (London), October 25. http://www.guardian.co.uk/world/2006/oct/25/usa.cuba (accessed May 16, 2010).

Canahuate, Margarita. 2006. "Ex presidentes señalados y acusados de corrupción." *Diario Horizonte,* November 10.

Carey, John M. 1996. *Term Limits and Legislative Representation.* Cambridge: Cambridge University Press.

Carey, John M., and Matthew Soberg Shugart. 1995. "Incentives to Cultivate a Personal Vote: A Rank Ordering of Electoral Formulas." *Electoral Studies* 14 (4): 417–39.

Carles Oberto, Rubén Darío. 1968. *Reminiscencias de los primeros años de la República de Panamá, 1903–1912.* Panama: La Estrella de Panamá.

Carrasco, Lisette. 1987. "Sí hubo fraude en las elecciones, declara magistrado César Quintero." *La Prensa,* June 9 (obtained through Brittmarie Janson Pérez).

Castillero Reyes, Ernesto. 1931. *Historia de la reorganización del Partido Conservador en Panamá.* Panama: Tipografía y Casa Editorial La Moderna.

Castillo, Norberto. 1994. "No hay peor ciego que el que no quiere ver." *La Prensa,* August 18. http://biblioteca.prensa.com/contenido/1994/batch10/ciego.000-0001352.html (accessed May 16, 2010).

Castrellón, Franklin. 2009. "Consulados, prueba de ácido." *La Prensa,* July 8. http://mensual.prensa.com/mensual/contenido/2009/07/08/hoy/opinion/1845631.asp (accessed May 16, 2010).

Castro, Isabel. 1999. "Darienitas denunciarán manipulación de elecciones." *El Panamá América,* May 15. http://www.pa-digital.com.pa/periodico/buscador/resultado.php?story_id=293347&page=103&texto=mar%EDn (accessed May 16, 2010).

Castro and Berguido. 2007. "Lawyers: Gabriel Castro Suárez." http://www.castroberguido.com/en/abogados/index.php#GabrielCastro (accessed May 16, 2010).

Center for Responsive Politics. 2010. "Reelection Rates over the Years." http://www.opensecrets.org/bigpicture/reelect.php?Cycle=2006&chamb=H (accessed May 16, 2010).

Chehabi, Houchang E., and Juan J. Linz. 1998a. "A Theory of Sultanism 1." In *Sultanistic Regimes,* ed. Houchang E. Chehabi and Juan J. Linz. Baltimore, MD: Johns Hopkins University Press.

———. 1998b. "A Theory of Sultanism 2." In *Sultanistic Regimes,* ed. Houchang E. Chehabi and Juan J. Linz. Baltimore, MD: Johns Hopkins University Press.

Chéry, Jean Marcel. 2000. "Nombran a ex presidente con B/.5 mil en la Asamblea." *El Panamá América,* September 29. http://www.pa-digital.com.pa/periodico/buscador/resultado.php?story_id=280915&page=13&texto=rigurosidad#axzz0o7zRvkif (accessed May 16, 2010).

———. 2001. "Corte rechaza pago de salario a legisladores." *El Panamá América,* January 26. http://www.pa-digital.com.pa/ (accessed May 16, 2010, through the electronic archive).

Cochez, Guillermo A. 1996. "Las partidas circuitales de los legisladores." *La Prensa,* December 23. http://biblioteca.prensa.com/contenido/1996/batch11/cochez-0000004.html (accessed May 16, 2010).

———. 1998. "¿Corrupción en manejo de fondos del FES?" *La Prensa,* February 5. http://biblioteca.prensa.com/contenido/1998/batch01/cochez-0000492.html (accessed May 16, 2010).

———. 1999. "¿Es todo el PRD un partido inmoral?" *La Prensa,* June 23. http://biblioteca.prensa.com/contenido/1999/06/26n25656.html (accessed May 16, 2010).

———. 2000. "El cinismo del ex ministro Jorge Eduardo Ritter." *El Universal,* June 15.

Cochez, Guillermo A., and Víctor Martínez. 2000. "Demanda de inconstitucionalidad presentada por Víctor Manuel Martínez Cedeño y Guillermo A. Cochez." Lawsuit press release, author's archive.

Comité de Apoyo a los Observadores Internacionales. 1989. *Panamá: testimonio de un proceso electoral.* Panama: Comité de Apoyo a los Observadores Internacionales.

Consejo General de Estado de la República de Panamá. 1989a. "Acuerdo #1 de 31 de agosto de 1989, por el cual se conforma [sic] un Gobierno Provisional." *Gaceta Oficial* no. 21,372, September 8. http://www.asamblea.gob.pa/APPS/LEGISPAN/PDF_GACETAS/1980/1989/21372_1989.PDF (accessed May 16, 2010).

———. 1989b. "Acuerdo #2 de 31 de agosto de 1989, por el cual se designa a los miembros del Gobierno Provisional de la República de Panamá." *Gaceta Oficial* no. 21,372, September 8. http://www.asamblea.gob.pa/APPS/LEGISPAN/PDF_GACETAS/1980/1989/21372_1989.PDF (accessed May 16, 2010).

Conte Porras, Jorge. 1990. *Réquiem por la revolución.* San José, Costa Rica: Litografía e Imprenta Lil.

———. 2004. *Procesos electorales y partidos políticos.* San José, Costa Rica: Litografía e Imprenta Lil.

Contraloría General de la República de Panamá. 1987. "Proyectos especiales de los legisladores: resumen del período 1985 a 1987." Panama: Contraloría General de la República, Dirección Nacional de Contabilidad, Departamento de Registro de Presupuesto.

———. 1994. "Resumen de compromisos por legislador de las iniciativas parlamentarias: vigencias 1993–1994." Panama: Contraloría General de la República, Dirección Nacional de Contabilidad, Departamento de Registro de Presupuesto.

————. 1998a. "Resumen de compromisos por legislador de las iniciativas parlamentarias: vigencias 1995–1998." Panama: Contraloría General de la República, Dirección Nacional de Contabilidad, Departamento de Registro de Presupuesto.

————. 1998b. *Informe del Contralor General de la República (1997)*. Panama: Contraloría General de la República.

————. 1999a. "Resumen de compromisos por legislador (1999)." Panama: Contraloría General de la República, Dirección de Métodos y Sistemas de Contabilidad, Registro de Presupuesto.

————. 1999b. *Informe del Contralor General de la República (1998)*. Panama: Contraloría General de la República.

————. 2000. *Informe del Contralor General de la República (1999)*. Panama: Contraloría General de la República.

————. 2006. "Algunas características de la división política-administrativa [sic] en la República de Panamá, por provincia, comarca indígena y distrito: año 2006." http://www.contraloria.gob.pa/dec/Publicaciones/17-03-01/caracteristicas.pdf (accessed May 16, 2010).

————. 2007. *Panamá en cifras: años 2002–2006*. Panama: Contraloría General de la República (Dirección de Estadística y Censo). http://www.contraloria.gob.pa/inec/ (accessed May 16, 2010).

Convención Nacional Constituyente de la República de Panamá. 1906. *Leyes expedidas por la Convención Nacional Constituyente de la República de Panamá en 1904*. Panama: Tipografía El Fanal.

Cordero, Carlos Anel. 1999. "Contraloría puede investigar legisladores por cuenta propia." *El Panamá América*, March 9. http://www.pa-digital.com.pa/periodico/edicion-anterior/nacion-interna.php?story_id=290382 (accessed May 16, 2010).

————. 2000a. "Legisladores devuelven finos obsequios." *El Panamá América*, January 5.

————. 2000b. "Asamblea debe pagar retroactivo a legisladores." *El Panamá América*, February 24. http://www.pa-digital.com.pa/periodico/edicion-anterior/nacion-interna.php?story_id=264873 (accessed May 16, 2010).

————. 2000c. "Eligen a Hugo Giraud presidente del PARLACEN." *El Panamá América*, October 23. http://www.pa-digital.com.pa/ (accessed May 17, 2010, through the electronic archive).

————. 2010. "Baruco: 'Martinelli designará al presidente de la Asamblea.'" *El Panamá América*, April 1. http://www.pa-digital.com.pa/periodico/edicion-anterior/nacion-interna.php?story_id=904631 (accessed May 16, 2010).

Cox, Gary W. 1987. *The Efficient Secret: The Cabinet and the Development of Political Parties in Victorian England*. Cambridge: Cambridge University Press.

Cox, Gary, and Scott Morgenstern. 2002. "Reactive Assemblies and Proactive Presidents: A Typology of Latin American Presidents and Legislatures." In *Legislative Politics in Latin America*, ed. Scott Morgenstern and Benito Nacif. Cambridge: Cambridge University Press.

Cuervo de Paredes, Maribel. 1999. "Botellas recicladas." *El Panamá América*, November 23.

Cumbrera, Santiago. 2007. "Partidas circuitales se manejaron sin control." *El Panamá América*, September 23. http://www.pa-digital.com.pa/periodico/edicion-anterior/nacion-interna.php?story_id=621984 (accessed May 16, 2010).

———. 2010. "Diputados evitan pagar más por importar autos de lujo." *El Panamá América*, April 6. http://www.pa-digital.com.pa/periodico/edicion-actual/autosdiputados2010-interna.php?story_id=905588 #ixzz0nfJNOkPC (accessed May 16, 2010).

Dahl, Robert A. 1971. *Polyarchy: Participation and Opposition*. New Haven, CT: Yale University Press.

———. 1989. *Democracy and Its Critics*. New Haven, CT: Yale University Press.

———. 1998. *On Democracy*. New Haven, CT: Yale University Press.

Dal Bó, Ernesto, Pedro Dal Bó, and Jason Snyder. 2009. "Political Dynasties." *Review of Economic Studies* 76:115–42.

Damián, Georgina. 2010. "Demanda de Wever sufre revés en la Corte." *El Panamá América*, April 2. http://www.pa-digital.com.pa/periodico/edicion-anterior/nacion-interna.php?story_id=904936 (accessed May 16, 2010).

Defensoría del Pueblo de la República de Panamá. 1998. "Informe especial sobre el referéndum constitucional del 30 de agosto de 1998, de la República de Panamá." Panama: Defensoría del Pueblo.

———. 1999. "Informe especial sobre las elecciones generales de dos (2) de mayo de 1999, en la República de Panamá." Panama: Defensoría del Pueblo.

Delgado, Tilcia. 1998. "Balbina Herrera defiende descuento por inasistencia." *La Prensa*, March 16. http://biblioteca.prensa.com/contenido/1998/batch02/balbina-0000124.html (accessed May 16, 2010).

Delgado Quintero, Hernán. 2009. "Carta a Martín Torrijos de Hernán Delgado." April 2. Electronic message distributed through the campaign office of Hernán Delgado (Centro de Campaña de Hernán Delgado).

Desposato, Scott. 2006. "Parties for Rent? Ambition, Ideology, and Party Switching in Brazil's Chamber of Deputies." *American Journal of Political Science* 50 (1): 62–80.

Deutsche Press-Agentur (DPA). 2005. "Panamá: Escándalo por autos libres de impuestos." *Diario Hoy* (Ecuador), July 22. http://www.hoy.com.ec/noticias-ecuador/panama-escandalo-por-autos-libres-de-impuestos-210107-210107.html (accessed May 16, 2010).

Díaz, Juan Manuel. 2000a. "Legisladores pueden equiparar su salario." *El Panamá América,* February 22. http://www.pa-digital.com.pa/periodico/ edicion-anterior/nacion-interna.php?story_id=264748 (accessed May 16, 2010).

———. 2000b. "Revocan sentencia condenatoria contra Miller." *El Panamá América,* July 4. http://www.pa-digital.com.pa/periodico/buscador/ resultado.php?story_id=274497&page=1&texto=sucari (accessed May 16, 2010).

Díaz, Ovidio. 2000. "Las partidas circuitales." Unpublished pamphlet.

Dinges, John. 1990. *Our Man in Panama: How General Noriega Used the United States and Made Millions in Drugs and Arms.* New York: Random House.

EFE. 2010. "Martinelli siente 'lástima' por Noriega y cree que ya pagó su pena." *Univisión San Diego,* May 12. http://www.univisionsandiego.com/ 171730-Martinelli-siente-l%C3%A1stima-por-Noriega-y-cree-que-ya-pag %C3%B3-su-pena.html (accessed May 16, 2010).

Ehrman, Dialys. 1999. "El voto de las comarcas indígenas." *La Prensa,* May 13. http://biblioteca.prensa.com/contenido/1999/05/25d32338.html (accessed May 16, 2010).

Encyclopædia Britannica Online. 2008. "Clientship." Accessed June 3, 2008, through the University of Nevada, Reno, Library.

Epstein, David F. 1984. *The Political Theory of* The Federalist. Chicago: University of Chicago Press.

Estrada, Carlos. 2005. "Diputados: Hasta B/.10 mil." *Crítica Libre,* November 2. http://www.critica.com.pa/archivo/11022005/ (accessed May 16, 2010).

Fábrega, Ramón E., and Mario Boyd Galindo, eds. 1981. *Constituciones de la República de Panamá.* Panama: Centro de Impresión Educativa.

Fenno, Richard F., Jr. 1973. *Congressmen in Committees.* Boston: Little, Brown, and Company.

Fernández, Jorge. 2004. "Fiscalía pide levantar la inmunidad de Alemán y Afú." *La Prensa,* June 22. http://biblioteca.prensa.com/contenido/2004/06/22/ 22-2a-not1.html (accessed May 16, 2010).

Figueroa, Vilma. 1994a. "Afirma R. Arosemena: Debe reglamentarse la exoneración a autos de legisladores." *La Prensa,* March 21. http://biblioteca .prensa.com/contenido/1994/batch03/ruben16-0000847.html (accessed May 16, 2010).

———. 1994b. "Remiten caso a la Corte: Decidirán pago a legisladores." *La Prensa,* July 19. http://biblioteca.prensa.com/contenido/1994/batch06/ chines-0000334.html (accessed May 16, 2010).

———. 1999. "Afirma la DRP: Fincas cauteladas en Chiriquí están en buenas condiciones." *La Prensa,* March 1. http://biblioteca.prensa.com/contenido/ 1999/03/23132026.html (accessed May 16, 2010).

Figueroa Navarro, Alfredo. 1982. *Dominio y sociedad en el Panamá colombiano (1821–1903): escrutinio sociológico.* 3rd ed. Panama: Editorial Universitaria.

Finer, Samuel E. 1997. *The Intermediate Ages.* Vol. 2 of *The History of Government from the Earliest Times.* Oxford: Oxford University Press.

Fiscalía General Electoral de Panamá. 2009a. "Procesos con motivo de la contienda electoral." http://www.fiscalia-electoral.gob.pa/wp-content/uploads/2009/07/reporte-denuncias.pdf (accessed May 16, 2010).

———. 2009b. "Fiscalías electorales abrieron 81 expedientes por denuncias del 3 de mayo." May 20. http://www.fiscalia-electoral.gob.pa/fiscalias-electorales-abrieron-81-expedientes-por-denuncias-del-3-de-mayo/ (accessed May 16, 2010).

Flores, Leonardo. 2007a. "Wever juega con dos ases." *La Prensa,* October 8. http://mensual.prensa.com/mensual/contenido/2007/10/08/hoy/panorama/1138113.html (accessed May 16, 2010).

———. 2007b. "Diputados renuevan sus vehículos." *La Prensa,* August 25. http://mensual.prensa.com/mensual/contenido/2007/08/25/hoy/panorama/1092840.html (accessed May 16, 2010).

———. 2008. "Ganan salarios excesivos." *La Prensa,* June 23. http://mensual.prensa.com/mensual/contenido/2008/06/23/hoy/panorama/1414474.html (accessed May 16, 2010).

———. 2009a. "Varela: 'salario es inmoral.'" *La Prensa,* June 1. http://mensual.prensa.com/mensual/contenido/2009/06/01/hoy/panorama/1804206.asp (accessed May 10, 2010).

———. 2009b. "Torrijos concede indultos al final de su mandato." *La Prensa,* July 2. http://mensual.prensa.com/mensual/contenido/2009/07/02/hoy/panorama/1839781.asp (accessed May 13, 2010).

———. 2009c. "Varela recorta los gastos de la Asamblea." *La Prensa,* July 3. http://mensual.prensa.com/mensual/contenido/2009/07/03/hoy/panorama/1842106.asp (accessed May 10, 2010).

Flores Cedeño, Jaime. 2008. "Parlamento [*sic*], sociedad y política en Panamá." *Revista Debate* 6 (14): 38–56. http://www.asamblea.gob.pa/debate/Ediciones_anteriores/JULIO2008/%DAltima_Edici%F3n/06-Parlamento_sociedad_politica_Panama.pdf (accessed May 16, 2010).

Flórez, Crisly. 2004. "Corro [*sic*] pide que se investiguen irregularidades en elecciones del 8–7." *La Prensa,* May 15. http://mensual.prensa.com/mensual/contenido/2004/05/15/uhora/uhora_nacional.shtml (accessed May 16, 2010).

Fonseca, Cecilia. 1994. "Reanuda labor la morgue del Hospital Obaldía de David." *La Prensa,* November 21. http://biblioteca.prensa.com/contenido/1994/batch09/morgue-0000933.html (accessed May 16, 2010).

Franco, Bolívar E. 2001. *Panamá: Los partidos políticos en los 90, entre elecciones y transformaciones.* Panamá: Universidad de Panamá y Tribunal Electoral de Panamá.

Freedom House. 2009a. "Freedom in the World Comparative and Historical Data: Country Ratings and Status, FIW 1973–2009." http://www.freedom house.org/template.cfm?page=439 (accessed May 17, 2010).

———. 2009b. "Freedom in the World Aggregate and Subcategory Scores." http://www.freedomhouse.org/template.cfm?page=276 (accessed May 17, 2010).

———. 2009c. "Freedom in the World: Methodology." http://www.freedom house.org/template.cfm?page=351&ana_page=354&year=2009 (accessed May 17, 2010).

———. 2009d. "Freedom in the World: Checklist Questions and Guidelines." http://www.freedomhouse.org/template.cfm?page=351&ana_page=355 &year=2009 (accessed May 17, 2010).

———. 2009e. "Map of Freedom in the World 2009: Panama." http://www .freedomhouse.org/template.cfm?page=22&year=2009&country=7680 (accessed December 29, 2010).

Freidenberg, Flavia. 2010. "Elecciones primarias en Panamá: Claves para el diagnóstico, buenas prácticas y estrategias de reforma (1994–2009)." In *Las reformas electorales en Panamá: claves de desarrollo humano para la toma de decisiones,* ed. Harry Brown Araúz, 73–138. Panama: United Nations Development Programme and Tribunal Electoral de Panamá.

Furlong, William F. 1993. "Panama's Difficult Transition Towards Democracy." *Journal of Interamerican Studies and World Affairs* 35 (Fall): 19–64.

Galindo Heurtematte, Mario. 1997. "Reelección: opción perniciosa." *El Panamá América,* October 13.

Gálvez, Florencio. 1999. "Investigaciones de partidas deben cumplir con requisitos." *Crítica Libre,* March 6. http://www.critica.com.pa/archivo/030699/nac3.html (accessed May 16, 2010).

———. 2007. "Denuncian a diputado por violencia intrafamiliar." *Crítica Libre,* December 7. http://www.critica.com.pa/archivo/12072007/politica.html (accessed May 16, 2010).

García Diez, Fátima. 2003. "Panamá." In *Partidos políticos de América Latina. Centroamérica, México y República Dominicana,* ed. Manuel Alcántara and Flavia Freidenberg, 527–614. Mexico: Fondo de Cultura Económica and Instituto Federal Electoral.

García Márquez, Gabriel. 2004. *Noticia de un secuestro.* Buenos Aires: Debolsillo.

García Rivas, Guillermo. 1996. "¿Inconstitucionalidad o inmoralidad?" *La Prensa,* February 15. http://biblioteca.prensa.com/contenido/1996/batch10/garcia-0000032.html (accessed May 16, 2010).

Garvin, Glenn. 1997a. "A Case That's Slipping Away: Suspect Being Tried in GI's Killing in Panama." *Miami Herald,* October 23.
———. 1997b. "3 Acquitted in Murder of U.S. Soldier." *Miami Herald,* November 2.
———. 1997c. "Ties with Panama Fray over Acquittal." *Miami Herald,* November 19.
Georgetown University Edmund A. Walsh School of Foreign Service. Center for Latin American Studies. 1995–2010. *Political Database of the Americas.* http://pdba.georgetown.edu/ (accessed May 16, 2010).
Gobierno de Chile. 2010. "Elecciones 2009, presidencial y parlamentarias." http://www.elecciones.gov.cl/Sitio2009_light/index_diputados.html (accessed May 16, 2010).
González Marcos, Miguel. 2004. "Diseño de Constituciones." *Boletín Mexicano de Derecho Comparado* 37 (110): 757–76. http://www.scielo.org.mx/pdf/bmdc/v37n110/n110a11.pdf (accessed May 16, 2010).
González Montenegro, Rigoberto, and Francisco Rodríguez Robles. 2001. "La objeción de inexequibilidad constitucional en Panamá." *Anuario Iberoamericano de Justicia Constitucional.* http://www.cepc.es/rap/Publicaciones/Revistas/8/AIB_005_125.pdf (accessed May 16, 2010).
Guardia, Gloria. 2006. *Lobos al anochecer.* Santafé de Bogotá: Alfaguara.
Guevara Mann, Carlos. 1996. *Panamanian Militarism: A Historical Interpretation.* Athens: Ohio University Center for International Studies.
———. 2003. "Las ideas políticas y los gobiernos republicanos: El liberalismo y el conservatismo en la consolidación del Estado panameño." *Istmo* 7 (November–December). http://www.denison.edu/collaborations/istmo/n07/articulos/ideas.html (accessed May 16, 2010).
———. 2004. "Calidad de la representación política tamaño de las circunscripciones electorales: una comparación de las Asambleas panameñas de 1945 y 1999." *Revista de Ciencia Política* 24 (2): 94–115.
———. 2007. *Hibridez y clientelismo: observaciones en torno al sistema de elección y las campañas electorales de los diputados panameños.* Panama: Editorial Cultural Portobelo.
———. 2010. "Observaciones sobre el rendimiento electoral de los partidos políticos panameños a partir de la transición democrática." *Revista Panameña de Política* 9 (January–June): 9–33.
Gutmann, Manfred, and Christian Frey, eds. 2000. *Prices and Earnings around the Globe: An International Comparison of Purchasing Power.* Zurich: Union Bank of Switzerland (UBS Switzerland). http://www.scarpaz.com/Documents/Prices%20and%20Earnings%20around%20the%20globe%202000.pdf (accessed May 16, 2010).
Harrington, Kevin. 1994. "Crónica de una muerte anunciada: El PDC persiste en hacer sonreír a Panamá." *La Prensa,* April 29. http://biblioteca

.prensa.com/contenido/1994/batch04/kevin.002-0001710.html (accessed May 16, 2010).

Hartlyn, Jonathan. 1988. *The Politics of Coalition Rule in Colombia.* Cambridge: Cambridge University Press.

Helmke, Gretchen, and Steve Levitsky. 2006. Introduction to *Informal Institutions and Democracy: Lessons from Latin America,* ed. Gretchen Helmke and Steve Levitsky. Baltimore, MD: Johns Hopkins University Press.

Henry, Melissa. 1999a. "Ex legislador está dispuesto a regalar cupos de operación." *La Prensa,* September 12. http://biblioteca.prensa.com/contenido/1999/09/29c32811.html (accessed May 16, 2010).

———. 1999b. "Salud ordena cierre de matadero municipal en Changuinola." *La Prensa,* September 14. http://biblioteca.prensa.com/contenido/1999/09/29e34228.html (accessed May 16, 2010).

———. 2000. "No negociarán cupos cancelados." *La Prensa,* February 8. http://biblioteca.prensa.com/contenido/2000/02/32841435.html (accessed May 16, 2010).

Hernández, Ismael. 1999. "Pedro Miguel González, nuevo presidente del PRD en Veraguas." *La Prensa,* August 2. http://biblioteca.prensa.com/contenido/1999/08/28232831.html (accessed May 16, 2010).

Herrera y Franco, Alfonso. 1996. "¿Legisladores responsables?: La minoría." *La Prensa,* December 22. http://biblioteca.prensa.com/contenido/1996/batch11/franco-0001697.html (accessed May 16, 2010).

Huntington, Samuel. 1968. *Political Order in Changing Societies.* New Haven, CT: Yale University Press.

Inter-American Development Bank (IDB). 1997. "Documentos sobre Proyectos Aprobados—Panamá." Discussion paper.

Inter-American Press Association (IAPA). 2002. "Midyear Meeting 2002: Information by Country, Panama." http://www.sipiapa.com/v4/index.php?page=det_informe&asamblea=15&infoid=257&idioma=us (accessed May 16, 2010).

Inter-Parliamentary Union (IPU). 2010a. *PARLINE Database on National Parliaments.* http://www.ipu.org/parline-e/parlinesearch.asp (accessed May 16, 2010).

———. 2010b. "Panama." In *PARLINE Database on National Parliaments.* Permanent link: http://www.ipu.org/parline-e/reports/2245.htm (accessed May 16, 2010).

Jackson, Eric. 2004. "Panama News Briefs." *Panama News,* December 5–18. http://www.thepanamanews.com/pn/v_10/issue_23/news_briefs.html (accessed May 16, 2010).

———. 2006. "Assault on BANISTMO Law Continues on More Than One Front." *Panama News,* September 17–October 7. http://www.thepanamanews.com/pn/v_12/issue_18/business_03.html (accessed May 26, 2010).

————. 2008. "Daniel Delgado Diamante Out of Cabinet, His Reforms Implemented in Administration Shuffle." *Panama News,* November 26. http://www.thepanamanews.com/pn/v_14/issue_22/news_01.html (accessed May 16, 2010).

————. 2009a. "Martinelli's Team." *Panama News,* May 18. http://www.thepanamanews.com/pn/v_15/issue_09/news_01.html (accessed May 16, 2010).

————. 2009b. "Years Later, High Court Reopens CEMIS Case." *Panama News,* July 28. http://www.thepanamanews.com/pn/v_15/issue_12/news_special_01.html (accessed May 16, 2010).

————. 2009c. "Panama's Prolonged and Messy Divorce from PARLACEN." *Panama News,* December 8. http://www.thepanamanews.com/pn/v_15/issue_18/news_01.html (accessed May 16, 2010).

Janson Pérez, Brittmarie. 1993. "The Process of Political Protest in Panama, 1968–1989." Ph.D. diss., University of Texas at Austin. [Published in Spanish as *En nuestras voces: Panamá protesta, 1968–1989* (Panama: Editorial La Prensa, 1993)].

————. 1997. *Golpes y tratados: piezas para el rompecabezas de nuestra historia.* Panama: Instituto de Estudios Políticos e Internacionales.

————. 1998a. "La dictadura de los partidos." *La Prensa,* January 14. http://biblioteca.prensa.com/contenido/1998/batch01/brity-0000307.html (accessed May 16, 2010).

————. 1998b. "El pueblo luchó y los políticos claudicaron." *La Prensa,* March 19. http://biblioteca.prensa.com/contenido/1998/batch02/brity2-0000659.html (accessed May 16, 2010).

————. 2000a. "La rosca infernal." *El Panamá América,* January 6.

————. 2000b. "El linchamiento de Mario Miller." *El Panamá América,* February 24.

Jones, Mark. 1998. "Explaining the High Level of Party Discipline in the Argentine Congress." Paper presented at the 21st International Congress of the Latin American Studies Association, Chicago, September 24–26. http://faculty.udesa.edu.ar/tommasi/cedi/dts/dt14.pdf (accessed May 17, 2010).

————. 2005. "The Role of Parties and Party Systems in the Policymaking Process." Paper prepared for the Inter-American Development Bank Workshop on State Reform, Public Policies and Policymaking Processes, Washington, DC, February 28–March 2. http://www.iadb.org/res/ipes2006/MarcJones-parties.pdf (accessed May 16, 2010).

————. 2010. "La representación de las mujeres en la Asamblea Nacional: Diagnóstico, buenas prácticas y propuestas de reforma." In *Las reformas electorales en Panamá: claves de desarrollo humano para la toma de decisiones,* ed. Harry Brown Araúz, 275–316. Panama: United Nations Development Programme and Tribunal Electoral de Panamá.

Jordán, Gionela. 1996. "Ley descontará el salario a los legisladores." *La Prensa,* December 30. http://biblioteca.prensa.com/contenido/1996/batch11/salarios-0001175.html (accessed May 17, 2010).

———. 1997a. "Entra en vigencia rebaja: salarial de los ministros." *La Prensa,* July 2. http://biblioteca.prensa.com/contenido/1997/batch06/rebaja1-0000143.html (accessed May 17, 2010).

———. 1997b. "Dice Gerardo González: Es un 'disparate' descontarles a los legisladores que falten." *La Prensa,* September 28. http://biblioteca.prensa.com/contenido/1997/batch03/descuento-0001893.html (accessed May 17, 2010).

———. 2000. "Aumentan salario a 142 legisladores suplentes." *La Prensa,* April 19. http://biblioteca.prensa.com/contenido/2000/04/34j31034.html (accessed May 17, 2010).

Jordán Serrano, Wilfredo. 1998a. "Intentan debatir anteproyecto que sanciona inasistencia de legisladores." *La Prensa,* September 16. http://biblioteca.prensa.com/contenido/1998/09-septiembre/19g40117.html (accessed May 17, 2010).

———. 1998b. "En primer debate: Aprueban descuento salarial a legisladores." *La Prensa,* October 23. http://biblioteca.prensa.com/contenido/1998/10-octubre/1an44112.html (accessed May 17, 2010).

———. 2000a. "Garrido dice que no hay 'botellas.'" *La Prensa,* April 25. http://biblioteca.prensa.com/contenido/2000/04/34p32423.html (accessed May 17, 2010).

———. 2000b. "Miller no tiene derecho a salarios caídos: Weeden." *La Prensa,* July 5. http://biblioteca.prensa.com/contenido/2000/07/37532405.html (accessed May 17, 2010).

Junta Provisional de Gobierno de Panama [Military Junta]. 1969. "Decreto de Gabinete #58 de 3 de marzo de 1969, por el cual se extinguen los partidos políticos vigentes." *Gaceta Oficial* no. 16,314, March 7. http://www.asamblea.gob.pa/APPS/LEGISPAN/PDF_GACETAS/1960/1969/16314_1969.PDF (accessed May 17, 2010).

Katz, Richard. 1980. *A Theory of Parties and Electoral Systems.* Baltimore, MD: Johns Hopkins University Press.

Koster, Richard M., and Guillermo Sánchez Borbón. 1990. *In the Time of the Tyrants: Panama, 1968–1990.* New York: W. W. Norton.

Krauss, Clifford. 2000a. "Argentine Vice President Quits to Protest Scandal." *New York Times,* October 7. http://www.nytimes.com/2000/10/07/world/argentine-vice-president-quits-to-protest-scandal.html (accessed December 29, 2010).

———. 2000b. "Argentine President Is Trying to Keep Coalition Together." *New York Times,* October 9. http://www.nytimes.com/2000/10/09/world/

argentine-president-is-trying-to-keep-coalition-together.html (accessed December 29, 2010).

———. 2000c. "Leader Denies Woes Amount to a Crisis in Argentina." *New York Times,* October 11. http://www.nytimes.com/2000/10/11/world/leader-denies-woes-amount-to-a-crisis-in-argentina.html?src=pm (accessed December 29, 2010).

———. 2000d. "Peruvian Talks to Set Election Are Suspended." *New York Times,* October 16. http://www.nytimes.com/2000/10/16/world/peruvian-talks-to-set-election-are-suspended.html (accessed December 29, 2010).

———. 2000e. "Fujimori Resignation Sets Off Succession Scramble in Peru." *New York Times,* November 21. http://www.nytimes.com/2000/11/21/world/fujimori-resignation-sets-off-succession-scramble-in-peru.html?src=pm (accessed December 29, 2010).

Kurian, George Thomas. 1998. "Glossary." In George Thomas Kurian, ed., *World Encyclopedia of Parliaments and Chambers,* vol. 2. Washington, DC: Congressional Quarterly.

Labrut, Michele. 1982. *Este es Omar Torrijos.* Panama: Litografía Enan.

Lakoff, Sanford A. 1996. *Democracy: History, Theory, Practice.* Boulder, CO: Westview Press.

Lara, Denise. 2010. "Doens: diputado Gabriel Méndez es un Caballo de Troya." *Telemetro,* April 4. http://www.telemetro.com/politica/2010/04/04/nota49810.html (accessed May 17, 2010).

Legislative Yuan of the Republic of China [Taiwan]. 2010. "Members of the Legislative Yuan." http://www.ly.gov.tw/en/01_introduce/introView.action?id=4 (accessed May 17, 2010).

Leis, Raúl. 1984. *Radiografía de los partidos.* Panamá: Centro de Capacitación Social.

———. 1999. "¿Qué hacemos con las partidas circuitales?" *El Panamá América,* February 24.

———. 2004. "Discretionary Funds and Patrimonialism." *Panama News,* November 7–20. http://www.thepanamanews.com/pn/v_10/issue_21/opinion_02.html (accessed May 17, 2010).

Lewis Galindo, Samuel. 1999. "Las partidas circuitales." *El Panamá América,* March 23.

Lijphart, Arend. 1984. *Democracies: Patterns of Majoritarian and Consensus Government in Twenty-One Countries.* New Haven, CT: Yale University Press.

———. 1999. *Patterns of Democracy: Government Forms and Performance in Thirty-Six Countries.* New Haven, CT: Yale University Press.

Linares Gutiérrez, Julio. 1989. *Enrique Linares en la historia política de Panamá, 1869–1949: calvario de un pueblo por afianzar su soberanía.* San José, Costa Rica: Litografía e Imprenta Lil.

Linares Herbruger, Francisco. 1978. "Democratización de la nación panameña." *La Estrella de Panamá,* October 6 (obtained through Brittmarie Janson Pérez).

Linz, Juan J. 1978. Introduction to *The Breakdown of Democratic Regimes,* ed. Juan J. Linz and Alfred Stepan. Baltimore, MD: Johns Hopkins University Press.

Loewenberg, Gerhard. 1995. "Legislatures and Parliaments." In *The Encyclopedia of Democracy,* vol. 3, ed. Seymour Martin Lipset. Washington, DC: Congressional Quarterly.

Loo Pinzón, Kemy. 2010. "CD ingresará al Parlacen." *La Prensa,* January 28. http://mensual.prensa.com/mensual/contenido/2010/01/28/hoy/panorama/2076742.asp (accessed May 17, 2010).

Loomis, Burdett. 1994. "The Motivations of Legislators." In *Encyclopedia of the American Legislative System,* vol. 1, ed. Joel H. Silbey. New York: Charles Scribner's Sons.

———. 1998. *The Contemporary Congress.* 2nd ed. New York: St. Martin's Press.

López, Jaime. 2005. "Control democrático de los privilegios." *Revista Probidad* (August).

Madison, James, Alexander Hamilton, and John Jay. 1987. *The Federalist Papers.* Ed. Isaac Kramnick. Harmondsworth, England: Penguin.

Mainwaring, Scott. 1999. *Rethinking Party Systems in the Third Wave of Democratization: The Case of Brazil.* Stanford: Stanford University Press.

Mainwaring, Scott, and Timothy Scully, eds. 1995. *Building Democratic Institutions: Party Systems in Latin America.* Stanford: Stanford University Press.

Manning, Jennifer E. 2010. "Membership of the 111th Congress: A Profile." CRS Report for Congress, R40086. http://www.senate.gov/CRSReports/crs-publish.cfm?pid=%260BL)PL%3B%3D%0A (accessed May 17, 2010).

Martínez, Eduardo. 2000a. "No hay dinero para pagar retroactivo a legisladores." *El Panamá América,* February 23. http://www.pa-digital.com.pa/periodico/edicion-anterior/nacion-interna.php?story_id=264822 (accessed May 17, 2010).

———. 2000b. "Legislador pide eliminar partidas circuitales." *El Panamá América,* July 3. Permanent link: http://www.pa-digital.com.pa/periodico/edicion-anterior/nacion-interna.php?story_id=274423 (accessed May 17, 2010).

Martínez Dettore, Juan Ramón. 1994a. "Los candidatos a legisladores se comprometen a eliminar privilegios." *La Prensa,* April 6. http://biblioteca.prensa.com/contenido/1994/batch03/valia2-0000020.html (accessed May 17, 2010).

———. 1994b. "Marco Ameglio con depuración legislativa." *La Prensa,* April 25. http://biblioteca.prensa.com/contenido/1994/batch04/depuracio-0001049.html (accessed May 17, 2010).

Martínez Peñate, Oscar. 1997. "Los diputados salvadoreños: condiciones y obligaciones." *Estudios Centroamericanos* 581–82 (March–April): 259–80.

Mateo Díaz, Mercedes, J. Mark Payne, and Daniel Zovatto. 2007. "Gauging Public Support for Democracy." In *Democracies in Development: Politics and Reform in Latin America,* ed. J. Mark Payne, Daniel Zovatto, and Mercedes Mateo Díaz. Washington, DC: Inter-American Development Bank, International Institute for Democracy and Electoral Assistance, and the David Rockefeller Center for Latin American Studies, Harvard University.

Mayhew, David. 1974. *Congress: The Electoral Connection.* New Haven, CT: Yale University Press.

McCubbins, Mathew D., and Frances M. Rosenbluth. 1995. "Party Provision for Personal Politics: Dividing the Vote in Japan." In *Structure and Policy in Japan and the United States,* ed. Peter F. Cowhey and Mathew D. McCubbins. Cambridge: Cambridge University Press.

McCullough, David. 1977. *The Path between the Seas: The Creation of the Panama Canal, 1870–1914.* New York: Simon and Schuster.

Mejía Acosta, Andrés. 1999. "Explaining 'camisetazos': The Logic of Party Switching in the Ecuadorian Congress (1979–1996)." Paper presented at the 57th Annual Meeting of the Midwest Political Science Association, Chicago, IL, April 15–17.

———. 2004. "La reelección legislativa en Ecuador: conexión electoral, carreras legislativas y partidos políticos (1979–1998)." *Ecuador debate* 62 (August). http://sala.clacso.org.ar/gsdl/cgi-bin/library?e=d-000-00---0debate--0 0-0-0Date--0prompt-10---4------0-1l--1-es-Zz-1---20-about---0003 1-001-0-0utfZz-8-00&a=d&c=debate&cl=CL1&d=HASH0102ad361348 ce5f95c672a0.14 (accessed May 17, 2010).

Méndez, J. Ignacio. 1980. "*Azul y rojo*: Panama's Independence in 1840." *Hispanic American Historical Review* 60 (2): 269–93.

Mendieta, Orlando. 1994a. "Ex legislador del PRD es condenado a tres años de cárcel por peculado." *La Prensa,* March 7. http://biblioteca.prensa.com/contenido/1994/batch02/lino-0000291.html (accessed May 17, 2010).

———. 1994b. "Vallarino denuncia campaña de descrédito contra legisladores." *La Prensa,* April 28. http://biblioteca.prensa.com/contenido/1994/batch04/exoner.001-0001447.html (accessed May 17, 2010).

Mendieta, Orlando, and José Otero. 1994. "César Quintero: Petición de legisladores carece de base." *La Prensa,* May 28. http://biblioteca.prensa.com/contenido/1994/batch05/vaca.003-0000322.html (accessed May 17, 2010).

Mendoza, Eduardo. 2010. "Indultan a policías acusados de homicidio." *La Prensa,* May 13. http://www.prensa.com/hoy/panorama/2186800.asp (accessed May 17, 2010).

Mill, John Stuart. 1861/1958. *Considerations on Representative Government.* Ed. and intro. Currin V. Shields. New York: Liberal Arts Press.

Ministerio de Gobierno y Justicia de Panamá. 1994a. "Decreto Ejecutivo #254 de 6 de junio de 1994." *Gaceta Oficial* no. 22,564, June 23. http://www .asamblea.gob.pa/APPS/LEGISPAN/PDF_GACETAS/1990/1994/ 22564_1994. PDF (accessed May 17, 2010).

———. 1994b. "Decreto Ejecutivo #255 de 6 de junio de 1994." *Gaceta Oficial* no. 22,564, June 23. http://www.asamblea.gob.pa/APPS/LEGI SPAN/PDF_GACETAS/1990/1994/22564_1994. PDF (accessed May 17, 2010).

———. 1994c. "Decreto Ejecutivo #256 de 6 de junio de 1994." *Gaceta Oficial* no. 22,564, June 23. http://www.asamblea.gob.pa/APPS/LEGI SPAN/PDF_GACETAS/1990/1994/22564_1994. PDF (accessed May 17, 2010).

———. 1994d. "Decreto Ejecutivo #257 de 6 de junio de 1994." *Gaceta Oficial* no. 22,564, June 23. http://www.asamblea.gob.pa/APPS/LEGISPAN/ PDF_GACETAS/1990/1994/22564_1994. PDF (accessed May 17, 2010).

———. 1994e. "Decreto Ejecutivo #469 de 23 de septiembre de 1994." *Gaceta Oficial* no. 22,632, September 28. http://www.asamblea.gob.pa/ APPS/LEGISPAN/PDF_GACETAS/1990/1994/22632_1994. PDF (accessed May 17, 2010).

———. 1995. "Decreto Ejecutivo #476 de 7 de septiembre de 1995." *Gaceta Oficial* no. 22,865, September 8. http://www.asamblea.gob.pa/APPS/ LEGISPAN/PDF_GACETAS/1990/1995/22865_1995. PDF (accessed May 17, 2010).

———. 2008. "Nuestras Gobernaciones" [list of provincial governors in 2008]. http://www.mingob.gob.pa/mingob/ (accessed December 26, 2008).

Ministerio de la Presidencia de Panamá. 2010. "Decreto Ejecutivo #464 de 14 de mayo de 2010, por el cual se eleva el salario mínimo a los servidores públicos del país." *Gaceta Oficial* no. 26,533-A, May 14. http://www .gacetaoficial.gob.pa/pdfTemp/26533_A/27525.pdf (accessed May 17, 2010).

Ministerio de Trabajo y Desarrollo Laboral de Panamá. 2009. "Tasa de salario mínimo: Decreto #263 de 21 de diciembre de 2009." http://www.mitradel .gob.pa/salrio%20minimo%20segun%20decreto%20263/CUADRO%20 x%20DIFERENTES%20JORNADAS%202009.pdf (accessed May 10, 2010).

Miranda, Inés. 2000. "El presidente del Congreso colombiano presenta su dimisión." *El Mundo,* March 27.

Mizrachi Angel, Flor. 2010. "Knockout: José Muñoz—¿Dónde está la corrupción en la Asamblea, que no la veo?" *La Prensa,* May 23. http://www .prensa.com/hoy/panorama/2193399.asp (accessed May 24, 2010).

Montesquieu, Charles-Louis de Secondat, Baron de la Brède et de. 1748/1966. *The Spirit of the Laws.* Trans. Thomas Nugent. New York: Hafner.

Morgenstern, Scott. 1998. "U.S. Models and Latin American Legislatures." Paper presented at the Annual Meeting of the American Political Science Association, Boston, September 3–6.

Morgenstern, Scott, Daniel Nielson, and Stephen Swindle. 1998. "The Electoral Disconnection? A Comparative Look at Reelection Rates." Paper presented at the Annual Meeting of the American Political Science Association, Boston, September 3–6.

Morice, Eugenio. 2000. "Polito, no esperes justicia." *La Prensa,* March 31. http://biblioteca.prensa.com/contenido/2000/03/33v25753.html (accessed May 17, 2010).

Moscoso, Antonio, Carlos Cabezas, and Rodolfo Aguilera Jr., eds. 1945. *Segunda Asamblea Nacional Constituyente de la República panameña.* Panama: Privately published by the authors.

Moscote, José Dolores. 1943. *El derecho constitucional panameño: antecedentes, doctrinas y soluciones.* Panama: Star and Herald Company.

Muñoz, Mario. 2000. "Dos ex presidentes son asesores en la Asamblea." *La Prensa,* September 29. http://biblioteca.prensa.com/contenido/2000/09/39t40605.html (accessed May 17, 2010).

Muñoz Aragón, Mariela. 2010. "Inician reuniones para adjudicar licitación del edificio de la Asamblea Nacional." National Assembly Press Release, April 26. http://www.asamblea.gob.pa/main/ComunicacionesyPrensa/tabid/84/articleType/ArticleView/articleId/333/Inician-reuniones-para-adjudicar-licitacion-del-edificio-de-la-Asamblea-Nacional.aspx (accessed May 17, 2010).

Murillo Muñoz, Lastenia. 1994a. "Asamblea decide hoy descuento salarial a legisladores." *La Prensa,* March 21. http://biblioteca.prensa.com/contenido/1994/batch03/descuento-0000836.html (accessed May 17, 2010).

———. 1994b. "Denuncian irregularidades en proceso electoral de Colón." *La Prensa,* May 11. http://biblioteca.prensa.com/contenido/1994/batch04/denuncio-0001501.html (accessed May 17, 2010).

———. 1994c. "Los legisladores insisten en el pago de sus vacaciones." *La Prensa,* July 12. http://biblioteca.prensa.com/contenido/1994/batch06/vaca.004-0000880.html (accessed May 17, 2010).

Murillo Muñoz, Lastenia, and Ibeth Vega. 1994. "La asamblea deja en 'suspenso' rebaja salarial a legisladores." *La Prensa,* March 22. http://biblioteca.prensa.com/contenido/1994/batch03/salari.000-0001205.html (accessed May 17, 2010).

Navarro, Sonia. 2010. "Diputados archivan expediente de soborno por falta de pruebas." *Mi Diario,* May 1. http://www.midiario.com/history/2010/05/01/mi_comunidad.asp (accessed May 17, 2010).

Naylor, R. Thomas. 1999. *Economic Warfare: Sanctions, Embargo Busting, and Their Human Cost.* Boston: Northeastern University Press.

Ng, Alex J. 2006. "Nueva modificación al ITBMS [Art.] 1057-v del Código Fiscal." Grant Thornton Cheng y Asociados, *Boletín Fiscal* No. 14, July 31. http://www.gt.com.pa/site/Boletines%20Fiscales/2006/2006-14.pdf (accessed May 17, 2010).

Nohlen, Dieter. 1993. *Enciclopedia electoral latinoamericana y del Caribe.* San José, Costa Rica: Instituto Interamericano de Derechos Humanos.

North, Douglass C. 1990. *Institutions, Institutional Change and Economic Performance.* Cambridge: Cambridge University Press.

Obaldía, Mario J. de. 1997. "Sin ton ni son: Cuestión de salarios." *La Prensa,* July 8. http://biblioteca.prensa.com/contenido/1997/batch06/sinton8-000 1296.html (accessed May 17, 2010).

O'Donnell, Guillermo. 1996. "Illusions about Consolidation." *Journal of Democracy* 7 (2): 34–51.

———. 1998a. "Polyarchies and the (Un)Rule of Law in Latin America." Working Paper No. 25. Madrid: Instituto Juan March de Estudios e Investigaciones.

———. 1998b. "Horizontal Accountability in New Democracies." *Journal of Democracy* 9 (3): 112–26.

———. 1999. "Polyarchies and the (Un)Rule of Law in Latin America: A Partial Conclusion." In *The (Un)Rule of Law and the Underprivileged in Latin America,* ed. Juan E. Méndez, Guillermo O'Donnell, and Paulo Sérgio Pinheiro. Notre Dame, IN: University of Notre Dame Press.

Organization of American States (OAS) and Inter-American Commission on Human Rights. 1978. *Resolución sobre la situación de los derechos humanos en Panamá.* 2nd ed. Washington, DC: OAS.

Órgano Judicial de la República de Panamá. 2010. "Corte Suprema declara inconstitucional decreto del Tribunal Electoral" [press release]. May 14. Accessed through http://www.organojudicial.gob.pa/ (May 20, 2010).

Ornstein, Norman J., Thomas E. Mann, Michael J. Malbin, Allen Schick, and John F. Bibby. 2000. *Vital Statistics on Congress, 1999–2000.* Washington, DC: AEI Press.

Ortega Luna, Aquilino. 2000. "Pérez B. afirma que Mireya regala Cartier 'y dice que no hay dinero.'" *El Panamá América,* January 25.

Otero, José. 1994a. "Opina Ballesteros: No se le debe pagar sueldo a Ramírez." *La Prensa,* January 14. http://biblioteca.prensa.com/contenido/1994/ batch01/dona.000-0001864.html (accessed May 17, 2010).

———. 1994b. "Contralor respalda descuento salarial a los legisladores." *La Prensa,* March 19. http://biblioteca.prensa.com/contenido/1994/batch03/ salario-0000456.html (accessed May 17, 2010).

———. 1994c. "Proclaman a 29 legisladores." *La Prensa,* May 12. http://biblio teca.prensa.com/contenido/1994/batch04/actas1-0001563.html (accessed May 17, 2010).

———. 1996. "En tercer debate: Aprueban más privilegios para legisladores y sus familiares." *La Prensa,* December 4. http://biblioteca.prensa.com/contenido/1996/batch11/privi5-0000510.html (accessed December 11, 2008).

———. 1997. "Entra hoy en vigor rebaja: salarial a funcionarios." *La Prensa,* July 15. http://biblioteca.prensa.com/contenido/1997/batch06/sala5-000 0624.html (accessed May 17, 2010).

———. 1999a. "Suplentes, encargados de hacer leyes en la asamblea." *La Prensa,* March 1. http://biblioteca.prensa.com/contenido/1999/03/2313 1716.html (accessed May 17, 2010).

———. 1999b. "Surgen nuevos implicados en el crimen de Hugo Spadafora." *La Prensa,* October 6. http://biblioteca.prensa.com/contenido/1999/10 /2a634155.html (accessed May 17, 2010).

———. 2000a. "Absuelven a Mario Miller." *La Prensa,* July 4. http://mensual .prensa.com/mensual/contenido/2000/07/04/hoy/portada/index.htm (accessed May 17, 2010).

———. 2000b. "Weeden reglamentará uso de las partidas." *La Prensa,* September 2. http://mensual.prensa.com/mensual/contenido/2000/09/02/hoy/nacionales/index.htm (accessed May 17, 2010).

———. 2005. "Sigue el litigio por el caso Alba." *La Prensa,* December 27. http://biblioteca.prensa.com/contenido/2005/12/27/27-8a-not2.html (accessed May 17, 2010).

———. 2010. "Bonissi se opone a cierre del caso Cemis." *La Prensa,* May 13. http://www.prensa.com/hoy/panorama/2186859.asp (accessed May 17, 2010).

Otero, José, and Ismael Hernández. 1995. "Arosemena pide a ministros que renuncien." *La Prensa,* November 20. http://biblioteca.prensa.com/contenido/1995/batch10/secte5-0001452.html (accessed May 17, 2010).

Otero, José, and Gionela Jordán. 1996. "'Pretensiones de legisladores causan asco': Endara." *La Prensa,* December 11. http://biblioteca.prensa.com/contenido/1996/batch11/yetu5-0001817.html (accessed May 17, 2010).

Otero, José, and José Quintero de León. 1997. "Por rebajar sueldos a ministros: Cigarruista califica de 'arbitrario' al presidente." *La Prensa,* July 3. http://biblioteca.prensa.com/contenido/1997/batch06/salarios-0000353.html (accessed May 17, 2010).

Otero Felipe, Patricia. 2006. "Partidos y sistemas de partidos en Panamá: un estudio de la estructuración ideológica." *Revista Panameña de Política* 1 (January–June): 47–118.

———. 2008. "Selección de candidatos en los partidos panameños: Las primarias y sus impactos en el Partido Revolucionario Democrático." *Política y Gobierno* 15 (2): 271–314.

Palm, Mónica. 2009. "116 denuncias y una sola condena." *La Prensa,* November 2. http://mensual.prensa.com/mensual/contenido/2009/11/02/hoy/panorama/1981661.asp (accessed May 17, 2010).

Paredes, Yureth. 2009. "Denuncian falta de transparencia en elecciones: Irregularidades en el circuito 8-1." *La Estrella de Panamá,* May 7. http://www.laestrella.com.pa/mensual/2009/05/07/contenido/95993.asp (accessed May 17, 2010).

PARLACÉN (Parlamento Centroamericano). 2010. "Historia del Parlamento Centroamericano." http://www.parlacen.org.gt/index-portada.html (accessed May 17, 2010).

Payne, J. Mark. 2006. "Sistemas de partidos y gobernabilidad democrática." In *La política importa: democracia y desarrollo en América Latina,* ed. J. Mark Payne, Daniel Zovatto, and Mercedes Mateo Díaz. Washington, DC: Inter-American Development Bank and International Institute for Democracy and Electoral Assistance.

———. 2007. "Party Systems and Democratic Governability." In *Democracies in Development: Politics and Reform in Latin America,* ed. J. Mark Payne, Daniel Zovatto, and Mercedes Mateo Díaz. Washington, DC: Inter-American Development Bank, International Institute for Democracy and Electoral Assistance, and the David Rockefeller Center for Latin American Studies, Harvard University.

Perea, Gabriel J. 2008. "¿Qué es ser Diputado de la República?" *El Panamá América,* May 29. http://www.pa-digital.com.pa/ (accessed May 17, 2010, through the electronic archive).

Pereira, Renato. 1979. *Panamá: fuerzas armadas y política.* Panama: Ediciones Nueva Universidad.

Pérez González, Rafael. 1999. "Proyectos penden ahora de la reelección: Asamblea decreta receso hasta el 3 de mayo." *La Prensa,* April 22. http://biblioteca.prensa.com/contenido/1999/04/24m41347.html (accessed May 17, 2010).

———. 2000a. "Legisladores del gobierno pasado no tienen derecho a salarios caídos." *La Prensa,* February 29. http://biblioteca.prensa.com/contenido/2000/02/32t33010.html (accessed May 17, 2010).

———. 2000b. "Eligio Salas solo dio su opinión personal, aclara la magistrada presidenta de la Corte." *La Prensa,* March 2. http://biblioteca.prensa.com/contenido/2000/03/33230526.html (accessed May 17, 2010).

———. 2000c. "Legisladores se quedarán sin sus salarios caídos." *La Prensa,* April 12. http://biblioteca.prensa.com/contenido/2000/04/34c32541.html (accessed May 17, 2010).

———. 2008. "Diputados con casos pendientes en la Corte." *La Prensa,* December 24. http://mensual.prensa.com/mensual/contenido/2008/12/24/hoy/panorama/1639925.html (accessed May 17, 2010).

Pérez González, Rafael, and Manuel Domínguez. 1999. "Según su hermana Berta: Omar Torrijos no está manchado con crímenes." *La Prensa,* October 11. http://biblioteca.prensa.com/contenido/1999/10/2ab32610.html (accessed May 17, 2010).

Pérez González, Rafael, and Omar Rodríguez. 2000. "Asegura frente contra la corrupción: Relojes Cartier no pagaron impuestos en la Zona Libre." *La Prensa,* January 9. http://mensual.prensa.com/mensual/contenido/2000/01/09/domingo/portada.html (accessed May 17, 2010).

Pérez Jaramillo, Rafael. 1998. "Partidas circuitales." *La Prensa,* October 30. http://biblioteca.prensa.com/contenido/1998/10-octubre/1au42057.html (accessed May 17, 2010).

———. 1999. "Partidas con 'P' de PRD." *El Panamá América,* March 10. http://www.pa-digital.com.pa/periodico/buscador/resultado.php?story_id=290432&page=257&texto=carreteras (accessed May 17, 2010).

———. 2000. "Partidas circuitales: historia de corrupción." *El Panamá América,* March 17. http://www.pa-digital.com.pa/periodico/buscador/resultado.php?story_id=266527&page=29&texto=cochez#axzz0oDCdImz7 (accessed May 17, 2010).

Pérez Liñán, Aníbal. 2007. *Presidential Impeachment and the New Political Instability in Latin America.* Cambridge: Cambridge University Press.

Pippin, Larry L. 1964. *The Remon Era: An Analysis of a Decade of Events in Panama, 1947–1957.* Stanford, CA: Institute of Hispanic-American and Luso-Brazilian Studies.

Pitkin, Hanna Fenichel. 1967. *The Concept of Representation.* Berkeley: University of California Press.

Pizzurno, Patricia, and Celestino Andrés Araúz. 1996. *Estudios sobre el Panamá republicano (1903–1989).* Panama: Manfer.

Priestley, George. 1986. *Military Government and Popular Participation in Panama: The Torrijos Regime, 1968–1975.* Boulder, CO: Westview Press.

Prieto Barreiro, Ereida. 2008. "Presidente de la Asamblea retornará partidas circuitales." *El Panamá América,* March 1. http://www.pa-digital.com.pa/periodico/edicion-anterior/nacion-interna.php?story_id=650016 (accessed May 17, 2010).

Putnam, Robert. 1993. *Making Democracy Work: Civic Traditions in Modern Italy.* Princeton, NJ: Princeton University Press.

Quijano, Guillermo. 1999. "La irresponsabilidad de nuestra Asamblea." *La Prensa,* July 4. http://biblioteca.prensa.com/contenido/1999/07/27430739.html (accessed May 17, 2010).

Quintero, César. 1967. *Derecho constitucional.* Vol. 1. San José: A. Lehmann.

Quintero Jiménez, Santiago. 1994. "Por sus hechos los conoceréis." *La Prensa,* April 21. http://biblioteca.prensa.com/contenido/1994/batch04/jimenez-0000495.html (accessed May 17, 2010).

Quintero de León, José. 1990. "Legisladores pensaron que presupuesto era botín: Iván Romero." *La Prensa,* April 26. http://biblioteca.prensa.com/contenido/1990/batch01/botin001.html (accessed May 17, 2010).

———. 1994a. "Reitera el Contralor: Legisladores no tienen derecho al pago de vacaciones." *La Prensa,* July 10. http://biblioteca.prensa.com/contenido/1994/batch06/chinito-0000437.html (accessed May 17, 2010).

———. 1994b. "Proponen reducir sueldos a legisladores." *La Prensa,* September 21. http://biblioteca.prensa.com/contenido/1994/batch07/hasamblea-0001322.html (accessed May 17, 2010).

———. 1996. "Se unen las bancadas: Reducción salarial no recibe buena acogida." *La Prensa,* December 14. http://biblioteca.prensa.com/contenido/1996/batch11/demagogo-0000427.html (accessed May 17, 2010).

———. 1998. "Denuncian abultamiento del padrón electoral." *La Prensa,* September 30. http://biblioteca.prensa.com/contenido/1998/09-septiembre/19u40212.html (accessed May 17, 2010).

———. 1999. "Pedro Miguel: 'Sólo muerto saldré de Panamá.'" *La Prensa,* May 23. http://biblioteca.prensa.com/contenido/1999/05/25n34627.html (accessed May 17, 2010).

Renka, Russell. 2007. "The Incumbency Advantage in the U.S. Congress." Class notes, Southeast Missouri State University, November 6. http://cstl-cla.semo.edu/renka/ps103/Fall2007/congressional_incumbency.htm (accessed May 17, 2010).

República de Panamá. 1992. "Ley No. 7 de 27 de mayo de 1992, por la cual se reforma la Ley No. 49 de 4 de diciembre de 1984, que dicta el Reglamento Orgánico del Régimen Interno de la Asamblea Legislativa." *Gaceta Oficial* no. 22,044, May 28. http://www.asamblea.gob.pa/APPS/LEGISPAN/PDF_GACETAS/1990/1992/22044_1992. PDF (accessed May 17, 2010).

———. 1994/1995. *Constitución política de la República de Panamá de 1972, reformada por los actos reformatorios de 1978, por el acto constitucional de 1983 y por los actos legislativos 1 de 1993 y 2 de 1994.* Panama: Instituto de Estudios Políticos e Internacionales.

———. 2002. "Ley #6 de 22 de enero de 2002, que dicta normas para la transparencia en la gestión pública, establece la acción de Hábeas Data y dicta otras disposiciones." *Gaceta Oficial* no. 24,476, January 23. http://www.presidencia.gob.pa/ley_n6_2002.pdf (accessed May 5, 2010).

———. 2003. *Código Electoral, reformado por la Ley #60 de 17 de diciembre de 2002.* Panama: Editora Pérez y Pérez.

———. 2004. *Constitución política de la República de Panamá de 1972, reformada por los actos reformatorios de 1978, por el acto constitucional de 1983 y los actos legislativos 1 de 1993, 2 de 1994 y 1 de 2004.* http://www.epasa.com/constitucion/constitu.html (accessed May 18, 2010).

———. 2005. "Ley #33 de 27 de octubre de 2005, que adopta el Código de Ética y Honor Parlamentario." *Gaceta Oficial* no. 25,418, October 31. http://www.asamblea.gob.pa/APPS/LEGISPAN/PDF_GACETAS/2000/2005/25418_2005.PDF (accessed May 17, 2010).

———. 2007. "Código Electoral." *Gaceta Oficial Digital* no. 25,875, September 12. http://www.tribunal-electoral.gob.pa/reformas/documentos/codigo-electoral.pdf (accessed May 17, 2010).

———. 2010a. "Texto único de la Ley 49 de 4 de diciembre de 1984, que dicta el Reglamento Orgánico del Régimen Interno de la Asamblea Nacional." *Gaceta Oficial Digital* no. 26,476D, February 24. http://www.asamblea.gob.pa/main/LinkClick.aspx?fileticket=t0euPFLTZoc%3d&tabid=123 (accessed May 17, 2010).

———. 2010b. "Ley #14 de 13 de abril de 2010, que dicta medidas sobre el Certificado de Información de Antecedentes Personales, reforma el Código Electoral y adiciona un artículo al Código Penal." *Gaceta Oficial* no. 26,510C, April 13. http://www.gacetaoficial.gob.pa/pdfTemp/26510_C/26933.pdf (accessed May 17, 2010).

Reyes, Herasto. 1994. "El colmo de una sinvergüenzura." *La Prensa,* May 30. http://biblioteca.prensa.com/contenido/1994/batch05/leggis.000-0000799.html (accessed May 17, 2010).

Ricord, Humberto E. 1983. *Los clanes de la oligarquía panameña y el golpe militar de 1968.* Panama: Privately published by the author.

———. 1989. *Panamá en la Guerra de los Mil Días.* Panama: Privately published by the author and Instituto Nacional de Cultura.

———. 1991. *Noriega y Panamá: orgía y aplastamiento de la narcodictadura.* México: Imprenta Eficiencia.

Rivera, Sandra. 1999. "El legislador Alvarado demandará a Otilio Miranda por calumnia e injuria." *La Prensa,* May 9. http://biblioteca.prensa.com/contenido/1999/05/25933348.html (accessed May 17, 2010).

———. 2004. "Por tercera ocasión, se reelige Carlos 'Titi' Alvarado en el 4–6." *La Prensa,* May 4. http://biblioteca.prensa.com/contenido/2004/05/04/4-10a-nota1a.html (accessed May 17, 2010).

Rodríguez, Omar. 1994. "Antón: Buscan pruebas para impugnar legislatura." *La Prensa,* May 14. http://biblioteca.prensa.com/contenido/1994/batch05/anton.000-0001266.html (accessed May 17, 2010).

———. 2000. "Señala Germán Vergara sobre los relojes Cartier: Iglesia no tiene autoridad para criticar." *La Prensa,* January 10. http://biblioteca.prensa.com/contenido/2000/01/31a24358.html (accessed May 17, 2010).

Rodríguez Bernal, Rolando. 1995. "Legisladores se niegan a rebajar su sueldo." *La Prensa,* October 19. http://biblioteca.prensa.com/contenido/1995/batch09/rebaja-0001653.html (accessed December 12, 2008).

————. 1996a. "Advierte Pérez Balladares: Legisladores ganan más que ministros." *La Prensa,* February 3. http://biblioteca.prensa.com/contenido/1996/batch01/roro-0001105.html (accessed May 17, 2010).

————. 1996b. "Proponen comisión que explique labor legislativa." *La Prensa,* December 17. http://biblioteca.prensa.com/contenido/1996/batch11/albert-0000999.html (accessed May 17, 2010).

Rodríguez Bernal, Rolando, and Hermes Sucre Serrano. 1996. "Opina Miguel Bush: Palabras de Chapman son 'irrespetuosas.'" *La Prensa,* February 3. http://biblioteca.prensa.com/contenido/1996/batch01/aumento-000 0010.html (accessed May 17, 2010).

Rodríguez Jované, Zoila. 1990. "Gobierno rebaja altos salarios." *La Prensa,* February 19. http://biblioteca.prensa.com/contenido/1990/batch04/rebaja .html (accessed May 17, 2010).

Rohter, Larry. 1995. "Some Familiar Faces Return to Power in Panama." *New York Times,* February 9. http://www.nytimes.com/1995/02/09/world/some-familiar-faces-return-to-power-in-panama.html (accessed December 30, 2010).

Romero, Simon. 2008. "President of Colombia Seeks Replay of '06 Vote." *New York Times,* June 28. http://www.nytimes.com/2008/06/28/world/americas/28colombia.html?fta=y (accessed May 17, 2010).

Ropp, Steve C. 1992. "Explaining the Long-Term Maintenance of a Military Regime: Panama before the U.S. Invasion." *World Politics* 44:222–26.

Rudolf, Gloria. 1999. *Panama's Poor: Victims, Agents, and Historymakers.* Gainesville: University Press of Florida.

Rujano, Elio. 1994. "Los candidatos a legisladores se comprometen a eliminar privilegios." *La Prensa,* April 6. http://biblioteca.prensa.com/contenido/1994/batch03/valia2-0000020.html (accessed May 17, 2010).

————. 1995. "PDC pide a la oposición que rechace el presupuesto." *La Prensa,* December 4. http://biblioteca.prensa.com/contenido/1995/batch10/veldes-0000447.html (accessed May 17, 2010).

Sabine, George H. 1973. *A History of Political Theory.* 4th ed., revised by Thomas Landon Thorson. Fort Worth, TX: Holt, Rinehart and Winston.

Sagel, Yuriela, and Juan Díaz. 2000. "Miller no recibirá pago por salarios caídos." *El Panamá América,* July 5. http://www.pa-digital.com.pa/ (accessed May 17, 2010, through the electronic archive).

Salas Céspedes, Aníbal. 1999. "Demanda para que el Tribunal Electoral, previo cumplimiento de los trámites legales, haga las investigaciones y rectificaciones que nuestro ordenamiento jurídico legal exige, dentro del proceso electoral que se llevó a cabo en el Circuito 8-4, especialmente en las materias reguladas en los títulos VI y VII del Código Electoral y sus reglamentaciones." Lawsuit documents, author's archive.

Samuels, David J. 1998. "Political Ambition in Brazil, 1945–95: Theory and Evidence." Paper presented at the 21st International Congress of the Latin American Studies Association, Chicago, September 24–26. http://lasa .international.pitt.edu/LASA98/Samuels.pdf (accessed May 17, 2010).

Samuels, David J., and Richard Snyder. 2001. "The Value of a Vote: Malapportionment in Comparative Perspective." *British Journal of Political Science* 31 (4): 651–71.

Sánchez, Peter. 2007. *Panama Lost? U.S. Hegemony, Democracy, and the Canal.* Gainesville: University Press of Florida.

Sánchez Borbón, Guillermo. 1992. "En pocas palabras." *La Prensa,* October 7.

———. 1994a. "En pocas palabras." *La Prensa,* October 9.

———. 1994b. "En pocas palabras." *La Prensa,* November 28.

Sánchez González, Salvador. 1996. *El financiamiento de los partidos políticos en Panamá.* Panamá: Fundación

———. 2004. "Cien años de labor legislativa." In *El siglo XX, capítulos 1–17,* vol. 1 of *Historia General de Panamá,* ed. Alfredo Castillero Calvo. Panama: Comité Nacional del Centenario.

Sanchiz, Miguel. 1994. "El que más organizado está y da más, es el que gana." *La Prensa,* February 19. http://biblioteca.prensa.com/contenido/1994/ batch02/sanchi.000-0001595.html (accessed May 17, 2010).

Santos Barrios, Angel. 2000a. "Posiciones encontradas en pago de salarios caídos a legisladores." *El Panamá América,* March 3. http://www.pa-digital .com.pa/ (accessed May 17, 2010, through the electronic archive).

———. 2000b. "Contralor no ha recibido petición para pagar a legisladores." *El Panamá América,* April 2. http://www.pa-digital.com.pa/ (accessed May 17, 2010, through the electronic archive).

Schemo, Diana Jean. 1997a. "Scandal Puts Brazil Leader Under Cloud." *New York Times,* May 21. http://www.nytimes.com/1997/05/21/world/scandal -puts-brazil-leader-under-cloud.html?src=pm (accessed December 30, 2010).

———. 1997b. "Brazil's Chief Wins Vote Despite Scandal." *New York Times,* May 22. http://www.nytimes.com/1997/05/22/world/brazil-s-chief-wins -vote-despite-scandal.html?pagewanted=1 (accessed May 17, 2010).

Schlesinger, Joseph A. 1966. *Ambition and Politics: Political Careers in the United States.* Chicago: Rand McNally.

Sepúlveda, Mélida Ruth. 1983. *Harmodio Arias Madrid: el hombre, el estadista y el periodista.* Panama: Editorial Universitaria.

Servicio Electoral de Chile. 2008. "Candidaturas desde 1989–2008" [*sic*]. http:// www.servel.cl/servel/index.aspx?channel=309 (accessed May 17, 2010).

Shields, Currin V. 1958. Introduction to *Considerations on Representative Government,* by John Stuart Mill. Ed. Currin V. Shields. New York: Liberal Arts Press.

Shugart, Matthew Soberg, and John M. Carey. 1992. *Presidents and Assemblies: Constitutional Design and Electoral Dynamics.* Cambridge: Cambridge University Press.

Simons, Lewis M. 1999. "Panama's Rite of Passage." *National Geographic* (November 1999).

Socialist International. 2008. "Member Parties of the Socialist International." http://www.socialistinternational.org/viewArticle.cfm?ArticlePageID= 927#b (accessed May 17, 2010).

Sonnleitner, Willibald. 2010. "Desproporcionalidad y malaporcionamiento legislativos en Panamá: reformas para mejorar el desempeño electoral." In *Las reformas electorales en Panamá: claves de desarrollo humano para la toma de decisiones,* ed. Harry Brown Araúz, 139–214. Panama: United Nations Development Programme and Tribunal Electoral de Panamá.

Stein, Ernesto, Mariano Tommasi, Koldo Echebarría, Eduardo Lora, and J. Mark Payne. 2005. *The Politics of Policies: Economic and Social Progress in Latin America (2006 Report).* Washington, DC: Inter-American Development Bank and David Rockefeller Center for Latin American Studies, Harvard University.

Srill, Jonathan. 1981. "Political Equality and Election Systems." *Ethics* 91:375–94.

Sucre Serrano, Hermes. 1994a. "En la A. Legislativa hubo total ausentismo de legisladores." *La Prensa,* May 10. http://biblioteca.prensa.com/contenido/ 1994/batch04/as.003-0001361.html (accessed May 17, 2010).

———. 1994b. "Asamblea espera fallo sobre vacaciones." *La Prensa,* September 4. http://biblioteca.prensa.com/contenido/1994/batch07/as.008-000 0187.html (accessed May 17, 2010).

———. 2001. "Corte falla contra legisladores." *La Prensa,* January 26. http:// ediciones.prensa.com/ (accessed May 17, 2010, through the electronic archive).

Sucre Serrano, Hermes, and Manuel Domínguez. 2000. "Pagué los Cartier de mi bolsillo: Moscoso." *La Prensa,* January 6. http://mensual.prensa.com/ mensual/contenido/2000/01/06/jueves/portada.html (accessed May 17, 2010).

Sucre Serrano, Hermes, and Gionela Jordán. 2000. "Por orden de la mandataria: Presidente del Partido Arnulfista pide disculpas al arzobispo." *La Prensa,* January 12. http://mensual.prensa.com/mensual/contenido/2000/01/12/ miercoles/portada.html (accessed May 17, 2010).

Szok, Peter. 2001. *"La última gaviota": Liberalism and Nostalgia in Early Twentieth-Century Panama.* Westport, CT: Greenwood Press.

Taagepera, Rein, and Matthew Soberg Shugart. 1989. *Seats and Votes: The Effects and Determinants of Electoral Systems.* New Haven, CT: Yale University Press.

Taylor, Philip. 1962. *Government and Politics of Uruguay.* New Orleans: Tulane University Press.

Taylor-Robinson, Michelle. 2006. "The Difficult Road from *Caudillismo* to Democracy: The Impact of Clientelism in Honduras." In *Informal Institutions and Democracy: Lessons from Latin America,* ed. Gretchen Helmke and Steve Levitsky, 106–24. Baltimore, MD: Johns Hopkins University Press.

Tejera, Aet. 2007. "Sopla Dios le regaló Biblia al MAN." *Crítica Libre,* September 16. http://www.critica.com.pa/archivo/09162007/relatos.html (accessed May 17, 2010).

Thirty-thousand.org. 2006. "Reelection Rates of Incumbents in the U.S. House by Congress and by State: First through 108th Congress. " *Quantitative Historical Analysis* No. 8. http://www.thirty-thousand.org/documents/QHA-08.pdf (accessed May 17, 2010).

Torres, Víctor. 1999a. "Defienden ausentismo de los legisladores." *La Prensa,* April 15. http://biblioteca.prensa.com/contenido/1999/04/24f42729.html (accessed May 17, 2010).

———. 1999b. "Con 10 mil dólares podrían multar alianzas de Mireya y Martín." *La Prensa,* May 3. http://biblioteca.prensa.com/contenido/1999/05/25330255.html (accessed December 17, 2010).

———. 1999c. "Alemán Boyd pide que se investigue a Franz Wever." *La Prensa,* May 6. http://biblioteca.prensa.com/contenido/1999/05/25634317.html (accessed December 17, 2010).

———. 1999d. "También se ausentan los que no se reeligieron: Legisladores reelectos no van a trabajar." *La Prensa,* May 20. http://biblioteca.prensa.com/contenido/1999/05/25k43855.html (accessed May 17, 2010).

Torres, Víctor, and Wilfredo Jordán. 1999. "No las entregan a tiempo: Piden cárcel para responsables de actas." *La Prensa,* May 4. http://biblioteca.prensa.com/contenido/1999/05/25433242.html (accessed May 17, 2010).

Transparency International. 2009. "Corruption Perceptions Index 2009." http://www.transparency.org/policy_research/surveys_indices/cpi/2009/cpi_2009_table (accessed May 17, 2010).

———. 2010. "Frequently Asked Questions about Corruption." http://www.transparency.org/news_room/faq/corruption_faq (accessed May 17, 2010).

Tribunal Electoral de Panamá. 1984a. "Cuadro completo de los candidatos electos en los distintos cargos de elección popular en las elecciones del 6 de mayo y 10 de junio de 1984." *Boletín del Tribunal Electoral* No. 286, November 9. http://129.171.91.238/tribpdf/BOLETIN03/alexsa0B/46L00FBB.pdf (accessed May 17, 2010).

———. 1984b. "Elecciones de 1984: cuadro estadístico" [report]. Panama: Tribunal Electoral, Dirección de Sistemas.

————. 1991a. "Cuadro completo de los candidatos electos en los distintos cargos de elección popular en las elecciones de 7 de mayo de 1989 y 27 de enero de 1991." *Boletín del Tribunal Electoral* No. 535, December 10. http://129.171.91.238/tribpdf/BOLETIN03/alexsa0R/46L00FHR.pdf (accessed May 17, 2010).

————. 1991b. "Elecciones generales 1989 y 1991" [report]. Panama: Tribunal Electoral, Dirección de Planificación, Departamento de Estadística.

————. 1994a. "Candidatos a legisladores, alcaldes, representantes de corregimiento y concejales: elecciones generales del 8 de mayo de 1994." *Boletín del Tribunal Electoral* No. 806, April 29.

————. 1994b. "Cuadro completo de los candidatos electos en los distintos cargos de elección popular en las elecciones celebradas el 8 de mayo de 1994." *Boletín del Tribunal Electoral* No. 885, December 9. http://129.171.91.238/tribpdf/BOLETIN02/alexsa0E/46L00EFE.pdf (accessed May 17, 2010).

————. 1994c. "Estadísticas electorales: elecciones generales del 8 de mayo de 1994" [report]. Panama: Tribunal Electoral (Dirección de Planificación).

————. 1999a. "Candidatos a presidente, vicepresidentes, diputados al Parlamento Centroamericano, legisladores, alcaldes, representantes de corregimiento y concejales: elecciones generales del 2 de mayo de 1999." *Boletín del Tribunal Electoral* No. 1,312, April 15. http://129.171.91.238/tribpdf/BOLETIN04/alexsa0F/46L00H0F.pdf (accessed May 17, 2010).

————. 1999b. "Cuadro completo de los candidatos electos a los distintos cargos de elección popular en las elecciones celebradas el 2 de mayo de 1999 y en las elecciones parciales del 15 y 22 de agosto de 1999." *Boletín del Tribunal Electoral* No. 1,409, August 30. http://129.171.91.238/tribpdf/BOLETIN04/alexsa1E/46L00HYE.pdf (accessed May 17, 2010).

————. 1999c. "Integración de la Asamblea Legislativa." http://www.tribunal-electoral.gob.pa/elecciones/elecciones1999/cuadros/elec-01.html (accessed May 17, 2010).

————. 1999d. "Elecciones: Documentos de interés electoral—Elecciones celebradas." http://www.tribunal-electoral.gob.pa/elecciones/docum_electoral/elec_celebradas.html (accessed May 17, 2010).

————. 1999e. "Elecciones: Elecciones 1999—Resultados." http://www.tribunal-electoral.gob.pa/elecciones/elecciones1999/cuadros/elec-01.html (accessed May 17, 2010).

————. 2004a. "Aviso en el que se hace del conocimiento público los nombres de los candidatos electos en las elecciones generales del 2 de mayo de 2004 y elecciones parciales del 8 de agosto y 12 de septiembre de 2004." *Boletín del Tribunal Electoral* No. 2005, October 15. http://129.171.91.238/tribpdf/BOLETIN05/alexsa1G/46L000WG.pdf (accessed May 17, 2010).

————. 2004b. "Elecciones 2004: candidatos proclamados—Cuadro #4: Mesas escrutadas, votos emitidos, votos válidos por partido político, votos en blanco y votos nulos en la República, según provincia, comarca y circuito electoral: elecciones populares para legisladores del 2 de mayo de 2004." http://www.tribunal-electoral.gob.pa/elecciones/elecciones-2004/candidatos-proclamados.html (accessed May 17, 2010).

————. 2004c. "Distribución de curules legislativas por partido y tipo de proclamación: Elecciones populares del 2 de mayo de 2004." www.tribunal-electoral.gob.pa/elecciones/elecciones-2004/doc/cuadro-07.xls (accessed May 17, 2010).

————. 2008. "Elecciones: Partidos desaparecido [*sic*] y los que subsistieron." http://www.tribunal-electoral.gob.pa/elecciones/partidos-pol/partidos_desap.html (accessed May 17, 2010).

————. 2009a. "Elecciones generales 2009: Ganadores oficiales—Diputados ganadores." http://www.tribunal-electoral.gob.pa/elecciones/elecciones-2009/resultados/diputados.ganadores.pdf (accessed May 17, 2010).

————. 2009b. "Elecciones generales de 2 de mayo de 2009: Resultados detallados." http://www.tribunal-electoral.gob.pa/elecciones/elecciones-2009/resultados/resultados.html (accessed May 17, 2010).

————. 2009c. "Elecciones: Configuración de los circuitos electorales y diputados a elegir, de acuerdo a la Ley #59 de 28 de diciembre de 2006." http://www.tribunal-electoral.gob.pa/elecciones/elecciones-2009/circuitos09.html (accessed May 17, 2010).

————. 2009d. "Cuadro #7: Distribución de curules legislativas por partido político y tipo de proclamación, elecciones populares del 3 de mayo de 2009." http://www.tribunal-electoral.gob.pa/elecciones/elecciones-2009/resultados/resultados.html (accessed May 17, 2010).

————. 2009e. "Cargos de elección popular elegidos en los comicios del 3 de mayo de 2009." http://www.tribunal-electoral.gob.pa/elecciones/elecciones-2009/cargo.eleccion.popular.html (accessed May 17, 2010).

————. 2010. "Elecciones: Partidos políticos—Estadístico de adherentes vigentes por partido político, al 28/febrero/2010." http://www.tribunal-electoral.gob.pa/elecciones/partidos-pol/adherentes-vigentes-pp/2010/100228.html (accessed May 17, 2010).

U. K. Review Body on Senior Salaries. 2008. "Report." Vol. 1 of *Report No. 64: Review of Parliamentary Pay, Pensions and Allowances 2007*. http://www.ome.uk.com/downloads/Review%20of%20Parliamentary%20pay%202007%20volume%201.pdf.pdf (accessed May 17, 2010).

Unidad Investigativa de *La Prensa*. 2010. "Entrega especial: millonario fraude en el FIS." http://www.prensa.com/especial/2010/escandalo_fis/index.html (accessed May 17, 2010).

United Nations Development Programme (UNDP). 2009. *Human Develop-ment Report 2009: Overcoming Barriers—Human Mobility and Develop-ment.* New York: UNDP. http://hdr.undp.org/en/media/HDR_2009_EN_Complete.pdf (accessed May 17, 2010).

United Nations Population Division. 2009. "World Population Prospects: The 2008 Revision Population Database." http://esa.un.org/unpp/index.asp (accessed May 17, 2010).

Universidad de Salamanca. Instituto Interuniversitario de Iberoamérica. 2008. "Datos de opinión: Elites parlamentarias latinoamericanas—Panamá (1999–2009)." Salamanca: Universidad de Salamanca. http://www.usal.es/~iberoame/pdfs/Boletin12.pdf (accessed May 17, 2010).

U.S. Central Intelligence Agency. 2010. "The World Factbook." https://www.cia.gov/library/publications/the-world-factbook/index.html (accessed May 17, 2010).

U.S. Department of State. 1972. *Treaties and Other International Agreements of the United States of America, 1776–1949.* Vol. 10. Washington, DC: Gov-ernment Printing Office.

———. 1998. *Panama Country Report on Human Rights Practices for 1997.* www.state.gov/www/global/human_rights/1997_hrp_report/panama.html (accessed May 17, 2010).

———. 2000. *1999 Country Reports on Human Rights Practices: Panama.* www.state.gov/www/global/human_rights/1999_hrp_report/panama.html (accessed May 17, 2010).

———. 2007. "Election of Panamanian National Assembly President Pedro Miguel Gonzalez-Pinzon." September 1. http://2001-2009.state.gov/r/pa/prs/ps/2007/sep/91670.htm (accessed May 17, 2010).

———. 2008. *2007 Country Reports on Human Rights Practices: Panama.* http://www.state.gov/g/drl/rls/hrrpt/2007/100648.htm (accessed May 17, 2010).

———. 2010. *2009 Country Reports on Human Rights Practices: Panama.* http://www.state.gov/g/drl/rls/hrrpt/2009/wha/136121.htm (accessed May 17, 2010).

U.S. National Security Council. 1977. "Information Memorandum: Brigadier General Omar Torrijos Herrera," October 14. Declassified document ob-tained through the National Security Archive, George Washington Uni-versity, Washington, DC.

Valdés, Evelio. 2009. "Denuncian a Miguel Fanovich." *El Siglo,* May 8. http://www.elsiglo.com/siglov2/Panama.php?idsec=33&fechaz=08-05-2009&idnews=100656 (accessed May 17, 2010).

Valdés Escoffery, Eduardo. 2006a. *Acontecer electoral panameño.* Vol. 1. Panama: Tribunal Electoral.

————. 2006b. "Regulación jurídica de los partidos politicos en Panamá." In *Regulación jurídica de los partidos políticos en América Latina,* ed. Daniel Zovatto. Stockholm: International Institute for Democracy and Electoral Assistance. http://www.bibliojuridica.org/libros/5/2144/19.pdf (accessed May 17, 2010).

Vargas Llosa, Mario. 2000. "La herencia maldita." *El País* (Madrid), October 5. http://www.aprodeh.org.pe/democracia/democracia1/c_oi_03oct2000.htm (accessed May 17, 2010).

Vásquez, Juan Materno. 1989. *Mi amigo Omar Torrijos.* Panama: Ediciones Olga Elena.

Vega, Ibeth. 1995. "Presidente no revocará aumento a los ministros." *La Prensa,* November 4. http://biblioteca.prensa.com/contenido/1995/batch10/toro -0000551.html (accessed May 17, 2010).

Vega, Ibeth, and Manuel Álvarez Cedeño. 1994. "Asamblea Legislativa: Logran consenso para limitar exoneraciones." *La Prensa,* March 23. http://biblio teca.prensa.com/contenido/1994/batch03/legis-0001178.html (accessed May 17, 2010).

————. 1995. "Presidente veta proyecto sobre telefonía celular." *La Prensa,* June 30. http://biblioteca.prensa.com/contenido/1995/batch06/phone .000-0000091.html (accessed May 17, 2010).

Velásquez, Osvaldo. 1993. *Historia de una dictadura: de Torrijos a Noriega.* Panama: Litho Editorial Chen.

Verbitsky, Horacio. 2000. "Una crítica democrática a la democracia: La muerte lenta." *Página 12,* October 15. http://www.pagina12.com.ar/2000/ 00-10/00-10-15/pag13.htm (accessed May 17, 2010).

Vergara, Gisela. 1994. "Legisladores dejan de pagar al fisco más de cuatro millones." *La Prensa,* March 19. http://biblioteca.prensa.com/contenido/ 1994/batch03/legisl-0000889.html (accessed May 17, 2010).

Vernaza, Vielka. 1990. "Sólo se ha despedido dos mil, revela viceministro Batista." *La Prensa,* February 23. http://biblioteca.prensa.com/contenido/ 1990/batch02/dosmil.html (accessed May 17, 2010).

Weber, Max. 1918/1978. "Parliament and Government in a Reconstructed Germany (A Contribution to the Political Critique of Officialdom and Party Politics)." In *Economy and Society: An Outline of Interpretive Sociology,* by Max Weber. Ed. Guenther Roth and Claus Wittich. Berkeley: University of California Press.

————. 1919/1946. "Politics as a Vocation." *From Max Weber: Essays in Sociology.* Trans. and ed. H. H. Gerth and C. Wright Mills. New York: Oxford University Press.

————. 1922/1978. *Economy and Society: An Outline of Interpretive Sociology.* Ed. Guenther Roth and Claus Wittich. Berkeley: University of California Press.

Williamson, Edwin. 1992. *The Penguin History of Latin America.* London: Penguin.

Wong, Edsel. 2001. "La verdad es sólo una." *El Panamá América,* January 19.

World Bank. 2010. "Data Catalog: World Development Indicators, Consumer Price Index Series, Panama, 1960–2008." http://data.worldbank.org/data-catalog (accessed May 17, 2010).

Yániz de Arias, Teresita. 2000. "Clientelismo y clientes." *La Prensa,* December 6. http://biblioteca.prensa.com/contenido/2000/12/3c631047.html (accessed May 17, 2010).

Zimbalist, Andrew, and John Weeks. 1991. *Panama at the Crossroads: Economic Development and Political Change in the Twentieth Century.* Berkeley: University of California Press.

Zúñiga, Carlos Iván. 1980. *El proceso Guizado (un alegato para la historia).* 2nd ed. Panama: Imprenta Bárcenas.

———. 2002. "Hacia unas navidades solidarias con los pobres." *La Prensa,* December 21. http://biblioteca.prensa.com/contenido/2002/12/21/21-11a-noti1.html (accessed May 17, 2010).

Other Works Consulted

Books and Articles

Alcántara, Manuel, and Flavia Freidenberg. *Partidos políticos de América Latina, Centroamérica, México y República Dominicana.* México: Fondo de Cultura Económica e Instituto Federal Electoral.

Ames, Barry. 1995. "Electoral Strategy under Open-List Proportional Representation." *American Journal of Political Science* 39 (2): 406–33.

Bernal, Miguel Antonio. 2000. "País político vs país nacional." *El Panamá América,* August 25.

———. 2000. "La reforma de la Asamblea." *El Panamá América,* September 19.

Bouche, Lidia. 1999. "¡Qué vida tan sufrida!" *La Prensa,* May 15. http://biblioteca.prensa.com/contenido/1999/05/25f32800.html (accessed May 16, 2010).

Flores, Leonardo. 2007. "Premiados por cambiar de toldas." *La Prensa,* October 27. http://mensual.prensa.com/mensual/contenido/2007/10/27/hoy/pdf/Portada.pdf (accessed April 7, 2008).

Galindo Heurtematte, Mario. 2000. "Mario J. Galindo H. solicita la declaratoria de inconstitucionalidad del artículo 16 de la Ley 35 de 30 de Julio de 1999." Lawsuit documents, author's archive.

Grant Thornton Cheng and Associates. 2008. *Boletín Fiscal.* http://www.gt.com.pa/site/boletinesind.php (accessed December 29, 2010).

International Monetary Fund (IMF). 1999. *International Financial Statistics (April 1999).* Washington, DC: IMF.

Jackson, Eric. 2006. "Panama's World Baseball Classic Team in Disarray." *Panama News,* February 19–March 4. http://www.thepanamanews.com/pn/v_12/issue_04/sports_02.html (accessed May 16, 2010).

Jaén, Néstor. 1996. "¿Votar en blanco en 1999?" *La Prensa,* December 31. http://biblioteca.prensa.com/contenido/1996/batch11/nestor-0001197.html (accessed May 16, 2010).

Janson Pérez, Brittmarie. 2000. "El reinado de la corrupción." *El Panamá América,* July 11.

Jong, Niek de, and Rob Vos. 2000. "Distribución de ingresos en Panamá." Panama: Ministerio de Economía y Finanzas. http://bdigital.binal.ac.pa/bdp/elingresoenpanama.pdf (accessed May 17, 2010).

Mata Kelly, Rainelda. 1992. Untitled Opinion Editorial. *La Prensa,* September 26. http://biblioteca.prensa.com/contenido/1992/batch02/tich25.000-0001620.html (accessed May 17, 2010).

O'Donnell, Guillermo. 1994. "Delegative Democracy." *Journal of Democracy* 5 (1): 56–69.

Otero, José. 1994. "Legisladores insisten en cobrar las vacaciones." *La Prensa,* June 13. http://biblioteca.prensa.com/contenido/1994/batch05/vallar.001-0001335.html (accessed May 17, 2010).

Quintero, César. 1989. *Evolución constitucional de Panamá.* 2nd ed. Panama: Privately published by the author.

Quintero de León, José. 2008. "Dominicana ya tiene su metro; Panamá espera." *La Prensa,* March 21. http://mensual.prensa.com/mensual/contenido/2008/03/21/hoy/panorama/1301041.html (accessed May 17, 2010).

Rae, Douglas W. 1971. *The Political Consequences of Electoral Laws.* New Haven, CT: Yale University Press.

República de Panamá. 1997. "Código Electoral." *Gaceta Oficial* no. 23,437, December 13. http://www.asamblea.gob.pa/APPS/LEGISPAN/PDF_GACETAS/1990/1997/23437_1997. PDF (accessed May 17, 2010).

———. 1998. "Ley No. 16 de 17 de febrero de 1998, por la que se reforma el Texto Único del Reglamento Orgánico del Régimen Interno de la Asamblea Legislativa." *Gaceta Oficial* no. 23,486, February 19. http://www.asamblea.gob.pa/APPS/LEGISPAN/PDF_GACETAS/1990/1998/23486_1998. PDF (accessed May 17, 2010).

Reyes, Herasto. 1994. "Composición de la nueva Asamblea Legislativa." *La Prensa,* August 31.

Reynolds, Andrew. 2005. *The International IDEA Handbook of Electoral System Design.* Stockholm: International Institute for Democracy and Electoral Assistance.

Rodríguez Bernal, Rolando. 1997. "Señala proyecto de ley: Descontarán salario a legisladores por sus ausencias injustificadas." *La Prensa,* March 4. http://

biblioteca.prensa.com/contenido/1997/batch09/mendez-0001261.html (accessed May 17, 2010).

Saiegh, Sebastián. 2005. "The Role of Legislatures in the Policymaking Process." Paper prepared for the Inter-American Development Bank Workshop on State Reform, Public Policies, and Policymaking Processes, Washington, DC, February 28–March 2. http://www.iadb.org/res/publications/pubfiles/pubS-302.pdf (accessed May 17, 2010).

Sánchez, Cynthia. 2004. "Limitarán las exoneraciones." *La Prensa,* February 13. http://mensual.prensa.com/mensual/contenido/2004/02/13/hoy/portada/1520169.html (accessed May 17, 2010).

Sánchez Borbón, Guillermo. 1984. "En pocas palabras." *La Prensa,* April 12.

———. 1990. "En pocas palabras." *La Prensa,* February 6.

Tribunal Electoral de Panamá. 1997. *La reforma electoral de 1997.* Panama: Tribunal Electoral.

———. 2006. "Propuesta de circuitos." http://www.tribunal-electoral.gob.pa/proyecto/propuesta-circuitos.html (accessed May 17, 2010).

———. 2008. "Estadístico de adherentes vigentes por partido político: inscripciones acumuladas de los partidos políticos constituidos y en formación (enero, octubre y noviembre de 2008)." http://www.tribunal-electoral.gob.pa/elecciones/partidos-pol/adherentes-vigentes-pp/2008/081130.html (accessed May 17, 2010).

———. 2009. "Elecciones: Partidos políticos vigentes." http://www.tribunal-electoral.gob.pa/elecciones/partidos-pol/index.html (accessed May 17, 2010).

U.S. Department of State. 2005. *2004 Country Reports on Human Rights Practices: Panama.* http://www.state.gov/g/drl/rls/hrrpt/2004/41769.htm (accessed May 17, 2010).

Personal Communications

Ameglio, Marco. 2008. Email to the author, June 13.

Brannan Jaén, Betty. 1998. Email to the author, October 31.

Cochez, Guillermo A. 2000. Email to the author, August 31.

Confidential source. 2007. Personal interview with the author.

Díaz, Ovidio. 2000. Telephone conversation with the author, July 25.

Guardia, Gloria. 2006. Personal interview with the author, August 15.

Jones, Mark. 1999. Email to the author, May 18.

Mejía Acosta, Andrés. 1999. Emails to the author, March 17 and May 4.

Méndez Fábrega, Víctor. 2000. Email to the author, May 5.

Quintero, César. 1999. Personal conversation with the author, August 18.

Ricord, Humberto E. 1999. Personal conversation with the author, August 18.

Samuels, David J. 1999. Email to the author, May 13.

Index

Capital letters in parentheses identify appendices.

Abad, Jaime, 248, 249, 250
Ábrego, Rafael, 167, 229, 283 (E), 303
  (I), 329 (K), 346 (L)
Ábrego, Roberto, 173, 204, 227–28, 283
  (E), 309 (I), 313 (I), 329 (K), 345
  (L), 363 (R)
Ábrego, Yanibel, 128, 158 (table 7.1), 283
  (E), 297 (F), 323 (J), 329 (K), 345 (L)
absolutism, 107
Afú, Carlos, 1, 128, 158 (table 7.1), 160
  (table 7.2), 163, 204, 222, 223, 283
  (E), 297 (F), 309 (I), 313 (I), 317
  (I), 322 (I), 323 (J), 329 (K), 345
  (L), 362 (R), 398n36
Aizpurúa, Edwin, 172, 283 (E), 313 (I),
  329 (K), 345 (L)
Alarcón, Fabián, 227
Alarcón, Marco, 125 (table 5.4), 157,
  283 (E), 303 (I), 329 (K), 346 (L)
Alba, Rogelio, 158 (table 7.1), 161
  (table 7.2), 183 (table 8.2), 186, 228,
  252, 283 (E), 297 (F), 309 (I), 313
  (I), 317 (I), 322 (I), 323 (J), 329
  (K), 347 (L), 363 (R), 394n19

Alemán, Francisco, 172, 202, 283 (E),
  313 (I), 317 (I), 323 (J), 329 (K),
  347 (L), 398n36
Alemán Boyd, Alberto, 171, 198, 206,
  220, 229, 231, 240, 241, 242, 245,
  253, 283 (E), 303 (I), 306 (I), 309
  (I), 346 (L), 347 (L), 263 (R),
  385n2, 396n10
Alfonso, Lorenzo, 229, 283 (E), 303 (I),
  329 (K), 344 (L)
Alianza Ciudadana Pro Justicia, 223
Altamirano Duque, Tomás, 50, 58–59,
  122 (table 5.2), 124 (table 5.3), 170,
  222, 283 (E), 303 (I), 309 (I), 312
  (I, note a), 320 (I, note a), 329 (K),
  344 (L), 345 (L), 379n15, 389n10
Altamirano Duque family, 58–59
Altamirano Mantovani, Tomás, 50,
  58–59, 170, 183 (table 8.2), 222,
  283 (E), 312 (I, note a), 313 (I), 317
  (I), 320 (I, note a), 323 (J), 329 (K),
  345 (L), 362 (R), 379n15
Alvarado, Carlos, 50, 143, 204, 222,
  224, 233–34, 283 (E), 309 (I), 317

(I), 320 (I, note b), 323 (J), 330 (K), 345 (L), 362 (R), 379n13

Álvarez, Carlos, 217

Alvarez, Edgardo, 144, 283 (E), 309 (I), 330 (K), 345 (L), 363 (R)

Amador Guerrero, Manuel, 27

Ameglio, Marco, 160 (table 7.2), 195, 283 (E), 306 (I), 309 (I), 313 (I), 321 (I), 330 (K), 346 (L), 347 (L), 364 (R), 396n10

Andorra, low levels of clientelism in, 377n13

Antinori Bolaños, Ítalo, 174

Antón, Coclé, Panama, 171

Antonío, Abelardo, 122 (table 5.2), 150, 183 (table 8.3), 284 (E), 306 (E), 309 (I), 313 (I), 323 (J), 330 (K), 344 (L), 345 (L), 363 (R), 381n36, 398n36

Aparicio, Héctor, 183 (table 8.3), 284 (E), 309 (I), 313 (I), 317 (I), 323 (J), 330 (K), 347 (L), 363 (R), 381n35, 398n36

Aprista Party, Peru (PAP), 42

Araúz, Rony, 183 (table 8.3), 284 (E), 323 (J), 330 (K), 345 (L)

Arce, Denis 284 (E), 309 (I), 313 (I), 317 (I), 323 (J), 330 (K), 345 (L), 362 (R), 398n36

Ardito Barletta, Nicolás, 134, 167, 375n13, 386n2

Arellano Lennox, Carlos, 241, 284 (E), 303 (I), 306 (I), 330 (K), 346 (L), 387n3, 396n8

Argentina: constituency funding in, 139, 140; difference between congressional and presidential votes in, 47; immunity of members of congress, 239; impunity in, 98; presidential reelection in, 262; reelection of members of congress in, 119; representatives' salaries in, 189, 190 (table 8.6)

Arias, Daniel, 77, 161 (table 7.2), 162, 226, 284 (E), 309 (I), 321 (I), 330 (K), 347 (L), 364 (R)

Arias Grimaldo, Gerardo, 125 (table 5.4), 284 (E), 309 (I), 330 (K), 345 (L), 363 (R), 380n28

Arias Madrid, Arnulfo, 2, 27, 28, 29, 39, 40, 41, 56, 95, 157, 165, 166, 167, 168, 280 (D), 377n8, 380n28, 381nn29, 32, 383n11

Arias Madrid, Harmodio, 56, 380n28, 381n29

Arias Paredes, Francisco, 378n3

Arosemena, Blas, 95

Arosemena, Gaspar, 95

Arosemena, Mariano, 95

Arosemena, Rodrigo, 204, 284 (E), 309 (I), 330 (K), 347 (L)

Arosemena, Rubén, 50, 123, 124 (table 5.3), 143, 198, 211, 284 (E), 309 (I), 313 (I), 317 (I), 331 (K), 347 (L), 364 (R), 378n5, 393n29

Arraiján, Panama, 57, 61 (table 2.6), 151, 170

Artola, Francisco, 157, 284 (E), 303 (I), 306 (I), 331 (K), 344 (L)

Assembly of County Representatives, 30–31, 35, 79–80, 81, 218, 377nn9 11

Austria, parliamentary immunity, 239

Baker, Eleuteria, 312 (I, note b), 379n18

Ballesteros, Donatilo, 194

Banco Hipotecario Nacional, 111

Banco Nacional de Panamá (National Bank of Panama), 232

Barrientos, José María, 95

Baruco, Rogelio, 186, 285 (E), 324 (J), 331 (K), 345 (L)

Batista, Arcelio, 161 (table 7.2), 163, 285 (E), 313 (I), 322 (I), 331 (K), 345 (L)

Batista, Fulgencio, 96

Bavarian Motors, 393n39

Belgium, parliamentary immunity, 239

Bendetti, Leopoldo, 122 (table 5.2), 161 (table 7.2), 285 (E), 309 (I), 317 (I), 321 (I), 324 (J), 331 (K), 345 (L), 364 (R)

Bidlack-Mallarino Treaty (1846) (Treaty of Peace, Amity, Commerce, and Navigation), 38, 378n2
Bocas del Toro Province, Panama, 216, 224, 247, 386n1
Bogotá, Colombia, 27, 95, 376n4
Bolívar, Simón, 376n4
Bolivia: as electoral democracy, 376n14; longevity of parties in, 48; non-programmatic politics in, 43; presidential reelection in, 262
Brazil: as large liberal democracy, 10; longevity of parties in, 48; party switching in, 154, 159, 164; political careers in, 119; presidential legislative powers in, 89; presidential reelection in, 262; reelection of members of congress in, 119; remuneration of representatives in, 190 (table 8.6); vote selling in, 216
Brin Martínez, Pedro, 167, 285 (E), 303 (I), 332 (K), 344 (L)
Budget Committee, National Assembly of Panama, 1, 142, 143, 202, 230
Bush, George H. W., 245, 247
Bush, Miguel, 94, 195, 198, 200, 210, 221, 227, 245, 246, 253, 285 (E), 306 (I), 309 (I), 313 (I), 332 (K), 344 (L), 345 (L), 363 (R)

Calidonia, Panama, 80
Cano, Felipe, 125 (table 5.4), 219, 285 (E), 313 (I), 332 (K), 347 (L)
Caracas, Venezuela, 103
Cárdenas, Miguel, 285 (E), 306 (I), 332 (K), 344 (L), 396n10
Cardoso, Fernando Henrique, 217
Carreño, José, 158 (table 7.1), 252, 285 (E), 297 (F), 312 (I, note c), 314 (I), 318 (I), 324 (J), 332 (K), 345 (L), 363 (R), 379n12
Cartier jewelry, 218–20
Castillero, Mateo, 1, 170, 222, 285 (E), 314 (I), 332 (K), 345 (L)

Castillo, Elías, 51, 169, 183 (table 8.2), 197, 212, 215, 220, 240–41, 244, 253, 286 (E), 306 (I), 309 (I), 314 (I), 318 (I), 324 (J), 332 (K), 346 (L), 347 (L), 362 (R), 398n36
Castillo, Geovany, 172, 813 (table 8.2), 286 (E), 318 (I), 324 (J), 332 (K), 345 (L)
Castillo, Leopoldo, 77
Castro, Fidel, 103
Castro, Gabriel, 146, 388n28
Catholic Church, Honduras, 236
Catholic Church, Panama, 197
Catholicism, 21
caudillismo, 38
Central American Parliament (PARLACÉN), 69, 212, 252, 382n5, 385n6, 395n23
Centro Multimodal Industrial y de Servicios (CEMIS), 1, 14, 128, 163, 222–23, 239, 251, 374n4, 398n36
Chavarría, Omar, 320 (I, note b), 379n13
Chen Barría, José, 194
Chepo, Panama, 58, 170
Chi, Ebén, 167, 229, 286 (E), 303 (I), 332 (K), 346 (L)
Chiari Remón, Roberto, 377n8, 378n3
Chiari Robles, Rodolfo, 378n3
Chile: Chamber of Deputies, 55; representatives' salaries in, 189, 190 (table 8.6)
Chiquita Brands, 221
Chiriquí Land Company, 221
Chiriquí Province, Panama, 172, 173, 231, 232, 233, 234
Christian Democratic Party, Italy, 46
Christian Democratic Party, Panama (Partido Demócrata Cristiano; Partido Popular), 41, 43, 162, 279 (D)
Cigarruista, Alberto, 125 (table 5.4), 196, 199, 222, 223, 251, 286 (E), 306, 309, 314 (I), 333 (K), 344 (L), 345 (L), 364 (R), 386n9

Clavel, Tomás, 166
clientelism, 1, 5, 7, 8, 9, 10, 13, 18, 25,
    33, 34, 57, 59, 64, 66, 71, 82, 84, 85,
    86, 90, 91, 98, 104–13, 139, 178,
    214, 215, 234, 235, 254, 255, 260,
    261, 264, 266, 377n13, 382n7,
    383n13, 393n3, 398n1
Coalición Nacional Revolucionaria, 40
Coalición Patriótica Nacional, 40
Cochez, Guillermo, 125 (table 5.4),
    207, 286 (E), 303, 306 (I), 333 (K),
    346 (L)
Coclé Province, Panama, 112, 171,
    388n30
Coco, Maribel, 173
Colegio Nacional de Abogados (National
    Bar Association of Panama), 144
Collado, Gustavo, 229, 286 (E), 303 (I),
    333 (K), 344 (L)
Colombia: border with Panama, 70, 210;
    Congress, 26, 86, 140, 227;
    constituency funding in, 139, 140,
    144; Constitution (1886), 27, 89;
    Constitution (1991), 140; electoral
    fraud in, 165; Liberal Party, 42;
    National Planning Office, 140;
    Panama's secession from, 27, 38, 108;
    Panama's union with, 26, 122, 165;
    party politics in, 43; political
    institutions, 37, 38; presidential
    reelection in, 262; representatives'
    wages in, 189, 190 (table 8.6); Treaty
    of 1846 with the United States, 38;
    vote buying in, 83
compadrazgo, 108
Comptroller-General's Office, Panama, 53,
    86, 87, 134, 135, 136, 145–48, 201,
    202, 211, 215, 228, 229, 230, 232,
    233, 235, 379n17, 384n18, 389n35
Constitutional Reform Commission,
    Panama (1983), 87, 88, 89
Correa, Omaira, 50, 124 (table 5.3), 125
    (table 5.4), 286 (E), 303 (I), 333
    (K), 346 (L)

corregidor, 245, 285n7
corregimientos (counties), 30, 79
Cortizo, Laurentino, 145, 169, 226, 286
    (E), 310, 314 (I), 333 (K), 345 (L),
    362 (R)
Costa Rica: constituency funding in,
    139, 140, 144; deputies' immunity,
    239; deputies' wages in, 189;
    difference between congressional
    and presidential votes in, 47;
    Legislative Assembly, 33; Otilio
    Miranda's escape to, 232; party
    institutionalization in, 47, 48;
    reelection of deputies in, 66, 119
Crítica, Panama (newspaper), 381
Cruz, Rogelio, 241, 242, 244, 245
Cuba: dictatorship of Batista in, 96;
    non-free status of, 376n14; Pedro
    González's escape to, 248
Cuervo, Maribel, 226
Culiolis, Edilberto, 210, 286 (E), 306
    (I), 333 (K), 344 (L)
Cunningham, Randy "Duke," 224
Curabo, Santiago, 167, 286 (E), 304 (I),
    333 (K), 344 (L)

Darién Province, Panama, 70, 170, 171,
    172, 173, 210, 215, 216, 246
Delgado, Hernán, 158 (table 7.1), 170,
    286 (E), 297 (F), 324 (J), 333 (K),
    335 (K), 345 (L)
Delgado Diamante, Daniel, 103
Delvalle, Eric, 376n13
Delvalle, Max, 29
Democratic Action, Venezuela (AD), 42
Democratic Labor Party, Brazil (PDT), 42
Denmark: low levels of clientelism in,
    377n13; parliamentary immunity,
    239; Socialist Party, 46
Díaz, Ovidio, 133–34, 286 (E), 304 (I),
    333 (K), 344 (L)
Díaz Arosemena, Domingo, 165, 378n3
district magnitude (M), 69, 71, 72
    (table 3.3), 75, 90

Doens, Mitchell, 164
Dominican Republic: deputies' salaries in, 189; dictatorship of Trujillo in, 96; electoral democracy in, 376n14; liberal democracy in, 375n10; membership in Central American Parliament, 382n5; party politics in, 43; presidential reelection in, 262
Dominican Revolutionary Party, 42
Duque, Carlos, 149, 388n29
Duque, José Gabriel, 58
Duque, Manuel Everardo, 58
Duvalier family, 97

Ecuador: constituency funding in, 139; deputies' salaries in, 190; party switching in, 154, 159; party system institutionalization in, 48; presidential reelection in, 262; presidential volatility in, 47
El Copé, Coclé, Panama, 110
El Panamá América, Panama, 99, 102, 174, 250, 263, 381n31
El Salvador: Corruption Perceptions Index of, 9; deputies' salaries in, 189, 190 (table 8.6); electoral democracy in, 376n14; Legislative Assembly, 189; liberal democracy in, 375n10; membership in Central American Parliament, 382n5; vehicle import exemption in, 208
El Siglo (Panama), 97, 225
Electoral Prosecutor's Office, Panama, 150, 172, 174
Electoral Tribunal of Panama, 31, 39, 41, 43, 44, 50, 54, 64, 70, 75, 77, 128, 144, 150, 155, 156, 158, 167, 168, 169, 170, 172, 174, 197, 215, 228, 235, 240, 249, 250
Emberá Indigenous Reserve, Panama, 230
Emergency Development Fund. See Fondo de Emergencia Social (FES); Fondo de Inversión Social (FIS)

Endara, Guillermo, 12, 41, 102, 120, 132, 136, 138, 168, 193, 220, 222, 225, 228, 235, 242, 282 (D), 375n12, 378n6, 383n8
Escobar Fornos, Iván, 189
Escudé, Agustín, 50, 287 (E), 318 (I), 320 (I, note e), 324 (J), 334 (K), 345 (L), 379n14
Esquivel, Roderick, 376n13
Esquivel, Romelia, 229, 287 (E), 304 (I), 334 (K), 346 (L)
Ex-Legislators Association, 225–27

Fábrega, José Luis, 160 (table 7.2), 163, 219, 287 (E), 314 (I), 318 (I), 322 (I), 325 (J), 334 (K), 347 (L), 398n36
Fanovich, Miguel, 172, 252, 287 (E), 318 (I), 325 (J), 334 (K), 345 (L)
Fernández Guardia, Alonso, 242, 287 (E), 307 (I), 321 (I), 334 (K), 396n12
Finland: low levels of clientelism in, 377n13; parliamentary immunity, 239
Fondo de Emergencia Social (FES) (Emergency Development Fund), 136–37, 139, 387n7
Fondo de Inversión Social (FIS) (Emergency Development Fund), 139, 387n7
France: electoral volatility in, 47; Noriega's trial in, 103; parliamentary immunity, 239; parliamentarians' wages in, 187, 188 (table 8.5)
Franco, Joaquín, 158, 287 (E), 310 (I), 334 (K), 345 (L), 364 (R)
Fujimori, Alberto, 217

Galindo Heurtematte, Mario, 88, 262–63
Gallego, Héctor, 231
Gálvez, Sergio, 160 (table 7.2), 163, 183 (tables 8.2, 8.3), 287 (E), 314 (I), 318 (I), 322 (I), 325 (J), 334 (K), 347 (L)
García Márquez, Gabriel, 83

Garrido, Enrique, 125 (table 5.4), 160
(table 7.2), 162, 201, 202, 206, 207,
226, 252, 287 (E), 310, 314, 318 (I),
321 (I), 322 (I), 325 (J), 335 (K),
347 (L), 364 (R)
General Council of State, Panama, 375n12
Giraud, Hugo, 124 (table 5.3), 167, 232,
288 (E), 304 (I), 335 (K), 346 (L),
395n23
Gómez, Ana, 223
Gómez, Osman, 252, 288 (E), 314 (I),
318 (I), 325 (J), 335 (K), 345 (L),
398n36
González, Jílmer, 124 (table 5.3, note b),
157, 288 (E), 308 (I, note a), 379n11
González, Leo, 161 (table 7.2), 288 (E),
307 (I), 321 (I), 335 (K), 346 (L),
396n10
González, Marcos, 122 (table 5.2), 172,
288 (E), 325 (J), 335 (K), 347 (L)
González, Pedro, 138, 146, 150, 169,
171, 183 (table 8.2), 247–51, 253,
288 (E), 314 (I), 318 (I), 325 (J),
335 (K), 347 (L), 389n34, 390n14
González, Yadira, 204, 288 (E), 310 (I),
335 (K), 345 (L), 363 (R)
González Vernaza, Gerardo, 150, 151,
167, 169, 201, 211, 224, 245, 247,
248, 288 (E), 310 (I), 335 (K), 346
(L), 347 (L), 362 (R), 389n33 (ch.
6), 389n5 (ch. 7), 390n14
González Vernaza family, 58
Gozaine, Camilo, 122 (table 5.2), 145,
232, 288 (E), 304 (I), 314 (I), 335
(K), 344 (L), 345 (L), 395n23
Great Britain. See United Kingdom
Guainora, Anselmo, 136, 215, 229, 230,
288 (E), 304 (I), 335 (K), 344 (L)
Guardia, Gloria, 381n33
Guardia Ponce, Aurelio, 380n28
Guardia Vieto, Aurelio, 380n28
Guatemala: Corruption Perceptions
Index of, 9; deputies' wages in, 190
(table 8.6); electoral democracy in,

376n14; membership in Central
American Parliament (PARLACÉN),
382n5
Guillén, Olmedo, 160 (table 7.2),
195–96, 198, 211, 288 (E), 310 (I),
321 (I), 335 (K), 347 (L), 364 (R)
Guizado, José Ramón, 29, 99

Haiti: Duvalier dictatorship in, 96;
electoral democracy in, 376n14
Harding, Kayra, 170
Hare, Thomas, 74, 77
Havana, Cuba, 103
Henríquez, Milton, 193, 288 (E), 307
(I), 336 (K), 346 (L)
Herrera, Balbina, 1, 53, 94, 125
(table 5.4), 143, 204, 221, 222,
224, 225, 240–42, 244, 245, 246,
253, 262, 263, 288 (E), 310 (I),
314 (I), 336 (K), 346 (L), 347 (L),
362 (R), 374n3
Herrera Province, Panama, 169, 170, 171
Hersh, Seymour M., 167
Hill, José, 124 (table 5.3), 200, 289 (E),
307, 318 (I), 336 (K), 344 (L)
Honduras: deputies' wages in, 190
(table 8.6); electoral democracy in,
376n14; membership in Central
American Parliament (PARLACÉN),
382n5
Hurtado, Raymundo, 125 (table 5.4),
161 (table 7.2), 196, 289 (E), 310 (I),
321 (I), 336 (K), 347 (L), 364 (R)

Icaza, Aristides de, 122 (table 5.2), 160
(table 7.2), 246, 289 (E), 310 (I), 319
(I), 321 (I), 322 (I), 325 (J), 336
(K), 345 (L), 363 (R)
Icaza, Harmodio, 167, 289 (E), 305 (I),
336 (K), 346 (L)
Iceland, low levels of clientelism in,
377n13
Iglesias, Frank, 206, 393n18
impugnaciones (legal objections), 173–74

India: clientelism in, 377n13;
Corruption Perceptions Index of, 9;
liberal democracy in, 10;
parliamentary immunity, 239
Indonesia: clientelism in, 377n13; liberal
democracy in, 10
Institute of Ibero-America, University of
Salamanca, 11
institutionalization: and clientelism,
104–13, 266; and corruption,
92–97, 214, 266; formal, 5, 6, 25,
34, 65–90, 374nn6–7; and
impunity, 97–104, 174, 214, 266;
informal, 5, 6, 7, 25, 26, 34, 113,
176, 214, 229, 266; party system,
46–49, 64, 91
Inter-American Commission on Human
Rights (IACHR), 77, 101
Inter-American Development Bank
(IDB), 149
Inter-Parliamentary Union (IPU), 199,
238
Iran, Reza Pahlevi's rule, 96
Israel, parliamentary immunity, 239
Italy: liberal democracy in, 10; multiparty
system in, 46; parliamentarians' wages
in, 188 (table 8.5), 189; prosecution
of Alfredo Oranges in, 226; Putnam's
study of, 24

Japan, parliamentary immunity, 239
Jiménez, Enrique A., 28, 378n3
Jiménez, Guillermo, 167, 229, 289 (E),
304 (I), 336 (K), 344 (L)
Jiménez, Mariela, 125 (table 5.4), 161
(table 7.2), 204, 226, 289 (E), 310 (I),
321 (I), 336 (K), 347 (L), 364 (R)
Jované, Rodrigo, 161 (table 7.2), 289
(E), 310 (I), 321 (I), 336 (K), 345
(L), 364 (R), 389n2
Juárez, Fabio, 229, 289 (E), 304 (I), 337
(K), 346 (L)

Kouri, Alberto, 217

La Chorrera, Panama, 61 (table 2.6), 173
La Guardia, Ricardo de, 27, 28
La Hora, Panama, 381n31
La Hoz, Manuel de, 161 (table 7.2), 163,
169, 289 (E), 310 (I), 314 (I), 322
(I), 337 (K), 347 (L), 362 (R)
La Prensa, Panama, 139, 184, 209, 210,
211, 218, 220, 231, 263
La Rúa, Fernando de, 217
Lakas, Demetrio, 377n9
Lanuza, Raquel, 289 (E), 307 (I), 337
(K), 344 (L), 396n10
Latin America: clientelism in, 107, 109;
congresses in, 33, 60; congressional
politics in, 154; constituency funding
in, 139; deputies in, 35, 62–63, 64;
deputies' wages in, 189, 190 (table
8.6); electoral democracies in, 13, 33,
34 (table 1.3), 53, 376n14; electoral
volatility in, 378n9; inequality in,
385n8; liberal democracies, 8, 375n10;
party system institutionalization
in, 46–49; policy making in, 21;
political institutions in, 6; political
parties in, 42; politics in, 12;
presidential democracies in, 13, 51,
85; presidential reelection in, 262;
republics in, 26, 33, 37, 129
Legislation Commission, Panama,
375n12
Legislative Council, Panama, 31, 58,
218, 377n11
León, Rubén de, 289 (E), 319 (I), 347
(L), 398n36
León de Pomares, Olivia de, 169, 289
(E), 310 (I), 315 (I), 337 (K), 347
(L), 362 (R)
Liberal Party (Partido Liberal, Panama),
30, 36, 37–39, 57, 157, 378n3,
381n33
Liechtenstein, 377n13
Linares Herbruger, Francisco, 80
Lleras Restrepo, Alberto, 140
Lobos al anochecer, 381n33

López, Ada, 232, 289 (E), 307 (I), 337 (K), 346 (L)

López, Cecilia, 151

López Tirone, Humberto, 167

Loré, Jaime, 158 (table 7.1), 204, 290 (E), 297 (F), 310 (I), 337 (K), 345 (L), 362 (R)

Los Santos Province, Panama, 133, 170

Lozada, José, 164, 183 (table 8.3), 290 (E), 326 (J), 337 (K), 345 (L)

Luxembourg, 377n13

Madison, John, 19–20, 22, 23, 71, 81, 90, 114, 120

Marcos, Ferdinand, 96

Márquez, Walter, 397n19

Martinelli, Ricardo, 12, 41, 103, 162, 233, 278 (D), 374n3, 387n11, 395n24

Martínez, Abraham, 160 (table 7.2), 163, 183 (table 8.3), 290 (E), 319 (I), 322 (I), 326 (J), 338 (K), 347 (L)

Martínez, Juvenal, 161 (table 7.2), 163, 290 (E), 319 (I), 322 (I), 326 (J), 337 (K), 345 (L)

Martínez, Victor, 207

Medina, Yidis, 217

Melamed, Moisés, 229, 290 (E), 304 (I), 338 (K), 346 (L)

Méndez, Gabriel, 164, 290 (E), 326 (J), 338 (K)

Méndez Fábrega, Víctor, 198, 200, 290 (E), 310 (I), 321 (I), 338 (K), 363 (R)

Mexico: deputies' wages in, 189, 190 (table 8.6); electoral democracy in, 376n14; liberal democracy in, 10, 375n10; PRI (Partido Revolucionario Institucional), 42; restrictions on reelection of deputies in, 66

Milanés, Haydée, 94, 160 (table 7.2), 163, 170, 172, 173, 202, 290 (E), 310 (I), 322 (I), 338 (K), 345 (L), 362 (R)

Mill, John Stuart, 18–19, 21, 75, 85, 90, 265

Miller, Mario, 50, 122 (table 5.2), 215, 216, 246–47, 253, 290 (E), 310 (I), 312 (I, note b), 326 (J), 338 (K), 345 (L), 379n18

Ministry of Public Works, Panama, 135, 136

Miranda, Nodier, 50, 134 (table 5.3, note b), 157, 158, 290 (E), 307 (I), 308 (I, note a), 338 (K), 344 (L)

Miranda, Otilio, 215, 230–34, 290 (E), 304 (I), 338 (K), 344 (L)

Misselis, Fausto, 252

Montemayor, Danis, 124 (table 5.3), 252, 290 (E), 319 (I), 326 (J), 338 (K), 347 (L)

Montenegro, Domiluis, 161 (table 7.2), 290 (E), 307 (I), 321 (I), 338 (K), 344 (L), 396n10

Montería, Treaty of (1980), 377n10

Montesinos, Vladimiro, 217

Montesquieu, Charles Marie de Secondat, Baron de, 22, 24, 90, 177–78

Monteza, Cecilia, 150–51

Montezuma, Enrique, 204, 345 (L)

Moreno, Gloria, 125 (table 5.4), 161 (table 7.2), 346 (L), 387n11, 396n10

Moscoso, Mireya, 2, 41, 94, 103, 138, 139, 146, 163, 172, 218–20, 222, 228, 233, 234, 249, 280 (D), 378n6, 387nn7, 11

Movimiento de Depuración Legislativa, 195

Movimiento de Renovación Nacional (MORENA), 45 (table 2.1), 155, 160 (table 7.2), 278 (D)

Movimiento de Unidad Nacional (MUN), 155

Movimiento Liberal Republicano Nacionalista (MOLIRENA), 39, 41, 45 (table 2.1), 88, 122 (table 5.2), 124 (table 5.3), 125 (table 5.4), 160 (table 7.2), 163, 222, 278 (D), 374n3, 391n1, 392n13, 396nn11–12, 397n20

Movimiento Papa Egoró (MPE), 143, 155
Multiagency Program. *See* Programa
  Multiagencial de Proyectos
  Comunitarios
multimember constituencies, 67, 69–78,
  83
Muñoz Molina, José, 184, 186

Namibia, parliamentary immunity, 239
National Bank of Panama (Banco
  Nacional de Panamá), 232
National Bar Association of Panama
  (Colegio Nacional de Abogados), 144
National Guard (Guardia Nacional de
  Panamá), 29, 30, 35, 55, 57, 95, 99,
  100, 101, 103, 166, 180, 377nn8,
  10, 384n4
National Liberation Party, Costa Rica
  (PLN)
National Vote Counting Board, Panama,
  165, 167
Netherlands: parliamentarians' wages in,
  188 (table 8.5), 189; parliamentary
  immunity, 239
New Granada, 26, 37, 38, 376n4,
  378n2. *See also* Colombia
New Orleans, 231
New Zealand: parliamentarians' wages
  in, 187, 188 (table 8.5); parliamentary
  immunity, 239
Noriega, Manuel, 42, 101, 102, 103,
  167, 215, 231, 232, 376n13, 378n7,
  386n2
Norway: Christian Democratic Party of,
  46; parliamentarians' wages in, 187,
  188 (table 8.5); parliamentary
  immunity, 239
Núñez, Rafael, 26

Obaldía, Mario J. de, 157, 291 (E), 305
  (I), 339 (K), 346 (L)
Ombudsman's Office, Panama
  (Defensoría del Pueblo de la República
  de Panamá), 11, 170, 173, 174

Oranges, Alfredo, 226, 291 (E), 305 (I),
  339 (K), 346 (L)
Organic Law, National Assembly of
  Panama, 138. *See also* Rules of
  Procedure, National Assembly
  of Panama
Ortiz, Manuel, 161 (table 7.2), 162, 291
  (E), 311 (I), 321 (I), 339 (K), 347
  (L), 364 (R)
Ossa, Raúl, 226, 242, 291 (E), 305 (I),
  308 (I), 339 (K), 344 (L), 396n10

padrinazgo, 108
Pahlevi, Mohammed Reza, 96
Panama, State of, 26, 376n4
Panama Canal, 377n10
Panama Canal Authority, 88
Panama Canal Treaty, 96
Panama City, 38, 58, 60, 61 (table 2.6),
  80, 93, 94, 95, 112, 123, 128, 151,
  169–70, 171, 173, 204, 216, 245,
  247, 247, 356 (O), 376n4, 386n9
Panamanian Defense Forces (Fuerzas
  de Defensa de Panamá), 101, 149,
  376n13, 384n4
Paraguay: deputies' wages in, 190
  (table 8.6); electoral democracy in,
  376n14
Pardo, César, 122 (table 5.2), 143, 149,
  196, 224, 291 (E), 305 (I), 311 (I),
  314 (I), 315 (I), 319 (I), 326 (J), 339
  (K), 344 (L), 345 (L), 325 (R),
  388n30, 392n7
Paredes, Rigoberto, 150, 168, 173, 215,
  231, 291 (E), 305 (I), 339 (K), 344
  (L), 389n32
Paredes, Rogelio, 150, 151, 170, 183
  (table 8.3), 291 (E), 319 (I), 326 (J),
  339 (K), 345 (L), 389n32, 393n4
Paredes, Rubén, 42
Paredes Robles family, 58
PARLACÉN (Central American
  Parliament), 69, 212, 252, 382n5,
  385n6, 395n23

Parliamentary Ethics and Honor Code, 199
partidas circuitales (constituency funds), 13, 113, 120, 132–48, 152, 187, 196, 218, 227, 229, 260, 261, 264, 387n11, 388n20, 398n1
Partido Arnulfista, 41, 157, 158, 280 (D), 396n12, 397n20. *See also* Partido Panameñista (PPAN)
Partido Cambio Democrático (CD), 12, 41, 45 (table 2.1), 103, 129, 150, 157, 162, 163, 164, 165, 184, 186, 216, 222, 247, 249, 278 (D)
Partido Demócrata Cristiano (PDC; Partido Popular; Christian Democratic Party), 41, 43, 48, 162, 279 (D)
Partido Laborista Agrario (PALA), 45 (table 2.1), 50, 57, 124 (table 5.3), 125 (table 5.4), 128, 155, 158 (table 7.1), 167, 194, 204, 205, 215, 216, 225, 229, 230, 231, 233, 246, 250, 253, 278 (D), 391n3, 397n18, 398n36
Partido Liberal (PL), 36, 37–39, 45 (table 2.1), 145, 155, 157, 158 (table 7.1), 159, 161 (table 7.2), 198, 204, 210, 279 (D), 389n2, 397n18
Partido Liberal Auténtico (PLA), 39, 41, 45 (table 2.1), 50, 124 (table 5.3), 125 (table 5.4), 155, 158 (table 7.1), 160 (table 7.2), 169, 195, 196, 222, 226, 251, 279 (D), 376n13, 378n3, 386n9, 391nn1, 3, 396nn10–12, 397n20
Partido Liberal Nacional (PLN), 38, 39, 43, 45 (table 2.1), 57, 154, 155, 158 (table 7.1), 161 (table 7.2), 183 (table 8.2), 186, 222, 228, 280 (D), 378n8, 392nn8, 13
Partido Liberal Republicano (LIBRE), 39, 45 (table 2.1), 155, 186, 228, 278 (D)
Partido Nacional Revolucionario, 40, 383n11

Partido Nacionalista Popular (PNP), 155, 226
Partido Panameñista (PPAN), 2, 36, 39–40, 41, 42, 43, 45 (table 2.1), 48, 122 (table 5.2), 124 (table 5.3), 125 (table 5.4), 129, 157, 158 (table 7.1), 160 (table 7.2), 162–63, 222, 280 (D), 378n8, 379n10, 391nn1, 3, 392n13, 396n12
Partido Panameñista Auténtico. *See* Partido Arnulfista; Partido Panameñista (PPAN)
Partido Panameñista Doctrinario (PPD), 155
Partido Popular (Partido Demócrata Cristiano; Christian Democratic Party), 41, 43, 124 (table 5.3), 125 (table 5.4), 162, 279 (D)
Partido Renovación Civilista (PRC), 45 (table 2.1), 155, 222, 226, 281 (D)
Partido Revolucionario Auténtico, 40
Partido Revolucionario Democrático (PRD), 1–2, 8–9, 31, 36, 41–42, 43, 44, 45 (table 2.1), 51, 62, 64, 73, 101, 102–3, 112, 122 (table 5.2), 124 (table 5.3), 125 (table 5.4), 129, 138, 154, 158 (table 7.1), 160 (table 7.2), 162–64, 167–68, 174, 214, 220, 222–23, 225, 226, 229, 242, 244, 263–63, 281 (D), 378n7, 379n10, 382n7, 391nn3, 5, 392nn8, 10, 396nn11–12, 397n18
Partido Revolucionario Institucional, Mexico (PRI), 42
Partido Solidaridad (PSOL), 43, 45 (table 2.1), 124 (table 5.3), 154, 158 (table 7.1), 160 (table 7.2), 222, 281 (D), 391nn3, 5, 392nn8, 10, 13
Partido Unión Patriótica (UP), 43, 154, 155, 282 (D)
party switching, 129, 153–64, 175–76, 260
Pastrana, Andrés, 141

patronage, 7, 11, 14, 25, 71, 81, 84, 86, 105–10, 112, 120, 131–32, 140, 147–48, 151–52, 176, 254, 259

Peláez, Humberto, 397n19

Penonomé, Coclé, Panama, 388n30

Pereira, Renato, 169

Pérez Balladares, Ernesto, 12, 43, 102, 132, 136–38, 141, 142, 144, 146, 149, 151, 163, 197–99, 204, 215, 220, 224, 225, 228, 230, 232–35, 247, 248, 250, 262–63, 388n28, 389n35, 393n18, 394n21

personalism, 66, 74, 79, 81, 82, 90, 95, 108, 261, 264

Peru: longevity of parties in, 48; non-programmatic politics in, 43; presidential reelection in, 262, 399n3; presidential volatility in, 47; vote buying under Fujimoro, 217

Philippines, dictatorship of Marcos, 96–97

Pitkin, Hannah, 17–18, 259

Planning Office, Panama, 135, 138

Playa Chiquita, Colón, Panama, 80

Poland, parliamentary practices, 218

Pomárico, Armando, 227

Porras, Belisario, 38

Portobello fairs, 94

Posada Carriles, Luis, 103

Pretto, Abraham, 173

Programa de Ayuda Rápida para Viviendas de Interés Social (PARVIS) (Rapid Help Program for Social Interest Housing), 149–50, 151, 388n31, 389n11

Programa Multiagencial de Proyectos Comunitarios (Multiagency Program), 134, 136, 229, 230, 233, 389n35

proportional representation, 67–68, 69, 71–79, 156

Prosecutor-General's Office (Panama), 2, 100, 150, 186–87, 215, 223, 228, 231–32, 235, 240, 241–46, 396n6

Provisional Government Junta (1903), 27

Provisional Government Junta (1969), 30, 39, 40, 79, 100

Provisional Government Statute, 100

proyectos de co-financiación, Colombia, 140–41

Public Works Committee, National Assembly of Panama, 133

Quiel, Mario, 145, 158 (table 7.1), 226, 291 (E), 297 (F), 311 (I), 340 (K), 345 (L), 363 (R)

Quintero, César, 86, 178–80

Quintero, Wigberto, 161 (table 7.2), 292 (E), 316 (I, note a), 319 (I), 322 (I), 327 (J), 340 (K), 347 (L), 381n34

Quintero Luna, Pablo, 126 (table 5.4), 169–70, 180, 292 (E), 311 (I), 340 (K), 345 (L), 364 (R)

Radical Civic Union, Argentina (UCR), 42

Ramírez, Anel, 50, 205–6, 215, 216, 246, 253, 292 (E), 308 (I), 340 (K), 344 (L), 379n17

Ramírez, Antonio, 379n17

Ramírez, Ezequiel, 172, 292 (E), 319 (I), 327 (J), 340 (K), 345 (L)

Ramírez Duque, Jorge, 58

Rapid Help Program for Social Interest Housing (PARVIS). See Programa de Ayuda Rápida para Viviendas de Interés Social

Real, Salvador, 172, 292 (E), 327 (J), 340 (K), 345 (I)

Refinería Panamá, 221

regidor, 112, 385n7

Remón, José Antonio, 29, 40, 99, 165

Richa, Susana, 51, 292 (E), 315 (I), 319 (I), 327 (J), 340 (K), 345 (L)

Riega, Melquíades, 210, 292 (E), 308 (I), 340 (K), 344 (L)

Riley, Enrique, 150, 161 (table 7.2), 169, 249–50, 292 (E), 311 (I), 321 (I), 340 (K), 347 (L), 363 (R)

Rivera, Alicio, 229, 292 (E), 305 (I), 340 (K), 346 (L)
Robinson, Benicio, 122 (table 5.2), 150, 183 (table 8.2), 201, 224, 292 (E), 308 (I), 311 (I), 319 (I), 327 (J), 340 (K), 344 (L), 345 (L), 362 (R), 389n33
Robles, Marco, 29–30, 133, 165–66, 377n8
Rodríguez, Abel, 224, 292 (E), 311 (I), 341 (K), 345 (L)
Rodríguez, Francisco, 226, 376n13
Rodríguez, Magdalena, 229, 292 (E), 305 (I), 341 (K), 344 (L)
Rognoni, Mario, 211, 292 (E), 308 (I), 341 (K), 346 (L), 396n6
Romero, Aristides, 136, 230, 388n28
Rosas, Jorge Alberto, 122 (table 5.2), 292 (E), 315 (I), 327 (J), 341 (K), 345 (L)
Rosas, Jorge Rubén, 292 (E), 305 (I), 308 (I), 341 (K), 344 (L), 386n9 (ch. 5), 386n1 (ch. 6), 398n36
Rosas, Olmedo, 386n1
Royo, Aristides, 377n9
Rules Committee, National Assembly of Panama, 200–201, 221, 223, 227–28, 241–43, 244–46, 253, 396n10
Rules of Procedure, National Assembly of Panama, 31, 66, 184, 196–99, 202–5, 207–9, 212, 240, 242–43, 244, 257–58, 390n4, 391n10, 395n4. See also Organic Law, National Assembly of Panama

Salerno, Noriel, 122 (table 5.2), 161 (table 7.2), 293 (E), 311 (I), 315 (I), 322 (I), 327 (J), 341 (K), 345 (L), 362 (R), 398n36
San Blas Indigenous Reservation, 70–71, 170
San Carlos-Chame constituency, Panama, 158
San Marino, low levels of clientelism in, 377n13

Sánchez, Miguel Peregrino, 50, 293 (E), 311 (I), 313 (I, note c), 341 (K), 345 (L), 363 (R), 379n12
Sánchez Borbón, Guillermo, 231
Sánchez Cárdenas, Francisco, 150
Sandinista National Liberation Front, Nicaragua (FSLN), 42
Sanjur, César, 224, 293 (E), 311 (I), 341 (K), 347 (L), 363 (R)
Santana, Carlos E., 160 (table 7.2), 162, 293 (E), 311 (I), 315 (I), 321 (I), 322 (I), 341 (K), 347 (L), 364 (R)
Schuverer, Virgilio, 386n1
Senate, Argentina, 217
Serracín, José, 77, 161 (table 7.2), 162, 226, 293 (E), 311 (I), 321 (I), 341 (K), 347 (L), 363 (R)
Serrano, Felipe, 224, 227, 293 (E), 311 (I), 342 (K), 345 (L)
Simons, Jorge, 229
single-member constituencies, 67, 69–76, 81
Smith, Carlos, 219, 293 (E), 312 (I), 315 (I), 342 (K), 345 (L), 362 (R)
Socialist International, 42, 378n7
Socialist Party, Chile, 42
Socialist Party, Panama. See Partido Revolucionario Democrático (PRD)
Solís, Francisco, 151, 229, 293 (E), 305 (I), 342 (K), 344 (L), 389n35
Solís, Gerardo, 144, 172, 250
Solís Palma, Manuel, 226, 375n13
Somoza family, 96
Sossa, José Antonio, 126 (table 5.4), 229, 248, 293 (E), 308 (I), 342 (K), 346 (L), 394n21
Spadafora, Hugo, 231
Spadafora, Winston, 222, 223, 251
Spain: Panama's independence from, 376n4; parliamentarians' wages in, 187, 188 (table 8.5); parliamentary immunity, 239
Statute of Immediate Return to Constitutional Order, Panama (1989), 193

Sucre, Lenín, 158 (table 7.1), 198, 293 (E), 297 (F), 312 (I), 315 (I), 342 (K), 345 (K), 364 (R)
Supreme Court of Panama, 1, 2, 4 (table 1.1), 29, 60–61, 100, 103, 123, 125 (table 5.4), 178, 188 (table 8.5, note c), 193, 194, 196–98, 201–2, 207, 208, 216, 217, 222–24, 237, 243, 247, 251–52, 379n16, 385n7, 386n9, 397n16
Sweden: low levels of clientelism in, 377n13; parliamentarians' wages in, 187, 188 (table 8.5); parliamentary immunity, 239; Socialist parties, 46
Switzerland, parliamentary immunity, 239

Tejeira, Gil Blas, 109, 385n6
Tejeira, Javier, 57, 161 (table 7.2), 183 (table 8.2), 252, 293 (E), 305 (I), 315 (I), 320 (I), 322 (I), 327 (J), 342 (K), 345 (L), 381n35
Texaco, 221
Thailand, Corruption Perceptions Index of, 9
Tócamo, Sergio, 170, 293 (E), 316 (I), 342 (K), 345 (L)
Torres, Freidi, 60–61, 183 (table 8.3), 293 (E), 316 (I), 320 (I), 327 (J), 342 (K), 347 (L), 398n36
Torres, José, 226, 293 (E), 308 (I), 342 (K), 344 (L)
Torrijos, Hugo, 168, 229, 293 (E), 305 (I), 342 (K), 344 (L)
Torrijos, Martín, 12, 97, 103, 126 (table 5.4, note c), 139, 163, 172, 229, 230, 235, 244, 251, 388n22, 389n10
Torrijos, Omar, 29, 30, 31, 41–42, 51, 89, 100, 111, 112, 281 (D), 377nn7, 9, 11
Transit Authority, Panama, 224
Transparency International, 9, 92, 146
Treaty of Peace, Amity, Commerce, and Navigation (1846) (Bidlack-Mallarino Treaty), 38, 378n2
Trujillo, Rafael, 96

UESAT antiterrorist unit, Panama, 103
Union Bank of Switzerland, 184
Unión Democrática Independiente (UDI), 155, 282 (D)
United Kingdom: allocation and service responsiveness in, 131; deviation from proportionality in elections, 77; House of Commons, 380n25; House of Lords, 380n25; parliamentarians' wages in, 189; parliamentary immunity, 239
United States: allocation and service responsiveness in, 131; congressional wages in, 187, 188 (table 8.5); deviation from proportionality in elections, 77; immunity of members of Congress, 239; reelection of members of Congress, 117–18, 379n19
University of Salamanca surveys, 11–12, 62, 64, 381n37
Uribe, Álvaro, 217
Uruguay: democracy in, 375n10, 376n14; difference between congressional and presidential votes in, 47; low ratio of representatives to population, 33; parliamentary immunity, 239; representatives' salaries in, 189, 190 (table 8.6); vehicle import exemption in, 208
U.S. Army 470th Counterintelligence Corps (CIC), 377n7
U.S. Congress, 32, 52 (table 2.4), 55, 117–19, 121, 178, 251, 387n11
U.S. Drug Enforcement Agency (DEA), 216, 246
U.S. National Security Council, 377n7

Valencia, Ricardo, 51, 183 (table 8.3), 294 (E), 329 (J), 342 (K), 345 (L)
Vallarino, Alberto, 162
Vallarino, Arturo, 50, 57, 123, 124 (table 5.3), 194, 200, 225, 294 (E), 305 (I), 308 (I), 312 (I), 316 (I), 342 (K), 346 (L), 347 (L), 363 (R), 381nn34–35, 391n3

Vallarino, Bolívar, 57
Vallarino, Carlos, 146
Vallarino, Carlota, 381n35
Vallarino, Ismael, 57, 381n33
Vallarino, Marylín, 57–58, 160 (table
    7.2), 294 (E), 320 (I), 322 (I), 328
    (J), 342 (K), 345 (L)
Vallarino Bartuano family, 57, 58
Vallarino Jiménez, Ramón, 95
Vanguardia Moral de la Patria (VMP),
    45 (table 2.1), 129, 155, 158
    (table 7.1), 161 (table 6.2), 282 (D)
Varela, José Luis, 160 (table 7.2), 162,
    184, 252, 294 (E), 312 (I), 316 (I),
    320 (I), 321 (I), 328 (J), 342 (K),
    345 (L), 363 (R), 398n36
Vásquez, Alcibíades, 294 (E), 316 (I),
    320 (I), 328 (J), 343 (K), 347 (L),
    398n36
Venezuela: longevity of parties in, 48;
    non-programmatic policies in, 43;
    presidential reelection in, 262, 382n1
Veraguas Province, Panama, 169, 171,
    231, 249, 250
Vienna Convention on Diplomatic
    Relations (1961), 203
Villarreal, Ramiro, 320 (I, note e), 379n14

War of the Thousand Days
    (1899–1902), 37, 38
Weber, Max, 20, 22, 23, 84–85, 90,
    96, 213, 264–65
Weeden, Alvin, 201–2, 211, 219,
    373 (T)
Wever, Franz, 60, 171, 173, 252, 294
    (E), 312 (I), 320 (I), 328 (J), 343
    (K), 347 (L), 362 (R)
Wilson, Jerry, 122 (table 5.2), 126
    (table 5.4), 212, 252, 294 (E), 305
    (I), 316 (I), 320 (I), 328 (J), 343
    (K), 346 (L), 347 (L), 386n9

Yániz, Teresita, 126 (table 5.4), 172,
    188 (table 8.5, note c), 219, 294 (E),
    316 (I), 320 (I), 328 (J), 343 (K),
    347 (L), 390n6, 398n1
Young, Gloria, 160 (table 7.2), 204, 294
    (E), 312 (I), 316 (I), 321 (I), 343
    (K), 347 (L), 364 (R)
Young, Ivonne, 219

Zarak, Lucas, 157, 158, 161 (table 7.2),
    162, 197, 226, 294 (E), 308 (I), 312
    (I), 321 (I), 343 (K), 346 (L), 347
    (L), 363 (R)

Carlos Guevara Mann

is an international consultant and teaches at Florida State University, Panama.

www.ingramcontent.com/pod-product-compliance
Lightning Source LLC
Chambersburg PA
CBHW020330270326
41926CB00007B/120